A TEXT BOOK OF

# STRENGTH OF MATERIALS

FOR
SEMESTER - I
SECOND YEAR (S.E.) DEGREE COURSE IN
MECHANICAL AND AUTOMOBILE ENGINEERING

Strictly According to New Revised Syllabus of
North Maharashtra University, Jalgaon, June 2013

ALSO USEFUL FOR ALL INDIAN UNIVERSITIES AND COMPETITIVE EXAMINATIONS

**Dr. SURESH R. PAREKAR**

*B. E. (Civil), M. E. (Structures), Ph. D.*

Professor, Civil Engg. Deptt.,
Sinhgad Academy of Engineering,
Kondhwa, PUNE 411048.

**NIRALI PRAKASHAN**

N3008

**S.E. STRENGTH OF MATERIALS (NMU : Mechanical and Automobile Engineering)**

| | | |
|---|---|---|
| First Edition | : August 2013 | ISBN 978-93-83525-03-4 |
| © | : Author | |

The text of this publication, or any part thereof, should not be reproduced or transmitted in any form or stored in any computer storage system or device for distribution including photocopy, recording, taping or information retrieval system or reproduced on any disc, tape, perforated media or other information storage device etc., without the written permission of Author with whom the rights are reserved. Breach of this condition is liable for legal action.

Every effort has been made to avoid errors or omissions in this publication. In spite of this, errors may have crept in. Any mistake, error or discrepancy so noted and shall be brought to our notice shall be taken care of in the next edition. It is notified that neither the publisher nor the author or seller shall be responsible for any damage or loss of action to any one, of any kind, in any manner, therefrom.

**Published By :**
**NIRALI PRAKASHAN**
Abhyudaya Pragati, 1312, Shivaji Nagar,
Off J.M. Road, PUNE – 411005
Tel - (020) 25512336/37/39, Fax - (020) 25511379
Email : niralipune@pragationline.com

**Printed at**
**Repro Knowledgecast Limited**
**Thane**

## DISTRIBUTION CENTRES

### PUNE

*Nirali Prakashan*
119, Budhwar Peth, Jogeshwari Mandir Lane
Pune 411002, Maharashtra
Tel : (020) 2445 2044, 66022708, Fax : (020) 2445 1538
Email : bookorder@pragationline.com

*Nirali Prakashan*
S. No. 28/25, Dhyari,
Near Pari Company, Pune 411041
Tel : (020) 24690204 Fax : (020) 24690316
Email : dhyari@pragationline.com
       bookorder@pragationline.com

### MUMBAI
*Nirali Prakashan*
385, S.V.P. Road, Rasdhara Co-op. Hsg. Society Ltd.,
Girgaum, Mumbai 400004, Maharashtra
Tel : (022) 2385 6339 / 2386 9976, Fax : (022) 2386 9976
Email : niralimumbai@pragationline.com

## DISTRIBUTION BRANCHES

**NAGPUR**
*Pratibha Book Distributors*
Above Maratha Mandir, Shop No. 3, First Floor,
Rani Jhanshi Square, Sitabuldi, Nagpur 440012,
Maharashtra, Tel : (0712) 254 7129

**BENGALURU**
*Pragati Book House*
House No. 1, Sanjeevappa Lane, Avenue Road Cross,
Opp. Rice Church, Bengaluru – 560002.
Tel : (080) 64513344, 64513355,
Mob : 9880582331, 9845021552
Email:bharatsavla@yahoo.com

**JALGAON**
*Nirali Prakashan*
34, V. V. Golani Market, Navi Peth, Jalgaon 425001,
Maharashtra, Tel : (0257) 222 0395
Mob : 94234 91860

**KOLHAPUR**
*Nirali Prakashan*
New Mahadvar Road,
Kedar Plaza, 1st Floor Opp. IDBI Bank
Kolhapur 416 012, Maharashtra. Mob : 9855046155

### CHENNAI
*Pragati Books*
9/1, Montieth Road, Behind Taas Mahal, Egmore,
Chennai 600008 Tamil Nadu, Tel : (044) 6518 3535,
Mob : 94440 01782 / 98450 21552 / 98805 82331, Email : bharatsavla@yahoo.com

## RETAIL OUTLETS

### PUNE

*Pragati Book Centre*
157, Budhwar Peth, Opp. Ratan Talkies,
Pune 411002, Maharashtra
Tel : (020) 2445 8887 / 6602 2707, Fax : (020) 2445 8887
*Pragati Book Centre*
Amber Chamber, 28/A, Budhwar Peth,
Appa Balwant Chowk, Pune : 411002, Maharashtra,
Tel : (020) 20240285 / 66281669
Email : pbcpune@pragationline.com

*Pragati Book Centre*
676/B, Budhwar Peth, Opp. Jogeshwari Mandir,
Pune 411002, Maharashtra
Tel : (020) 6601 7784 / 6602 0855
*PBC Book Sellers & Stationers*
152, Budhwar Peth, Pune 411002, Maharashtra
Tel : (020) 2445 2254 / 6609 2463

### MUMBAI
*Pragati Book Corner*
Indira Niwas, 111 - A, Bhavani Shankar Road, Dadar (W), Mumbai 400028, Maharashtra
Tel : (022) 2422 3526 / 6662 5254, Email : pbcmumbai@pragationline.com

# PREFACE

The subject **'Strength of Materials'** is a foundation stone for any Engineering Course. Today, Engineering applications are mostly interdisciplinary, involving basics of various fundamental subjects. One of such subject of vital importance is **"Strength of Materials"**. The present text is aimed at catering the needs of students appearing for Second Year Degree Course in Mechanical and Automobile Engineering of North Maharashtra University, Jalgaon.

The text gives fundamental and simple treatment to the subject with a clear and distinct presentation of theoretical concepts and well graded numerous examples from different universities.

Main feature of this book is, **complete coverage** of the new syllabus revised in June 2013 with large number of **Worked (Solved) Examples, Exercises** at the end of each chapter.

We are sincerely thankful to **Shri Dineshbhai Furia, Shri. Jignesh Furia, Shri. M. P. Munde** and Team of workers who really have taken keen interest and untiring efforts in publishing this text. We are also thankful to **Shri. Santosh Bare, Mrs. Prachi Sawant, Mrs. Manasi Pingle and Shri. Ramesh Pandya** for their kind co-operation throughout the work. We take this opportunity to express our deep sense of gratitude towards all the dear friends and students for their direct or indirect help in making this venture a success.

Inspite of having taken all the precautions, it is possible that some errors may have escaped our attention. The readers are kindly requested to bring to our notice such corrections for being rectified in the next edition.

26th **August 2013**

**PUNE**

**Dr. S. R. Parekar**

# SYLLABUS

### Unit I : Introduction to Strength of Material       (12 Hours, 16 Marks)
(a) Concept of stresses and strain (linear, lateral, shear and volumetric), Hook's law, Poisson's ratio, modulus of elasticity, modulus of rigidity, stress-strain diagram for ductile and brittle materials, factor of safety and working stress, concept of 3-D stress state, bulk modulus, in relation between elastic modulus.
(b) Axial force diagram, stress-strain, deformations in determinate, homogeneous and composite bars of following types : (1) Prismatic. (2) Linearly varying. (3) Steeped section under concentration loads and self-weights.
(c) Axial stresses and strain in determinate members – axial stress, strain and deformation in following indeterminate, homogenous and composite bars.
(1) Prismatic. (2) Linearly varying. (3) Stepped section under concentrated loads, self-weights.
(d) Temperature stresses and strain for prismatic, linearly varying and composite bars.

### Unit II : Principal Stresses and Strains       (08 Hours, 16 Marks)
(a) Introduction to normal and shear stress on any oblique plane, concept and principal plane.
(b) Derivation of expression for principal stresses and planes and plane of maximum shear stress position of principal plane and plane of maximum shear.
(c) Graphical solution using Mohr's circle of stresses.
(d) Combined effect of shear and bending in beams.
(e) Strain energy and impact-concept of strain energy, derivation and use of expression for deformation of axially loaded members under gradual, sudden and impact loads. Strain energy due to self-weight.

### Unit III : Shear Force and Bending Moment Diagram       (07 Hours, 16 Marks)
(a) Introduction to different types of beams, different types of supports and loads.
(b) Concept and definition of shear force bending moment in determinant beams due to concentrated loads, UDL, UVL and couple.
(c) Relation between SF, BM and intensity of loading, construction of shear force and bending moment diagram for cantilever, simple and compound beams, defining critical and maximum value and position of point of contra flexure.
(d) Construction of BMD and load diagram from SFD, construction of load diagram and SFD and BMD.

### Unit IV : Bending Stresses       (07 Hours, 16 Marks)
(a) Theory of simple bending, assumptions in bending theory, derivation of flexural formula.
(b) Area center and moment of inertia of common cross-section (regular section, T-section, channel section, I-section) with respect to centroidal and parallel axis, bending stress distribution diagram, moment of resistance and section modulus calculations.
(c) Direct and bending stresses in short column with eccentric point loads, concept of core section, middle third rule.
(d) Shear stresses : Concept, derivation of shear stress distribution formula, shear stress distribution diagram for common cross-section, maximum and average shear stresses, shear connection between flange and web.

### Unit V : Torsion in Circular Shafts       (08 Hours, 16 Marks)
(a) Stresses, strains and deformations in solid and hollow shafts, homogeneous and composite circular cross-sections subjected to torsion.
(b) Derivation of torsion equation. Stress due to combined torsion, bending and axial force on shafts.
(c) Thin and thick walled pressure vessels : Stress, strain and deformation in thin wall seamless cylindrical and spherical vessel due to internal fluid pressure, change in volume, constants, effects of additional compressible and incompressible fluid injected under pressure.

•••

# CONTENTS

### Unit - I

1. SIMPLE STRESSES AND STRAINS (PART-I) — 1.1 – 1.36
2. SIMPLE STRESSES AND STRAINS (PART-II) — 2.1 – 2.68

### Unit - II

3. PRINCIPAL STRESSES AND STRAINS — 3.1 – 3.40
4. STRAIN ENERGY — 4.1 – 4.36

### Unit - III

5. SHEAR FORCE AND BENDING MOMENT (PART-A) — 5.1 – 5.94
6. SHEAR FORCE AND BENDING MOMENT (PART-B) — 6.1 – 6.16

### Unit - IV

7. BENDING STRESSES IN BEAMS — 7.1 – 7.52
8. DIRECT AND BENDING STRESSES — 8.1 – 8.56
9. SHEAR STRESS DISTRIBUTION IN BEAMS — 9.1 – 9.42

### Unit - V

10. TORSION — 10.1 – 10.54
11. COMBINED LOADING — 11.1 – 11.26
12. PRESSURE VESSELS — 12.1 – 12.38

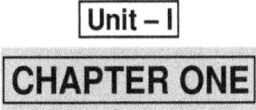

# SIMPLE STRESSES AND STRAINS
# (PART - I)

## 1.1 INTRODUCTION

The group of studies known as mechanics may be divided and classified in many ways, one of which is indicated below :

Mechanics $\begin{cases} \text{Particle and Rigid Bodies} \\ \text{(Applied Mechanics)} \\ \text{Deformable Bodies} \end{cases}$ − $\begin{cases} \text{Elastic (Strength of Materials)} \\ \text{Plastic (Advanced Course in Plasticity)} \\ \text{Fluid (Hydraulics, Fluid Mechanics, Aerodynamics)} \end{cases}$

In the usual Applied or Engineering mechanics, all the bodies studied are considered to be particles or rigid bodies - particles when the dimensions of the body are neglected, rigid bodies when the dimensions are considered but the deformations are neglected.

There are many cases in which the distortions of different dimensions of the body must be considered. Structural members, machine parts and springs are usually made of solid materials that deform considerably under the action of external loads, but regain their original shape after the load is removed. Such materials are said to be *elastic*.

In all the studies to follow, the free body concept as used in earlier studies in mechanics, will be found indispensable, as well as equations of equilibrium, because the subject "Strength of Materials" is built upon previous knowledge of mechanics with the addition of only a few new concepts.

To illustrate the distinction between the problems of Applied Mechanics and those of Strength of Materials, consider the beam of Fig. 1.1.

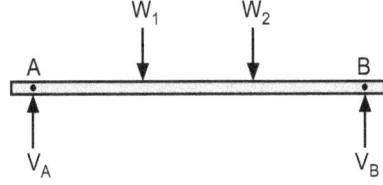

Fig. 1.1

In Applied Mechanics, we learned how to apply the equations of equilibrium to the free body in order to determine the unknown reactions $V_A$ and $V_B$, having given the magnitude and spacing of loads. Although the beam does deform due to applied loads, the changes in the dimensions are so small that it has no appreciable effect on the reactions. That is, we consider the beam to be a rigid body.

In Strength of Materials, we shall continue to neglect these deformations while determining the reactions, but we shall be concerned with these deformations while doing other calculations like we may wish to determine how much the beam will deflect or we may be interested in the deformations as a step in determining the internal stresses. Magnitude of these internal stresses must be known in order to proportion a member for a given length and loading.

Throughout this text, we study the principles that govern two fundamental concepts, strength and rigidity. In this first chapter, we start with the simple axial loading, later we consider bending loads, twisting loads and finally we discuss simultaneous combinations of these three basic types of loadings.

## 1.2 LOADS AND THEIR CLASSIFICATION

Loads may be classified in two ways :

**(a) According to manner to their application :** As per this classification, loads may be classified as (i) Dead load, (ii) Live load, (iii) Wind load, (iv) Seismic loads, (v) Temperature loads, (vi) Impact loads, (vii) Erection loads etc.

**(b) According to effect they produce :** Variety of loads acting on structural member produce different types of effects. For convenience these forces are resolved into components that are normal and tangential to the cross-section as shown in Fig. 1.2. The origin of the reference axis is always taken at the centroid of the cross-section. Each of these components have different structural effect and produces different structural deformation.

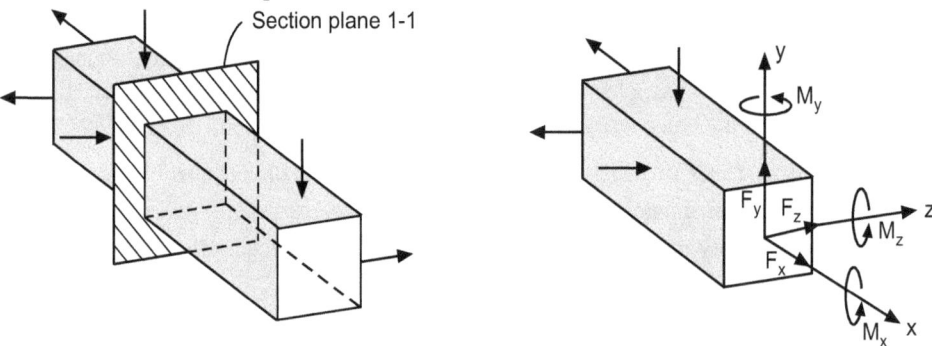

(a) General loading on member     (b) Internal forces at cross-section 1-1

**Fig. 1.2**

Various components and their structural names are as follows :

(i) $F_x$ : **Axial Force :** The force acting *normal to the cross-section and passing through CG* is called as axial force. The primary effect of axial force is to change the length of member. Axial force may be tensile in nature (pull) which causes increase in the length of a member or compressive in nature (push) which causes decrease in the length of a member.

(ii) $F_y$ ; $F_z$ : **Shear Forces :** The force acting *tangential to the cross-section* is called as shear force. The primary effect of these forces is to cause sliding of one cross-section with respect to other.

(iii) $M_x$ : **Torsional Moment :** Net moment vector acting *normal to the cross-section* is called as torsional moment or torque or torsion. The primary effect of torsional moment is to cause rotation of different cross-sections of member with respect to each other about polar axis. This rotation is called as twist.

(iv) $M_y$ ; $M_z$ : **Bending Moment :** Net moment vector acting *tangential to the cross-section* is called as bending moment. These moments cause bending of the member about an axis parallel to the cross-section and ultimately produce slopes and deflection.

The subject Strength of Materials is the study of all above structural actions, corresponding deformations and stresses produced by an individual action or combination thereof.

## 1.3 STRESS

When as elastic body is subjected to loads, it undergoes deformation. While undergoing deformations, the particles of the material offer a resisting force. When this resisting force equals the applied loads, equilibrium is attained and further deformation stops. This internal resistance is called as *stress*. The resistance per unit area is called as intensity of stress. Generally, the word stress refers to *intensity of stress*. Thus, stress is *resistance per unit area*.

### 1.3.1 Types of Stresses

Stresses are of two types : (i) Normal Stresses and (ii) Shear Stresses.

Stresses which act normal to the section are called as normal stresses while that acting tangential to the section are called shear stresses. It should be noted that *axial force* produces *uniform normal stresses* over the section while *bending moment* produces *linearly varying stresses* over the section within elastic limit, as discussed later in the text. Shear force and torsional moment produces shear stresses over the section. Thus, type of stress produced depends on the type of action the cross-section is subjected to.

Normal stresses can further be classified as tensile or compressive in nature, depending on kind of deformation the member undergoes.

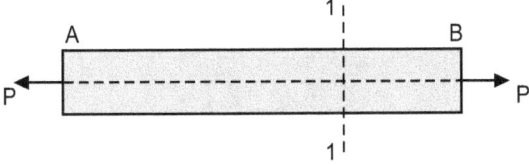

(a) Member subjected to axial tension (Pull)

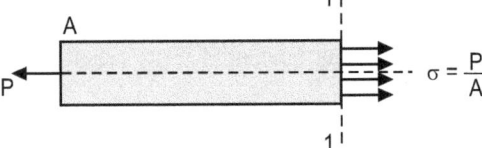

(b) Uniform normal tensile stresses produced by axial pull

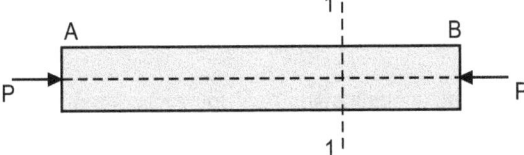

(c) Member subjected to axial compression (Push)

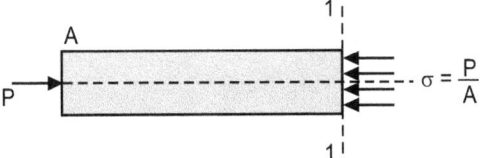

(d) Uniform normal compressive stresses produced by axial push

**Fig. 1.3**

Fig. 1.3 (a) shows member subjected to axial tensile force. Consider section 1-1 and FBD of part of the member as shown in Fig. 1.3 (b). For equilibrium, cross-section must offer a resistive force = applied force = P. This resistive force per unit area is called as *normal stress*.

Thus, for axial force, normal stress $= \sigma_n = \dfrac{P}{A}$ ... (1.1)

where, A = cross-sectional area of member.

Fig. 1.3 (c) and 1.3 (d) respectively show compressive force and corresponding normal stresses.

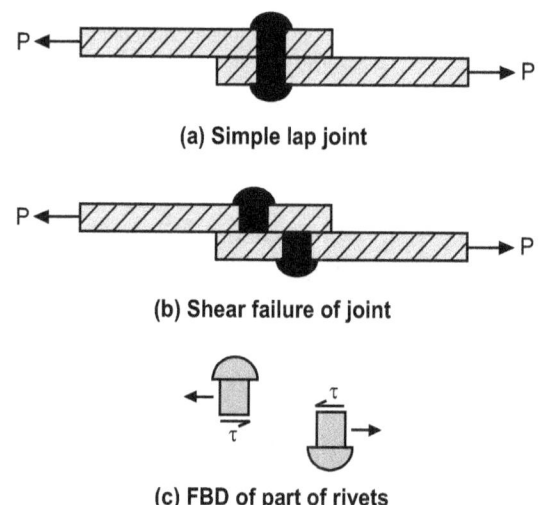

(a) Simple lap joint

(b) Shear failure of joint

(c) FBD of part of rivets

**Fig. 1.4**

Fig. 1.4 shows a simple riveted lap joint and its shear failure. It should be noted that, the force which causes failure of rivet is acting tangential to its cross-section and hence produces shear stress ($\tau$).

$$\text{Shear stress} = \tau = \dfrac{\text{Shear force}}{\text{Cross-sectional area}} \quad \text{... (1.2)}$$

### 1.3.2 Sign Convention and Unit of Stress

Normal tensile stress is considered positive while normal compressive stress is considered negative.

Shear stress '$\tau$' which produces clockwise couple is considered positive and that producing anticlockwise couple is considered negative as shown in Fig. 1.5.

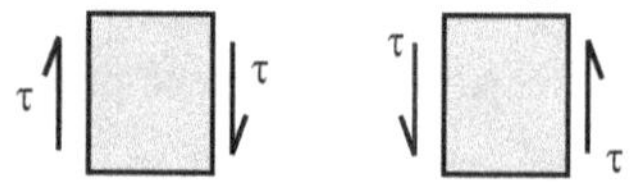

+ ve shear     − ve shear

**Fig. 1.5**

Unit of stress is MPa or GPa (mega or gega Pascal).

**Note :**  1 MPa = 1 N/mm²
            1 GPa = 1 kN/mm²
∴           1 GPa = $10^3$ MPa

## 1.4 STRAIN

When an elastic body is subjected to loads, it undergoes deformation. Strain is a *measure of deformation produced by application of external forces.*

### 1.4.1 Types of Strains

Strains are of two types : (i) Linear strain and (ii) Shear strain.

1. **Linear Strain :** It is the ratio of alteration in any dimension of the body to the respective original dimension.

Thus, Linear strain = $\varepsilon$ = $\dfrac{\text{Change in dimension}}{\text{Original dimension}}$ ... (1.3)

In case of an axial force, linear strain produced along the length is called as *longitudinal strain* while that produced along cross-section is called as *lateral strain*.

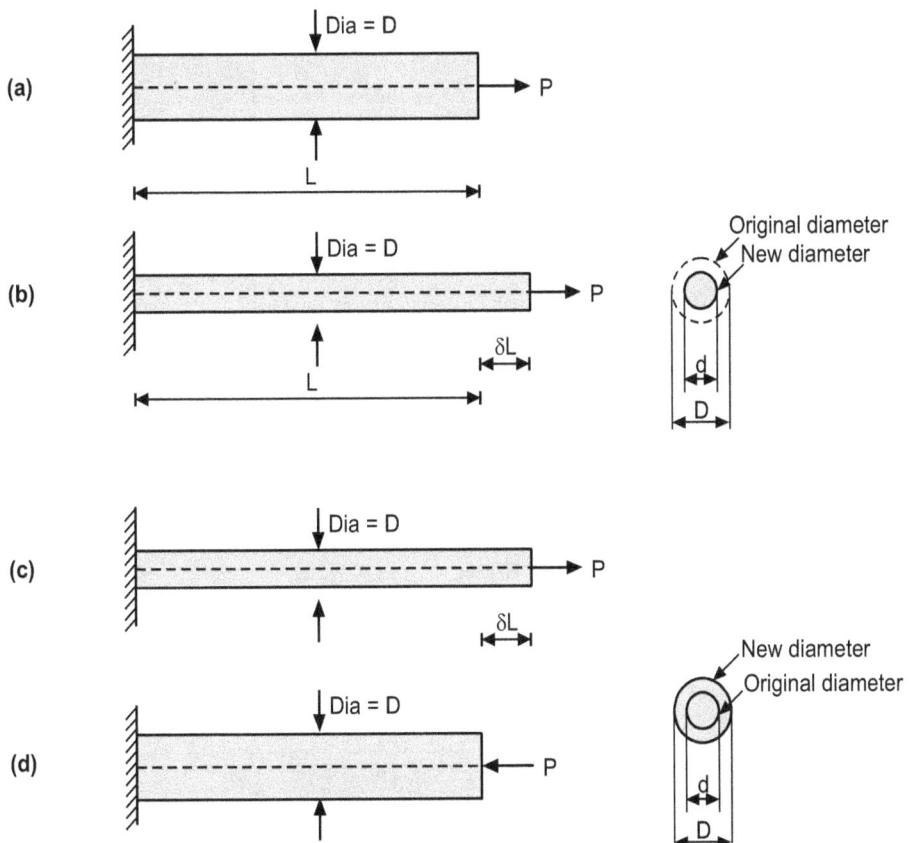

**Fig. 1.6 : Longitudinal and Lateral strains**

Linear strain may be tensile or compressive in nature. Axial pull causes increase in length while decrease in cross-sectional dimensions and axial push causes decrease in length while increase in cross-sectional dimensions as shown in Fig. 1.6.

Thus,

$$\text{Longitudinal strain} = \varepsilon_L = \frac{\text{Change in length}}{\text{Original length}}$$

∴
$$\varepsilon_L = \frac{\delta L}{L} \qquad \text{... (1.4)}$$

$$\text{Lateral strain} = \varepsilon_{Lt} = \frac{\text{Change in cross-sectional dimensions}}{\text{Original cross-sectional dimensions}} \qquad \text{... (1.5)}$$

For the example of circular bar considered in Fig. 1.6,

$$\text{Lateral strain} = \varepsilon_{Lt} = \frac{\text{Change in diameter}}{\text{Original diameter}}$$

**(ii) Shear strain :** If an element ABCD shown in Fig. 1.7 is subjected to shear stress $\tau$ on faces AB and CD, then it undergoes angular deformation $\phi$ as shown.

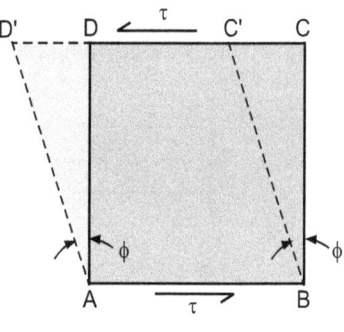

$$\text{Shear strain} = \gamma = \tan \phi = \frac{DD'}{AD} \qquad \text{... (1.6)}$$

Shear strain being very small,

$$\tan \phi \approx \phi$$

**Fig. 1.7**

### 1.4.2 Sign Convention and Unit of Strain

Linear strain tensile in nature is considered positive while that compressive in nature is considered negative.

Shear strain sign convention is same as explained in article 1.3.2.

Strain does not have any unit.

## 1.5 POISSON'S RATIO ($\mu$)

It is the ratio of lateral strain to linear strain.

Thus,
$$\mu = \frac{\text{Lateral strain}}{\text{Linear strain}} = \frac{\varepsilon_{Lt}}{\varepsilon_L} \qquad \text{... (1.7)}$$

The value of Poisson's ratio depends on type of material and for most metals it is 0.25 to 0.35.

## 1.6 HOOKE'S LAW AND MODULUS OF ELASTICITY (E)

By experiment it has been established for many structural materials that, within elastic limit, the elongation of the bar is proportional to tensile force. This linear relationship between the force and the elongation produced by it was formulated by Robert Hooke and hence known as Hooke's law.

If bars of same material but different lengths and different cross-sectional areas are experimented, it is observed that its elongation is proportional to tensile force, length and inversely proportional to the cross-sectional area.

Thus,
$$\delta L \propto \frac{PL}{A}$$

OR
$$\delta L = \frac{PL}{AE} \quad \ldots (1.8)$$

where, E = constant for any given material and is called as **Modulus of elasticity or Young's modulus.**

From equation (1.8), we can further write,
$$E = \frac{\sigma_n}{\varepsilon_L} \quad \ldots (1.9)$$

as
$$\sigma = \frac{P}{A} \text{ and } \varepsilon_L = \frac{\delta L}{L}$$

Thus, Hooke's law states that **stress is proportional to strain.** It should be noted that unit of Modulus of elasticity is same as that of stress.

## 1.7 MODULUS OF RIGIDITY OR SHEAR MODULUS (G)

The shear stress ($\tau$) is proportional to shear strain ($\gamma$) as long as proportional limit in shear is not exceeded.

Thus,
$$\tau \propto \gamma$$

i.e.
$$\tau = G\gamma$$

or
$$G = \frac{\tau}{\gamma} \quad \ldots (1.10)$$

where, G = Modulus of rigidity or Shear modulus

It should be noted that the unit of modulus of rigidity is same as that of stress.

## 1.8 VOLUMETRIC STRESS AND VOLUMETRIC STRAIN

When an elastic body is subjected to three mutually perpendicular equal direct stresses as shown in Fig. 1.8, it undergoes a change in volume without distortion of shape. Such a stress is called as *volumetric stress* ($\sigma_v$). Such a state of stress occurs when a cube is at a large depth in a liquid. The intensity of compressive pressure will have the same magnitude on all the faces. Such a state of stress is also called as *hydrostatic* state of stress.

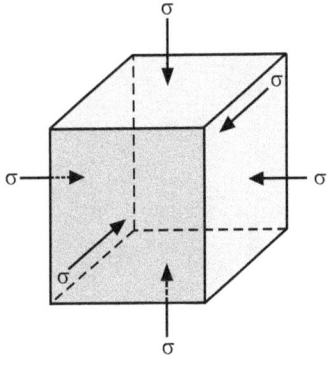

Fig. 1.8

The ratio of change in volume to original volume of a body is called as volumetric strain.
$$\varepsilon_v = \frac{\delta V}{V} \quad \ldots (1.11)$$

where,
$$\delta V = \text{Change in volume}$$
$$V = \text{Original volume}$$

Let L, b and d be the length, width and depth of an elastic member subjected to external force.

$$\text{Original volume} = V = L \cdot b \cdot d$$
$$\text{Change in volume} = \delta V = \delta L \cdot bd + \delta b \cdot L \cdot d + \delta d \cdot L \cdot b$$
$$\therefore \quad \text{Volumetric strain} = \varepsilon_v = \frac{\delta V}{V}$$
$$= \frac{\delta L \cdot bd + \delta b \cdot L \cdot d + \delta d \cdot L \cdot b}{L\,b\,d}$$
$$\frac{\delta V}{V} = \frac{\delta L}{L} + \frac{\delta b}{b} + \frac{\delta d}{d} \qquad \ldots (1.12)$$

*Volumetric strain is thus equal to algebraic sum of linear strains of the three sides.*

Thus, for axial loading,
$$\varepsilon_v = \varepsilon_L + \varepsilon_{Lt} + \varepsilon_{Lt}$$
$$= \varepsilon_L - \mu\,\varepsilon_L - \mu\,\varepsilon_L$$
$$= \varepsilon_L (1 - 2\mu) \qquad \ldots (1.13)$$

It should be noted that, lateral strain is of opposite sense to that of longitudinal strain.

## 1.9 BULK MODULUS (K)

It is defined as 'the ratio of volumetric stress ($\sigma_v$) to volumetric strain ($\varepsilon_v$)'.

Thus, $\quad$ Bulk modulus $= K = \dfrac{\sigma_v}{\varepsilon_v} \qquad \ldots (1.14)$

It should be noted that, the unit of Bulk modulus is same as that of stress.

## 1.10 STRESS-STRAIN CURVE

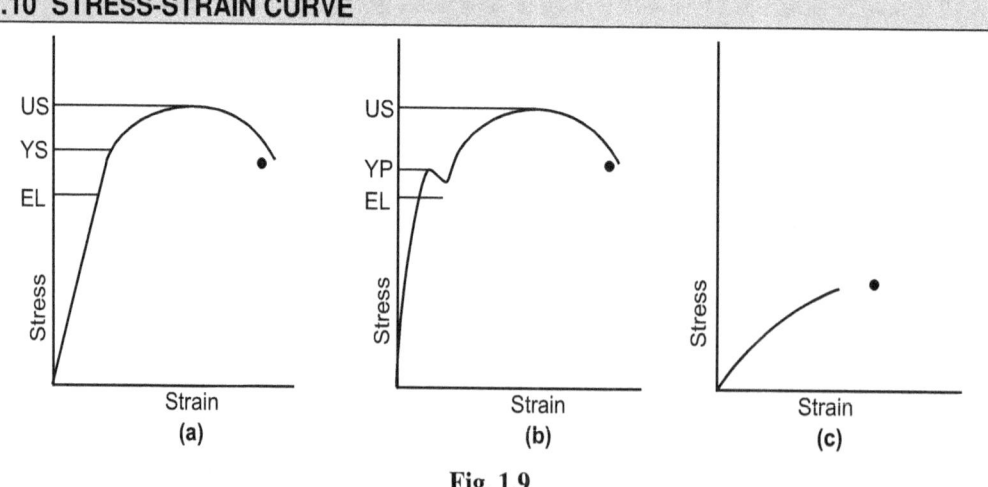

Fig. 1.9

In Fig. 1.9, typical stress-strain curves are shown for several common materials. Such curves are obtained by loading a specimen of the material in tension and recording simultaneous observations of both load and elongation. From these readings, stresses and strains are computed and curves are plotted.

**The Elastic Limit (EL)** is that stress below which the ratio of stress to strain is constant. See Fig. 1.9 (a) and 1.9 (b). More precisely we have defined the proportional limit or proportional elastic limit but the words are often used interchangeably.

**The Yield Point (YP)** is that stress at which elongation continues without increase in the load. See Fig. 1.9 (b). Low carbon steel is one of the few materials which exhibits a true yield point. For the majority of ductile materials, those which do not exhibit this characteristic, a corresponding value called yield strength is determined.

**Yield Strength (YS)** is that stress at which a predetermined permanent set is produced. See Fig. 1.9 (a). The yield point or yield strength each indicates the stress below which a given increment of stress will produce a small strain and above which the same increment of stress will produce a very much larger increment of strain.

The **Ultimate Strength (US)** is the ratio of maximum load sustained during a tensile test divided by the original cross-sectional area.

One or the other of the curves of Fig. 1.9 (a) and 1.9 (b) is a representative of most structural materials. However, the brittle materials, such as concrete and ordinary cast iron, usually exhibit tensile curves similar to Fig. 1.9 (c), breaking with negligible elongation.

The values of yield point, elastic limit and modulus of elasticity are generally determined from tension tests, the results may be applied to problems of compression as well.

## 1.11 ALLOWABLE STRESS AND FACTOR OF SAFETY

The factor of safety allows for errors in estimating design loads, some variations in material quality and perhaps most important of all, errors in the assumptions used in the design calculations. There are two ways of defining factor of safety :

(i) **Based on ultimate stress :** It is the ratio of ultimate stress to working stress.

(ii) **Based on yield stress :** It is the ratio of yield stress to working stress.

It is obvious that the factor of safety based on ultimate stress has larger value than that based on yield stress.

The factor of safety may vary depending upon the judgement of designers and depending upon their experience.

## 1.12 RELATION BETWEEN MODULUS OF ELASTICITY (E) AND MODULUS OF RIGIDITY (G)

Consider an elementary rectangular block ABCD of unit thickness, having shear stresses '$\tau$' acting on faces AD and BC as shown in Fig. 1.10. Assuming AD to be fixed, block ABCD will deform to AB'C'D. Let $\phi$ be the shear strain.

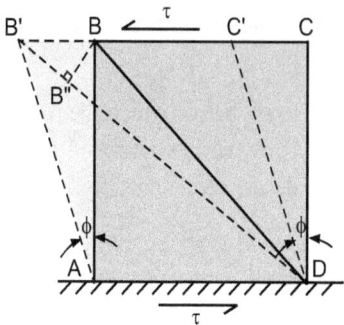

**Fig. 1.10**

$$\text{Linear strain of diagonal BD} = \frac{DB' - DB}{DB}$$

$$= \frac{B'B''}{DB}$$

$$= \frac{(BB')\cos 45}{\sqrt{2}\,AB}$$

$$\varepsilon_{BD} = \frac{1}{2}\left(\frac{BB'}{AB}\right) = \frac{1}{2}(\phi) \text{ (Tensile)} \qquad \ldots (1.15)$$

Similarly, the linear strain of the diagonal AC is also $\frac{1}{2}(\phi)$, but it is compressive in nature.

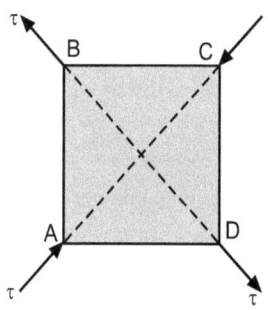

**Fig. 1.11**

Linear strain of diagonal BD can also be derived by considering direct tensile stress $\tau$ across the plane AC, accompanied by the direct compressive stress across the plane BD as shown in Fig. 1.11. This is an equivalent of stress system considered in Fig. 1.10. The combined effect of the two direct stresses on diagonal BD will therefore be tensile strain of magnitude

$$\varepsilon_{BD} = \frac{\tau}{E}(1+\mu) \qquad \ldots (1.16)$$

This linear strain is already found to be $\frac{1}{2}(\phi)$.

∴ Equating equations (1.15) and (1.16), we get

$$\frac{\tau}{E}(1+\mu) = \frac{1}{2}(\phi)$$

$$\frac{\tau}{E}(1+\mu) = \frac{1}{2}\left(\frac{\tau}{G}\right)$$

∴ $$\mathbf{E = 2\,G\,(1+\mu)} \qquad \ldots (1.17)$$

## 1.13 RELATION BETWEEN MODULUS OF ELASTICITY (E) & BULK MODULUS (K)

Consider a cube of side 'L' with its faces subjected to direct stresses of intensity ($\sigma$) as shown in Fig. 1.12.

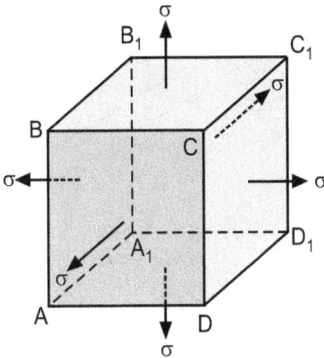

**Fig. 1.12**

The linear strain in any one direction is given by generalised Hooke's law,

Thus, $\dfrac{\delta L}{L} = \dfrac{1}{E}(\sigma - \mu\sigma - \mu\sigma)$

$$= \dfrac{\sigma}{E}(1 - 2\mu) \qquad \text{... (1.18)}$$

where, $\mu$ = Poisson's ratio

Original volume of cube, $V = L^3$

$\therefore \qquad \delta V = 3L^2\, \delta L$

$\therefore \qquad$ Volumetric strain $= \varepsilon_V = \dfrac{\delta V}{V} = \dfrac{3L^2\, \delta L}{L^3} = 3 \cdot \dfrac{\delta L}{L} \qquad \text{... (1.19)}$

Substituting for $\dfrac{\delta L}{L}$ from equation (1.18), we get

$$\varepsilon_V = 3 \cdot \left[\dfrac{\sigma}{E}(1 - 2\mu)\right] \qquad \text{... (1.20)}$$

Bulk modulus, $\quad K = \dfrac{\sigma}{\varepsilon_V} = \dfrac{\sigma}{\dfrac{3\sigma}{E}(1 - 2\mu)}$

$\therefore \qquad E = 3K(1 - 2\mu) \qquad \text{... (1.21)}$

From equations (1.17) and (1.21), the relation between four elastic constants is given by

$$E = 2G(1 + \mu) = 3K(1 - 2\mu) \qquad \text{... (1.22)}$$

### SOLVED EXAMPLES

**Example 1.1 :** A 2.8 m long member is 60 mm deep and 40 mm wide in cross-section. It is subjected to axial tensile force of 210 kN as shown in Fig. 1.13. Determine (i) change in length, (ii) change in cross-sectional dimensions, (iii) change in volume. Assume E = 200 GPa, $\mu$ = 0.3.

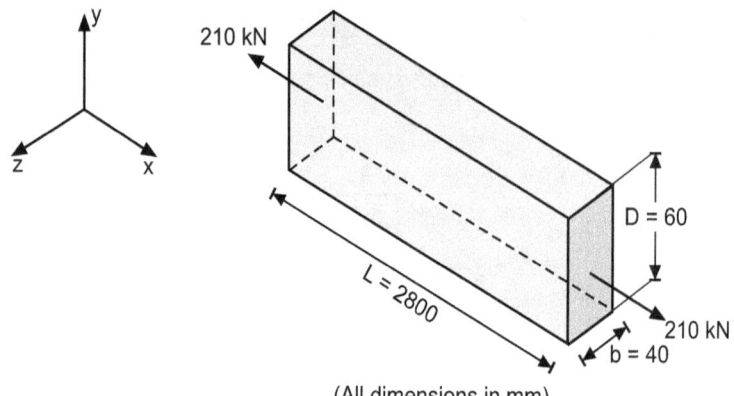

(All dimensions in mm)

**Fig. 1.13 : Given member**

**Data :** As shown in Fig. 1.13, E = 200 GPa, $\mu$ = 0.3.

**Required :** $\delta L$, $\delta b$, $\delta D$, $\delta V$.

**Concept :** Standard formulae.

**Solution :** (i) Geometric properties :

$$\text{Cross-sectional area} = A = 60 \times 40 = 2400 \text{ mm}^2.$$

(ii) Stresses and strains :

$$\text{Normal stress} = \sigma = \frac{P}{A} = \frac{210 \times 10^3}{2400} = 87.5 \text{ MPa (Tensile)}$$

$$\text{Longitudinal strain} = \varepsilon_L = \frac{\sigma}{E} = \frac{87.5}{200 \times 10^3} = 4.375 \times 10^{-4} \text{ (Tensile)}$$

$$\text{Lateral strain} = \varepsilon_{Lt} = \mu \cdot \varepsilon_L = 0.3 \times 4.375 \times 10^{-4}$$
$$= 1.3125 \times 10^{-4} \text{ (Compressive)}$$

(iii) Change in dimensions :

$$\text{Change in length,} \quad \delta L = \varepsilon_L \cdot L$$
$$= 4.375 \times 10^{-4} \times 2800$$
$$= \textbf{1.225 mm (increase)}$$

$$\text{Change in depth,} \quad \delta D = \varepsilon_{Lt} \cdot D$$
$$= 1.3125 \times 10^{-4} \times 60$$
$$= \textbf{0.0078 mm (decrease)}$$

$$\text{Change in width,} \quad \delta b = \varepsilon_{Lt} \cdot b$$
$$= 1.3125 \times 10^{-4} \times 40$$
$$= \textbf{0.0052 mm (decrease)}$$

**(iv) Change in volume :**

$$\text{Volumetric strain, } \varepsilon_v = \varepsilon_x + \varepsilon_y + \varepsilon_z$$
$$= \varepsilon_L + \varepsilon_{Lt} + \varepsilon_{Lt}$$
$$= \varepsilon(1 - 2\mu)$$
$$= 4.375 \times 10^{-4} (1 - 2 \times 0.3)$$
$$= 1.75 \times 10^{-4}$$
$$\delta V = \varepsilon_v \cdot V = (1.75 \times 10^{-4})(2800 \times 60 \times 40)$$
$$= \mathbf{1176 \text{ mm}^3 \text{ (increase)}}$$

**Example 1.2 :** Determine the change in volume of 25 mm cube of aluminium (E = 70 GPa) and $\mu = \frac{1}{3}$ when dropped at a distance of 8 km in the ocean.

Assume density of water = 10 kN/m³.

**Data :** Cube size : 25 mm, E = 70 GPa, $\mu = \frac{1}{3}$, $\gamma_{water}$ = 10 kN/m³, h = 8 km

**Required :** Change in volume.

**Concept :** Water pressure = Volumetric stress = $\sigma_v = \gamma_h$

$$\text{Bulk modulus} = K = \frac{E}{3(1 - 2\mu)}$$

$$\text{Volumetric strain} = \varepsilon_v = \frac{\sigma_v}{K}$$

**Solution :** (i) Volumetric stress :
$$\sigma_v = \gamma_h = 10 \times 8000 = 8 \times 10^4 \text{ kN/m}^2 = 80 \text{ MPa}$$

(ii) Bulk modulus (K) :
$$K = \frac{E}{3(1 - 2\mu)} = \frac{70 \times 10^3}{3\left(1 - 2 \times \frac{1}{3}\right)} = 70 \times 10^3 \text{ MPa}$$

(iii) Change in volume ($\delta V$) :
$$\text{Volumetric strain} = \varepsilon_v = \frac{\delta V}{V} = \frac{\sigma_v}{K}$$

$$\therefore \quad \delta V = \frac{\sigma_v}{K} \cdot V$$
$$= \frac{80}{70 \times 10^3} \times (25)^3$$
$$= \mathbf{17.85 \text{ mm}^3 \text{ (decrease)}}$$

**Example 1.3 :** A bar of certain material is 60 mm × 60 mm in cross-section is subjected to an axial pull of 230 kN. The extension over a length of 120 mm is 0.07 mm and decrease in each side is 0.007 mm. Calculate all the elastic constants for material.

**Data :** Cross-section of member = 60 mm × 60 mm, P = 230 kN (Tensile)

$\delta L$ = 0.07 mm increase, L = 120 mm, $\delta b$ = 0.007 mm (decrease)

**Required :** Elastic constants.

**Concept :** Standard formulae.

**Solution :** (i) Geometric properties :

Cross-sectional area, A = 60 × 60 = 3600 mm²

(ii) Stresses and strains :

$$\text{Normal stress} = \sigma = \frac{P}{A} = \frac{230 \times 10^3}{3600} = 63.89 \text{ MPa}$$

$$\text{Longitudinal strain} = \varepsilon_L = \frac{\delta L}{L} = \frac{0.07}{120} = 5.83 \times 10^{-4}$$

$$\text{Lateral strain} = \varepsilon_{Lt} = \frac{\delta b}{b} = \frac{0.007}{60} = 1.167 \times 10^{-4}$$

(iii) Elastic constants :

$$\text{Young's modulus,} \quad E = \frac{\sigma}{\varepsilon_L} = \frac{63.89}{5.83 \times 10^{-4}} = 109.58 \times 10^3 \text{ MPa} = \mathbf{109.58 \text{ GPa}}$$

$$\text{Poisson's ratio,} \quad \mu = \frac{\varepsilon_{Lt}}{\varepsilon_L} = \frac{1.167 \times 10^{-4}}{5.83 \times 10^{-4}} = \mathbf{0.2}$$

$$\text{Shear modulus,} \quad G = \frac{E}{2(1+\mu)} = \frac{109.58}{2(1+0.2)} = \mathbf{45.66 \text{ GPa}}$$

$$\text{Bulk modulus,} \quad K = \frac{E}{3(1-2\mu)} = \frac{109.58}{3(1-2 \times 0.2)} = \mathbf{60.87 \text{ GPa}}$$

**Example 1.4 :** When a metal tube of external diameter 20 mm and internal diameter 15 mm was subjected to an axial load of 23 kN, the extension on gauge length of 60 mm was 0.05 mm and decrease in outer diameter was 0.005 mm. Find Young's modulus of elasticity (E), Poisson's ratio ($\mu$) and change in volume ($\delta V$) assuming length of tube = 700 mm.

**Data :** D = 20 mm, d = 15 mm, P = 23 kN, $\delta L$ = 0.05 mm for gauge length of 60 mm,

$\delta D$ = 0.005 mm (decrease), Length of tube = L = 700 mm.

**Required :** E, $\mu$ and change in volume ($\delta V$).

**Concept :** Standard formulae.

**Solution :** (i) Geometric properties :

$$\text{Cross-sectional area,} \quad A = \frac{\pi}{4}(D^2 - d^2)$$

$$= \frac{\pi}{4}(20^2 - 15^2)$$

$$= 137.44 \text{ mm}^2$$

(ii) Stress and strain :

$$\text{Normal stress,} \quad \sigma = \frac{P}{A} = \frac{23 \times 10^3}{137.44} = 167.34 \text{ MPa}$$

Longitudinal strain, $\varepsilon_L = \dfrac{\delta L}{L} = \dfrac{0.05}{60} = 8.33 \times 10^{-4}$

Lateral strain, $\varepsilon_{Lt} = \dfrac{\delta D}{D} = \dfrac{0.005}{20} = 2.5 \times 10^{-4}$

(iii) Young's modulus (E) and Poisson's ratio ($\mu$):

$$E = \dfrac{\text{Normal stress}}{\text{Longitudinal strain}} = \dfrac{167.34}{8.33 \times 10^{-4}}$$

$$= 200.89 \times 10^3 \text{ MPa} = 200.89 \text{ GPa}$$

$$\mu = \dfrac{\text{Lateral strain}}{\text{Longitudinal strain}} = \dfrac{2.5 \times 10^{-4}}{8.33 \times 10^{-4}} = 0.3$$

(iv) Change in volume ($\delta V$):

Volumetric strain, $\varepsilon_V = \varepsilon_L (1 - 2\mu)$

$$= 8.33 \times 10^{-4} (1 - 2 \times 0.3)$$

$$= 3.332 \times 10^{-4}$$

Change in volume, $\delta V = \varepsilon_V \cdot V$

$$= 3.332 \times 10^{-4} (137.44 \times 700)$$

$$= \mathbf{32.05 \text{ mm}^3 \text{ (increase)}}$$

**Example 1.5 :** A bar of cross-section 8 mm × 8 mm is subjected to axial pull of 7 kN. The lateral dimensions of the bar are found to have reduced by $1.5 \times 10^{-3}$ mm. Find Poisson's ratio and Modulus of elasticity, assuming G = 80 GPa.

**Data :** Cross-section of member = 8 mm × 8 mm, axial force = 7 kN, change in cross-sectional dimension = $1.5 \times 10^{-3}$ mm, G = 80 GPa.

**Required :** Modulus of elasticity (E) and Poisson's ratio ($\mu$).

**Concept :** Standard formulae.

**Solution :** (i) Stresses and strains :

Normal stress, $\sigma = \dfrac{P}{A} = \dfrac{7 \times 10^3}{8 \times 8} = 109.375 \text{ MPa}$

Longitudinal strain, $\varepsilon_L = \dfrac{\sigma}{E} = \dfrac{109.375}{E}$

Lateral strain, $\varepsilon_{Lt} = $ Change in c/s dimension / Original dimension

$$= \dfrac{1.5 \times 10^{-3}}{8}$$

$$= 1.875 \times 10^{-4}$$

(ii) Modulus of elasticity and Poisson's ratio :

We have, $\varepsilon_{Lt} = \mu \, \varepsilon_L$

$$1.875 \times 10^{-4} = \mu \times \dfrac{109.375}{E}$$

$$E = 583.33 \times 10^3 \, \mu \qquad \text{...(i)}$$

Also, $\quad E = 2G(1+\mu)$

∴ $\quad E = 2 \times 80 \times 10^3 (1+\mu)$
$$= 160 \times 10^3 (1+\mu) \qquad \text{...(ii)}$$

Equating equations (i) and (ii),
$$583.33 \times 10^3 \, \mu = 160 \times 10^3 (1+\mu)$$

∴ $\quad \mu = 0.377$, put in (i)
$$E = 220.47 \times 10^3 \text{ MPa}$$
$$= \mathbf{220.47 \text{ GPa}}$$

**Example 1.6 :** A steel punch can be stressed to a maximum compressive stress of 800 MPa. Find the least diameter of hole which can be punched through a plate of 16 mm thickness if its ultimate shear strength is 300 MPa.

**Data :** Ultimate compressive and shear stress = 800 MPa and 300 MPa respectively, thickness of plate = 16 mm

**Required :** Diameter of hole which can be punched.

**Concept :** Normal and shear stress.

**Solution :** Let $\phi$ be the diameter of hole in mm.

Maximum force on punch $= \dfrac{\pi}{4} \phi^2 \cdot \sigma$

$$= \dfrac{\pi}{4} (\phi)^2 \times 800 \qquad \text{...(i)}$$

Punching shear strength $= (\pi \phi t) \tau$
$$= \pi \phi \times 16 \times 300 \qquad \text{...(ii)}$$

Equating (i) and (ii),
$$\dfrac{\pi}{4} (\phi)^2 \times 800 = \pi \phi \times 16 \times 300$$

∴ $\quad \phi = \mathbf{24 \text{ mm}}$

**Example 1.7 :** A flat plate is connected to gusset plate by four rivets as shown in Fig. 1.14. The normal stress for the flat plate is 120 MPa due to the force P. Find suitable diameter of rivets if permissible shear stress for rivets is 90 MPa. Neglect weakening of plate due to rivet holes.

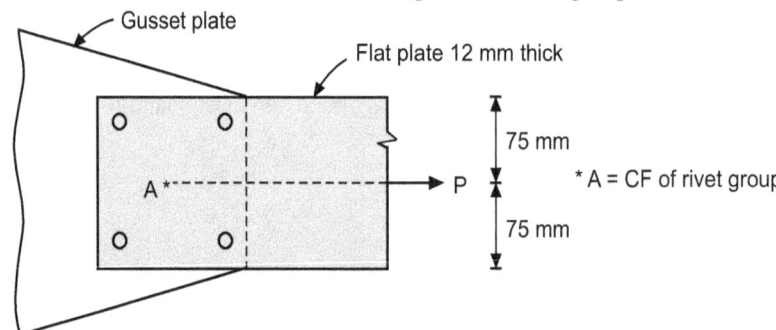

Fig. 1.14

**Data :** $\sigma_{flat}$ = 120 MPa, $\tau_{rivets}$ = 90 MPa

**Required :** Diameter of rivets.

**Concept :** Normal and shear stress.

**Solution :** (i) Axial force for flat plate,
$$P = (\sigma)_{flat} \times c/s \text{ area}$$
$$= 120 \times (150 \times 12)$$
$$= 216000 \text{ N}$$

(ii) Shear stress for rivets :
$$\text{Force on each rivet} = \frac{216000}{4} = 54000 \text{ N}$$

Let $\phi$ be the diameter of rivets in mm.
$$\text{Shear stress for each rivet} = \frac{\text{Force on rivet}}{c/s \text{ area}}$$
$$90 = \frac{54000}{\frac{\pi}{4}(\phi)^2}$$

$\therefore \quad \phi$ = **27.63 mm**

**Example 1.8 :** Two wooden pieces are joined as shown in Fig. 1.15. Find the safe value of axial load P if the normal stress for wood is limited to 20 MPa and shear stress for joint is limited to 5 MPa.

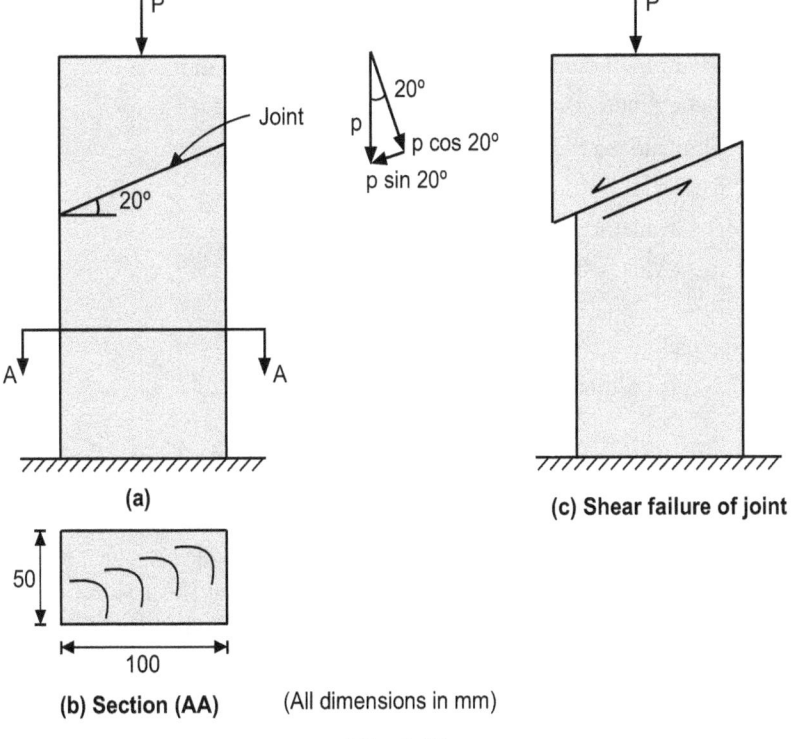

(All dimensions in mm)

**Fig. 1.15**

**Data :** Normal stress $\sigma > 20$ MPa, shear stress of joint $\tau > 5$ MPa.

**Required :** Safe value of load P.

**Concept :** Normal stress and shear stress.

**Solution :** (i) Magnitude of 'P' from normal stress criteria :

Let P be the value of load in kN.

$$\sigma = \frac{P}{A}$$

$$20 = \frac{P \times 10^3}{50 \times 100}$$

$$\therefore \quad P = 100 \text{ kN} \quad \ldots \text{(i)}$$

(ii) Magnitude of 'P' from shear stress criteria :

$$\tau = \frac{\text{Shear force for joint}}{\text{c/s area of joint}}$$

$$5 = \frac{P \sin 20° \times 10^3}{100 \sec 20° \times 50}$$

$$P = \mathbf{77.78 \text{ kN}} \quad \ldots \text{(ii)}$$

Safe value of P = **77.78 kN** (least of (i) and (ii)).

**Example 1.9 :** A solid cylinder 100 mm high and 50 mm in diameter is inserted in another cylinder of 50 mm inner diameter and the surfaces of the two cylinders in contact are glued together. If the ultimate shear stress of the glue is 2.6 N/mm², calculate the ultimate load under which the joint will fail.

**Data :** h = 100 mm, for outer cylinder inner diameter d = 50 mm,

for inner cylinder, d = 50 mm, $\tau_{max}$ = 2.6 N/mm²

**Required :** Ultimate load.

**Concept :** Shear stress.

**Solution :** (i) Geometric properties :

$$\text{Area under shear} = 100 \times \pi \times 50$$

$$= 5000 \pi \text{ mm}^2$$

(ii) Ultimate load :

$$\text{Ultimate load} = \text{Area under shear} \times \tau_{max}$$

$$= 5000 \pi \times 2.6$$

$$= 40840.7 \text{ N}$$

$$= \mathbf{40.84 \text{ kN}}$$

**Example 1.10 :** A forked end carries an axial pin 25 mm diameter which is in double shear. Calculate the ultimate and safe loads for this pin if the ultimate shear stress of the material is 200 MPa and the ratio between the ultimate and safe stress is to be 5 : 1.

**Data :** $\phi_{pin}$ = 25 mm, $\tau_{max}$ = 200 MPa, $\frac{\tau_{max}}{\tau_{safe}} = \frac{5}{1}$

**Required :** Ultimate and safe loads for the pin.

**Concept :** Normal and shear stress.

**Solution :** (i) Geometric properties :

$$\text{Cross-sectional area of the pin, } A_p = \frac{\pi}{4}(25)^2$$
$$= 490 \text{ mm}^2$$

(ii) $\quad$ Area under shear $= 2 \cdot A_p$
$$= 2 \times 490$$
$$= 980 \text{ mm}^2$$

(iii) $\quad$ Ultimate load $= 980 \times 200$
$$= 196 \times 10^3 \text{ N}$$
$$= 196 \text{ kN}$$

(iv) $\quad$ Safe load $= \dfrac{196}{5} = \mathbf{39.2 \text{ kN}}$

## 1.14 GENERALISED HOOKE'S LAW

When an elastic body is subjected to normal stresses in x, y and z directions as shown in Fig. 1.16, the corresponding strains in these directions are given by

$$\left. \begin{array}{l} \varepsilon_x = \dfrac{1}{E}(\sigma_x - \mu\sigma_y - \mu\sigma_z) \\[4pt] \varepsilon_y = \dfrac{1}{E}(\sigma_y - \mu\sigma_x - \mu\sigma_z) \\[4pt] \varepsilon_z = \dfrac{1}{E}(\sigma_z - \mu\sigma_x - \mu\sigma_y) \end{array} \right\} \quad \dots (1.23)$$

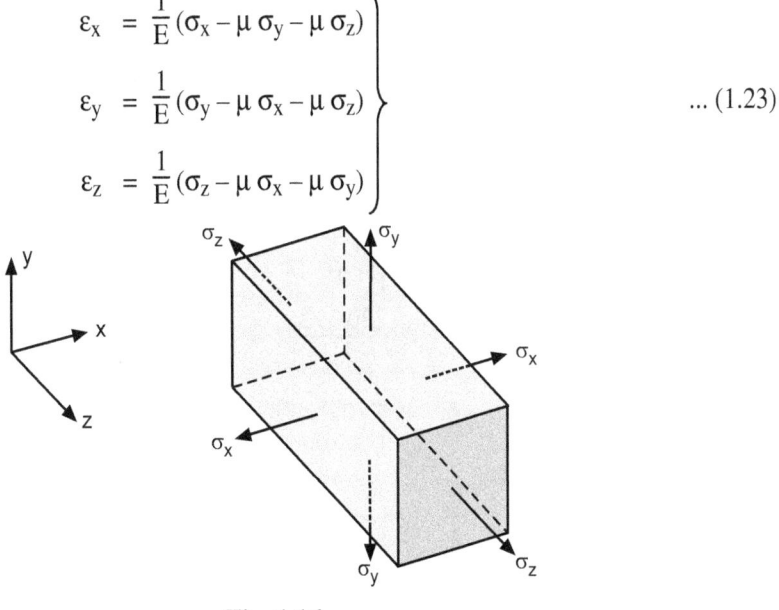

**Fig. 1.16**

**Example 1.11 :** A rectangular bar 200 mm long, 70 mm wide and 20 mm thick is loaded with an axial tensile load of 150 kN; together with a normal compressive force of 1500 kN on 70 mm × 200 mm face and tensile force of 250 kN on 20 mm × 200 mm face. Calculate change in length, width, thickness and volume. Assume E = 200 GPa and μ = 0.3.

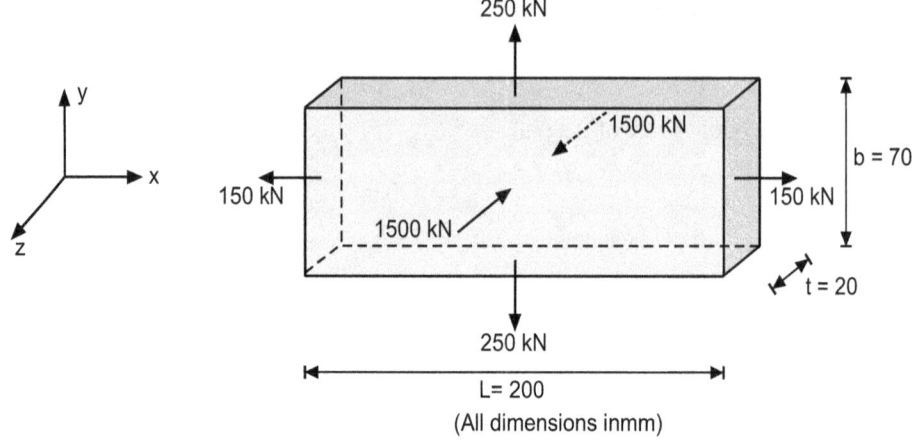

Fig. 1.17

**Data :** As shown in Fig. 1.17, E = 200 GPa, μ = 0.3.
**Required :** Change in length, width, thickness and volume.
**Concept :** Generalised Hooke's law.
**Solution :** (i) Normal stresses :

$$\sigma_x = \frac{150 \times 10^3}{20 \times 70} = 107.14 \text{ MPa}$$

$$\sigma_y = \frac{250 \times 10^3}{200 \times 20} = 62.5 \text{ MPa}$$

$$\sigma_z = -\frac{1500 \times 10^3}{200 \times 70} = -107.14 \text{ MPa}$$

**Note :** – ve sign for $\sigma_z$ is due to its compressive nature.

(ii) Strains :

$$\varepsilon_x = \frac{1}{E}(\sigma_x - \mu\sigma_y - \mu\sigma_z)$$

$$= \frac{1}{E}(107.14 - 0.3 \times 62.5 - 0.3(-107.14))$$

$$= \frac{120.532}{E}$$

$$\varepsilon_y = \frac{1}{E}(\sigma_y - \mu\sigma_x - \mu\sigma_z)$$

$$= \frac{1}{E}(62.5 - 0.3 \times 107.14 - 0.3(-107.14))$$

$$= \frac{62.5}{E}$$

$$\varepsilon_z = \frac{1}{E}(\sigma_z - \mu\sigma_x - \mu\sigma_y)$$

$$= \frac{1}{E}(-107.14 - 0.3 \times 107.14 - 0.3 \times 62.5)$$

$$= -\frac{158.03}{E}$$

(iii) Change in dimensions :

$$\delta L = \varepsilon_x \cdot L = \frac{120.532}{E} \times 200$$

$$= \frac{120.532}{200 \times 10^3} \times 200 = \textbf{0.12 mm (increase)}$$

$$\delta b = \varepsilon_y \cdot b = \frac{62.5}{E} \times 70$$

$$= \frac{62.5}{200 \times 10^3} \times 70 = \textbf{0.0218 mm (increase)}$$

$$\delta t = \varepsilon_z \cdot t = \frac{-158.03}{E} \times 20 = \frac{-158.03}{200 \times 10^3} \times 20$$

$$= -0.0158 \text{ mm} = \textbf{0.0158 mm (decrease)}$$

(iv) Change in volume :

Volumetric strain, $\varepsilon_v = \varepsilon_x + \varepsilon_y + \varepsilon_z$

$$= \frac{1}{E}(120.532 + 62.5 - 158.03)$$

$$= \frac{25.002}{E}$$

Change in volume $= \varepsilon_v \cdot V$

$$= \frac{25.002}{200 \times 10^3} \times (200 \times 70 \times 20)$$

$$= \textbf{35 mm}^3 \textbf{ (increase)}$$

**Example 1.12 :** A mild steel bar 250 mm long and 100 mm × 100 mm in cross-section is subjected to longitudinal axial compressive force of 1000 kN. Determine the values of lateral forces necessary to prevent any transverse strain. Also find change in length and volume. Assume E = 200 GPa and $\mu$ = 0.3.

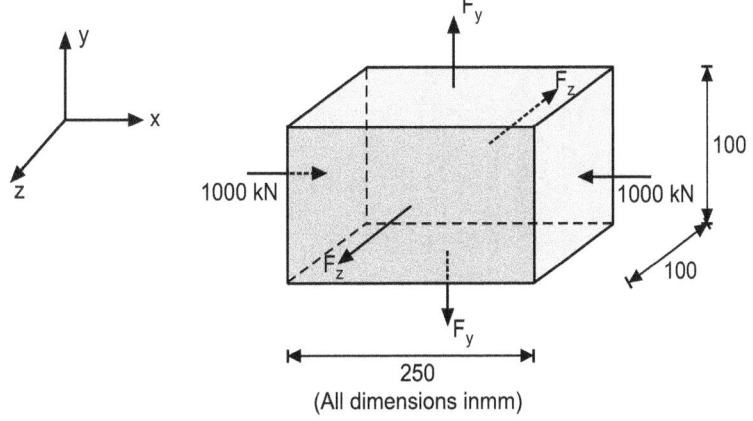

**Fig. 1.18**

**Data :** As shown in Fig. 1.18, E = 200 GPa, μ = 0.3.

**Required :** Forces $F_y$ and $F_z$ in y and z directions respectively such that there is no transverse strain. Let these forces be tensile in nature as shown.

**Concept :** Generalised Hooke's law.

**Solution :** (i) Normal stresses :

$$\sigma_x = \frac{-1000 \times 10^3}{100 \times 100} = -100 \text{ MPa}$$

$$\sigma_y = \frac{F_y \times 10^3}{250 \times 100} = \frac{F_y}{25} \text{ MPa}$$

$$\sigma_z = \frac{F_z \times 10^3}{250 \times 100} = \frac{F_z}{25} \text{ MPa}$$

where, $F_y$ and $F_z$ are forces assumed in kN.

(ii) Strains :

$$\varepsilon_x = \frac{1}{E}(\sigma_x - \mu\sigma_y - \mu\sigma_z)$$

$$= \frac{1}{E}\left(-100 - 0.3 \times \frac{F_y}{25} - 0.3 \times \frac{F_z}{25}\right)$$

$$= -\frac{1}{E}(100 + 0.012\, F_y + 0.012\, F_z)$$

$$\varepsilon_y = \frac{1}{E}(\sigma_y - \mu\sigma_x - \mu\sigma_z)$$

$$= \frac{1}{E}\left(\frac{F_y}{25} - 0.3 \times (-100) - 0.3 \times \frac{F_z}{25}\right)$$

$$= \frac{1}{E}(0.04\, F_y + 30 - 0.012\, F_z)$$

$$\varepsilon_z = \frac{1}{E}(\sigma_z - \mu\sigma_x - \mu\sigma_y)$$

$$= \frac{1}{E}\left(\frac{F_z}{25} - 0.3 \times (-100) - 0.3 \times \frac{F_y}{25}\right)$$

$$= \frac{1}{E}(0.04\, F_z + 30 - 0.012\, F_y)$$

(iii) Magnitudes of $F_y$ and $F_z$ for no transverse strains :

It is given that transverse strains $\varepsilon_y$ and $\varepsilon_z$ are zero.

$$\therefore \quad \frac{1}{E}(0.04\, F_y + 30 - 0.012\, F_z) = 0 \quad \ldots \text{(i)}$$

$$\frac{1}{E}(0.04\, F_z + 30 - 0.012\, F_y) = 0 \quad \ldots \text{(ii)}$$

Solving equations (i) and (ii), we get

$$F_y = -1071.42 \text{ kN}$$
$$F_z = -1071.42 \text{ kN}$$

**Note :** –ve sign indicates compression.

(iv) Change in length :

$$\varepsilon_x = -\frac{1}{E}(100 + 0.012 \times (-1071.42) + 0.012 \times (-1071.42))$$

$$= \frac{-74.28}{E}$$

$$\delta L = \varepsilon_x \cdot L$$

$$\delta L = \frac{-74.28}{200 \times 10^3} \times 250$$

$$= -0.093 \text{ mm} = \mathbf{0.093 \text{ mm (decrease)}}$$

(v) Change in volume :

Volumetric strain $= \varepsilon_v = \varepsilon_x + \varepsilon_y + \varepsilon_z$

$$= \frac{-74.28}{E} + 0 + 0$$

$$= \frac{-74.28}{E}$$

Change in volume $= \delta V = \varepsilon_v \cdot V$

$$= \frac{-74.28}{200 \times 10^3}(250 \times 100 \times 100)$$

$$= -928.5 \text{ mm}^3$$

$$= \mathbf{928.5 \text{ mm}^3 \text{ (decrease)}}$$

**Example 1.13 :** A plate of uniform thickness is subjected to stresses $\sigma_x$ and $\sigma_y$ as shown in Fig. 1.19. Due to these stresses length of the plate increases by 0.6 mm while width increases by 0.09 mm. Assuming E = 200 GPa and $\mu$ = 0.25, find (i) stresses $\sigma_x$ and $\sigma_y$, (ii) change in thickness, (iii) change in volume.

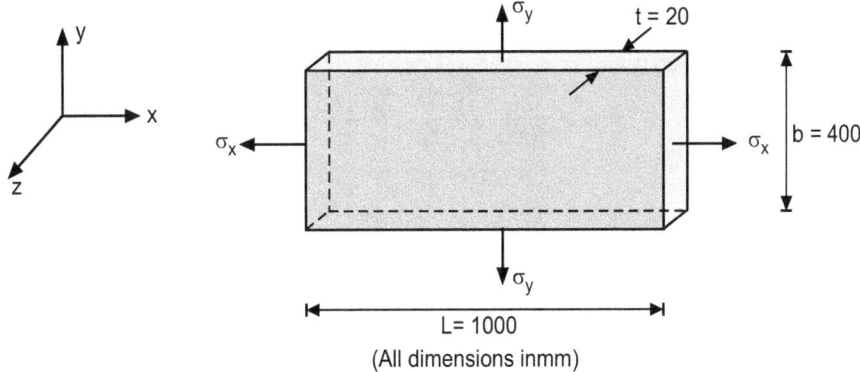

Fig. 1.19

**Data :** As shown in Fig. 1.19, E = 200 GPa, $\mu$ = 0.25, $\delta L$ = 0.6 mm, $\delta b$ = 0.09 mm

**Required :** (i) $\sigma_x$, $\sigma_y$, (ii) $\delta t$, (iii) $\delta V$.

**Concept :** Generalised Hooke's law.

**Solution :** (i) Stresses $\sigma_x$ and $\sigma_y$.

From generalised Hooke's law,

$$\varepsilon_x = \frac{1}{E}(\sigma_x - \mu\,\sigma_y)$$

$$\frac{0.6}{1000} = \frac{1}{E}(\sigma_x - 0.25\,\sigma_y) \quad \ldots \text{(i)}$$

$$\varepsilon_y = \frac{1}{E}(\sigma_y - \mu\,\sigma_x)$$

$$\frac{0.09}{400} = \frac{1}{\varepsilon}(\sigma_y - 0.25\,\sigma_x) \quad \ldots \text{(ii)}$$

Substituting the value of E, we get

$$\sigma_x - 0.25\,\sigma_y = 120 \quad \ldots \text{(i)}$$
$$\sigma_y - 0.25\,\sigma_x = 45 \quad \ldots \text{(ii)}$$

Solving equations (i) and (ii),

$$\sigma_x = 140 \text{ MPa} \quad \text{and} \quad \sigma_y = 80 \text{ MPa}$$

(ii) Change in thickness :

$$\varepsilon_z = \frac{\delta t}{t} = \frac{1}{E}(\sigma_z - \mu\,\sigma_x - \mu\,\sigma_y)$$

$$= \frac{1}{200 \times 10^3}(0 - 0.25 \times 140 - 0.25 \times 80)$$

$$= -2.75 \times 10^{-4}$$

$\therefore \quad \delta t = -2.75 \times 10^{-4} \times 20$

$$= \mathbf{0.0055 \text{ mm (decrease)}}$$

(iii) Change in volume :

Volumetric strain $= \varepsilon_v = \varepsilon_{xx} + \varepsilon_{yy} + \varepsilon_{zz}$

$$= \frac{0.6}{1000} + \frac{0.09}{400} - \frac{0.0055}{20}$$

$$= 5.5 \times 10^{-4}$$

Change in volume $= \delta V = \varepsilon_v \cdot V$

$$= 5.5 \times 10^{-4} (1000 \times 400 \times 20)$$

$$= \mathbf{4400 \text{ mm}^3 \text{ (increase)}}$$

---

**Example 1.14 :** A bar 30 mm diameter was subjected to tensile load of 54 kN. Measured extension on 300 mm gauge length was 0.112 mm and change in diameter was 0.00366 mm. Calculate Poisson's ratio and values of three elastic moduli.

**Data :** $d = 30$ mm, $P = 54$ kN, $l = 300$ mm, $\delta l = 0.112$ mm, $\delta d = 0.00366$ mm

**Required :** $\mu$, E, K and G.

**Concept :** Generalised Hooke's law.

**Solution :**

(i) $\quad$ Poisson's ratio $= \dfrac{\text{Lateral strain}}{\text{Linear strain}}$

$$\mu = \dfrac{(\delta d/d)}{\left(\dfrac{\delta l}{l}\right)} = \dfrac{(0.0036/30)}{(0.112/300)} = 0.32$$

(ii) $\quad \delta l = \dfrac{PL}{AE}$

$$0.112 = \dfrac{54 \times 10^3 \times 300}{\dfrac{\pi}{4} \times (30)^2 \times E}$$

∴ $\quad$ **E = 204627.78 N/mm²**

(iii) $\quad$ E = 3K (1 – 2μ)

$\quad$ 204627.78 = 3K (1 – 2 × 0.32)

∴ $\quad$ **K = 189470.17 N/mm²**

(iv) $\quad$ E = 2G (1 + μ)

$\quad$ 204627.78 = 2G (1 + 0.32)

∴ $\quad$ **G = 77510.52 N/mm²**

**Example 1.15 :** A metallic piece is subjected to forces as shown in Fig. 1.20. Determine the change in volume if E = 200 kN/mm² and Poisson's ratio μ = 0.25.

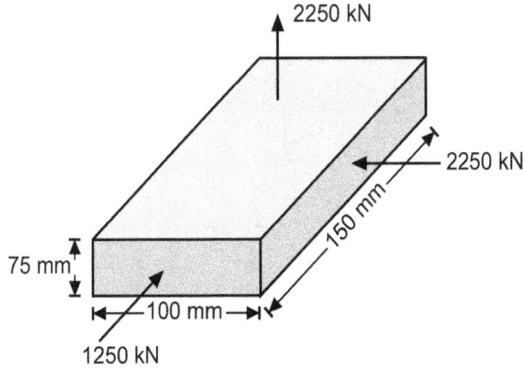

**Fig. 1.20**

**Data :** As shown in Fig. 1.20.

**Required :** Change in volume.

**Concept :** Generalised Hooke's law.

**Solution :**

(i) Normal stresses : $\sigma_x = \dfrac{-2250 \times 10^3}{75 \times 150} = -200$ MPa

$\sigma_y = \dfrac{2250 \times 10^3}{150 \times 100} = 150$ MPa

$\sigma_z = \dfrac{-1250 \times 10^3}{75 \times 100} = -166.67$ MPa

**Note :** – ve sign is due to its compressive stress.

(ii) Strains :
$$\varepsilon_x = \dfrac{1}{E}(\sigma_x - \mu \sigma_y - \mu \sigma_z)$$

$$= \dfrac{1}{E}[-200 - 0.25 \times 150 - 0.25 \times (-166.67)]$$

$$= -\dfrac{195.83}{200 \times 10^3} = 9.79 \times 10^{-4}$$

$$\varepsilon_y = \dfrac{1}{E}(\sigma_y - \mu\sigma_x - \mu\sigma_z)$$

$$= \dfrac{1}{E}[150 - 0.25 \times (-200) - 0.25 (-166.67)]$$

$$= \dfrac{241.67}{E} = \dfrac{241.67}{200 \times 10^3}$$

$$= 1.208 \times 10^{-3}$$

$$\varepsilon_z = \dfrac{1}{E}(\sigma_z - \mu\sigma_x - \mu\sigma_y)$$

$$= \dfrac{1}{E}[-166.67 - 0.25 \times 150 - 0.25 \times (-200)]$$

$$= -\dfrac{154.17}{200 \times 10^3} = -7.71 \times 10^{-4}$$

(iii) Change in volume :

Volumetric strain $= \varepsilon_v = \varepsilon_x + \varepsilon_y + \varepsilon_z$

$$= \dfrac{1}{E}(-195.83 + 241.67 - 154.17)$$

$$= -\dfrac{108.33}{200 \times 10^3} = -5.42 \times 10^{-4}$$

$\therefore \quad \delta V = -5.42 \times 10^{-4} \times 75 \times 100 \times 150$

$\quad = -609.75$ mm³

Change in volume, $\delta V$ = **609.75 mm³ (decrease)**

**Example 1.16 :** The following observations were made while testing a mild steel specimen, during tension test of original diameter 20 mm and gauge length 50 mm.

(a) Load at limit of proportionality = 80 kN
(b) Corresponding extension = 0.06 mm
(c) Yield point load = 85 kN
(d) Ultimate load = 150 kN
(e) Diameter at the neck = 15.80 mm
(f) After fitting the two broken parts neatly together, length between gauge points = 69.50 mm

Calculate :
(i) Young's modulus
(ii) Stress at the limit of proportionality
(iii) Yield stress
(iv) Ultimate tensile stress
(v) Percentage elongation
(vi) Percentage contraction

**Data :**  Load at limit of proportionality = 80 kN
Corresponding extension = 0.06 mm
Yield point load = 85 kN
Ultimate load = 150 kN
Diameter at the neck = 15.80 mm
Total length = 69.50 mm
Gauge length ($l$) = 50 mm
Cross-sectional area = $\frac{\pi}{4} \times (20)^2$ = 314.16 mm²

**Required :** Stress at different condition, elongation and contraction.
**Concept :** Standard formulae.

**Solution :** (i)
$$\delta l = \frac{PL}{AE}$$
$$0.06 = \frac{80 \times 10^3 \times 50}{314.16 \, E}$$
∴ $E = 212206.06 \text{ N/mm}^2$

(ii) Stress at limit of proportionality,
$$\sigma = \frac{P}{A} = \frac{80 \times 10^3}{314.16} = 254.65 \text{ N/mm}^2$$

(iii) Stress at yield point,
$$\sigma = \frac{P}{A} = \frac{85 \times 10^3}{314.16} = 270.56 \text{ N/mm}^2$$

(iv) Ultimate tensile stress,

$$\sigma = \frac{P}{A} = \frac{150 \times 10^3}{314.16} = 477.46 \text{ N/mm}^2$$

(v) Percentage elongation,

$$\delta l = 69.50 - 50 = 19.50 \text{ mm}$$

$$\% \text{ elongation} = \frac{\delta l}{l} \times 100$$

$$= \frac{19.50}{50} \times 100 = \mathbf{39\ \%}$$

(vi) Percentage contraction,

$$\delta d = 20 - 15.80 = 4.20 \text{ mm}$$

$$\% \text{ contraction} = \frac{\delta d}{d} \times 100$$

$$= \frac{4.20}{20} \times 100$$

Percentage contraction = **21 %**

**Example 1.17 :** A surveyor's steel tape 30 m long has a cross-section of 6 mm × 0.75 mm. Determine the elongation when the full length is held taut by applying a force of 100 N. The modulus of elasticity is 200 GPa.

**Data :** $l$ = 30 m, cross-sectional area = 6 × 0.75 mm², P = 100 N, E = 200 × 10³ MPa

**Required :** $\delta l$

**Concept :** Standard formula.

**Solution :**

$$\delta l = \frac{PL}{AE}$$

∴

$$\delta l = \frac{100 \times 30.000}{6 \times 0.75 \times 200 \times 10^3}$$

∴  Elongation = $\delta l$ = **3.33 mm**

**Example 1.18 :** For a certain material, E = 210 MPa. The Poisson's ratio is 0.3. State the relationship to calculate the values of other two elastic constants and find their values.

**Data :** E = 210 × 10³ MPa, μ = 0.3.

**Required :** K and G.

**Concept :** Standard formulae.

**Solution :**

(i) Bulk Modulus (K) :

$$E = 3K(1 - 2\mu)$$

∴

$$K = \frac{210 \times 10^3}{3(1 - 2 \times 0.3)}$$

∴  K = **175 × 10³ MPa**

(ii) Modulus of rigidity :

$$E = 2G(1+\mu)$$

$$\therefore \quad G = \frac{210 \times 10^3}{2(1+0.3)}$$

$$\therefore \quad G = 80.77 \times 10^3 \text{ MPa}$$

**Problem 1.19 :** A cylinder 150 mm in diameter, 300 mm in length is subjected to axial compressive load of 180 kN which causes increase in diameter 0.0952 mm and a decrease in length by 0.64 mm. Calculate Poisson's ratio and modulus of elasticity.

**Data :** d = 150 mm, l = 300 mm, P = 180 kN, δd = 0.0952 mm, δl = 0.64 mm (decrease)

**Required :** μ, E.

**Concept :** Generalised Hooke's law.

**Solution :**

(i) Poisson's ratio (μ) :

$$\mu = \frac{\text{Lateral strain}}{\text{Linear strain}}$$

$$\text{Linear strain} = \frac{\delta l}{l} = \frac{0.64}{300} = 0.0021$$

$$\text{Lateral strain} = \frac{\delta d}{d} = \frac{0.0952}{150} = 0.00063$$

$$\therefore \quad \mu = \frac{0.00063}{0.0021} = 0.3$$

(ii) Modulus of elasticity :

$$\delta l = \frac{PL}{AE}$$

$$0.64 = \frac{180 \times 10^3 \times 300}{\frac{\pi}{4} \times (150)^2 \times E}$$

$$\therefore \quad E = 4774.65 \text{ MPa}$$

$$\therefore \quad E = 4.77 \text{ GPa}$$

**Example 1.20 :** In a tensile test on a steel tube of external diameter 18 mm and internal diameter 12 mm, an axial pull of 2 kN produced a stretch of $6.72 \times 10^{-3}$ mm in a length of 100 mm and a lateral contraction of $3.62 \times 10^{-4}$ mm in the outer diameter. Calculate the three moduli and Poisson's ratio for the material of the tube.

**Data :** $D_o$ = 18 mm, $D_i$ = 12 mm, P = 2 kN, l = 100 mm,

$\delta l = 6.72 \times 10^{-3}$ mm, $\delta d = 3.62 \times 10^{-4}$ mm

**Required :** E, μ, K and G.

**Concept :** (i) $\delta l = \dfrac{PL}{AE}$, (ii) Standard formulae.

**Solution :**

(i) Geometric properties :

$$A = \dfrac{\pi}{4} \times [D_o^2 - D_i^2]$$

$$= \dfrac{\pi}{4}[(18)^2 - (12)^2]$$

$$= 141.37 \text{ mm}^2$$

(ii) Calculation for E :

$$\delta l = \dfrac{PL}{AE}$$

$$6.72 \times 10^{-3} = \dfrac{2 \times 10^3 \times 100}{141.37 \times E}$$

∴ $E = 210.52 \times 10^3$ MPa = **210.52 GPa**

(iii) Calculation for μ :

$$\mu = \dfrac{\text{Lateral strain}}{\text{Linear strain}} = \dfrac{(\delta d / d)}{(\delta l / l)}$$

∴ $$\mu = \dfrac{(3.62 \times 10^{-4} / 18)}{(6.72 \times 10^{-3} / 100)}$$

∴ $\mu = \mathbf{0.299}$

(iv) Calculation for K : $K = \dfrac{E}{3(1 - 2\mu)}$

$$= \dfrac{210.52 \times 10^3}{3(1 - 2 \times 0.299)}$$

$K = 117.35 \times 10^3$ MPa

∴ $K = \mathbf{117.35 \text{ GPa}}$

(v) Calculation for G :

$$G = \dfrac{E}{2(1 + \mu)}$$

$$= \dfrac{210.52 \times 10^3}{2(1 + 0.299)}$$

∴ $G = 81.03 \times 10^3$ MPa = **81.03 GPa**

**Example 1.21 :** A rectangular steel plate 1 m long, 0.4 m wide and 20 mm thick is subjected to biaxial stresses $\sigma_x$ and $\sigma_y$ acting along length and width respectively. If the increase in length is 0.6 mm and the increase in width is 0.09 mm, find :

(i) $\sigma_x$ and $\sigma_y$,

(ii) Change in thickness of the plate,

(iii) Change in volume of the plate.

E = 200 GPa, Poisson's ratio = 0.25

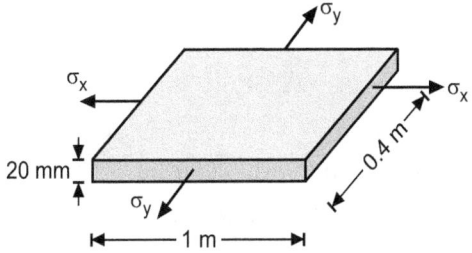

**Fig. 1.21**

**Data :** As shown in Fig. 1.21, E = 200 GPa, μ = 0.25, δl = 0.6 mm, δb = 0.09 mm

**Required :** $\sigma_x$, $\sigma_y$, δt and δV.

**Concept :** Generalised Hooke's law.

**Solution :**

(i) Calculation for $\sigma_x$ and $\sigma_y$ :

$$\varepsilon_x = \frac{\sigma_x}{E} - \frac{\mu\sigma_y}{E} - \frac{\mu\sigma_z}{E}$$

$$\sigma_z = 0$$

$$\varepsilon_x = \frac{\delta l}{l}$$

∴ $$\frac{0.6}{1000} = \frac{\sigma_x - 0.25\,\sigma_y}{200 \times 10^3}$$

∴ $$\sigma_x - 0.25\,\sigma_y = 120 \qquad \ldots (1)$$

$$\varepsilon_y = \frac{\sigma_y}{E} - \mu\frac{\sigma_x}{E} \qquad (\text{as } \sigma_z = 0)$$

$$\varepsilon_y = \frac{\delta b}{b} = \frac{0.09}{400}$$

∴ $$\frac{0.09}{400} = \frac{\sigma_y - \mu\sigma_x}{200 \times 10^3}$$

∴ $$\sigma_y - 0.25\,\sigma_x = 45 \qquad \ldots (2)$$

Solving equations (1) and (2),

$$\sigma_x = \mathbf{140 \text{ MPa}}$$
$$\sigma_y = \mathbf{80 \text{ MPa}}$$

(ii) Change in thickness δt :

$$\frac{\delta t}{t} = \frac{\sigma_z}{E} - \frac{\mu\sigma_x}{E} - \frac{\mu\sigma_y}{E}$$

$$\frac{\delta t}{20} = -\frac{0.25}{200 \times 10^3}(140 + 80)$$

∴ $$\delta t = -5.5 \times 10^{-3} \text{ mm}$$

$$\delta t = \mathbf{5.5 \times 10^{-3} \text{ mm (decrease)}}$$

(iii) Change in volume $\delta V$ :

$$\frac{\delta V}{V} = \varepsilon_x + \varepsilon_y + \varepsilon_z$$

$$\frac{\delta V}{V} = \left(\frac{0.6}{1000}\right) + \left(\frac{0.09}{400}\right) - \left(\frac{5.5 \times 10^{-3}}{20}\right)$$

∴ $\delta V = 4400$ mm³ **(increase)**

**Example 1.22 :** Two rectangular pieces of wood, 100 mm × 50 mm are glued together along the joint, as shown in Fig. 1.22. Determine the maximum safe axial force P, that can be applied to the block if :
  (i) The compressive stress in wood is limited to 20 MPa.
  (ii) Shear stress of the joint is limited to 5 MPa.

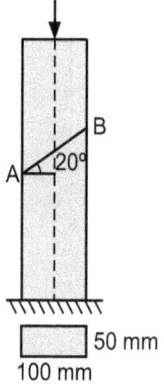

**Fig. 1.22**

**Data :** As shown in Fig. 1.22, compressive stress = 20 MPa, shear stress = 5 MPa
**Required :** Value of P.
**Concept :** Minimum from two.
**Solution :**
(i) P from compression :

Cross-sectional area = $100 \times 50 = 5000$ mm²
P = Compressive stress × Area
  = $20 \times 5000$
  = $100 \times 10^3$ N = 100 kN

(ii) P from shear on plane AB :
∴ Shear force along AB is P sin 20.

Cross-sectional area = $50 \times \frac{100}{\cos 20}$
  = 5320.89 mm²

∴ P sin 20 = Shear stress × Area along force

∴ $P = \frac{5 \times 5320.89}{\sin 20} = 77786.21$ N

∴ P = 77.79 kN
∴ Maximum axial force is **77.79 kN**

**Example 1.23 :** A plate 2 m × 2 m × 20 mm is subjected to stresses $\sigma_x = 100$ MPa tensile and $\sigma_y = 50$ MPa compressive in the plane of the plate. Modulus of elasticity of the plate is 200 GPa and Poisson's ratio is 0.25. Calculate the volume of the plate.

**Solution :**

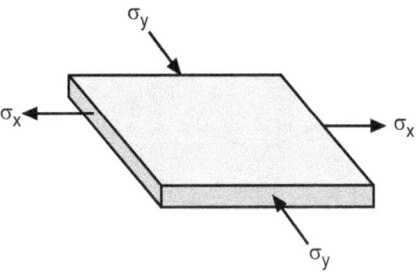

Fig. 1.23

(i) Strains :
$$\varepsilon_x = \frac{1}{E}(\sigma_x - \mu\sigma_y - \mu\sigma_z) = \frac{1}{E}(100 + 0.25 \times 50) = \frac{112.5}{E}$$

$$\varepsilon_y = \frac{1}{E}(\sigma_y - \mu\sigma_x - \mu\sigma_z) = \frac{-75}{E}$$

$$\varepsilon_z = \frac{1}{E}(\sigma_z - \mu\sigma_x - \mu\sigma_y) = \frac{-12.5}{E}$$

$$\varepsilon_v = \varepsilon_x + \varepsilon_y + \varepsilon_z = \frac{25}{E}$$

(ii) Change in volume $\delta V = \varepsilon_v \cdot V = 10^4$ mm³ **(increase)**

**Example 1.24 :** A bar of 30 mm diameter was subjected to tensile force of 53 kN and measured extension on 300 mm gauge length was 0.112 mm and change in the diameter was 0.00366 mm. Calculate Poisson's ratio and the values of three moduli.

**Solution :** (i) $\quad A = \frac{\pi}{4}(30)^2 = 706.86$ mm²

$$\delta L = \frac{PL}{AE}$$

∴ $\quad 0.112 = \dfrac{53 \times 300}{706.86 \, E}$

$E = 200.838 \times 10^3$ MPa

∴ $\quad E = 200.838$ GPa

(ii) $\quad \mu = \dfrac{\left(\dfrac{\delta D}{D}\right)}{\left(\dfrac{\delta L}{L}\right)} = \dfrac{0.00366}{30} \times \dfrac{300}{0.112} = \mathbf{0.326}$

(iii) $\quad E = 2G(1+\mu) = 3K(1-2\mu)$

∴ $\quad G = \mathbf{75.73 \text{ GPa}}$

$E = 3K(1-2\mu)$

$K = \mathbf{192.37 \text{ GPa}}$

**Example 1.25 :** A bar of steel is 40 mm × 40 mm in section and is 120 mm long. It is subjected to loads as shown in Fig. 1.24. Find the change in dimensions of bar and change in volume. Also find what axial longitudinal load alone can produce the same longitudinal strain as in first part ?

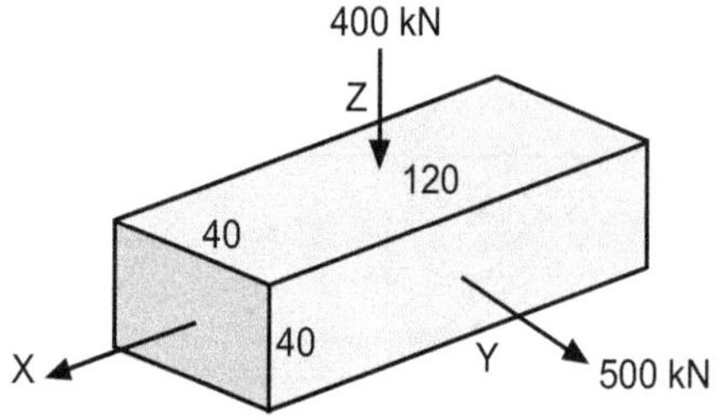

Fig. 1.24

$$\sigma_x = \frac{P}{A} = \frac{200 \times 10^3}{40 \times 40} = 125 \text{ N/mm}^2$$

$$\sigma_y = \frac{P}{A} = \frac{500 \times 10^3}{120 \times 40} = 104.17 \text{ N/mm}^2$$

$$\sigma_z = \frac{P}{A} = \frac{400 \times 10^3}{120 \times 40} = -83.33 \text{ N/mm}^2$$

$$\varepsilon_x = \frac{\sigma_x}{E} - \frac{\mu\sigma_y}{E} - \frac{\mu\sigma_z}{E} = \frac{125}{2 \times 10^5} - \frac{0.3 \times 104.17}{2 \times 10^5} + \frac{0.3 \times 83.33}{2 \times 10^5}$$

$$\varepsilon_x = 5.94 \times 10^{-4}$$

∴ $\delta l = 0.0712$

$$\varepsilon_y = \frac{104.17}{2 \times 10^5} - \frac{0.3 \times 125}{2 \times 10^5} + \frac{0.3 \times 83.33}{2 \times 10^5} = 4.58 \times 10^{-4}$$

$$\varepsilon_z = -\frac{83.33}{2 \times 10^5} - \frac{0.3 \times 125}{2 \times 10^5} - \frac{0.3 \times 104.17}{2 \times 10^5} = -7.6 \times 10^{-4}$$

$$\frac{\delta V}{V} = (\varepsilon_x + \varepsilon_y + \varepsilon_z)$$

∴ $\delta V = (5.94 + 4.58 - 7.6) \times 10^{-4} \times 40 \times 40 \times 120 = 56.06 \text{ mm}^3$

$\varepsilon_x = 5.94 \times 10^{-4}$

$$\varepsilon = \frac{\sigma}{E}$$

$\sigma_x = 5.94 \times 10^{-4} \times E = 5.94 \times 10^{-4} \times 2 \times 10^5 = 118.8$

∴ $P_x = 118.8 \times 40 \times 40 = 190.08 \text{ kN}$

190.08 kN force can produce same longitudinal strain as in first part.

**Example 1.26 :** A mild steel bar 200 mm long and 80 mm × 60 mm in cross-section is subjected to a longitudinal axial compression of 720 kN. Determine the value of lateral forces necessary to prevent any transverse strain. Evaluate the resultant alternation in length. E = 200 GPa and μ = 0.25.

**Data :** $l = 200$ m, b = 80 mm, t = 60 mm, E = 200 × $10^3$ N/mm², μ = 0.25.
**Required :** Lateral forces to prevent transverse strain and resultant change in length.
**Concept :** Standard formula.

**Solution :** $\dfrac{\delta b}{b} = \dfrac{\delta t}{t} = \mu \times \dfrac{\delta l}{l} = 0.25 \times \dfrac{P}{AE} = \dfrac{0.25 \times 720 \times 10^3}{80 \times 60 \times 200 \times 10^3}$

$\dfrac{\delta b}{b} = \dfrac{\delta t}{t} = 1.875 \times 10^{-4}$

$\delta b = 1.875 \times 10^{-4} \times 80 = 0.015$ mm

$\delta b = \dfrac{P_b b}{AE}$

$0.015 = \dfrac{P_b \times 80}{200 \times 60 \times 200 \times 10^3}$

$P_b = 450 \times 10^3$ N $= 450$ kN

Force along width $= 450$ kN (Compression)

$\delta t = \dfrac{P_t \cdot t}{AE}$

$0.015 = \dfrac{P_t \times 60}{200 \times 80 \times 200 \times 10^3}$

$P_t = 800 \times 10^3$ N $= 800$ kN

Force along thickness $= 800$ kN (Compression)

$\varepsilon_x = \dfrac{\sigma_x}{E} - \dfrac{\mu \sigma_y}{E} - \dfrac{\mu \sigma_z}{E}$

$= -\dfrac{720 \times 10^3}{80 \times 60 \times 200 \times 10^3} + \dfrac{450 \times 10^3 \times 0.25}{200 \times 60 \times 200 \times 10^3} + \dfrac{800 \times 10^3 \times 0.25}{200 \times 80 \times 200 \times 10^3}$

$= -7.5 \times 10^{-4} + 4.69 \times 10^{-5} + 6.25 \times 10^{-5}$

$\varepsilon_x = \dfrac{\delta l}{l} = -6.406 \times 10^{-4}$

$\dfrac{\delta l}{200} = -6.406 \times 10^{-4}$

$\delta l = -1.23$ mm

∴ Reduction in length by 1.23 mm.

**Example 1.27 :** A 50 mm square steel bar is subjected to an axial tensile load of 250 kN. Determine the decrease in lateral dimension if E = 200 GPa and V = 0.30.

**Data :** Square bar 50 mm side, P = 250 kN
**Required :** Decrease in lateral dimension.
**Concept :** Standard formula.
**Solution :**

$A = (50)^2 = 2500$ mm$^2$

$\dfrac{\delta l}{l} = \dfrac{P}{AE} = \dfrac{250 \times 10^2}{2500 \times 200 \times 10^3}$

$\dfrac{\delta l}{l} = 5 \times 10^{-4}$

$V = \dfrac{\text{Lateral strain}}{\text{Linear strain}}$

$$0.3 = \frac{5 \times 10^{-4}}{\left(\dfrac{\delta b}{b}\right)}$$

$$\delta b = 0.083 \text{ mm}$$

Lateral dimension is decreased by 0.083 mm.

## EXERCISE

1. A member 1 m long, 20 mm × 20 mm in cross-section is subjected to axial pull of 20 kN. If modulus of elasticity of material is 200 GPa, find the elongation of member.
   ($\delta L = 0.25$ mm)

2. Two steel rods AB and BC each 5 m long are connected at B as shown in Fig. 1.25. A load of 200 kN is supported at B as shown.
   (a) Determine the diameter of each member if allowable stress is 100 MPa.
   (b) Determine the vertical displacement of joint B assuming E = 200 GPa.
   (d = 50.46 mm, $\delta B = 5$ mm ($\rightarrow$))

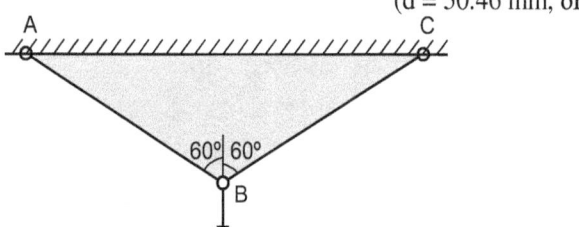

Fig. 1.25

3. A hollow circular member is 3 m long, 300 mm outside diameter and thickness of metal 50 mm is subjected to axial load such that stress produced is 75 MPa. If E = 150 GPa, find (i) magnitude of load, (ii) change in length. (P = 2945.2 kN, $\delta L = 1.5$ mm)

4. The following observations were made during a tensile test on a mild steel specimen 30 mm diameter and 200 mm long.
   Elongation with 40 kN load = 0.054 mm
   Yield load = 90 kN
   Maximum load = 140 kN
   Length of specimen at fracture = 241 mm.
   Determine (i) Young's modulus of elasticity, (ii) Yield stress, (iii) Ultimate stress, (iv) Percentage elongation.
   (E = 209.56 GPa, Yield stress = 127.32 MPa, Ultimate stress = 198 MPa, Percentage elongation = 20.5 %)

5. A prismatic steel bar 800 mm long is stretched by 0.7 mm by axial tensile force 'P'. Find the magnitude of force P if the volume of the bar is 450 × 10³ mm³ and E = 210 GPa.
   (P = 103.35 kN)

6. A steel rod 30 mm in diameter, 300 mm long is subjected to axial forces alternating between 18 kN compression and 8 kN tension. Find the difference between the greatest and the least lengths of the rod. Take E = 210 GPa. (0.0524 mm)

7. A short cast iron block of rectangular section 50 mm × 20 mm is subjected to an axial compressive load of 49 kN. Calculate the shear and the normal stresses on a section inclined at 30° to the line of action of load. ($\sigma = 12.25$ MPa, $\tau = 21.21$ MPa)

# CHAPTER TWO

# SIMPLE STRESSES AND STRAINS (PART-II)

## 2.1 AXIAL FLEXIBILITY (f)

Axial flexibility (f) is defined as the change in length produced by unit axial force.

We have, $\delta L = \dfrac{PL}{AE}$

$\therefore \quad f = \dfrac{L}{AE}$ ... (2.1)

*Axial flexibility is directly proportional to length (L) of a member and inversely proportional to product of cross-sectional area and Young's modulus of elasticity* called as **axial rigidity (EA).**

Unit of axial flexibility is mm/N or m/N etc.

## 2.2 AXIAL STIFFNESS (S)

Axial stiffness (S) is defined as the axial force required to cause unit change in length.

We have, $\delta L = \dfrac{PL}{AE}$

$\therefore \quad S = \dfrac{AE}{L}$ ... (2.2)

*Axial stiffness is directly proportional to axial rigidity (EA) and inversely proportional to length (L).*

Unit of axial stiffness is N/mm or N/m etc.

It should be noted that axial flexibility and stiffness are reciprocals of each other.

**Example 2.1 :** Find the position of load 'W' for the arrangement shown such that member AB remains horizontal.

**Data :** As shown in Fig. 2.1 (a).

**Required :** Position of load 'W' for the arrangement shown such that member AB remains horizontal.

**Concept :** Elongation of both, copper and steel wires must be same for member AB to remain horizontal.

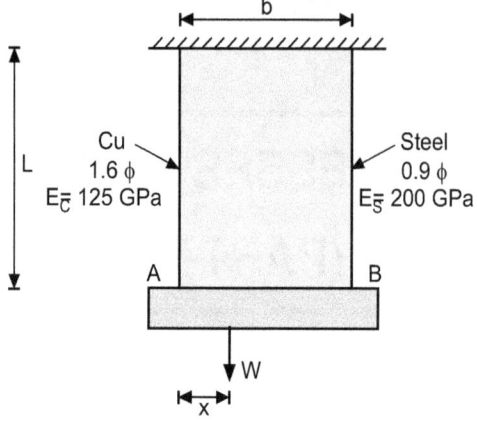

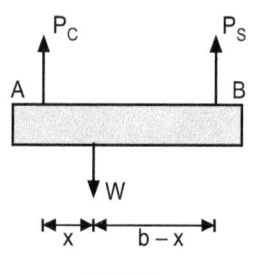

(b) FBD

Fig. 2.1

**Solution :** (i) Equation of statics :

$$P_C = \frac{W(b-x)}{b} \quad \ldots \text{(i)}$$

$$P_S = \frac{Wx}{b} \quad \ldots \text{(ii)}$$

(ii) For AB to remain horizontal,

$$(\delta L)_{cu} = (\delta L)_{st}$$

$$\left(\frac{PL}{AE}\right)_{cu} = \left(\frac{PL}{AE}\right)_{st}$$

$$\frac{P_C}{\frac{\pi}{4} \times (1.6)^2 \times 125 \times 10^3} = \frac{P_S}{\frac{\pi}{4} \times (0.9)^2 \times 200 \times 10^3} \quad \ldots \text{(iii)}$$

$$P_C = 1.97 \, P_S$$

Put equations (i) and (ii) in (iii),

$$\frac{W(b-x)}{b} = 1.97 \times \frac{W \cdot x}{b}$$

∴ $\quad b - x = 1.97 \, x$

∴ $\quad x = \dfrac{b}{2.97}$

## 2.3 STRESS AND ELONGATION PRODUCED IN A BAR DUE TO ITS OWN WEIGHT

Let a bar of length 'L' and diameter 'D' be rigidly fixed at the upper end and hanging vertically as shown in Fig. 2.2. Let w be the weight per unit volume of the bar.

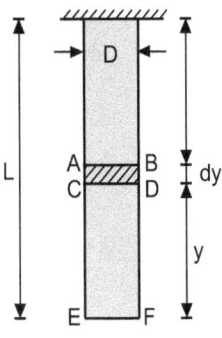

**Fig. 2.2**

Consider a small strip of the bar between the sections AB and CD at a distance 'y' of thickness 'dy' as shown in Fig. 2.2.

Downward force acting at CD is equal to the weight of the bar CDEF = $\frac{\pi}{4} D^2 yw$

$$\text{Stress at section CD} = \sigma = \frac{\text{Force at CD}}{\text{c/s area}}$$

$$= \frac{\left(\frac{\pi}{4}\right) D^2 yw}{\left(\frac{\pi}{4}\right) D^2}$$

$$\sigma = yw \quad \ldots (2.3)$$

Thus, stress at any section due to self weight of the bar is directly proportional to y i.e. the distance of the section from the lower end. Stress at the lower end of the bar is zero and at the top it is maximum = wL.

Stresses at the sections AB and CD can be assumed same, since dy is very small. The elongation of length 'dy' = $\frac{\sigma}{E} \cdot dy = \frac{yw}{E} \cdot dy$.

Elongation of entire length of the bar,

$$\delta L = \int_0^L \frac{yw}{E} \cdot dy = \frac{w}{E} \left(\frac{y^2}{2}\right)_0^L$$

$$\therefore \quad \delta L = \frac{wL^2}{2E} \quad \ldots (2.4)$$

**Note :** Elongation produced by the self weight of the bar is equal to that produced by a load of half its weight applied at the end.

**Example 2.2 :** A vertical tie bar of 20 mm$\phi$, 2 m long is fixed at the top and supports a downward load of 20 kN at bottom. Calculate the maximum stress and elongation of the bar assuming density = 78 kN/m³ and E = 200 GPa.

**Data :** $\phi = 20$ mm, L = 2 m, P = 20 kN, w = 78 kN/m³, E = 200 GPa.

**Required :** Maximum stress and elongation due to applied load and self weight.

**Concept :** Standard formulae.

**Solution :** (i) Maximum stress :

$$\sigma = \frac{P}{A} + wL$$

$$= \frac{20 \times 10^3}{\frac{\pi}{4}(20)^2} + 7.8 \times 10^{-5} \times 2000 \qquad (\geq 78 \text{ kN/m}^3 = 7.8 \times 10^{-5} \text{ N/mm}^3)$$

$$= 63.67 + 0.156$$

$$= \mathbf{63.826 \text{ MPa (Tensile)}}$$

(ii) Maximum elongation :

$$\delta L = \frac{\sigma L}{E} + \frac{wL^2}{2E} = \frac{63.67 \times 2000}{200 \times 10^3} + \frac{7.8 \times 10^{-5} \times (2000)^2}{2 \times 200 \times 10^3}$$

$$= \mathbf{0.637 \text{ mm (increase)}}$$

## 2.4 ELONGATION OF CONICAL BAR DUE TO ITS OWN WEIGHT

A conical rod of length L and base diameter D is rigidly fixed at BC as shown in Fig. 2.3.

Let w be the weight per unit volume of the bar. Consider a small length 'dy' at distance 'y' from A as shown in Fig. 2.3.

$$\text{Weight of portion AFG} = \left(\frac{\pi}{4} d^2 \cdot \frac{y}{3}\right) w$$

where, $d$ = Diameter of cross-section FG

$$\text{Stress at section FG} = \sigma = \frac{\text{Force at FG}}{\text{Area at FG}} = \frac{\left(\frac{\pi}{4} d^2 \cdot \frac{y}{3}\right) w}{\frac{\pi}{4} d^2}$$

$$\sigma = \frac{wy}{3} \qquad \qquad \ldots (2.5)$$

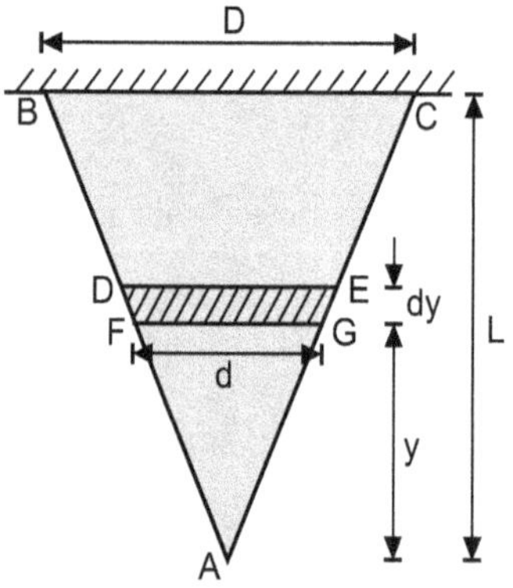

**Fig. 2.3**

$$\text{Elongation of length 'dy'} = \frac{\sigma}{E} \cdot dy$$

$$= \frac{wy}{3E} \cdot dy$$

∴ Elongation of the bar due to self weight

$$= \int_0^L \frac{wy}{3E} \cdot dy$$

$$= \frac{w}{3E} \left(\frac{y^2}{2}\right)_0^L$$

$$= \frac{wL^2}{6E} \qquad \text{... (2.6)}$$

## 2.5 LINEARLY VARYING SECTIONS

For these members, cross-sectional area changes linearly as a function of length of member. Change in length of these members can be computed with the help of integration.

**Example 2.3 :** A plate of uniform thickness is 60 mm wide at one end and 120 mm wide at other end and 500 mm long. Assuming uniform thickness of 8 mm, find the elongation of plate when subjected to axial tensile force of 50 kN. Take E = 200 GPa.

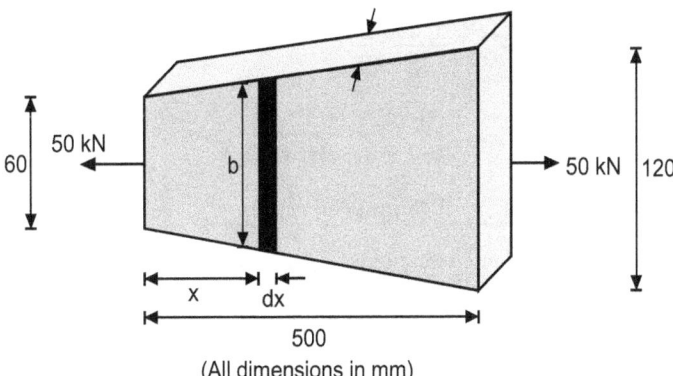

**Fig. 2.4**

**Data :** As shown in Fig. 2.4, E = 200 GPa.

**Required :** Change in length '$\delta L$'.

**Concept :** Member of varying cross-section.

**Solution :** (i) Consider an elementary strip of length 'dx' at a distance 'x' from left end. Let 'b' be the width of the section at x from left end.

Since, width of plate varies linearly,

$$\frac{120 - 60}{500} = \frac{b - 60}{x}$$

∴ $\qquad b = 60 + 0.12\,x$

∴ Cross-sectional area for strip $= A = bt$

$$= (60 + 0.12\,x) \times 8$$

Change in length of strip $= \dfrac{PL}{AE}$

$= \dfrac{P\,dx}{(60 + 0.12x)\,8E}$

(ii) Change in length of member :

$$\delta L = \int_0^{500} \dfrac{P\,dx}{(60 + 0.12x) \times 8E}$$

$$= \dfrac{P}{8E} \int_0^{500} \dfrac{dx}{(60 + 0.12x)}$$

$$= \dfrac{P}{8E}\left[\log_e(60 + 0.12x) \times \dfrac{1}{0.12}\right]_0^{500}$$

$$= \dfrac{P}{0.12 \times 8E}\left[\log_e(60 + 0.12 \times 500) - \log_e(60)\right]$$

$$= \dfrac{0.693\,P}{0.12 \times 8E}$$

$$= \dfrac{0.693 \times 50 \times 10^3}{0.12 \times 8 \times 200 \times 10^3}$$

$$= \mathbf{0.18\ mm\ (increase)}$$

**Example 2.4 :** For a member having solid circular cross-section, diameter is 'd' at one end and it linearly increases to 'D' at other end over the length 'L'. Show that its change in length under the action of axial force is given by $\delta L = \dfrac{4\,PL}{\pi\,D\,d\,E}$.

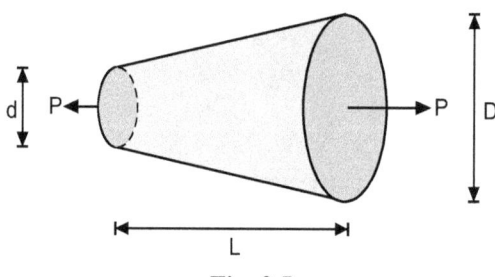

**Fig. 2.5**

**Data :** As shown in Fig. 2.5.

**Required :** Change in length $\delta L$.

**Concept :** Member of varying cross-section.

**Solution :** (i) Consider an elementary strip of length 'dx' at a distance x from left end. Let $\phi$ be the diameter of section at a distance x from left end as shown in Fig. 2.6.

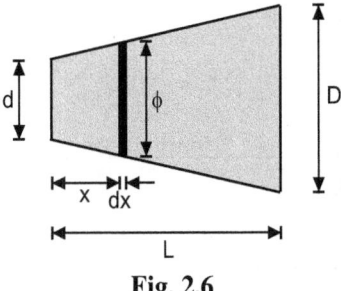

**Fig. 2.6**

Since diameter of bar varies linearly,

$$\frac{D-d}{L} = \frac{\phi - d}{x}$$

$$\therefore \quad \phi = d + \frac{(D-d)x}{L}$$

Cross-sectional area of strip $= A = \frac{\pi}{4}\phi^2 = \frac{\pi}{4}\left[d + \left(\frac{D-d}{L}\right)x\right]^2$

Change in length of strip $= \frac{PL}{AE} = \frac{P\,dx}{\frac{\pi}{4}\left[d + \left(\frac{D-d}{L}\right)x\right]^2 E}$

(ii) Change in length of member :

$$\delta L = \int_0^L \frac{P\,dx}{\frac{\pi}{4}\left[d + \left(\frac{D-d}{L}\right)x\right]^2 E} = \frac{4P}{\pi E}\left[\frac{-1}{d + \left(\frac{D-d}{L}\right)x} \div \frac{D-d}{L}\right]_0^L$$

$$= \frac{-4PL}{\pi E(D-d)}\left[\frac{1}{d+(D-d)} - \frac{1}{d}\right]$$

$$= \frac{-4PL}{\pi E(D-d)}\left[\frac{1}{D} - \frac{1}{d}\right] = \frac{-4PL}{\pi E(D-d)}\left[\frac{d-D}{Dd}\right]$$

$$\delta L = \frac{4PL}{\pi D\,dE} \qquad \text{... Hence proved.}$$

**Example 2.5 :** A circular bar 2.5 m long tapers uniformly from 2.5 cm diameter to 1.2 cm diameter. Determine extension of a rod under a pull of 30 kN. Take E = 200 GPa.

**Solution :**

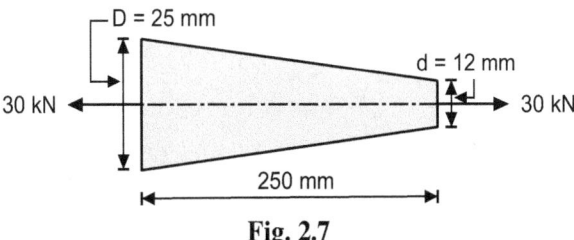

**Fig. 2.7**

Refer derivation proved in Example 2.4.

$$\delta L = \frac{4PL}{\pi E Dd} = \frac{4 \times 30 \times 2500}{\pi \times 200 \times 25 \times 12}$$

$$= 1.59 \text{ mm (increase)}$$

## 2.6 COMPOUND SECTIONS

When a member consists of *segments or components of different cross-sectional area but of same material,* it is called as compound section. Fig. 2.8 shows a compound section subjected to axial tensile force P.

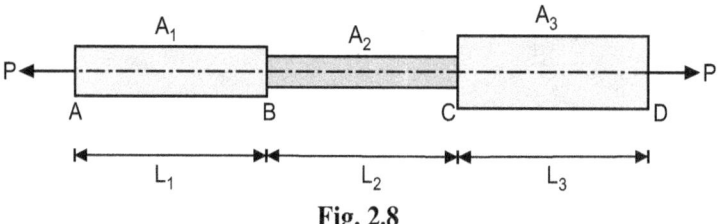

**Fig. 2.8**

Axial force 'P' is constant throughout the length of member but normal stresses are different because of different cross-sectional areas of components. For these sections, change in normal stresses from one component to other is sudden because of sudden change in cross-sectional areas.

Thus, for the compound section considered,

$$\left.\begin{array}{l}(\sigma)_{AB} = \dfrac{P}{A_1} \\[6pt] (\sigma)_{BC} = \dfrac{P}{A_2} \\[6pt] (\sigma)_{CD} = \dfrac{P}{A_3}\end{array}\right\} \quad \ldots (2.7)$$

Change in length of complete member can be obtained by,

$$\delta L = (\delta L)_{AB} + (\delta L)_{BC} + (\delta L)_{CD}$$

$$= \left(\frac{PL}{AE}\right)_{AB} + \left(\frac{PL}{AE}\right)_{BC} + \left(\frac{PL}{AE}\right)_{CD}$$

Since, axial force P is constant throughout the length of member,

$$\delta L = P\left[\left(\frac{L}{AE}\right)_{AB} + \left(\frac{L}{AE}\right)_{BC} + \left(\frac{L}{AE}\right)_{CD}\right]$$

$$= P \text{ [Sum of flexibility coefficients of components]} \quad \ldots (2.8)$$

However, material being same throughout,

$$\delta L = \frac{P}{E}\left[\left(\frac{L}{A}\right)_{AB} + \left(\frac{L}{A}\right)_{BC} + \left(\frac{L}{A}\right)_{CD}\right] \quad \ldots (2.9)$$

**Axial Force Diagram (AFD) :** It is the *diagram which shows variation of axial force along the length of member.* For knowing axial force in different components, method of section is used. Method of section consists of following steps :

(i) Take a section which cuts the component of our interest.

(ii) Take algebraic addition of all the forces either to the left or to the right of section with due care of signs. Sign convention to be followed is axial tension positive and axial compression negative. The force going away from the section represents tension, while towards the section represents compression.

The above procedure is explained further with a numerical example as under :

Let, a compound section be subjected to axial forces as shown in Fig. 2.9 (a).

To find axial forces in components AB, BC and CD, consider sections 1-1, 2-2 and 3-3 respectively. It should be remembered that, member as a whole with given external forces and FBD of components with external and internal forces (shown dotted) must maintain the equilibrium.

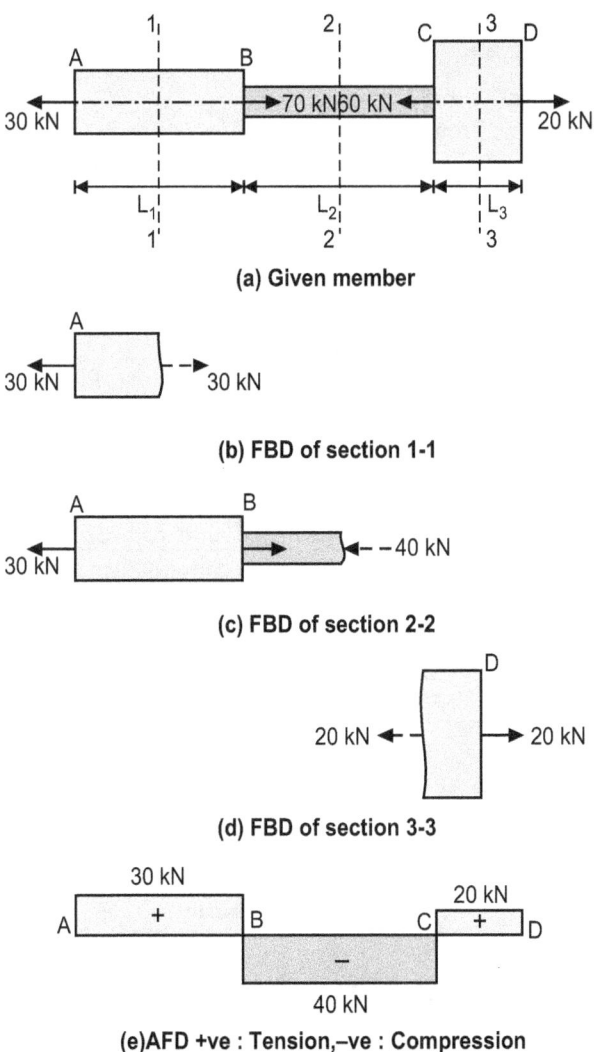

Fig. 2.9

Thus, Axial force for component AB = $P_{AB}$ = 30 kN (Tensile)
Axial force for component BC = $P_{BC}$ = 30 − 70 = − 40 kN
= 40 kN (Compressive)
Axial force for component CD = $P_{CD}$ = 20 kN (Tensile)
AFD is as shown in Fig. 2.9 (e).

**Example 2.6 :** A compound bar shown in Fig. 2.10 elongates by 0.45 mm when subjected to an axial pull of 150 kN. Calculate Young's modulus of elasticity.

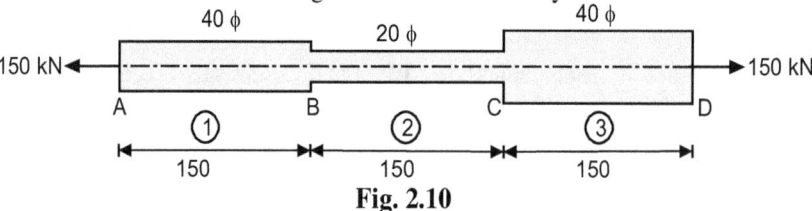

Fig. 2.10

**Data :** $\delta L$ = 0.45 mm, Refer Fig. 2.10.
**Required :** Young's modulus of elasticity (E).
**Concept :** $\delta L = \delta L_1 + \delta L_2 + \delta L_3$
**Solution :** (i) Geometric properties :

$$A_1 = A_3 = \frac{\pi}{4}(40)^2 = 1256.63 \text{ mm}^2$$

$$A_2 = \frac{\pi}{4}(20)^2 = 314.16 \text{ mm}^2$$

(ii) Modulus of elasticity (E) :

$$\delta L = \delta L_1 + \delta L_2 + \delta L_3$$

$$= \left(\frac{PL}{AE}\right)_1 + \left(\frac{PL}{AE}\right)_2 + \left(\frac{PL}{AE}\right)_3 = \frac{PL}{E}\left(\frac{1}{A_1} + \frac{1}{A_2} + \frac{1}{A_3}\right)$$

Substituting, $0.45 = \frac{150 \times 10^3 \times 150}{E}\left(\frac{1}{1256.63} + \frac{1}{314.16} + \frac{1}{1256.63}\right)$

∴ E = 238.732 × 10³ MPa = **238.732 GPa**

**Example 2.7 :** A 1.75 m long steel bar is having uniform diameter of 30 mm for a length of 750 mm; for next 500 mm length its diameter gradually reduces to 'd' mm; and for remaining 500 mm length, diameter 'd' remains constant. When a load of 100 kN is applied, the extension observed is 2 mm. Assuming E = 200 GPa, find 'd'.

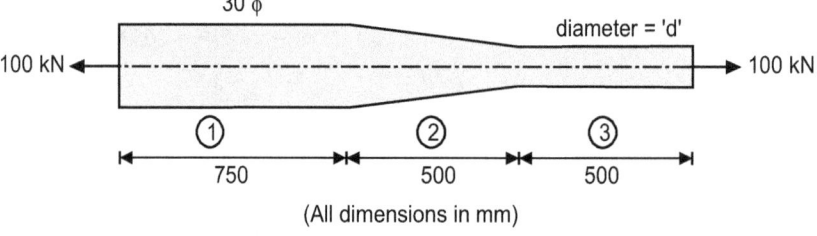

(All dimensions in mm)

Fig. 2.11

**Data :** As shown in Fig. 2.11, E = 200 GPa, $\delta L$ = 2 mm
**Required :** Diameter 'd'.
**Concept :** $\delta L = \delta L_1 + \delta L_2 + \delta L_3$

**Solution :** (i) Geometric properties :

$$A_1 = \frac{\pi}{4}(30)^2 = 706.85 \text{ mm}^2$$

$$A_3 = \frac{\pi}{4}(d)^2$$

(ii) Diameter 'd' :
We have, $\delta L = \delta L_1 + \delta L_2 + \delta L_3$
where, $\delta L = 2$ mm

$$\delta L_1 = \left(\frac{PL}{AE}\right)_1 = \frac{P \times 750}{706.85 \, E} = 1.061 \frac{P}{E}$$

$$\delta L_2 = \frac{4 \, PL}{\pi \, D \, dE} = \frac{4P \times 500}{\pi \times 30 \, dE} = \frac{21.22 \, P}{dE}$$

$$\delta L_3 = \left(\frac{PL}{AE}\right)_3 = \frac{P \times 500}{\frac{\pi}{4}(d)^2 \, E} = \frac{636.62 \, P}{d^2 \, E}$$

Substituting,
$$2 = \frac{P}{E}\left(1.061 + \frac{21.22}{d} + \frac{636.62}{d^2}\right)$$

$$= \frac{100 \times 10^3}{200 \times 10^3}\left(1.061 + \frac{21.22}{d} + \frac{636.62}{d^2}\right)$$

$2.939 \, d^2 - 21.22 \, d - 636.62 = 0$
Solving, $d = 18.76$ mm

**Example 2.8 :** A mild steel bar 40 mm in diameter and 3 m long is subjected to an axial pull of 50 kN. To what length, bar should be centrally bored so that the total extension will increase by 25 % under same axial pull ? Assume diameter of bore as 20 mm and E = 200 GPa.

**Data :** As shown in Fig. 2.12, E = 200 GPa, $(\delta L)_{case\,(ii)} = 1.25 \, (\delta L)_{case\,(i)}$

**Required :** Length of bore 'x'.

**Concept :** $\delta L = (\delta L)_1 + (\delta L)_2$ for case (ii).

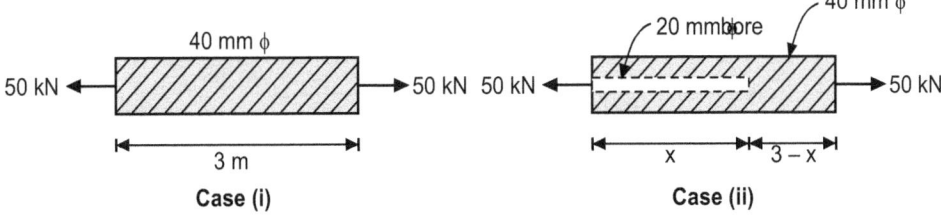

Fig. 2.12

**Solution :** (i) Analysis of case (i) :

$$\delta L = \frac{PL}{AE}$$

where, $P = 50 \times 10^3$ N
$L = 3000$ mm

$$A = \frac{\pi}{4}(40)^2 = 1256.63 \text{ mm}^2$$

$$E = 200 \times 10^3 \text{ MPa}$$

Substituting, $\quad \delta L = \dfrac{50 \times 10^3 \times 3000}{1256.63 \times 200 \times 10^3} = 0.5968 \text{ mm}$

(ii) Analysis of case (ii) :

$$\delta L = (\delta L)_1 + (\delta L)_2 = \left(\dfrac{PL}{AE}\right)_1 + \left(\dfrac{PL}{AE}\right)_2 = \dfrac{P}{E}\left(\dfrac{L_1}{A_1} + \dfrac{L_2}{A_2}\right)$$

where, $\quad L_1 = \text{x metres}$

$\quad L_2 = (3 - x) \text{ metres}$

$$A_1 = \frac{\pi}{4}(40^2 - 20^2) = 942.47 \text{ mm}^2$$

$$A_2 = \frac{\pi}{4}(40)^2 = 1256.63 \text{ mm}^2$$

Substituting, $\quad \delta L = \dfrac{50 \times 10^3}{200 \times 10^3}\left(\dfrac{x \times 10^3}{942.47} + \dfrac{(3-x) \, 10^3}{1256.63}\right)$

$\quad\quad\quad = (0.2652)\,x + 0.5968 - (0.1989)\,x$

$\quad\quad\quad = (0.0663)\,x + 0.5968 \text{ mm}$

(iii) Length of bore (x) :

We have, $\quad (\delta L)_{\text{case (ii)}} = 1.25\,(\delta L)_{\text{case (i)}}$

$\quad (0.0663)\,x + 0.5968 = 1.25 \times 0.5968$

$\therefore \quad\quad\quad x = \mathbf{2.25 \text{ m}}$

**Example 2.9 :** For the compound bar ABC shown in Fig. 2.13, (i) Determine the magnitude of P for equilibrium, (ii) Draw axial force diagram, (iii) Find total change in length, (iv) Find displacement of B with respect to A. Assume E = 200 GPa.

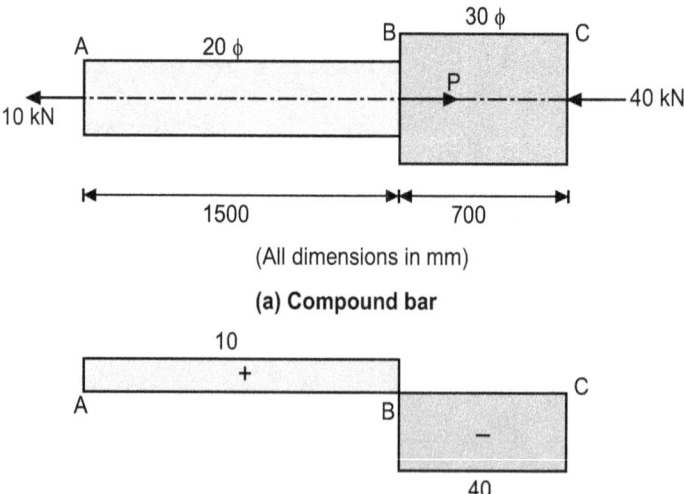

(a) Compound bar

(b) AFD (kN)

Fig. 2.13

**Data :** As shown in Fig. 2.13 (a), E = 200 GPa.

**Required :** (i) P, (ii) δL, (iii) δB/A.

**Concept :** (i) $\Sigma F_X = 0$ gives magnitude of P.

(ii) $\delta L = (\delta L)_{AB} + (\delta L)_{BC}$

(iii) Displacement of B with respect to A = $(\delta L)_{AB}$

**Solution :** (i) Magnitude of 'P' :

$\Sigma F_X = 0, -10 + P - 40 = 0$

∴ $\quad P = 50$ kN

(ii) Axial force diagram (AFD) :

Taking vertical sections for members AB and BC, we get

Axial force for member AB = $P_{AB}$ = 10 kN (Tensile)

Axial force for member BC = $P_{BC}$ = 40 kN (Compressive)

Axial force diagram is as shown in Fig. 2.13 (b).

(iii) Total change in length :

$$\delta L = (\delta L)_{AB} + (\delta L)_{BC} = \left(\frac{PL}{AE}\right)_{AB} + \left(\frac{PL}{AE}\right)_{BC}$$

$$= \frac{1}{200 \times 10^3} \left[\frac{10 \times 10^3 \times 1500}{\frac{\pi}{4}(20)^2} + \frac{(-40) \times 10^3 \times 700}{\frac{\pi}{4}(30)^2}\right]$$

$= 0.238 - 0.198$

= **0.04 mm (increase)**

(iv) Displacement of B with respect to A :

$$\delta B/A = (\delta L)_{AB} = \left(\frac{PL}{AE}\right)_{AB}$$

= **0.238 mm (→)**

**Example 2.10 :** For member ABC shown in Fig. 2.14, find the diameter of portion BC if displacement of C with respect to A is 2 mm. Assume E = 200 GPa.

**Data :** As shown in Fig. 2.14 (a), E = 200 GPa, δL = 2 mm

**Required :** Diameter of portion BC (φ) mm.

**Concept :** $\delta L = (\delta L)_{AB} + (\delta L)_{BC}$

**Solution :** (i) Geometric properties :

Cross-sectional area of AB = $A_{AB} = \frac{\pi}{4}(30)^2 = 706.85$ mm²

Cross-sectional area of BC = $A_{BC} = \frac{\pi}{4}(\phi)^2$ mm²

(ii) Analysis :

Let $H_A$ ($\rightarrow$) be the reaction at A.

$\Sigma F_x = 0$,

$$H_A + 150 + 75 = 0$$

$\therefore \quad H_A = -225 \text{ kN} = 225 \text{ kN} (\leftarrow)$

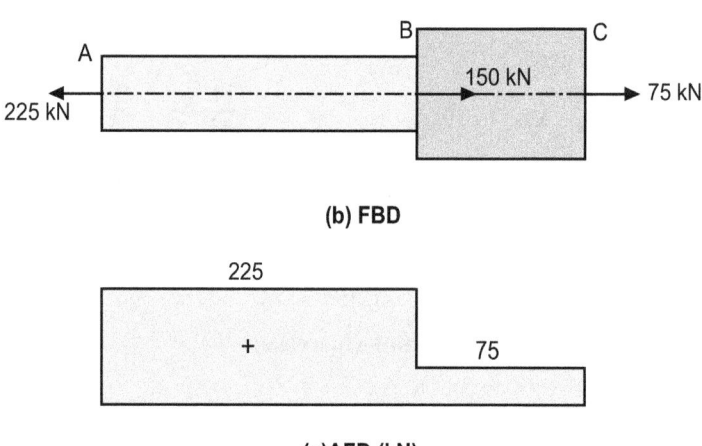

Fig. 2.14

FBD of member is as shown in Fig. 2.14 (b).

Axial force diagram is as shown in Fig. 2.14 (c).

**Note :** Axial forces are obtained by taking sections in portions AB and BC.

(iii) Diameter of portion BC :

$$\delta L = (\delta L)_{AB} + (\delta L)_{BC}$$

$$2 = \left(\frac{PL}{AE}\right)_{AB} + \left(\frac{PL}{AE}\right)_{BC}$$

$$= \frac{1}{200 \times 10^3} \left[ \frac{225 \times 10^3 \times 1200}{706.85} + \frac{75 \times 10^3 \times 900}{\frac{\pi}{4}(\phi)^2} \right]$$

$$\phi = 69.05 \text{ mm}$$

**Example 2.11 :** A member 36 mm$\phi$ is subjected to axial forces as shown in Fig. 2.15. Find the total change in length of the bar assuming E = 200 GPa.

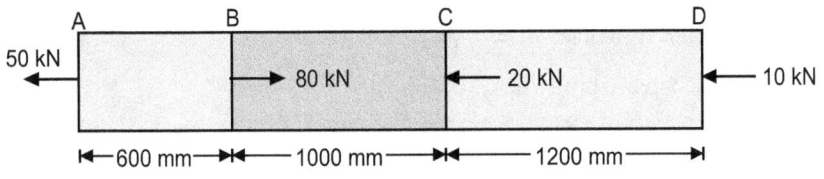

Fig. 2.15

**Data :** As shown in Fig. 2.15, E = 200 × 10³ MPa.
**Required :** $\delta l$
**Concept :** Standard formulae.
**Solution :** (i) Geometric properties :

$$A = \frac{\pi}{4} \times d^2 = \frac{\pi}{4} \times (36)^2 = 1017.88 \text{ mm}^2$$

(ii) Change in length :

$$\delta l = \left(\frac{Pl}{AE}\right)_{AB} + \left(\frac{Pl}{AE}\right)_{BC} + \left(\frac{Pl}{AE}\right)_{CD}$$

$$= \frac{1}{AE}[(Pl)_{AB} + (Pl)_{BC} + (Pl)_{CD}]$$

$$= \frac{[(50 \times 10^3 \times 600) - (30 \times 10^3 \times 1000) - (10 \times 10^3 \times 1200)]}{1017.88 \times 200 \times 10^3}$$

$$= -0.118 \text{ mm}$$

∴ $\delta l = -0.118 \text{ mm} = $ **0.118 mm (decrease)**

**Example 2.12 :** A member is framed by connecting a steel bar to aluminium bar as shown in Fig. 2.16. Assuming that bars are prevented from buckling sidewise, calculate the magnitude of force P that will cause the total length of member to decrease by 0.33 mm.
$E_{st}$ = 210 GPa, $E_{Al}$ = 70 GPa.

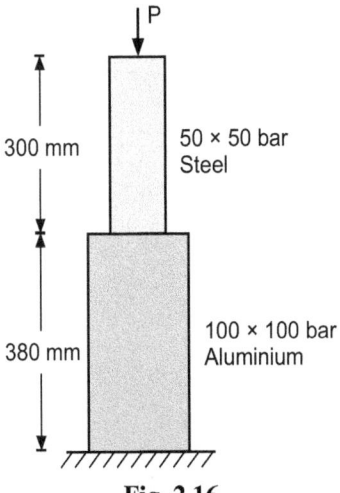

Fig. 2.16

**Data :** As shown in Fig. 2.16, $E_{st} = 210 \times 10^3$ MPa, $E_{Al} = 70 \times 10^3$ MPa, $\delta l = 0.33$ mm
**Required :** P.

**Concept :** Standard formulae, $\delta l = \dfrac{Pl}{AE}$

**Solution :** (i) Geometric properties :
$$A_{st} = 50 \times 50 = 2500 \text{ mm}^2$$
$$A_{Al} = 100 \times 100 = 10000 \text{ mm}^2$$

(ii) Calculation for P :
$$\delta l = \left(\dfrac{Pl}{AE}\right)_{st} + \left(\dfrac{Pl}{AE}\right)_{Al}$$

As both bars are in compression, so there is decrease in total length.
∴ $\delta l = -0.33$

Substituting, $-0.33 = -\left(\dfrac{P \times 300 \times 10^3}{2500 \times 210 \times 10^3}\right) - \left(\dfrac{P \times 380 \times 10^3}{10000 \times 70 \times 10^3}\right)$

∴ $P = 296.15$ kN (Compression)

**Example 2.13 :** A member ABCD is loaded as shown in Fig. 2.17. Determine (a) total deformation of rod, (b) displacement of 'C'. Assume E = 70 GPa.

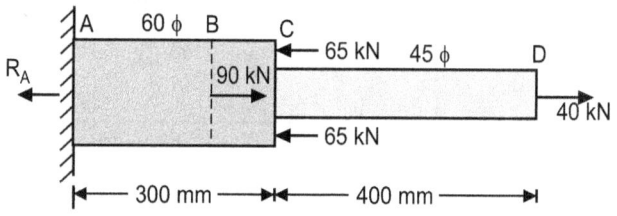

Fig. 2.17

**Data :** As shown in Fig. 2.17, $E = 70 \times 10^3$ MPa
**Required :** $\delta l$, displacement of C.

**Concept :** Equilibrium equation, $\delta l = \dfrac{Pl}{AE}$

**Solution :** (i) Geometric properties :
$$A_{AB} = \dfrac{\pi}{4} \times (60)^2 = 2827.43 \text{ mm}^2$$

$$A_{BC} = \dfrac{\pi}{4} \times (60)^2 = 2827.43 \text{ mm}^2$$

$$A_{CD} = \dfrac{\pi}{4} \times (45)^2 = 1590.43 \text{ mm}^2$$

(ii) Equilibrium equation :
$$\Sigma F_X = 0$$
$$-R_A + 90 - 130 + 40 = 0$$
∴ $R_A = 0$

(iii) Total deformation :
$$\delta l = \left(\dfrac{Pl}{AE}\right)_{AB} + \left(\dfrac{Pl}{AE}\right)_{BC} + \left(\dfrac{Pl}{AE}\right)_{CD}$$

Substituting, $\delta l = 0 - \left(\dfrac{90 \times 10^3 \times 200}{2827.43 \times 70 \times 10^3}\right) + \left(\dfrac{40 \times 10^3 \times 400}{1590.43 \times 70 \times 10^3}\right)$

$= -0.091 + 0.1437$

$\therefore \quad \delta l = 0.0527$ mm

(iv) Displacement of point C :

As there is no force on AB, so point B remains on the same point and so C will be displaced by 0.091 mm towards left.

**Example 2.14 :** A stepped rod is as shown in Fig. 2.18. Find the value of P that will not exceed a maximum overall deformation of 2 mm or a stress in steel of 140 MPa, that in Aluminium 80 MPa and in Brass 120 MPa.

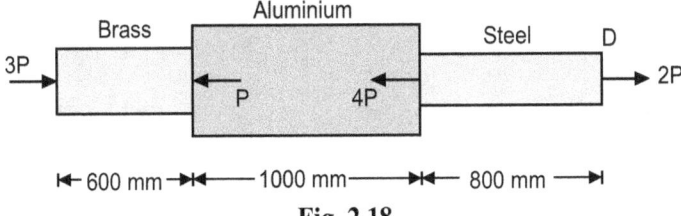

Fig. 2.18

**Data :** As shown in Fig. 2.18.

**Required :** P

**Concept :** Standard formulae.

**Solution :** (i) P due to Brass :

$\left(\sigma = \dfrac{3P}{A}\right)_{Br}$ $\therefore$ $P = \dfrac{\sigma A}{3} = \dfrac{120 \times 450}{3}$

$P = 18000$ N ... (i)

(ii) P due to Aluminium :

$\left(\sigma = \dfrac{2P}{A}\right)_{Al}$ $\therefore$ $P = \dfrac{\sigma A}{2} = \dfrac{80 \times 600}{2}$

$P = 24000$ N ... (ii)

(iii) P due to Steel :

$\left(\sigma = \dfrac{2P}{A}\right)_{Steel}$ $\therefore$ $P = \dfrac{\sigma A}{2} = \dfrac{140 \times 300}{2}$

$P = 21000$ N ... (iii)

(iv) P due to overall deformation :

$\delta l = \left(\dfrac{Pl}{AE}\right)_{Br} + \left(\dfrac{Pl}{AE}\right)_{Al} + \left(\dfrac{Pl}{AE}\right)_{st}$

Substituting, $2 = \dfrac{3P \times 600 \times 10^3}{450 \times 83 \times 10^3} + \dfrac{2P \times 1000 \times 10^3}{600 \times 70 \times 10^3} - \dfrac{2P \times 800 \times 10^3}{300 \times 200 \times 10^3}$

$2 = 0.048 P + 4.76 \times 10^{-3} P - 0.0267 P$

$P = 76.745$ kN

$P = 76745$ N ... (iv)

$\therefore$ Value of P = **18000 N** = **18 kN** [Least of (i), (ii), (iii) and (iv)]

**Example 2.15 :** A member ABCD is subjected to point loads $P_1$, $P_2$, $P_3$ and $P_4$ as shown in Fig. 2.19. Calculate the force $P_3$ necessary for equilibrium if $P_1 = 120$ kN, $P_2 = 220$ kN and $P_4 = 160$ kN. Determine also the net change in length of the member. Take $E = 200$ GN/m².

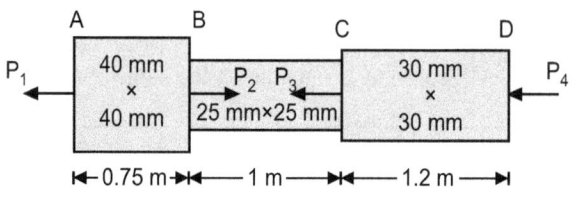

Fig. 2.19

**Data :** As shown in Fig. 2.19, $P_1 = 120$ kN, $P_2 = 220$ kN, $P_4 = 160$ kN,

$$E = 200 \text{ GN/m}^2 = 200 \times 10^3 \text{ N/mm}^2$$

**Required :** $P_3$, $\delta l$.

**Concept :** $\Sigma F_x = 0$, standard formulae.

**Solution :**

(i) $\qquad \Sigma F_x = 0$

$\therefore \qquad -P_1 + P_2 - P_3 + P_4 = 0$

$\qquad P_1 + P_3 = P_2 + P_4$

$\therefore \qquad 120 + P_3 = 220 + 160$

$\therefore \qquad P_3 = 260 \text{ kN}$

(ii) $\qquad \delta l = \left(\dfrac{Pl}{AE}\right)_{AB} + \left(\dfrac{Pl}{AE}\right)_{BC} + \left(\dfrac{Pl}{AE}\right)_{CD}$

Substituting, $\quad \delta l = \left(\dfrac{120 \times 10^3 \times 750}{40 \times 40 \times 200 \times 10^3}\right) - \left(\dfrac{100 \times 10^3 \times 1000}{25 \times 25 \times 200 \times 10^3}\right)$

$$+ \left(\dfrac{160 \times 10^3 \times 1200}{30 \times 30 \times 200 \times 10^3}\right)$$

$$= 0.28 - 0.8 + 1.067$$

$\therefore \qquad \delta l = 0.547 \text{ mm}$

**Example 2.16 :** Rod AB has diameter 25 mm, length 800 mm and modulus of elasticity $E_1$; while rod BC has diameter 25 mm, length 550 mm and modulus of elasticity $E_2$. $P_1$, $P_2$ and $P_3$ are axial forces acting on the rod ABC as shown in Fig. 2.20. When $P_1 = 0$, $P_2 = 20$ kN, $P_3 = 20$ kN, elongation of the rod is 1 mm and when $P_1 = 20$ kN, $P_2 = 0$, $P_3 = 20$ kN, elongation of rod ABC is 1.8 mm. Determine the values of $E_1$ and $E_2$.

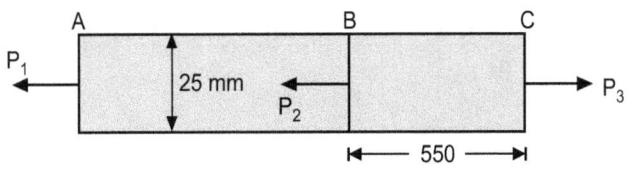

**Fig. 2.20**

**Data :** (i) As shown in Fig. 2.20, $P_1 = 0$, $P_2 = 20$ kN, $P_3 = 20$ kN, $\delta l_1 = 1$ mm

(ii) $P_1 = 20$ kN, $P_2 = 0$, $P_3 = 20$ kN, $\delta l_2 = 1.8$ mm

**Required :** (i) $E_1$, (ii) $E_2$.

**Concept :** $\delta l = \delta l_{AB} + \delta l_{AC}$

**Solution :** (i) Geometric properties :

Cross-sectional area of AB = cross-sectional area of BC

$$A_{AB} = A_{BC} = \frac{\pi}{4} \times (25)^2 = 490.87 \text{ mm}^2$$

(ii) Modulus of elasticity $E_1$ and $E_2$ :

$$\delta l_1 = \left(\frac{Pl}{AE}\right)_{AB} + \left(\frac{Pl}{AE}\right)_{BC}$$

$$1 = 0 + \frac{20 \times 10^3 \times 550}{490.87 \times E_2}$$

∴ $\qquad E_2 = 22409.19 \text{ N/mm}^2$

$$\delta l_2 = \left(\frac{Pl}{AE}\right)_{AB} + \left(\frac{Pl}{AE}\right)_{BC}$$

$$1.8 = \frac{20 \times 10^3 \times 800}{490.87 \times E_1} + \frac{20 \times 10^3 \times 550}{490.87 \times 22409.19}$$

$$1.8 = \frac{32595.19}{E_1} + 1$$

∴ $\qquad \frac{32595.19}{E_1} = 0.8$

∴ $\qquad E_1 = 40743.99 \text{ N/mm}^2$

**Example 2.17 :** For a member ABC as shown in Fig. 2.21, find the diameter of the portion BC, if the total deformation of the member is 3 mm. Diameter of portion AB is 30 mm. Use E = 200 GPa.

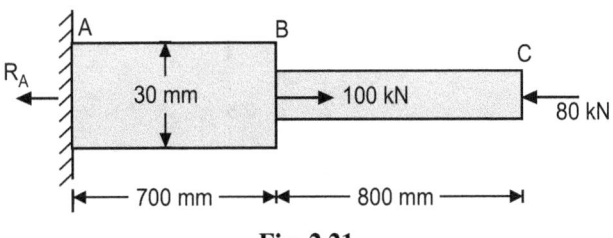

**Fig. 2.21**

**Data :** As shown in Fig. 2.21, $E = 200 \times 10^3$ MPa, $\delta l = 3$ mm
**Required :** Diameter of BC.
**Concept :** $\delta l = \dfrac{Pl}{AE}$

**Solution :** (i) Geometric properties :

$$A_{AB} = \dfrac{\pi}{4} \times (30)^2 = 706.86 \text{ mm}^2$$

$$A_{BC} = \dfrac{\pi}{4} \times d^2$$

(ii) Analysis : $\Sigma F_x = 0$
$- H_A + 100 - 80 = 0$
$\therefore \qquad H_A = 20$ kN ($\leftarrow$)

**Note :** As BC member has force larger than AB, so there is decrease in total length of the member.

(iii) Diameter of portion BC :

$$\delta l = \left(\dfrac{Pl}{AE}\right)_{AB} + \left(\dfrac{Pl}{AE}\right)_{BC}$$

Substituting, $\quad -3 = \dfrac{20 \times 10^3 \times 700}{706.86 \times 200 \times 10^3} - \dfrac{80 \times 10^3 \times 800}{A \times 200 \times 10^3}$

$\therefore \qquad A = 103.25$ mm$^2$

$\therefore \qquad \dfrac{\pi}{4} D^2 = 103.25$

$\therefore \qquad D = \mathbf{11.466}$ **mm**

**Example 2.18 :** A steel bar (E = 200 GPa) is supported and loaded as shown in Fig. 2.22. The cross-sectional area of the bar is 250 mm². Determine the force P, so that the lower end D of the bar does not move vertically when the loads are applied.

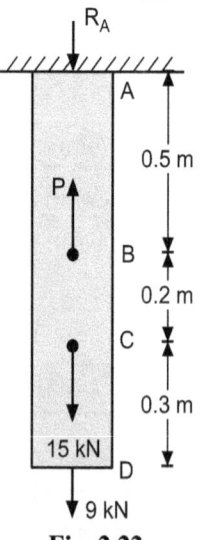

Fig. 2.22

**Data :** As shown in Fig. 2.22, A = 250 mm², E = 200 GPa, $\delta l = 0$.
**Required :** P.

**Concept :** (i) $\Sigma F_x = 0$ gives $R_A$, (ii) $\delta l = \dfrac{Pl}{AE}$

**Solution :** (i) Magnitude of reaction :
$$\Sigma F_x = 0$$
$$- R_A + P - 24 = 0$$
$$\therefore \quad R_A = (P - 24)$$

(ii) Total change in length :
$$\delta l = 0 = \delta l_{AB} + \delta l_{BC} + \delta l_{CD}$$
$$= \left(\dfrac{Pl}{AE}\right)_{AB} + \left(\dfrac{Pl}{AE}\right)_{BC} + \left(\dfrac{Pl}{AE}\right)_{CD}$$

Substituting, $\quad 0 = \dfrac{[-(P-24) \times 10^3 \times 500] + (24 \times 10^3 \times 200) + (9 \times 10^3 \times 300)}{AE}$

$$(P - 24) \times 10^3 \times 500 = (24 \times 10^3 \times 200) + (9 \times 10^3 \times 300)$$
$$\therefore \quad P = 39 \text{ kN}$$

**Example 2.19 :** A 30 kN weight is supported by means of a pulley as shown in Fig. 2.23. The pulley is supported by a frame ABC. Find the cross-sectional areas for members AC and BC if the allowable stress in tension is 140 MPa and in compression 96 MPa.

**Solution :**

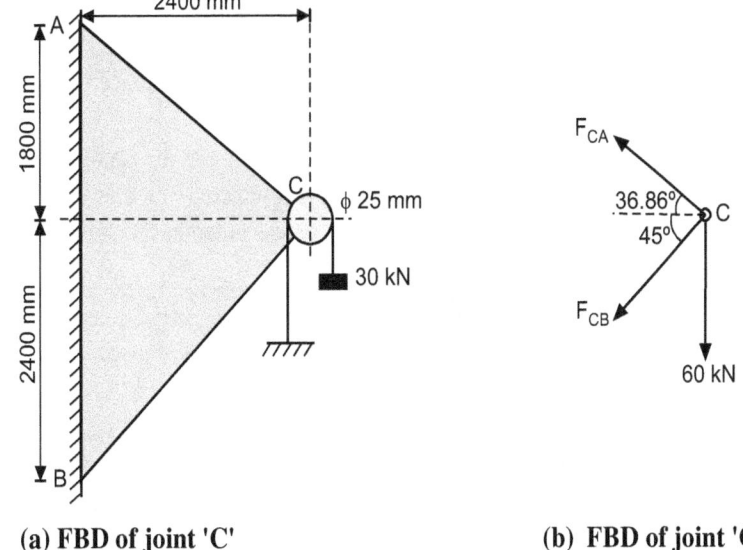

(a) FBD of joint 'C'      (b) FBD of joint 'C'

**Fig. 2.23**

(i) $\quad F_{CA} = 42.85$ kN (Tension)
$\quad F_{CB} = 48.48$ kN (Compression)

(ii) For AC,
$$\sigma = \frac{P}{A}$$
$$140 = \frac{42.85 \times 10^3}{A_{AC}}$$
∴ $A_{AC} = \mathbf{306.07 \ mm^2}$

For BC,
$$\sigma = \frac{P}{A}$$
$$96 = \frac{48.48 \times 10^3}{A_{BC}}$$
∴ $A_{BC} = 505 \ mm^2$

## 2.7 STATICALLY INDETERMINATE PROBLEMS

When laws of static equilibrium, $\sum F_x = 0$, $\sum F_y = 0$ and $\sum M_z = 0$ (3 equations for 2D analysis) are not sufficient enough to evaluate the unknown forces, it is called as statically indeterminate problem. For solution of such problems, additional equations are required to be employed called as equations of **compatibility**.

## 2.8 COMPATIBILITY

In addition to the static equilibrium conditions, it is necessary in any structural analysis, that all conditions of compatibility be satisfied. These conditions refer to continuity of displacements throughout the structure, and are sometimes referred as conditions of geometry. As an example, compatibility conditions must be satisfied at all points of support, where it is necessary that the displacements of the structure be consistent with the support conditions. For instance, at a fixed support, there can be no rotation as well as translation of member.

Compatibility conditions must also be satisfied at all points throughout the interior of structure / structural member. Usually it is compatibility conditions at the joints that are of interest. For example, at a rigid joint between two members, the displacements (translation and rotation) of both members must be the same.

The condition of compatibility required to be employed for the analysis of indeterminate problem must be corresponding to the unknown force selected for analysis i.e. condition of translation must be considered if force is considered as unknown and condition of rotation must be considered if moment is considered as unknown.

## 2.9 PRINCIPLE OF SUPERPOSITION

*The principle states that, the effects produced by several causes can be obtained by combining the effect due to individual causes (forces /actions).*

The principle of superposition is valid whenever linear relations exist between actions and displacements. This occurs whenever following three requirements are satisfied : (i) The material of structure follows Hooke's law; (ii) The displacements of the structure are small; and (iii) There is no interaction between axial and flexural effects in the member. The first of these requirements means that the material is perfectly elastic and has a linear relationship between stress and strain. The second requirement means that, all calculations involving overall dimensions of the structure can be based upon the original dimension of the structure. The third requirement implies that, the effect of axial force on bending of the member is neglected. This requirement refers to the fact that, axial forces in a member, in combination with even small deflections of the member, will have an effect on the bending moments. The effect is non-linear and can be omitted from the analysis when the axial forces are not large. When all three of these requirements are satisfied, the structure is said to be *linearly elastic*.

**Example 2.20 :** A steel bar 20 mm diameter is enclosed in a brass tube of 25 mm external diameter and 2 mm thickness. Assuming $\frac{E_s}{E_b} = 2$ and initial length of both components = 400 mm, determine the stresses in the steel and brass if the composite section is subjected to an axial compressive force of 50 kN. Assuming $E_s = 200$ GPa, find change in length of composite section.

**Data :** As shown in Fig. 2.24, $\frac{E_s}{E_b} = 2$, $E_s = 200$ GPa.

**Required :** Stresses in steel and brass, change in length.

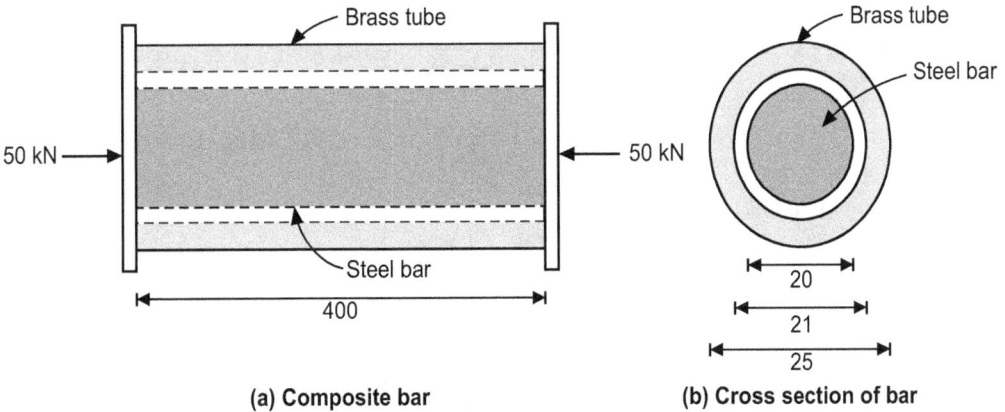

(a) Composite bar     (b) Cross section of bar

**Fig. 2.24**

**Concept :** Statically indeterminate.

(i) Equation of statics : $P_b + P_s = P$

i.e. Force in brass tube + Force in steel bar = Total force applied

(ii) Equation of compatibility.

$(\delta L)_b = (\delta L)_s$ i.e. change in length for brass and steel is equal.

**Solution :** (i) Geometric properties :

$$\text{Cross-sectional area of brass tube} = A_b = \frac{\pi}{4}[(25)^2 - (21)^2]$$

$$= 144.51 \text{ mm}^2$$

$$\text{Cross-sectional area of steel bar} = A_s = \frac{\pi}{4}(20)^2 = 314.15 \text{ mm}^2$$

(ii) Equation of statics :

$$P_b + P_s = P$$
$$P_b + P_s = 50 \qquad \qquad \text{... (i)}$$

(iii) Equation of compatibility :

$$(\delta L)_b = (\delta L)_s$$

$$\left(\frac{PL}{AE}\right)_b = \left(\frac{PL}{AE}\right)_s$$

$$\frac{P_b}{A_b} = \left(\frac{E_b}{E_s}\right)\left(\frac{P_s}{A_s}\right)$$

$$P_b = 144.51 \times \frac{1}{2} \times \frac{P_s}{314.15}$$

$$P_b = 0.23 \, P_s \qquad \ldots \text{(ii)}$$

(iv) Solution of equations :

Solving equations (i) and (ii),

$$P_s = 40.65 \text{ kN}$$
$$P_b = 9.35 \text{ kN}$$

(v) Stresses :

$$\sigma_b = \left(\frac{P}{A}\right)_b = \frac{9.35 \times 10^3}{144.51} = 64.7 \text{ MPa (Compressive)}$$

$$\sigma_s = \left(\frac{P}{A}\right)_s = \frac{40.65 \times 10^3}{314.15} = 129.39 \text{ MPa (Compressive)}$$

(vi) Change in length :

$$\delta L = (\delta L)_b \text{ OR } (\delta L)_s$$

$$= \left(\frac{\delta L}{E}\right)_s = \frac{129.39 \times 400}{200 \times 10^3} = 0.25 \text{ mm (decrease)}$$

**Example 2.21 :** A mild steel bar of cross-sectional area 380 mm² is surrounded by copper tube of area 175 mm² as shown in Fig. 2.25. This composite section is carrying a load of 50 kN. It is found that steel bar is longer by 0.2 mm. Find the stresses in each bar.
Assume $E_s$ = 200 GPa, $E_c$ = 100 GPa.

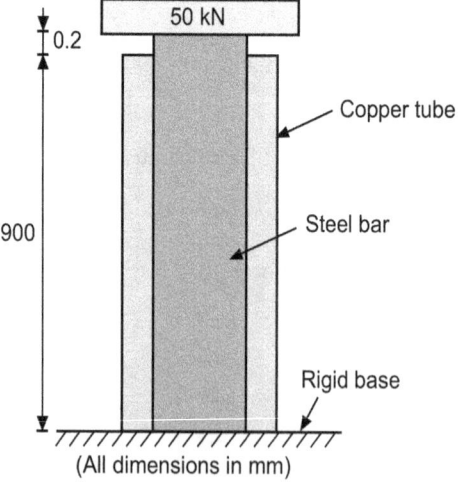

Fig. 2.25

**Data :** $A_s = 380$ mm², $A_c = 175$ mm², $P = 50$ kN, $E_s = 200$ GPa, $E_c = 100$ GPa

**Required :** Stresses in each bar.

**Concept :** Load applied = Load required to produce 0.2 mm shortening of steel bar (stage I) + Load resisted by composite action (stage II)

Let, $P_I$ = Load corresponding to stage I

and $P_{II}$ = Load corresponding to stage II

**Solution :** (i) Stage I :

$$(\delta L)_s = 0.2 = \left(\frac{PL}{AE}\right)_s$$

$$0.2 = \frac{P_I \times 900.2}{380 \times 200 \times 10^3}$$

$$P_I = 16885.13 \text{ N} = 16.88 \text{ kN}$$

Stresses at the end of stage I :

$$\sigma_s = \frac{16.88 \times 10^3}{380} = 44.42 \text{ MPa and } \sigma_c = 0$$

(ii) Stage II : Equation of statics :

$$P_{II} = P_c + P_s$$

$$(50 - 16.88) \times 10^3 = \sigma_c A_c + \sigma_s A_s$$

∴ $\quad 33.12 \times 10^3 = \sigma_c A_c + \sigma_s A_s \quad \ldots$ (i)

Equation of compatibility :

$$(\delta L)_c = (\delta L)_s$$

$$\left(\frac{\sigma L}{E}\right)_c = \left(\frac{\delta L}{E}\right)_s$$

$$\sigma_c = \frac{E_c}{E_s} \cdot \sigma_s$$

$$= \frac{100}{200} \times \sigma_s$$

$$\sigma_c = 0.5 \, \sigma_s \quad \ldots \text{(ii)}$$

Putting equation (ii) in equation (i),

$$33.12 \times 10^3 = 0.5 \, \sigma_s \times 175 + \sigma_s \times 380$$

$$\sigma_s = 70.84 \text{ MPa}$$

∴ $\quad \sigma_c = 35.42$ MPa

(iii) Final stresses :

$$\sigma_s = 44.42 + 70.84 = \mathbf{115.26 \text{ MPa}}$$

$$\sigma_c = 0 + 35.42 = \mathbf{35.42 \text{ MPa}}$$

**Example 2.22 :** Two bars having geometric properties as shown in Fig. 2.26 are rigidly connected at ends. Find stresses in each bar when 40 kN load is applied axially on composite section. Assume $E_1 = 200$ GPa and $E_2 = 100$ GPa.

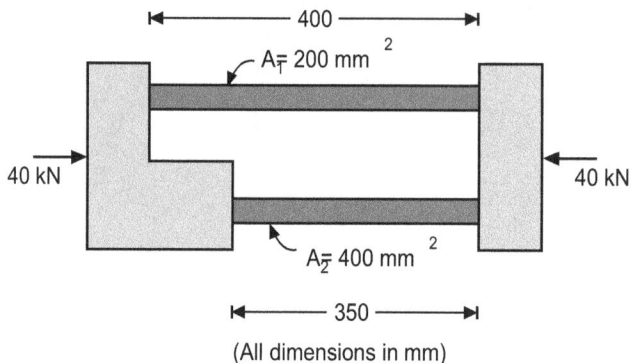

Fig. 2.26

**Data :** As shown in Fig. 2.26.

**Required :** Stresses in each bar.

**Concept :** Composite section, statically indeterminate, statics and compatibility.

**Solution :** (i) Equation of statics :

$$P = P_1 + P_2$$
$$40 \times 10^3 = \sigma_1 A_1 + \sigma_2 A_2 \quad \ldots (i)$$

(ii) Equation of compatibility :

$$(\delta L)_1 = (\delta L)_2$$

**Note :** Shortening of the bars is same but not the strain.

$$\left(\frac{\sigma L}{E}\right)_1 = \left(\frac{\sigma L}{E}\right)_2$$

$$\frac{\sigma_1 \times 400}{200 \times 10^3} = \frac{\sigma_2 \times 350}{100 \times 10^3}$$

$$\sigma_1 = 1.75 \, \sigma_2 \quad \ldots (ii)$$

(iii) Solution of equations :

Put equation (ii) in equation (i),

$$40 \times 10^3 = (1.75 \, \sigma_2)(200) + \sigma_2 \times 400$$

$$\therefore \quad \sigma_2 = \mathbf{53.33 \text{ MPa}}$$

$$\therefore \quad \sigma_1 = 1.75 \times 53.33$$

$$= \mathbf{93.33 \text{ MPa}}$$

**Example 2.23 :** For the compound section fixed at both ends as shown in Fig. 2.33 (a), find (i) Reactions at both the ends, (ii) Stresses in individual components.

| Material | Component | | |
|---|---|---|---|
| | AB | BC | CD |
| Material | Copper | Aluminium | Brass |
| Length (mm) | 500 | 400 | 600 |
| c/s area (mm²) | 400 | 300 | 550 |
| E (GPa) | 120 | 70 | 100 |

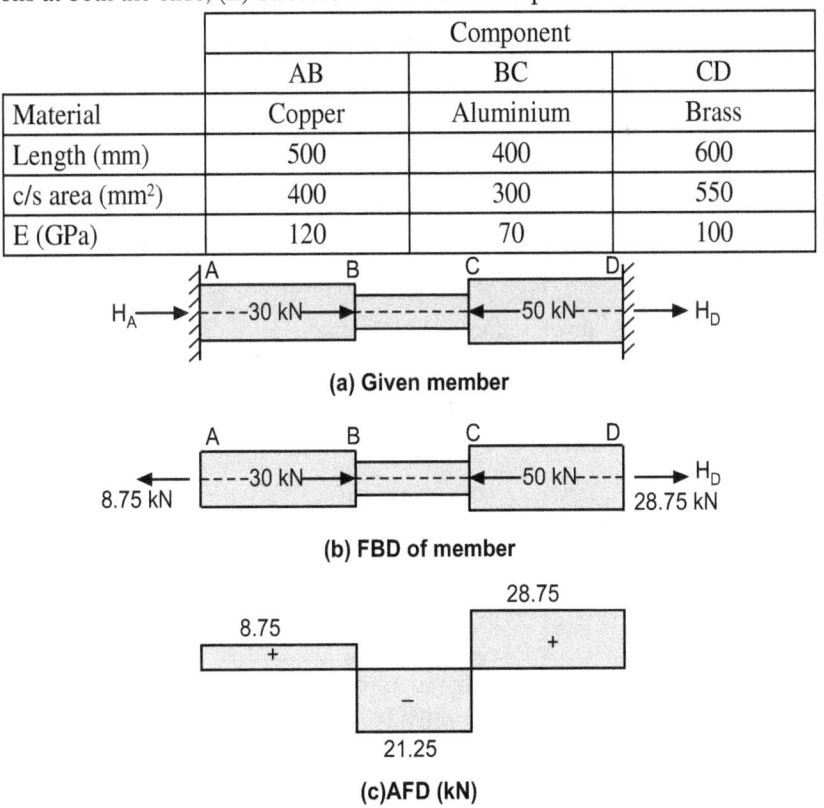

(a) Given member

(b) FBD of member

(c) AFD (kN)

Fig. 2.27

**Data :** As shown in Fig. 2.27 (a).
**Required :** (i) Reactions at both fixed ends and (ii) Stresses in individual components.
**Concept :** Statically indeterminate.

(i) Equation of statics : $\Sigma F_x = 0$

(ii) Equation of compatibility : $\delta L = (\delta L)_{AB} + (\delta L)_{BC} + (\delta L)_{CD} = 0$

**Solution :** (i) Equation of statics :
Assuming $H_A$ and $H_D$ both towards right,

$\Sigma F_x = 0, \quad H_A + 30 - 50 + H_D = 0$

$$H_A + H_D = 20 \quad \ldots \text{(i)}$$

(ii) Equation of compatibility :

$$\delta L = (\delta L)_{AB} + (\delta L)_{BC} + (\delta L)_{CD} = 0$$

$$\therefore \left(\frac{PL}{AE}\right)_{AB} + \left(\frac{PL}{AE}\right)_{BC} + \left(\frac{PL}{AE}\right)_{CD} = 0$$

$$\frac{H_A \times 500}{400 \times 120} + \frac{(H_A + 30) \times 400}{300 \times 70} + \frac{(H_A + 30 - 50) \times 600}{550 \times 100} = 0$$

$$0.0403 \, H_A + 0.353 = 0 \quad \ldots \text{(ii)}$$

(iii) Solution of equations :

Solving equations (i) and (ii),  $H_A = -8.75$ kN $= 8.75$ kN ($\leftarrow$)

$H_D = 28.75$ kN $= 28.75$ kN ($\rightarrow$)

FBD of member is as shown in Fig. 2.27 (b).

(iv) Axial force diagram :

Considering sections in portions AB, BC and CD,

$$P_{AB} = 8.75 \text{ kN (Tensile)}$$
$$P_{BC} = 8.75 - 30 = -21.25 \text{ kN} = 21.25 \text{ kN (Compressive)}$$
$$P_{CD} = 28.75 \text{ kN (Tensile)}$$

Axial force diagram is as shown in Fig. 2.27 (c).

(v) Stresses :

$$(\sigma)_{AB} = \left(\frac{P}{A}\right)_{AB} = \frac{8.75 \times 10^3}{400} = 21.87 \text{ MPa (Tensile)}$$

$$(\sigma)_{BC} = \left(\frac{P}{A}\right)_{BC} = \frac{21.25 \times 10^3}{300} = 70.83 \text{ MPa (Compressive)}$$

$$(\sigma)_{CD} = \left(\frac{P}{A}\right)_{CD} = \frac{28.75 \times 10^3}{550} = 52.27 \text{ MPa (Tensile)}$$

**Example 2.24 :** A 20 mm diameter bar is fixed at ends A and B. Two collars weighing 12 kN and 20 kN are placed at C and D respectively as shown in Fig. 2.28. Find
(i) Reactions at ends A and B, (ii) Stresses in each portion and
(iii) Distance through which each collar moves.
Assume E = 200 GPa.

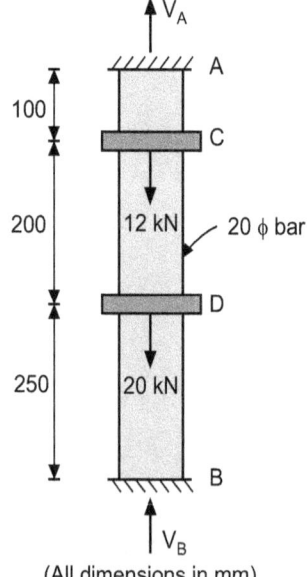

(All dimensions in mm)

**Fig. 2.28**

**Data :** As shown in Fig. 2.28. E = 200 GPa.

**Required :** (i) Reactions at A and B,
(ii) Stresses in each portion and
(iii) Displacement of each collar.

**Concept :** Statically indeterminate problem. Equations of statics and compatibility.

**Solution :** (i) Geometric properties of bar :

$$A = \frac{\pi}{4}(20)^2 = 314.16 \text{ mm}^2$$

(ii) Equation of statics :
Assuming $V_A$ and $V_B$ both upwards,
$\Sigma F_y = 0$,  $V_A + V_B - 12 - 20 = 0$
$\therefore$   $V_A + V_B = 32$   ... (i)

(iii) Equation of compatibility :
$\delta L = (\delta L)_{AC} + (\delta L)_{CD} + (\delta L)_{DB} = 0$

$\therefore \left(\frac{PL}{AE}\right)_{AC} + \left(\frac{PL}{AE}\right)_{CD} + \left(\frac{PL}{AE}\right)_{DB} = 0$

$\therefore \frac{1}{AE} [V_A \times 100 + (V_A - 12) \times 200 + (V_A - 12 - 20) \times 250] = 0$

$\therefore \frac{1}{AE} [550 V_A - 10400] = 0$   ... (ii)

(iv) Solution of equations :
From equation (ii),
$550 V_A - 10400 = 0$
$\therefore$   $V_A = 18.9$ kN ($\uparrow$)
Put in (i),   $V_B = 13.1$ kN ($\uparrow$)

(v) FBD of member and axial force diagram (AFD) :

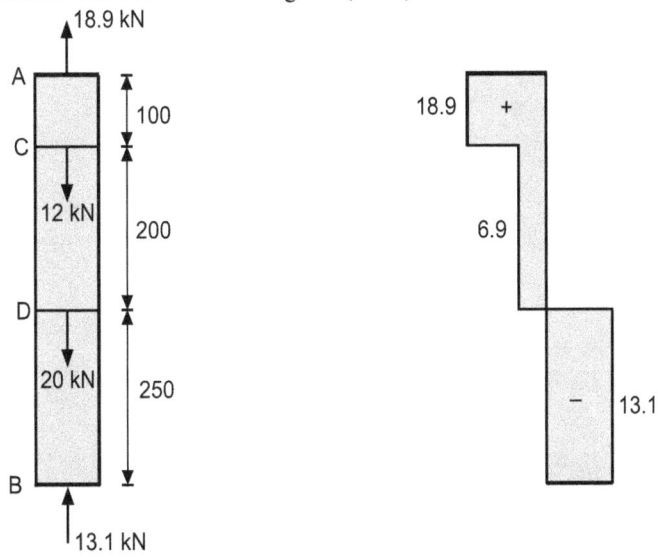

(a) FBD of member   (All dimensions in mm)   (b) AFD (kN)

Fig. 2.29

**(vi) Stresses in components :**

$$\sigma_{AC} = \left(\frac{P}{A}\right)_{AC} = \frac{18.9 \times 10^3}{314.16} = 60.16 \text{ MPa (Tensile)}$$

$$\sigma_{CD} = \left(\frac{P}{A}\right)_{CD} = \frac{6.9 \times 10^3}{314.16} = 21.96 \text{ MPa (Tensile)}$$

$$\sigma_{DB} = \left(\frac{P}{A}\right)_{DB} = \frac{13.1 \times 10^3}{314.16} = 41.69 \text{ MPa (Compressive)}$$

**(vii) Displacements of collars :**

$$\text{Displacement of collar C} = (\delta L)_{AC} = \left(\frac{\sigma L}{E}\right)_{AC} = \frac{60.16 \times 100}{200 \times 10^3} = 0.03 \text{ mm } (\downarrow)$$

$$\begin{aligned}
\text{Displacement of collar D} &= (\delta L)_{AD} \\
&= (\delta L)_{AC} + (\delta L)_{CD} = \left(\frac{\sigma L}{E}\right)_{AC} + \left(\frac{\sigma L}{E}\right)_{CD} \\
&= \frac{1}{E}(60.16 \times 100 + 21.96 \times 200) = \frac{10408}{200 \times 10^3} \\
&= \mathbf{0.052 \text{ mm } (\downarrow)}
\end{aligned}$$

**Example 2.25 :** A composite bar ABC is rigidly fixed at A and 1 mm above the lower support is loaded as shown in Fig. 2.30. Determine the reactions at the end and the stresses in the two components. Assume E = 200 GPa.

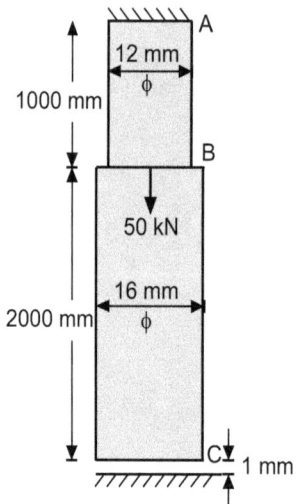

**Fig. 2.30**

**Data :** As shown in Fig. 2.30, E = 200 × 10³ MPa.

**Required :** Stresses in the bar.

**Concept :** $\delta l = \dfrac{Pl}{AE}$

**Solution :** (i) Geometric properties :

$$A_{AB} = \frac{\pi}{4} \times (12)^2 = 113.10 \text{ mm}^2$$

$$A_{BC} = \frac{\pi}{4} \times (16)^2 = 201.06 \text{ mm}^2$$

(ii) Force required to touch the support 'C' :

**Note :** Bar AB is in tension and bar BC is in compression, so stresses are developed in AB due to increase in length.

$$\therefore \quad \delta l = \left(\frac{Pl}{AE}\right)_{AB}$$

$$1 = \frac{P \times 10^3 \times 1000}{113.10 \times 200 \times 10^3}$$

$$\therefore \quad P = 22.62 \text{ kN}$$

$$\therefore \quad \text{Force balanced} = 50 - 22.62$$

$$= 27.380 \text{ kN}$$

(iii) Calculation of stresses :

$$P_{AB1} + P_{BC} = 27.381 \text{ kN} \quad \ldots (i)$$

$$\delta l_{AB} = \delta l_{BC}$$

$$\left(\frac{Pl}{AE}\right)_{AB} = \left(\frac{Pl}{AE}\right)_{BC}$$

$$\frac{P_{AB1} \times 1000}{113.10 \times E} = \frac{P_{BC} \times 2000}{201.06 \times E}$$

$$P_{AB1} = 1.125 \, P_{BC} \quad \ldots (ii)$$

Solving (i) and (ii),

$$P_{BC} = 12.89 \text{ kN}$$

$$P_{AB1} = 14.50 \text{ kN}$$

$$\therefore \quad P_{AB} = P + P_{AB1}$$

$$= 22.62 + 14.50 = 37.12 \text{ kN}$$

$$P_{BC} = 12.89 \text{ kN}$$

$$\therefore \quad \text{Stress in AB} = \frac{P_{AB}}{A_{AB}}$$

$$\sigma_{AB} = \frac{37.12 \times 10^3}{113.10} = \mathbf{328.21 \text{ MPa}}$$

$$\text{Stress in BC} = \frac{P_{BC}}{A_{BC}}$$

$$\sigma_{BC} = \frac{12.89 \times 10^3}{201.06} = \mathbf{64.11 \text{ MPa}}$$

**Example 2.26 :** Two steel rods and one copper rod each of 20 mm diameter, together support a load of 20 kN as shown in Fig. 2.31. Find the stresses in rods. Take $E_{st}$ and $E_{Cu}$ as 205 GN/m² and 110 GN/m² respectively.

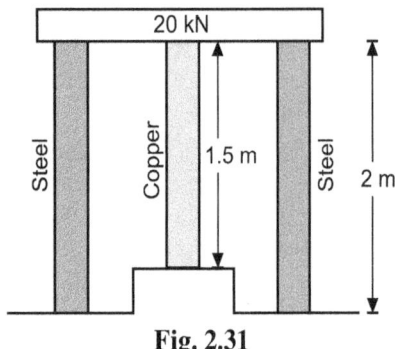

**Fig. 2.31**

**Data :** As shown in Fig. 2.31, $D_{st}$ = 20 mm, $D_{Cu}$ = 20 mm,

$$E_{st} = 205 \times 10^3 \text{ N/mm}^2, \quad E_{Cu} = 110 \times 10^3 \text{ N/mm}^2$$

**Required :** Stresses in rods.

**Concept :** Statically indeterminate.

(a) Forces in rods = Total load

(b) $\delta_{st} = \delta_{Cu}$

**Solution :** (i) Geometric properties : $A_{st} = A_{Cu} = \dfrac{\pi}{4} \times (20)^2 = 314.16 \text{ mm}^2$

(ii) Equation of equilibrium :

$$P_{st} + P_{Cu} + P_{st} = 20 \text{ kN}$$

∴ $\quad 2 P_{st} + P_{Cu} = 20 \quad$ ... (i)

(iii) $\quad \delta l_{st} = \delta l_{Cu}$

$$\left(\dfrac{Pl}{AE}\right)_{st} = \left(\dfrac{Pl}{AE}\right)_{Cu}$$

$$\dfrac{P_{st} \times 10^3 \times 2000}{\dfrac{\pi}{4} \times (20)^2 \times 205 \times 10^3} = \dfrac{P_{Cu} \times 10^3 \times 1500}{\dfrac{\pi}{4} \times (20)^2 \times 110 \times 10^3}$$

$$P_{st} = 1.4 \, P_{Cu} \quad \text{... (ii)}$$

Solving equations (i) and (ii),

$$P_{Cu} = 5.26 \text{ kN}$$
$$P_{st} = 7.36 \text{ kN}$$

∴ $\quad$ Stress in steel $= \dfrac{P_{st}}{A_{st}} = \dfrac{7.36 \times 10^3}{314.16}$

∴ $\quad \sigma_{st} = \mathbf{23.43 \text{ MPa}}$

$\quad$ Stress in copper $= \dfrac{P_{Cu}}{A_{Cu}} = \dfrac{5.26 \times 10^3}{314.16}$

∴ $\quad \sigma_{Cu} = \mathbf{16.74 \text{ MPa}}$

**Example 2.27 :** Fig. 2.32 shows a round steel rod supported and surrounded by co-axial brass tube. The upper end of the rod is 0.1 mm below that of the tube and axial load is applied to a rigid plate resting on the top of the tube.

(i) Determine the magnitude of the maximum permissible load if the compressive stress in the rod is not to exceed 110 MPa and that in the tube not to exceed 80 MPa.

(ii) Find the amount by which the tube will be shortened by the load if the compressive stress in the tube is same as that in the rod. $E_s = 210$ GPa, $E_b = 90$ GPa.

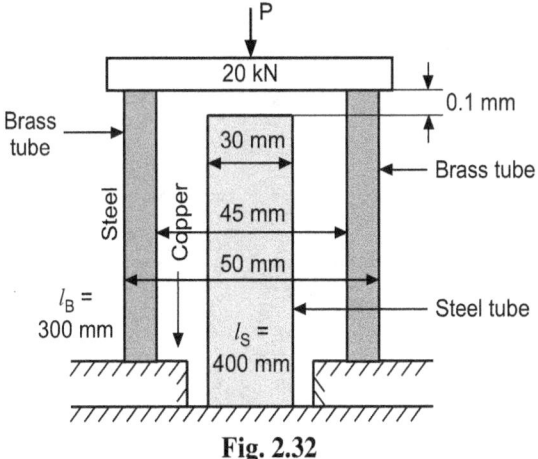

**Fig. 2.32**

**Data :** As shown in Fig. 2.32, $\sigma_{br\ max} = 110$ MPa,

$\sigma_{st\ max} = 80$ MPa, $E_{st} = 210 \times 10^3$ MPa, $E_b = 90 \times 10^3$ MPa.

**Required :** (i) Maximum value of P.
(ii) Amount of tube to be shorten.

**Concept :** (a) Force in rods + Force in tube = Total force
(b) $\delta_{br} + 0.1 = \delta_{st}$

**Solution :** (i) Geometric properties :

$$A_{br} = \frac{\pi}{4}[(50)^2 - (45)^2] = 373.06 \text{ mm}^2$$

$$A_{st} = \frac{\pi}{4} \times 30^2 = 706.86 \text{ mm}^2$$

(ii) Stress developed in brass to shorten by 0.1 mm

$$\delta l = \left(\frac{Pl}{AE}\right)_{Br}$$

$$0.1 = \frac{\sigma_{Brl} \times 300}{90 \times 10^3}$$

∴ $\sigma_{Brl} = 30$ MPa

(iii) $\delta l_{Br} = \delta l_{st}$

$$\left(\frac{Pl}{AE}\right)_{Br} = \left(\frac{Pl}{AE}\right)_{st}$$

$$\frac{\sigma_{Br} \times 300}{90 \times 10^3} = \frac{\sigma_{st} \times 400}{210 \times 10^3}$$

$$\sigma_{Br} = 0.57 \, \sigma_S$$

∴ $\sigma_{st} = \dfrac{50}{0.57} = 87.22 \text{ MPa} < 110 \text{ MPa}$

∴ Force taken by brass $= \sigma_{Br} \times A_{Br}$
$= 80 \times 373.06$
$P_{Br} = 29.84 \text{ kN}$

Force taken by steel $= \sigma_{st} \times A_{st}$
$P_{st} = 87.22 \times 706.85 = 62 \text{ kN}$
$P = P_{Br} + P_{st} = 29.84 + 62 = \mathbf{91.84 \text{ kN}}$

(iv) Amount of tube shorten: $\delta l = \left(\dfrac{Pl}{AE}\right)_{Br} = \dfrac{\sigma_{Br} \times l}{E} = \dfrac{80 \times 300}{90 \times 10^3}$

$= 0.267 \text{ mm}$

**Example 2.28 :** A rigid member ABCD is supported as shown in Fig. 2.33. Find stresses in steel wires at 'B' and 'C'.

**Data :** As shown in Fig. 2.33 (a).

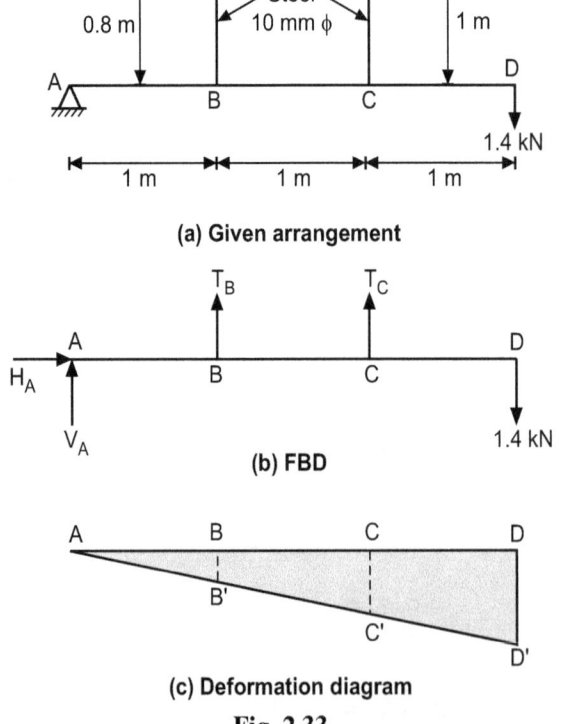

(a) Given arrangement

(b) FBD

(c) Deformation diagram

**Fig. 2.33**

**Required :** Stresses in steel wires at 'B' and 'C'.
**Concept :** Statically indeterminate, statics and compatibility.
**Solution :** (i) Equation of statics :

$$\Sigma M_A = 0$$
$$T_B \times 1 + T_C \times 2 - 1.4 \times 3 = 0$$
$$\therefore \quad T_B + 2T_C = 4.2 \qquad ...(i)$$

(ii) From compatibility,
$$\frac{CC'}{2} = \frac{BB'}{1}$$
$$\therefore \quad CC' = 2\,BB'$$
$$\therefore \quad \left(\frac{PL}{AE}\right)_C = \left(\frac{2PL}{AE}\right)_B$$
$$\frac{T_C \times 1000}{(AE)} = \frac{2\,T_B \times 800}{(AE)}$$
$$\therefore \quad T_C = 1.6\,T_B \qquad ...(ii)$$

(iii) Solving (i) and (ii),
$$T_B = 1 \text{ kN}$$
$$T_C = 1.6 \text{ kN}$$

(iv) Stresses :
$$\sigma_B = \frac{1 \times 10^3}{\frac{\pi}{4} \times 10^2} = 12.7 \text{ MPa (Tensile)}$$

$$\sigma_C = \frac{1.6 \times 10^3}{\frac{\pi}{4} \times 10^2} = 20.37 \text{ MPa (Tensile)}$$

---

**Example 2.29 :** Find the safe value of 'P' if stresses in steel and brass are restricted to 150 MPa and 70 MPa respectively.

**Data :** As shown in Fig. 2.34 (a).
**Required :** Safe value of P.
**Concept :** Governing stresses shall be obtained from geometry of deformation.
**Solution :** (i) Geometry of deformation :

$$\frac{CC'}{1.5} = \frac{DD'}{3}$$
$$CC' = 0.5\,DD'$$
$$\left(\frac{\sigma L}{E}\right)_S = 0.5 \left(\frac{\sigma L}{E}\right)_D$$
$$\frac{\sigma_s \times 1500}{200 \times 10^3} = 0.5 \left(\frac{\sigma_b \times 2000}{83 \times 10^3}\right)$$
$$\sigma_s = 1.606\,\sigma_b \qquad ...(i)$$

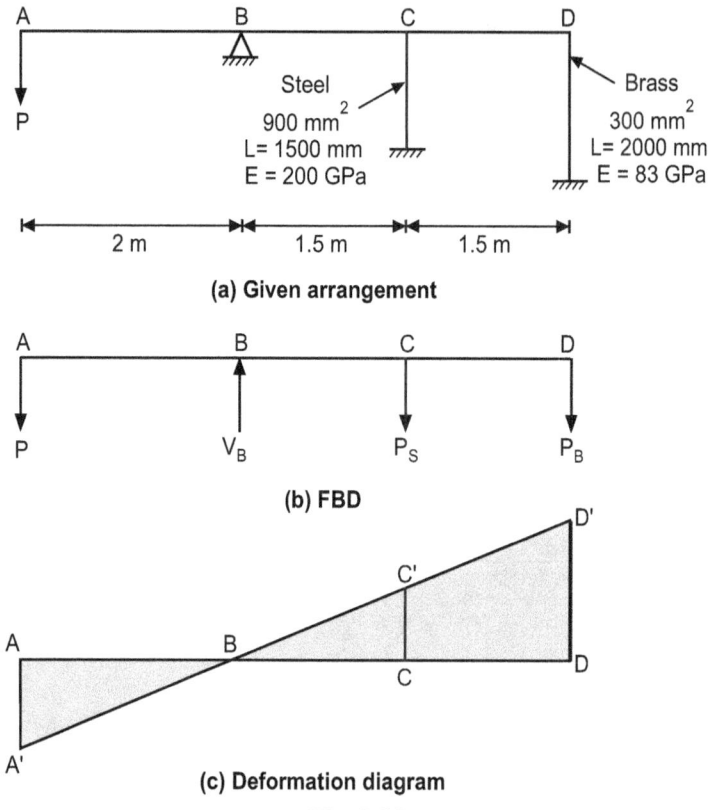

(a) Given arrangement

(b) FBD

(c) Deformation diagram

**Fig. 2.34**

(ii) Stresses :

Let,          $\sigma_s$ = 150 MPa     put in (i)

∴          $\sigma_b$ = 93.4 MPa > 70 MPa     ∴ Not allowed

Let,          $\sigma_b$ = 70 MPa     put in (i)

∴          $\sigma_s$ = 112.42 MPa < 150 MPa    ∴ OK

(iii) Forces :     $P_s = \sigma_s A_s = 112.42 \times 900 \times 10^{-3} = 101.78$ kN   ... (ii)

$P_b = \sigma_b A_b = 70 \times 300 \times 10^{-3} = 21$ kN

(iv) Safe value of (P),

From FBD,      $\Sigma M_B = 0$

$2P - 1.5 P_s - 3 P_b = 0$         ... (iii)

Put $P_s$ and $P_b$ from (ii) in (iii),

$2P - 1.5 \times 101.78 - 3 \times 21 = 0$

∴          P = **107.835 kN**

**Example 2.30 :** A uniform bar AB of length L is suspended in a horizontal position under its own weight by two vertical wires attached to it's ends. Both wires are made of same material and have the same cross-sectional area, but the lengths are $L_1$ and $L_2$. Derive a formula for the distance x (from A) to the point on the bar where a vertical load P should be applied if the bar is to remain horizontal.

**Solution :** Data : $A_{AC} = A_{BD}$, $E_{AC} = E_{BD}$.

**Required :** Expression for distance 'x'.

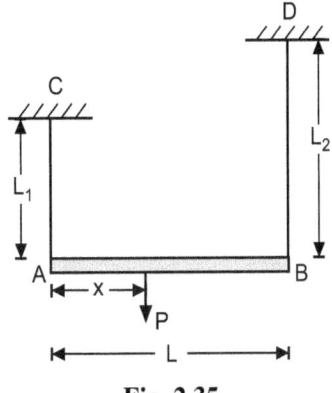

Fig. 2.35

Let $P_1$ and $P_2$ be the forces in wires CA and DB.

∴ Moment @ CA = 0.

∴
$$P \times x = P_2 \times L$$
$$P_1 + P_2 = P$$

As bar remains horizontal,
$$\delta l_{AC} = \delta l_{BD}$$
$$\frac{P_1 L_1}{AE} = \frac{P_2 L_2}{AE}$$
$$P_1 L_1 = P_2 L_2$$

∴
$$\frac{P_1}{P_2} = \frac{L_2}{L_1}$$

$$P_1 = P - P_2 = P - \frac{P_1 L_1}{L_2} \quad \text{from (i)}$$

∴
$$P_1 = \frac{PL_2 - P_1 L_1}{L_2}$$

$$P(L_2 + L_1) = PL_2$$

$$\frac{P_1(L_2 + L_1)}{L_2} \ x = P_2 \times L$$

$$\frac{P_1}{P_2} \ x = \frac{L_2 \times L}{(L_2 + L_1)}$$

$$\frac{L_2}{L_1} \ x = \frac{L_2 \times L}{(L_2 + L_1)}$$

$$x = \left(\frac{LL_1}{L_2 + L_1}\right)$$

**Example 2.31:** Three wires of same material and same cross-sectional area supports load 'P' as shown. Wire no. 1 is 1 m long while wires 2 and 3 are longer by 0.5 mm and 1 mm respectively. Determine the load P which will induce the tensile stress of 250 MPa in wire no. 1. Take c/s area = 10 mm², E = 200 GPa.

**Data:** $A = 10 \text{ mm}^2$, $\sigma_1 = 250$ MPa,

$L_1 = 1\text{m}$, $E = 200$ GPa.

**Required:** Load P.

**Concept:** Find elongation of each wire and hence forces in them. $P = P_1 + P_2 + P_3$

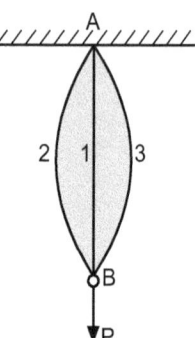

**Fig. 2.36 : Given arrangement**

**Solution:** (i) $\quad P_1 = \sigma_1 A_1 = 250 \times 10 = 2500$ N

$\therefore \quad (\delta L)_1 = \left(\dfrac{\sigma L}{E}\right)_1 = \left(\dfrac{250 \times 1000}{200 \times 10^3}\right) = 1.25$ mm

$\therefore \quad (\delta L)_2 = 1.25 - 0.5 \text{ mm} = 0.75$ mm

$(\delta L)_3 = 1.25 - 1 = 0.25$ mm

(ii) $\quad (\delta L)_2 = \left(\dfrac{\sigma L}{E}\right)_2$

$0.75 = \dfrac{\sigma_2 \times 1000}{200 \times 10^3}$

$\therefore \quad \sigma_2 = 150$ MPa

$\therefore \quad P_2 = \sigma_2 A_2 = 150 \times 10 = 1500$ N

$(\delta L)_3 = \left(\dfrac{\sigma L}{E}\right)_3$

$0.25 = \dfrac{\sigma_3 \times 1000}{200 \times 10^3}$

$\therefore \quad \sigma_3 = 50$ MPa

$\therefore \quad P_3 = \sigma_3 A_3 = 50 \times 10 = 500$ N

$\therefore \quad$ Total $P = P_1 + P_2 + P_3$

$= 2500 + 1500 + 500$

$= 4500$ N

$= 4.5$ kN

**Example 2.32 :** Four G.I. wires of 4 mm diameter spaced at an interval of 500 mm as shown in Fig. 2.37 (a) are jointly supporting a rigid bar. Assuming negligible weight of the bar, find stresses in each rod due to load of 3 kN supported at C.

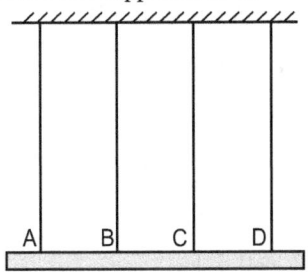

**(a) Right bar supported by wires**

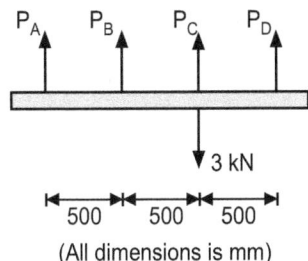

(All dimensions is mm)

**(b) FBD of rigid bar**

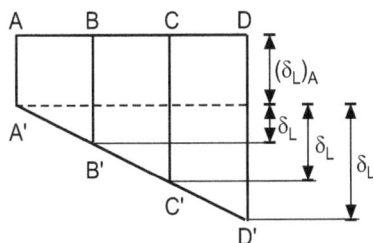

**(c) Deformation of wires**

**Fig. 2.37**

**Data :** As shown in Fig. 2.37 (a).

**Required :** Stresses in each wire.

**Concept :** Statically indeterminate. Equations of statics and compatibility.

**Solution :** (i) Equations of statics :

Let $P_A, P_B, P_C$ and $P_D$ be the forces in wires A, B, C and D respectively.

Taking moments @ $P_A$,

$$P_B \times 500 + P_C \times 1000 - 3 \times 1000 + P_D \times 1500 = 0$$

∴  $\quad P_B + 2 P_C + 3 P_D = 6$ ... (i)

And $\Sigma F_y = 0$, $\quad P_A + P_B + P_C + P_D = 3$ ... (ii)

(ii) Equation of compatibility :

Let,  $(\delta L)_A$ = Elongation of wire A from geometry of Fig. 2.37 (b)

$\delta L_A + \delta L$ = Elongation of wire B

$\delta L_A + 2\delta L$ = Elongation of wire C

$\delta L_A + 3\delta L$ = Elongation of wire D

Also, $P_A$ is the force which causes elongation = $\delta L_A$

Let, P' be the force which causes elongation = $\delta L$

$\therefore$
$$\left.\begin{array}{l} P_B = P_A + P' \\ P_C = P_A + 2P' \\ P_D = P_A + 3P' \end{array}\right\} \qquad \ldots \text{(iii)}$$

(iii) Solution of equations : Putting equation (iii) in equation (i), we get

$P_A + P' + 2(P_A + 2P') + 3(P_A + 3P') = 6$

$6P_A + 14 P' = 6$ ... (iv)

Putting equation (iii) in equation (ii), we get

$P_A + (P_A + P') + (P_A + 2P') + (P_A + 3P') = 3$

$\therefore \qquad 4P_A + 6P' = 3$ ... (v)

Solving equations (iv) and (v),

$P_A$ = 0.3 kN

$P'$ = 0.3 kN

(iv) Stresses in each wire :

Area of each wire = $A = \frac{\pi}{4}(4)^2$ = 12.56 mm²

$\sigma_A = \dfrac{P_A}{A} = \dfrac{0.3 \times 10^3}{12.56}$ = **23.89 MPa**

$\sigma_B = \dfrac{P_B}{A} = \dfrac{P_A + P'}{A} = \dfrac{(0.3 + 0.3) \times 10^3}{12.56}$ = **47.77 MPa**

$\sigma_C = \dfrac{P_C}{A} = \dfrac{P_A + 2P'}{A} = \dfrac{(0.3 + 2 \times 0.3) \times 10^3}{12.56}$ = **71.65 MPa**

$\sigma_D = \dfrac{P_D}{A} = \dfrac{P_A + 3P'}{A} = \dfrac{(0.3 + 3 \times 0.3) \times 10^3}{12.56}$ = **95.54 MPa**

**Example 2.33 :** A load of 5 kN is suspended from (i) a frictionless pulley and placed on a continuous rope as shown in Fig. 2.38 (a) and (ii) a rigid platform supported by two ropes as shown in Fig. 2.38 (b). The platform remaining horizontal before and after being loaded. If the area of cross-section of each rope is 50 mm², find the stresses in the ropes and the vertical displacement of the load in each case. Assume E = 200 GPa.

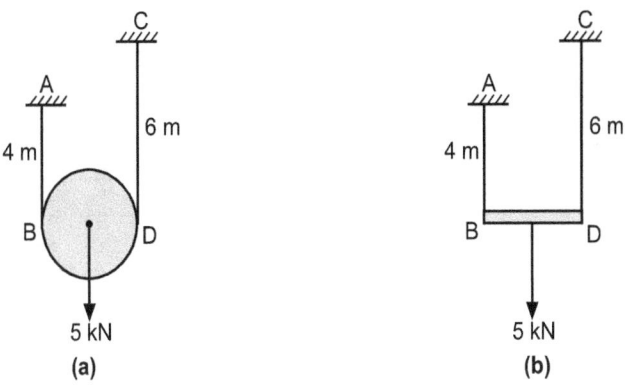

Fig. 2.38

**Data :** As shown in Fig. 2.38 (a) and (b), cross-sectional area = 50 mm², 

E = 200 × 10³ MPa and vertical displacement of the platform.

**Concept :** $\delta l_{AB} = \delta l_{CD}$, $P_{AB} + P_{CD} = 50$ kN

**Solution : Case (i) :** $\delta l_{AB} = \left(\dfrac{Pl}{AE}\right)_{AB}$, $\delta l_{CD} = \left(\dfrac{Pl}{AE}\right)_{CD}$

∴ $\left(\dfrac{Pl}{AE}\right)_{AB} = \left(\dfrac{Pl}{AE}\right)_{CD}$

$\dfrac{P_{AB} \times 4000}{50 \times 200} = \dfrac{P_{CD} \times 6000}{50 \times 200}$

∴ $P_{AB} = 1.5 \, P_{CD}$

∴ $P_{AB} = 30$ kN

$P_{CD} = 20$ kN

∴ $\sigma_{AB} = \dfrac{P_{AB}}{A_{AB}} = \dfrac{30 \times 10^3}{50} = 600$ mm²

$\sigma_{CD} = \dfrac{P_{CD}}{A_{CD}} = \dfrac{20 \times 10^3}{50} = 400$ mm²

Vertical displacement of pulley,

$\delta = \left(\dfrac{Pl}{AE}\right)_{AB} = \dfrac{30 \times 10^3 \times 4000}{50 \times 200 \times 10^3}$

∴ $\delta = 12$ mm

**Case (ii) :** Same as case (i).

**Example 2.34 :** The bar AB held between rigid supports, has cross-sectional area $A_1$ from A to C and $2A_1$ from C to B. Find the displacement at point D where the load P acts. What are the reactions at supports A and B ? Refer Fig. 2.39.

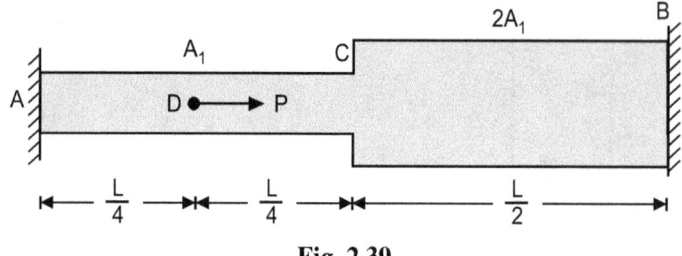

**Fig. 2.39**

**Data :** As shown in Fig. 2.39.
**Required :** Displacement at point D.
**Concept :** Standard formulae.
**Solution :**

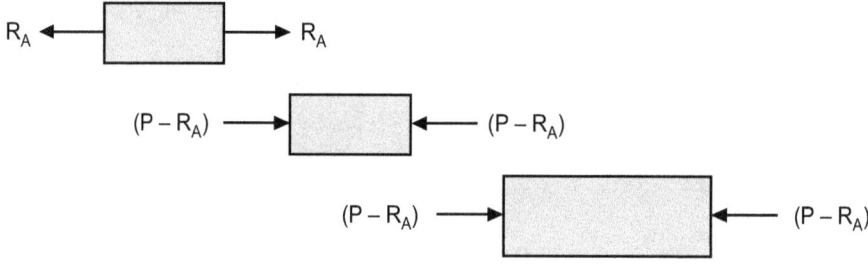

**Fig. 2.40**

Bar AB is in tension, and DC and CB are in compression.

$$\therefore \quad \delta l_{AB} = \delta l_{DC} + \delta l_{CB}$$

$$\therefore \quad \frac{R_A \times 10^3}{A_1 \times E} \times \frac{L}{4} = \frac{(P - R_A) \times 10^3}{A_1 \times E} \times \frac{L}{4} + \frac{(P - R_A) \times 10^3}{2 A_1 \times E} \times \frac{L}{2}$$

$$R_A = P - R_A + P - R_A$$

$$\therefore \quad 3 R_A = 2P$$

$$\therefore \quad R_A = \frac{2P}{3}$$

$$\therefore \quad R_A = \frac{2P}{3} \; (\leftarrow)$$

$$R_B = \frac{P}{3} \; (\leftarrow)$$

$$\text{Displacement at point D} = \frac{Pl}{AE}$$

$$= \frac{R_A \times 10^3}{A_1 \times E} \times \frac{L}{4}$$

$$= \frac{2P \times 10^3}{3 A_1 E} \times \frac{L}{4} = \frac{PL \times 10^3}{6 A_1 E}$$

where P is in kN.

**Example 2.35 :** Two horizontal rigid bars AB and CD are connected by wires of length L, modulus of elasticity E and diameters $d_1$ and $d_2$. Refer Fig. 2.41. What is the increase ($\delta$) in the distance between points E and F where vertical load P act ?

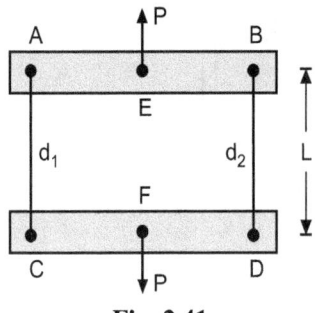

Fig. 2.41

**Data :** As shown in Fig. 2.41
**Required :** Increase ($\delta$) in distance between E and F.
**Solution :** Let $P_A$ and $P_B$ be the forces in wires AC and BD respectively.

∴ Moment @ AC = 0

∴ $$P \times \frac{L}{2} = P_B \times L$$

∴ $$P_B = \frac{P}{2}$$

∴ $$P_A = \frac{P}{2}$$

Let $\delta l_{AB}$ and $\delta l_{BD}$ be the displacements in members AC and BD.

∴ $$\delta l_{AB} = \frac{P_A L}{\frac{\pi}{4} d_1^2 \times E} = \frac{2PL}{\pi d_1^2 E}$$

$$\delta l_{BD} = \frac{P_B \times L}{\frac{\pi}{4} \times d_2^2 E} = \frac{2PL}{\pi d_2^2 E}$$

As point E is between AB, so deflection at E is half that of at A and at B.

∴ $$\delta l_{EF} = \frac{1}{2}[\delta l_{AB} + \delta l_{BD}] = \frac{1}{2}\left[\frac{2PL}{\pi d_1^2 E} + \frac{2PL}{\pi d_2^2 E}\right]$$

$$= \frac{PL}{\pi E}\left[\frac{1}{d_1^2} + \frac{1}{d_2^2}\right]$$

**Example 2.36 :** A rigid bar is suspended by two vertical rods and hangs in a horizontal position by its own weight (Refer Fig. 2.42 (a)). The rod at 'A' is brass, length 3 m, cross-sectional area 1000 mm² and modulus of elasticity 1 × 10⁵ N/mm². The rod at B is steel, length 5 m, cross-sectional area 445 mm², modulus of elasticity 2 × 10⁵ N/mm². At what distance from A may a vertical load P be applied if the bar is to remain horizontal after the load is applied ?

**Solution :**

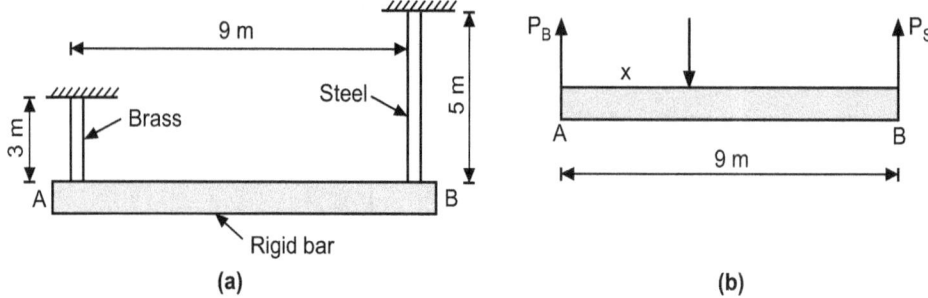

Fig. 2.42

(i) Statics : $\quad \Sigma F_y = P_B + P_S - P = 0 \quad$ ... (i)

$$\Sigma M_A = -P(x) + P_S(9) = 0 \quad \text{... (ii)}$$

(ii) Compatibility : $(\delta L)_B = (\delta L)_S$

$$\left(\frac{PL}{AE}\right)_B = \left(\frac{PL}{AE}\right)_S$$

$$\frac{P_B \times 3}{1000 \times 1 \times 10^5} = \frac{P_S \times 5}{445 \times 2 \times 10^5}$$

$\therefore \qquad P_B = 1.87 \, P_S \quad$ ... (iii)

From (i) and (ii), $\quad P_S = 0.348 \, P$

$$P_B = 0.652 \, P$$

Put $P_S = 0.348 \, P$ in (ii),

$\therefore \qquad x = 3.132 \text{ m}$

## 2.10 TEMPERATURE STRESSES

When a member is subjected to temperature change, it is likely to expand or contract. This free expansion or contraction ($\delta L$) is given by

$$\delta L = \alpha t \cdot L \quad \text{... (2.10)}$$

where, $\qquad \alpha$ = Coefficient of thermal expansion

$t$ = Change in temperature

$L$ = Length of member

$\alpha$ is usually expressed in units of per °C.

When this free expansion or contraction is prevented then only member will be subjected to temperature stresses. In other words, only *statically indeterminate systems* will be subjected to temperature stresses. This temperature stress is given by

$$\sigma = \frac{\delta L \cdot E}{L}$$

$$\sigma = \alpha t E \qquad \ldots (2.11)$$

It should be noted that, when number is subjected to temperature **rise**, it is likely to expand, and if this expansion is prevented, it is subjected to temperature stress which is **compressive** in nature. Similarly, temperature **fall** will cause **tensile** stresses in a member.

Following are the two situations that we generally come across.

**(i) Members of different cross-sectional areas arranged in series and fixed at both ends :**

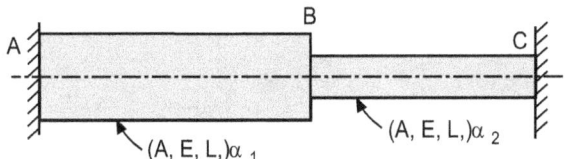

**Fig. 2.43 : Members in series**

If such a member is subjected to temperature change, free expansion or contraction being prevented, it will be subjected to temperature stresses. To evaluate these stresses is a statically indeterminate problem.

The force of internal resistance developed, to prevent the change in length of member as a whole, must be same for both components.

Thus, equation of statics can be written as :

$$P_1 = P_2$$

i.e. $\qquad \sigma_1 A_1 = \sigma_2 A_2 \qquad \ldots (2.12)$

Equation of compatibility can be written as,

(Free change in length possible) − (Change in length prevented) = 0

$$[(\alpha t L)_1 + (\alpha t L)_2] - \left[\left(\frac{\sigma L}{E}\right)_1 + \left(\frac{\sigma L}{E}\right)_2\right] = 0 \qquad \ldots (2.13)$$

(∵ change in length of a member as a whole is zero.)

Solving equations (2.12) and (2.13), required temperature stresses can be obtained.

In case if any of the support yields, equation (2.13) of compatibility is to be modified as,

$$[(\alpha t L)_1 - (\alpha t L)_2] - \left[\left(\frac{\sigma L}{E}\right)_1 + \left(\frac{\sigma L}{E}\right)_2\right] = \text{Amount of yielding of support} \qquad \ldots (2.14)$$

## (ii) Members of two or more materials joined in parallel :

(a) Members in parallel

(b) Free expansion of individual members :

(c) Actual expansion of composite member :

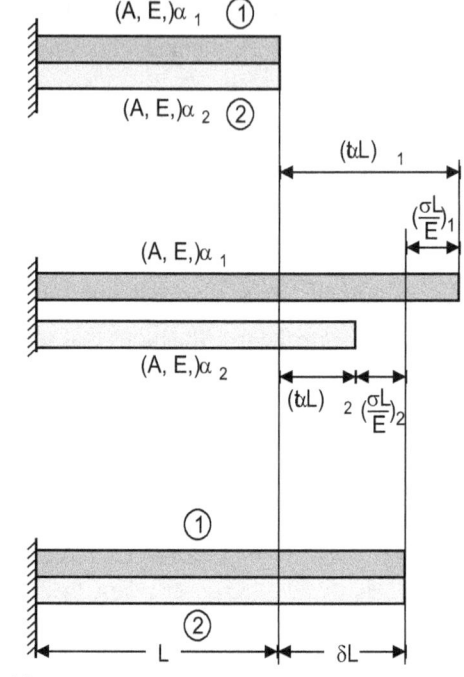

Fig. 2.44

When such a member is subjected to temperature change, actual expansion or contraction of each of the member must be the same.

This actual change in length is different from free change in length as shown in Fig. 2.44.

Hence, members will be subjected to temperature stresses. This is also a statically indeterminate problem.

Equation of statics is the same as that of equation (2.12). Since both the components must undergo equal amount of change in length, equation of compatibility can be written as,

$$(\delta L)_1 = (\delta L)_2$$

$$\left(\alpha t L - \frac{\sigma L}{E}\right)_1 = \left(\alpha t L + \frac{\sigma L}{E}\right)_2$$

The above equation assumes $\alpha_1 > \alpha_2$ as indicated by larger free expansion of member 1 in Fig. 2.44.

Thus, in general, equation of compatibility will be written as,

$$\left(\sigma t L \pm \frac{\sigma L}{E}\right)_1 = \left(\alpha t L \pm \frac{\sigma L}{E}\right)_2 \qquad \ldots (2.15)$$

It should be noted that, material having relatively higher value of $\alpha$ will be subjected to compressive stresses, hence the term $\sigma L/E$ for the corresponding material must be assigned $-$ve sign.

Solving equations (2.12) and (2.15), required temperature stresses can be obtained.

**Example 2.37 :** A steel rod 1 m long of uniform cross-section is fixed at ends. It is subjected to initial tensile stress of 48 MPa. Find,
(a) Rise in temperature required to make the rod stress free.
(b) Stress in rod if temperature is increased further by 16°C.
$\alpha = 12 \times 10^{-6}/°C$, $E = 200$ GPa.

**Data :** $L = 1$ m, $\sigma = 48$ MPa, $\alpha = 12 \times 10^{-6}/°C$, $E = 200$ GPa.

**Required :** (a) Rise in temperature required to make the rod stress free.
(b) Stress in rod if temperature is increased further by 16°C.

**Concept :** (i) To make the rod stress free, temperature stress = 48 MPa, compressive should be developed. (ii) Temperature stress = $\sigma = \alpha t E$.

**Solution :** (i) Rise in temperature :

$$\sigma = \alpha t E$$
$$48 = 12 \times 10^{-6} \times t \times 2 \times 10^5$$
$$\therefore \quad t = 20°C \text{ ... (Rise)}$$

(ii) Stress in rod :
$$\sigma = \alpha t E$$
$$= 12 \times 10^{-6} \times 16 \times 2 \times 10^5$$
$$\therefore \quad \sigma = \textbf{38.4 MPa (Compressive)}$$

**Example 2.38 :** A steel rod 10 mm φ and 1 mm long is fixed at ends. If temperature of rod is increased by 50°C, what will be reaction at supports ? If the rod remains unchanged in length, and if the temperature stress in the rod is to be reduced by 40 %, what should be the yielding of support ? Take $E = 100$ GPa, $\alpha = 10^{-5}/°C$.

**Data :** $d = 10$ mm, $L = 1$ m, $t = 50°C$, $E = 100$ GPa, $\alpha = 10^{-5}/°C$.

**Required :** Reaction at supports; yielding of supports.

**Concept :** (i) Reaction at supports = Temperature stress in the member × Cross-sectional area of member.
(ii) Yielding of support causes decrease in temperature stress.

**Solution :** (i) Geometric properties :

$$\text{Area of steel rod} = A = \frac{\pi}{4}(10)^2 = 78.54 \text{ mm}^2$$

(ii) Reaction at supports :
$$\sigma = \alpha t E$$
$$= 10^{-5} \times 50 \times 100 \times 10^3$$
$$= 50 \text{ MPa (Compressive)}$$
$$\text{Reaction} = R = \sigma \cdot A$$
$$= 50 \times 78.54 = \textbf{3.9 kN}$$

(iii) Yielding of support :
Stress consumed in yielding of support = 40 % of 50 MPa
$$= 20 \text{ MPa}$$

$$\therefore \quad \text{Yielding of support} = \Delta L = \frac{\sigma L}{E} = \frac{20 \times 1000}{100 \times 10^3} = \textbf{0.2 mm}$$

**Example 2.39 :** Rails of 10 m length are laid on the track in the morning. The atmospheric temperature then was 12°C. A gap of 1.5 mm was kept between two consecutive rails. At what maximum temperature the rails will remain stress free ? If the temperature is raised further by 10°C, what will be the magnitude and nature of the stresses induced in the rails ?

Take $\alpha = 12 \times 10^{-6}$ /°C, $E = 200$ GPa.

**Data :** $L = 10$ m, $\Delta L = 1.5$ mm, $\alpha = 12 \times 10^{-6}$ /°C, $E = 200$ GPa.

**Required :** Maximum temperature the rails will remain stress free, find magnitude and nature of the stresses induced in the rails when temperature is further raised by 10°C.

**Concept :** Till the time there is a gap between consecutive rails, no temperature stresses are induced.

**Solution :** (i) Let t be the temperature at stress free condition.

Extension for individual rail = 1.5 mm

$$\Delta L = \alpha t L$$

$$\therefore \quad 1.5 = 12 \times 10^{-6} \times (t - 12) \times 10 \times 10^3$$

$$\therefore \quad t = 24.5 \text{ °C}$$

(ii)
$$\sigma = \alpha t E = 12 \times 10^{-6} \times 10 \times 200 \times 10^3$$
$$= 24 \text{ MPa (Compressive)}$$

**Example 2.40 :** Data as shown in Fig. 2.45 below. Find the thermal stresses if the temperature rises by 10°K. Assume $L_1 = L_2 = L$, $A_1 = 2A_2$. Take $\alpha = 11.7 \times 10^{-6}$ /°K, $E = 200$ GPa.

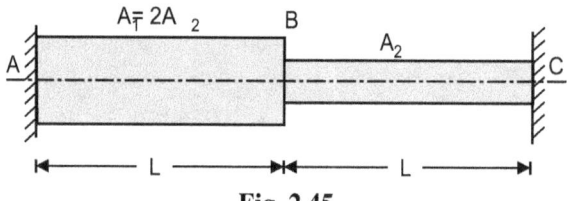

Fig. 2.45

**Data :** As shown in Fig. 2.45.
**Required :** Thermal stresses.
**Concept :** Statically indeterminate : Statics and Compatibility.
**Solution :** (i) Equation of statics :

$$\sigma_1 A_1 = \sigma_2 A_2$$
$$\sigma_1 (2A_2) = \sigma_2 A_2$$
$$\therefore \quad \sigma_1 = \frac{\sigma_2}{2} \qquad \ldots \text{(i)}$$

(ii) Compatibility :

$$(\alpha t L)_1 + (\alpha t L)_2 - \left[\left(\frac{\sigma L}{E}\right)_1 + \left(\frac{\sigma L}{E}\right)_2\right] = 0$$

$$\therefore \quad 2\alpha t = \frac{\sigma_1}{E_1} + \frac{\sigma_2}{E_2}$$

$$\therefore \quad (2 \times 11.7 \times 10^{-6} \times 10) E = \sigma_1 + \sigma_2$$

$$\therefore \quad \sigma_1 + \sigma_2 = 46.8 \text{ MPa} \qquad \ldots \text{(ii)}$$

(iii) Thermal stresses :

Solving equations (i) and (ii), $\sigma_1 = \dfrac{\sigma_2}{2}$ from (i) and (ii)

$\sigma_1$ = **15.6 MPa (Compressive)**

$\sigma_2$ = **31.2 MPa (Compressive)**

---

**Example 2.41 :** Data as shown in Fig. 2.46 below. If the temperature of the bar is raised through 14°K, find force exerted on supports.

$\alpha_S = 11 \times 10^{-6} /°K$, $E_S = 210$ GPa; $\alpha_B = 20 \times 10^{-6} /°K$, $E_B = 85$ MPa.

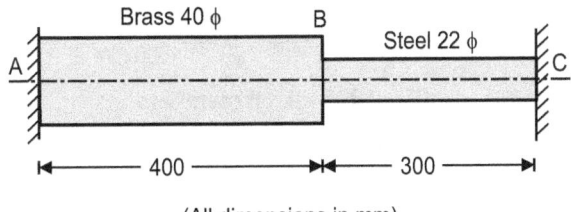

(All dimensions in mm)

**Fig. 2.46 : Given member**

**Data :** As shown in Fig. 2.46.
**Required :** Force exerted on supports.
**Concept :** Statically indeterminate : Statics and Compatibility.
**Solution :** (i) Geometric properties :

Area of steel, $A_S = \dfrac{\pi}{4}(22)^2 = 380.12$ mm²

Area of brass, $A_B = \dfrac{\pi}{4}(40)^2 = 1256.63$ mm²

(ii) 
$(\sigma \cdot A)_S = (\sigma \cdot A)_B$

$\sigma_S \times 380.12 = \sigma_B \times 1256.63$

∴ $\sigma_S = 3.30 \, \sigma_B$ ... (i)

(iii) Compatibility :

$$(\alpha \, t \, L)_S + (\alpha \, t \, L)_B - \left[\left(\dfrac{\sigma L}{E}\right)_S + \left(\dfrac{\sigma L}{E}\right)_B\right] = 0$$

$(11 \times 10^{-6} \times 14 \times 300) + (20 \times 10^{-6} \times 14 \times 400) = \dfrac{\sigma_S \times 300}{210 \times 10^3} + \dfrac{\sigma_B \times 400}{85 \times 10^3}$

∴ $0.1582 = \dfrac{\sigma_S}{700} + \dfrac{\sigma_B}{212.5}$ ... (ii)

(iv) Thermal stresses : Solving equations (i) and (ii),

$\sigma_B$ = **16.79 MPa (Compressive)**

$\sigma_S$ = **55.42 MPa (Compressive)**

(v) Force at supports :
$F = \sigma_S A_S = \sigma_B A_B$
$= 55.42 \times 380 \times 10^{-3}$ kN
= **21.059 kN**

**Example 2.42 :** Data as shown in Fig. 2.47 below. Find the stress in each rod when temperature of aluminium rod only is increased by 50°C.

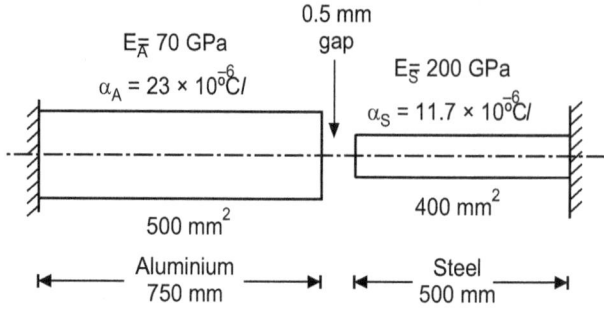

Fig. 2.47 : Given members

**Data :** $A_A = 500$ mm², $A_S = 400$ mm², $\alpha_A = 23 \times 10^{-6}$ /°C

$E_A = 70$ GPa, $E_S = 200$ GPa, $\alpha_S = 11.7 \times 10^{-6}$ /°C

**Required :** Stress in each rod.

**Concept :** Till the time gap is present, no stresses are developed.

**Solution :** (i) Equation of statics :

$$\sigma_A \cdot A_A = \sigma_S \cdot A_S$$

$$\sigma_A (500) = \sigma_S (400)$$

$$\sigma_A = 0.8 \, (\sigma_S) \qquad \ldots (i)$$

(ii) Equation of compatibility :

$$(\alpha \, t \, L)_A + (\alpha \, t \, L)_S - \left[ \left(\frac{\sigma L}{E}\right)_A + \left(\frac{\sigma L}{E}\right)_S \right] = 0.5$$

Substituting,

$$23 \times 10^{-6} \times 50 \times 750 - \left[ \frac{\sigma_A \times 750}{70 \times 10^3} + \frac{\sigma_S \times 500}{200 \times 10^3} \right] = 0.5 \qquad (\geq (\alpha \, t \, L)_S = 0)$$

$$\therefore \qquad 0.3625 = \frac{\sigma_A}{93.34} + \frac{\sigma_S}{400} \qquad \ldots (ii)$$

(iii) Thermal stresses :

Solving equations (i) and (ii),   $\sigma_S$ = **32.74 MPa (Compressive)**

$\sigma_A$ = **26.2 MPa (Compressive)**

**Example 2.43 :** A compound member is supported as shown in Fig. 2.48 below. Initially the system is stress free. If the temperature is then dropped by 20°K, find (i) stress in each bar if the supports are unyielding, (ii) stress in each bar, if the right hand support yield by 0.1 mm. Assume $\alpha_B = 20 \times 10^{-6}$ /°C, $\alpha_A = 25 \times 10^{-6}$ /°C, $E_B = 90$ GPa and $E_A = 70$ GPa.

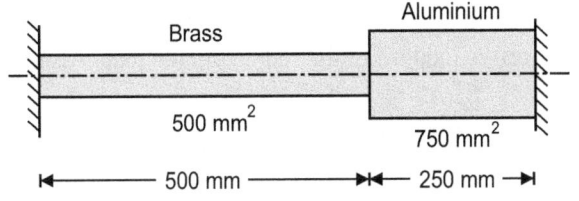

Fig. 2.48

**Data :** $A_B = 500 \text{ mm}^2$, $A_A = 750 \text{ mm}^2$, $\alpha_B = 20 \times 10^{-6} / ^\circ C$.
$\alpha_A = 25 \times 10^{-6} / ^\circ C$, $E_B = 90$ MPa, $E_A = 70$ GPa.

**Required :** (i) Stress in each bar if the supports are unyielding.
(ii) Stress in each bar if the right hand support yield by 0.1 mm.

**Concept :** Statically indeterminate : Statics and Compatibility.

**Solution :** (i) Equation of statics :

$$(\sigma A)_B = (\sigma A)_A$$
$$\sigma_B \times 500 = \sigma_A \times 750$$
$$\sigma_B = 1.5 \sigma_A \qquad \ldots \text{(i)}$$

(ii) Equation of compatibility :

$$(\alpha t L)_B + (\alpha t L)_A - \left[\left(\frac{\sigma L}{E}\right)_B + \left(\frac{\sigma L}{E}\right)_A\right] = 0$$

$$(20 \times 10^{-6} \times 20 \times 500) + (25 \times 10^{-6} \times 20 \times 250) = \frac{\sigma_B \times 500}{90 \times 10^3} + \frac{\sigma_A \times 250}{70 \times 10^3}$$

$$0.325 = \frac{\sigma_B}{180} + \frac{\sigma_A}{280} \qquad \ldots \text{(ii)}$$

(iii) Thermal stresses :
Solving equations (i) and (ii),

$$\sigma_B = 40.95 \text{ MPa (Tensile)}$$
$$\sigma_A = 27.3 \text{ MPa (Tensile)}$$

(iv) When support yields by 0.1 mm, equation of statics remains the same.

$$\sigma_B = 1.5 \sigma_A \qquad \ldots \text{(iii)}$$

(v) Compatibility :

$$(\alpha t L)_B + (\alpha t L)_A - \left[\left(\frac{\sigma L}{E}\right)_B + \left(\frac{\sigma L}{E}\right)_A\right] = 0.1$$

$$0.325 = \frac{\sigma_B}{180} + \frac{\sigma_A}{280} + 0.1$$

$$0.225 = \frac{\sigma_B}{180} + \frac{\sigma_A}{280} \qquad \ldots \text{(iv)}$$

(vi) Thermal stresses :
Solving equations (i) and (iii),

$$\sigma_B = 28.55 \text{ MPa (Tensile)}$$
$$\sigma_A = 19.03 \text{ MPa (Tensile)}$$

**Example 2.44 :** Data as shown in Fig. 2.49. The temperature of the combination is increased by 30°C. Calculate the stresses induced in the rod and in the tube. Also find actual expansion of composite member.

Take $\alpha_S = 12 \times 10^{-6}$ /°C, $E_S = 200$ GPa, $\alpha_{Cu} = 16 \times 10^{-6}$ /°C, $E_C = 100$ GPa.

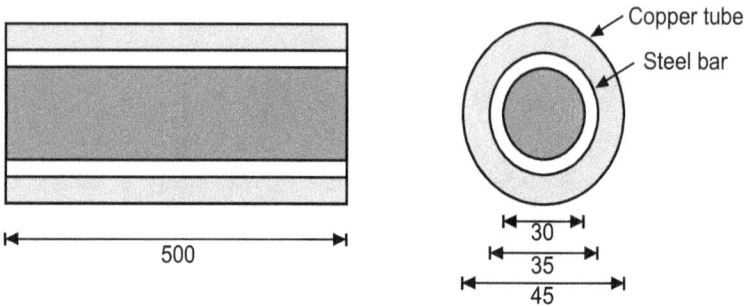

(a) Given member    (b) Cross-section of member

**Fig. 2.49**

**Data :** As shown in Fig. 2.49.

**Required :** Stresses induced in the rod and in the tube; actual expansion of composite member.

**Concept :** Statically indeterminate : Statics and Compatibility.

**Solution :** (i) Geometric properties :

$$\text{Area of steel} = A_S = \frac{\pi}{4}(30)^2 = 706.8 \text{ mm}^2$$

$$\text{Area of copper} = A_C = \frac{\pi}{4}[(45)^2 - (35)^2] = 628.3 \text{ mm}^2$$

(ii) Equation of statics :

$$P_C = P_S$$

$\therefore \qquad \sigma_C A_C = \sigma_S A_S$

$\therefore \qquad \sigma_C = 1.124 \, \sigma_S$ ... (i)

(iii) Equation of compatibility :

$$\left(\alpha t L - \frac{\sigma L}{E}\right)_{Cu} = \left(\frac{\sigma L}{E} + \alpha t L\right)_{st}$$

As $\alpha_C > \alpha_{st}$ ; Cu will be subjected to compression.

$$\left(16 \times 10^{-6} \times 30 - \frac{\sigma_C}{100 \times 10^3}\right) = \left(12 \times 10^{-6} \times 30 + \frac{\sigma_S}{200 \times 10^3}\right)$$

Substituting, $\qquad \sigma_S + 2\sigma_C = 24$ ... (ii)

**(iv) Thermal stresses :**

Solving equations (i) and (ii),

$$\sigma_S = 7.38 \text{ MPa (Tensile)}$$
$$\sigma_C = 8.31 \text{ MPa (Compressive)}$$

**(v) Actual expansion :**

$$(\delta L)_C = (\delta L)_{st}$$

$$\left(\alpha t L - \frac{\sigma L}{E}\right)_C = \left(16 \times 10^{-6} \times 30 \times 500 - \frac{8.31 \times 500}{100 \times 10^3}\right)$$

∴ $(\delta L)_C = 0.198 \text{ mm}$

**Example 2.45 :** Three wires as shown in Fig. 2.50 are supporting a load of 18 kN. The cross-sectional area of each wire is 150 mm². If the lengths of wires are adjusted so as to share the load equally at 20°C, find the stresses in wires at 50°C temperature.

Take $E_S = 2 \times 10^5$ MPa, $\alpha_S = 12 \times 10^{-6}$ /°C, $E_C = 1 \times 10^5$ MPa, $\alpha_C = 18 \times 10^{-6}$ /°C.

**Data :** P = 18 kN, $A_S = A_C = 150$ mm².

**Required :** Stresses in wires at 50°C.

**Concept :** (i) Statically indeterminate

(ii) Superposition of stresses.

**Solution :** (i) Geometric properties :

Area of steel ($A_S$) = Area of copper ($A_C$) = 150 mm²

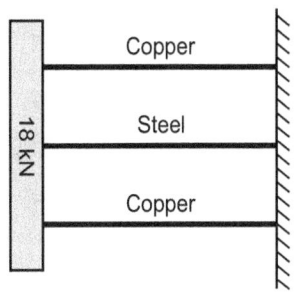

Fig. 2.50

**(ii) Equation of statics :**

Due to temperature change,

$$\text{Compressive force in copper wires} = \text{Tensile force in steel wire}$$
$$2(\sigma_C \times A_C) = (\sigma_S \times A_S)$$
$$2\sigma_C = \sigma_S$$
$$\sigma_C = 0.5 \sigma_S \qquad \ldots (i)$$

**(iii) Equation of compatibility :**

$$\left(\alpha t L - \frac{\sigma L}{E}\right)_C = \left(\alpha t L + \frac{\sigma L}{E}\right)_S$$

∴ $$18 \times 10^{-6} \times (50 - 20) - \frac{\sigma_C}{1 \times 10^5} = 12 \times 10^{-6} \times (50 - 20) + \frac{\sigma_S}{2 \times 10^5}$$

$$1.8 \times 10^{-4} = \frac{\sigma_S}{2 \times 10^5} + \frac{\sigma_C}{1 \times 10^5}$$

$$36 = \sigma_S + 2\sigma_C \qquad \ldots (ii)$$

**(iv) Solution of equations :** Solving equations (i) and (ii),

$$\sigma_S = 18 \text{ MPa (Tensile)}$$
$$\sigma_C = 9 \text{ MPa (Compressive)}$$

(v) Stresses due to load :
At 20°C, the load is shared equally by three wires.

$$\therefore \quad \text{Load taken by each wire} = \frac{18 \times 10^3}{3} = 6 \times 10^3$$

$$\therefore \quad \text{Tensile stress in each wire} = \frac{6 \times 10^3}{150} = 40 \text{ MPa (Tensile)}$$

(vi) Final stresses :

$$\text{Stress in steel} = \sigma_S = 18 + 40 = \mathbf{58 \text{ MPa (Tensile)}}$$

$$\text{Stress in copper} = \sigma_C = -9 + 40 = \mathbf{31 \text{ MPa (Tensile)}}$$

**Example 2.46 :** A copper flat 60 mm × 30 mm is joined to another 60 mm × 60 mm steel flat as shown in Fig. 2.51. If the combination is heated through 100°C, determine :

(i) stress produced in each bar,

(ii) the shear force between the flats,

(iii) shear stress.

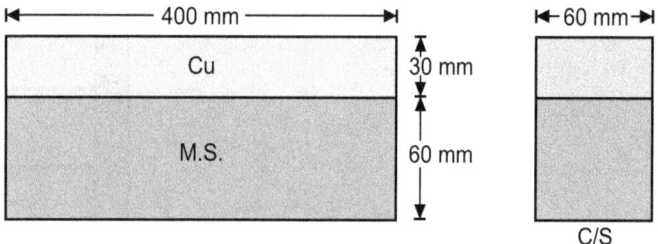

**Fig. 2.51**

**Given :** $\alpha_C = 18.5 \times 10^{-6}$ /°C, $\alpha_S = 12 \times 10^{-6}$ /°C, $E_C = 101$ GPa, $E_S = 220$ GPa.

**Data :** As shown in Fig. 2.51.

**Required :** Stresses induced in the bar, shear force and shear stress.

**Concept :** Statically indeterminate : Statics and compatibility.

**Solution :** (i) Geometric properties :

$$A_{Cu} = 60 \times 30 = 1800 \text{ mm}^2$$

$$A_{MS} = 60 \times 60 = 3600 \text{ mm}^2$$

(ii) Equation of statics :

$$P_{Cu} = P_{MS}$$

$$\sigma_{Cu} A_{Cu} = \sigma_{MS} A_{MS}$$

$$\sigma_{Cu} \times 1800 = \sigma_{MS} \times 3600$$

$$\sigma_{Cu} = 2 \times \sigma_{MS} \quad \ldots \text{(i)}$$

(iii) Equation of compatibility :

$$\left(\alpha t L - \frac{\sigma L}{E}\right)_{Cu} = \left(\frac{\sigma L}{E} + \alpha t L\right)_{MS}$$

As $\alpha_{Cu} > \alpha_{MS}$ ; Cu will be subjected to compression.

$$\left(18.5 \times 10^{-6} \times 100 \times 400 - \frac{\sigma_{Cu} \times 400}{101 \times 10^3}\right) = \left(\frac{\sigma_{st} \times 400}{220 \times 10^3} + 12 \times 10^{-6} \times 100 \times 400\right)$$

$$0.74 - 3.96 \times 10^{-3} \sigma_{Cu} = \sigma_{MS} \times 1.82 \times 10^{-3} + 0.48$$

$$1.82 \times 10^{-3} \sigma_{MS} + 3.96 \times 10^{-3} \sigma_{Cu} = 0.26$$

$$1.82 \times 10^{-3} \sigma_{MS} + 2 \times 3.96 \times 10^{-3} \sigma_{MS} = 0.26 \quad \ldots \text{(ii)}$$

Putting equation (i) in (ii), $\quad \sigma_{MS} = 26.69 \text{ N/mm}^2$

∴ $\quad \sigma_{Cu} = 53.39 \text{ N/mm}^2$

**(iv) Shear force between flats :**

$$S = \sigma_{Cu} \times A_{Cu} = 53.39 \times 1800$$

∴ $\quad S = 96102 \text{ N}$

**Example 2.47 :** Rails of 15 m length were laid on the track in the morning when the temperature was 16°C. A gap of 1.8 mm was kept between the two rails. At what maximum temperature the rails will remain stress free ? If temperature is further increased by 15°C, what will be the magnitude and nature of stresses induced in the rails ?

Assume $\alpha = 12 \times 10^{-6}$ /°C and E = 200 GPa. Assume that rails can expand in one direction.

**Data :** $l = 15$ m, $\delta l = \dfrac{1.8}{2} = 0.9$ mm (for each)

$t = 16°C$, $t = (16 + 15) = 31°C$, $\alpha = 12 \times 10^{-6}$ /°C, E = 200 GPa = $200 \times 10^3$ MPa.

**Required :** Maximum temperature for which rails are stress free and stress at 31°C.

**Concept :** $\delta l = l\alpha t$ and $\sigma = \alpha t E$

**Solution : Case (i) :** $\quad \delta l = l\alpha t$

$$0.9 = 15000 \times 12 \times 10^{-6} \times t$$

∴ $\quad t = $ Change in temperature $= 5°C$

∴ Maximum temperature at which rails are stress free $= (16 + 5) = $ **21°C**

**Case (ii) :** Change in temperature $= 31 - 21 = 10°C$

∴ $\quad \sigma = \alpha t E$

$$= 12 \times 10^{-6} \times 10 \times 200 \times 10^3$$

∴ $\quad \sigma = $ **24 N/mm² (Compressive)**

**Example 2.48 :** A compound strut consists of a brass portion AB of diameter 75 mm and a steel portion BC 40 mm diameter as shown in Fig. 2.52. Supports at A and C are rigid. If temperature is raised through 140°C, find

(i) Nature and magnitude of stresses developed in brass and steel.

(ii) Force exerted on the supports and

(iii) The relative movement at the junction B.

**Given :** $\alpha_{Br} = 20 \times 10^{-6}$ /°C, $\alpha_{st} = 11 \times 10^{-6}$ /°C, $E_{Br} = 85$ GPa, $E_{st} = 210$ GPa

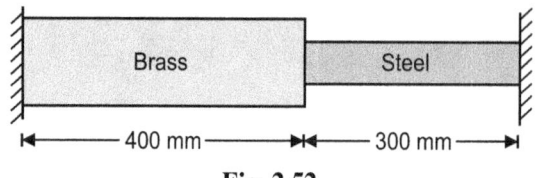

Fig. 2.52

**Data :** Brass : $d = 75$ mm, $l = 400$ mm, $\alpha = 20 \times 10^{-6}$ /°C, $E = 85$ GPa,

Steel : $d = 40$ mm, $l = 300$ mm, $\alpha = 11 \times 10^{-6}$ /°C, $E = 210$ GPa, $t = 140$°C

**Required :** Stresses, reaction and relative movement of junction B.

**Concept :** Statically indeterminate, statics and compatibility.

**Solution :**

(i) Geometric properties :

$$A_{Br} = \frac{\pi}{4} \times (75)^2 = 4417.86 \text{ mm}^2$$

$$A_{st} = \frac{\pi}{4} \times (40)^2 = 1256.64 \text{ mm}^2$$

(ii)
$$(\sigma \cdot A)_{Br} = (\sigma \cdot A)_{st}$$
$$\sigma_{Br} \times 4417.86 = \sigma_{st} \times 1256.64$$

∴ $\sigma_{st} = 3.52 \, \sigma_{Br}$

(iii) Compatibility :

$$(\alpha \, t \, l)_{st} + (\alpha \, t \, l)_{Br} - \left[\left(\frac{\sigma l}{E}\right)_{st} + \left(\frac{\sigma l}{E}\right)_{Br}\right] = 0$$

$$11 \times 10^{-6} \times 140 \times 400 + 20 \times 10^{-6} \times 140 \times 300 - \left[\frac{\sigma_{st} \times 300}{210 \times 10^3} + \frac{\sigma_{Br} \times 400}{85 \times 10^3}\right] = 0$$

$$0.616 + 0.84 - \left[1.43 \times 10^{-3} \sigma_{st} + 4.706 \times 10^{-3} \times \sigma_{Br}\right] = 0$$

$$9.7396 \times 10^{-3} \sigma_{Br} = 1.456$$

$$\sigma_{Br} = 149.49 \text{ N/mm}^2$$

$$\sigma_{st} = 526.21 \text{ N/mm}^2$$

(iv) $\sigma_{st} = \dfrac{P_{st}}{A}$

∴ $P_{st} = \sigma_{st} A = 526.21 \times 1256.64$

∴ $P_{st} = \mathbf{661.25 \text{ kN}}$

**Example 2.49 :** The steel wire in Fig. 2.53 is stretched between two rigid supports. The initial stress in the wire is 30 MPa, when the temperature is 20°C. What is the stress in the wire when temperature drops to 0°C ? At what temperature will the stress be zero ? $\alpha = 14 \times 10^{-6}/°C$ and E = 210 GPa.

**Fig. 2.53**

**Data :** As shown in Fig. 2.53, $\alpha = 14 \times 10^{-6}/°C$, E = 210 GPa, $t_1 = 20°C$, $\sigma = 30$ MPa.

**Required :** Stress at zero temperature, temperature at zero stress.

**Concept :** Compressive force will be developed due to decrease in temperature and tensile force will be developed due to increase in temperature.

**Solution :** (i) Temperature drops from 20°C to 0°C.

∴
$$\sigma = \alpha t E$$
$$= 14 \times 10^{-6} \times 20 \times 210 \times 10^3$$
$$= 58.8 \text{ MPa}$$

∴ Stress in wire $= -30 + 58.8 = 28.8$ MPa (Compressive)

(ii) $\sigma = 30$ MPa tensile should be developed to neutralize compressive force.

$$\sigma = \alpha t E$$
$$30 = 14 \times 10^{-6} \times t \times 210 \times 10^3$$
∴ $$t = 10.2°C$$

When temperature is 9.8°C, stress in bar will be zero.

---

**Example 2.50 :** A square r.c.c. column is 300 mm × 300 mm in cross-section. It is reinforced with 4 bars of 20 mm diameter. Determine the load carrying capacity of column if allowable stresses in concrete and steel are 7 MPa and 140 MPa respectively. $E_s$ = 200 GPa and modular ratio m is 13.

**Data :** Size of column = 300 × 300 mm, $A_{st}$ = 4 bars of 20 mm $\phi$. Allowable stress in concrete = 7 MPa and in steel = 140 MPa, m = 13, $E_s$ = 200 GPa

**Required :** Load carrying capacity of column.

**Concept :** Standard formula.

**Solution :** Area of column $= 300 \times 300 = 90000$ mm²

Area of steel $= 4 \times \frac{\pi}{4} d^2 = 4 \times \frac{\pi}{4} \times (20)^2 = 1256.64$ mm²

Area of concrete = Area of column − Area of steel
$$= 90000 - 1256.64 \text{ mm}^2$$
$$= 88743.36 \text{ mm}^2$$

$$P = \left[\frac{E_c}{E_s} A_c + A_s\right] \sigma_s = \left[\frac{1}{13} \times 88743.36 + 1256.64\right] \times 140$$

$$= 1131.63 \times 10^3 \text{ N} = 1131.63 \text{ kN}$$

$$P = \left[\frac{E_s}{E_c} A_s + A_c\right] \sigma_c = [13 \times 1256.64 + 88743.36] \times 7$$

$$= 735.56 \times 10^3 \text{ N} = 735.56 \text{ kN}$$

Load carrying capacity of column is 785.56 kN

**Example 2.51 :** The rigid bar ABC shown in Fig. 2.54 is hinged at A and supported by steel rod at B. Determine largest load P that can be applied at C if the stress in the steel rod is limited to 260 MPa and the vertical movement of end C must not exceed 40 mm.

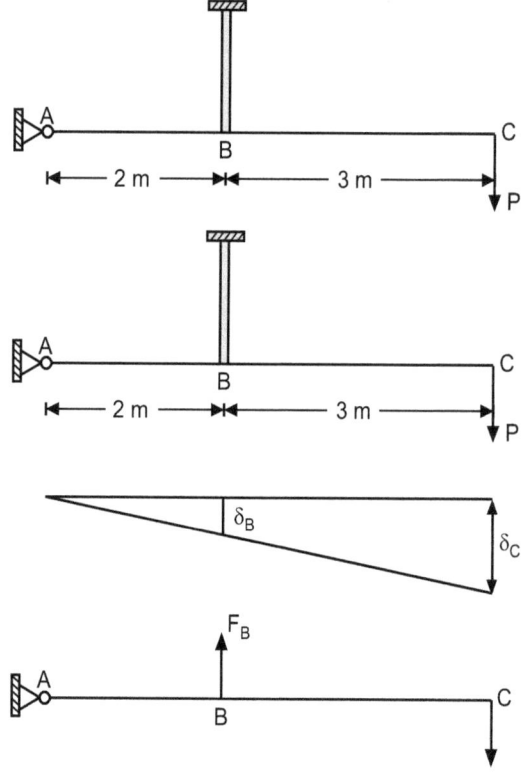

Fig. 2.54

**Data :** As shown in Fig. 2.54, maximum bending stress = 260 MPa and vertical displacement allowed = 40 mm

**Required :** Largest load P that can be applied at C.

**Concept :** Standard formula.

**Solution :**

$$A = \frac{\pi}{4} \times 5^2 = 19.63 \text{ mm}^2$$

$$F_B = \sigma_B \times A = 260 \times 19.63 = 5103.8 \text{ N}$$

$$\Sigma M @ A = 0$$
$$-F_B \times 2 + P \times 5 = 0$$
$$P = 2041.52 \text{ N}$$
$$\frac{\delta l_B}{2} = \frac{\delta l_C}{5}$$
$$\delta l_B = 16 \text{ mm}$$
$$\delta l_B = 16 \text{ mm} = \frac{F_B \times l}{AE}$$
$$F_B = \frac{16 \times 19.63 \times 200 \times 10^3}{2000} = 31408 \text{ N}$$

The largest value of P is 5103.8 N.

**Example 2.52 :** Two wires AB and CD are connected to a right horizontal bar BD shown in Fig. 2.55. Wire AB has cross-sectional area of 100 mm² and E = 130 GPa. Length of wire AB is 1 m. Wire CD has cross-sectional area of 50 mm² and E = 200 GPa. If load W of 6 kN is applied as shown, find out the deflection of rigid bar BD.

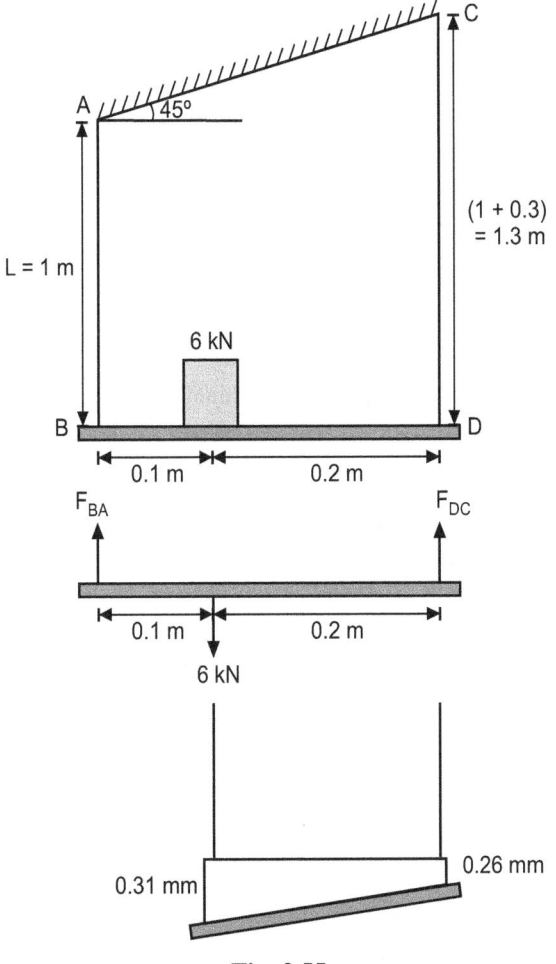

**Fig. 2.55**

**Data :** As shown in Fig. 2.55, $A_{AB} = 100 \text{ mm}^2$, $A_{CD} = 50 \text{ mm}^2$,
$E_{AB} = 130 \text{ GPa}$, $E_{CD} = 200 \text{ GPa}$.

**Required :** Deflection of rigid bar BD.

**Concept :** Standard formula.

**Solution :** $\Sigma M$ @ wire AB = 0

$$- F_{BA} \times 0 - F_{DC} \times 0.3 + 6 \times 0.1 = 0$$

$$F_{DC} = 2 \text{ kN}$$

$$\Sigma F_y = 0$$

$$F_{BA} + F_{DC} = 6$$

$$F_{BA} = 4 \text{ kN}$$

$$\delta_B = F_{BA} \times \left(\frac{L}{AE}\right)_{BA}$$

$$= 4000 \times \frac{1000}{100 \times 130000}$$

$$= 0.31 \text{ mm}$$

$$\delta_D = F_{DC} \times \left(\frac{L}{AE}\right)_{CD}$$

$$= 2000 \times \frac{1300}{50 \times 200000}$$

$$= 0.26 \text{ mm}$$

**Example 2.53 :** An elastic bar ABC is held at both the ends and is loaded as shown in Fig. 2.56. Cross-sectional area of part AB is 'A' and that of part BC is '2A'. Find out the reactions at A and C. Also draw AFD.

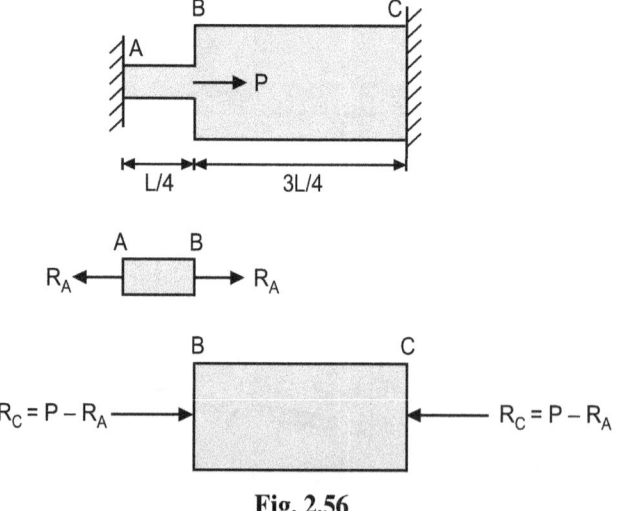

**Fig. 2.56**

**Data :** As shown in Fig. 2.56, $A_{AB} = A$, $A_{BC} = 2A$.
**Required :** Reactions at A and C.
**Concept :** Standard formula.
**Solution :**

$$\frac{R_A \times (L/4)}{AE} - \frac{(P-R_A) \times (3L)}{2AE} = 0$$

$$\frac{R_A \times (L/4)}{AE} = \frac{(P-R_A) \times (3L)}{2AE}$$

$$\frac{R_A}{4} = \frac{(P-R_A) \times 3}{8}$$

$$2R_A = 3P - 3R_A$$

$$R_A = 0.6P$$

$$R_C = 0.4P$$

**Example 2.54 :** Determine the temperature change that will cause a compressive stress of 36 MPa in the composite bar shown in Fig. 2.57, if $E_S = 210$ GPa, $E_A = 70$ GPa and $\alpha_S = 12 \times 10^{-6}$ /°C, $\alpha_A = 23 \times 10^{-6}$ /°C.

**Data :** Compressive stress = 36 MPa, $E_S = 210$ GPa, $E_A = 70$ GPa,
$\alpha_S = 12 \times 10^{-6}$ /°C and $\alpha_A = 23 \times 10^{-6}$ /°C

**Required :** Temperature change that will cause a compressive stress of 36 MPa in the composite bar.

**Concept :** Standard formula.

**Solution :** Temperature is calculated to elongated 0.3 mm. Till 0.3 mm expansion, stress will not develop.

$$\delta l_S + \delta l_{Al} = (l\alpha t)_S + (l\alpha t)_{Al}$$
$$0.3 = 250 \times 12 \times 10^{-6} \, t_1 + 300 \times 23 \times 10^{-6} \, t_1$$
$$t_1 = 30.3°C$$
$$\sigma_S A_S = \sigma_{Al} A_{Al}$$

As area is same, stress is always same. Now aluminium bar touch the other support and displacement is not possible now.

$$(l\alpha t)_S + (l\alpha t)_{Al} = \left(\frac{Pl}{AE}\right)_S + \left(\frac{Pl}{AE}\right)_{AL}$$

$$(250 \times 12 \times 10^{-6} \times t_2) + (300 \times 23 \times 10^{-6} \times t_2)$$
$$= \left[\frac{\sigma_S \times 250}{210 \times 10^3}\right] + \left[\frac{\sigma_{AL} \times 300}{70 \times 10^3}\right]$$

$$\sigma_S = \sigma_{Al} = 36 \text{ MPa}$$
$$9.9 \times 10^{-3} \, t_2 = 0.197$$
$$t_2 = 19.90°C$$
$$t = t_1 + t_2 = 30.30 + 19.90$$

Compressive stress in the composite bar occurs at 50.20°C.

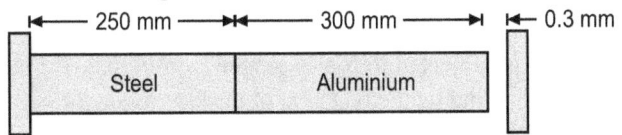

**Fig. 2.57**

## EXERCISE

1. A compound bar ABCD is subjected to an axial compressive load of 30 kN as shown in Fig. 2.58. Find stresses in individual components and total change in length of bar. Assume E = 200 GPa.

($\sigma_{AB}$ = 23.87 MPa, $\sigma_{BC}$ = 95.49 MPa, $\sigma_{CD}$ = 42.44 MPa, $\delta L$ = 0.364 mm)

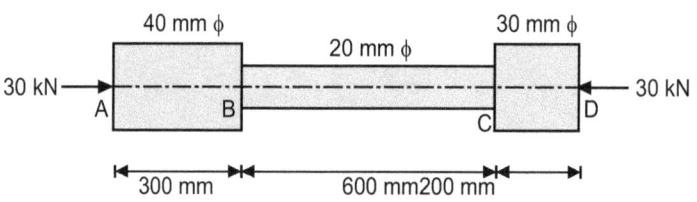

Fig. 2.58

2. A compound bar ABCD shown in Fig. 2.59 is subjected to axial compressive load which causes maximum stress of 100 MPa. Find total contraction of member if E = 150 GPa. ($\delta L$ = 0.28 mm)

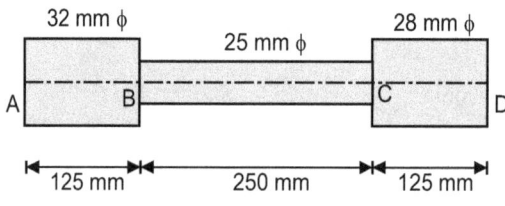

Fig. 2.59

3. A member 36 mm$\phi$ is subjected to axial forces as shown in Fig. 2.60. Find the total change in length of the bar assuming E = 100 GPa. (0.1178 mm contraction)

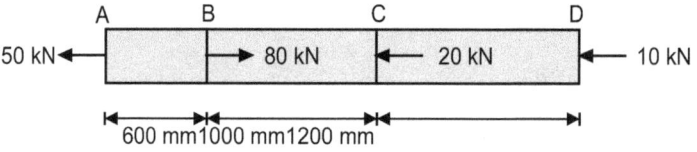

Fig. 2.60

4. A straight bar of steel 3 m long has rectangular cross-section which varies uniformly from 100 mm × 12 mm at one end to 25 mm × 12 mm at other end. Find change in length of member when subjected to axial load of 35 kN. Assume E = 200 GPa.

(0.807 mm)

5. A rod tapers uniformly from 40 mm to 22 mm in diameter in a length of 400 mm. If the rod is subjected to an axial load of 40 kN, find the extension of the rod assuming E = 200 GPa. (0.115 mm)

6. A member ABCD is subjected to forces as shown in Fig. 2.61. Find force 'P' necessary for equilibrium. Also find total elongation of the bar. Assume E = 210 GPa.

(P = 280 kN, $\delta L$ = 0.476 mm)

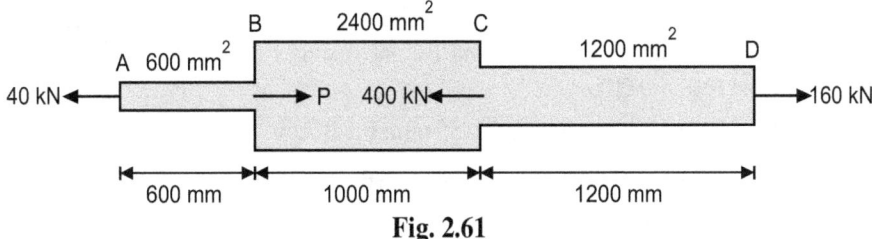

Fig. 2.61

7. A cylinder 150 mm in diameter, 300 mm in length is subjected to axial compressive load of 180 kN which causes increase in diameter by 0.0952 mm and a decrease in length by 0.64 mm. Compute the values of Poisson's ratio and modulus of elasticity.

($\mu = 0.295$, E = 4.78 GPa)

8. A square bar of 20 mm side is held between two rigid supports and loaded as shown in Fig. 2.62. Find the reactions at the supports A and C and the extension of portion AB.

Assume E = 200 GPa.  ($H_A = \overleftarrow{60}$ kN, $H_C = \overleftarrow{90}$ kN, $\delta L_{AB} = 0.225$ mm)

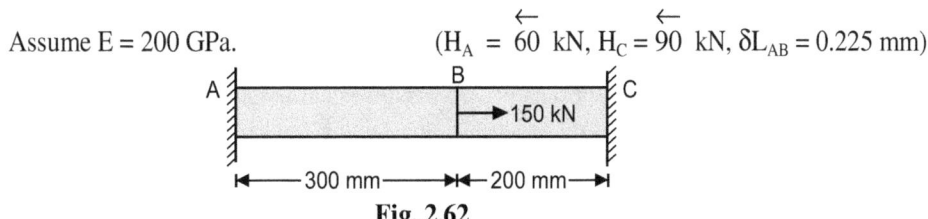

Fig. 2.62

9. A member ABCD is loaded as shown in Fig. 2.63. Determine (i) total deformation of rod, (ii) displacement of 'C'. Assume E = 70 GPa.

($\delta L = 0.0528$ mm, $\delta C = 0.09$ mm ($\leftarrow$))

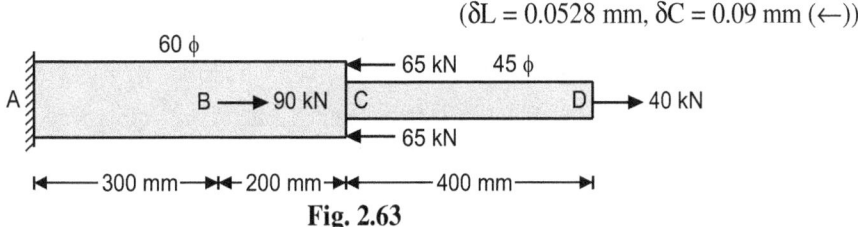

Fig. 2.63

10. A square bar is subjected to axial compressive stress $\sigma_x$ in the longitudinal direction. The lateral strains in the direction at right angles are completely prevented by suitable external pressure. Evaluate this external pressure. $\left(p = \left(\dfrac{\mu}{1-\mu}\right)\sigma_x, \dfrac{\sigma_x}{\epsilon_x} = \dfrac{E}{\mu^2 - 1}\right)$

11. A short piece of steel pipe is to carry an axial compressive force of 1200 kN with a factor of safety of 1.8 against yielding. If thickness t of the pipe is $\dfrac{1}{8}$th of its outside diameter, find minimum required outside diameter. Assume yield stress = 270 MPa.

(153 mm)

12. A metal rod 10 mm diameter when tested under axial pull of 10 kN was found to reduce its diameter by 0.003 mm. Modulus of rigidity for the material is G = 51 GPa. Find other elastic constants. ($\mu = 0.317$, E = 134.3 GPa, K = 122.3 GPa)

13. A steel bar ABC transmits an axial tensile force such that, total change in length is 0.6 mm. Determine for parts AB and BC the changes in length and diameter. Assume $\mu = 0.3$ and $E = 200$ GPa.

(For AB, $\delta L = 0.232$ mm, $\delta d = 0.00185$ mm; for BC, $\delta L = 0.368$ mm, $\delta d = 0.00286$ mm)

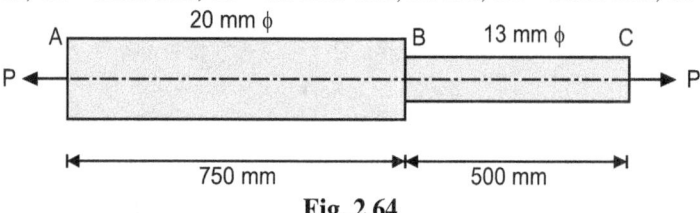

Fig. 2.64

14. A column 3 m high has a hollow circular cross-section of external diameter 300 mm and carries an axial compressive load of 500 kN. If stress in the column is limited to 150 MPa and shortening of column is restricted to 2 mm, find the internal diameter required. Also calculate maximum shortening of column, $E = 200$ GPa.

(205.5 mm, 2 mm)

15. A composite section consists of two bars of equal lengths connected together by sides. If $A_1$ and $A_2$ are their cross-sectional areas and $E_1$ and $E_2$ are their respective modulii of elasticity, show that the equivalent or apparent modulus of elasticity of composite bar is given by $E = \dfrac{E_1 A_1 + E_2 A_2}{A_1 + A_2}$, when loaded axially.

16. A copper bar 36 mm$\phi$ is enclosed in a steel tube having 50 mm external diameter and 5 mm metal thickness. The composite section is subjected to an axial pull of 120 kN. Find stresses induced in both materials and extension of member assuming $L = 1.5$ m, $E_C = 110$ GPa and $E_S = 200$ GPa.  ($\sigma_C = 52$ MPa, $\sigma_S = 94.7$ MPa, $\delta L = 0.7$ mm)

17. Three vertical rods, equal in lengths, each 12 mm$\phi$ are equispaced in a vertical plane and jointly support of load of 12 kN; the rods being so adjusted to share the load equally. If a further load of 13 kN is added, find the stresses in each rod. Assume $E_C = 110$ GPa, $E_S = 200$ GPa.  ($\sigma_C = 60.18$ MPa, $\sigma_S = 80.47$ MPa)

18. A compound bar consists of a central steel strip 25 mm wide and 6 mm thick placed between two strips of brass each 25 mm wide and t mm thick. The strips are firmly fixed together, to form a compound bar of rectangular section 25 mm wide and (6 + 2t) mm thick. Determine (a) the thickness t of the brass strips which will make apparent modulus of elasticity of the compound bar 140 GPa and (b) the maximum axial pull the bar can then carry if the stress is not to exceed 140 MPa in either the brass or the steel. Assume $E_S = 200$ GPa, $E_b = 110$ GPa  (t = 5.92 mm, P = 43.7 kN)

19. A solid steel cylinder 500 mm long and 70 mm diameter is placed inside an aluminium cylinder having 75 mm inside diameter and 100 mm outside diameter. The aluminium cylinder is 0.15 mm longer than the steel cylinder. An axial load of 400 kN is applied to the composite section through rigid cover plates. Find stresses developed in each material assuming $E_S = 220$ GPa, $E_A = 70$ GPa.  ($\sigma_S = 66.34$ MPa, $\sigma_A = 42.1$ MPa)

20. A steel rod 20 mm diameter passes centrally through a steel tube 25 mm internal diameter and 40 mm external diameter. The tube is 800 mm long and is closed by rigid

washers of negligible thickness which are fastened by nuts threaded on the rod. The nuts are tightened until the compressive load on the tube is 20 kN. Calculate the stresses in the tube and the rod. Also find the increase in these stresses when one nut is tightened by one quarter of a turn relative to other. There are 0.4 threads per mm length. Assume E = 210 GPa.

(For 20 kN load on tube, $\sigma_{st}$ = 26.1 MPa compressive, $\sigma_{sr}$ = 63.6 MPa tensile,

When nut is tightened by one quarter, $\sigma_{st}$ = 47.72 MPa compressive,

$\sigma_{sr}$ = 116.34 MPa tensile)

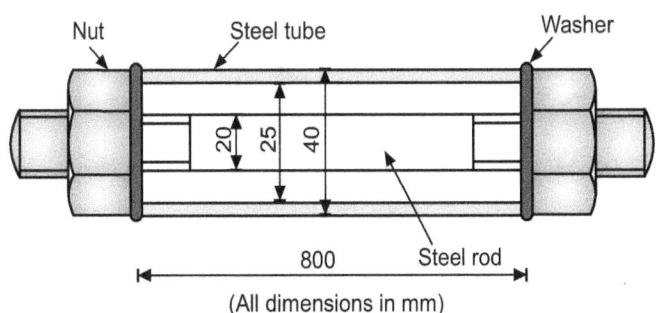

(All dimensions in mm)

Fig. 2.65

21. A copper sleeve 21 mm internal and 27 mm external diameter, surrounds a 20 mm steel bolt, one end of the sleeve being in contact with the shoulder of the bolt. The sleeve is 70 mm long. After putting a rigid washer on the other end of the sleeve, a nut is screwed on the bolt through 10 degrees. If the pitch of the threads is 2.5 mm, find the stresses induced in the copper sleeve and steel bolt.
    Take $E_S$ = 210 GPa and $E_C$ = 80 GPa. ($\sigma_S$ = 44.78 MPa, $\sigma_C$ = 62.25 MPa)

22. A bar of 2 m length and 20 mm × 15 mm in cross-section is subjected to an axial tensile load of 35 kN. Find the final volume of the bar if $\mu$ = 0.25 and E = 200 GPa.
    ($700.175 \times 10^3$ mm$^3$)

23. A steel block in the form of rectangular parallelopiped has sides 100 mm along x-axis and 50 mm along y and z axes. The block carries a tensile load of 25 kN along x-axis passing through C.G. of block. (i) Find strains along x, y, and z axes. (ii) What load should be applied along z-axis so that strain along y-axis is zero under the action of combined loading ? Take E = 200 GPa, $\mu$ = 0.3.
    ($\varepsilon_x = 5 \times 10^{-5}$ tensile, $\varepsilon_y = \varepsilon_z = 1.5 \times 10^{-5}$ compressive, $P_z$ = 50 kN compressive)

24. A mild steel flat 150 mm wide and 20 mm thick is 6 m long. It carries an axial pull of 325 kN. If E = 200 GPa and $\mu$ = 0.26, calculate the change in length, width, thickness and volume of the flat.
    ($\delta L$ = 3.25 mm, $\delta b$ = 0.021 mm, $\delta t$ = 0.0028 mm, $\delta V$ = 4680 mm$^3$)

25. A rigid member ABCD is supported and loaded as shown in Fig. 2.66. Find stresses developed in steel and brass. ($\sigma_C$ = 107.7 MPa, $\sigma_S$ = 107.7 MPa)

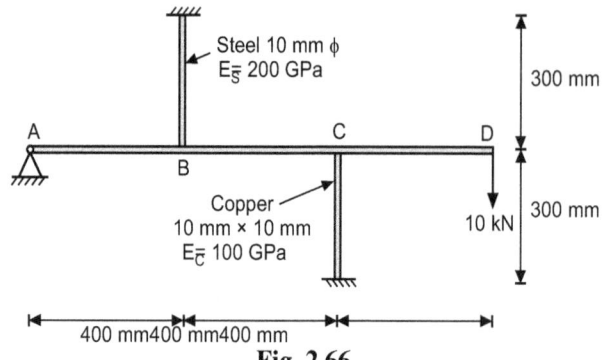

Fig. 2.66

26. A rigid bar 3.5 m in length is hinged at A and supported by wires as shown in Fig. 2.67. Determine (i) stresses in each rod, (ii) elongation of the steel rod. Assume $E_C = 120$ GPa, $E_S = 200$ GPa.  $(\sigma_S = 140.7$ MPa, $\sigma_C = 64.32$ MPa, $\delta L_S = 0.7$ mm$)$

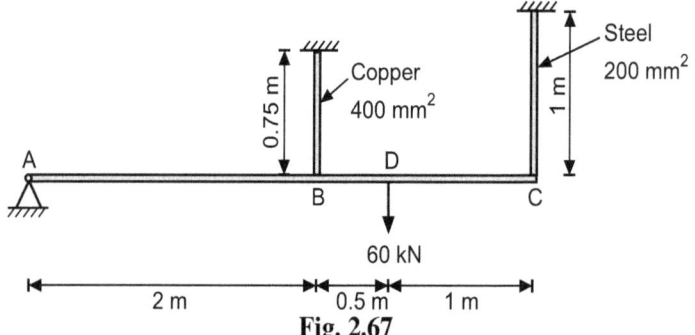

Fig. 2.67

27. A rigid beam weighing 200 N is held in horizontal position by three vertical wires as shown in Fig. 2.68. The outer wires of brass are 1.25 mm in diameter and the central steel wire is 0.6 mm in diameter. If the wires are stress free before the beam is attached, estimate the stresses induced in each wire. Assume $E_S = 210$ GPa, $E_b = 86$ GPa.
$(\sigma_b = 63.59$ MPa, $\sigma_S = 154.48$ MPa$)$

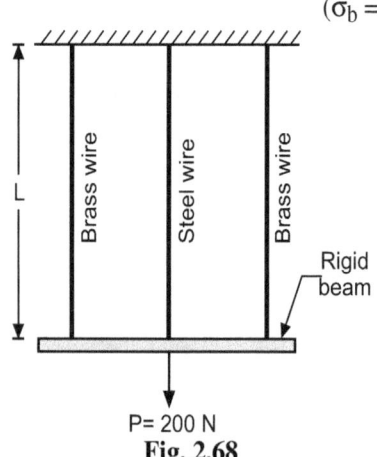

Fig. 2.68

28. A steel rod 15 m long is subjected to temperature change of 50°C. Find the temperature stress produced (i) when the expansion of the rod is prevented, (ii) the rod is permitted to expand by 5 mm. Assume $\alpha_S = 1.2 \times 10^{-6}$ /°C and E = 200 GPa.
(120 MPa, 53.33 MPa)

29. A cartwheel of 1.2 m diameter is to be provided with a thin steel tyre. Assuming the wheel to be rigid if the stress in steel is not to exceed 150 MPa, calculate the minimum diameter of the tyre and the minimum temperature to which it should be heated before slipping on to wheel. Assume E = 200 GPa, $\alpha_s = 12 \times 10^{-6}$ /°C. (1199.1 mm, 62.5°C)

30. A surveyor steel tape, nominally 30 metres is 12 mm wide and 1 mm thick. Its length is correct when used at a temperature of 16°C and under a pull of 100 N. By how much it will be in error when used at a temperature of 50°C and under a pull of 50 N ? E = 200 GPa and $\alpha = 11 \times 10^{-6}$ /°C. (10.595 mm longer)

31. A bar of steel and two bars of copper, each of the same area and length, have their ends rigidly connected together when a temperature of 25°C so that the steel bar lies between the two copper bars. When the temperature is raised to 275°C, the length of the bar increases by 2 mm. Determine the original length and final stresses in the bar. Take $E_s$ = 200 GPa, $E_C$ = 110 GPa, $\alpha_C = 17.5 \times 10^{-6}$/°C, $\alpha_s = 12 \times 10^{-6}$ /°C.
($\sigma_C$ = 71.98 MPa, $\sigma_S$ = 143.97 MPa, $l$ = 537.55 mm)

32. A mild steel bar 20 mm in diameter and 300 mm long is encased in a brass tube whose external diameter is 30 mm and internal diameter is 25 mm. The composite bar is heated through 40°C. Calculate the stresses induced in each material. $\alpha_s = 11.2 \times 10^{-6}$ /°C, $\alpha_b = 16.5 \times 10^{-6}$ /°C, $E_s$ = 200 GPa, $E_C$ = 100 GPa.
($\sigma_b$ = 15.77 MPa, $\sigma_s$ = 10.84 MPa)

33. A steel rod, 20 mm diameter, 200 mm long is heated through 120°K and at the same time subjected to a pull P. If the total extension of the rod is 0.3 mm, what should be the magnitude of P ? $\alpha_s = 12 \times 10^{-6}$ /°K, E = 215 GPa. (P = 3.769 kN)

34. A steel rod 25 mm diameter passes through a brass tube of 25 mm internal diameter and 35 mm external diameter. The nut on the rod is tightened until a stress of 15 MPa is developed in the rod. The temperature of the tube is then raised by 60°K. What are the final stresses in the rod and the tube ?
$E_s$ = 200 GPa, $E_b$ = 80 GPa, $\alpha_s = 11.7 \times 10^{-6}$ /°K, $\alpha_b = 19 \times 10^{-6}$ /°K.
($\sigma_s$ = 39.16 MPa tensile; $\sigma_b$ = 40.79 MPa compressive)

35. A copper flat 60 mm × 30 mm is joined to another 60 mm × 60 mm steel flat as shown in Fig. 2.69. If the combination is heated through 100°C, determine
    (i) stress produced in each of the bar,
    (ii) shear force between the flats, and (iii) shear stress.
    $\alpha_c = 18.5 \times 10^{-6}$ /°C; $\alpha_s = 12 \times 10^{-6}$ /°C; $E_c$ = 110 GPa; $E_s$ = 220 GPa.
    ($\sigma_c$ = 57.2 MPa; $\sigma_s$ = 28.6 MPa, Shear force = 102.96 kN; Shear stress = 4.29 MPa)

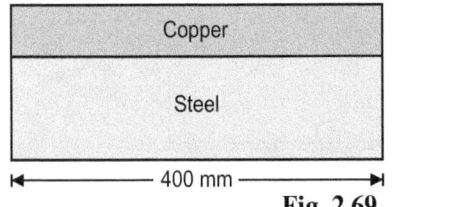
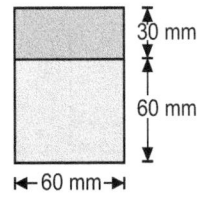

Fig. 2.69

36. A composite bar made up of aluminium and steel is held between two supports as shown in Fig. 2.70. What will be the stresses in the two bars when the temperature is dropped by 30°C if (i) supports are non-yielding, (ii) one of the support yields by 0.1 mm.
$E_s$ = 210 GPa; $E_a$ = 74 GPa, $\sigma_s = 11.7 \times 10^{-6}$ /°C; $\alpha_a = 23.4 \times 10^{-6}$ /°C

(For non-yielding supports ; $\sigma_s$ = 22.09 MPa; $\sigma_a$ = 88.38 MPa;
For yielding of supports; $\sigma_s$ = 16.85 MPa, $\sigma_a$ = 67.41 MPa)

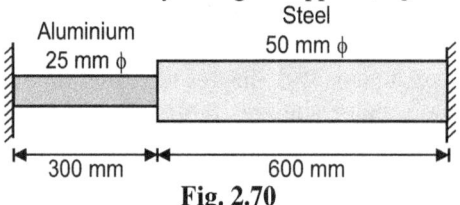

Fig. 2.70

37. A compound bar is made up by connecting a steel member and a copper member as shown in Fig. 2.71.
   Take $\alpha_s = 12 \times 10^{-6}$ /°C; $\alpha_c = 15.6 \times 10^{-6}$ /°C; $E_s$ = 200 GPa; $E_c$ = 100 GPa.
   Estimate the stress induced in the members due to temperature rise of 100°C.
   ($\sigma_c$ = 26.16 MPa; $\sigma_s$ = 26.16 MPa and 13.08 MPa)

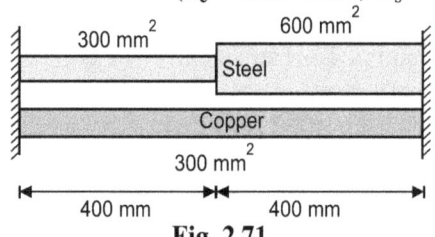

Fig. 2.71

38. A circular section tapered bar is rigidly fixed at both ends as shown in Fig. 2.72. If the temperature is raised by 30°C, calculate the maximum stress in the bar. E = 200 GPa, $\alpha = 12 \times 10^{-6}$/°C. (126 MPa)

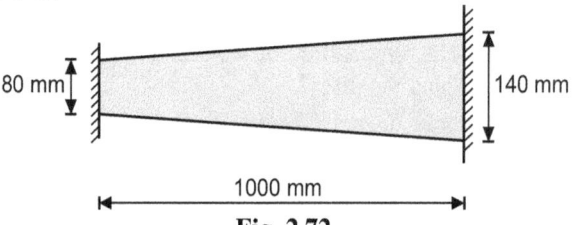

Fig. 2.72

39. A rigid bar of negligible weight is supported as shown in Fig. 2.73. If W = 80 kN, compute the temperature change that will cause the stress in the steel rod to be 55 MPa. Take $\alpha_s = 11.7 \times 10^{-6}$/°C, $\alpha_b = 18.9 \times 10^{-6}$/°C. (28.3°C)

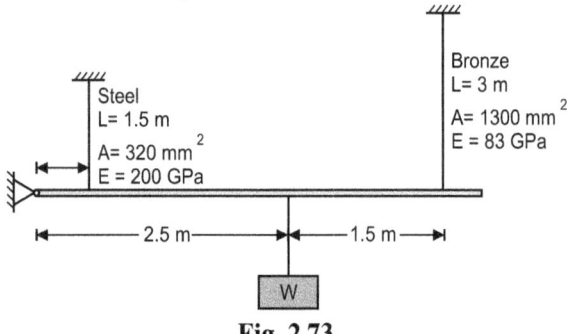

Fig. 2.73

❑❑❑

| Unit – II |

| CHAPTER THREE |

# PRINCIPAL STRESSES AND STRAINS

## 3.1 INTRODUCTION

The problems studied so far include direct tension, compression and shear separately, but there are many structures in which these various stresses occur in combination. Hence, it is of practical importance to find the resultant stresses which may be greater than the applied ones and also the planes on which they act when subjected to complex stress system.

In general, a three dimensional state of stress is as shown in Fig. 3.1 (a) which indicates nine stress components.

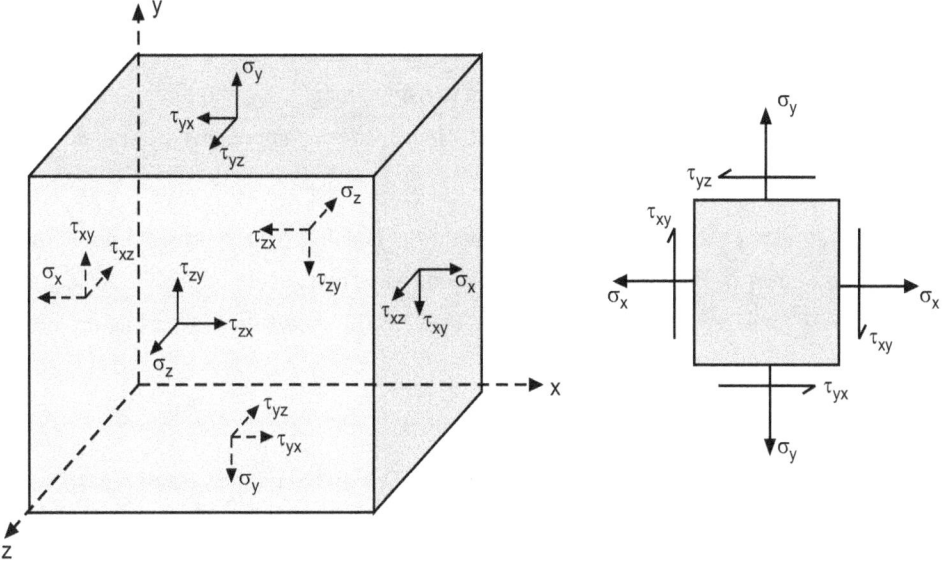

(a) Three dimensional state of stress          (b) State of plane stress

Fig. 3.1

The notation used here defines a normal stress by means of single subscript corresponding to the face on which it acts. A face takes the name of the axis normal to it; for example, the x face is perpendicular to x-axis. A shear stress is indicated by double subscript, the first letter corresponding to the face on which it acts and second indicating its direction. Thus, the shear stress on x face acting in the y direction is denoted by $\tau_{xy}$. It should be noted that $\tau_{xy} = \tau_{yx}$ since, the shear stresses on perpendicular planes are equal.

(3.1)

In this text, we consider only plane stress i.e. state of stress that can be represented by components that act parallel to a single plane i.e. stress components normal to the plane of body are zero. State of plane stress is shown in Fig. 3.1 (b).

## 3.2 TRANSFORMATION OF PLANE STRESS

The stress acting at a point is represented by the stresses acting on the faces of the element enclosing the point. These stresses will change as a function of the inclination of the planes passing through that point. Thus, the stresses on the faces of the element vary as the angular position of the element changes.

Two algebraic expressions, one for the normal stress and one for the shear stress, can be developed to give these stresses in terms of the initially known stresses and of an angle of inclination of the plane being investigated. These equations are called equations of *stress transformation*. The derivatives of these algebraic equations with respect to the angle of inclination, when equated to zero, locate the planes on which either the normal or the shear stress reaches maximum or minimum values.

Stress components are vectorial in nature but mathematically they do not obey the laws of vector addition and subtraction, since in addition to having magnitude and direction, they are also associated with unit of area over which they act. Hence, stress components are first converted to forces and then added or subtracted vectorially.

Consider an elementary area of uniform thickness isolated from a stressed body on which stresses are as shown in Fig. 3.2 (a). Let, it be required to investigate normal and shear stresses on any plane AC making an angle $\theta$ as shown. Fig. 3.2 (b) shows the stresses acting on wedge ABC.

Let  A = Area of wedge face AC

∴  A cos $\theta$, A sin $\theta$ = Areas of vertical face AB and horizontal face BC respectively.

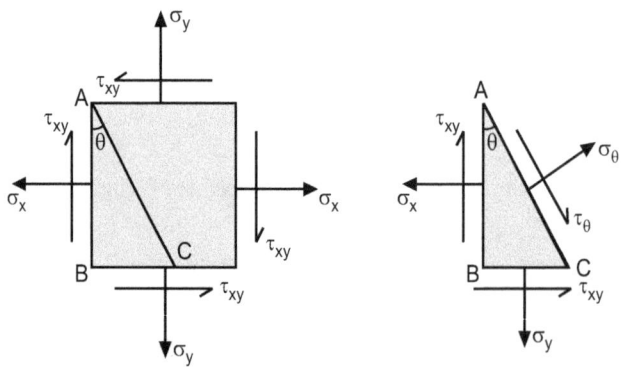

(a) State of plane stress        (b) Stresses on wedge ABC

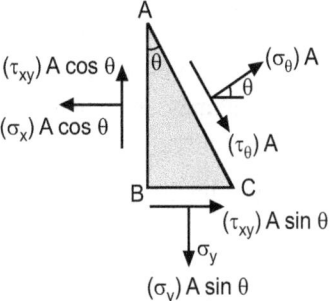

**(c) FBD of wedge ABC**

**Fig. 3.2**

Stresses acting on the wedge having converted to forces, FBD of wedge ABC can be drawn as shown in Fig. 3.2 (c).

Using equations of statics ;

Algebraic sum of all the forces acting normal to the face AC $= \sum F_\theta = 0$

$\therefore \quad (\sigma_\theta) A = (\sigma_x A \cos \theta) \cos \theta + (\sigma_y A \sin \theta) \sin \theta$

$\quad - (\tau_{xy} \cdot A \cos \theta) \sin \theta - (\tau_{xy} A \sin \theta) \cos \theta$

$\therefore \quad \sigma_\theta = \sigma_x \cdot \cos^2 \theta + \sigma_y \cdot \sin^2 \theta - 2 \tau_{xy} \sin \theta \cos \theta \qquad \ldots (3.1)$

Algebraic sum of all the forces acting tangential to the face AC $= \sum F_t = 0$

$\therefore \quad (\tau_\theta) A = (\sigma_x A \cos \theta) \sin \theta - (\sigma_y A \sin \theta) \cos \theta$

$\quad + (\tau_{xy} A \cos \theta) \cos \theta - (\tau_{xy} A \sin \theta) \sin \theta$

$\therefore \quad \tau_\theta = (\sigma_x - \sigma_y) \sin \theta \cos \theta + \tau_{xy} (\cos^2 \theta - \sin^2 \theta) \qquad \ldots (3.2)$

We have, $\quad \cos^2 \theta = \dfrac{1 + \cos 2\theta}{2}$

$\quad \sin^2 \theta = \dfrac{1 - \cos 2\theta}{2}$

$\quad \sin \theta \cos \theta = \dfrac{\sin 2\theta}{2}$

Using these relations for equations (3.1) and (3.2),

$\sigma_\theta = \dfrac{\sigma_x + \sigma_y}{2} + \dfrac{\sigma_x - \sigma_y}{2} \cos (2\theta) - \tau_{xy} \sin (2\theta) \qquad \ldots (3.3)$

$\tau_\theta = \dfrac{\sigma_x - \sigma_y}{2} \sin (2\theta) + \tau_{xy} \cos (2\theta) \qquad \ldots (3.4)$

These equations (3.3) and (3.4) are called as the *equations of stress transformation*.

The angle that the line of action of resultant stress makes with the normal to the plane is called the *obliquity* ($\phi$).

$\tan \phi = \dfrac{\tau_\theta}{\sigma_\theta} \qquad \ldots (3.5)$

## 3.3 PRINCIPAL STRESSES

The planes on which maximum or minimum normal stresses occur, there is no shear stress. These planes are called as **principal planes** and the stresses acting on these planes - the maximum and minimum normal stresses – are called as the **principal stresses.**

To locate the planes of maximum and minimum normal stresses, differentiate equation (3.3) with respect to '$\theta$' and equate it to zero

i.e. $\quad \dfrac{d}{d\theta}(\sigma_\theta) = -\dfrac{\sigma_x - \sigma_y}{2} \cdot 2 \cdot \sin(2\theta) - 2\,\tau_{xy} \cdot \cos(2\theta) = 0$

$\therefore \quad -(\sigma_x - \sigma_y)\sin(2\theta) - 2\,\tau_{xy}\cos(2\theta) = 0$

$\therefore \quad -(\sigma_x - \sigma_y)\tan(2\theta) = 2\,\tau_{xy}$

$\therefore \qquad \tan(2\theta_n) = -\dfrac{2\,\tau_{xy}}{\sigma_x - \sigma_y} \qquad \ldots (3.6)$

where, $\theta_n$ = Orientation of plane of maximum normal stress.

**Note :** These planes can also be located by setting $\tau_\theta$ equal to zero from equation (3.4) which indicates that there is no shear stress on the plane of maximum or minimum normal stress. Equation (3.6) gives two values of $(2\theta_n)$ that differ by 180°, hence *principal planes are 90° apart.*

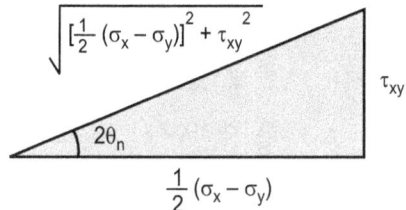

**Fig. 3.3**

From equation (3.6), we can write

$$\left. \begin{aligned} \sin(2\theta_n) &= \dfrac{\tau_{xy}}{\sqrt{\left[\dfrac{1}{2}(\sigma_x - \sigma_y)\right]^2 + (\tau_{xy})^2}} \\[1em] \cos(2\theta_n) &= \dfrac{\dfrac{1}{2}(\sigma_x - \sigma_y)}{\sqrt{\left[\dfrac{1}{2}(\sigma_x - \sigma_y)\right]^2 + (\tau_{xy})^2}} \end{aligned} \right\} \qquad \ldots (3.7)$$

Substituting these values of $\sin(2\theta_n)$ and $\cos(2\theta_n)$ from equation (3.7) in equation (3.3), we get principal stresses as,

$$\sigma_1, \sigma_2 = \dfrac{\sigma_x + \sigma_y}{2} \pm \sqrt{\left(\dfrac{\sigma_x - \sigma_y}{2}\right)^2 + (\tau_{xy})^2} \qquad \ldots (3.8)$$

where; $\qquad \sigma_1, \sigma_2$ = Major and minor principal stresses.

**Note :** + ve sign shall be used to get major principal stress, while – ve sign shall be used to get minor principal stress.

## 3.4 MAXIMUM SHEAR STRESS

To locate the plane of maximum shear stress, differentiate equation (3.4) with respect to $\theta$ and equate it to zero.

i.e. $\quad \dfrac{d}{d\theta}(\tau_\theta) = \left(\dfrac{\sigma_x - \sigma_y}{2}\right) 2 \cdot \cos(2\theta) - (\tau_{xy}) 2 \sin(2\theta) = 0$

$\therefore \quad (\sigma_x - \sigma_y) \cos(2\theta) = 2 \tau_{xy} \sin(2\theta)$

$\therefore \quad \tan(2\theta_s) = \dfrac{\sigma_x - \sigma_y}{2 \tau_{xy}} \qquad \ldots (3.9)$

where, $\theta_s$ = Orientation of plane of maximum shear stress.

Equation (3.9) is a negative reciprocal of equation (3.6). That means values of $(2\theta_n)$ defined by equation (3.6) and that of $(2\theta_s)$ defined by equation (3.9) differ by 90°. In other words, *planes of maximum shear stress are inclined at 45° to the principal planes.*

From equation (3.8), we can write,

$$\left. \begin{aligned} \sin(2\theta_s) &= \dfrac{\frac{1}{2}(\sigma_x - \sigma_y)}{\sqrt{\left[\frac{1}{2}(\sigma_x - \sigma_y)\right]^2 + (\tau_{xy})^2}} \\[2mm] \cos(2\theta_s) &= \dfrac{\tau_{xy}}{\sqrt{\left[\frac{1}{2}(\sigma_x - \sigma_y)\right]^2 + (\tau_{xy})^2}} \end{aligned} \right\} \qquad \ldots (3.10)$$

Substituting these values of $\sin(2\theta_s)$ and $\cos(2\theta_s)$ from equation (3.10) in equation (3.4), we get

$$\tau_{max} \; ; \; \tau_{min} = \pm \sqrt{\left(\dfrac{\sigma_x - \sigma_y}{2}\right)^2 + (\tau_{xy})^2} \qquad \ldots (3.11)$$

If $\sigma_x$ and $\sigma_y$ are principal stresses of $\sigma_1$ and $\sigma_2$ then $\tau_{xy}$ is zero and equation (3.11) simplifies to

$$\tau_{max} = \pm \dfrac{\sigma_1 - \sigma_2}{2} \qquad \ldots (3.12)$$

Thus, the maximum shear stress differs from minimum shear stress only in sign.

On the principal planes, shear stresses are zero but on the planes of maximum shear stress, normal stress is not zero. Substituting equation (3.10) in equation (3.3), the magnitude of normal stress ($\sigma'$) on the plane of maximum shear stress is obtained as ;

$$\sigma' = \dfrac{\sigma_x + \sigma_y}{2} \qquad \ldots (3.13)$$

Therefore, normal stress ($\sigma'$) acts simultaneously with the maximum shear stress.

## SOLVED EXAMPLES

**Example 3.1 :** A circular bar 40 mm diameter carries an axial tensile load of 100 kN. What is the value of shear stress on the plane on which normal stress has value of 50 MPa, tensile ?

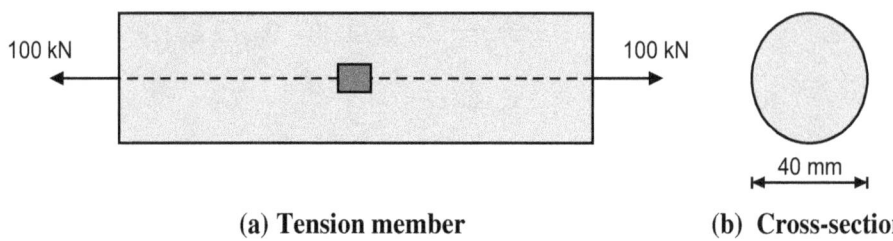

(a) Tension member  (b) Cross-section

Fig. 3.4

**Data**       : As shown in Fig. 3.4.
**Required**   : Value of shear stress on the plane on which normal stress is 50 MPa, tensile.
**Concept**    : Considering an element as shown in Fig. 3.4 find normal stress $\sigma_x$ and then use standard formulae.
**Solution**   : (i) State of stress :

$$\text{Normal stress} = \sigma_x = \frac{P}{A} = \frac{100 \times 10^3}{\frac{\pi}{4}(40)^2}$$

$$= 79.57 \text{ MPa (Tensile)}$$

State of stress is as shown in Fig. 3.5.

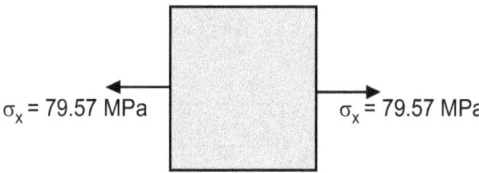

Fig. 3.5 : State of stress on element

(ii) Plane on which normal stress is 50 MPa, tensile :

$$\sigma_\theta = \frac{\sigma_x}{2} + \frac{\sigma_x}{2}\cos(2\theta) \qquad (\because \sigma_y = \tau_{xy} = 0)$$

$$50 = \frac{79.57}{2} + \frac{79.57}{2}\cos(2\theta)$$

$$\theta = 37.56°$$

(iii) Shear stress :

$$\tau_\theta = \frac{\sigma_x}{2}\sin(2\theta) \qquad \left(\because \sigma_y = \tau_{xy} = 0\right)$$

$$\tau_{37.56°} = \frac{79.57}{2} \cdot \sin(2 \times 37.56)$$

$$= 38.45 \text{ MPa}$$

**Example 3.2 :** If an element is subjected to state of stress as shown in Fig. 3.6, find the principal stresses. Also find the stress components on a plane at 30° anticlockwise from x face.

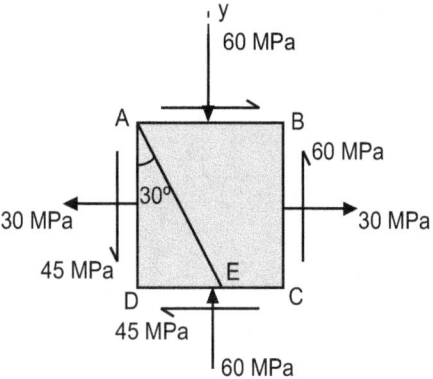

**Fig. 3.6 : Given state of stress**

**Data**       : As shown in Fig. 3.6.
**Required**   : Principal stresses, stress components on plane AE.
**Concept**    : Standard formulae.
**Solution**   : (i) Principal stresses :

$$\sigma_1, \sigma_2 = \frac{\sigma_x + \sigma_y}{2} \pm \sqrt{\left(\frac{\sigma_x - \sigma_y}{2}\right)^2 + (\tau_{xy})^2}$$

$$= \frac{30 - 60}{2} \pm \sqrt{\left[\frac{30 - (-60)}{2}\right]^2}$$

$$= -15 \pm 63.63$$

$$\sigma_1 = -78.63 \text{ MPa} = \mathbf{78.63 \text{ MPa (Compressive)}}$$

$$\sigma_2 = \mathbf{48.63 \text{ MPa (Tensile)}}$$

(ii) Stress components on plane AE :

$$\sigma_\theta = \frac{\sigma_x + \sigma_y}{2} + \frac{\sigma_x - \sigma_y}{2} \cos(2\theta) - \tau_{xy} \sin(2\theta)$$

$$= \frac{30 - 60}{2} + \frac{30 - (-60)}{2} \cos(2 \times 30) - (-45) \sin(2 \times 30)$$

$$\sigma_{30°} = 46.47 \text{ MPa (Tensile)}$$

$$\tau_\theta = \frac{\sigma_x - \sigma_y}{2} \sin(2\theta) + \tau_{xy} \cos(2\theta)$$

$$= \frac{30 - (-60)}{2} \sin(2 \times 30) + (-45) \cos(2 \times 30)$$

$$\tau_{30°} = \mathbf{16.47 \text{ MPa}}$$

**Example 3.3 :** The principal tensile stresses at a point on two perpendicular planes are 60 MPa and 30 MPa. Find normal, tangential and resultant stress and its obliquity on a plane at 20° with the major principal plane as shown in Fig. 3.7. Also find the intensity of stress which acting alone can produce the same maximum strain. Assume Poisson's ratio $\mu = 0.3$.

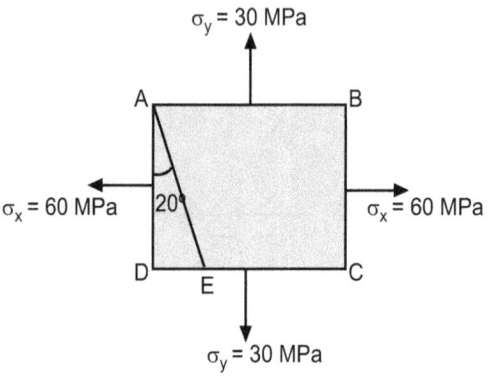

**Fig. 3.7 : Given state of stress**

Data        :  As shown in Fig. 3.7.

Required    :  Normal, tangential, resultant stress and its obliquity on a plane at 20° to major principal plane.

Concept     :  Transformation of stress.

Solution    :  (i) Normal stress on plane AE :

$$\sigma_\theta = \frac{\sigma_x + \sigma_y}{2} + \frac{\sigma_x - \sigma_y}{2} \cos(2\theta) - \tau_{xy} \sin 2\theta$$

$$= \frac{60 + 30}{2} + \frac{60 - 30}{2} \cos(2 \times 20) - 0$$

$$\sigma_{20°} = 56.49 \text{ MPa} \quad \text{(Tensile)}$$

(ii) Shear stress on plane AE :

$$\tau_\theta = \frac{\sigma_x - \sigma_y}{2} (\sin 2\theta) + \tau_{xy} \cos(2\theta)$$

$$= \frac{60 - 30}{2} \sin(2 \times 20) + 0$$

$$\tau_{20°} = 9.64 \text{ MPa}$$

(iii) Resultant stress and its obliquity :

$$\text{Resultant stress} = \sqrt{\sigma_\theta^2 + \tau_\theta^2}$$

$$= \sqrt{(56.49)^2 + (9.64)^2}$$

$$= 57.30 \text{ MPa}$$

$$\text{Obliquity} = \phi = \tan^{-1}\left(\frac{\tau_\theta}{\sigma_\theta}\right)$$

$$= \tan^{-1}\left(\frac{9.64}{56.49}\right)$$

$$= \mathbf{9.68°}$$

(iv) Stress ($\sigma$) which produces the same principal strain :

$$\text{Principal strain} = \varepsilon_1 = \frac{1}{E}(\sigma_1 - \mu\sigma_2)$$

$$= \frac{1}{E}(60 - 0.3 \times 30)$$

$$= \frac{51}{E}$$

$$\therefore \quad \frac{\sigma}{E} = \frac{51}{E}$$

$$\therefore \quad \sigma = \mathbf{51\ MPa}$$

**Example 3.4 :** At a point in a strained material, the state of stress is as shown in Fig. 3.8. Determine : (i) principal stresses, (ii) principal planes, (iii) maximum shear stress and plane on which it acts, (iv) the tensile stress which acting alone will produce same maximum shear stress, and (v) the shear stress which acting alone will produce same maximum tensile principal stress.

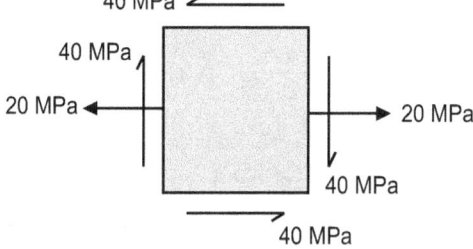

**Fig. 3.8 : Given state of stress**

**Data** : As shown in Fig. 3.8.
**Required** : As given above in the example.
**Concept** : Standard formulae.
**Solution** : (i) Principal stresses ($\sigma_1, \sigma_2$) :

$$\sigma_1, \sigma_2 = \frac{\sigma_x}{2} \pm \sqrt{\left(\frac{\sigma_x}{2}\right)^2 + (\tau_{xy})^2} \qquad (\because \sigma_y = 0)$$

$$\sigma_1, \sigma_2 = \frac{20}{2} \pm \sqrt{\left(\frac{20}{2}\right)^2 + (40)^2}$$

$$= 10 \pm 41.23$$

$$\sigma_1 = \mathbf{51.23\ MPa\ (Tensile)}$$

$$\sigma_2 = -31.23\ \text{MPa} = \mathbf{31.23\ MPa\ (Compressive)}$$

(ii) Principal planes:

$$\tan(2\theta) = -\frac{2\tau_{xy}}{\sigma_x} \qquad (\because \sigma_y = 0)$$

$$\tan(2\theta) = -\frac{2 \times 40}{20} = -4$$

$$\theta = -37.98° \text{ and } -127.98°$$

(iii) Maximum shear stress ($\tau_{max}$):

$$\tau_{max} = \frac{\sigma_1 - \sigma_2}{2} = \frac{51.23 - (-31.23)}{2} = 41.23 \text{ MPa}$$

(iv) Planes of maximum shear:

$$\tan(2\theta) = \frac{\sigma_x}{2\tau_{xy}} \qquad (\because \sigma_y = 0)$$

$$= \frac{20}{2 \times 40} = 0.25$$

$$\therefore \theta = 7° \text{ and } 97°$$

(v) The tensile stress which acting alone will produce same maximum shear stress:

$$\tau_{max} = \frac{\sigma_1 - \sigma_2}{2} = \frac{\sigma_1}{2} \qquad (\because \sigma_2 = 0)$$

$$41.23 = \frac{\sigma_1}{2} \quad \therefore \sigma_1 = 82.46 \text{ MPa (Tensile)}$$

(vi) The shear stress which acting alone will produce same maximum principal tensile stress:

$$\sigma_1 = \frac{\sigma_x + \sigma_y}{2} \pm \sqrt{\left(\frac{\sigma_x - \sigma_y}{2}\right)^2 + (\tau_{xy})^2}$$

$$51.23 = 0 + \tau_{xy}$$

$$\therefore \tau_{xy} = 51.23 \text{ MPa}$$

**Example 3.5**: At a point in a piece of strained material, there are two planes at right angles on which the shear stress intensity is '$\tau$' along with normal stress intensity of 40 MPa, tensile on one plane and 24 MPa, compressive on the other. If the major principal stress is 56 MPa, tensile, evaluate the smaller principal stress and shear stress $\tau$. Also evaluate maximum shear stress $\tau_{max}$ and normal stress on plane of maximum shear.

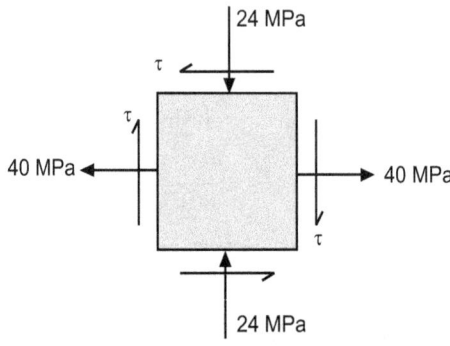

**Fig. 3.9 : Given state of stress**

**Data** : As shown in Fig. 3.9 ; $\sigma_1 = 56$ MPa, tensile

**Required** : Shear stress ($\tau$); minor principal stress ($\sigma_2$); $\tau_{max}$ and normal stress ($\sigma$) on the plane of maximum shear.

**Concept** : Standard formulae.

**Solution** : (i) Shear stress ($\tau$) :

$$\sigma_1 = \frac{\sigma_x + \sigma_y}{2} + \sqrt{\left(\frac{\sigma_x - \sigma_y}{2}\right)^2 + (\tau_{xy})^2}$$

$$56 = \frac{40 + (-24)}{2} + \sqrt{\left(\frac{40 - (-24)}{2}\right)^2 + (\tau_{xy})^2}$$

∴ $\tau_{xy}$ = **35.78 MPa**

(ii) Minor principal stress ($\sigma_2$) :

$$\sigma_2 = \frac{\sigma_x + \sigma_y}{2} - \sqrt{\left(\frac{\sigma_x - \sigma_y}{2}\right)^2 + (\tau_{xy})^2}$$

$$= \frac{40 + (-24)}{2} - \sqrt{\left(\frac{40 - (-24)}{2}\right)^2 + (35.78)^2}$$

$$= -40 \text{ MPa}$$

$$= \textbf{40 MPa (Compressive)}$$

(iii) Maximum shear stress ($\tau_{max}$) :

$$\tau_{max} = \frac{\sigma_1 - \sigma_2}{2} = \frac{56 - (-40)}{2} = \textbf{48 MPa}$$

(iv) Normal stress ($\sigma$) on the plane of maximum shear :

$$\sigma = \frac{\sigma_x + \sigma_y}{2} = \frac{40 - 24}{2} = \textbf{8 MPa (tensile)}$$

---

**Example 3.6** : At a point in a strained material subjected to two dimensional state of stress, one of the principal stress is 78 MPa, tensile on a plane at 60° to this principal plane, the normal stress is zero. Determine : (i) the other principal stress, (ii) the shear stress on the plane of zero normal stress, and (iii) the planes on which the normal and shear stresses are equal in magnitude.

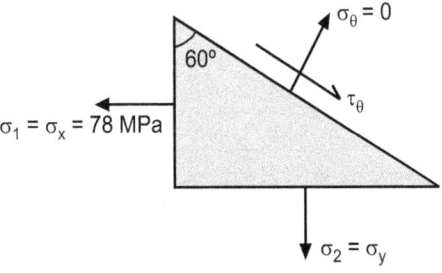

**Fig. 3.10 : Given state of stress**

**Data** : As shown in Fig. 3.10.

**Required** : (i) Other principal stress ($\sigma_2$)
(ii) Shear stress ($\tau_\theta$)
(ii) Plane on which $\sigma_\theta = \tau_\theta$.

**Concept** : Standard formulae.

**Solution** : (i) Principal stress $\sigma_2$ :

Let, other principal stress $\sigma_2$ be tensile in nature. See Fig. 3.10.

We have,

$$\sigma_\theta = 0 = \frac{\sigma_x + \sigma_y}{2} + \frac{\sigma_x - \sigma_y}{2} \cos(2\theta) \qquad (\because \tau_{xy} = 0)$$

$$\therefore \quad 0 = \frac{78 + \sigma_2}{2} + \frac{78 - \sigma_2}{2} \cdot \cos(2 \times 60)$$

$$0 = 39 + 0.5\sigma_2 + 0.25\sigma_2 - 19.5$$

$$\therefore \quad \sigma_2 = -26 \text{ MPa} = \mathbf{26 \text{ MPa} \text{ (Compressive)}}$$

(ii) Shear stress ($\tau_\theta$) :

$$\tau_\theta = \frac{\sigma_x - \sigma_y}{2} \cdot \sin(2\theta)$$

$$= \frac{78 - (-26)}{2} \sin(2 \times 60)$$

$$\therefore \quad \tau_{60} = \mathbf{45 \text{ MPa}}$$

(iii) The inclination of plane for which normal and shear stresses are equal in magnitude :
Equating $\sigma_\theta$ and $\tau_\theta$ from equations (3.1) and (3.2),

$$\sigma_x \cdot \cos^2\theta + \sigma_y \cdot \sin^2\theta = (\sigma_x - \sigma_y) \sin\theta \cos\theta$$

$$78 \cdot \cos^2\theta - 26 \sin^2\theta = (78 - (-26)) \cdot \sin\theta \cdot \cos\theta$$

$$78 \cos^2\theta - 26 \sin^2\theta = 104 \cdot \sin\theta \cos\theta$$

$$\frac{78}{\tan\theta} - 26 \tan\theta = 104$$

$$78 - 26 \tan^2\theta = 104 \tan\theta$$

$$\tan^2\theta + 4\tan\theta - 3 = 0$$

Solving, $\tan\theta = 0.646 \text{ or } -4.646$

$$\therefore \quad \theta = \mathbf{32.87^\circ} \text{ or } \mathbf{-77.87^\circ}$$

**Example 3.7** : At a point in a stressed elastic plate, following information is known :
(i) Maximum shearing strain = $\phi_{max} = 5 \times 10^{-4}$.
(ii) The sum of the normal stresses on two perpendicular planes passing through the point = 27.5 MPa.

(iii) Modulus of elasticity E = 200 GPa and Poisson's ratio $\mu$ = 0.25. Compute the magnitude of principal stresses at the point.

**Data** : $\phi_{max} = 5 \times 10^{-4}$; E = 200 GPa; $\mu = 0.25$; $\sigma_1 + \sigma_2 = 27.5$ MPa.

**Required** : Principal stresses $\sigma_1$ and $\sigma_2$.

**Concept** : (i) Knowing maximum shear strain, find $\tau_{max}$.

(ii) $\tau_{max} = \dfrac{\sigma_1 - \sigma_2}{2}$ and $\sigma_1 + \sigma_2 = 27.5$.

Solving these two equations, principal stresses can be obtained.

**Solution** : (i) Maximum shear stress ($\tau_{max}$).

$$E = 2G(1 + \mu)$$
$$200 = 2G(1 + 0.25)$$
$$\therefore \quad G = 80 \text{ GPa}$$
$$\tau_{max} = \phi_{max} \cdot G = 5 \times 10^{-4} \times 80 \times 10^3 = 40 \text{ MPa}$$

(ii) Principal stresses ($\sigma_1, \sigma_2$).

$$\sigma_1 - \sigma_2 = 2 \times 40 \quad \ldots \text{(i)}$$
$$\sigma_1 + \sigma_2 = 27.5 \quad \ldots \text{(ii)}$$

Solving equations (i) and (ii),

$$\sigma_1 = 53.75 \text{ MPa (Tensile)}$$
$$\sigma_2 = -26.25 \text{ MPa} = 26.25 \text{ MPa (Compressive)}$$

**Example 3.8 :** At certain element; plane AB carries direct tensile stress of 30 MPa and shear stress of 20 MPa while other plane BC carries direct tensile stress of 20 MPa and a shear stress as shown in Fig. 3.11 (a). If the planes AB and BC are inclined at 30° and plane AC at right angles to plane AB which carries direct stress of unknown magnitude and nature, find : (i) shear stress on BC, (ii) magnitude and nature of direct stress on AC and (iii) principal stresses.

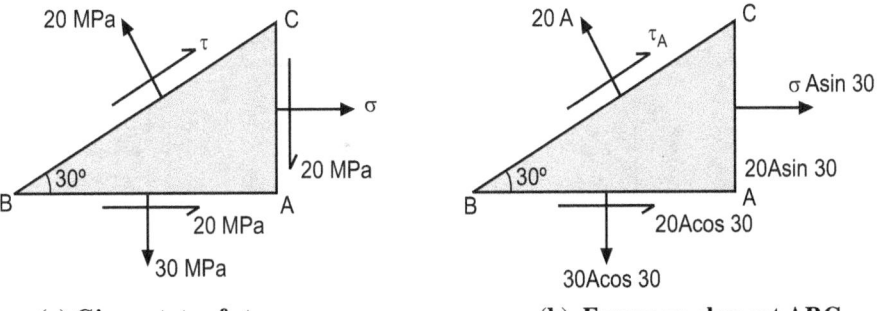

(a) Given state of stress     (b) Forces on element ABC

**Fig. 3.11**

**Data** : As shown in Fig. 3.11 (a).

**Required :** (i) Shear stress ($\tau$) on BC, (ii) Magnitude and nature of direct stress ($\sigma$) on AC and (iii) Principal stresses.

**Concept :** Equilibrium and standard formulae.

**Solution :** (i) Equilibrium : Let A be the area along the plane BC.

∴ Area of plane AC = A sin 30 and area of plane AB = A cos 30. Forces on element ABC are as shown in Fig. 3.11 (b).

$\Sigma F_x = 0$ ;

$$\sigma A \sin 30 + 20 A \cos 30 + \tau A \cos 30 - 20 A \sin 30 = 0$$

$$0.5 \sigma + 0.86 \tau + 7.32 = 0 \quad \ldots (i)$$

$\Sigma F_y = 0$ ;

$$- 20 A \sin 30 - 30 A \cos 30 + \tau A \sin 30 + 20 A \cos 30 = 0 \quad \ldots (ii)$$

∴ $\tau = 37.32$ MPa   put this value in equation (i)

∴ $\sigma = -79.28$ MPa = **79.28 MPa (Compressive)**

(ii) Principal stresses ($\sigma_1, \sigma_2$) :

$$\sigma_1, \sigma_2 = \frac{\sigma_x + \sigma_y}{2} \pm \sqrt{\left(\frac{\sigma_x - \sigma_y}{2}\right)^2 + (\tau_{xy})^2}$$

$$= \frac{-79.28 + 30}{2} \pm \sqrt{\left(\frac{-79.28 - 30}{2}\right)^2 + (20)^2}$$

$$= -24.64 \pm 58.18$$

$\sigma_1 = -82.82$ MPa = **82.82 MPa (Compressive)**

$\sigma_2 =$ **33.54 MPa (Tensile)**

**Example 3.9 :** At a point in a strained material, the state of stress is as shown in Fig. 3.12 (a). Locate the principal planes and evaluate the principal stresses.

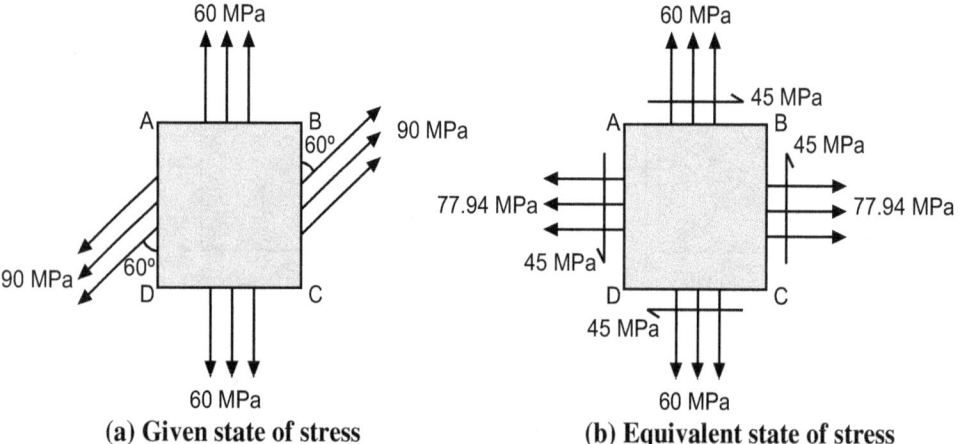

(a) Given state of stress          (b) Equivalent state of stress

Fig. 3.12

**Data** : As shown in Fig. 3.12 (a).

**Required** : Principal planes and principal stresses.

**Concept** : Standard formulae.

**Solution** : (i) Equivalent state of stress :

Stress normal to faces BC and AD = $90 \times \sin 60 = 77.94$ MPa

and shear stress = $90 \times \cos 60 = 45$ MPa

Equivalent state of stress is as shown in Fig. 3.12 (b).

(ii) Principal stresses ($\sigma_1, \sigma_2$) :

$$\sigma_1, \sigma_2 = \frac{\sigma_x + \sigma_y}{2} \pm \sqrt{\left(\frac{\sigma_x - \sigma_y}{2}\right)^2 + (\tau_{xy})^2}$$

$$\sigma_1, \sigma_2 = \frac{77.94 + 60}{2} \pm \sqrt{\left(\frac{77.94 - 60}{2}\right)^2 + (45)^2}$$

$$= 68.97 \pm 45.88$$

$\sigma_1$ = **114.85 MPa (Tensile)**

$\sigma_2$ = **23.09 MPa (Tensile)**

(iii) Principal planes :

$$\tan(2\theta) = -\frac{2\tau_{xy}}{\sigma_x - \sigma_y}$$

$$= \frac{2 \times 45}{77.94 - 60} \qquad (\because \tau_{xy} \text{ is } -ve)$$

$$= 5.016$$

∴ $\theta_1$ = **39.36°**, $\theta_2 = \theta_1 + 90° = $ **129.36°**

**Example 3.10** : At a point in a strained material under two-dimensional stress condition, the normal stress on a certain plane is 80 MPa compressive and the shear stress is 56 MPa. On a plane at right angles to this plane, there is no normal stress. If the maximum permissible stresses for the material are 150 MPa in compression, 130 MPa in tension and 65 MPa in shear; examine the safety of section giving reasons.

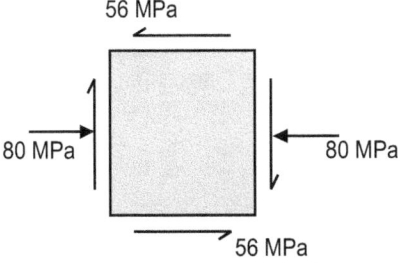

Fig. 3.13 : Given state of stress

**Data** : State of stress as shown in Fig. 3.13.

Allowable stresses : In compression : 150 MPa, In tension : 130 MPa

In shear : 65 MPa.

**Required** : To check safety of the section.

**Concept** : If actual stresses induced are less than respective allowable stresses, section is safe.

**Solution** : (i) Principal stresses ($\sigma_1$, $\sigma_2$) :

$$\sigma_1, \sigma_2 = \frac{\sigma_x}{2} \pm \sqrt{\left(\frac{\sigma_x}{2}\right)^2 + (\tau_{xy})^2} \qquad (\because \sigma_y = 0)$$

$$\sigma_1, \sigma_2 = \frac{-80}{2} \pm \sqrt{\left(\frac{-80}{2}\right)^2 + (56)^2}$$

$$= -40 \pm 68.82 \text{ MPa}$$

$$\sigma_1 = -108.82 \text{ MPa}$$

= **108.82 MPa (Compressive) < 150 MPa** ... (Safe)

$\sigma_2$ = **28.82 MPa (Tensile) < 130 MPa** ... (Safe)

(ii) Maximum shear stress ($\tau_{max}$) :

$$\tau_{max} = \frac{\sigma_1 - \sigma_2}{2} = \pm 68.82 \text{ MPa} > 65 \text{ MPa} \qquad \text{... (Unsafe)}$$

∴ The section is unsafe in shear.

**Example 3.11** : At a point in a strained material, the resultant stress on vertical plane is 100 MPa, tensile, making 30° angle with normal. On horizontal plane through the point, the resultant compressive stress makes an angle of 60° with the normal as shown in Fig. 3.14 (a). Determine : (i) the principal stresses and principal planes, (ii) maximum shear stress and (iii) on properly oriented element, show principal stresses.

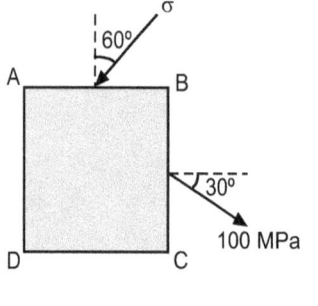
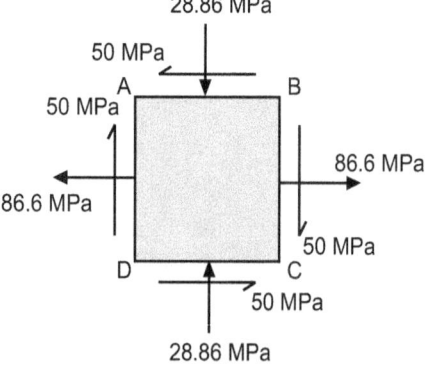

(a) Given state of stress      (b) Equivalent state of stress

**Fig. 3.14**

**Data** : As shown in Fig. 3.14 (a).
**Required** : (i) Principal planes and principal stresses, (ii) Maximum shear stress.
**Concept** : Standard formulae.
**Solution** : (i) Equivalent state of stress :

Normal stress on faces BC and AD = 100 cos 30 = 86.6 MPa (Tensile)

Shear stress = 100 sin 30 = 50 MPa (on all faces)

Compressive stress $\sigma$ on face AB $= \dfrac{50}{\sin 60} = 57.73$ MPa.

Normal stress on faces AB and CD = 57.73 cos 60 = 28.86 MPa (Compressive)

Equivalent state of stress is as shown in Fig. 3.14 (b).

(ii) Principal stresses ($\sigma_1, \sigma_2$) :

$$\sigma_1, \sigma_2 = \dfrac{\sigma_x + \sigma_y}{2} \pm \sqrt{\left(\dfrac{\sigma_x - \sigma_y}{2}\right)^2 + (\tau_{xy})^2}$$

$$= \dfrac{86.6 - 28.86}{2} \pm \sqrt{\left(\dfrac{86.6 - (-28.86)}{2}\right)^2 + (50)^2}$$

$$= 28.87 \pm 76.37$$

$\sigma_1 = $ **105.24 MPa (Tensile)**

$\sigma_2 = -47.50$ MPa = **47.5 MPa (Compressive)**

(iii) Principal planes : $\tan(2\theta) = -\dfrac{2\tau_{xy}}{\sigma_x - \sigma_y}$

$$= -\dfrac{2 \times 50}{86.6 - (-28.86)}$$

$$= -0.866$$

$\theta = $ **−20.44°** and **−110.44°**

(iv) Maximum shear stress ($\tau_{max}$) :

$$\tau_{max} = \dfrac{\sigma_1 - \sigma_2}{2} = \dfrac{105.24 - (-47.5)}{2} = 76.37 \text{ MPa}$$

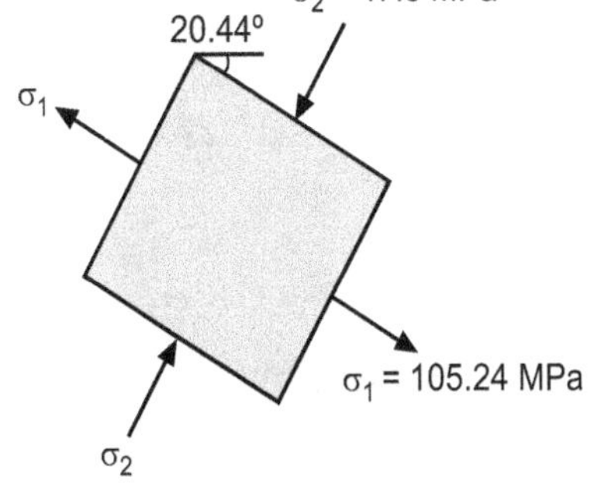

**Fig. 3.14 (c) : Principal stresses on oriented element**

**Example 3.12 :** A circle 40 mm in diameter is marked on a steel plate before it is stressed as shown in Fig. 3.15. As a result of these stresses, the circle deforms to an ellipse. Calculate the lengths of the major and minor axes of the ellipse and their directions. Assume E = 200 GPa and μ = 0.25.

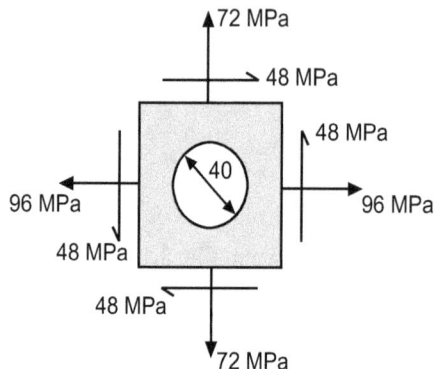

**Fig. 3.15 : State of stress on a plate**

**Data** : State of stress as shown in Fig. 3.15.
**Required** : Lengths and directions of major and minor axes of the ellipse.
**Concept** : Principal stresses and principal strains.
**Solution** : (i) Principal stresses ($\sigma_1$, $\sigma_2$) :

$$\sigma_1, \sigma_2 = \frac{\sigma_x + \sigma_y}{2} \pm \sqrt{\left(\frac{\sigma_x - \sigma_y}{2}\right)^2 + (\tau_{xy})^2}$$

$$= \frac{96 + 72}{2} \pm \sqrt{\left(\frac{96 - 72}{2}\right)^2 + (48)^2}$$

$$= 84 \pm 49.47$$

$$\sigma_1 = 133.47 \text{ MPa (Tensile)}$$

$$\sigma_2 = 34.53 \text{ MPa (Tensile)}$$

(ii) Principal planes :

$$\tan(2\theta) = \frac{2\tau_{xy}}{\sigma_x - \sigma_y} \qquad (\because \tau_{xy} \text{ is } -\text{ve})$$

$$= \frac{2 \times 48}{96 - 72} = 4$$

$$\theta = 37.98° \text{ and } 127.98°$$

(iii) Principal strains ($\varepsilon_1$, $\varepsilon_2$) :

$$\varepsilon_1 = \frac{1}{E}(\sigma_1 - \mu\sigma_2) = \frac{1}{200 \times 10^3}(133.47 - 0.25 \times 34.53)$$

$$= 6.24 \times 10^{-4}$$

$$\varepsilon_2 = \frac{1}{E}(\sigma_2 - \mu\sigma_1) = \frac{1}{200 \times 10^3}(34.53 - 0.25 \times 133.47)$$

$$= 5.81 \times 10^{-6}$$

Increase in diameter = $\delta d_1$ = 6.24 × 10⁻⁴ × 40 = **0.0249 mm**

∴ Length of major axis = 40 + 0.0249 = **40.0249 mm**

Increase in diameter = $\delta d_2$ = 5.81 × 10⁻⁶ × 40 = **2.32 × 10⁻⁴ mm**

Length of minor axis = 40 + 2.32 × 10⁻⁴ = **40.000232 mm**

**Example 3.13 :** A small block is 60 mm long, 40 mm wide and 5 mm thick. It is subjected to uniformly distributed tensile forces having the resultant values as shown in Fig. 3.16. Compute the stress components developed along the diagonal AB.

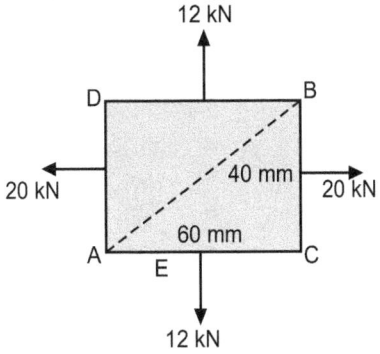

**Fig. 3.16 : State of stress on a block**

**Data** : As shown in Fig. 3.16.

**Required** : Stress components on diagonal AB.

**Concept** : FBD and equations of statics.

**Solution** : (i) FBD of wedge ABC :

Let $F_n$ and $F_t$ be the forces normal and tangential to diagonal AB for equilibrium as shown in Fig. 3.17.

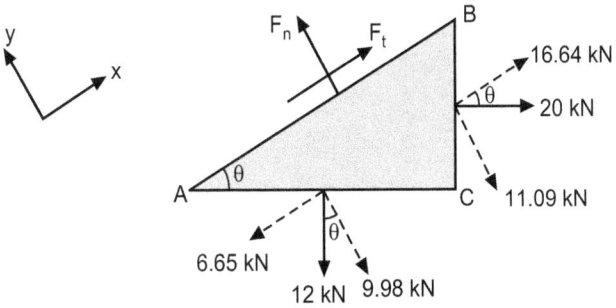

**Fig. 3.17 : Forces on wedge ABC**

$$\theta = \tan^{-1}\left(\frac{40}{60}\right) = 33.7°$$

Resolving forces normal and tangential to plane AB, the components are obtained as shown in Fig. 3.17.

$\Sigma F_x = 0$;
$$F_t + 16.64 - 6.65 = 0$$
$$\therefore \quad F_t = 10 \text{ kN}$$
$\Sigma F_y = 0$;
$$F_n - 11.09 - 9.98 = 0$$
$$F_n = 21.07 \text{ kN}$$

(ii) Stress components :

$$l(AB) = \sqrt{(60)^2 + (40)^2} = 72.11 \text{ mm}$$
$$\therefore \quad \text{Area of plane } AB = A = l(AB) \times \text{Thickness}$$
$$= 72.11 \times 5$$
$$A = 360.55 \text{ mm}^2$$
$$\therefore \quad \text{Normal stress} = \sigma_n = \frac{F_n}{A} = \frac{21.07 \times 10^3}{360.55}$$
$$= 58.43 \text{ MPa (Tensile)}$$
$$\text{Shear stress} = \tau = \frac{F_t}{A} = \frac{10 \times 10^3}{360.55}$$
$$= 27.73 \text{ MPa}$$

**Example 3.14 :** The principal strains at a point in a two-dimensional stress system were observed to be 0.00035 extension and 0.00025 contraction. Determine the principal stresses. Also find the maximum shear stress.

$$E = 200 \text{ GPa}, \quad \mu = \frac{1}{m} = 0.3$$

**Data :** $\varepsilon_1 = 0.00035$, $\varepsilon_2 = -0.00025$, $E = 200$ GPa, $\mu = \frac{1}{m} = 0.3$

**Required :** $\sigma_1$, $\sigma_2$, $\tau_{max}$ and plane on which maximum shear stress acts.

**Concept :** Generalised Hooke's law.

**Solution :** (i) Principal stresses :

We have,
$$\varepsilon_1 = \frac{1}{E}(\sigma_1 - \mu \sigma_2)$$
$$0.00035 = \frac{1}{200 \times 10^3}(\sigma_1 - 0.3 \sigma_2)$$
$$\sigma_1 - 0.3 \sigma_2 = 70 \quad \ldots \text{(i)}$$
$$\varepsilon_2 = \frac{1}{E}(\sigma_2 - \mu \sigma_1)$$
$$-0.00025 = \frac{1}{200 \times 10^3}(\sigma_2 - 0.3 \sigma_1)$$
$$\sigma_2 - 0.3 \sigma_1 = -50 \quad \ldots \text{(ii)}$$

Solving equations (i) and (ii),

$$\sigma_1 = 60.44 \text{ MPa (Tensile)}$$
$$\sigma_2 = -31.87 \text{ MPa} = 31.87 \text{ MPa (Compressive)}$$

(ii) Maximum shear stress :

$$\tau_{max} = \frac{\sigma_1 - \sigma_2}{2}$$
$$= \frac{60.44 - (-31.87)}{2}$$

∴ $\tau_{max} = 46.155$ MPa (Tensile)

**Example 3.15 :** At a point in a strained material, direct stresses of 102 MPa (tensile) and 76.5 MPa (compressive) exist on two perpendicular planes. These planes also carry shear stresses. The major principal stress is 127.5 MPa. Find shear stresses on these planes. Also find the maximum shear stress.

**Data :** $\sigma_x = 102$ MPa, $\sigma_y = -76.5$ MPa, $\sigma_1 = 127.5$ MPa.

**Required :** $\tau_{xy}$, $\tau_{max}$.

**Concept :** Standard formulae.

**Solution :** (i) $\tau_{xy}$ :

$$\sigma_1 = \frac{\sigma_x + \sigma_y}{2} + \sqrt{\left(\frac{\sigma_x - \sigma_y}{2}\right)^2 + \tau_{xy}^2}$$

$$127.5 = \frac{102 - 76.5}{2} + \sqrt{\left(\frac{102 + 76.5}{2}\right)^2 + \tau_{xy}^2}$$

$$= 12.75 + \sqrt{7965.56 + \tau_{xy}^2}$$

$$13167.56 = 7965.56 + \tau_{xy}^2$$

∴ $\tau_{xy} = 72.12$ MPa

(ii)
$$\sigma_2 = \frac{\sigma_x + \sigma_y}{2} - \sqrt{\left(\frac{\sigma_x - \sigma_y}{2}\right)^2 + \tau_{xy}^2}$$

$$= 12.75 - 114.74$$

$$\sigma_2 = -101.99 \text{ MPa} = 101.99 \text{ MPa (Compressive)}$$

(iii) Maximum shear stress :

$$\tau_{max} = \frac{\sigma_1 - \sigma_2}{2} = \frac{127.5 - (-101.99)}{2}$$

∴ $\tau_{max} = 114.745$ MPa (Tensile)

**Example 3.16 :** A piece of material is subjected to a tensile stress of 80 MPa in one direction, a compressive stress of 60 MPa in a direction at right angle to the tensile stress, and a shearing stress of 50 MPa. Find the normal, tangential and resultant component of the stress on the plane, the normal of which makes an angle of 30° with the tensile stress.

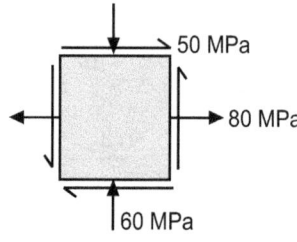

Fig. 3.18

**Data :** As shown in Fig. 3.18, θ = 60°.

**Required :** Normal, tangential and resultant component of the stress.

**Concept :** Standard formulae.

**Solution :** (i) Normal stress :

$$\sigma_\theta = \frac{\sigma_x + \sigma_y}{2} + \frac{\sigma_x - \sigma_y}{2} \cos 2\theta - \tau_{xy} \sin 2\theta$$

$$= \frac{80 - 60}{2} + \frac{80 - (-60)}{2} \cos 120 - 50 \sin 120$$

$$= 10 - 35 - 43.30$$

∴ $\sigma_\theta = -68.3$ MPa = **68.3 MPa (Compressive)**

(ii) Shear stress :

$$\tau_\theta = \frac{\sigma_x - \sigma_y}{2} \sin 2\theta + \tau_{xy} \cos 2\theta$$

$$= \frac{80 - (-60)}{2} \sin 120 + 50 \cos 120$$

$$= 60.62 - 25 = 35.62$$

$\tau_\theta = $ **35.62 (Tensile)**

(iii) Resultant stress and its obliquity :

$$\text{Resultant stress} = \sqrt{\sigma_\theta^2 + \tau_\theta^2}$$

$$= \sqrt{(-68.3)^2 + (35.62)^2}$$

$$= \mathbf{77.03 \text{ MPa}}$$

$$\text{Obliquity} = \phi = \tan^{-1}\left(\frac{\tau_\theta}{\sigma_\theta}\right)$$

$$= \tan^{-1}\left(\frac{35.62}{-68.3}\right) = \mathbf{-27.54°}$$

**Example 3.17 :** A steel bolt of 30 mm diameter is subjected to direct tension of 20 kN and shearing force of 15 kN. Determine the intensities of normal and shear stresses across a plane at an angle of 70° to the axis of bolt. Also calculate the principal stresses.

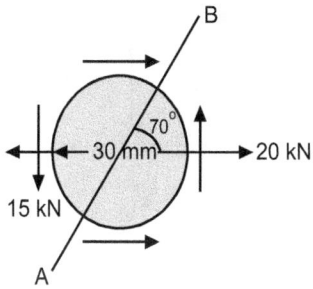

Fig. 3.19

**Data :** As shown in Fig. 3.19, $\theta = 20°$.
**Required :** Stress component on plane AB and principal stresses.
**Concept :** Standard formulae.
**Solution :** (i) State of stress :

$$\text{Normal stress} = \frac{P}{A} = \frac{20 \times 10^3}{\frac{\pi}{4} \times (30)^2} = 28.29 \text{ MPa}$$

$$\text{Shear stress} = \frac{S}{A} = \frac{15 \times 10^3}{\frac{\pi}{4} \times (30)^2} = 21.22 \text{ MPa}$$

(ii) Principal stresses :

$$\sigma_1, \sigma_2 = \frac{\sigma_x}{2} \pm \sqrt{\left(\frac{\sigma_x}{2}\right)^2 + \tau_{xy}^2}$$

$$= \frac{28.29}{2} \pm \sqrt{\left(\frac{28.29}{2}\right)^2 + (21.22)^2}$$

$$= 14.145 \pm 25.50$$

$\sigma_1 = $ **39.645 MPa (Tensile)**
$\sigma_2 = -11.355$ MPa $= $ **11.355 (Compressive)**

(iii) Stress component on plane AE :

$$\sigma_\theta = \frac{\sigma_x}{2} + \frac{\sigma_x}{2} \cos 2\theta - \tau_{xy} \sin 2\theta$$

$$= \frac{28.29}{2} + \frac{28.29}{2} \cos 40 - 21.22 \sin 40$$

$\sigma_\theta = $ **11.34 MPa (Tensile)**

$$\tau_\theta = \frac{\sigma_x}{2} \sin 2\theta + \tau_{xy} \cos 2\theta$$

$$= \frac{28.29}{2} \sin 40 + 21.22 \cos 40$$

$\tau_\theta = $ **25.35 MPa (Tensile)**

**Example 3.18 :** An element in a plane stress is subjected to stresses as shown in Fig. 3.20. Obtain the principal stresses and show them on a properly oriented element.

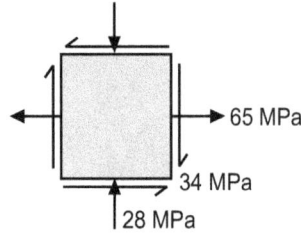

Fig. 3.20

**Data :** As shown in Fig. 3.20.

**Required :** $\sigma_1, \sigma_2$.

**Concept :** Standard formulae.

**Solution :** Principal stresses :

$$\sigma_1, \sigma_2 = \frac{\sigma_x + \sigma_y}{2} \pm \sqrt{\left(\frac{\sigma_x - \sigma_y}{2}\right)^2 + \tau_{xy}^2}$$

$$= \frac{65 - 28}{2} \pm \sqrt{\left(\frac{65 + 28}{2}\right)^2 + (34)^2}$$

$$= 18.5 \pm 57.60$$

$$\sigma_1 = 76.10 \text{ MPa (Tensile)}$$

$$\sigma_2 = -39.10 \text{ MPa} = 39.10 \text{ MPa (Compressive)}$$

$$\tan 2\theta = -\frac{2\tau_{xy}}{\sigma_x - \sigma_y} = \frac{-2 \times 34}{(65 - (-28))} = -0.73$$

$$\therefore \quad \theta = -18.08, \quad \theta = -108.09°$$

**Example 3.19 :** At a particular point in a wooden member, the state of stress is as shown in Fig. 3.21. The direction of grain in the wood makes a 30° angle with the horizontal.

If the allowable shearing stress parallel to the grain is 1 MPa, verify that, this state of stress is permissible.

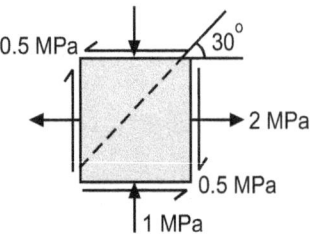

Fig. 3.21

**Data :** As shown in Fig. 3.21, $\tau_\theta = 1$ MPa, $\theta = 60°$.

**Required :** Check for shearing stress.

**Solution :** Standard formulae.

$$\tau_\theta = \frac{\sigma_x - \sigma_y}{2} \sin 2\theta + \tau_{xy} \cos 2\theta$$

$$= \frac{2-(-1)}{2} \sin 120 + 0.5 \cos 120$$

$$= 1.3 + 0.25 = 1.55 \text{ MPa} > 1 \text{ MPa}$$

State of stress is not permissible.

## 3.5 MOHR'S CIRCLE

Mohr's circle is a graphical representation of a general state of stress at a point. It is a graphical method used for evaluation of principal stresses, maximum shear stress, normal and tangential stresses on any given plane.

Equations (3.3) and (3.4) are rewritten as

$$\sigma_\theta - \frac{\sigma_x + \sigma_y}{2} = \frac{\sigma_x - \sigma_y}{2} \cos(2\theta) - \tau_{xy} \cdot \sin(2\theta)$$

$$\tau_\theta = \frac{\sigma_x - \sigma_y}{2} \sin(2\theta) + \tau_{xy} \cdot \cos(2\theta)$$

Squaring and adding these equations we get,

$$\left(\sigma_\theta - \frac{\sigma_x + \sigma_y}{2}\right)^2 + \tau_\theta^2 = \left(\frac{\sigma_x - \sigma_y}{2}\right)^2 + (\tau_{xy})^2 \qquad \ldots (3.14)$$

It should be noted that, $\sigma_x$, $\sigma_y$ and $\tau_{xy}$ are constants for a given state of stress, while $\sigma_\theta$ and $\tau_\theta$ are variables. Equation (3.13) is the equation of circle of the form

$$(\sigma_\theta - a)^2 + \tau_\theta^2 = R^2 \qquad \ldots (3.15)$$

where, $$a = \frac{\sigma_x + \sigma_y}{2}$$

and $$R = \sqrt{\left(\frac{\sigma_x - \sigma_y}{2}\right)^2 + (\tau_{xy})^2}$$

The centre of Mohr's circle lies at (a, 0) i.e. $\left(\frac{\sigma_x + \sigma_y}{2}, 0\right)$.

Following important points must be noted for graphical analysis by Mohr's circle :

(1) The normal stresses $\sigma_x$, $\sigma_y$ are plotted along the abscissa. The tensile stresses are considered positive and the compressive stresses are considered negative.

(2) The shear stress $\tau$ is plotted as ordinates. Shear stress which causes clockwise rotation of element is considered positive while the one which causes anticlockwise rotation is considered negative.

(3) Co-ordinates of various points on Mohr's circle represent the state of stress at different planes.

(4) The radius of the circle to any point on its circumference represents the axis directed normal to the plane whose stress components are given by the co-ordinates of that point.

(5) The angle between radii to points on Mohr's circle is twice the angle between the normals to the actual planes represented by these points. The rotational sense of this angle is same as that of rotational sense of the actual angle between the normals to the plane.

**Example 3.20 :** At a certain point in a stressed body, the principal stresses are as shown in Fig. 3.22 (a). Determine normal and shear stress components on the planes whose normals are at 20° and 110° with x-axis. Show your result on properly oriented element.

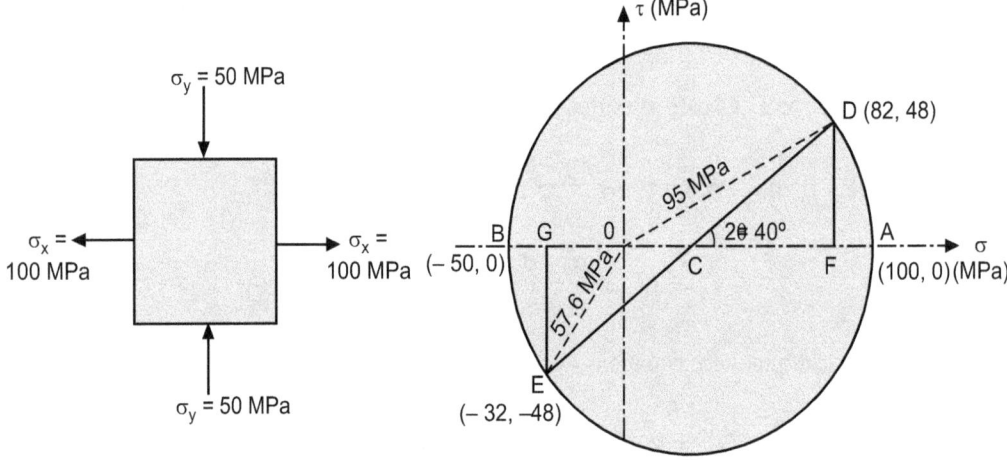

(a) State of stress at a given element        (b) Mohr's circle

**Fig. 3.22**

**Data** : State of stress as shown in Fig. 3.22 (a).

**Required** : Normal and shear stress components on the planes whose normals are at 20° and 110° with x-axis.

**Concept** : Mohr's circle.

**Solution** :

(i) Draw a set of rectangular axes and label them as $\sigma$ and $\tau$ axes as shown in Fig. 3.22 (b).

(ii) Along the x-axis, OA and OB are set-off equal in length to $\sigma_x$ and $\sigma_y$ respectively. Please note that $\sigma_x$ is + ve while $\sigma_y$ is – ve.

(iii) AB represents the diameter of Mohr's circle. Mark centre 'C' of AB and with 'C' as centre and AC as radius, draw Mohr's circle.

(iv) Normal and tangential stress components are required on the planes whose normals are at 20° and 110° with x-axis. Hence, draw CD and CE at 40° and 220° anticlockwise as shown in Fig. 3.22 (b).
(v) The co-ordinates of points D and E represent state of stress on the planes whose normals are at 20° and 110° with x-axis respectively.

**Ans. :** On plane, whose normal is at 20° to x axis, $\sigma = 82$ MPa (Tensile) and $\tau = 48$ MPa (clockwise)

On plane, whose normal is at 110° to x-axis, $\sigma = -32$ MPa $= 32$ MPa (Compressive) and $\tau = -48$ MPa $= 48$ MPa (anticlockwise), as shown in Fig. 3.23.

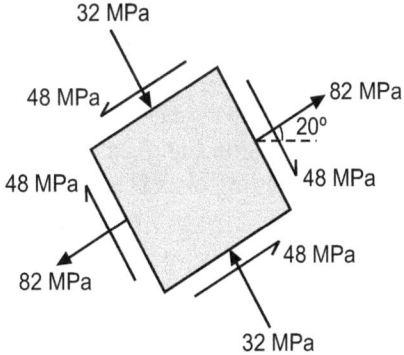

**Fig. 3.23 : State of stress on oriented element**

**Note :** It should be noted that OD and OE represent the resultant stresses on planes whose normals are at 20° and 110° with x-axis respectively. Thus, resultant stress on plane whose normal is at 20° = 95 MPa (Tensile) and resultant stress on plane whose normal is at 110° = 57.6 MPa (Compressive).

**Example 3.21 :** At a point in a strained material, two-dimensional state of stress is as shown in Fig. 3.24 (a). Determine graphically : (i) Principal stresses, (ii) Principal planes, (iii) Maximum shear stress, (iv) Planes of maximum shear, (v) Normal and shear stress components on planes whose normals are at 35° and 125° with x-axis.

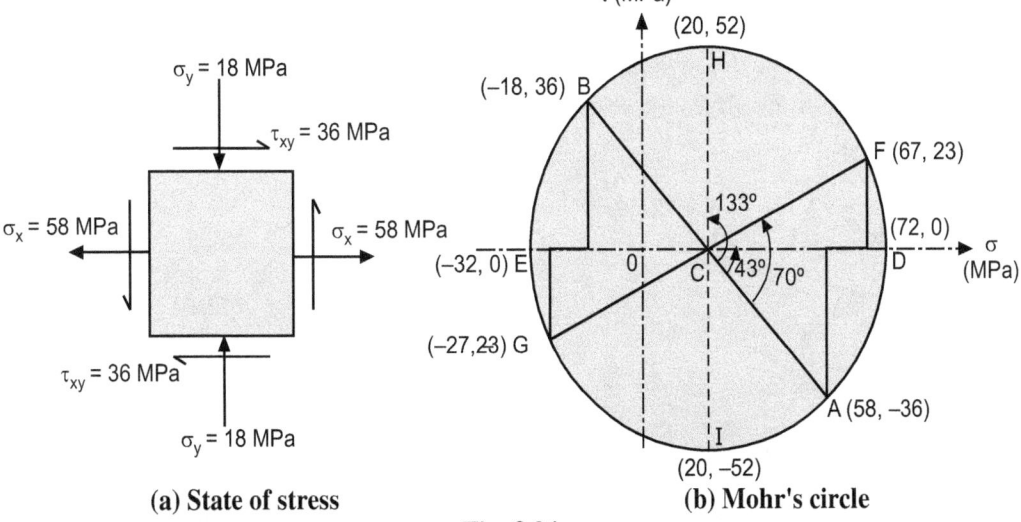

(a) State of stress   (b) Mohr's circle

**Fig. 3.24**

**Data** : State of stress as shown in Fig. 3.24 (a).

**Required** : (i) Principal planes and principal stresses, (ii) Maximum shear stress and its plane, (iii) Normal and shear stress components on plane whose normals are at 35° and 125° with x-axis.

**Concept** : Mohr's circle.

**Solution** :

(i) Draw a set of rectangular axes and label them as $\sigma$ and $\tau$ axes.

(ii) Locate points A (58, – 36) and B (– 18, 36) representing state of stress on x and y planes respectively. It should be noted that shear on x plane is negative while that on y plane is positive.

(iii) AB is the diameter of Mohr's circle whose centre lies at C. With 'C' as centre and CA as radius draw Mohr's circle as shown in Fig. 3.24 (b); which cuts the x-axis at D and E. Measure and write the co-ordinates of points D and E which represent principal planes.

Thus, $\sigma_1$ = 72 MPa (Tensile) and $\sigma_2$ = – 32 MPa = 32 MPa (Compressive)

(iv) Measure $\angle ACD = 2\theta_n = 43°$.

$\therefore$ $\theta_1 = 21.5°$ and $\theta_2 = 111.5°$ represent directions of principal planes. See Fig. 3.25 (a).

(v) Locate points H (20, 52) and I (20, – 52) on vertical diameter. These are the planes of maximum shear stress.

Thus, maximum shear stress = $\tau_{max}$ = $\pm 52$ MPa and normal stress on the plane of maximum shear is 20 MPa (Tensile).

(vi) Measure $\angle ACH = 2\theta_s = 133°$

$\therefore$ $\theta_3 = 66.5°$ and $\theta_4 = 156.5°$ represent the directions of planes of maximum shear. See Fig. 3.25 (b).

(vii) Normal and tangential stress components are required on planes whose normals are at 35° and 125° with x-axis. Hence, draw CF and CG at 70° and 250° anticlockwise with respect to CA as shown in Fig. 3.24 (b). The co-ordinates of points F and G represent the state of stress on planes whose normals are at 35° and 125° with x-axis, respectively.

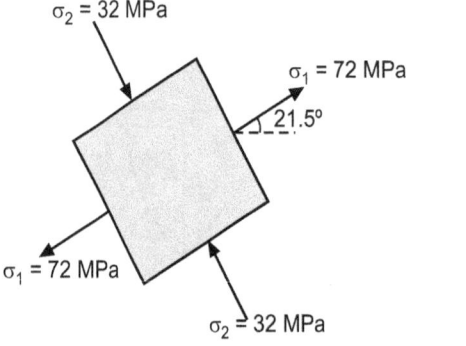

(a) Principal stresses

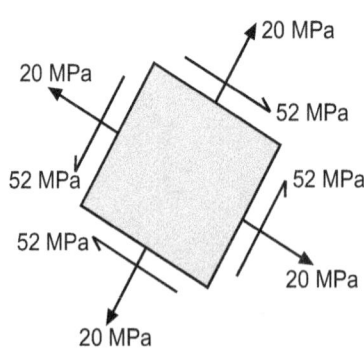

(b) Maximum shear stress

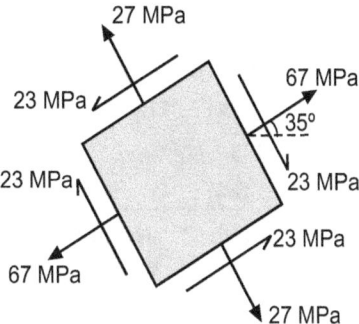

**(c) State of stress on element whose normals are at 35° and 125° to x-axis**

**Fig. 3.25**

Thus, on plane whose normal is at 35° with x-axis, normal stress = σ = 67 MPa (Tensile) and shear stress = τ = 23 MPa (clockwise).

On plane whose normal is at 125° with x-axis, normal stress = σ = – 27 MPa = 27 MPa (Compressive) and shear stress = τ = – 23 MPa = 23 MPa (anticlockwise). See Fig. 3.25 (c).

**Example 3.22 :** At a point in a strained material, the normal and tangential stresses, on a plane inclined at 40° to the plane carrying major principal tensile stress, are 68 N/mm² tensile and 158 N/mm² respectively. Find the magnitude and nature of principal stresses. Also find the resultant stress on the given inclined plane.

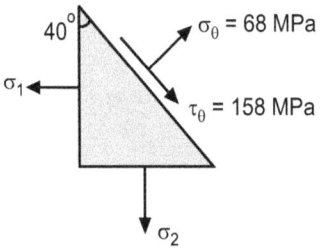

**Fig. 3.26**

**Solution :** (i)

$$\sigma_\theta = 68 = \frac{\sigma_1 + \sigma_2}{2} + \left\{\frac{\sigma_1 - \sigma_2}{2}\right\} \cos(2 \times 40)$$

∴ $\quad 136 = 1.1736\,\sigma_1 + 0.8264\,\sigma_2 \qquad \ldots \text{(i)}$

$$\tau_\theta = 156 = \left\{\frac{\sigma_1 - \sigma_2}{2}\right\} \sin(2 \times 40)$$

∴ $\quad 316.81 = \sigma_1 - \sigma_2 \qquad \ldots \text{(ii)}$

Solving (i) and (ii),

$$\sigma_1 = 198.9 \text{ MPa}, \quad \sigma_2 = 117.9 \text{ MPa}$$

(ii) Resultant stress on inclined plane,

$$\sigma_R = \sqrt{(68)^2 + (156)^2}$$
$$= 170.17 \text{ MPa}$$
$$\phi = \tan^{-1}(\tau_\theta/\sigma_\theta)$$
$$= 66.41°$$

**Example 3.23 :** At a point in an strained material, stress pattern is as shown in Fig. 3.27. Determine (i) magnitude of principal stresses and their orientation, (ii) maximum shear stress and its orientation.

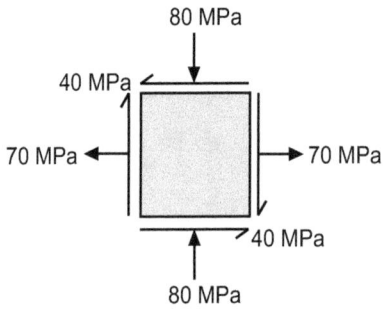

**Fig. 3.27**

**Solution :** (i) Principal stresses and its planes :

$$\sigma_1, \sigma_2 = \frac{\sigma_x + \sigma_y}{2} \pm \sqrt{\left(\frac{\sigma_x - \sigma_y}{2}\right)^2 + \tau_{xy}^2}$$

$$= \frac{70 - 80}{2} \pm \sqrt{\frac{(70 + 80)^2}{2} + (40)^2}$$

$$\sigma_1 = -90 \text{ MPa and } \sigma_2 = 80 \text{ MPa}$$

$$\tan(2\theta_1) = -\frac{2\tau_{xy}}{\sigma_x - \sigma_y}$$

$$\theta_1 = 14.03°, \ \theta_2 = 104.03°$$

(ii) Maximum shear stresses and its planes :

$$\tau_{max} = \pm(\sigma_1 - \sigma_2)/2 = \pm 85 \text{ MPa}$$

$$\theta_3 = -30.96° \text{ and } \theta_4 = -120.96°$$

**Example 3.24 :** $\sigma_x$, $\sigma_y$ and $\tau_{xy}$ are the stress components along the rectangular axes x and y, whereas $\sigma_x'$, $\sigma_y'$ and $\tau_{xy}'$ are the components along the rectangular axes x' and y' as shown in Fig. 3.28. Prove that $\sigma_x' \cdot \sigma_y' - \tau_{x'y'}^2$ is independent of the orientation, as defined by $\theta$, of x' and y'. Using this invariance property, express the shear stress $\tau_{xy}$ in terms of $\sigma_x$, $\sigma_y$ and the principal stresses $\sigma_1$, $\sigma_2$.

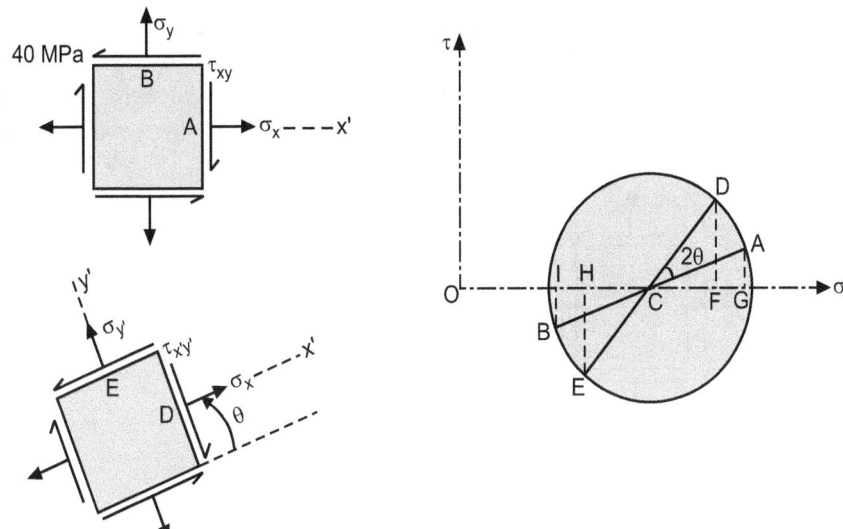

**Fig. 3.28**

**Solution :** Required : $\sigma_x \cdot \sigma_y - \sigma_{xy}^2 = \sigma_x' \cdot \sigma_y' - \tau_{x'y'}^2 =$ constant.

$$(OG)(OI) - AG^2 = (OF)(OH) - DF^2$$
$$(OC + CG)(OC - CI) - AG^2 = (OC + CF)(OC - CH) - DF^2$$
$$OC^2 - CG^2 - AG^2 = OC^2 - CF^2 - DF^2$$
$$CG^2 + AG^2 = CF^2 + DF^2 = R^2 = \text{constant. Hence proved.}$$

Also
$$\sigma_x \cdot \sigma_y - \tau_{xy}^2 = \sigma_1 \cdot \sigma_2$$

$$\tau_{xy} = \sqrt{\sigma_x \cdot \sigma_y - \sigma_1 \cdot \sigma_2}$$

**Example 3.25 :** If $\sigma_x = 60$ MPa, $\sigma_y = -120$ MPa, $\tau_{xy} = 100$ MPa and $\theta = 30°$, obtain the values of $\sigma_x'$, $\sigma_y'$ and $\tau_{xy}'$. Locate the planes of principal stresses and the planes of maximum shear stresses. Find the magnitude of these stresses.

**Solution :**
$$\sigma_x' = \sigma_\theta = \frac{\sigma_x + \sigma_y}{2} + \frac{\sigma_x - \sigma_y}{2}\cos(2\theta) - \tau_{xy}\sin(2\theta)$$
$$= -71.6 \text{ MPa}$$

$$\sigma_y' = \frac{\sigma_x + \sigma_y}{2} + \frac{\sigma_x - \sigma_y}{2}\cos[2(\theta + 90)] - \tau_{xy}\sin[2(\theta + 90)]$$
$$= 11.6 \text{ MPa}$$

$$\tau_{xy}' = \frac{\sigma_x - \sigma_y}{2}\sin(2\theta) + \tau_{xy}\cos(2\theta)$$
$$= \pm 127.94 \text{ MPa}$$

$\sigma_1 = 104.5$ MPa, $\sigma_2 = -164.5$ MPa

$\theta_1 = 24°$, $\theta_2 = 114°$, $\theta_3 = -21°$, $\theta_4 = -111°$

$\tau_{max} = \pm 134.5$ MPa

**Example 3.26 :** At a point in a structure subjected to plane stress, the stresses have magnitude and directions shown acting on element A in the first part of Fig. 3.29. Element B, located at the same point, is rotated through an angle θ of such magnitude that the stresses have the values shown in the second part of Fig. 3.29. Calculate the normal stress σ and the angle θ.

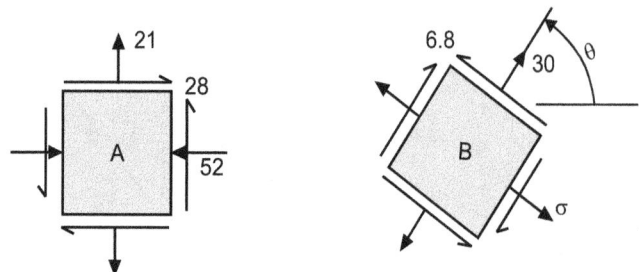

Fig. 3.29

**Solution :**

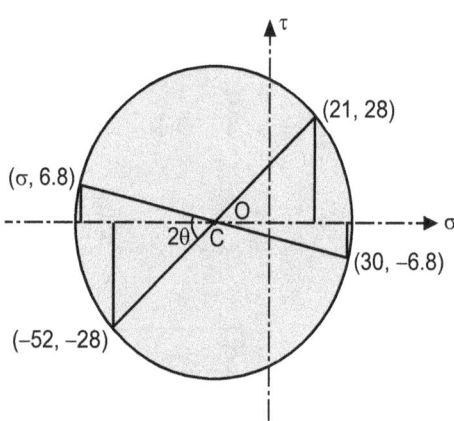

Fig. 3.30

From Mohr's circle, σ = –61 MPa, θ = 24°.

**Example 3.27 :** The state of stress at a point is the result of the three separate actions that produce the three states of stresses as shown in Fig. 3.31. Determine the principal stresses caused by the superposition of these three stress states.

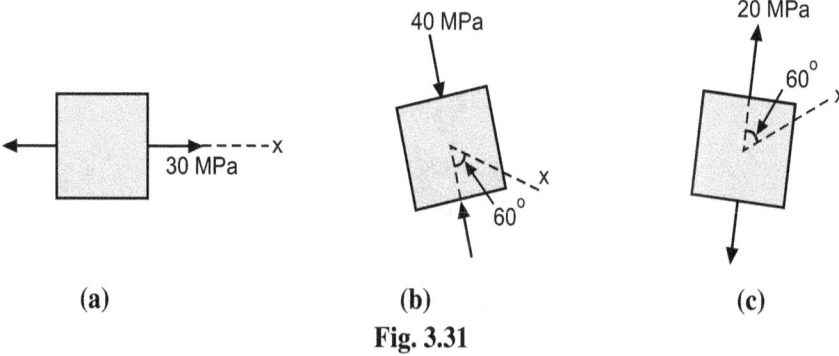

Fig. 3.31

## Solution :

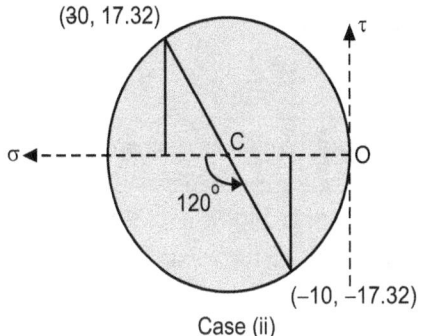
Case (ii)

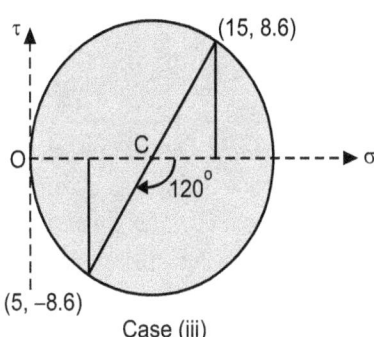
Case (iii)

**Fig. 3.32**

Case (i) :  $\sigma_x = 30$ MPa,  $\sigma_y = 0$,  $\tau_{xy} = 0$

Case (ii) :  $\sigma_x = -10$ MPa,  $\sigma_y = -30$ MPa,  $\tau_{xy} = -17.32$ MPa

Case (iii) :  $\sigma_x = 5$ MPa,  $\sigma_y = 15$ MPa,  $\tau_{xy} = -8.6$ MPa

∴ Resultant,  $\sigma_x = 25$ MPa,  $\sigma_y = -15$ MPa,  $\tau_{xy} = -25.92$ MPa

$$\sigma_1, \sigma_2 = \frac{\sigma_x + \sigma_y}{2} \pm \sqrt{\left(\frac{\sigma_x - \sigma_y}{2}\right)^2 + \tau_{xy}^2}$$

$$= (25 - 15)/2 \pm \sqrt{((25 + 15)/2)^2 + (25.92)^2}$$

$$\sigma_1 = \mathbf{37.73 \text{ MPa}} \quad \text{and} \quad \sigma_2 = \mathbf{-27.7 \text{ MPa}}$$

**Example 3.28 :** At a point in a strained material the normal and tangential stresses on a plane inclined at 40° to the vertical plane are 68 N/mm² and 158 N/mm² respectively. Find the magnitude and nature of principal stresses. Also find the resultant stresses on the given inclined plane.

**Data** : $\sigma_\theta = 68$ N/mm², $\tau_\theta = 158$ N/mm², $\theta = 40°$

**Required** : Principal stresses and resultant stresses.

**Concept** : Standard formula.

**Solution** :

$$\sigma_\theta = \frac{\sigma_x + \sigma_y}{2} + \frac{\sigma_x - \sigma_y}{2} \cos 2\theta$$

$$68 = \frac{\sigma_x + \sigma_y}{2} + \frac{\sigma_x - \sigma_y}{2} \cos 80$$

$$\tau_\theta = \frac{\sigma_x - \sigma_y}{2} \sin 2\theta$$

$$158 = \frac{\sigma_x - \sigma_y}{2} \sin 80$$

$\sigma_x - \sigma_y = 320.87$

$\sigma_x + \sigma_y = 80.28$

$\sigma_x = \mathbf{200.58 \text{ N/mm}^2 \text{ (T)}}$

$\sigma_y = -120.29$ N/mm²

$$\sigma_y = 120.29 \text{ N/mm}^2 \text{ (C)}$$

$$\sigma_R = \sqrt{\sigma_\theta^2 + \tau_\theta^2} = \sqrt{68^2 + 158^2}$$

$$\sigma_R = 172 \text{ N/mm}^2$$

**Example 3.29 :** Direct stresses of 160 N/mm² tensile and 120 N/mm² compressive, exist on two perpendicular planes at a certain point in a body. They are also accompanied by shear stresses on the planes. The greatest principal stress at the point is 200 N/mm². What must be the magnitude of shearing stresses on the two planes and what will be the maximum shearing stress at the point ?

**Data**      : $\sigma_x = 160 \text{ N/mm}^2 \text{ (T)}$, $\sigma_y = 120 \text{ N/mm}^2 \text{ (C)}$, $\sigma_1 = 200 \text{ N/mm}^2$
**Required** : Shearing stress on planes and maximum shear stress.
**Concept**  : Standard formula

**Solution** :

$$\sigma_1; \sigma_2 = \frac{\sigma_x + \sigma_y}{2} \pm \left[\sqrt{\left(\frac{\sigma_x - \sigma_y}{2}\right)^2 + \tau_{xy}^2}\right]$$

$$\sigma_1; \sigma_2 = \frac{160 - 120}{2} \pm \left[\sqrt{\left(\frac{160-(-120)}{2}\right)^2 + \tau_{xy}^2}\right]$$

$$200 = 20 \pm \left[\sqrt{(140)^2 + \tau_{xy}^2}\right]$$

$$(140)^2 + \tau_{xy}^2 = 180^2$$

$$\tau_{xy} = 113.14 \text{ N/mm}^2$$

$$\sigma_2 = -160 \text{ N/mm}^2$$

$$\tau_{max} = \frac{200 - (-160)}{2} = 180 \text{ N/mm}^2$$

**Example 3.30 :** For the stress condition on an element as shown in Fig. 3.33, determine the principal planes and stresses. Also determine the maximum shear stress and the planes on which they act.

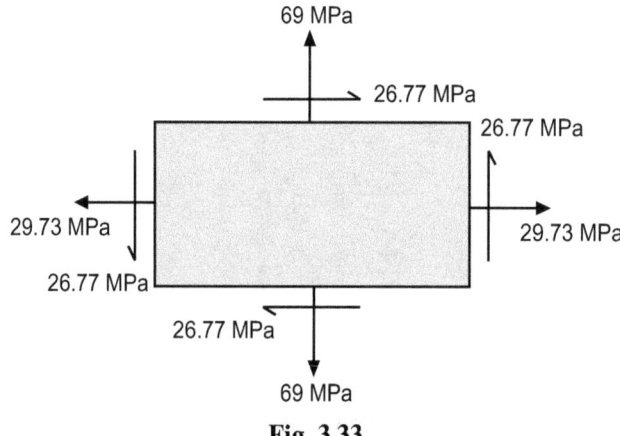

**Fig. 3.33**

**Data** : As shown in Fig. 3.33.

**Required** : Principal stresses and their planes and maximum shear stress.

**Concept** : Standard formula.

**Solution** :
$$\sigma_1; \sigma_2 = \frac{\sigma_x + \sigma_y}{2} \pm \left[\sqrt{\left(\frac{\sigma_x - \sigma_y}{2}\right)^2 + \tau_{xy}^2}\right]$$

$$\sigma_1; \sigma_2 = \frac{29.73 - (-69)}{2} \pm \left[\sqrt{\left(\frac{29.73 - 69}{2}\right)^2 + (26.67)^2}\right]$$

$$\sigma_1; \sigma_2 = 49.37 \pm \left[\sqrt{(-19.64)^2 + (26.67)^2}\right]$$

$$\sigma_1; \sigma_2 = 49.37 \pm 33.12$$

$$\sigma_1 = \mathbf{41.25 \ N/mm^2}$$

$$\sigma_2 = \mathbf{8.13 \ N/mm^2}$$

$$\tan 2\theta = \frac{-2\tau_{xy}}{(\sigma_x - \sigma_y)} = -\frac{2(26.77)}{(29.73) - (69)}$$

$$\theta_1 = 14.24, \quad \theta_2 = 104.24$$

$$\tau_{max} = \frac{41.25 + 8.13}{2} = \mathbf{49.38 \ N/mm^2}$$

$$\tan 2\theta_s = \frac{(\sigma_x - \sigma_y)}{2\tau_{xy}} = \frac{(29.73 - 69)}{2(26.77)}$$

$$\theta_{s_1} = -36.25, \quad \theta_{s_2} = 53.75$$

**Example 3.31** : The principal tensile stresses at a point are 100 N/mm² and 60 N/mm². Find normal, tangential and resultant stress on a plane at 30° with vertical plane. What is the angle of obliquity ?

**Data** : $\sigma_x = 100 \ N/mm^2$, $\sigma_y = 60 \ N/mm^2$, $\theta = 30°$

**Required** : Normal stress, tangential stress, resultant stress and angle of obliquity.

**Concept** : Standard formula.

**Solution** :

Normal stress, $\sigma_n = \sigma_1 \cos^2 \theta + \sigma_2 \sin^2 \theta + \tau_{xy} \sin 2\theta$
$= 100 \cos^2 30 + 60 \sin^2 30 + 0$
$= 75 + 15 = \mathbf{90 \ MPa}$

Tangential stress, $\sigma_t = \left[\frac{\sigma_1 - \sigma_2}{2}\right] \sin 2\theta - \tau_{xy} \cos 2\theta$

$= \left(\frac{100 - 60}{2}\right) \sin(2 \times 30) - 0$

$$= \frac{40}{2} \sin 60$$

$$= 13.32 \text{ MPa}$$

Resultant stress, $\sigma_R = \sqrt{\sigma_n^2 + \sigma_t^2}$

$$= \sqrt{90^2 + 17.32^2}$$

$$\sigma_R = 91.65 \text{ MPa}$$

Angle of obliquity, $\tan \theta = \dfrac{\sigma_t}{\sigma_n}$

$$\theta = \tan^{-1}\left[\dfrac{\sigma_t}{\sigma_n}\right]$$

$$\theta = 10.76°$$

## EXERCISE

1. A circular bar is subjected to an axial pull of 80 kN. If the maximum intensity of shear stress on any oblique plane is not to exceed 50 MPa, determine the diameter of the bar.
   (31.91 mm)

2. A short metallic column of 500 mm² cross-sectional area carries an axial compressive load of 80 kN. For a plane inclined at 60° with the direction of load, calculate (i) normal stress, (ii) shear stress, (iii) resultant stress, (iv) maximum shear stress, and (v) obliquity of the resultant stress.
   ($\sigma_n$ = 120.08 MPa ; $\tau$ = 69.28 MPa, $\sigma$ = 138.63 MPa, $\tau_{max}$ = 80 MPa, $\phi$ = 30°)

3. The principal tensile stresses at a point across two perpendicular planes are 100 MPa and 50 MPa. Find the normal and shear stresses and the resultant stress and its obliquity on a plane at 20° with the major principal plane. Find also the intensity of stress which acting alone can produce the same strain assuming $\mu$ = 0.25.
   ($\sigma_n$ = 94.15 MPa, $\tau$ = 16.08 MPa ; Resultant $\sigma$ = 95.51 MPa, $\phi$ = 9.68° ; $\sigma$ = 87.5 MPa)

4. The principal stresses at a point are 150 MPa (tensile) and 75 MPa (compressive). Determine the resultant stress in magnitude and direction on a plane inclined at 60° to the axis of major principal stress. Also determine the maximum intensity of shear stress.
   ($\sigma_n$ = 93.75 MPa, $\tau$ = 97.425 MPa, Resultant $\sigma$ = 135.2 MPa ;
   $\phi$ = 46.1°; $\tau_{max}$ = 112.5 MPa)

5. A prismatic bar carrying an axial tensile stress $\sigma_x$ is cut by an oblique section. If the normal and shear stresses on this section are 73.8 MPa and 24.6 MPa respectively, find values of $\sigma_x$ and angle $\theta$ defining the aspect of the section.
   ($\sigma_x$ = 83.0 MPa; $\theta$ = 18.43°)

6. The principal stresses acting on an element subjected to plane stresses are 12 MPa and 4.5 MPa (both tensile) respectively. Find out the position of the plane AA when the resultant stress makes the maximum angle with the normal to the plane.   ($\phi$ = 27°)

7. A piece of material is subjected to two compressive stresses at right angles, their values being 60 MPa and 90 MPa. Find the position of plane across which the resultant stress is most inclined to the normal and determine the value of this resultant stress.

($\theta = 39.14°$; Resultant $\sigma = 73.5$ MPa)

8. At a point in a strained material, state of stress is as shown in Fig. 3.34. Find (i) The direction of principal planes, (ii) The magnitude of principal stresses, (iii) The magnitude of greatest shear stress. ($\sigma_1 = 116.1$ MPa ; $\sigma_2 = 6.3$ MPa ; $\theta_1 = 31.6°$ ; $\theta_2 = 121.6°$ ; $\tau_{max} = 54.9$ MPa ; $\theta_3 = 76.6°$ , $\theta_4 = 166.6°$)

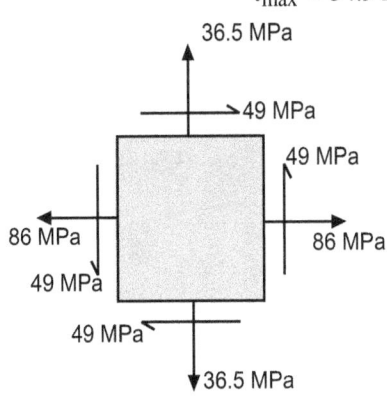

Fig. 3.34

9. State of stress at a point in a strained material is as shown in Fig. 3.35.

Determine : (i) The resultant stress on plane AB.

(ii) The principal stresses and their directions.

(iii) The maximum shear stresses and their planes.

(Normal stress on AB = 86.6 MPa; shear stress on AB = 50 MPa, $\sigma_1 = 131.13$ MPa; $\sigma_2 = 30.46$ MPa, $\theta_1 = 41.69°$, $\theta_2 = 131.69°$, $\tau_{max} = 50.33$ MPa, $\theta_3 = 86.69°$, $\theta_4 = 176.69°$)

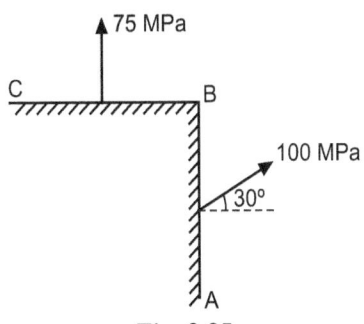

Fig. 3.35

10. Direct stresses of 102 MPa (tensile) and 76.5 MPa (compressive) exist on two perpendicular planes at a point in a strained material. These planes are also carrying shear stresses. The major principal stress is 127.5 MPa.

(i) Find the shear stresses on these planes.

(ii) Find also the maximum shear stress. ($\tau = 72.12$ MPa, $\tau_{max} = 114.75$ MPa)

11. Draw Mohr's circles for the elements subjected to state of stress as shown in Fig. 3.36.

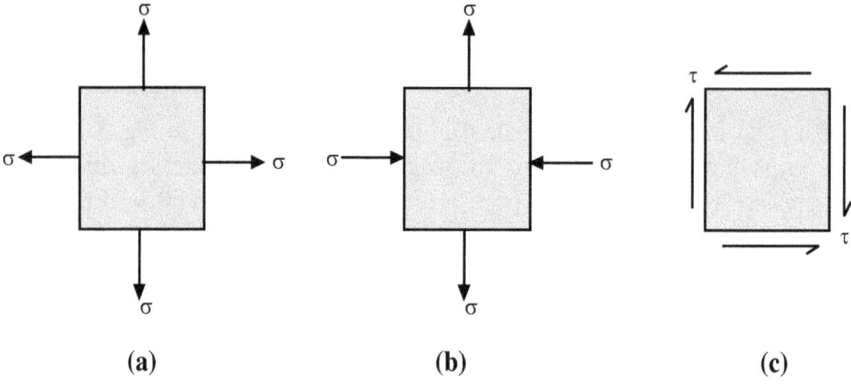

Fig. 3.36

(a) No Mohr's circle

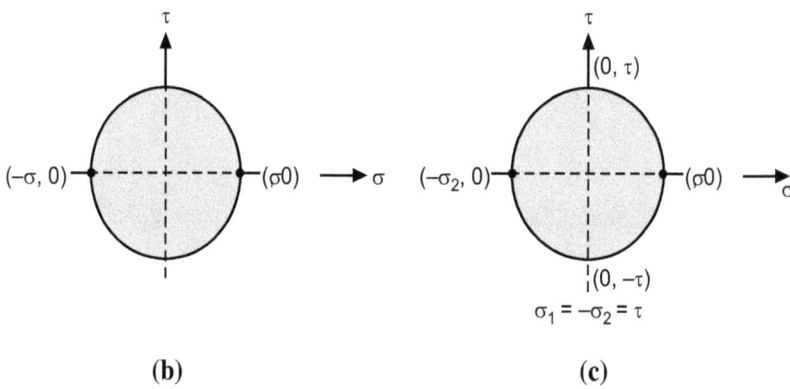

Fig. 3.37

12. At a point in a strained material, one of the principal stress is 60 MPa tensile. On a plane at 60° to this principal plane, the normal stress is zero. Determine (i) the other principal stress, (ii) the shear stress on the above plane of zero normal stress, (iii) the planes on which the normal and shear stresses are equal in magnitude.

($\sigma_2 = -20$ MPa = 20 MPa (compressive), $\tau_{60}° = 34.64$ MPa, $\theta = 32.85°$)

13. An element in a two-dimensional stress system is subjected to $\sigma_x = 150$ MPa tensile, $\sigma_y = 100$ MPa compressive and $\tau_{xy} = \tau_{yx} = 50$ MPa. Determine the planes of zero shear and maximum shear. Also find the normal and shear stress intensities on these planes. ($\theta_1 = 10.9°$, $\theta_2 = 100.9°$, $\theta_3 = 55.9°$, $\theta_4 = 145.9°$, $\sigma_1 = 159.63$ MPa (tensile), $\sigma_2 = 109.63$ MPa (compressive), $\tau_{max} = 134.63$ MPa)

14. Fig. 3.38 shows the normal and tangential stresses on two planes. Determine the principal stresses. $(\sigma_1 = 53.73 \text{ MPa}, \sigma_2 = 22.4 \text{ MPa})$

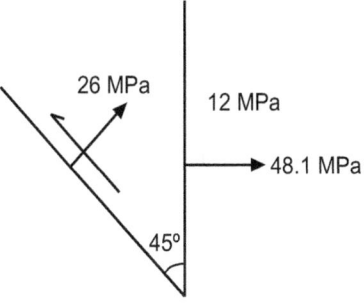

Fig. 3.38

15. At a point in a strained material, the principal stresses are 135 MPa and 54 MPa, both tensile. Locate graphically the planes for which the resultant stress is inclined at 15° to the normal. Find this resultant stress. Find also the planes for which the resultant stress is most inclined with the normal.

   $(\theta_1 = 26°, \theta_2 = 79°, \theta_3 = 101°, \theta_4 = 154°$, Resultant stresses = 92 MPa, 43.5 MPa, Angular position of planes of maximum obliquity = 125°)

16. A thin plate is under a state of stress as shown in Fig. 3.39. Find the principal stresses and their directions by using the Mohr's circle method.

   $(\sigma_1 = 121.42 \text{ MPa (tensile)}, \sigma_2 = 21.43 \text{ MPa (compressive)})$

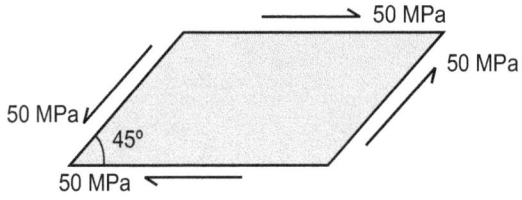

Fig. 3.39

17. A triangular prism of material is subjected to two-dimensional state of stress as shown in Fig. 3.40. Determine (i) the angle '$\theta$' between the planes AC and BC, (ii) the tangential, normal and resultant stress on BC, and (iii) other principal stress. [(i) $\theta = 33.34°$; (ii) On plane BC; $\sigma_n = 69.7$ MPa (tensile), $\tau = 19.13$ MPa (clockwise), Resultant stress = 72.29 MPa, (iii) $\sigma_2 = 39.71$ MPa (tensile)].

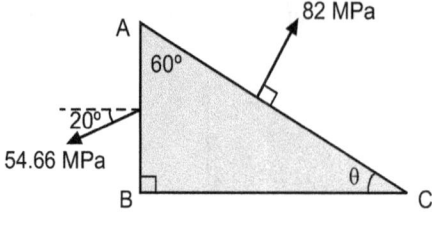

Fig. 3.40

# CHAPTER FOUR

# STRAIN ENERGY

## 4.1 INTRODUCTION

When a load is applied on any elastic member, there is deformation. The kind of deformation, that the member undergoes, depends on the type of load applied. For example, axial load causes elongation or contraction of the member depending on whether the axial load is tensile or compressive in nature. Similarly, torsional moment causes angular deformation called as twist. Bending moment also causes angular deformation. Thus, the applied load does some work on a member. When the external loads are removed, member has a capacity to regain its original shape, provided the loads were applied within elastic limit. Thus, the work done on a member is stored in the body as energy and that is why body has capacity to regain its original size and shape. This stored energy, which is by virtue of strain, is called as *strain energy*. Our main interest in this chapter is to study strain energy due to axial force.

## 4.2 STRAIN ENERGY DUE TO AXIAL FORCE

When a member is subjected to axial load, it undergoes axial deformation i.e. change in length. Also, resistance is set up in the member gradually. Within the limit of proportionality, the relation between resistance set up and deformation is always linear as shown in Fig. 4.1.

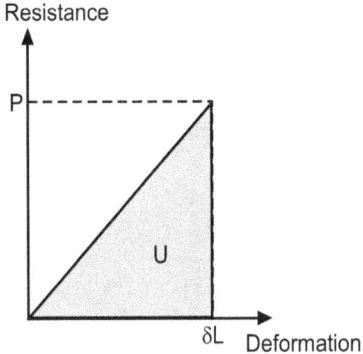

**Fig. 4.1 : Relation between resistance and deformation within elastic limit**

Symbols :  
R = Resistance  
σ = Normal stress  
A = Cross-sectional area  
δL = Axial deformation  
L = Length of member  
E = Young's modulus of elasticity  
P = Applied load  
U = Strain energy  

(4.1)

From Fig. 4.1, area under resistance deformation diagram indicates strain energy U.

$$\therefore \quad U = \frac{1}{2} R \cdot \delta L$$

$$= \frac{1}{2} (\sigma A) \delta L \qquad (\because R = \sigma A)$$

$$= \frac{1}{2} (\sigma A) \left(\frac{\sigma L}{E}\right) \qquad \left(\because \delta L = \frac{\sigma L}{E}\right)$$

$$= \frac{\sigma^2}{2E} \cdot (AL)$$

$$= \frac{\sigma^2}{2E} \cdot \text{Volume} \qquad (\because \text{Volume} = AL)$$

OR
$$U = \frac{1}{2} \sigma A \cdot \delta L \times \frac{L}{L} \qquad \text{(multiply and divide by L)}$$

$$= \frac{1}{2} \cdot \sigma \cdot \varepsilon \cdot AL \qquad \left(\because \text{linear strain} = \varepsilon = \frac{\delta L}{L}\right)$$

$$= \frac{1}{2} \sigma \cdot \varepsilon \cdot \text{Volume}$$

Thus, various forms of expression of strain energy are,

$$U = \frac{1}{2} \sigma A \cdot \delta L \qquad \text{... (4.1 a)}$$

OR $$U = \frac{\sigma^2}{2E} \cdot \text{Volume} \qquad \text{... (4.1 b)}$$

OR $$U = \frac{1}{2} \sigma \cdot \varepsilon \cdot \text{Volume} \qquad \text{... (4.1 c)}$$

Unit of strain energy is Nm.

## 4.3 PROOF RESILIENCE

It is defined as the *maximum strain energy which can be stored by a body without undergoing permanent deformation*. Obviously, it is the strain energy at elastic limit.

Let $\quad F_y = $ Stress at elastic limit

$$\therefore \quad \textbf{Proof resilience} = \frac{F_y^2}{2E} \cdot \text{Volume} \qquad \text{... (4.2)}$$

Unit of proof resilience is same as that of strain energy i.e. Nm.

## 4.4 MODULUS OF RESILIENCE

It is defined as *proof resilience per unit volume*.

$$\therefore \quad \textbf{Modulus of resilience} = \frac{F_y^2}{2E} \qquad \text{... (4.3)}$$

Unit of Modulus of resilience is MPa.

## 4.5 STRESS DUE TO VARIOUS TYPES OF AXIAL LOADS

### 4.5.1 Gradually Applied Load

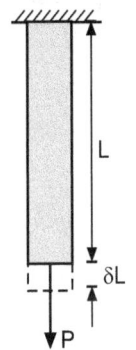

(a) Gradually applied axial load

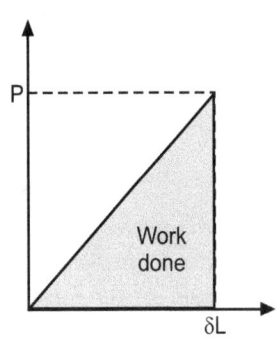

(b) Relation between gradual load and deformation within elastic limit

**Fig. 4.2**

Let the load P be gradually applied to a member of uniform cross-sectional area A and length L which means magnitude of P increases from zero to final value P. Initially, when load P is zero, the corresponding deformation is also zero. When the magnitude of load is equal to P, the corresponding deformation is $\delta L$. Fig. 4.2 (b) shows this relation of gradually applied load and corresponding deformation.

Equating work done to strain energy,

$$\frac{1}{2} P \cdot \delta L = \frac{1}{2} \sigma A \cdot \delta L$$

$$\therefore \quad \sigma = \frac{P}{A} \quad \ldots (4.4)$$

### 4.5.2 Suddenly Applied Load

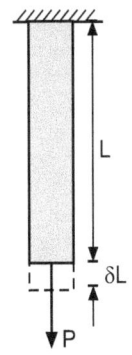

(a) Suddenly applied axial load

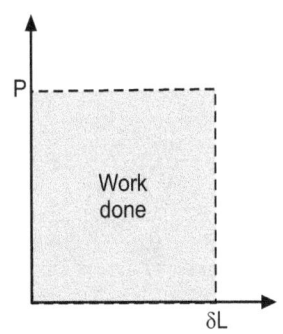

(b) Relation between suddenly applied load and deformation within elastic limit

**Fig. 4.3**

Let, the load P be suddenly applied to a member of uniform cross-sectional area A and length L. In this case, magnitude of load P is constant throughout the process of extension. Fig. 4.3 (b) shows this relation of gradually applied load and corresponding deformation.

Equating work done to strain energy,

$$\therefore \quad P \cdot \delta L = \frac{1}{2} \sigma \cdot A \cdot \delta L$$

$$\therefore \quad \sigma = \frac{2P}{A} \quad \ldots (4.5)$$

It is important here to note that stress produced by suddenly applied load is twice that of gradually applied load. After the instantaneous extension due to suddenly applied load, the state of equilibrium is not reached. As the force of resistance is double the applied load, it sets the motion of vibration into a member like suddenly loaded spring. The equation (4.5) gives maximum instantaneous stress developed in a member due to suddenly applied load.

### 4.5.3 Impact Load

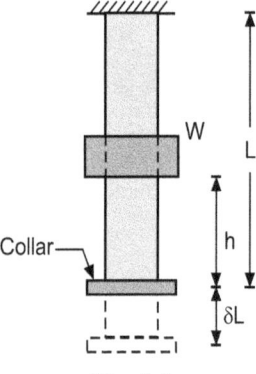

Fig. 4.4

Let the load W fall freely through a distance h before it strikes the rigid collar attached at the bottom of the bar as shown in Fig. 4.4. This is the case of impact loading.

Work done $= W(h + \delta L)$

Strain energy $= \frac{1}{2} \sigma A \cdot \delta L$

Equation of instantaneous stress produced by impact load can be derived by equating work done to strain energy and substituting $\delta L = \frac{\sigma L}{E}$.

$$W\left(h + \frac{\sigma L}{E}\right) = \frac{1}{2} \sigma A \cdot \frac{\sigma L}{E}$$

$$\therefore \quad \frac{\sigma^2}{2E} \cdot AL - \left(\frac{WL}{E}\right) \sigma = Wh$$

$$\sigma^2 - \left(\frac{2W}{A}\right) \sigma = \frac{2WhE}{AL}$$

$$\therefore \quad \left(\sigma - \frac{W}{A}\right)^2 = \frac{2WhE}{AL} + \frac{W^2}{A^2}$$

$$\therefore \quad \sigma - \frac{W}{A} = \pm \sqrt{\frac{2WhE}{AL} + \frac{W^2}{A^2}}$$

$$\therefore \quad \sigma = \frac{W}{A} \pm \sqrt{\frac{2WhE}{AL} + \frac{W^2}{A^2}} \quad \ldots (4.6)$$

Other form of equation (4.6) can be derived as,

$$\sigma = \frac{W}{A} \pm \sqrt{\frac{2\,WhE}{AL} \cdot \frac{WA}{WA} + \frac{W^2}{A^2}}$$

$$= \frac{W}{A} \pm \sqrt{\frac{2h}{WL/AE} \cdot \frac{W^2}{A^2} + \frac{W^2}{A^2}}$$

$$= \frac{W}{A}\left[1 \pm \sqrt{\frac{2h}{\delta_{st}} + 1}\right] \qquad \ldots (4.7)$$

where, $\delta_{st}$ = Axial deformation produced by gradually applied load called as axial deformation produced by static load = $\frac{WL}{AE}$

It should be noted that, in equation (4.7) if $h = 0$,

$$\sigma = \frac{2W}{A} = \text{Instantaneous stress produced by suddenly applied load.}$$

## SOLVED EXAMPLES

**Example 4.1 :** A vertical steel bar 1.5 m long is fixed at top. A weight can slide freely along the rod and its fall is arrested at the bottom by collar. When weight falls through 40 mm, the maximum instantaneous stress developed in the bar is 200 MPa. Determine the stress in the same bar when same weight is (i) gradually applied; (ii) suddenly applied; (iii) with free fall of 50 mm.

**Data** : $L = 1.5$ m $= 1500$ mm ; $h = 40$ mm which produces $\sigma_{max} = 200$ MPa ; $E = 200$ GPa.

**Required** : Maximum stress for gradually applied; suddenly applied load and maximum stress with the same weight falling through height of 50 mm.

**Concept** : Knowing instantaneous stress $\sigma_{max} = 200$ MPa for $h = 40$ mm, find $\frac{W}{A}$ and then evaluate stresses for different types of loads applied.

**Solution** : (i) For $h = 40$ mm ; $\sigma_{max} = 200$ MPa

$$\sigma_{max} = \frac{W}{A} \pm \sqrt{\frac{2\,WhE}{AL} + \frac{W^2}{A^2}}$$

$$200 = \frac{W}{A} \pm \sqrt{\frac{2 \times W \times 40 \times 200 \times 10^3}{A \times 1500} + \frac{W^2}{A^2}}$$

Let, $\frac{W}{A} = x$

∴ $200 = x \pm \sqrt{10.67 \times 10^3 (x) + x^2}$

$(200 - x)^2 = 10.67 \times 10^3 (x) + x^2$

$40 \times 10^3 - 400\,x + x^2 = 10.67 \times 10^3 (x) + x^2$

$40 \times 10^3 - 400\,x = 10.67 \times 10^3 (x)$

∴ $x = 3.62$ MPa

$\frac{W}{A} = 3.62$ MPa

(ii) $\sigma_{max}$ when load is gradually applied :

$$\sigma_{max} = \frac{W}{A} = 3.62 \text{ MPa}$$

(iii) $\sigma_{max}$ when load is suddenly applied :

$$\sigma_{max} = \frac{2W}{A} = 2 \times 3.62$$
$$= 7.24 \text{ MPa}$$

(iv) $\sigma_{max}$ when load falls through height of 50 mm :

$$\sigma_{max} = \frac{W}{A} \pm \sqrt{\frac{2 \text{ WhE}}{AL} + \frac{W^2}{A^2}}$$

$$= 3.62 \pm \sqrt{\frac{2 \times 3.62 \times 50 \times 200 \times 10^3}{(1500)} + (3.62)^2}$$

$$= 223.35 \text{ MPa}$$

**Example 4.2 :** Water under pressure of 10 MPa is suddenly admitted on to a plunger of 100 mm diameter, attached to a rod 28 mm diameter, 3 m long. Find the maximum instantaneous stress and deformation of the rod if E = 210 GPa.

**Data** : Water pressure p = 10 MPa ; Diameter of plunger = 100 mm; Diameter of rod = 28 mm ; Length of rod = L = 3000 mm ; E = 210 GPa.

**Required** : Maximum instantaneous stress and elongation for rod.

**Concept** : Knowing pressure intensity and area of plunger, find force on the rod.

Stress due to suddenly applied load $= \sigma = \frac{2P}{A}$.

**Solution** : (i) Geometric properties :

Cross-sectional area of plunger $= \frac{\pi}{4} (100)^2 = 7853.98 \text{ mm}^2$

Cross-sectional area of rod $= \frac{\pi}{4} (28)^2 = 615.75 \text{ mm}^2$

(ii) Force on rod 'P'     P = Water pressure × C/s area of plunger
$$= 10 \times 7853.98$$
$$= 78539.8 \text{ N}$$

(iii) Maximum instantaneous stress for rod,

$$\sigma_{max} = \frac{2P}{A} \qquad \text{... (\textbf{Note} : Sudden application of force)}$$

$$= \frac{2 \times 78539.8}{615.75}$$

$$= 255.1 \text{ MPa}$$

(iv) Maximum instantaneous elongation,

$$\delta L = \frac{\sigma \cdot L}{E} = \frac{255.1 \times 3000}{210 \times 10^3}$$

$$= 3.64 \text{ mm}$$

**Example 4.3 :** A bar 50 mm in diameter, 2 m long has to transmit shock energy of 100 joules. Calculate maximum instantaneous stress developed and maximum elongation if E = 200 GPa.

**Data** : $d = 50$ mm ; $L = 2000$ mm ; $U = 100$ joules

∴ $U = 100$ Nm $= 100 \times 10^3$ Nmm; $E = 200$ GPa

**Required** : $\sigma_{max}$ and $\delta L_{max}$.

**Concept** : Equate shock energy to strain energy and find maximum instantaneous stress and hence elongation.

**Solution** : (i) Maximum instantaneous stress :

$$\text{Strain energy} = \frac{\sigma_{max}^2}{2E} \times \text{Volume}$$

$$100 \times 10^3 = \frac{\sigma_{max}^2}{2 \times 200 \times 10^3} \times \frac{\pi}{4} (50)^2 \times 2000$$

∴ $\sigma_{max} = 100.9$ MPa

(ii) Maximum elongation :

$$\delta L_{max} = \frac{\sigma_{max} \cdot L}{E}$$

$$= \frac{100.9 \times 2000}{200 \times 10^3}$$

$$= 1 \text{ mm}$$

**Example 4.4 :** A vertically suspended steel bar, circular in cross-section, is subjected to load of 5 kN which falls by 20 mm on rigid collar provided at lower end of bar. If maximum allowable strain for bar is $\frac{1}{1250}$, find suitable diameter of rod.

Assume E = 200 GPa and length of bar = 2 m.

**Data** : $W = 5$ kN ; $h = 20$ mm ; Strain $= \frac{1}{1250}$ ;

$E = 200$ GPa; $L = 2000$ mm as shown in Fig. 4.5

**Required** : Diameter of bar.

**Concept** : Knowing strain, elongation and stress for the bar can be obtained, then use basic work equation.

**Solution** : (i) Work equation :

$$W(h + \delta L) = \frac{\sigma^2}{2E} \times \text{Volume}$$

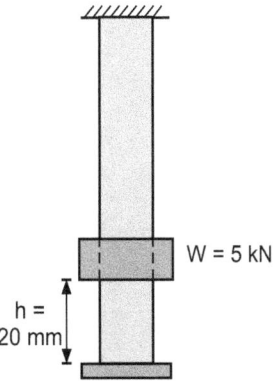

Fig. 4.5

where
$$\delta L = \text{Strain} \times L$$
$$= \frac{1}{1250} \times 2000$$
$$= 1.6 \text{ mm}$$
$$\sigma = \text{Strain} \times E$$
$$= \frac{1}{1250} \times 200 \times 10^3 = 160 \text{ MPa}$$

Substituting,
$$5 \times 10^3 \times (20 + 1.6) = \frac{(160)^2}{2 \times 200 \times 10^3} \times \frac{\pi}{4} (\phi)^2 \times 2000$$
$$\phi = 32.78 \text{ mm}$$

**Example 4.5 :** A bar of 25 mm diameter stretches 2 mm under gradually applied load of 65 kN. If a weight of 2 kN is dropped on to a collar at the lower end of this bar, through a height of 40 mm, calculate maximum instantaneous stress and elongation of bar. Assume E = 200 GPa.

**Data** : $\phi = 25$ mm ; $\delta L = 2$ mm for gradually applied load of 65 kN; W = 2 kN ; h = 40 mm ; E = 200 GPa as shown in Fig. 4.6.

**Required** : Maximum instantaneous stress and elongation.

**Concept** : Length of bar can be obtained by knowing elongation due to gradually applied load ; then use standard formulae for impact loading.

**Solution** : (i) Geometric properties :
$$A = \frac{\pi}{4} (25)^2 = 490.87 \text{ mm}^2$$

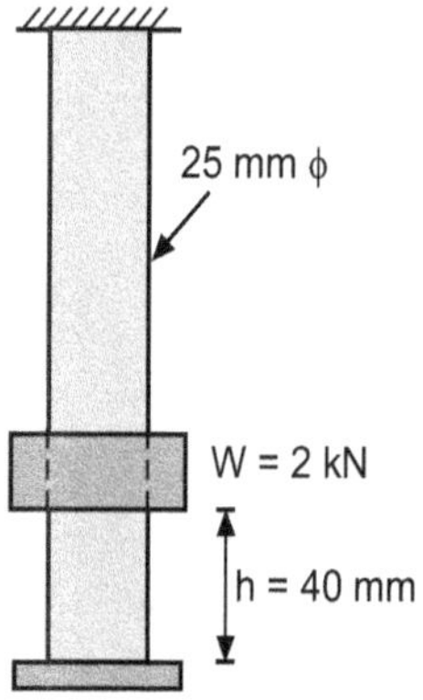

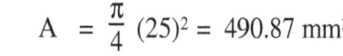

Fig. 4.6

(ii) Gradually applied load :
$$\delta L = \frac{PL}{AE}$$
$$2 = \frac{65 \times 10^3 \times L}{490.87 \times 200 \times 10^3}$$
$$\therefore L = 3020.76 \text{ mm}$$

(iii) Stress for impact loading,
$$\sigma = \frac{W}{A} \pm \sqrt{\frac{2 \text{ WhE}}{AL} + \frac{W^2}{A^2}}$$
$$= \frac{2 \times 10^3}{490.87} \pm \sqrt{\frac{2 \times 2 \times 10^3 \times 40 \times 200 \times 10^3}{490.87 \times 3020.76} + \left(\frac{2000}{490.87}\right)^2}$$
$$= 151.03 \text{ MPa}$$

(iv) Elongation for impact loading,

$$\delta L = \frac{\sigma L}{E} = \frac{151.03 \times 3020.76}{200 \times 10^3}$$

$$\delta L = 2.281 \text{ mm}$$

**Example 4.6 :** A vertical steel bar 16 mm diameter; 1.5 m long is provided with a collar at lower end. Find the maximum weight that can be dropped through a height of 100 mm over the collar if maximum permissible tensile stress is 150 MPa. Assume E = 200 GPa.

**Data** : $\phi = 16$ mm ; L = 1500 mm ; h = 100 mm ;

$\sigma_{max} = 150$ MPa ; E = 200 GPa

as shown in Fig. 4.7.

**Required :** Weight W.

**Concept :** Standard formulae.

**Solution :** (i) Geometric properties :

$$A = \frac{\pi}{4}(16)^2 = 201.06 \text{ mm}^2$$

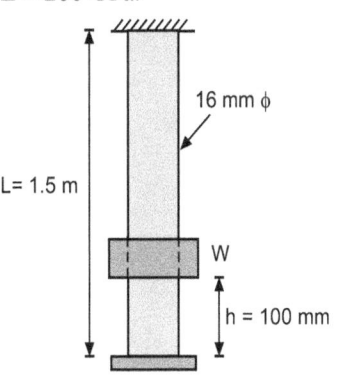

Fig. 4.7

(ii) Maximum weight : $\sigma_{max} = \frac{W}{A} \pm \sqrt{\frac{2 WhE}{AL} + \frac{W^2}{A^2}}$

Let $\frac{W}{A} = x$

$$150 = x \pm \sqrt{\frac{2x \times 100 \times 200 \times 10^3}{1500} + x^2}$$

$$150 = x \pm \sqrt{26.67 \times 10^3 x + x^2}$$

$(150 - x)^2 = 26.67 \times 10^3 x + x^2$

$22500 - 300 x + x^2 = 26.67 \times 10^3 x + x^2$

$$x = 0.834 = \frac{W}{A}$$

∴ W = 0.834 × 201.06

**W = 167.75 N**

**Example 4.7 :** A solid vertical prismatic steel bar of equilateral triangular section of side 25 mm is firmly fixed at top. A rigid collar is attached at the lower end at a distance of 600 mm from top. Compute the strain energy in each of the following cases :

(i) When a pull of 10 kN is applied gradually.

(ii) When a force of 8 kN is suddenly applied.

(iii) When a weight of 4 kN falls through 120 mm. Assume E = 210 GPa.

**Data** : Cross-section of bar; equilateral triangular section with 25 mm side; L = 600 mm; E = 210 GPa.

**Required** : Strain energy for different given cases.

**Concept** : Standard formulae.

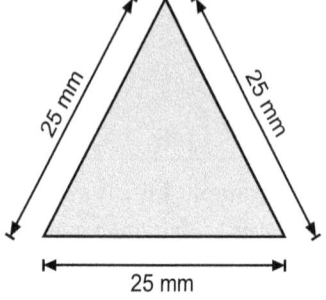

**Fig. 4.8 : c/s of bar**

**Solution** : (i) Geometric properties :

$$A = \frac{1}{2} \times \text{Base} \times \text{Height} = \frac{1}{2} \times 25 \times \left(\frac{25}{2} \times \tan 60\right)$$

$$= 270.63 \text{ mm}^2$$

(ii) Strain energy, when pull of 10 kN is applied gradually :

$$\sigma_{max} = \frac{P}{A} = \frac{10 \times 10^3}{270.63}$$

$$= 36.95 \text{ MPa}$$

$$U = \frac{\sigma_{max}^2}{2E} \times \text{Volume}$$

$$= \frac{(36.95)^2}{2 \times 210 \times 10^3} \times 270.63 \times 600$$

$$= 527.85 \text{ Nmm}$$

(ii) Strain energy, when a force of 8 kN is suddenly applied :

$$\sigma_{max} = \frac{2P}{A} = \frac{2 \times 8 \times 10^3}{270.63}$$

$$= 59.12 \text{ MPa}$$

$$U = \frac{\sigma_{max}^2}{2E} \times \text{Volume}$$

$$= \frac{(59.12)^2}{2 \times 210 \times 10^3} \times 270.63 \times 600$$

$$= 1351.28 \text{ Nmm}$$

(iii) When a weight of 4 kN falls through 120 mm,

$$\sigma_{max} = \frac{W}{A} \pm \sqrt{\frac{2WhE}{AL} + \frac{W^2}{A^2}}$$

$$= \frac{4 \times 10^3}{270.63} \pm \sqrt{\frac{2 \times 4 \times 10^3 \times 120 \times 210 \times 10^3}{270.63 \times 600} + \left[\frac{4 \times 10^3}{270.63}\right]^2}$$

$$= 14.78 \pm 1114.3$$

$$= 1129.125 \text{ MPa}$$

$$\text{Strain energy, } U = \frac{\sigma_{max}^2}{2E} \times \text{Volume}$$

$$= \frac{(1129.125)^2}{2 \times 210 \times 10^3} \times 270.63 \times 600$$

$$= 492.90 \times 10^3 \text{ Nmm}$$

---

**Example 4.8 :** A steel specimen 16 mm φ stretches by 0.12 mm over 150 mm length under an axial load of 35 kN. Calculate the strain energy stored in the specimen at this stage. If the load at the elastic limit for the specimen is 50 kN, calculate the elongation at elastic limit and the proof resilience.

**Data** : φ = 16 mm ; for W = 35 kN; δL = 0.12 mm ;

L = 150 mm ; for elastic limit W = 50 kN.

**Required** : Strain energy of bar for W = 35 kN; elongation at elastic limit; proof resilience.

**Concept** : Standard formula.

**Solution** : (i) Geometric properties :

$$A = \frac{\pi}{4}(16)^2 = 201.06 \text{ mm}^2$$

(ii) Strain energy of bar for W = 35 kN

$$U = \frac{1}{2} W \cdot \delta L$$

$$= \frac{1}{2} \times 35 \times 10^3 \times 0.12$$

$$= 2100 \text{ Nmm}$$
$$= 2.1 \text{ Nm}$$
$$= 2.1 \text{ J}$$

(iii) Elongation at elastic limit :

Elongation due to 35 kN load = 0.12 mm

∴ Elongation due to 50 kN load $= 0.12 \times \frac{50}{35}$

$$= 0.171 \text{ mm}$$

(iv) Proof resilience = Maximum strain energy stored in the member at elastic limit

$$= \frac{1}{2} \cdot W \cdot \delta L$$

$$= \frac{1}{2} \times 50 \times 10^3 \times 0.171$$

$$= 4275 \text{ Nmm}$$
$$= \mathbf{4.275 \text{ Nm}} = \mathbf{4.275 \text{ J}}$$

**Example 4.9 :** A uniform bar of cross-sectional area 500 mm² is 2.5 m long. Find the proof resilience and modulus of resilience, if the elastic limit for the bar material is 250 MPa. Also find maximum value of suddenly applied load that the member can carry. Assume = E = 200 GPa.

**Data**     : $A = 500$ mm² ; $L = 2.5$ m $= 2500$ mm ; $F_y = 250$ MPa ; $E = 200$ GPa.

**Required** : Proof resilience, modulus of resilience and suddenly applied load.

**Concept**  : Standard formulae.

**Solution** : (i) Proof resilience :

$$U_{max} = \frac{\sigma_{max}^2}{2E} \times \text{Volume}$$

$$= \frac{(250)^2}{2 \times 200 \times 10^3} (500 \times 2500)$$

$$= 195312.5 \text{ Nmm}$$

$$= 195.312 \text{ Nm}$$

$$= 195.312 \text{ J}$$

(ii) Modulus of resilience = Maximum strain energy per unit volume

$$= \frac{\sigma_{max}^2}{2E}$$

$$= \frac{(250)^2}{2 \times 200 \times 10^3}$$

$$= 0.156 \text{ MPa}$$

(iii) Maximum suddenly applied load,

$$\sigma_{max} = \frac{2P}{A}$$

$$250 = \frac{2P}{500}$$

∴      $P = 62500$ N

$$= 62.5 \text{ kN}$$

**Example 4.10 :** A uniform rod AB is made of brass for which yield stress $F_y = 125$ MPa and $E = 105$ GPa. Collar 'D' moves along the rod and has a speed of 3 m/s as it strikes a small plate attached to end B of the rod. Using factor of safety of 4, determine the largest allowable mass of collar if the rod is not to be permanently deformed. Will the answer be different, if rod is held vertical and mass is moving downward ? Why ?

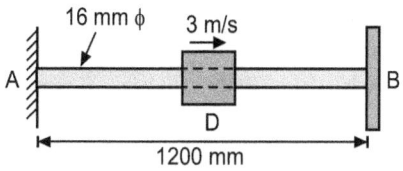

Fig. 4.9

**Data** : $F_y = 125$ MPa ; $E = 105$ GPa ; $V = 3$ m/s ; Factor of safety = 4.

**Required** : Mass of collar.

**Concept** : Kinetic energy of collar will get converted to strain energy of rod. If the rod is held vertically, the answer will be different because then the motion of collar is with uniform acceleration due to gravity.

**Solution** : (i) K.E. of collar :

Let mass of collar be 'm' kg.

$$\text{K.E.} = \frac{1}{2} mV^2$$

$$= \frac{1}{2} m \times 3^2$$

$$= 4.5 \text{ m N.m}$$

(ii) Strain energy of rod, $U = \dfrac{\sigma_{max}^2}{2E} \times \text{Volume}$

With factor of safety = 4 ;

$$\sigma_{max} = \frac{F_y}{4} = \frac{125}{4} = 31.25 \text{ MPa}$$

∴ $$U = \frac{(31.25)^2}{2 \times 105 \times 10^3} \times \frac{\pi}{4} (16)^2 \times 1200$$

$$U = 1121.986 \text{ Nmm}$$

(iii) Mass of collar :

Equating kinetic energy to strain energy, we get

$$4.5 \text{ m} = 1121.98 \times 10^{-3}$$

$$m = \mathbf{0.249 \text{ kg}}$$

**Example 4.11 :** A wagon weighing 20 kN is attached to a wire rope and is moving at the speed of 5.4 kmph. The rope suddenly jams and wagon is brought to rest. If length of rope is 50 m and diameter is 36 mm, find maximum instantaneous stress and elongation of rope assuming $E = 200$ GPa.

**Data** : $W = 20$ kN ; $V = 5.4$ kmph = 1.5 m/s; $L = 50$ m ; $\phi = 36$ mm ; $E = 200$ GPa.

**Required** : Maximum instantaneous stress and elongation of rope.

**Concept** : Kinetic energy of wagon will be converted to strain energy of rope.

**Solution** : (i) Kinetic energy of wagon :

$$\text{K.E.} = \frac{1}{2} mV^2$$

$$= \frac{1}{2}\left(\frac{20 \times 10^3}{9.81}\right) \times (1.5)^2$$

$$= 2293.58 \text{ Nm}$$

$$= 2293.58 \times 10^3 \text{ Nmm}$$

(ii) Strain energy of rope : 
$$U = \frac{\sigma_{max}^2}{2E} \times \text{Volume}$$

$$= \frac{\sigma_{max}^2}{2 \times 200 \times 10^3} \left(\frac{\pi}{4}(36)^2 \times 50 \times 10^3\right)$$

$$= 127.23 \ \sigma_{max}^2$$

(iii) Maximum instantaneous stress :

Equating kinetic energy and strain energy, we get

$$2293.58 \times 10^3 = 127.23 \ \sigma_{max}^2$$

$$\sigma_{max} = \mathbf{134.26 \ MPa}$$

(iv) Maximum instantaneous elongation,

$$\delta L_{max} = \frac{\sigma_{max} \cdot L}{E} = \frac{134.26 \times 50 \times 10^3}{200 \times 10^3}$$

$$= \mathbf{33.56 \ mm}$$

**Example 4.12** : A lift weighing 20 kN is to function at a speed of 1 m/s. Length of rope connecting lift is 40 m. If yield stress for rope material is 300 MPa, find suitable diameter of rope assuming factor of safety of 2. Assume E = 200 GPa.

**Data** : $W = 20$ kN ; $V = 1$ m/s ; $L = 40$ m ; $F_y = 300$ MPa ;

Factor of safety = 2 ; E = 200 GPa.

**Required** : Diameter of rope.

**Concept** : Same as Example 4.11. In the following analysis, static stress due to self weight of lift is neglected. However, for the exact analysis, see Example 4.13.

**Solution** : (i) Kinetic energy of lift :

$$\text{K.E.} = \frac{1}{2} mV^2$$

$$= \frac{1}{2}\left(\frac{20 \times 10^3}{9.81}\right) \times (1)^2$$

$$= 1019.36 \text{ Nm}$$

$$= 1019.36 \times 10^3 \text{ Nmm}$$

(ii) Strain energy of rope :

$$U = \frac{\sigma_{max}^2}{2E} \cdot \text{Volume}$$

$$\text{Maximum safe stress} = \sigma_{max} = \frac{\text{Yield stress}}{\text{Factor of safety}}$$

$$\therefore \quad \sigma_{max} = \frac{300}{2} = 150 \text{ MPa}$$

$$\therefore \quad U = \frac{(150)^2}{2 \times 200 \times 10^3} \left(\frac{\pi}{4}(\phi)^2 \times 40 \times 10^3\right)$$

$$= 1767.14 \, \phi^2$$

(iii) Diameter of rope :

Equating kinetic energy and strain energy, we get

$$1019.36 \times 10^3 = 1761.14 \, \phi^2$$

$$\therefore \quad \phi = 24 \text{ mm}$$

**Example 4.13 :** A crane chain lowers a load of 8 kN at uniform rate of 0.6 m/s. When length of chain unwound is 10 m, it suddenly gets jammed. Estimate the instantaneous stress induced in it due to the sudden stoppage and the maximum elongation, if each link is 'O' shaped and made of 10 mm $\phi$ steel rod. Also find impulsive force on each link. Assume E = 200 GPa.

**Data** : $W = 8$ kN ; $V = 0.6$ m/s ; $L = 10$ m ; $\phi = 10$ mm for O shaped link.

**Required** : Maximum instantaneous stress ; elongation and impulsive force.

**Concept** : Maximum instantaneous stress = Stress due to impulsive force
+ Stress due to static load.

**Solution** : (i) Geometric properties :

Cross-sectional area of each O-shaped link

$$= 2 \times \frac{\pi}{4} \times (10)^2$$

$$= 157.08 \text{ mm}^2$$

(ii) Kinetic energy : 

$$\text{K.E.} = \frac{1}{2} mV^2$$

$$\text{K.E.} = \frac{1}{2} \left(\frac{8 \times 10^3}{9.81}\right) \times (0.6)^2$$

$$= 146.79 \text{ Nm}$$

$$= 146.79 \times 10^3 \text{ Nmm}$$

(iii) Strain energy :

$$U = \frac{\sigma^2}{2E} \cdot \text{Volume}$$

$$= \frac{\sigma^2}{2 \times 200 \times 10^3} \times (157.08 \times 10 \times 10^3)$$

$$U = 3.927 \, \sigma^2$$

(iv) Instantaneous stress :

Equating kinetic energy to strain energy, we get

$$146.79 \times 10^3 = 3.927 \sigma^2$$
$$\sigma = 193.34 \text{ MPa} \qquad \text{(Stress due to impulse)}$$

In addition to above impulsive stress, static stress due to load of 8 kN

$$= \frac{8 \times 10^3}{157.08}$$
$$= 50.93 \text{ MPa}$$

Maximum instantaneous stress,

$$\sigma_{max} = \text{Stress due to impulse + Static stress}$$
$$= 193.34 + 50.93$$
$$= 244.27 \text{ MPa}$$

(v) Maximum instantaneous elongation,

$$\delta L = \sigma_{max} \cdot \frac{L}{E}$$
$$= \frac{244.27 \times 10 \times 10^3}{200 \times 10^3}$$
$$= \mathbf{12.21 \text{ mm}}$$

(vi) Impulsive force :

$$\text{Impulsive force} = F = \sigma_{max} \times A$$
$$= 244.27 \times 157.08$$
$$= 38.37 \times 10^3 \text{ N}$$
$$= \mathbf{38.37 \text{ kN}}$$

**Example 4.14 :** A load P is supported at B by two rods of same material and the same cross-sectional area A as shown in Fig. 4.10. Determine the strain energy of system. Let 'E' be the modulus of elasticity.

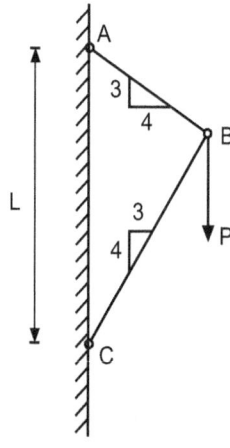

**Fig. 4.10**

**Data** : As shown in Fig. 4.10.

**Required** : Strain energy of system.

**Concept** : Analyse joint P and get the forces in members AB and BC and then find total strain energy of system.

**Solution** : (i) Force in members :

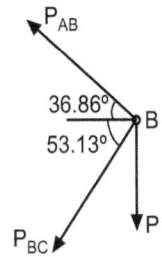

Fig. 4.11 : FBD of joint B

$$\frac{P}{\sin(90)} = \frac{P_{AB}}{\sin(36.86)} = \frac{P_{BC}}{\sin(233.14)}$$

$$P_{AB} = 0.6\,P$$
$$P_{BC} = -0.8\,P = 0.8\,P \quad \ldots \text{(Compressive)}$$

(ii) Strain energy of system :

$$U = \left(\frac{\sigma^2}{2E} \times \text{Volume}\right)_{AB} + \left(\frac{\sigma^2}{2E} \times \text{Volume}\right)_{BC}$$

where $\quad \sigma_{AB} = \dfrac{0.6\,P}{A}$ and $\sigma_{BC} = \dfrac{0.8\,P}{A}$

By geometry,

$$\frac{L}{\sin(90)} = \frac{L_{AB}}{\sin(36.86)} = \frac{L_{BC}}{\sin(53.13)}$$

∴ $\quad L_{AB} = 0.6\,L$ and $L_{BC} = 0.8\,L$

∴ Volume of AB $= A \times (0.6\,L) = 0.6\,AL$

and Volume of BC $= A \times (0.8\,L) = 0.8\,AL$

Substituting, $\quad U = \left(\dfrac{0.6\,P}{A}\right)^2 \times \dfrac{0.6\,AL}{2E} + \left(\dfrac{0.8\,P}{A}\right)^2 \times \dfrac{0.8\,AL}{2E}$

$$U = 0.364 \,\frac{P^2\,L}{AE}$$

**Example 4.15** : Show that for a member subjected to principal stresses $\sigma_1$ and $\sigma_2$, the strain energy per unit volume is given by $\dfrac{1}{2E}\left(\sigma_1^2 + \sigma_2^2 - 2\mu\,\sigma_1\sigma_2\right)$

where, $\quad E = $ Young's modulus

and $\quad \mu = $ Poisson's ratio

**Data** : Principal stresses are $\sigma_1$ and $\sigma_2$.

**Required** : Strain energy per unit volume.

**Concept** : Generalised Hook's law and $U = \dfrac{1}{2} \sigma \cdot \varepsilon$

**Solution** : (i) Principal strains :

$$\varepsilon_1 = \dfrac{1}{E}(\sigma_1 - \mu\, \sigma_2)$$

$$\varepsilon_2 = \dfrac{1}{E}(\sigma_2 - \mu\, \sigma_1)$$

(ii) Strain energy per unit volume :

$$U = \dfrac{1}{2}\sigma_1 \varepsilon_1 + \dfrac{1}{2}\sigma_2 \varepsilon_2$$

$$= \dfrac{1}{2}\sigma_1 \left[\dfrac{1}{E}(\sigma_1 - \mu\,\sigma_2)\right] + \dfrac{1}{2}\sigma_2 \left[\dfrac{1}{E}(\sigma_2 - \mu\,\sigma_1)\right]$$

$$U = \dfrac{1}{2E}\left[\sigma_1^2 + \sigma_2^2 - 2\mu\,\sigma_1 \sigma_2\right]$$

**Example 4.16 :** Determine the diameter of aluminium shaft designed to store same amount of strain energy per unit volume as that of 50 mm ϕ steel bar of same length, when both shafts are subjected to same axial load.

Take $E_S = 200$ GPa and $E_A = 67$ GPa.

Also find the ratio of stresses developed in two bars.

**Data** : Diameter of steel shaft = 50 mm ; $E_S = 200$ GPa ; $E_A = 67$ GPa ; $U_A = U_S$

**Required** : Diameter of aluminium shaft and ratio of stresses developed.

**Concept** : Equate strain energy of aluminium and steel shaft and get relation between stresses and then find diameter of aluminium shaft.

**Solution** : (i) Ratio of stresses :

$$U_A = U_S \text{ for unit volume}$$

$$\therefore \quad \left(\dfrac{\sigma_{max}^2}{2E}\right)_A = \left(\dfrac{\sigma_{max}^2}{2E}\right)_S$$

$$\dfrac{(\sigma_{max}^2)_A}{2 \times 67 \times 10^3} = \dfrac{(\sigma_{max}^2)_S}{2 \times 200 \times 10^3}$$

$$(\sigma_{max})_A = (0.578)(\sigma_{max})_S$$

$$\therefore \quad \dfrac{(\sigma_{max})_A}{(\sigma_{max})_S} = 0.578$$

OR $\quad \dfrac{(\sigma_{max})_S}{(\sigma_{max})_A} = 1.727$

(ii) Diameter of aluminium shaft :

$$\left(\frac{P}{A}\right)_A = 0.578 \left(\frac{P}{A}\right)_S \qquad (\because P_A = P_S)$$

$$\therefore \quad \frac{1}{\frac{\pi}{4}(\phi)_A^2} = 0.578 \left(\frac{1}{\frac{\pi}{4}(50)^2}\right)$$

$$\therefore \quad \phi_A = 65.76 \text{ mm}$$

**Example 4.17 :** A copper rod 30 mm diameter is enclosed in a steel tube 45 mm internal diameter and 5 mm thickness. The length of composite member is 2 m. It is fixed at top and provided with a rigid collar at bottom. A body of mass 50 kg is allowed to slide down freely through a height (h). If maximum instantaneous stress developed in copper is not to exceed 75 MPa, find height and elongation of composite bar. Take $E_S$ = 200 GPa and $E_c$ = 120 GPa.

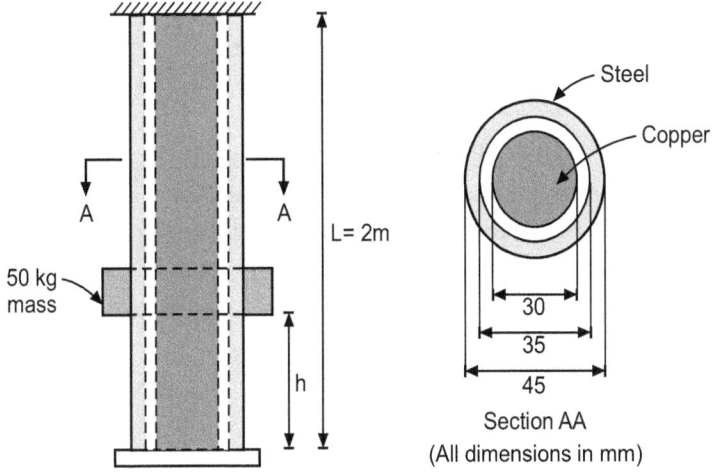

**Fig. 4.12**

**Data** : As shown in Fig. 4.12.

**Required** : h and δL.

**Concept** : Use basic work equation along with compatibility as $(\delta L)_S = (\delta L)_c$.

**Solution** : (i) Geometric properties :

$$A_c = \frac{\pi}{4}(30)^2 = 706.85 \text{ mm}^2$$

$$A_S = \frac{\pi}{4}[(45)^2 - (35)^2] = 628.32 \text{ mm}^2$$

(ii) Work equation :

$$W(h + \delta L) = \left(\frac{\sigma_{max}^2}{2E} \times \text{Volume}\right)_c + \left(\frac{\sigma_{max}^2}{2E} \times \text{Volume}\right)_S$$

We have,    $(\delta L)_c = (\delta L)_s$

∴    $\sigma_s = \dfrac{E_s}{E_c} \times \sigma_c$

$= \dfrac{200}{120} \times 75$

$= 125$ MPa

Also,    $W = 50$ kg $= 50 \times 9.81 = 490.5$ N

Instantaneous elongation $= \delta L = \left(\dfrac{\sigma L}{E}\right)_c = \left(\dfrac{\sigma L}{E}\right)_s$

$= \dfrac{75 \times 2000}{120 \times 10^3} = 1.25$ mm

Substituting,

$490.5\,(h + 1.25) = \dfrac{(75)^2}{2 \times 120 \times 10^3} \times 706.85 \times 2000 + \dfrac{(125)^2}{2 \times 200 \times 10^3} \times 628.32 \times 2000$

$490.5\,(h + 1.25) = 82.22 \times 10^3$

∴    $h = \mathbf{166.37}$ **mm**

**Example 4.18 :** A copper bar is enclosed in a steel tube 36 mm external diameter and 4 mm thickness. A composite bar is held vertically fixed at top and provided with a collar at bottom. A weight of 2.5 kN falls freely through height of 20 mm. Length of composite section is 1.5 m. Find diameter of copper bar if maximum instantaneous stress developed in steel is 150 MPa. Assume $E_c = 100$ GPa ; $E_s = 200$ GPa.

**Data**      : As shown in Fig. 4.13.
**Required** : Diameter of copper bar and maximum elongation of composite section.
**Concept**  : Same as Example 4.17.
**Solution** :

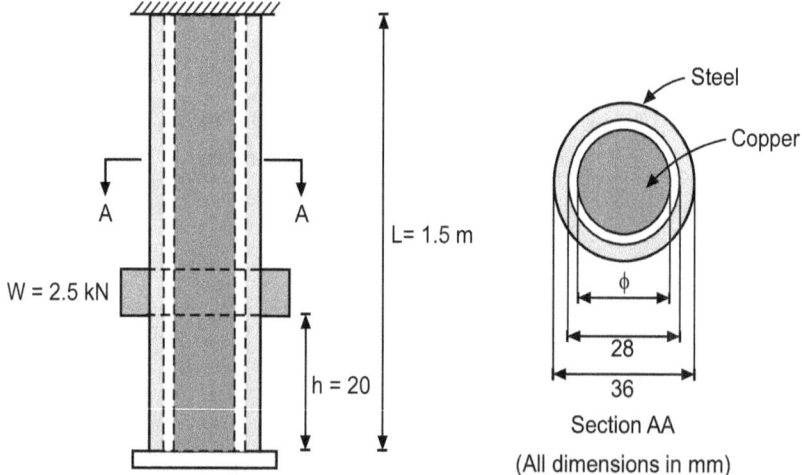

Fig. 4.13

(i) Geometric properties :

$$A_s = \frac{\pi}{4}[(36)^2 - (28)^2] = 402.12 \text{ mm}^2$$

$$A_c = \text{Unknown}$$

(ii) Work equation :

$$W(h + \delta L) = \left(\frac{\sigma^2}{2E} \cdot \text{Volume}\right)_c + \left(\frac{\sigma^2}{2E} \cdot \text{Volume}\right)_s$$

We have, $(\delta L)_c = (\delta L)_s$

$$\left(\frac{\sigma L}{E}\right)_c = \left(\frac{\sigma L}{E}\right)_s$$

$$\sigma_c = \frac{E_c}{E_s} \cdot \sigma_s$$

$$= \frac{100}{200} \cdot \sigma_s$$

$$\sigma_c = 0.5\sigma_s = 0.5 \times 150 = 75 \text{ MPa}$$

$$W(h + \delta L) = \frac{(75)^2}{2 \times 100 \times 10^3} \times A_c \times 1500 + \frac{(150)^2}{2 \times 200 \times 10^3}(402.12 \times 1500)$$

$$W(h + \delta L) = 42.18 A_c + 33928.875$$

Substituting, $W = 2.5 \text{ kN} = 2500 \text{ N}$

$h = 20 \text{ mm}$

$$\delta L = \left(\frac{\sigma L}{E}\right)_s = \frac{150 \times 1500}{200 \times 10^3}$$

$$= 1.125 \text{ mm}$$

∴ $2500(20 + 1.125) = 42.18 A_c + 33928.875$

$$A_c = 447.69 \text{ mm}^2$$

$$\frac{\pi}{4}(\phi)^2 = 447.69$$

∴ $\phi = \mathbf{23.87 \text{ mm}}$

**Example 4.19 :** A copper bar 20 mm $\phi$ is enclosed in a steel tube 30 mm external diameter and 3 mm thickness. The composite bar is held vertically, fixed at top and provided with a collar at bottom. A weight of 2 kN falls freely through height of 20 mm. If length of bar is 2 m, find :

(i) Maximum instantaneous stress developed in each material.

(ii) Maximum instantaneous elongation.

Assume $E_s = 200$ GPa ; $E_c = 110$ GPa.

**Data** : As shown in Fig. 4.14.

**Required** : $\sigma_{max}$ for copper and steel, $\delta L$.

**Concept** : Same as Example 4.17.

**Solution :**

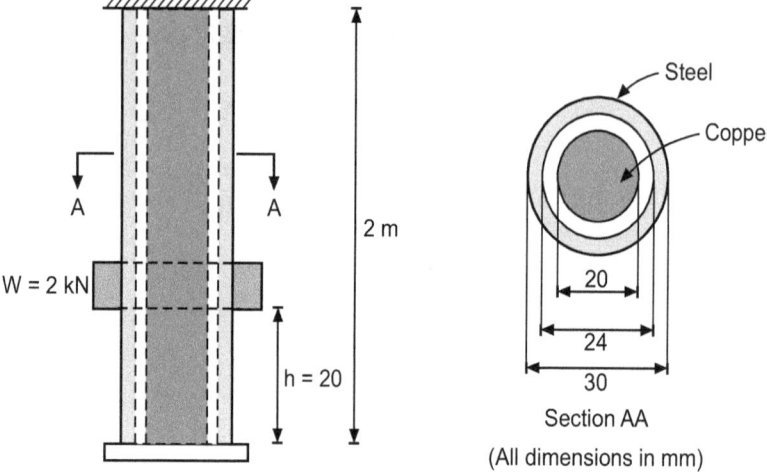

Fig. 4.14

(i) Geometric properties :

$$A_c = \frac{\pi}{4}(20)^2 = 314.16 \text{ mm}^2$$

$$A_s = \frac{\pi}{4}[(30)^2 - (24)^2] = 254.47 \text{ mm}^2$$

(ii) Work equation :

$$W(h + \delta L) = U_c + U_s$$

$$= \left[\frac{\sigma_{max}^2}{2E} \times \text{Volume}\right]_c + \left[\frac{\sigma_{max}^2}{2E} \times \text{Volume}\right]_s$$

We have, $(\delta L)_c = (\delta L)_s$

$$\left(\frac{\sigma L}{E}\right)_c = \left(\frac{\sigma L}{E}\right)_s$$

$$\frac{\sigma_c}{E_c} = \frac{\sigma_s}{E_s}$$

∴ $$\sigma_c = \frac{E_c}{E_s} \cdot \sigma_s$$

$$= \frac{110}{200} \cdot \sigma_s$$

$$\sigma_c = 0.55 \, \sigma_s$$

∴ $$W(h + \delta L) = \frac{(0.55 \, \sigma_s)^2}{2 \times 110 \times 10^3} \times 314.16 \times 2000 + \frac{\sigma_s^2}{2 \times 200 \times 10^3} \times 254.47 \times 2000$$

∴ $$W(h + \delta L) = 2.136 \, \sigma_s^2$$

Substituting for $\delta L = \dfrac{\sigma_s L_s}{E_s}$

$$= \dfrac{\sigma_s \times 2000}{200 \times 10^3}$$

$$= 0.01\ \sigma_s$$

and $W = 2\text{ kN} = 2000\text{ N}$ ; $h = 20\text{ mm}$

$$2000\,(20 + 0.01\,\sigma_s) = 2.136\,\sigma_s^2$$

Solving, $\sigma_s = 141.6\text{ MPa}$

$\sigma_c = 0.55 \times \sigma_s$

$= 0.55 \times 141.6$

$= 77.88\text{ MPa}$

**(iii) Maximum elongation $\delta L$ :**

$$\delta L = \left(\dfrac{\sigma L}{E}\right)_c = \left(\dfrac{\sigma L}{E}\right)_s$$

$$= \dfrac{77.88 \times 2000}{110 \times 10^3}$$

$$= \mathbf{1.416\text{ mm}}$$

**Example 4.20 :** A vertical steel rod 1.5 m long is fixed at top and provided with collar at bottom. The upper 900 mm length of bar is 28 mm $\phi$, while the lower 600 mm bar is 16 mm $\phi$. A weight of magnitude 150 N falls freely through a height of 60 mm. Find

(i) Maximum instantaneous stress,

(ii) Maximum elongation,

(iii) Total strain energy stored.

Assume $E = 200$ GPa

**Data** : As shown in Fig. 4.15.

**Required** : $\sigma_{max}$, $\delta L_{max}$ and U

**Concept** : Use of equation (4.7) where,

$$\delta_{st} = \left(\dfrac{PL}{AE}\right)_1 + \left(\dfrac{PL}{AE}\right)_2$$

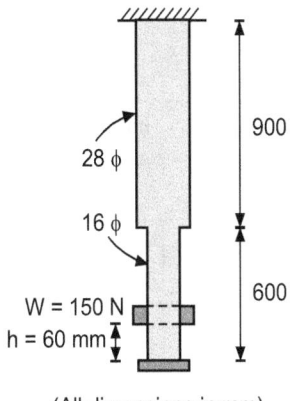

(All dimensions in mm)

**Fig. 4.15**

**Solution** : (i) Geometric properties :

Let, $A_1 = \dfrac{\pi}{4}(28)^2 = 615.75\text{ mm}^2$

$A_2 = \dfrac{\pi}{4}(16)^2 = 201.06\text{ mm}^2$

(ii) Maximum instantaneous stress,

$$\sigma_{max} = \frac{W}{A}\left[1 \pm \sqrt{1 + \frac{2h}{\delta_{st}}}\right]$$

where
$$\delta_{st} = \left(\frac{PL}{AE}\right)_1 + \left(\frac{PL}{AE}\right)_2$$

$$= \left[\frac{150 \times 900}{615.75} + \frac{150 \times 600}{201.06}\right] \times \frac{1}{200 \times 10^3}$$

$$= 3.33 \times 10^{-3} \text{ mm}$$

$$\therefore \quad \sigma_{max} = \frac{150}{201.06}\left[1 \pm \sqrt{1 + \frac{2 \times 60}{3.33 \times 10^{-3}}}\right]$$

$$= 142.28 \text{ MPa}$$

**Note :** Maximum stress occurs in the portion of relatively smaller area.

(iii) Maximum instantaneous elongation :

We have,
$$\sigma_1 A_1 = \sigma_2 A_2$$
$$\sigma_1 \times 615.75 = 142.28 \times 201.06$$
$$\sigma_1 = 46.46 \text{ MPa}$$

Now,
$$\delta L = \frac{1}{E}(\sigma_1 L_1 + \sigma_2 L_2)$$

$$= \frac{1}{200 \times 10^3}(46.46 \times 900 + 142.28 \times 600) = 0.6359 \text{ mm}$$

(iv) Total strain energy, U :

$$U = W(h + \delta L)$$
$$= 150(60 + 0.6359) = 9095.3 \text{ Nmm}$$
$$= \mathbf{9.09 \text{ J}}$$

**Example 4.21 :** A hammer of weight 75 N falls freely through a distance of 100 mm on a bar as shown in Fig. 4.16. Assuming E = 200 GPa, find instantaneous stress developed in bar at top and bottom.

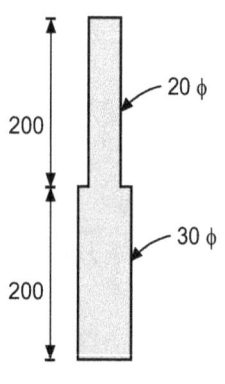

(All dimensions in mm)

**Fig. 4.16**

**Data :** W = 75 N ; h = 100 mm ;

E = 200 GPa

**Required :** Instantaneous stress at top and bottom.

**Concept :** Same as Example 4.20.

**Solution :** (i) Geometric properties :

$$A_1 = \frac{\pi}{4}(20)^2 = 314.16 \text{ mm}^2;$$

$$A_2 = \frac{\pi}{4}(30)^2 = 706.86 \text{ mm}^2$$

(ii) Stresses :

$$\sigma_{max} = \sigma_1 = \frac{W}{A}\left[1 + \sqrt{1 + \frac{2h}{\delta_{st}}}\right] \quad \{\text{Note}: \sigma_1 > \sigma_2\}$$

where

$$\delta_{st} = \left(\frac{WL}{AE}\right)_1 + \left(\frac{WL}{AE}\right)_2$$

$$= \frac{75}{200 \times 10^3}\left[\frac{200}{314.16} + \frac{200}{706.86}\right] = 3.448 \times 10^{-4}$$

$$\therefore \quad \sigma_{max} = \sigma_1 = \frac{75}{314.16}\left[1 + \sqrt{1 + \frac{2 \times 100}{3.448 \times 10^{-4}}}\right]$$

$$\sigma_1 = 182 \text{ MPa}$$

Also 
$$\sigma_1 A_1 = \sigma_2 A_2$$
$$182 \times 314.16 = \sigma_2 \times 706.86$$

$$\therefore \quad \sigma_2 = \mathbf{80.91 \text{ MPa}}$$

**Example 4.22 :** A steel bar 4 m long has details as shown in Fig. 4.17. This bar is given an axial blow transmitting a shock energy of 100 Nm. Calculate the maximum instantaneous stress induced and maximum instantaneous elongation of the bar. E = 210 GPa.

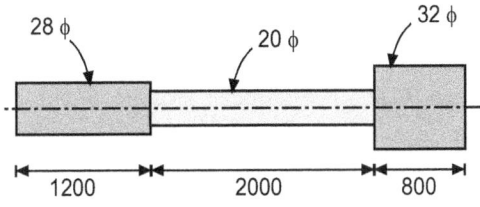

(All dimensions in mm)

Fig. 4.17

**Data** : Shock energy = 100 Nm ; E = 210 GPa.
**Required** : Maximum instantaneous stress and elongation.
**Concept** : Shock energy shall be equated to strain energy of compound bar.
**Solution** : (i) Geometric properties :

$$A_1 = \frac{\pi}{4}(28)^2 = 615.75 \text{ mm}^2 \; ; \; L_1 = 1200 \text{ mm}$$

$$\therefore \quad \text{Volume}_1 = A_1 \times L_1 = 615.75 \times 1200 = 738.9 \times 10^3 \text{ mm}^3$$

$$A_2 = \frac{\pi}{4}(20)^2 = 314.16 \text{ mm}^2 \; ; \; L_2 = 2000 \text{ mm}$$

$$\text{Volume}_2 = A_2 \times L_2 = 314.16 \times 2000 = 628.32 \times 10^3 \text{ mm}^3$$

$$A_3 = \frac{\pi}{4}(32)^2 = 804.25 \text{ mm}^2 \; ; \; L_3 = 800 \text{ mm}$$

$$\text{Volume}_3 = A_3 \times L_3 = 804.25 \times 800 = 643.39 \times 10^3 \text{ mm}^3$$

(ii) Instantaneous stress :

$$U = \left(\frac{\sigma^2}{2E} \cdot \text{Volume}\right)_1 + \left(\frac{\sigma^2}{2E} \cdot \text{Volume}\right)_2 + \left(\frac{\sigma^2}{2E} \cdot \text{Volume}\right)_3$$

We have $\sigma_1 A_1 = \sigma_2 A_2 = \sigma_3 A_3$

$\sigma_1 \times 615.75 = \sigma_2 \times 314.16 = \sigma_3 \times 804.25$

∴ $\sigma_1 = 0.51 \sigma_2$ and $\sigma_3 = 0.39 \sigma_2$  (∵ $\sigma_2$ = Maximum stress)

Substituting,

$$100 \times 10^3 = \frac{1}{2E} [(0.51 \sigma_2)^2 \times 738.9 \times 10^3 + \sigma_2^2 \times 628.32 \times 10^3 + (0.39 \sigma_2)^2 \times 643.39 \times 10^3]$$

$$100 \times 10^3 = 459.18 \times 10^3 \cdot \frac{\sigma_2^2}{E} = \frac{459.18 \times 10^3}{210 \times 10^3} \cdot \sigma_2^2$$

∴ $\sigma_2 = 213.85$ MPa

∴ $\sigma_1 = 109.06$ MPa and $\sigma_3 = 83.4$ MPa

(iii) Instantaneous elongation :

$$\delta L = \delta L_1 + \delta L_2 + \delta L_3$$

$$= \left(\frac{\sigma L}{E}\right)_1 + \left(\frac{\sigma L}{E}\right)_2 + \left(\frac{\sigma L}{E}\right)_3 = \frac{1}{E}[\sigma_1 L_1 + \sigma_2 L_2 + \sigma_3 L_3]$$

$$= \frac{1}{210 \times 10^3} [109.06 \times 1200 + 213.85 \times 2000 + 83.4 \times 800]$$

$$= \mathbf{2.977 \text{ mm}}$$

**Example 4.23** : Two bars A and B of circular cross-section and of the same material have dimensions as shown in Fig. 4.18. An axial blow given to 'A', produces maximum instantaneous stress of 100 MPa in it.

(i) Calculate the maximum instantaneous stress produced by same axial blow given to 'B' assuming $U_A = U_B$.

(ii) If each bar is stressed to elastic limit, calculate the ratio of resilience of 'A' to that of 'B'.

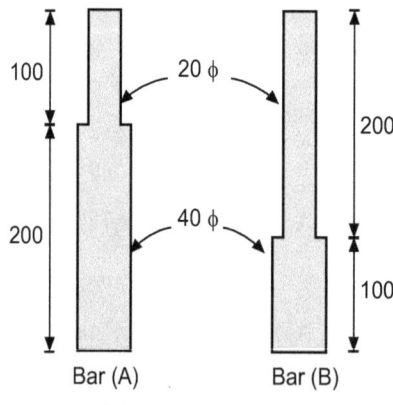

Bar (A)   Bar (B)

(All dimensions in mm)

**Fig. 4.18**

**Data** : As shown in Fig. 4.18.
**Required** : $\sigma_{max}$ for bar B and ratio of resilience of A to B.
**Concept** : Standard formulae.
**Solution** : (i) Geometric properties :

Let $A_1$ and $A_2$ be the cross-sectional areas of bar 'A' for 20 mm $\phi$ and 40 mm $\phi$ components respectively. $A_3$ and $A_4$ be the cross-sectional areas of bar 'B' for 20 mm $\phi$ and 40 mm $\phi$ components respectively.

$\therefore$ 
$$A_1 = \frac{\pi}{4}(20)^2 = 314.16 \text{ mm}^2 = A_3$$

$$A_2 = \frac{\pi}{4}(40)^2 = 1256.64 \text{ mm}^2 = A_4$$

$V_1$ and $V_2$ = Volumes of bar 'A' for components of 20 mm $\phi$ and 40 mm $\phi$ respectively.

$$V_1 = 314.16 \times 100 = 31.416 \times 10^3 \text{ mm}^3$$
$$V_2 = 1256.64 \times 200 = 251.328 \times 10^3 \text{ mm}^3$$

$V_3$ and $V_4$ = Volumes of bar 'B' for components of 20 mm $\phi$ and 40 mm $\phi$ respectively.

$$V_3 = 314.16 \times 200 = 62.832 \times 10^3 \text{ mm}^3$$
$$V_4 = 1256.64 \times 100 = 125.664 \times 10^3 \text{ mm}^3$$

$\sigma_1, \sigma_2$ = Stresses developed in bar 'A' for components of 20 mm $\phi$ and 40 mm $\phi$ respectively.

and $\sigma_3, \sigma_4$ = Stresses developed in bar 'B' for components of 20 mm $\phi$ and 40 mm $\phi$ respectively.

(ii) Strain energy of bar 'A' :

$$U_A = \left(\frac{\sigma^2}{2E} \cdot \text{Volume}\right)_1 + \left(\frac{\sigma^2}{2E} \cdot \text{Volume}\right)_2$$

We have, 
$$\sigma_1 A_1 = \sigma_2 A_2$$
$$100 \times 314.16 = \sigma_2 \times 1256.64$$

$\therefore$ 
$$\sigma_2 = 25 \text{ MPa}$$

$\therefore$ 
$$U_A = \frac{(100)^2}{2E} \times 31.416 \times 10^3 + \frac{(25)^2}{2E} \times 251.328 \times 10^3$$

$$= \frac{235.62 \times 10^6}{E}$$

(iii) Strain energy of bar 'B' :

$$U_B = \left(\frac{\sigma^2}{2E} \cdot \text{Volume}\right)_3 + \left(\frac{\sigma^2}{2E} \cdot \text{Volume}\right)_4$$

We have,
$$\sigma_3 A_3 = \sigma_4 A_4$$
$$\sigma_3 \times 314.16 = \sigma_4 \times 1256.64$$
$$\sigma_3 = 4 \cdot \sigma_4$$

OR
$$\sigma_4 = 0.25 \sigma_3$$

$$U_B = \frac{\sigma_3^2}{2E} \times 62.832 \times 10^3 + \frac{(0.25\sigma_3)^2}{2E} \times 125.664 \times 10^3$$

$$U_B = 35343 \cdot \frac{\sigma_3^2}{E} \qquad \text{(Note : } \sigma_3 > \sigma_4\text{)}$$

(iv) Maximum instantaneous stress for bar 'B' :

Equating strain energy of 'A' to that of 'B',

$$\frac{235.62 \times 10^6}{E} = 35343 \frac{\sigma_3^2}{E}$$

$$\therefore \quad \sigma_3 = 81.65 \text{ MPa}$$

(v) Ratio of resilience when each bar is stressed to elastic limit :

Let, $F_y$ = Yield stress

**Note :** Material for bar 'A' and bar 'B' being same, yield stress is same for both the bars. Also for bar 'A', $\sigma_1 > \sigma_2$, hence $\sigma_1 = F_y$ and for bar B, $\sigma_3 > \sigma_4$, hence $\sigma_3 = F_y$.

$$\text{Resilience of 'A'} = \left(\frac{\sigma^2}{2E} \cdot \text{Volume}\right)_1 + \left(\frac{\sigma^2}{2E} \cdot \text{Volume}\right)_2$$

where $\sigma_1 = F_y$ and $\sigma_2 = 0.25 F_y$

Substituting,

$$\text{Resilience of 'A'} = \frac{1}{2E} (F_y^2 \times 31.416 \times 10^3 + (0.25 F_y)^2 \times 251.328 \times 10^3)$$

$$= 23562 \frac{F_y^2}{E}$$

$$\text{Resilience of 'B'} = \left(\frac{\sigma^2}{2E} \cdot \text{Volume}\right)_3 + \left(\frac{\sigma^2}{2E} \cdot \text{Volume}\right)_4$$

where $\sigma_3 = F_y$ and $\sigma_4 = 0.25 F_y$

Substituting,

$$\text{Resilience of B} = \frac{1}{2E} [F_y^2 \times 62.832 \times 10^3 + (0.25 F_y)^2 \times 125.664 \times 10^3]$$

$$= 35343 \frac{F_y^2}{E}$$

$$\frac{\text{Resilience of A}}{\text{Resilience of B}} = 23562 \frac{F_y^2}{E} \times \frac{E}{35343 F_y^2}$$

$$= \frac{1}{1.5}$$

**Example 4.24 :** A 300 mm long stepped bar 'A' has a diameter of 20 mm for a length of 100 mm and a diameter of 40 mm for the remaining length. Another bar 'B' made of same material has a diameter of 30 mm throughout the entire length of 300 mm. Compare the values of maximum strain energy stored in them, if permissible stresses for the material are same.

**Data** : As shown in Fig. 4.19.

**Required** : $\dfrac{U_A}{U_B}$.

**Concept** : Standard formulae.

**Solution** :

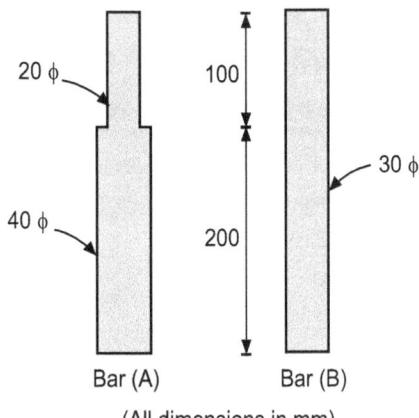

Bar (A)  Bar (B)
(All dimensions in mm)

**Fig. 4.19**

**Solution** : (i) Strain energy of bar A :

Let $\sigma_1$ and $\sigma_2$ be the stresses developed in portions 20 mm $\phi$ and 40 mm $\phi$ of bar A respectively.

We have,
$$U_A = \left(\dfrac{\sigma^2}{2E} \cdot \text{Volume}\right)_1 + \left(\dfrac{\sigma^2}{2E} \cdot \text{Volume}\right)_2$$

where
$$\text{Volume}_1 = \dfrac{\pi}{4}(20)^2 \times 100 = 31.42 \times 10^3 \text{ mm}^3$$

$$\text{Volume}_2 = \dfrac{\pi}{4}(40)^2 \times 200 = 251.33 \times 10^3 \text{ mm}^3$$

Now,
$$\sigma_1 A_1 = \sigma_2 A_2$$

$$\sigma_1 \times \dfrac{\pi}{4}(20)^2 = \sigma_2 \times \dfrac{\pi}{4}(40)^2$$

∴ $\sigma_1 = 4\sigma_2$  OR  $\sigma_2 = 0.25\sigma_1$

Substituting,
$$U_A = \dfrac{\sigma_1^2}{2E} \times 31.42 \times 10^3 + \dfrac{(0.25\sigma_1)^2}{2E} \times 251.33 \times 10^3$$

$$= \left(\dfrac{23.56 \times 10^3}{E}\right)\sigma_1^2$$

Note that $\sigma_1 > \sigma_2$, hence $U_A$ is obtained in terms of $\sigma_1$.

(ii) Strain energy of bar B :

Let $\sigma_3$ be the stress developed in bar B.

$$U_B = \frac{\sigma_3^2}{2E} \times \text{Volume} = \frac{\sigma_3^2}{2E} \times \frac{\pi}{4} (30)^2 \times 300$$

$$= \left(\frac{106.02 \times 10^3}{E}\right) \sigma_3^2$$

(iii) Comparison of $U_A$ and $U_B$ :

$$\frac{U_A}{U_B} = \left(\frac{23.56 \times 10^3}{E}\right) \sigma_1^2 \times \frac{E}{106.02 \times 10^3 \sigma_3^2}$$

$$= \frac{1}{4.5}$$

**Note :** Material for bars A and B being same, E = constant and $\sigma_1 = \sigma_3$.

**Example 4.25 :** A uniform rod of cross-sectional area = A ; length = L is held vertically as shown in Fig. 4.20. Derive the expression for strain energy due to self weight. Assume Young's modulus of elasticity 'E' and mass density '$\rho$'.

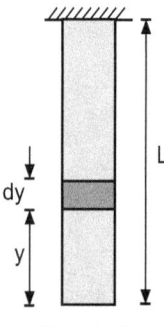

**Data :** A, L, E, $\rho$.

**Required :** Expression for strain energy due to self weight.

**Concept :** Strain energy due to self weight by integration.

Fig. 4.20

**Solution :** Consider an elementary strip of thickness 'dy' at a distance 'y' from bottom as shown in Fig. 4.20.

Axial force on elementary strip = F = Volume below the strip × Weight density
$$= A \cdot y \cdot \rho \cdot g$$

Normal stress on elementary strip = $\sigma$ = $\dfrac{F}{\text{Cross-sectional area of strip}} = \dfrac{A \cdot y \cdot \rho \cdot g}{A}$

$$\sigma = y \cdot \rho \cdot g$$

Strain energy of strip = dU = $\dfrac{\sigma^2}{2E} \times$ Volume of strip

$$= \frac{(y \cdot \rho \cdot g)^2}{2E} \times (A \cdot dy)$$

Strain energy of member = U = $\displaystyle\int_0^L dU = \int_0^L \frac{y^2 \cdot \rho^2 \cdot g^2 \cdot A}{2E} \cdot dy$

$$= \frac{\rho^2 \cdot g^2 \cdot A \cdot L^3}{6E}$$

**Example 4.26 :** A solid right circular cone is held vertically as shown in Fig. 4.21. Derive the expression for strain energy stored in it due to self weight using standard notation.

**Data** : As shown in Fig. 4.21.

**Required** : Expression for strain energy due to self weight.

**Concept** : Same as Example 4.25.

**Solution** : Consider an elementary strip of thickness 'dy' at a distance 'y' from bottom as shown in Fig. 4.21.

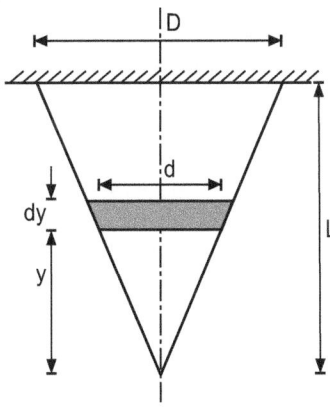

**Fig. 4.21**

Let,
- $D$ = Diameter of cone at fixed end
- $d$ = Diameter of cone at 'y' from bottom
- $L$ = Height of cone
- $\rho$ = Mass density of cone material
- $g$ = Gravitational acceleration
- $E$ = Modulus of elasticity

Axial force on elementary strip = Volume below the strip × Weight density

$$= \left(\frac{1}{3} A_y \cdot y\right) \cdot \rho \cdot g$$

where $A_y$ = Area of cross-section at 'y' from bottom.

∴ Normal stress on elementary strip $= \sigma = \dfrac{F}{A_y} = \dfrac{y \cdot \rho \cdot g}{3}$

∴ Strain energy of elementary strip $= dU$

$$= \frac{\sigma^2}{2E} \times \text{Volume of strip}$$

∴ $$dU = \left(\frac{y \cdot \rho \cdot g}{3}\right)^2 \cdot \frac{1}{2E} \cdot (A_y \cdot dy)$$

∴ $$dU = \frac{y^2 \cdot \rho^2 \cdot g^2}{18 E} \cdot (A_y \cdot dy)$$

where, $$A_y = \frac{\pi}{4} d^2 = \frac{\pi}{4}\left[\frac{D}{L} \cdot y\right]^2$$

Total strain energy for cone = $U = \int_0^L dU$

$\therefore \quad U = \int_0^L \dfrac{y^2 \rho^2 g^2}{18 E} \left[\dfrac{\pi}{4}\left(\dfrac{D}{L} \cdot y\right)^2\right] dy = \dfrac{\rho^2 g^2 \pi D^2}{72 E L^2} \cdot \left[\dfrac{L^5}{5}\right]$

$= \dfrac{\rho^2 g^2 \cdot \pi D^2}{360 E} \cdot L^3$

**Example 4.27 :** For the two bars of same material shown in Fig. 4.22 (a) and (b), find the ratio of maximum stress of bar (a) to that of bar (b). If the two bars are stressed to proportional limit, find the ratio of their proof resilience.

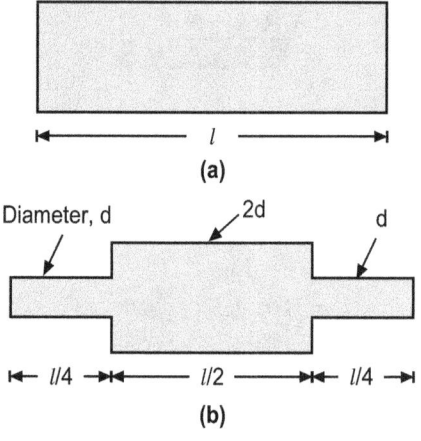

Fig. 4.22

**Data** : As shown in Fig. 4.22.

**Required** : Ratio of maximum stress of bar (a) to that of bar (b) and ratio of their proof resilience.

**Concept** : Standard formula.

**Solution** :

Maximum stress (Fig. 4.22 (a)) $= \dfrac{P}{A} = \dfrac{P}{\dfrac{\pi}{4} \times d^2}$

Maximum stress (Fig. 4.22 (b)) $= \dfrac{P}{A} = \dfrac{P}{\dfrac{\pi}{4} \times d^2}$

Ratio of stress $= \dfrac{\text{Maximum stress (Fig. 4.22 (a))}}{\text{Maximum stress (Fig. 4.22 (b))}} = 1$

Proof resilience (Fig. 4.22 (a)) $= \dfrac{f_y^2}{2E} \times \text{Volume}$

$= \dfrac{f_y^2}{2E} \times \dfrac{\pi}{4} \times d^2 \times l$

Proof resilience (Fig. 4.22 (b)) $= \dfrac{f_y^2}{2E} \times 2 \times \dfrac{\pi}{4} \times d^2 \times \dfrac{l}{4} + \dfrac{f_y^2}{2E} \times \dfrac{\pi}{4} \times 4d^2 \times \dfrac{l}{2}$

$= \dfrac{f_y^2}{2E} \times \dfrac{\pi}{4} \times d^2 \left[\dfrac{l}{2} + 2l\right]$

$= \dfrac{f_y^2}{2E} \times \dfrac{\pi}{4} \times d^2 \times \dfrac{5l}{2}$

Ratio of resilience $= \dfrac{\text{Proof resilience of Fig. 4.22 (a)}}{\text{Proof resilience of Fig. 4.22 (b)}}$

$= \dfrac{\dfrac{f_y^2}{2E} \times \dfrac{\pi}{4} \times d^2 \times l}{\dfrac{f_y^2}{2E} \times \dfrac{\pi}{4} \times d^2 \times \dfrac{5l}{2}} = \dfrac{2}{5}$

---

**Example 4.28 :** A load of 50 N falls by gravity through a vertical distance of 2000 mm. When it is suddenly stopped by a coller at end of vertical rod of length 6 m and diameter 20 mm, calculate the maximum stress and strain induced in the bar. The top of the bar is rigidly fixed to the ceiling. Assume $E = 1.96 \times 10^5$ N/mm².

**Data** : $W = 50$ N, $h = 2000$ mm, $l = 6000$ mm, $E = 1.96 \times 10^5$ N/mm², $\phi = 20$ mm

**Required** : Maximum stress and strain induced in bar.

**Concept** : Standard formula.

**Solution** : $A = \dfrac{\pi}{4} \times d^2 = \dfrac{\pi}{4} (20)^2 = 314.16$ mm²

$\sigma_{max} = \left[\dfrac{W}{A} + \sqrt{\dfrac{W^2}{A^2} + \dfrac{2hEA}{WL}}\right]$

$= \dfrac{50}{314.16} + \sqrt{\left(\dfrac{50}{314.16}\right)^2 + \left(\dfrac{2 \times 2000 \times 1.96 \times 10^5 \times 314.16}{50 \times 6000}\right)}$

$= 0.16 + \sqrt{(0.16)^2 + 821 \times 10^3}$

$= 0.16 + 906.25$

$\delta l = \dfrac{\sigma_{max} \times L}{E} = \dfrac{906.25 \times 6000}{1.96 \times 10^5} = 27.74$ mm

$\delta l = \mathbf{27.74 \text{ mm}}$

---

**Example 4.29 :** A load of 500 N falls freely through a height of 150 mm onto a coller attached to end of vertical rod of 50 mm diameter and 2 m long, the upper end of rod being fixed to the ceiling. Calculate the maximum instantaneous extension of the bar. Also calculate the maximum stress in the bar. Assume $E = 200$ GPa.

**Data** : $W = 500$ N, $h = 150$ mm, $D = 50$ mm, $E = 200$ GPa

**Required** : Maximum instantaneous extension and stress.

**Concept** : Standard formula.

**Solution** :
$$\sigma_{max} = \frac{W}{A} \pm \left[\sqrt{\left(\frac{2WhE}{AL}\right)^2 + \frac{W^2}{A^2}}\right]$$

$$\therefore \sigma_{max} = \frac{500}{19635} \pm \left[\sqrt{\left(\frac{2 \times 500 \times 150 \times 200 \times 10^3}{1963.5 \times 2000}\right)^2 + \frac{500^2}{1963.5^2}}\right]$$

$$\sigma_{max} = 0.255 \pm \sqrt{(7639.42 + 0.065)}$$

$$\sigma_{max} = 0.255 + 87.40 = 87.655 \text{ N/mm}^2$$

$$\delta l = \frac{\sigma l}{E} = \frac{87.655 \times 2000}{200 \times 10^3} = 0.88 \text{ mm}$$

## EXERCISE

1. A bar 75 mm in diameter, 3.2 m long has to transmit shock energy of 175 joules. Calculate maximum instantaneous stress developed and maximum elongation if $E = 200$ GPa. ($\sigma_{max} = 70.36$ MPa ; $\delta L_{max} = 1.125$ mm)

2. A vertical steel bar 1.75 m long is fixed at top. A weight can slide freely along the rod and its fall is arrested at the bottom by collar. When weight falls through 50 mm, the maximum instantaneous stress developed in the bar is 200 MPa. Determine the stress in the same bar when weight is (i) gradually applied, (ii) suddenly applied, (iii) applied with free fall of 60 mm.

((i) $\sigma_{max} = 3.38$ MPa, (ii) $\sigma_{max} = 6.76$ MPa, (iii) $\sigma_{max} = 218.706$ MPa)

3. A uniform bar of cross-sectional area 485 mm² is 8.85 m long. Find the proof resilience and modulus of resilience if the elastic limit for the bar material is 250 MPa. Also find the maximum value of suddenly applied load, the member can carry. Assume $E = 200$ GPa. (Proof resilience = 215.976 joules, Modulus of resilience = 0.156 MPa, Suddenly applied load = 60.625 kN)

4. A vertical steel rod 1.7 m long is fixed at top and provided with collar at bottom. The upper 1000 mm length of bar is 30 mm $\phi$, while the lower 700 mm is of 15 mm $\phi$. A weight of magnitude 175 N falls freely through a height of 75 mm. Find (i) maximum instantaneous stress, (ii) maximum elongation, (iii) total strain energy stored. Assume $E = 200$ GPa.

((i) $\sigma_{max} = 177.84$ MPa, (ii) $\delta L = 0.848$ mm (iii) $U = 13.273$ joules)

5. A vertical steel bar 15 mm diameter, 1.4 m long is provided with a collar at lower end. Find the maximum weight that can be dropped through a height of 95 mm over the collar if maximum permissible tensile stress is 150 MPa. Assume $E = 200$ GPa.

($W = 144.88$ N)

6. A bar of 20 mm diameter stretches 1 mm under gradually applied load of 50 kN. If a weight of 1.5 kN is dropped on to a collar at the lower end of this bar through a height of 35 mm, calculate the maximum instantaneous stress and elongation of the bar. Take $E = 200$ GPa. ($\sigma_{max} = 235.46$ MPa ; $\delta L = 1.479$ mm)

7. Water under pressure of 10 MPa is suddenly admitted on to a plunger of 125 mm diameter attached to a rod 30 mm diameter, 4 m long. Find the maximum instantaneous stress and deformation of the rod if E = 210 GPa. ($\sigma_{max}$ = 347.22 MPa ; $\delta L$ = 6.9 mm)

8. A steel specimen 15 mm $\phi$ stretches by 0.1 mm over 175 mm length under an axial load of 40 kN. Calculate the strain energy stored in the specimen at this stage. If the load at the elastic limit for the specimen is 50 kN, calculate the elongation at elastic limit and proof resilience. (U = 2 joules ; $\delta L$ = 0.125 mm, Proof resilience = 3.125 joules)

9. A vertically suspended steel bar, circular in cross-section, is subjected to load of 7.5 kN, which falls by 15 mm on rigid collar provided at lower end of the bar. If maximum allowable strain for the bar is $\frac{1}{1300}$, find suitable diameter of bar. Assume E = 200 GPa and length of bar = 3 m. (30.512 mm)

10. A wagon weighing 25 kN is attached to a wire rope and is moving at the speed of 5.5 kmph. The rope suddenly jams and the wagon is brought to rest. If length of the rope is 45 m and diameter 40 mm, find maximum instantaneous stress and elongation of rope assuming E = 200 GPa. ($\sigma_{max}$ = 145.04 MPa ; $\delta L_{max}$ = 32.63 mm)

11. A lift weighing 22 kN is connected by 24 mm diameter and 42 m long rope. If yield stress for the rope material is 300 MPa and factor of safety = 2.1, E = 200 GPa, find the safe working speed for the lift. (0.9 m/s)

12. A copper rod 25 mm diameter is enclosed in a steel tube 30 mm internal diameter and 3 mm thickness. The length of composite member is 2.4 m. It is fixed at top and provided with a rigid collar at bottom. A body of mass 44 kg is allowed to slide down freely through a height 'h'. If maximum instantaneous stress developed in copper is not to exceed 70 MPa, find height and elongation of composite bar.
Take $E_s$ = 200 GPa, $E_c$ = 120 GPa. (h = 113.17 mm ; $\delta L$ = 1.4 mm)

13. A copper bar 18 mm $\phi$ is enclosed in a steel tube 28 mm external diameter and 3.2 mm thickness. The composite bar is held vertically and provided with a rigid collar at bottom. A weight of 1.75 kN falls freely through a height of 22 mm. If length of the bar is 2.5 m, find (i) Maximum instantaneous stress developed in each material and (ii) Maximum instantaneous elongation. Take $E_s$ = 200 GPa, $E_c$ = 110 GPa.
($\sigma_s$ = 130.36 MPa, $\sigma_c$ = 71.7 MPa, $\delta L$ = 1.629 mm)

14. A copper tube is enclosed in a steel tube 35 mm external diameter and 5 mm thickness. This composite bar is held vertically fixed at top and provided with a rigid collar at bottom. A weight of 3 kN falls freely through a height of 25 mm. Length of composite member is 3 m. Find diameter of copper bar if maximum instantaneous stress developed in steel is 150 MPa. Assume $E_c$ = 100 GPa, $E_s$ = 200 GPa. (21.1 mm)

15. A 500 mm long stepped bar 'A' has a diameter of 25 mm for a length of 200 mm and a diameter of 45 mm for the remaining length. Another bar 'B' made of same material has a diameter of 30 mm throughout the entire length of 500 mm. Compare the values of maximum strain energy stored in them if permissible stress for the material is same.
(1 : 2.46)

16. A vertical steel bar is fixed at top and provided with rigid collar at bottom as shown in Fig. 4.23. Compute maximum stress induced in a member if 30 N weight falls through a height of 200 mm. E = 200 × $10^3$ MPa. ($\sigma_{max}$ = 107.4 MPa)

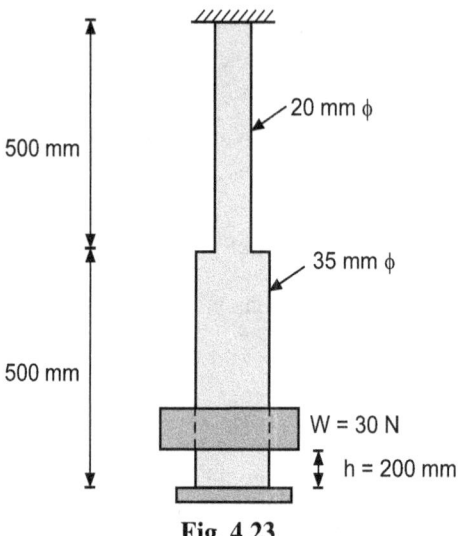

Fig. 4.23

17. An unknown weight 'W' falls through a height of 10 mm on a collar rigidly attached to the lower end of a vertical bar 5 m long and 600 mm² in section. If the maximum extension of the rod is to be 3 mm, what is the corresponding stress and magnitude of unknown weight ? E = 200 GPa. (W = 8.3 kN)

18. A vertical steel rod of 25 mm diameter checks the fall on its end of weight 2.5 kN which drops through a distance of 4 mm before it strikes the rod. Find the shortest length of rod which will bear the impact if the stress is not to exceed 150 MPa. E = 210 GPa.
(407.9 mm)

19. A bar 1 m long as shown in Fig. 4.24 is subjected to an axial pull such that the maximum stress is equal to 160 MPa. If E = 200 GPa, calculate the strain energy stored in the bar.
(3.359 Nm)

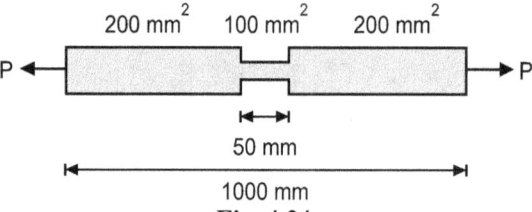

Fig. 4.24

20. Two circular bars of some material have the same length L. One bar has diameter 'd' for a length $\frac{L}{3}$ and diameter '2d' for the remaining length. The other bar has a diameter '2d' for a length $\frac{2L}{3}$ and the diameter '3d' for the remaining length. The bars are subjected to same axial loads. Compare the amount of strain energy in the bar. Compare also the amount of strain energy in them when the maximum stress induced in both the bars is the same, the stress being within elastic limit. $\left(\frac{27}{11}, \frac{27}{176}\right)$

❏❏❏

# Unit – III

## CHAPTER FIVE

# SHEAR FORCE AND BENDING MOMENT (PART-A)

## 5.1 INTRODUCTION

We have so far studied stresses set up in a member due to axial force. As discussed in chapter 1, the axial force may or may not be constant along the length of member. When axial force is not constant along the length of member, we had used method of section to evaluate the axial force at a section of our interest and axial force diagrams were drawn to study the variation of axial force along the length of member. In this chapter, our interest is to study the effect of transverse loading on the member.

*Beam is a structural member which carries lateral or transverse forces i.e. forces at right angles to the axis of the member.* The study of these transverse loads, however, is complicated by the fact that the loading effects vary from section to section of the beam. As a preliminary to study the stresses in beams, we shall study the variation of shear and bending moment at various cross-sections of the beam. Beams may be straight or curved, but we shall study only straight beams in this chapter. Also the forces applied to the beam will be assumed to lie in the same plane. All the beams discussed will be *statically determinate* i.e. unknown reactions can be determined by applying equations of static equilibrium.

## 5.2 TYPES OF SUPPORTS

In making sketches of structures or structural members it will be convenient to make use of symbols to show the manner in which it is supported. The various types of supports commonly employed in structural arrangements and their description are given in Table 5.1.

**Table 5.1**

| Sr. No. | Support type | Symbol | Description |
|---|---|---|---|
| 1. | Hinged or pinned | | Horizontal or vertical movement of the point of support, A, is prevented, but free rotation about the point of support is possible. |
| 2. | Roller/Link | Rollers / Link | Movement normal to the plane on which rollers are supported is prevented, but movement parallel to the surface of support and rotation about the point of support is possible. |
| 3. | Fixed | | Movement or rotation in any direction is absolutely prevented. |

From the above discussion of various types of supports, it must be clear that, a hinged or a pinned support is capable of resisting a force acting in any direction of the plane. Hence, in general, the reaction at such a support may have two components, one in the horizontal and one in the vertical direction. The roller or link support is capable of resisting a force only in the direction normal to the plane on which it is supported. The fixed support is capable of resisting a force in any direction and is also capable of resisting a couple or a moment.

Thus, two reaction components are possible at hinged end, one reaction component is possible at roller end and three reaction components are possible at the fixed end as shown in Fig. 5.1.

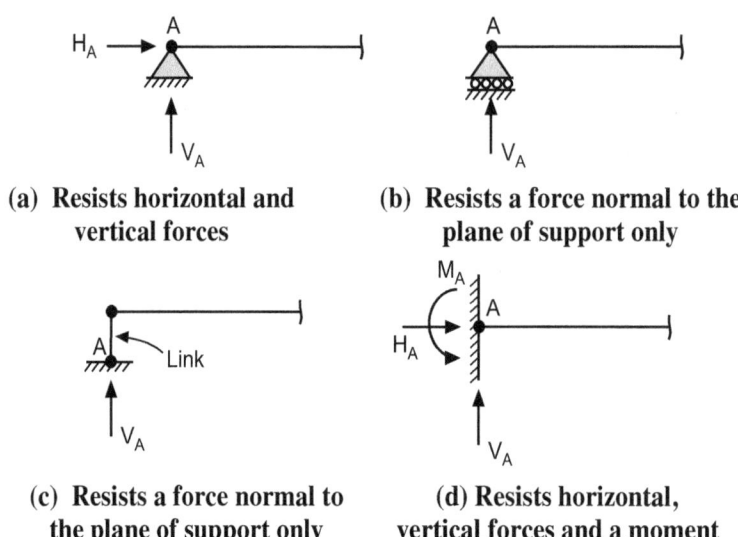

(a) Resists horizontal and vertical forces

(b) Resists a force normal to the plane of support only

(c) Resists a force normal to the plane of support only

(d) Resists horizontal, vertical forces and a moment

Fig. 5.1

## 5.3 TYPES OF LOADS

A beam may be subjected to the following types of loads :

(i) **Concentrated or Point Loads** : These loads act on a very small area and hence it can be assumed to act at a point as shown in Fig. 5.2 (a). Magnitude of the point load is expressed in **N or kN.**

(ii) **Uniformly Distributed Load (UDL)** : A load which is spread over a length of beam such that, each unit length is loaded to the same extent is known as uniformly distributed load (UDL), as shown in Fig. 5.2 (b). The intensity of UDL is expressed in **N/m or kN/m.**

(iii) **Uniformly Varying Load (UVL)** : A load which is spread over a length of beam such that, its extent varies uniformly on each unit length is known as uniformly varying load (UVL); as shown in Fig. 5.2 (c), (d). The intensity of UVL is expressed in **N/m or kN/m.**

(iv) **Couple or Moment :** A beam may be subjected to couple or moment at a point as shown in Fig. 5.2 (d). The magnitude of couple or moment is expressed in **Nm** or **kNm**.

(v) **Bracket Loads :** A beam may be subjected to a bracket load as shown in Fig. 5.2 (g) which ultimately result in **point load** and **couple** at the point of attachment of bracket with the beam.

The reactions from secondary beams, columns, brackets etc. are generally idealized as concentrated or point loads. The self weight of beam, live load etc. are generally uniformly distributed over the length of beam. Loading on side walls of water tanks, lintels, retaining walls etc. is uniformly varying load. Point loads on brackets or point loads eccentric to the axis of the member result in couples.

There may also be various combinations of these loadings. All these loads are assumed to act in one plane, called as plane of loading. To get the reactions set up by various *distributed loads,* one needs only to consider the load replaced by an *equivalent concentrated load acting at its centre of gravity.*

## 5.4 REACTIONS

If a body, subjected to forces acting in a plane, is at rest, there are three conditions of equilibrium which must be satisfied.

$$\Sigma F_x = 0 \, ; \quad \Sigma F_y = 0 \quad \text{and} \quad \Sigma M_z = 0$$

It follows that, in determining the reactions acting on the body, the loads being known, not more than three unknown quantities can be found. There are three things which must be known about each force in order to have it fully determined : *its magnitude, its direction, and its point of application or line of action.* If knowledge of all these concerning one reaction is lacking, then the magnitude, direction and point of application or line of action of all other forces acting on the structure must be known. This reaction would then hold the body at equilibrium.

It must be remembered that, the number of unknowns which can be determined is fixed by the number of equations available, and it makes no difference whether they pertain to one reaction or to several reactions as long as the unknown quantities do not exceed in number of independent equations.

To find the reactions of given beam or structure, first of all we remove the supports and show the respective reaction components in their places and draw complete free body diagram (FBD). Then apply laws of statics to get the required unknown reactions. *Sign convention* used for applying laws of *statics* is as under :

(i) All horizontal forces to the right are considered positive.

(ii) All vertical forces acting upwards are considered positive.

(iii) All anticlockwise moments are considered positive.

Forces, moments, opposite of above are considered negative.

## 5.5 TYPES OF BEAMS

Beams are basically classified as statically determinate and statically indeterminate beams. When unknown reactions can be obtained by use of equations of static equilibrium alone, it is called as statically determinate. The various types of statically determinate beams are (i) Simply supported beam, (ii) Simple beam, (iii) Cantilever beam, (iv) Overhanging beam etc. While the various types of statically indeterminate beams are (i) Fixed beams, (ii) Continuous beams, (iii) Propped cantilevers etc. These various types of beams are shown in Fig. 5.2.

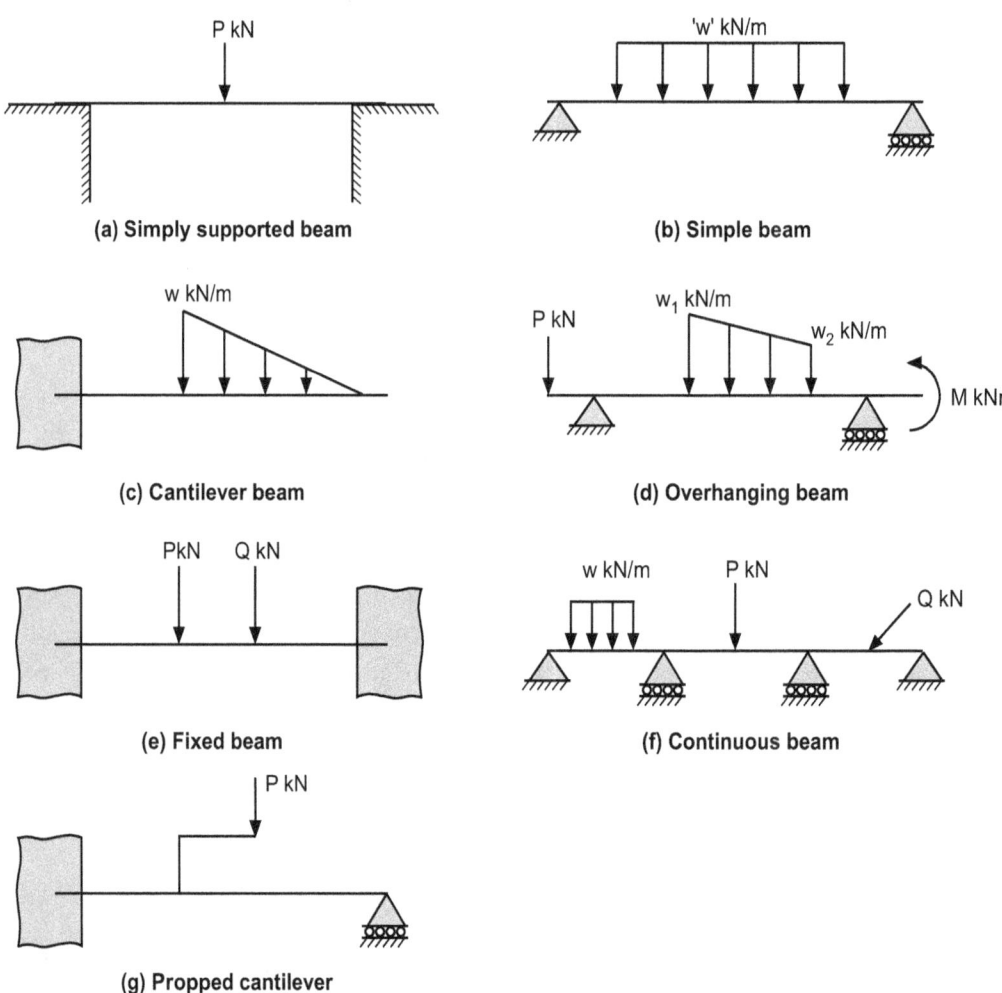

Fig. 5.2 : Various types of beams

## 5.6 SHEAR FORCE AND BENDING MOMENT

Consider a FBD of beam as shown in Fig. 5.3 (a). The unknown reactions are determined by equations of laws of statics and having obtained the unknown reactions, *method of section* is used to find shear force and bending moment at a cross-section.

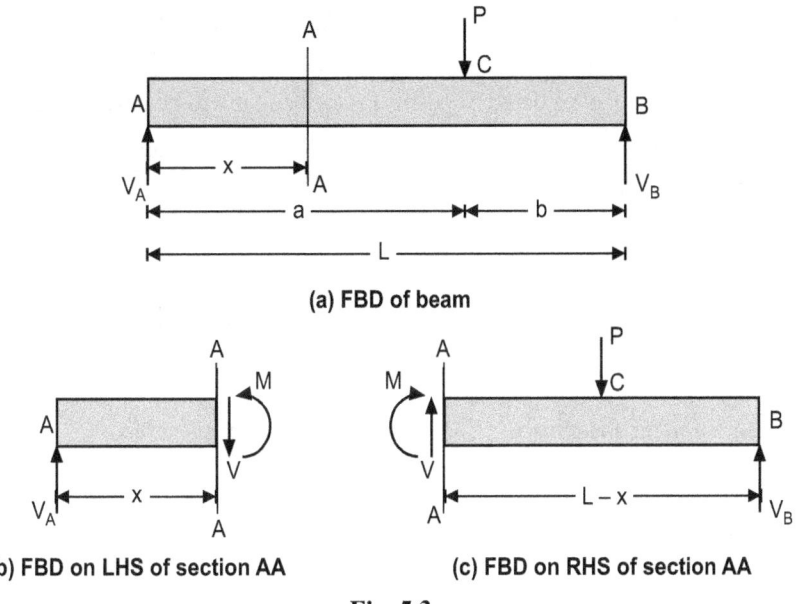

**Fig. 5.3**

Fig. 5.3 (b) shows the FBD of part of the beam on left hand side of the section considered at a distance x from A. Since the beam and all its parts are in equilibrium, this section of the beam must be in equilibrium. First consider the equilibrium of the vertical forces i.e. $\sum F_y = 0$. This equation shows that, there must be a downward vertical force equal in magnitude to the reaction at left support. The only surface on which such a force can act is that on the right end of the free body. This downward force is called as the shear force and is designated as V or SF. Since, there are no horizontal forces, a moment equation is all that remains to be satisfied for equilibrium of the element shown. We can, of course, write a moment equation about any point in the plane of the diagram, but it is convenient to write it with respect to the right hand end of the section. Assuming unknown couple at this section of magnitude M, we have

$$M - V_A(x) = 0$$

∴
$$M = V_A(x)$$

This quantity is known as the bending moment and is designated as M or BM.

Fig. 5.3 (c) shows FBD of part of the beam on right hand side of the section considered. *It should be noted that magnitude and nature of the shear force and bending moment at a section whether computed from left or right hand side of the section remains the same.* The side to be chosen for calculation is that side on which fewer external forces are acting and the *section is to be considered normal to the axis of the beam.*

Thus, shear force and bending moment at a section can be defined as follows :

**Shear force :** It is the algebraic sum of all the external forces acting parallel to the section, on any one side of the section.

**Bending moment :** It is the algebraic sum of the moments of all the external forces acting on any one side of the section taken about the centre of gravity of section.

## 5.6.1 Sign Conventions for Shear Force and Bending Moment

**(a) Shear Force :** An upward shear force to the left of the section or downward shear force to the right of the section is considered as positive; otherwise it will be negative. See Fig. 5.4 (a).

This sign convention of shear force leads to the shear effect as shown in Fig. 5.4 (b).

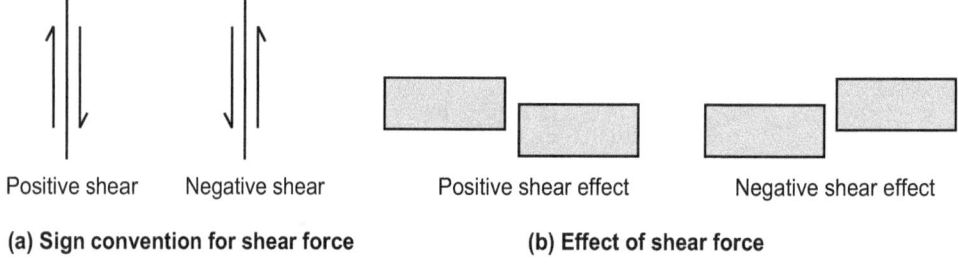

(a) Sign convention for shear force     (b) Effect of shear force

Fig. 5.4

**(b) Bending Moment :** The bending moment which produces the deformation of the beam **concave upwards** is called **sagging** bending moment and it is considered **positive**. The bending moment which produces the deformation of the beam **convex upwards** is called **hogging** bending moment and it is considered **negative**. See Fig. 5.5 (a). This sign convention of bending moment leads to the bending effect as shown in Fig. 5.5 (b).

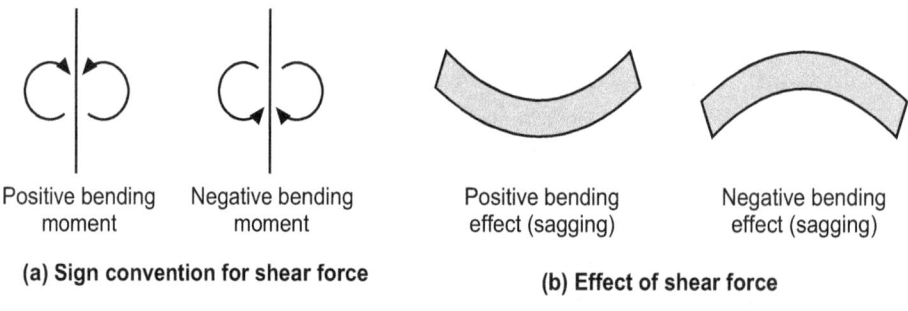

(a) Sign convention for shear force     (b) Effect of shear force

Fig. 5.5

It should be noted that, for a horizontal beam, upward external forces cause positive bending moments with respect to any section, while the downward external forces cause negative bending moments.

## 5.7 SHEAR FORCE AND BENDING MOMENT DIAGRAMS (SFD AND BMD)

The shear force and bending moment can be calculated numerically at any particular section. But from the design point of view, we are interested in knowing the manner in which these values vary, along the length of beam. This can be done by plotting the shear force or the bending moment as ordinate and the position of the cross-section as abscissa to give shear force diagram (SFD) and bending moment diagram (BMD) respectively. While plotting these diagrams, positive values are plotted above the reference line and negative values below it. The shear force and bending moment diagrams can be plotted from shear force and bending moment equations written for respective zones. The nature of these curves depends on the type of loading the beam is subjected to. This is illustrated in following simple examples.

# SOLVED EXAMPLES

**Example 5.1 :** Draw SFD and BMD for the following cantilever beams.

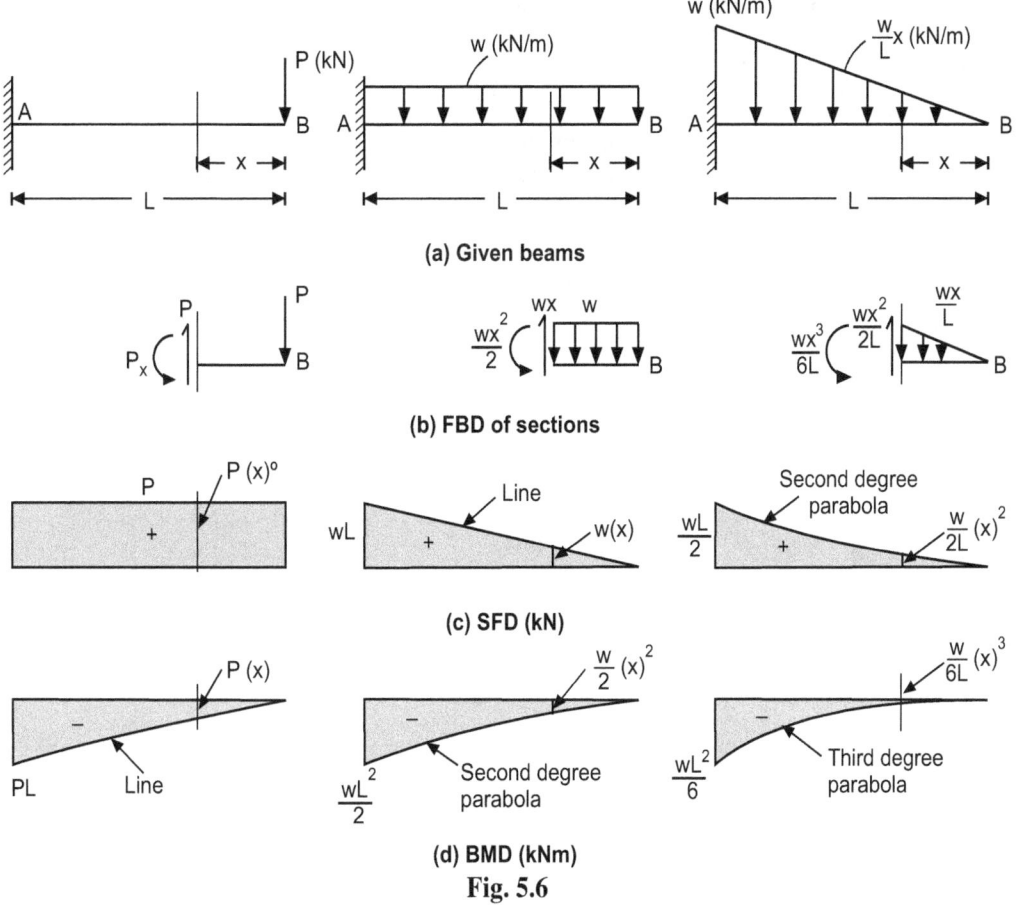

(a) Given beams
(b) FBD of sections
(c) SFD (kN)
(d) BMD (kNm)
Fig. 5.6

**Data** : Given beams as shown in Fig. 5.6 (a).

**Required** : SFD and BMD.

**Concept** : Consider a section at a distance 'x' from free end B as shown in Fig. 5.6 (a) and write the equations of SF and BM for the respective beams.

**Solution** : **(i) Case I :** Cantilever beam with point load at free end.

| Zone | Origin | Limits | $SF_{(x)}$ | $BM_{(x)}$ | SF at $x = 0$ | SF at $x = L$ | BM at $x = 0$ | BM at $x = L$ |
|------|--------|--------|------------|------------|---------------|---------------|---------------|---------------|
| BA | B | 0 – L | P | – Px | P | P | 0 | – PL |

**Note :** (i) Shear force is independent of position of section defined by distance 'x'. Therefore, shear force is constant throughout the beam; and SFD is as shown in Fig. 5.6 (c).

(ii) Bending moment is linear function of 'x'. Therefore, bending moment is zero at free end and maximum at fixed end. The variation of BM is linear along the length of beam as shown in Fig. 5.6 (d).

**(ii) Case II : Cantilever beam with UDL throughout the span.**

| Zone | Origin | Limits | SF$_{(x)}$ | BM$_{(x)}$ | SF at x = 0 | SF at x = L | BM at x = 0 | BM at x = L |
|---|---|---|---|---|---|---|---|---|
| BA | B | 0 – L | wx | $-\dfrac{wx^2}{2}$ | 0 | wL | 0 | $-\dfrac{wL^2}{2}$ |

**Note :** (i) Shear force is linear function of 'x'. Therefore, shear force is zero at free end and maximum at fixed end. The variation of shear is linear along the length of beam as shown in Fig. 5.6 (c).

(ii) Bending moment is function of (x)². Therefore, bending moment is zero at free end and maximum at fixed end. The variation of bending moment is second degree parabolic along the length of beam as shown in Fig. 5.6 (d).

**(iii) Case III : Cantilever beam carrying triangular load (UVL) as shown in Fig. 5.6 (a).** Intensity of triangular load at a distance 'x' from free end is given by $\dfrac{wx}{L}$ from similar triangles.

| Zone | Origin | Limits | SF$_{(x)}$ | BM$_{(x)}$ | SF at x = 0 | SF at x = L | BM at x = 0 | BM at x = L |
|---|---|---|---|---|---|---|---|---|
| BA | B | 0 – L | $\dfrac{1}{2} \times \left(\dfrac{wx}{L}\right) x = \dfrac{wx^2}{2L}$ | $-\dfrac{wx^2}{2L}\left(\dfrac{x}{3}\right) = -\dfrac{wx^3}{6L}$ | 0 | $\dfrac{wL}{2}$ | 0 | $-\dfrac{wL^2}{6}$ |

**Note :** (i) Shear force is a function of (x)². Therefore, shear force is zero at free end and maximum at fixed end. The variation of shear force is second degree parabolic along the length of beam as shown in Fig. 5.6 (c).

(ii) Bending moment is a function of (x)³. Therefore, bending moment is zero at free end and maximum at fixed end. The variation of bending moment is third degree parabolic along the length of beam as shown in Fig. 5.6 (d).

**Example 5.2 :** Draw SF and BM diagrams for following simple beams.

**Data** : As shown in Fig. 5.7 (a).

**Required** : SFD and BMD.

**Solution** : (i) **Case I :** Simple beam with single point load.

**Reactions :** $\Sigma M_A = 0$;  $V_B \times L - Pa = 0$  $\therefore$  $V_B = \dfrac{Pa}{L}$ (↑)

$\Sigma F_y = 0$;  $\therefore$  $V_A + V_B - P = 0$

$\therefore$  $V_A = P - \dfrac{Pa}{L} = \dfrac{Pb}{L}$ (↑)

FBD of beam is as shown in Fig. 5.7 (b).

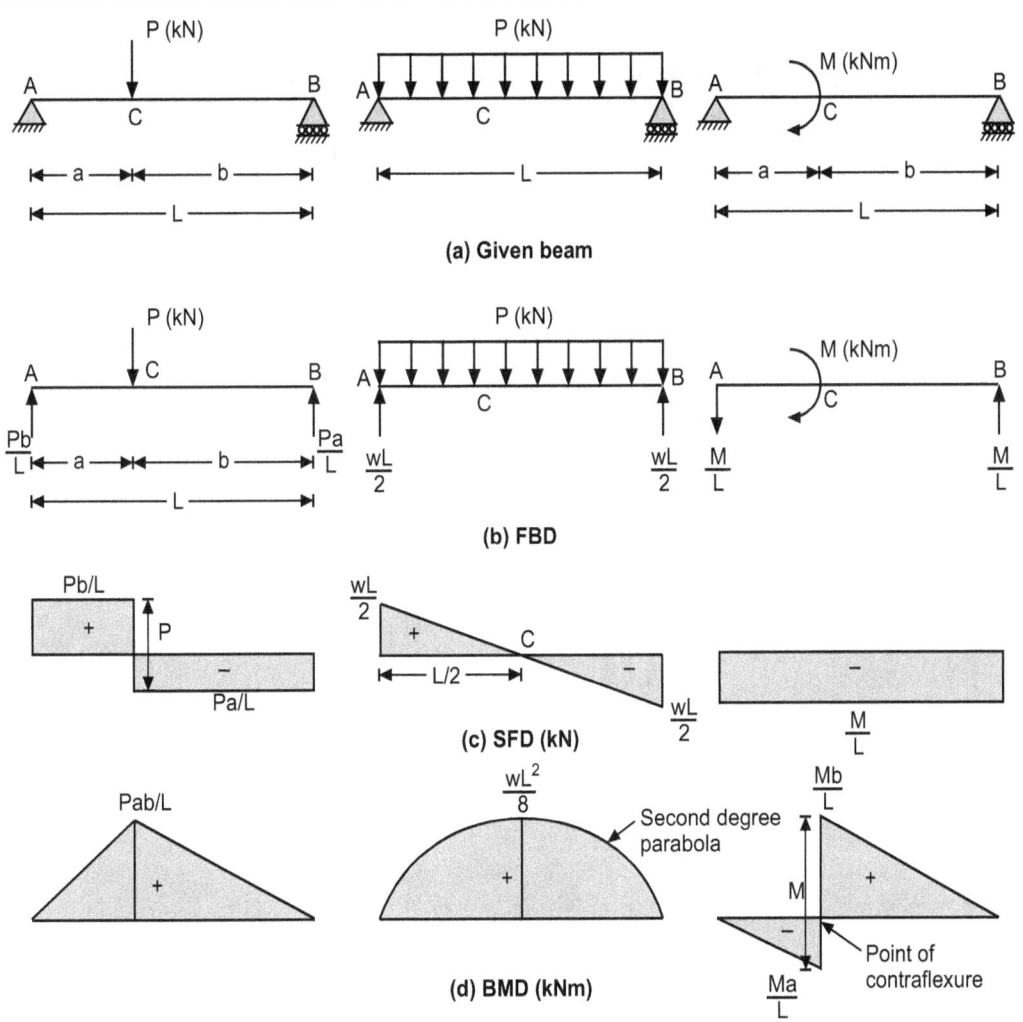

**Fig. 5.7**

**SF calculations :** $SF_A = \dfrac{Pb}{L}$

$$SF \text{ (just to the left of C)} = \dfrac{Pb}{L}$$

$$SF \text{ (just to the right of C)} = \dfrac{Pb}{L} - P = -\dfrac{Pa}{L}$$

$$SF_B = -\dfrac{Pa}{L}$$

**Note :** It is important to find shear force on either side of the concentrated force. SFD is as shown in Fig. 5.7 (c).

**BM Calculations :** $BM_A = BM_B = 0$

$$BM_C = \left(\dfrac{Pb}{L}\right) a = \dfrac{Pab}{L}$$

BMD is as shown in Fig. 5.7 (d).

**Note :** (i) SFD is parallel to the reference line.
(ii) Bending moment variation is linear along the length of beam.
(iii) Vertical drop in SFD indicates sudden change in the value of shear force at a section. The magnitude of drop in SF diagram is equal to the magnitude of point load acting at a section.
(iv) Bending moment is maximum at 'C' where, shear force changes the sign.

**(ii) Case II : Simple beam with UDL.**

**Reactions :** By symmetry ; $V_A = V_B = \dfrac{wL}{2}$ (↑)

FBD of beam is as shown in Fig. 5.6 (b).

**SF Calculations :** Consider a section at a distance 'x' from A; FBD of part of the beam is as shown in Fig. 5.8.

Shear force at a distance 'x' = $SF_x = V = \dfrac{wL}{2} - wx$ ... (i)

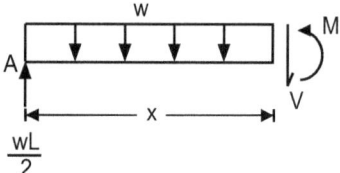

**Fig. 5.8**

Put x = 0 for shear force at A, $SF_A = \dfrac{wL}{2}$

Put x = L for shear force at B, $SF_B = \dfrac{wL}{2} - wL = \dfrac{-wL}{2}$

Equating equation (i) to zero, we can locate the section of zero shear force as,

$$\dfrac{wL}{2} - wx = 0 \quad \therefore \quad x = \dfrac{L}{2}$$

SFD is as shown in Fig. 5.7 (c).

**BM Calculations :** From Fig. 5.8, BM at a distance x

$$= BM_x = M = \dfrac{wL}{2}(x) - \dfrac{wx^2}{2} \quad \text{... (ii)}$$

Put x = 0 for bending moment at A, $BM_A = 0$

Put x = L for bending moment at B, $BM_B = \dfrac{wL^2}{2} - \dfrac{wL^2}{2} = 0$

Put x = $\dfrac{L}{2}$ for BM at point of zero SF i.e. at C, $BM_C = \dfrac{wL}{2}\left(\dfrac{L}{2}\right) - \dfrac{w}{2}\left(\dfrac{L}{2}\right)^2$

$$BM_C = \dfrac{wL^2}{4} - \dfrac{wL^2}{8} = \dfrac{wL^2}{8}$$

BMD is as shown in Fig. 5.7 (d).

**Note :** (i) Shear force variation is linear along the length of beam.

(ii) Bending moment variation is second degree parabolic along the length of beam.

(iii) Bending moment is maximum at C where shear force changes the sign. *For locating the section of zero shear force, shear force equation for the respective zone shall be equated to zero.*

**(iii) Case III :** Simple beam carrying a couple.

**Reaction :** $\sum M_A = 0$; $\quad V_B \times L - M = 0 \quad \therefore \quad V_B = \dfrac{M}{L}$ (↑)

$\sum F_y = 0$; $\quad V_A + V_B = 0 \quad \therefore \quad V_A = -\dfrac{M}{L} = \dfrac{M}{L}$ (↓)

FBD of beam is as shown in Fig. 5.7 (b).

**SF Calculations :** Since there is no vertical loading on the beam, shear force is constant throughout and $SF = -\dfrac{M}{L}$.

SFD is as shown in Fig. 5.7 (c).

**BM Calculations :** $\quad BM_A = BM_B = 0$

$$BM \text{ (just to the left of C)} = -\dfrac{M}{L} a$$

$$BM \text{ (just to the right of C)} = \dfrac{M}{L} b.$$

**Note :** It is important to find bending moment on either side of a couple.

BMD is as shown in Fig. 5.7 (d).

**Note :** (i) SFD is parallel to the reference line.

(ii) Bending moment variation is linear along the length of beam.

(iii) At a section where couple is acting, shear force does not change.

(iv) Section where bending moment changes its sign is called as point of *contraflexure*. Since change of sign is possible, only when bending moment at point of contraflexure is zero, it is also called as point of zero bending moment or point of **inflection**. It should be understood that a point of contraflexure is necessarily a point of inflection, but point of inflection need not be a point of contraflexure. *For locating point of contraflexure, bending moment equation in the respective zone shall be equated to zero.*

(v) Vertical drop in the BMD indicates sudden change in the value of bending moment at a section. The magnitude of drop in the BM diagram is equal to the magnitude of couple acting at a section.

## 5.8 RELATIONSHIP BETWEEN LOAD, SHEAR AND BENDING MOMENT

The relationship between load, shear and bending moment can be derived as under. Consider a beam supported and loaded as shown in Fig. 5.9 (a).

Let $V_x$ and $M_x$ be the shear and bending moment on a section at a distance 'x' from A. Likewise $V_x + dV_x$ and $M_x + dM_x$ are the shear and bending moment on a section at a distance x + dx from A. The free body diagram of the segment of the beam which is dx in length is shown in Fig. 5.9 (b).

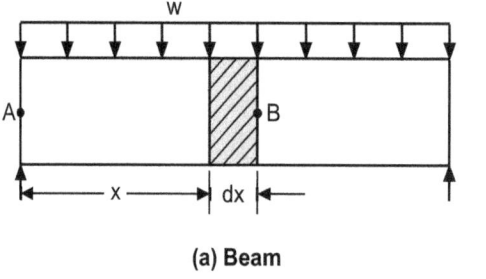
(a) Beam

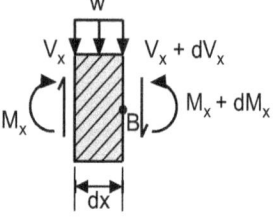
(b) FBD of beam segement

Fig. 5.9

Applying equations of equilibrium to FBD of segment as under :

$\Sigma F_y = 0 \Rightarrow \quad V_x - (V_x + dV_x) - w \cdot dx = 0$

$$dV_x = -w \cdot dx$$

$\therefore \quad \dfrac{dV_x}{dx} = -w \qquad \ldots (5.1)$

Thus, *the rate of decrease of shear force with respect to x, on any section at a distance 'x' from left end of the beam is equal to the intensity of load at the section.*

$\Sigma M_B = 0 \Rightarrow \quad V_x \cdot dx + M_x = M_x + dM_x + w\dfrac{dx^2}{2}$

The term $w\dfrac{dx^2}{2}$ being very small; can be neglected.

$$dM_x = V_x \cdot dx$$

$\dfrac{dM_x}{dx} = V_x \qquad \ldots (5.2)$

Thus, *the rate of increase of bending moment with respect to 'x', on any section at a distance 'x' from left end of the beam, is equal to shear at the section.*

**Example 5.3** : The beam is supported and loaded as shown in Fig. 5.10 (a). Draw SFD and BMD indicating all the important values.

**Data** : As shown in Fig. 5.10 (a).

**Required** : SFD, BMD.

**Solution** : (i) Reactions :

$\Sigma F_y = 0;$   $V_A - 20 - 30 = 0$   $\therefore$   $V_A = 50$ kN (↑)

$\Sigma M_A = 0;$   $M_A - 20 \times 1 - 30 \times 2.5 = 0$   $\therefore$   $M_A = 95$ kNm (↺)

$\Sigma F_x = 0;$   $H_A = 0$

FBD of beam is as shown in Fig. 5.10 (b).

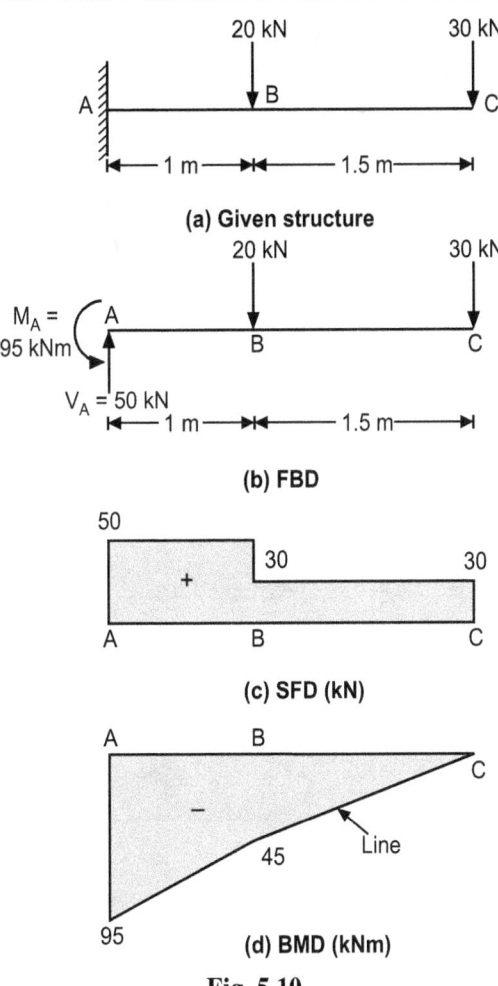

Fig. 5.10

(ii) SF calculations :

$$SF_A = 50 \text{ kN}$$
$$SF_B \text{ (just to the left)} = 50 \text{ kN}$$
$$SF_B \text{ (just to the right)} = 50 - 20 = 30 \text{ kN}$$
$$SF_C = 30 \text{ kN}$$

SFD is as shown in Fig. 5.10 (c).

(iii) BM calculations :

$$BM_A = -95 \text{ kNm}$$
$$BM_B = -30 \times 1.5 = -45 \text{ kNm}$$
$$BM_C = 0$$

BMD is as shown in Fig. 5.10 (d).

**Example 5.4 :** The beam is supported and loaded as shown in Fig. 5.11 (a). Draw SFD and BMD indicating all important values.

**Data** : As shown in Fig. 5.11 (a).

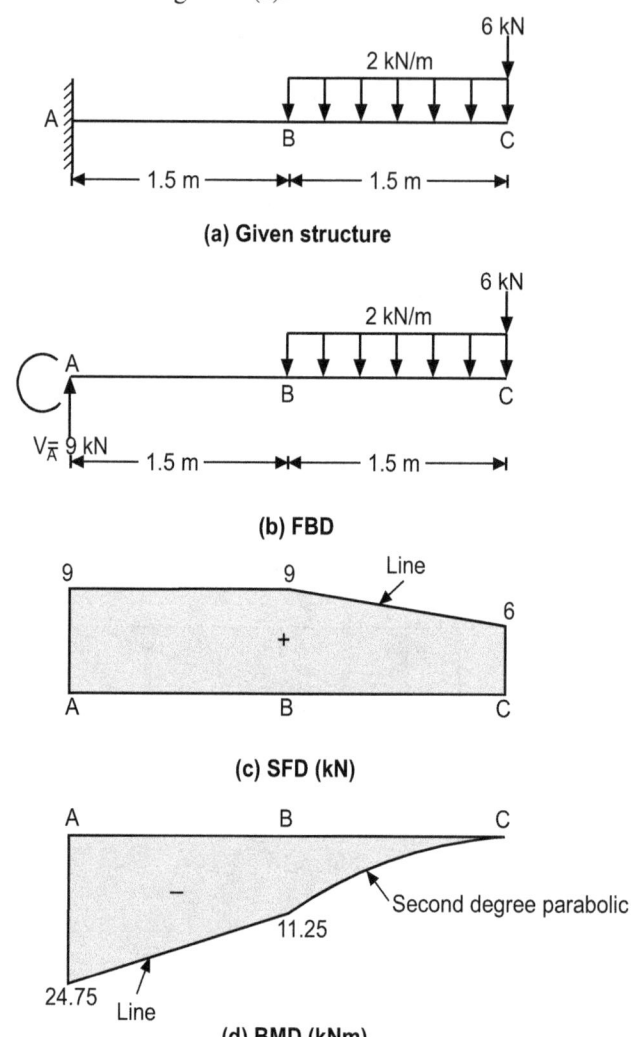

Fig. 5.11

**Required** : SFD, BMD.

**Solution** : (i) Reactions :

$\Sigma F_y = 0$ ;  $V_A - 2 \times 1.5 - 6 = 0$

∴  $V_A = 9$ kN (↑)

$\Sigma M_A = 0$ ;  $M_A - 2 \times 1.5 \times 2.25 - 6 \times 3 = 0$

  $M_A = 24.75$ kN.m (↻)

$\Sigma F_x = 0$ ;  $H_A = 0$

FBD of beam is as shown in Fig. 5.11 (b).

(ii) SF calculations :

$$SF_A = SF_B = 9 \text{ kN}$$
$$SF_C = 6 \text{ kN}$$

SFD is as shown in Fig. 5.11 (c).

(iii) BM calculations :

$$BM_A = -24.75 \text{ kN.m}$$
$$BM_B = -24.75 + 9 \times 1.5 = -11.25 \text{ kN.m}$$
$$BM_C = 0$$

BMD is as shown in Fig. 5.11 (d).

**Example 5.5 :** The beam is supported and loaded as shown in Fig. 5.12 (a). Draw SFD and BMD indicating all the important values.

**Data** : As shown in Fig. 5.12 (a).

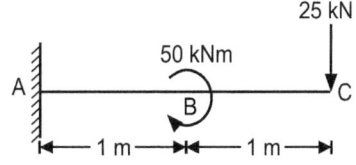

(a) Given structure

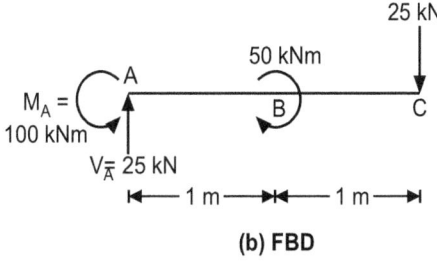

(b) FBD

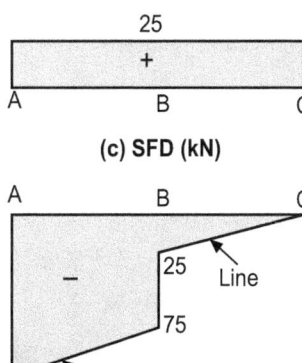

(c) SFD (kN)

(d) BMD (kN.m)

Fig. 5.12

**Required :** SFD, BMD.

**Solution** : (i) Reactions :

$\Sigma F_y = 0$;  $V_A - 25 = 0$   $\therefore$  $V_A = 25$ kN ($\uparrow$)

$\Sigma M_A = 0$;  $M_A - 50 - 25 \times 2 = 0$

$\therefore$  $M_A = 100$ kN.m ($\circlearrowleft$)

$\Sigma F_x = 0$;  $H_A = 0$

FBD of beam is as shown in Fig. 5.12 (b).

(ii) SF calculations :

$$SF_A = SF_B = SF_C = 25 \text{ kN}$$

SFD is as shown in Fig. 5.12 (c).

(iii) BM calculations :

$BM_A = -100$ kN.m

$BM_B$ (just to the left) $= -100 + 25 \times 1 = -75$ kN.m

$BM_B$ (just to the right) $= -75 + 50 = -25$ kN.m

$BM_C = 0$

BMD is as shown in Fig. 5.12 (d).

**Example 5.6** : The beam is supported and loaded as shown in Fig. 5.13 (a). Draw SFD and BMD indicating all the important values.

**Data** : As shown in Fig. 5.13 (a).

**Required** : SFD, BMD.

**Solution** : (i) Reactions :

$\Sigma F_y = 0$;  $V_A - 10 \times 2 = 0$   $\therefore$  $V_A = 20$ kN ($\uparrow$)

$\Sigma M_A = 0$;  $M_A - 25 - 10 \times \frac{2^2}{2} = 0$   $\therefore$  $M_A = 45$ kN.m ($\circlearrowleft$)

$\Sigma F_x = 0$;  $H_A = 0$

FBD of beam is as shown in Fig. 5.13 (b).

(ii) SF calculations :

$SF_A = 20$ kN

$SF_C = 0$

SFD is as shown in Fig. 5.13 (c).

(iii) BM calculations :

$BM_A = -45$ kN.m

$BM_B$ (just to the left) $= -45 + 20 \times 1 - 10 \times \frac{1^2}{2} = -30$ kN.m

$BM_B$ (just to the right) $= -30 + 25 = -5$ kN.m

$BM_C = 0$

BMD is as shown in Fig. 5.13 (d).

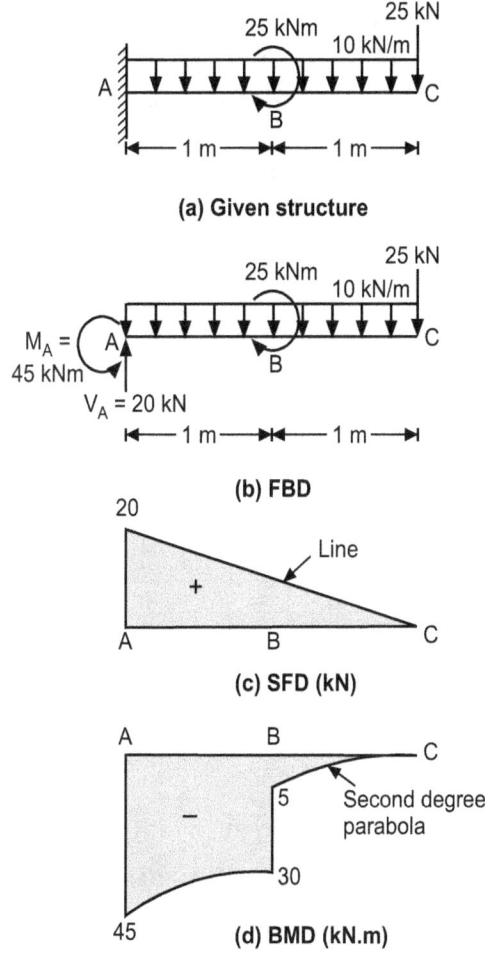

Fig. 5.13

**Example 5.7 :** The beam is supported and loaded as shown in Fig. 5.14 (a). Draw SFD and BMD indicating all the important values.

**Data**   :   As shown in Fig. 5.14 (a).

**Required** :   SFD, BMD.

**Solution** :   (i) Reactions :

$\Sigma F_y = 0$;     $V_A = 0$

$\Sigma M_A = 0$;    $M_A - 75 + 25 - 50 = 0$

∴     $M_A = 100$ kN.m (↺)

FBD of beam is as shown in Fig. 5.14 (b).

(ii)   SF calculations :

Beam is not subjected to any shear force.

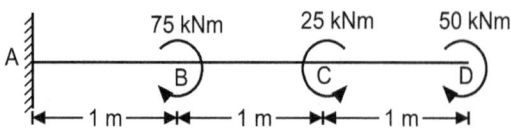

(a) Given structure

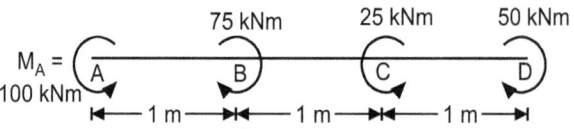

(b) FBD

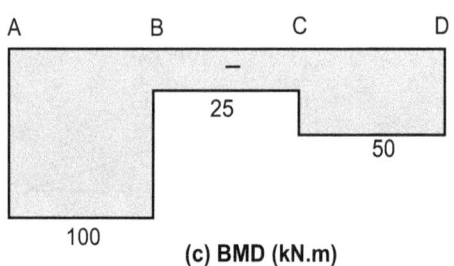

(c) BMD (kN.m)

Fig. 5.14

(iii) BM calculations :

$$BM_A = -100 \text{ kN.m}$$

$BM_B$ (just to the left) $= -100$ kN.m

$BM_B$ (just to the right) $= -100 + 75 = -25$ kN.m

$BM_C$ (just to the left) $= -25$ kN.m

$BM_C$ (just to the right) $= -25 - 25 = -50$ kN.m

$BM_D = -50$ kN.m

BMD is as shown in Fig. 5.14 (c).

**Example 5.8 :** Draw SFD and BMD for the cantilever beam shown in Fig. 5.15 (a).

**Data** : As shown in Fig. 5.15 (a).

**Required** : SFD, BMD.

**Solution** : (i) Reactions :

$\Sigma F_y = 0$;    $V_A - \frac{1}{2} \times w \times L = 0$    $\therefore V_A = \frac{wL}{2}$ (↑)

$\Sigma M_A = 0$;    $M_A - \frac{wL}{2} \times \frac{2L}{3} = 0$    $\therefore M_A = \frac{wL^2}{3}$ (↺)

FBD of beam is as shown in Fig. 5.15 (b).

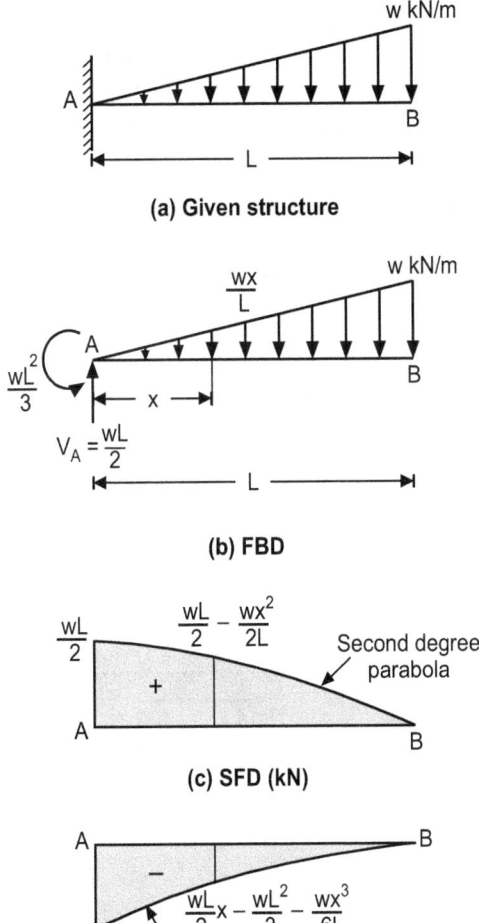

**Fig. 5.15**

(ii) SF and BM :

| Zone | Origin | Limits | SF(x) | BM(x) | SF at x = 0 | SF at x = L | BM at x = 0 | BM at x = L |
|---|---|---|---|---|---|---|---|---|
| AB | A | 0 – L | $\dfrac{wL}{2} - \dfrac{wx^2}{2L}$ | $\dfrac{wL}{2}x - \dfrac{wL^2}{3} - \dfrac{wx^3}{6L}$ | $\dfrac{wL}{2}$ | 0 | $\dfrac{wL^2}{3}$ | 0 |

SFD and BMD are as shown in Fig. 5.15 (c) and Fig. 5.15 (d) respectively.

**Example 5.9 :** The beam is supported and loaded as shown in Fig. 5.16 (a). Draw SFD and BMD indicating all the important values.

**Data** : As shown in Fig. 5.16 (a).

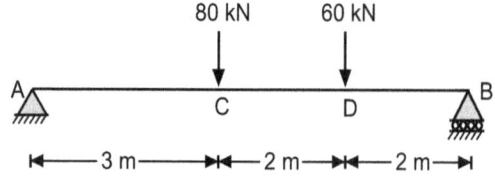

(a) Given structure

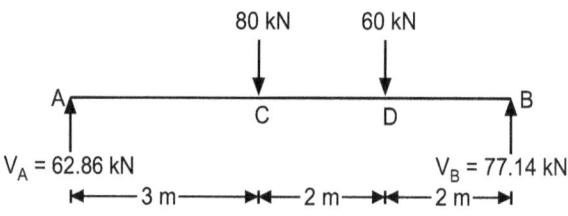

(b) FBD

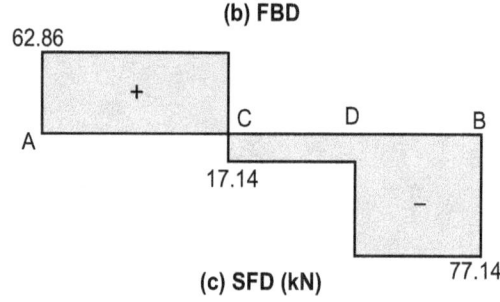

(c) SFD (kN)

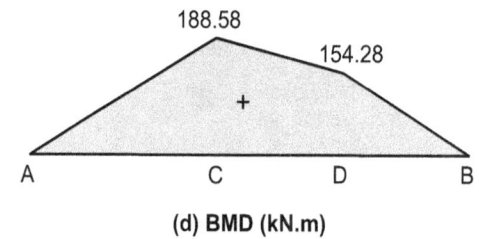

(d) BMD (kN.m)

Fig. 5.16

**Required** : SFD, BMD.

**Solution** : (i) Reactions :

$\Sigma M_A = 0$ ;   $V_B \times 7 - 60 \times 5 - 80 \times 3 = 0$

$\therefore$   $V_B = 77.14$ kN ($\uparrow$)

$\Sigma F_y = 0$ ;   $V_A + V_B - 80 - 60 = 0$

$\therefore$   $V_A = 62.86$ kN ($\uparrow$)

$\Sigma F_x = 0$ ;   $H_A = 0$

FBD of beam is as shown in Fig. 5.16 (b).

(ii) SF calculations :   $SF_A = 62.86$ kN

$SF_C$ (just to the left) = 62.86 kN

$SF_C$ (just to the right) = 62.86 − 80 = − 17.14 kN

$SF_D$ (just to the left) = − 17.14 kN

$SF_D$ (just to the right) = − 17.14 − 60 = − 77.14 kN

$SF_B$ = − 77.14 kN

SFD is as shown in Fig. 5.16 (c).

(iii) BM calculations : $BM_A = BM_B = 0$

$BM_C = 62.86 \times 3 = 188.58$ kN.m

$BM_D = 77.14 \times 2 = 154.28$ kN.m

BMD is as shown in Fig. 5.16 (d).

**Example 5.10 :** The beam is supported and loaded as shown in Fig. 5.17 (a). Draw SFD and BMD indicating all the important values.

**Data :** As shown in Fig. 5.17 (a).

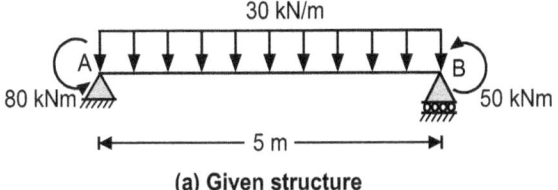

(a) Given structure

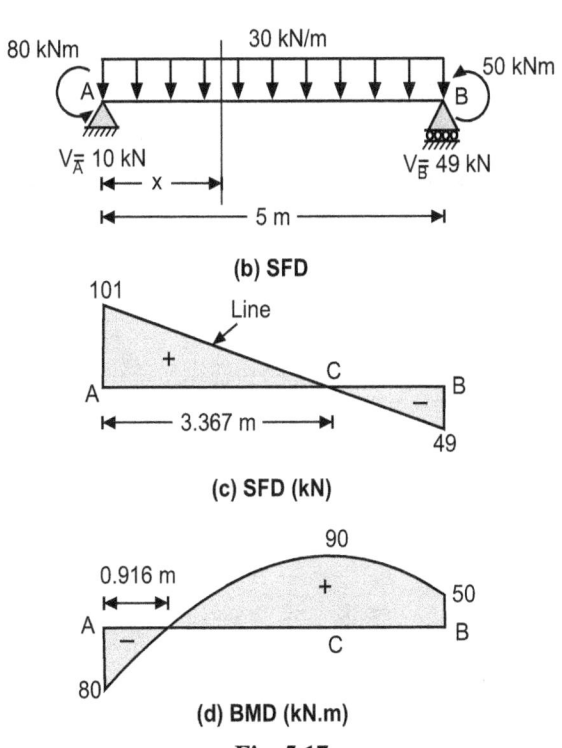

Fig. 5.17

**Required :** SFD, BMD.

**Solution** : (i) Reactions :

$\Sigma M_A = 0$; $\quad V_B \times 5 + 50 - 30 \times \dfrac{5^2}{2} + 80 = 0.$

$\therefore \qquad V_B = 49$ kN $(\uparrow)$

$\Sigma F_y = 0$; $\quad V_A + V_B - 30 \times 5 = 0$

$\therefore \qquad V_A = 101$ kN $(\uparrow)$

FBD of beam is as shown in Fig. 5.17 (b).

(ii) SF calculations :

Consider a section at a distance 'x' from 'A'.

$\qquad SF_x = 101 - 30 x$ ... (i)

put x = 0; $\qquad SF_A = 101$ kN

put x = 5 m; $\qquad SF_B = 101 - 30 \times 5 = -49$ kN

To locate point of zero SF, equate equation (i) to zero.

$\qquad 101 - 30 x = 0$

$\therefore \qquad x = 3.367$ m from A

SFD is as shown in Fig. 5.17 (c).

(iii) BM calculations :

$BM_x = 101 x - 80 - \dfrac{30 x^2}{2} = 101 x - 80 - 15 x^2$ ... (ii)

put x = 0; $\qquad BM_A = -80$ kN.m

x = 3.367 m ; $\qquad BM_C = 101 \times 3.367 - 80 - 15 (3.367)^2 = 90$ kN.m

x = 5 m ; $\qquad BM_B = 101 \times 5 - 80 - 15 (5)^2 = 50$ kN.m

To locate point of contraflexure, equate equation (ii) to zero.

$\qquad BM_x = 101 x - 80 - 15 x^2 = 0$

Solving $\qquad x = 0.916$ m from A

BMD is as shown in Fig. 5.17 (d).

**Example 5.11 :** The beam is supported and loaded as shown in Fig. 5.18 (a). Draw SFD and BMD indicating all the important values.

**Data** : As shown in Fig. 5.18 (a).

**Required** : SFD, BMD.

**Solution** : (i) Reactions :

Couple at D = $5 \times 2 \times 0.375 = 3.75$ kN.m $(\circlearrowleft)$

$\Sigma M_A = 0$; $\quad V_B \times 3 - 5 \times 2.625 - 3.75 - 5 \times 0.375 = 0$

$\therefore \qquad V_B = 6.25$ kN $(\uparrow)$

$\Sigma F_y = 0$; $\quad V_A + V_B - 5 - 5 = 0$

$\qquad V_A = 3.75$ kN $(\uparrow)$

$\Sigma F_x = 0 \qquad H_A = 0$

FBD of beam is as shown in Fig. 5.18 (b).

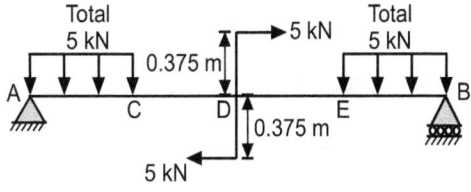

(a) Given structure

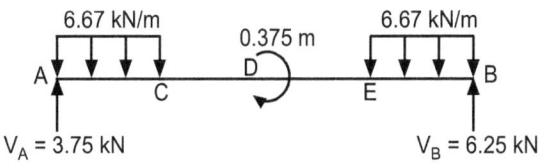

(b) FBD

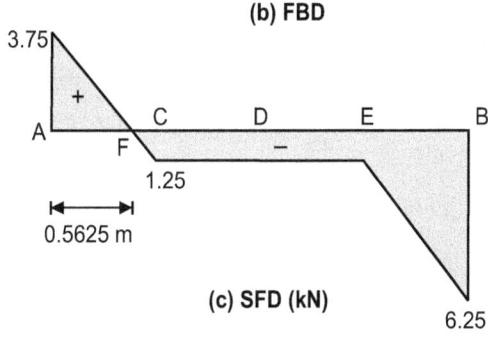

(c) SFD (kN)

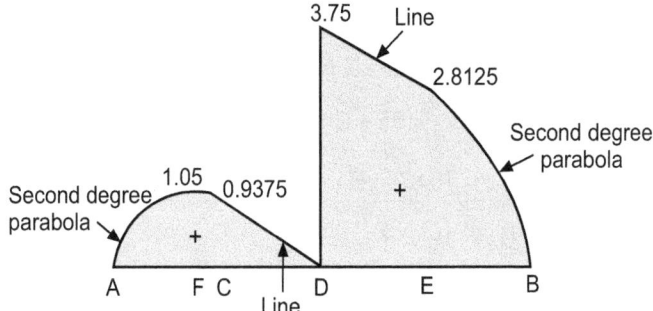

(d) BMD (kN.m)

Fig. 5.18

(ii) SF calculations :   $SF_A = 3.75$ kN

$SF_C = 3.75 - 5 = -1.25$ kN

$SF_B = -6.25$ kN

To locate point of zero SF, consider a section at a distance 'x' from A in zone AC.

$$SF_x = 3.75 - 6.67 x = 0$$

∴ $\qquad x = 0.5625$ m from A

SFD is as shown in Fig. 5.18 (c).

(iii) BM calculations :

$$BM_A = BM_B = 0$$

$$BM_C = 3.75 \times 0.75 - 5 \times \frac{0.75}{2} = 0.9375 \text{ kN.m}$$

$$\text{BM at point of zero SF} = BM_F = 3.75 \times 0.5625 - 6.67 \times \frac{(0.5625)^2}{2} = 1.05 \text{ kN.m}$$

$$BM_D \text{ (just to the left)} = 3.75 \times 1.5 - 5 \times 1.125 = 0$$

$$BM_D \text{ (just to the right)} = 0 + 3.75 = 3.75 \text{ kN.m}$$

$$BM_E = 6.25 \times 0.75 - 5 \times \frac{0.75}{2} = \mathbf{2.8125 \text{ kN.m}}$$

**Example 5.12 :** The beam is supported and loaded as shown in Fig. 5.19 (a). Draw SFD, BMD indicating all important values.

**Data** : As shown in Fig. 5.19 (a).

**Required** : SFD, BMD.

**Solution** : (i) Reactions :

$\sum M_A = 0;  \qquad V_B \times 8 - 100 - 50 - 75 \times 1 = 0$

$\qquad\qquad\qquad V_B = 28.125$ kN (↑)

$\sum F_y = 0;  \qquad V_A + V_B - 75 = 0$

$\qquad\qquad\qquad V_A = 46.875$ kN (↑)

$\sum F_x = 0;  \qquad H_A = 0$

FBD of beam is as shown in Fig. 5.19 (b).

(ii) SF calculations : $\quad SF_A = 46.875$ kN

$\qquad\qquad\qquad SF_C$ (just to the left) $= 46.875$ kN

$\qquad\qquad\qquad SF_C$ (just to the right) $= 46.875 - 75 = -28.125$ kN

$\qquad\qquad\qquad SF_D = SF_E = SF_B = -28.125$ kN

SFD is as shown in Fig. 5.19 (c).

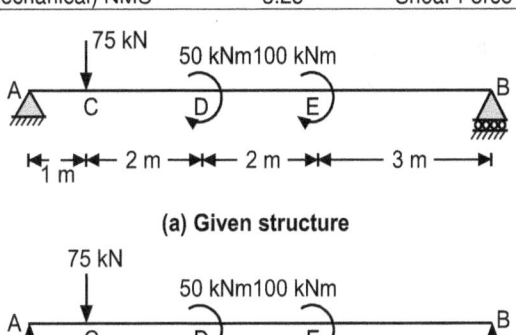

(a) Given structure

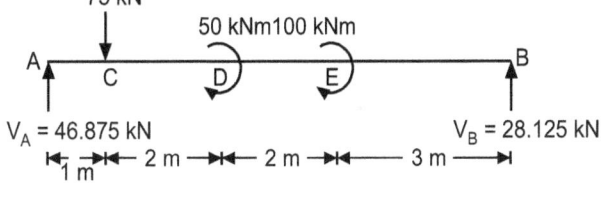

(b) FBD

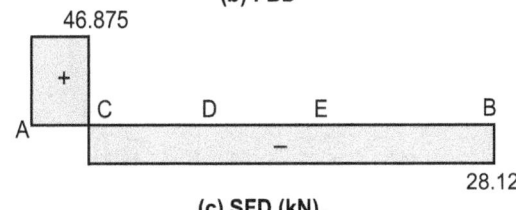

(c) SFD (kN)

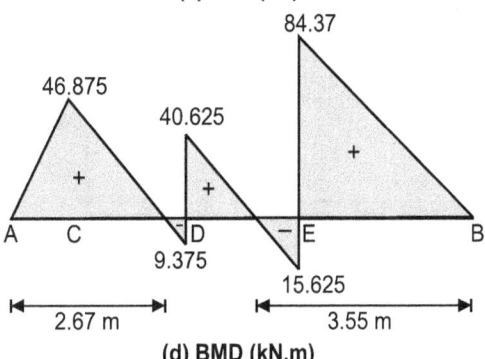

(d) BMD (kN.m)

Fig. 5.19

(iii) BM calculations :

$$BM_A = BM_B = 0$$
$$BM_C = 46.875 \times 1 = 46.875 \text{ kN.m}$$
$$BM_D \text{ (just to the left)} = 46.875 \times 3 - 75 \times 2$$
$$= -9.375 \text{ kN.m}$$
$$BM_D \text{ (just to the right)} = -9.375 + 50$$
$$= 40.625 \text{ kN.m}$$
$$BM_E \text{ (just to the right)} = 28.125 \times 3$$
$$= 84.375 \text{ kN.m}$$
$$BM_E \text{ (just to the left)} = 84.375 - 100$$
$$= -15.625 \text{ kN.m}$$

To locate point of contraflexure in zone CD, consider a section at a distance 'x' from 'A' in zone CD.

$$BM_x = 46.875 \, x - 75 \, (x - 1) = 0$$

$$\therefore \quad x = 2.67 \text{ m from 'A'}$$

To locate point of contraflexure in zone DE, consider a section at a distance 'x' from B in zone DE.

$$BM_x = 28.125 \, x - 100 = 0$$

$$\therefore \quad x = 3.55 \text{ m from B}$$

BMD is as shown in Fig. 5.19 (d).

**Example 5.13 :** The beam is supported and loaded as shown in Fig. 5.20 (a). Draw SFD and BMD indicating all the important values.

**Data** : As shown in Fig. 5.20 (a).

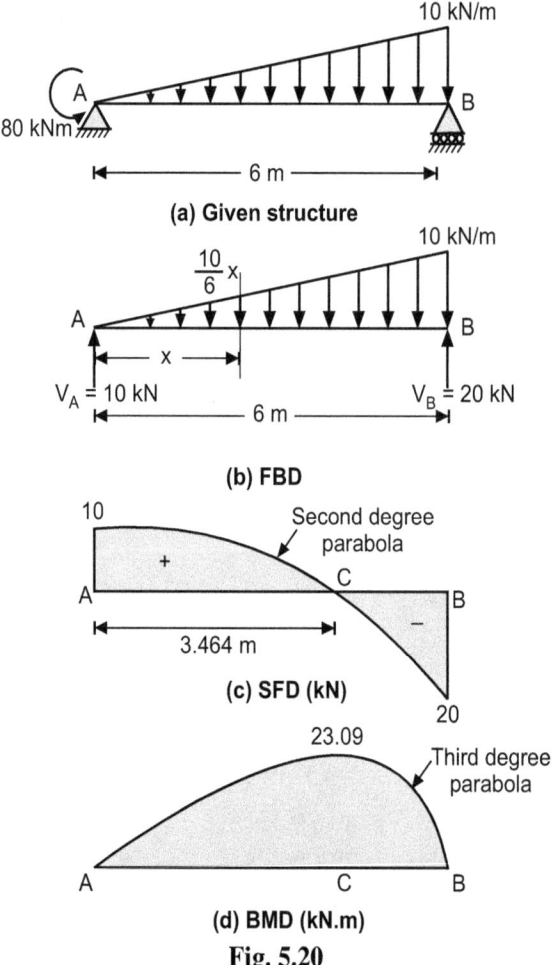

Fig. 5.20

**Required :** SFD, BMD.

**Solution** : (i) Reactions :

$\Sigma M_A = 0$ ;  $V_B \times 6 - \frac{1}{2} \times 6 \times 10 \times \frac{2}{3} \times 6 = 0$

∴  $V_B = 20$ kN (↑)

$\Sigma F_y = 0$ ;  $V_A + V_B - \frac{1}{2} \times 6 \times 10 = 0$

∴  $V_A = 10$ kN (↑)

$\Sigma F_x = 0$ ;  $H_A = 0$

FBD of beam is as shown in Fig. 5.20 (b).

(ii) SF calculations :

Intensity of UVL at 'x' from A $= \frac{10}{6} x$

SF at a distance 'x' from A, $SF_x = 10 - \frac{1}{2} \times x \times \frac{10}{6} x$

∴  $SF_x = 10 - \frac{5}{6} x^2$ ... (i)

put x = 0 ;  $SF_A = 10$ kN

put x = 6 m ;  $SF_B = 10 - \frac{5}{6} (6)^2 = -20$ kN

To locate point of zero SF, equate equation (i) to zero.

$10 - \frac{5}{6} x^2 = 0$  ∴  x = 3.464 m from A.

SFD is as shown in Fig. 5.20 (c).

(iii) BM calculations :

BM at a distance 'x' from A = $BM_x$

$= 10 x - \frac{5}{6} x^2 \times \frac{x}{3}$

$= 10 x - \frac{5x^3}{18}$ ... (ii)

put x = 0 ;  $BM_A = 0$
put x = 0 ;  $BM_B = 0$

put x = 3.464 m;  $BM_C = 10 \times 3.464 - \frac{5 \times (3.464)^3}{18} = $ **23.09 kN.m**

BMD is as shown in Fig. 5.20 (d).

**Example 5.14 :** The beam is supported and loaded as shown in Fig. 5.21 (a). Draw SFD and BMD indicating all the important values.

**Data** : As shown in Fig. 5.21 (a).
**Required** : SFD, BMD.

**Solution :** (i) Reactions :

$$V_A = V_B = \frac{1}{2}\left[\frac{1}{2} \times L \times w\right] = \frac{wL}{4} \; (\uparrow)$$

FBD of beam is as shown in Fig. 5.21 (b).

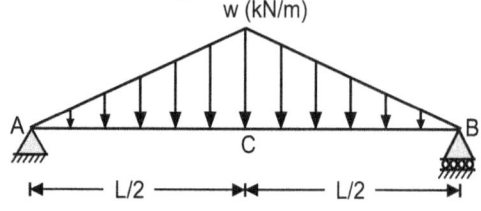

(a) Given structure

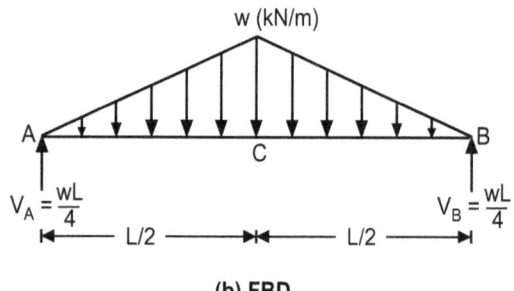

(b) FBD

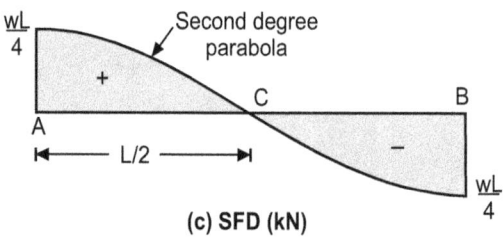

(c) SFD (kN)

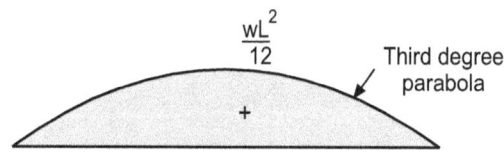

(c) BMD (kN.m)

Fig. 5.21

(ii) SF calculations :

$$SF_A = \frac{wL}{4}$$

$$SF_B = -\frac{wL}{4}$$

$$SF_C = 0. \text{ (By symmetry)}$$

SFD is as shown in Fig. 5.21 (c).

(iii) BM calculations :

$$BM_A = BM_B = 0$$

$$BM_C = \frac{wL}{4} \times \frac{L}{2} - \frac{1}{2} \times \frac{L}{2} \times w \times \frac{1}{3} \times \frac{L}{2} = \frac{wL^2}{8} - \frac{wL^2}{24} = \frac{wL^2}{12}$$

BMD is as shown in Fig. 5.21 (d).

**Example 5.15 :** The beam is supported and loaded as shown in Fig. 5.22 (a). Draw SFD and BMD indicating all the important values.

**Data** : As shown in Fig. 5.22 (a).

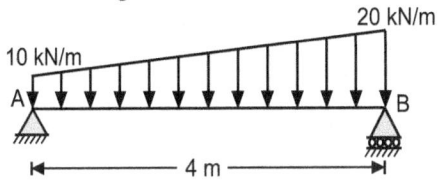

(a) Given structure

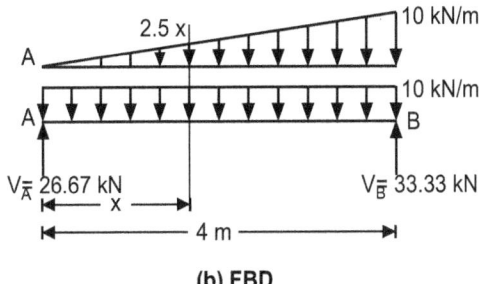

(b) FBD

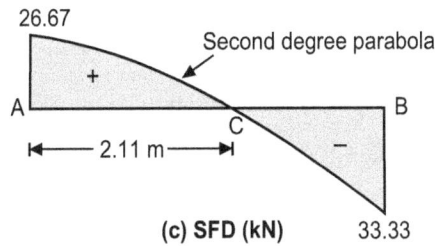

(c) SFD (kN)

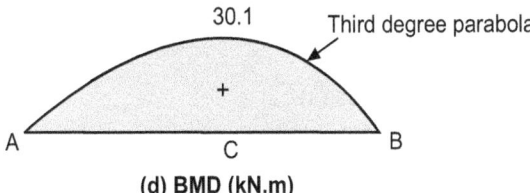

(d) BMD (kN.m)

Fig. 5.22

**Required** : SFD, BMD.
**Solution** : (i) Reactions :

$\Sigma M_A = 0$ ;  $\quad V_B \times 4 - 10 \times \frac{4^2}{2} - \frac{1}{2} \times 10 \times 4 \times \frac{2}{3} \times 4 = 0$

$\therefore \quad V_B = 33.33 \text{ kN} (\uparrow)$

$\Sigma F_y = 0$ ;  $\quad V_A + V_B = 10 \times 4 + \frac{1}{2} \times 10 \times 4$

$\quad V_A = 26.67 \text{ kN} (\uparrow)$

$\Sigma F_x = 0$ ;   $H_A = 0$

FBD of beam is as shown in Fig. 5.22 (b).

(ii) SF calculations :

Consider a section at a distance 'x' from 'A'.

$$SF_x = 26.67 - 10x - \frac{1}{2} \times x \times 2.5x$$

$$= 26.67 - 10x - 1.25x^2 \qquad \ldots \text{(i)}$$

put x = 0 ;   $SF_A = 26.67$ kN

put x = 4 m ;   $SF_B = 26.67 - 10 \times 4 - 1.25 \times 4^2 = -33.33$ kN

To locate point of zero SF, equate equation (i) to zero.

$$SF_x = 26.67 - 10x - 1.25x^2 = 0$$

Solving ;   x = 2.11 m from A

SFD is as shown in Fig. 5.22 (c).

(iii) BM calculations :

$$BM_x = 26.67x - 10\frac{x^2}{2} - 1.25x^2 \times \frac{x}{3}$$

$$= 26.67x - 5x^2 - \frac{x^3}{2.4} \qquad \ldots \text{(ii)}$$

put x = 0 ;   $BM_A = 0$

put x = 4 m ;   $BM_B = 0$

put x = 2.11 m ;   $BM_C = 26.67 \times 2.11 - 5(2.11)^2 - \frac{(2.11)^3}{2.4} = 30.1$ kN.m

BMD is as shown in Fig. 5.22 (d).

**Example 5.16 :** The beam is supported and loaded as shown in Fig. 5.23 (a). Draw SFD and BMD indicating all the important values.

**Data**   : As shown in Fig. 5.23 (a).

**Required** : SFD, BMD.

**Solution** : (i) Reactions :

$\Sigma M_A = 0$ ;   $V_B \times 6 - \frac{1}{2} \times 3 \times 10 \times \frac{2}{3} \times 3 + \frac{1}{2} \times 3 \times 10 \times \left(3 + \frac{1}{3} \times 3\right) = 0$

∴   $V_B = -5$ kN = 5 kN (↓)

$\Sigma F_y = 0$ ;   $V_A + V_B - \frac{1}{2} \times 3 \times 10 + \frac{1}{2} \times 3 \times 10 = 0$

∴   $V_A = 5$ kN (↑)

$\Sigma F_x = 0$ ;   $H_A = 0$

FBD of beam is as shown in Fig. 5.23 (b).

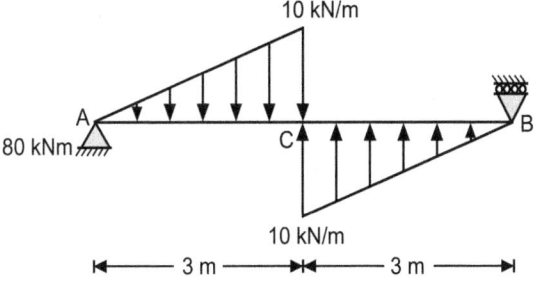

(a) Given structure

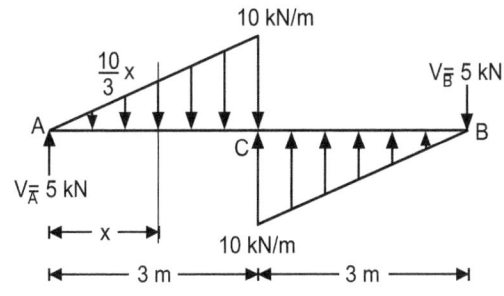

(b) FBD

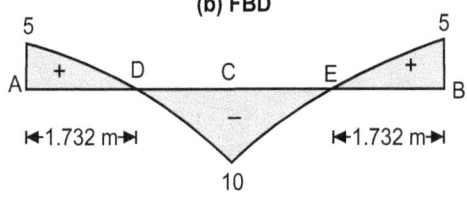

(c) SFD (kN)

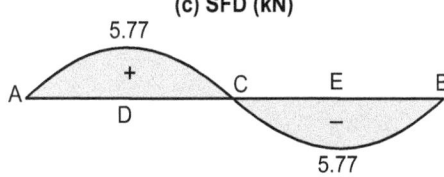

(d) BMD (kN.m)
Fig. 5.23

(ii) SF calculations :
Consider a section at a distance 'x' from A in zone AC.

$$SF_x = 5 - \frac{1}{2} \times x \times \frac{10}{3} x = 5 - \frac{5}{3} x^2 \qquad \ldots (i)$$

put x = 0 ; $\quad SF_A = 5$ kN

put x = 3 m ; $\quad SF_C = 5 - \frac{5}{3} (3)^2 = -10$ kN

To locate point of zero SF, equate equation (i) to zero.

$$5 - \frac{5}{3} x^2 = 0 \quad \therefore \quad x = 1.732 \text{ m from A}$$

SFD for zone BC will be same as that of zone AC by symmetry.
SFD is as shown in Fig. 5.23 (c).

(iii) BM calculations :

$$BM_x = 5x - \frac{5}{3} x^2 \times \frac{x}{3} = 5x - \frac{5}{9} x^3 \quad \ldots \text{(ii)}$$

put x = 0 ;  $BM_A = 0$

put x = 3 m ;  $BM_C = 5 \times 3 - \frac{5}{9} (3)^3 = 0$

put x = 1.732 m ;  $BM_D = 5 \times 1.732 - \frac{5}{9} (1.732)^3 = 5.77$ kN.m

BMD for zone BC will be same as that of zone AC by symmetry.

BMD is as shown in Fig. 5.23 (d).

**Example 5.17 :** The beam PQ is supported and loaded as shown in Fig. 5.24 (a). Determine the magnitude of couple 'M' at C such that reaction at P is zero. Draw SFD and BMD.

**Data** : As shown in Fig. 5.24 (a).

**Required** : Magnitude of couple 'M' and SFD, BMD.

**Solution** : (i) Reactions and magnitude of couple 'M' :

$\Sigma F_y = 0;$   $V_P + V_Q - \frac{1}{2} \times 1.8 \times 2.4 = 0$

∴   $V_Q = 2.16$ kN (↑)   $(\because V_P = 0)$

$\Sigma M_P = 0;$   $V_Q \times 3 - M - \frac{1}{2} \times 1.8 \times 2.4 \times \frac{1}{3} \times 1.8 = 0$

$M = 5.184$ kN.m

FBD of beam is as shown in Fig. 5.24 (b).

(ii) SF calculations :

$SF_P = 0$

$SF_D = -\frac{1}{2} \times 1.8 \times 2.4 = -2.16$ kN.m

$SF_Q = -2.16$ kN.m

SFD is as shown in Fig. 5.24 (c).

(iii) BM calculations :

$BM_P = BM_Q = 0$

$BM_C$ (just to the right) $= 2.16 \times 0.6 = 1.296$ kN.m

$BM_C$ (just to the left) $= 1.296 - 5.184 = -3.888$ kN.m

$BM_D = -\frac{1}{2} \times 1.8 \times 2.4 \times \frac{2}{3} \times 1.8 = -2.592$ kN.m

BMD is as shown in Fig. 5.24 (d).

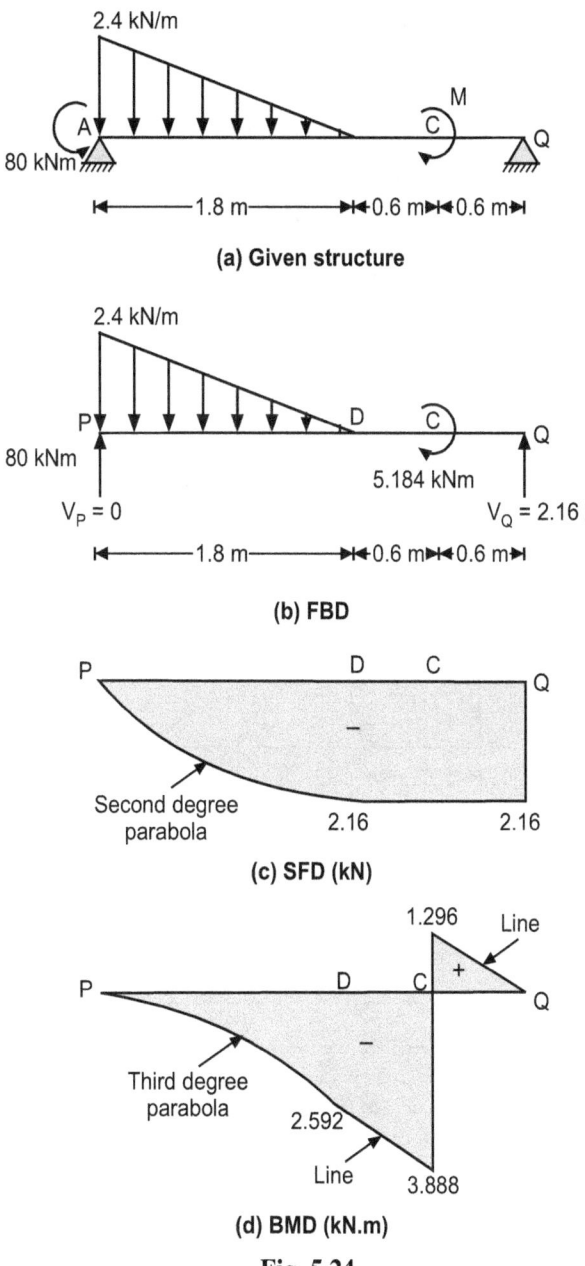

**Fig. 5.24**

**Example 5.18 :** The beam is supported and loaded as shown in Fig. 5.25 (a). Draw SFD and BMD indicating all the important values.

**Data :** As shown in Fig. 5.25 (a).
**Required :** SFD, BMD.
**Solution :** (i) Reactions :

$\Sigma M_A = 0$ ;  $\qquad -10 \times 5.5 \times \dfrac{5.5}{2} + V_B \times 4 = 0$

∴ $V_B = 37.8$ kN (↑)

$\sum F_y = 0$ ; $V_A + V_B - 10 \times 5.5 = 0$

∴ $V_A = 17.2$ kN (↑)

FBD of beam is as shown in Fig. 5.25 (b).

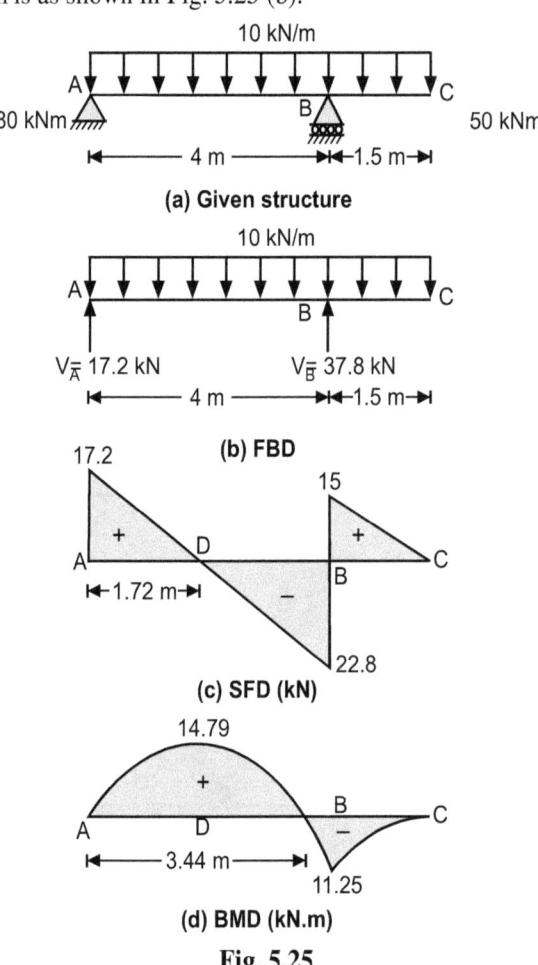

Fig. 5.25

(ii) SF calculations :

$SF_A = 17.2$ kN

$SF_B$ (just to the left) $= 17.2 - 10 \times 4 = -22.8$ kN

$SF_B$ (just to the right) $= -22.8 + 37.8 = 15$ kN

$SF_C = 0$

To locate point of zero SF, consider a section at a distance x from A in zone AB.

$SF_x = 17.2 - 10x = 0$

∴ $x = 1.72$ m from A

SFD is as shown in Fig. 5.25 (c).

(iii) BM calculations :

$$BM_A = BM_C = 0$$

$$BM_B = -10 \times \frac{(1.5)^2}{2} = -11.25 \text{ kN.m}$$

BM at point of zero SF $= BM_D$

$$= 17.2 \times 1.72 - 10 \times \frac{(1.72)^2}{2}$$

$$= 14.79 \text{ kN.m}$$

To locate point of contraflexure, consider a section at a distance x from A in zone AB.

$$BM_x = 17.2 x - 10 \frac{x^2}{2} = 0$$

$$x = 3.44 \text{ m from A.}$$

BMD is as shown in Fig. 5.25 (d).

**Example 5.19 :** The beam is supported and loaded as shown in Fig. 5.26 (a). Draw SFD and BMD indicating all the important values.

**Data** : As shown in Fig. 5.26 (a).
**Required** : SFD, BMD.
**Solution** : (i) Reactions :

$\Sigma M_A = 0$ ;  $V_B \times 20 - 10 \times \frac{10^2}{2} - 20 \times 15 - 30 \times 25 = 0$

∴  $V_B = 77.5 \text{ kN} (\uparrow)$

$\Sigma F_y = 0$ ;  $V_A + V_B - 10 \times 10 - 20 - 30 = 0$

∴  $V_A = 72.5 \text{ kN} (\uparrow)$

$\Sigma F_x = 0$ ;  $H_A = 0$

FBD of beam is as shown in Fig. 5.26 (b).

(ii) SF calculations :

$$SF_A = 72.5 \text{ kN}$$
$$SF_C = 72.5 - 10 \times 10 = -27.5 \text{ kN}$$
$$SF_D \text{ (just to the left)} = -27.5 \text{ kN}$$
$$SF_D \text{ (just to the right)} = -27.5 - 20 = -47.5 \text{ kN}$$
$$SF_B \text{ (just to the right )} = 30 \text{ kN}$$
$$SF_B \text{ (just to the left)} = 30 - 77.5 = -47.5 \text{ kN}$$
$$SF_E = 30 \text{ kN}$$

To locate point of zero SF, consider a section at a distance x from A in zone AC.

$$SF_x = 72.5 - 10 x = 0$$

∴  $x = 7.26 \text{ m from A}$

SFD is as shown in Fig. 5.26 (c).

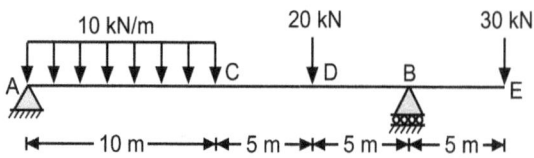

(a) Given structure

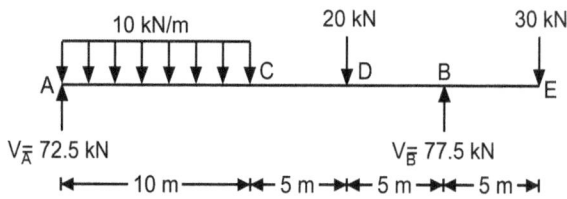

(b) FBD

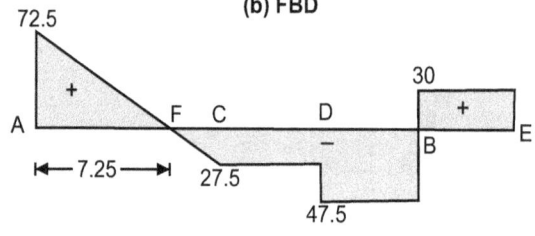

(c) SFD (kN)

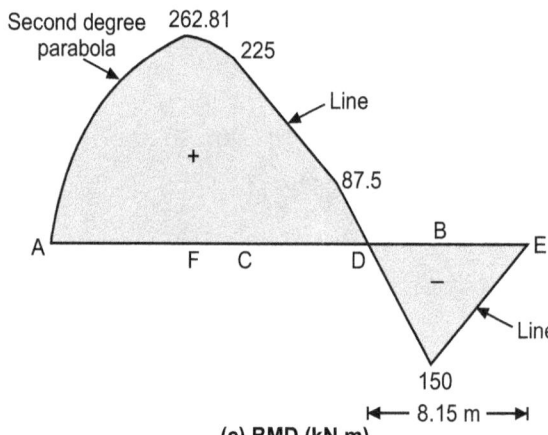

(c) BMD (kN.m)

Fig. 5.26

(iii) BM calculations :

$$BM_A = BM_E = 0$$

$$BM_C = 72.5 \times 10 - 10 \times \frac{10^2}{2} = 225 \text{ kN.m}$$

$$\text{BM at a point of zero SF} = BM_F = 72.5 \times 7.25 - 10 \times \frac{(7.25)^2}{2}$$

$$= 262.81 \text{ kN.m}$$

$$BM_D = 77.5 \times 5 - 30 \times 10 = 87.5 \text{ kN.m}$$

$$BM_B = -30 \times 5 = -150 \text{ kN.m}$$

To locate point of contraflexure, consider a section at a distance 'x' from E in zone DB.

$$BM_x = -30x + 77.5(x-5) = 0$$

∴ $x = 8.15$ m from E

BMD is as shown in Fig. 5.26 (d).

**Example 5.20 :** The beam is supported and loaded as shown in Fig. 5.27 (a). Draw SFD and BMD indicating all the important values.

**Data** : As shown in Fig. 5.27 (a).

**Required** : SFD, BMD.

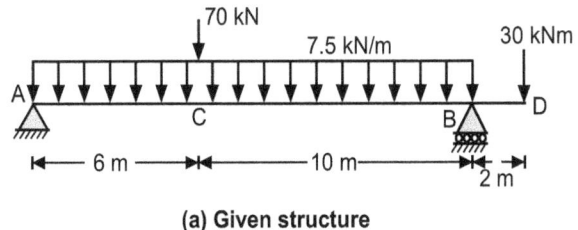
(a) Given structure

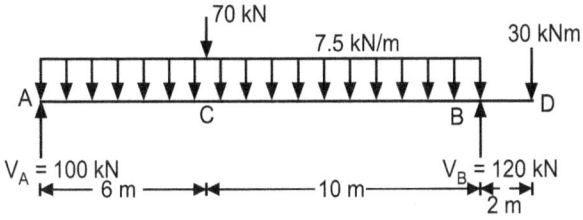
(b) FBD

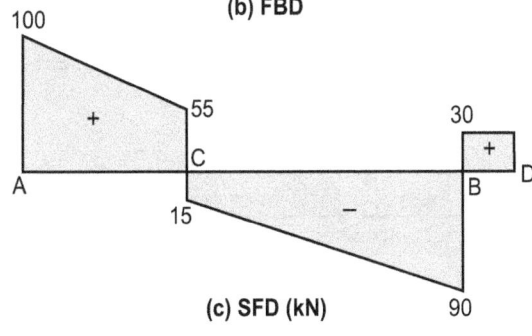
(c) SFD (kN)

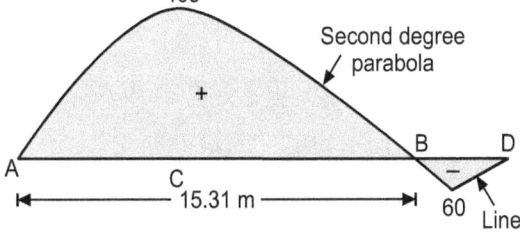
(c) BMD (kN.m)

**Fig. 5.27**

**Solution :** (i) Reactions :

$\sum M_A = 0$ ;  $V_B \times 16 - 30 \times 18 - 7.5 \times \dfrac{(16)^2}{2} - 70 \times 6 = 0$

∴  $V_B = 120$ kN (↑)

$\sum F_y = 0$ ;  $V_A + V_B - 70 - 30 - 7.5 \times 16 = 0$

∴  $V_A = 100$ kN (↑)

$\sum F_x = 0$ ;  $H_A = 0$

FBD of beam is as shown in Fig. 5.27 (b).

(ii) SF calculations :

$SF_A = 100$ kN

$SF_C$ (just to the left) $= 100 - 7.5 \times 6 = 55$ kN

$SF_C$ (just to the right) $= 55 - 70 = -15$ kN

$SF_B$ (just to the left) $= 30 - 120 = -90$ kN

$SF_B$ (just to the right) $= 30$ kN

$SF_D = 30$ kN

SFD is as shown in Fig. 5.27 (c).

(iii) BM calculations :

$BM_A = BM_D = 0$

$BM_C = 100 \times 6 - 7.5 \times \dfrac{6^2}{2} = 465$ kN.m

$BM_B = -30 \times 2 = -60$ kN.m

To locate point of contraflexure, consider a section at a distance x from A in the zone CB.

$BM_x = 100x - 7.5\dfrac{x^2}{2} - 70(x-6) = 0$

∴  $x^2 - 8x - 112 = 0$

Solving ;  $x = 15.31$ m  or  $-7.31$ m

Neglecting negative value, x = 15.31 m from A.

**Example 5.21 :** The beam is supported and loaded as shown in Fig. 5.28 (a). Draw SFD and BMD indicating all the important values.

**Data** : As shown in Fig. 5.28 (a).

**Required :** SFD, BMD.

**Solution :** (i) Reactions :

$\sum M_A = 0$ ;  $V_D \times 8 - 7.5 \times 10 - 10 \times 6 - 10 \times 2 - 15 \times \dfrac{10^2}{2} = 0$

∴  $V_D = 113.125$ kN (↑)

$\sum F_y = 0$ ;  $V_A + V_D = 10 + 10 + 7.5 + 15 \times 10$

∴  $V_A = 64.375$ kN (↑)

$\sum F_x = 0$ ;  $H_A = 0$

FBD of beam is as shown in Fig. 5.28 (b).

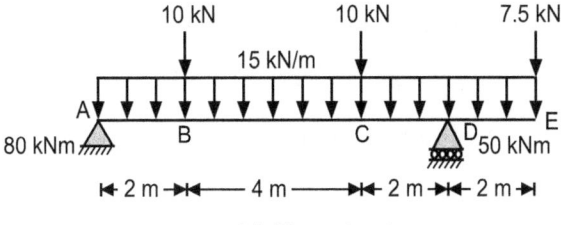

**(a) Given structure**

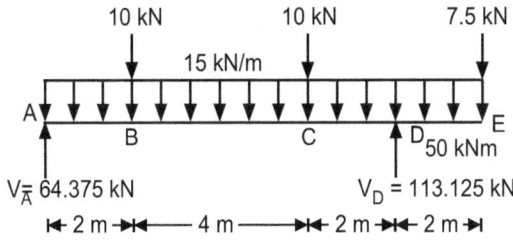

**(b) FBD**

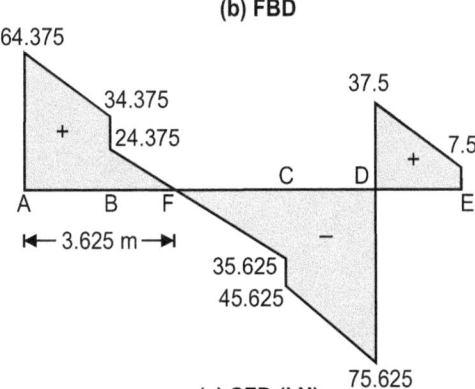

**(c) SFD (kN)**

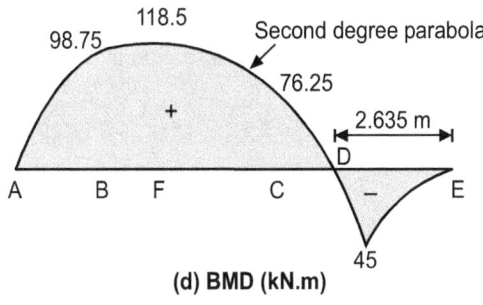

**(d) BMD (kN.m)**

**Fig. 5.28**

(ii) SF calculations :

$$SF_A = 64.375 \text{ kN}$$

$$SF_B \text{ (just to the left)} = 64.375 - 15 \times 2 = 34.375 \text{ kN}$$

$$SF_B \text{ (just to the right)} = 34.375 - 10 = 24.375 \text{ kN}$$

$$SF_C \text{ (just to the left)} = 64.375 - 10 - 15 \times 6 = -35.625 \text{ kN}$$

$SF_C$ (just to the right) = $-35.625 - 10 = -45.625$ kN

$SF_D$ (just to the right) = $7.5 + 15 \times 2 = 37.5$ kN

$SF_D$ (just to the left) = $37.5 - 113.125 = -75.625$ kN

$SF_E = 7.5$ kN

To locate point of zero SF, consider a section at a distance x from A in zone BC.

$$SF_x = 64.375 - 15x - 10 = 0$$

$\therefore \quad x = 3.625$ m from A

(iii) BM calculations :

$$BM_A = BM_E = 0$$

$$BM_B = 64.375 \times 2 - 15 \times \frac{2^2}{2} = 98.75 \text{ kN.m}$$

BM at point of zero SF = $BM_F$

$$= 64.375 \times 3.625 - 15 \times \frac{(3.625)^2}{2} - 10 \times 1.625$$

$$= 118.55 \text{ kN.m}$$

$$BM_C = -7.5 \times 4 - 15 \times \frac{4^2}{2} + 113.125 \times 2 = 76.25 \text{ kN.m}$$

$$BM_D = -7.5 \times 2 - 15 \times \frac{2^2}{2} = -45 \text{ kN.m}$$

To locate point of contraflexure, consider a section at a distance x from 'E' in zone CD.

$$BM_x = -7.5x - 15\frac{x^2}{2} + 113.125(x-2) = 0$$

$$-7.5x^2 + 105.625x - 226.25 = 0$$

Solving, $\quad x = 2.635$ m from E.

BMD is as shown in Fig. 5.28 (d).

**Example 5.22 :** The beam is supported and loaded as shown in Fig. 5.29 (a). Locate the position of support 'C' such that mid-point of the beam 'E' is point of contraflexure. Also draw SFD and BMD.

**Data** : As shown in Fig. 5.29 (a).
**Required** : SFD, BMD.

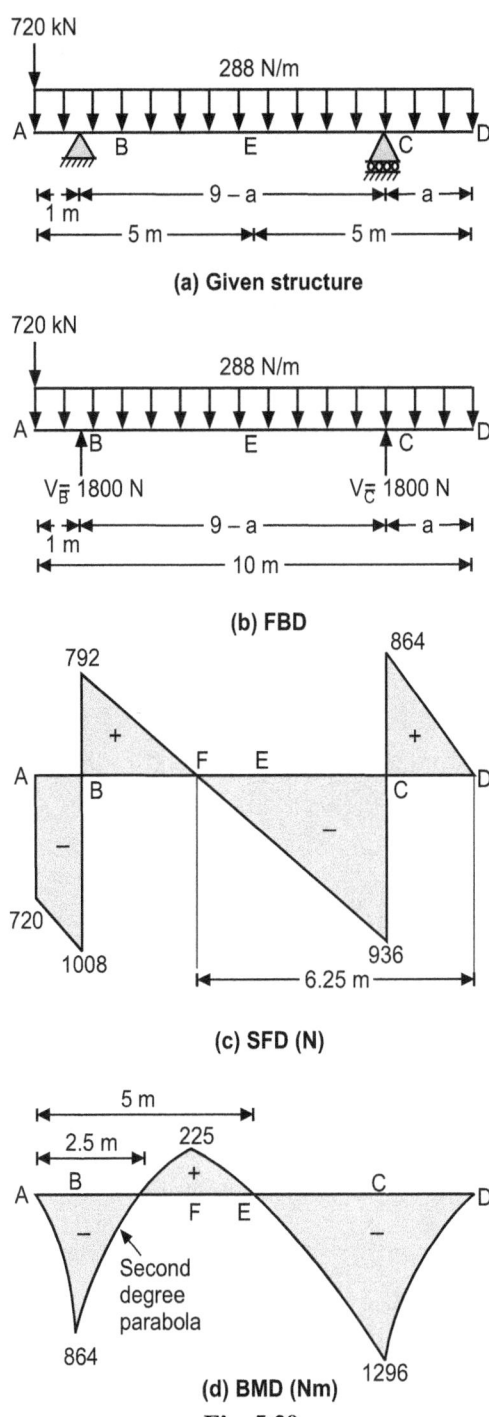

(a) Given structure

(b) FBD

(c) SFD (N)

(d) BMD (Nm)

Fig. 5.29

**Solution** : (i) Reactions and position of support 'C'.

As mid-point of the beam, 'E' is a point of contraflexure.

$\sum M_{E \text{ (LHS)}} = \sum M_{E \text{ (RHS)}} = 0$

$\sum M_{E\,(LHS)} = 0$ ;    $- V_B \times 4 + 720 \times 5 + 288 \times \dfrac{5^2}{2} = 0$

∴    $V_B = 1800 \text{ N } (\uparrow)$

$\sum F_y = 0$ ;    $V_B + V_C - 720 - 288 \times 10 = 0$

∴    $V_C = 1800 \text{ N } (\uparrow)$

$\sum M_{E\,(RHS)} = 0$ ;    $V_C (5 - a) - 288 \times \dfrac{5^2}{2} = 0$

∴    $1800 (5 - a) - 288 \times \dfrac{5^2}{2} = 0$

∴    $a = 3 \text{ m}$

$\sum F_x = 0$ ;    $H_B = 0.$

FBD of beam is as shown in Fig. 5.29 (b).

(ii) SF calculations :

$SF_A = -720 \text{ N}$

$SF_B$ (just to the left) $= -720 - 288 \times 1 = -1008 \text{ N}$

$SF_B$ (just to the right) $= -1008 + 1800 = 792 \text{ N}$

$SF_D = 0$

$SF_C$ (just to the right) $= 288 \times 3 = 864 \text{ N}$

$SF_C$ (just to the left) $= 864 - 1800 = -936 \text{ N}$

To locate point of zero SF, consider a section at a distance 'x' from D in zone BC.

$SF_x = 288 x - 1800 = 0$

$x = 6.25 \text{ m from D.}$

SFD is as shown in Fig. 5.29 (c).

(iii) BM calculations :

$BM_A = BM_E = BM_D = 0$

$BM_B = -720 \times 1 - 288 \times \dfrac{1^2}{2} = -864 \text{ Nm}$

$BM_F = -288 \times \dfrac{(6.25)^2}{2} + 1800 (6.25 - 3) = 225 \text{ Nm}$

$BM_C = -288 \times \dfrac{3^2}{2} = -1296 \text{ Nm}$

To locate point of contraflexure, consider a section at a distance x from A in zone BE.

$BM_x = -720 x - 288 \dfrac{x^2}{2} + 1800 (x - 1) = 0$

$x^2 - 7.5 x + 12.5 = 0$

Solving,    $x = 2.5 \text{ m and 5 m.}$

BMD is as shown in Fig. 5.29 (d).

**Example 5.23 :** The beam is supported and loaded as shown in Fig. 5.30 (a). Draw SFD and BMD indicating all the important values.

**Data**    : As shown in Fig. 5.30 (a).

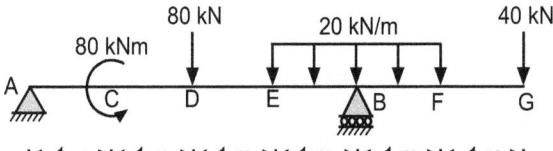

**(a) Given structure**

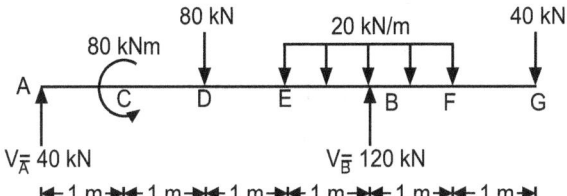

**(b) FBD**

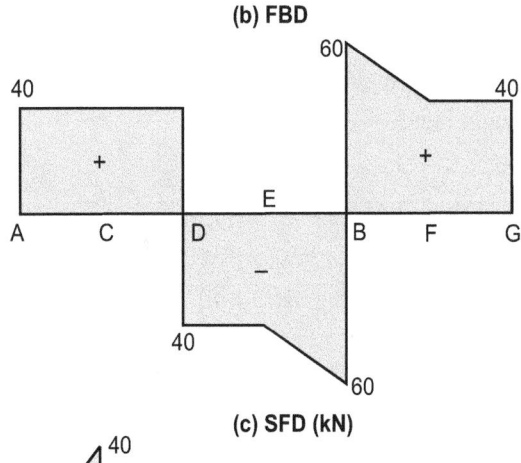

**(c) SFD (kN)**

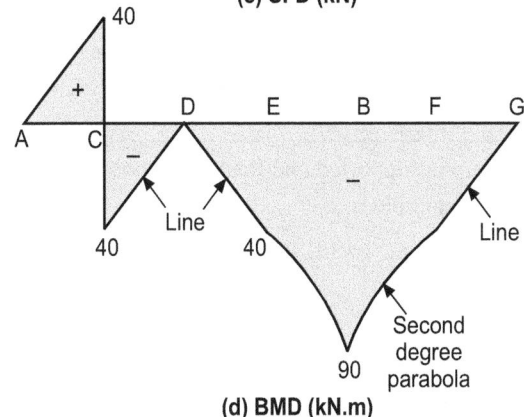

**(d) BMD (kN.m)**

**Fig. 5.30**

**Required :** SFD, BMD.

**Solution :** (i) Reactions :

$\Sigma M_A = 0$ ; $\quad V_B \times 4 - 40 \times 6 - 20 \times 2 \times 4 - 80 \times 2 + 80 = 0$

$\qquad V_B = 120 \text{ kN } (\uparrow)$

$\Sigma F_y = 0$ ;   $V_A + V_B - 80 - 20 \times 2 - 40 = 0$

∴   $V_A = 40$ kN (↑)

$\Sigma F_x = 0$ ;   $H_A = 0$.

FBD of beam is as shown in Fig. 5.30 (b).

(ii) SF calculations :

$SF_A = 40$ kN

$SF_C = 40$ kN

$SF_D$ (just to the left) $= 40$ kN

$SF_D$ (just to the right) $= 40 - 80 = -40$ kN

$SF_E = 40 - 80 = -40$ kN

$SF_B$ (just to the left) $= 40 - 80 - 20 \times 1 = -60$ kN

$SF_B$ (just to the right) $= -60 + 120 = 60$ kN

$SF_F = SF_G = 40$ kN

SFD is as shown in Fig. 5.30 (c).

(iii) BM calculations :

$BM_A = BM_G = 0$

$BM_C$ (just to the left) $= 40 \times 1 = 40$ kN.m

$BM_C$ (just to the right) $= 40 - 80 = -40$ kN.m

$BM_D = 40 \times 2 - 80 = 0$

$BM_E = 40 \times 3 - 80 - 80 \times 1 = -40$ kN.m

$BM_B = -40 \times 2 - 20 \times \dfrac{1^2}{2} = -90$ kN.m

$BM_F = -40 \times 1 = -40$ kN.m

BMD is as shown in Fig. 5.30 (d).

**Example 5.24 :** The beam is supported and loaded as shown in Fig. 5.31 (a). Draw SFD and BMD indicating all the important values.

**Data**    : As shown in Fig. 5.31 (a).
**Required** : SFD, BMD.
**Solution** : (i) Reactions :

$\Sigma M_B = 0$ ;   $V_E \times 6 - 40 \times 7.8 - 40 - 100 \times 1.8 - 15 \times \dfrac{(1.8)^2}{2} + 15 \times \dfrac{(1.2)^2}{2} = 0$

∴   $V_E = 90.92$ kN (↑)

$\Sigma F_y = 0$ ;   $V_B + V_E - 15 \times 3 - 100 - 40 = 0$

∴   $V_B = 94.08$ kN (↑)

$\Sigma F_x = 0$ ;   $H_A = 0$.

FBD of beam is as shown in Fig. 5.31 (b).

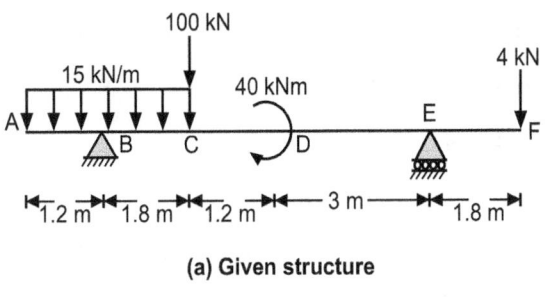

(a) Given structure

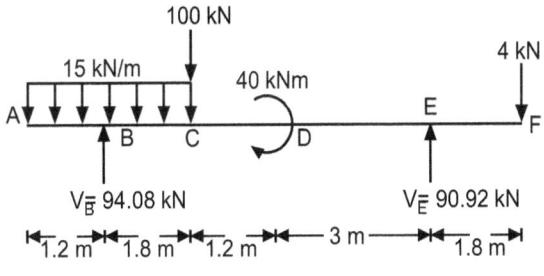

(b) FBD

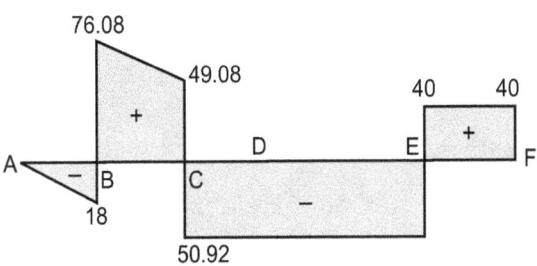

(c) SFD (kN)

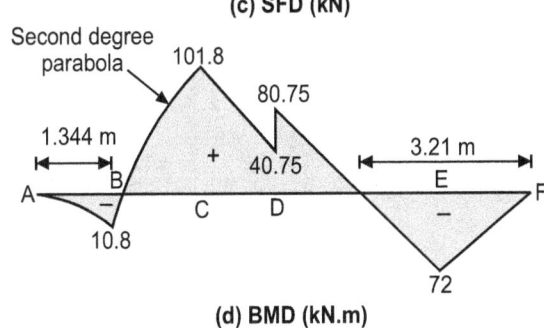

(d) BMD (kN.m)

Fig. 5.31

(ii) SF calculations :

$SF_A = 0$

$SF_B$ (just to the left) $= -15 \times 1.2 = -18$ kN

$SF_B$ (just to the right) $= -18 + 94.08 = 76.08$ kN

$SF_C$ (just to the left) = 94.08 − 15 × 3 = 49.08 kN

$SF_C$ (just to the right) = 49.08 − 100 = − 50.92 kN

$SF_F$ = 40 kN

$SF_E$ (just to the right) = 40 kN

$SF_E$ (just to the left) = 40 − 90.92 = − 50.92 kN

SFD is as shown in Fig. 5.31 (c).

(ii) BM calculations :

$$BM_A = BM_F = 0$$

$$BM_B = -15 \times \frac{(1.2)^2}{2} = -10.8 \text{ kN.m}$$

$$BM_C = -15 \times \frac{3^2}{2} + 94.08 \times 1.8 = 101.8 \text{ kN.m}$$

$$BM_D \text{ (just to the left)} = 94.08 \times 3 - 15 \times 3 \times \left(1.2 + \frac{3}{2}\right) - 100 \times 1.2$$

$$= 40.75 \text{ kN.m}$$

$$BM_D \text{ (just to the right)} = 40.75 + 40$$

$$= 80.75 \text{ kN.m}$$

$$BM_E = -40 \times 1.8 = -72 \text{ kN.m}$$

To locate point of contraflexure, consider a section at a distance x from 'F' in zone ED.

$$BM_x = -40x + 90.92(x - 1.8) = 0$$

∴ x = 3.21 m from F.

To locate another point of contraflexure, consider a section at a distance 'x' from A in zone BC.

$$BM_x = -15 \frac{x^2}{2} + 94.08(x - 1.2) = 0$$

∴ x = 1.344 m from A.

BMD is as shown in Fig. 5.31 (d).

**Example 5.25 :** The beam is supported and loaded as shown in Fig. 5.32 (a). Find the magnitude of load W such that support reactions at A and B are equal. Draw SFD and BMD.

**Data** : As shown in Fig. 5.32 (a).

**Required** : Magnitude of load W and SFD; BMD.

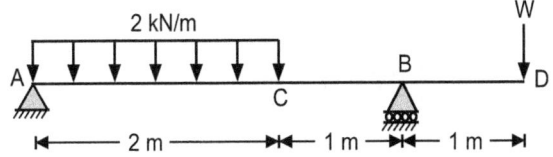

**(a) Given structure**

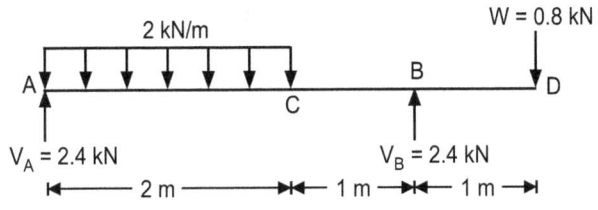

**(b) FBD**

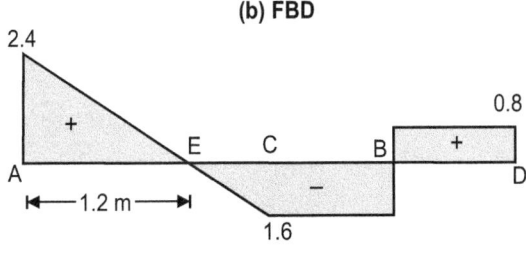

**(c) SFD (kN)**

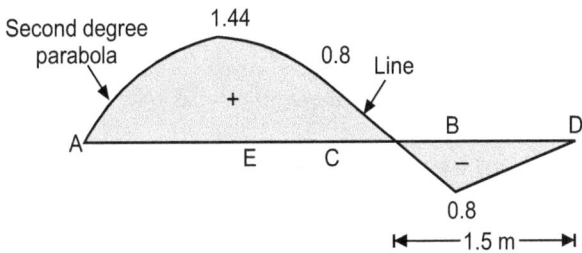

**(d) BMD (kN.m)**

**Fig. 5.32**

**Solution :** (i) Reactions and magnitude of load 'W' :

Let ; $\quad V_A = V_B = V$ (say)

$\Sigma M_A = 0$ ; $\quad V \times 3 - W \times 4 - 2 \times \dfrac{2^2}{2} = 0$

$\therefore \quad V = \dfrac{4}{3}(W + 1)$ ... (i)

$\Sigma F_y = 0$ ; $\quad 2V - 2 \times 2 - W = 0$

$V = \dfrac{W}{2} + 2$ ... (ii)

Equating (i) and (ii),

$$\frac{4}{3}(W+1) = \frac{W}{2} + 2$$

∴ $W = 0.8$ kN

Reactions $= V_A = V_B = \frac{W}{2} + 2 = 2.4$ kN (↑)

FBD of beam is as shown in Fig. 5.32 (b).

(ii) SF calculations :

$SF_A = 2.4$ kN

$SF_C = 2.4 - 2 \times 2 = -1.6$ kN

$SF_B$ (just to the left) $= -1.6$ kN

$SF_B$ (just to the right) $= -1.6 + 2.4 = 0.8$ kN

$SF_D = 0.8$ kN

To locate point of zero SF, consider a section at a distance 'x' from A in zone AC,

$SF_x = 2.4 - 2x = 0$

∴ $x = 1.2$ m from A.

SFD is as shown in Fig. 5.32 (c).

(iii) BM calculations :

$BM_A = BM_D = 0$

$BM_C = 2.4 \times 2 - 2 \times \frac{2^2}{2} = 0.8$ kN.m

BM at point of zero SF $= BM_E = 2.4 \times 1.2 - 2 \times \frac{(1.2)^2}{2} = 1.44$ kN.m

$BM_B = -0.8 \times 1 = -0.8$ kN.m

To locate point of contraflexure, consider a section at a distance x from D in zone CB.

$BM_x = -0.8x + 2.4(x-1) = 0$

∴ $x = 1.5$ m from D.

BMD is as shown in Fig. 5.32 (d).

**Example 5.26 :** For the beam ABCD shown in Fig. 5.33 (a), find the position of supports at B and C such that, the maximum BM is minimum possible. Also draw SFD and BMD.

**Data** : As shown in Fig. 5.33 (a).

**Required** : Position of supports SFD, BMD.

**Solution** : (i) Position of supports :

Hogging moments at supports B and C $= \frac{wa^2}{2}$ ... (i)

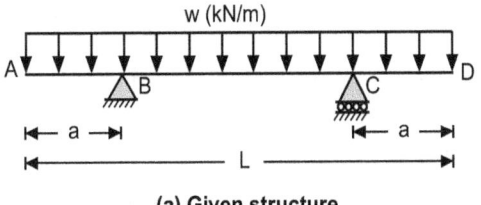

**(a) Given structure**

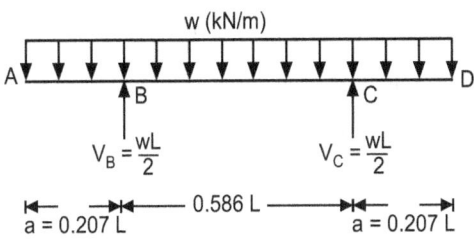

**(b) FBD**

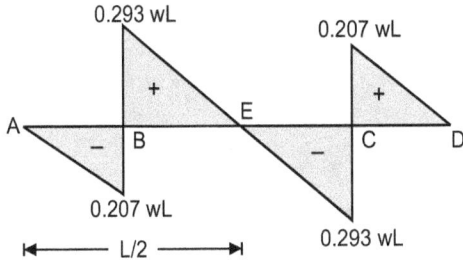

**(c) SFD (kN)**

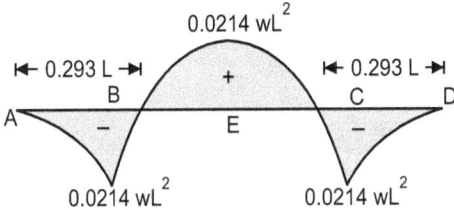

**(d) BMD (kN.m)**

Fig. 5.33

Maximum sagging moment at

$$\text{midspan} = \frac{w}{8}(L-2a)^2 - \frac{wa^2}{2} \quad \ldots \text{(ii)}$$

For maximum bending moment to be minimum, equating (i) and (ii),

$$\therefore \quad \frac{wa^2}{2} = \frac{w}{8}(L-2a)^2 - \frac{wa^2}{2}$$

$$\therefore \quad a^2 = \frac{(L-2a)^2}{4} - a^2$$

$$\therefore \quad a^2 + La - \frac{L^2}{4} = 0$$

Solving ;  a = 0.207 L

$$\text{Reactions} = V_A = V_B = \frac{wL}{2} \;(\uparrow) \text{ by symmetry.}$$

FBD of beam is as shown in Fig. 5.33 (b).

(ii) SF calculations :

$$SF_A = SF_D = 0$$

$$SF_B \text{ (just to the left)} = -0.207 \, wL$$

$$SF_B \text{ (just to the right)} = -0.207 \, wL + 0.5 \, wL = 0.293 \, wL$$

By symmetry, SF is zero at midspan.

SFD is drawn using symmetry as shown in Fig. 5.33 (c).

(iii) BM calculations :

$$BM_A = BM_D = 0$$

Hogging moment at supports B and C

= Sagging moment at midspan.

$$= \frac{wa^2}{2} \text{ where } a = 0.207 \, L = \frac{w\,(0.207\,L)^2}{2}$$

$$= 0.0214 \, wL^2$$

To locate point of contraflexure, consider a section at a distance 'x' from A in zone BC.

$$BM_x = -\frac{wx^2}{2} + \frac{wL}{2}\,(x - 0.207\,L) = 0$$

$$\therefore \quad x^2 - Lx + 0.207 \, L^2 = 0$$

Solving,  x = 0.293 L

BMD is as shown in Fig. 5.33 (d).

**Example 5.27 :** The beam is supported and loaded as shown in Fig. 5.34 (a). Draw AFD, SFD and BMD for beam ABC indicating all the important values.

**Data** : As shown in Fig. 5.34 (a).

**Required :** AFD, SFD, BMD.

**Solution :** (i) Reactions :

Vertical component of 50 kN force at D

$$= 50 \times \frac{3}{5} = 30 \text{ kN } (\uparrow)$$

Horizontal component of 50 kN force at D

$$= 50 \times \frac{4}{5} = 40 \text{ kN } (\rightarrow)$$

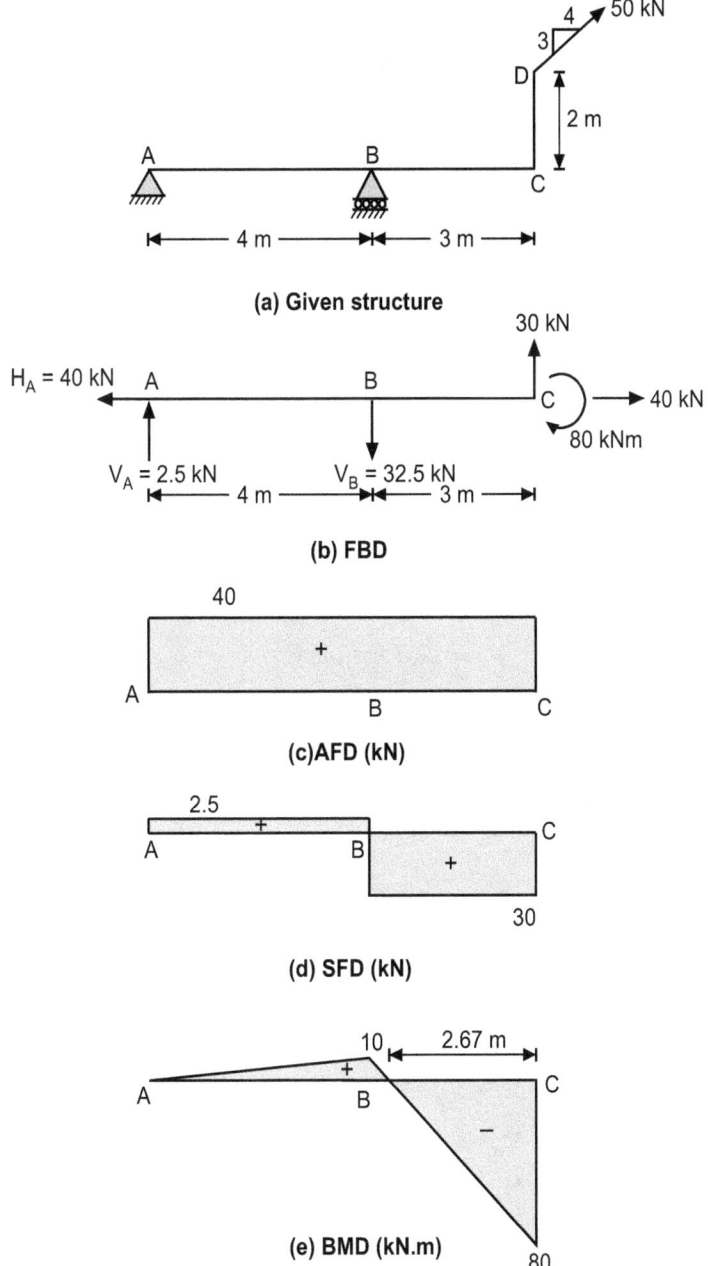

Fig. 5.34

Force components at D are transferred at C as shown in Fig. 5.34 (b).

$\Sigma M_A = 0$;   $V_B \times 4 - 80 + 30 \times 7 = 0$

$\therefore$   $V_B = -32.5$ kN $= 32.5$ kN $(\downarrow)$

$\Sigma F_y = 0$;   $V_A + V_B + 30 = 0$

$\therefore$   $V_A = 2.5$ kN $(\uparrow)$

$\Sigma F_x = 0$;   $H_A = 40$ kN $(\leftarrow)$

FBD of beam is as shown in Fig. 5.34 (b).

(ii) Axial force :

Member ABC is subjected to axial tension of 40 kN. AFD is as shown in Fig. 5.34 (c).

(iii) SF calculations :

$$SF_A = 2.5 \text{ kN}$$
$$SF_B \text{ (just to the left)} = 2.5 \text{ kN}$$
$$SF_B \text{ (just to the right)} = 2.5 - 32.5 = -30 \text{ kN}$$
$$SF_C = -30 \text{ kN}$$

SFD is as shown in Fig. 5.34 (d).

(iv) BM calculations :

$$BM_A = 0$$
$$BM_B = 2.5 \times 4 = 10 \text{ kN.m}$$
$$BM_C = -80 \text{ kN.m}$$

To locate point of contraflexure, consider a section at a distance 'x' from 'C' in zone BC.

$$BM_x = 30x - 80 = 0$$
$$x = 2.67 \text{ m from C.}$$

BMD is as shown in Fig. 5.34 (e).

**Example 5.28 :** The beam is supported and loaded as shown in Fig. 5.35 (a). Draw SFD and BMD indicating all the important values.

**Data** : As shown in Fig. 5.35 (a).

**Required** : SFD, BMD.

**Solution** : (i) Reactions :

$$\Sigma M_A = 0; \quad V_B \times 7 - 10 \times \frac{3^2}{2} + 50 - 30 \times 1 \times 7.5 = 0$$

$$\therefore \quad V_B = 31.43 \text{ kN } (\uparrow)$$

$$\Sigma F_y = 0; \quad V_A + V_B - 10 \times 3 - 30 \times 1 = 0$$

$$V_A = 28.57 \text{ kN } (\uparrow)$$

$$\Sigma F_x = 0; \quad H_A = 0$$

FBD of beam is as shown in Fig. 5.35 (b).

(ii) SF calculations :

$$SF_A = 28.57 \text{ kN}$$
$$SF_C = 28.57 - 10 \times 3 = -1.43 \text{ kN}$$
$$SF_B \text{ (just to the right)} = 30 \text{ kN}$$
$$SF_B \text{ (just to the left)} = 30 - 31.43 = -1.43 \text{ kN}$$
$$SF_E = 0$$

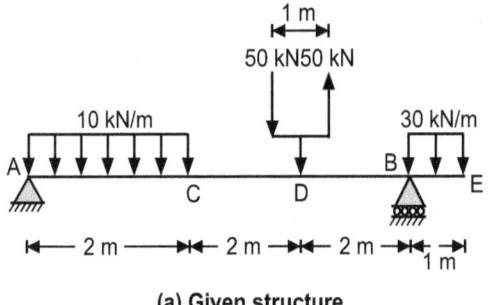

**(a) Given structure**

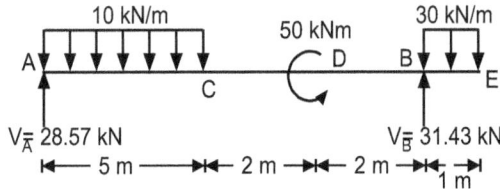

**(b) FBD**

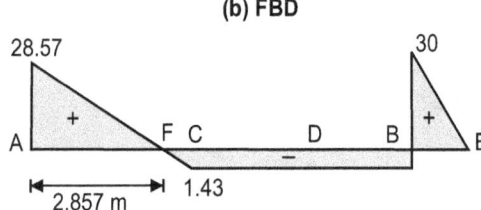

**(c) SFD (kN)**

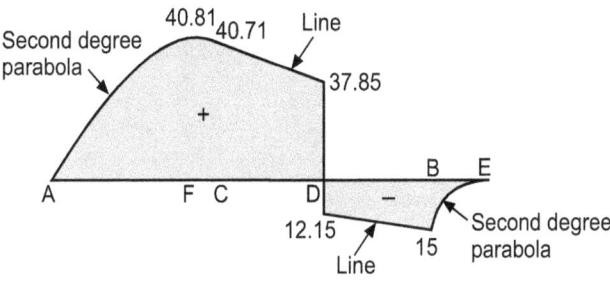

**(d) BMD (kN.m)**

**Fig. 5.35**

To locate point of zero SF, consider a section at a distance 'x' from A in zone AC.

$$SF_x = 28.57 - 10x = 0$$

∴ $x = 2.857$ m from A.

SFD is as shown in Fig. 5.35 (c).

(iii) BM calculations :

$$BM_A = BM_E = 0$$

BM at point of zero SF = $BM_F$

$$= 28.57 \times 2.857 - 10 \times \frac{(2.857)^2}{2}$$

$$= 40.81 \text{ kN.m}$$

$BM_C = 28.57 \times 3 - 10 \times \frac{3^2}{2} = 40.71 \text{ kN.m}$

$BM_D$ (just to the left) $= 28.57 \times 5 - 10 \times 3 \times 3.5$

$$= 37.85 \text{ kN.m}$$

$BM_D$ (just to the right) $= 37.85 - 50 = -12.15 \text{ kN.m}$

$BM_B = -30 \times \frac{1^2}{2} = -15 \text{ kN.m}$

BMD is as shown in Fig. 5.35 (d).

**Example 5.29 :** The beam is supported and loaded as shown in Fig. 5.36 (a). Draw AFD, SFD, BMD indicating all the important values.

**Data** : As shown in Fig. 5.36 (a).

**Required** : AFD, SFD, BMD.

**Solution** : (i) Reactions :

$\Sigma M_A = 0$; $V_D \times 3.4 - 21.21 \times 1 + 21.21 - 20 \times 2.2 - 15 \times 2.4 \times 3.4 = 0$

∴ $V_D = 48.94 \text{ kN } (\uparrow)$

$\Sigma F_y = 0$; $V_A + V_D - 21.21 - 20 - 15 \times 2.4 = 0$

$V_A = 28.27 \text{ kN } (\uparrow)$

$\Sigma F_x = 0$; $H_A = 21.21 \text{ kN } (\rightarrow)$

(ii) Axial force :

Portion AB has axial compressive force of 21.21 kN.

AFD is as shown in Fig. 5.36 (c).

(iii) SF calculations :

$SF_A = 28.27 \text{ kN}$

$SF_B$ (just to the left) $= 28.27 \text{ kN}$

$SF_B$ (just to the right) $= 28.27 - 21.21 = 7.06 \text{ kN}$

$SF_C$ (just to the left) $= 7.06 \text{ kN}$

$SF_C$ (just to the right) $= 7.06 - 20 = -12.94 \text{ kN}$

$SF_D$ (just to the right) $= 15 \times 1.2 = 18 \text{ kN}$

$SF_D$ (just to the left) $= 18 - 48.94 = -30.94 \text{ kN}$

SFD is as shown in Fig. 5.36 (d).

Shear Force & Bending Moment (Part - A)

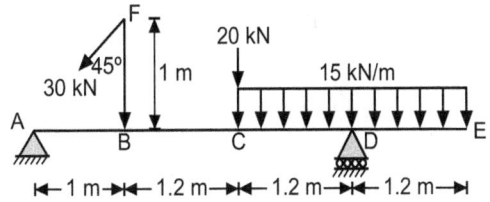

(a) Given structure

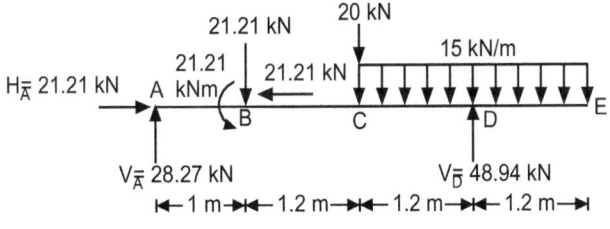

(b) FBD

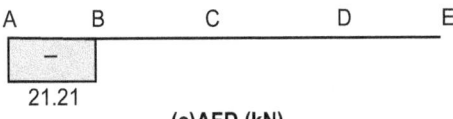

(c) AFD (kN)

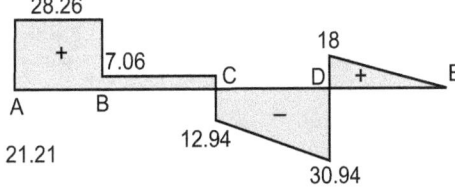

(d) SFD (kN)

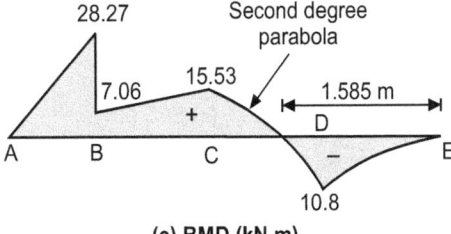

(e) BMD (kN.m)

Fig. 5.36

(iv) BM calculations : $BM_A = BM_E = 0$

$BM_B$ (just to the left) $= 28.27 \times 1 = 28.27$ kN.m

$BM_B$ (just to the right) $= 28.27 - 21.21 = 7.06$ kN.m

$BM_C = 28.27 \times 2.2 - 21.21 - 21.21 \times 1.2 = 15.53$ kN.m

$BM_D = -15 \times \dfrac{(1.2)^2}{2} = -10.8$ kN.m

To locate point of contraflexure, consider a section at a distance 'x' from 'E' in zone CD,

$$BM_x = -15\frac{x^2}{2} + 48.94(x - 1.2) = 0$$

Solving,  $x = 1.585$ m from E.

BMD is as shown in Fig. 5.36 (e).

**Example 5.30 :** The beam is supported and loaded as shown in Fig. 5.37 (a). Draw SFD and BMD indicating all the important values.

**Data** : As shown in Fig. 5.37 (a).

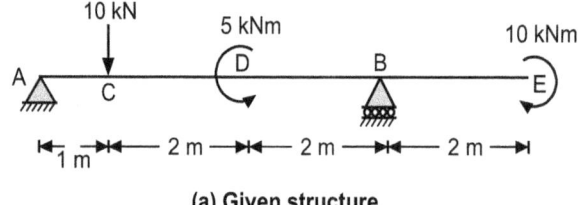

(a) Given structure

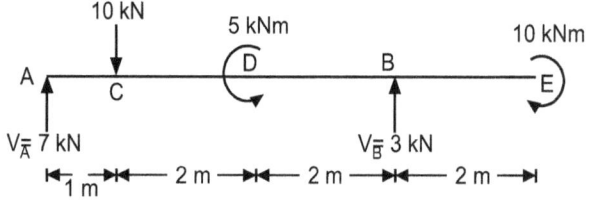

(b) FBD

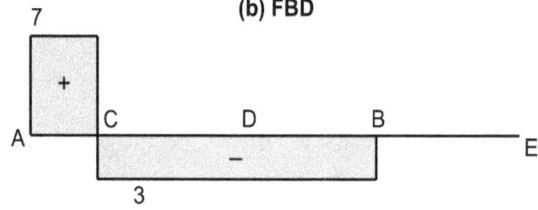

(c) SFD (kN)

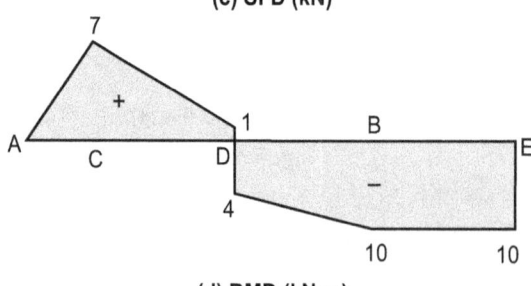

(d) BMD (kN.m)

Fig. 5.37

**Required** : SFD, BMD.

**Solution** : (i) Reactions :

$\sum M_A = 0$ ;   $V_B \times 5 - 10 \times 1 + 5 - 10 = 0$

∴   $V_B = 3$ kN (↑)

$\sum F_y = 0$ ;   $V_A + V_B - 10 = 0$

∴   $V_A = 7$ kN (↑)

$\sum F_x = 0$ ;   $H_A = 0$

FBD of beam is as shown in Fig. 5.37 (b).

(ii) SF calculations :

$SF_A = 7$ kN

$SF_C$ (just to the left) $= 7$ kN

$SF_C$ (just to the right) $= 7 - 10 = -3$ kN

$SF_B$ (just to the left) $= -3$ kN

$SF_B$ (just to the right) $= -3 + 3 = 0$

$SF_E = 0$

SFD is as shown in Fig. 5.37 (c).

(iii) BM calculations :

$BM_A = 0$

$BM_C = 7 \times 1 = 7$ kN.m

$BM_D$ (just to the left) $= 7 \times 3 - 10 \times 2 = 1$ kN.m

$BM_D$ (just to the right) $= 1 - 5 = -4$ kN.m

$BM_D = BM_E = -10$ kN.m

BMD is as shown in Fig. 5.37 (d).

**Example 5.31** : The beam is supported and loaded as shown in Fig. 5.38 (a). Find the magnitude of couple 'M' such that reaction at A will be $\frac{1}{4}^{th}$ of the reaction at B. Draw SFD and BMD indicating all the important values.

**Data** : As shown in Fig. 5.38 (a).

**Required** : Magnitude of couple 'M' and SFD, BMD.

**Solution** : (i) Magnitude of couple 'M' and reactions :

Let $V_A$ and $V_B$ be the vertical reaction components at A and B respectively.

We have,

$$V_A = \frac{1}{4} V_B \quad \ldots (i)$$

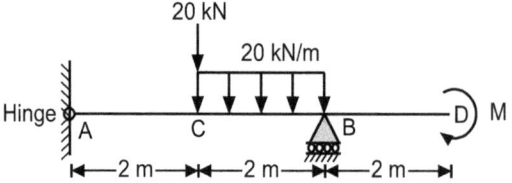

**(a) Given structure**

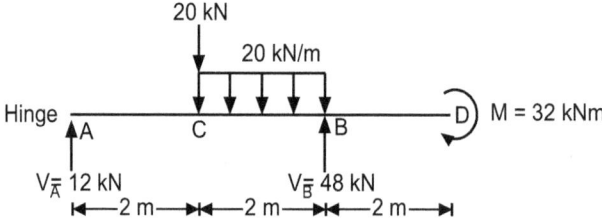

**(a) Given structure**

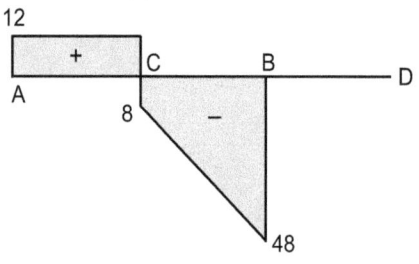

**(c) SFD (kN)**

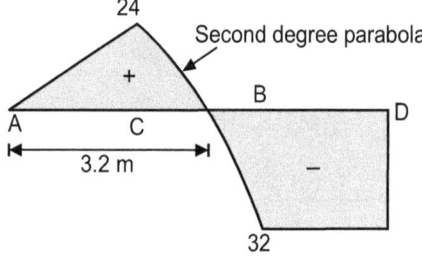

**(d) BMD (kN.m)**

**Fig. 5.38**

$\Sigma M_A = 0$;  $\quad V_B \times 4 - M - 20 \times 2 \times 3 - 20 \times 2 = 0$

$$V_B = \frac{M}{4} + 40 \qquad \ldots \text{(ii)}$$

$\Sigma F_y = 0$;  $\quad V_A + V_B - 20 \times 2 - 20 = 0$

$$V_A + V_B = 60 \qquad \ldots \text{(iii)}$$

Put equation (i) in equation (ii),

$$\frac{1}{4} V_B + V_B = 60$$

$$\therefore \quad V_B = 48 \text{ kN } (\uparrow)$$
$$\therefore \quad V_A = 12 \text{ kN } (\uparrow)$$
$$\therefore \quad M = 32 \text{ kN.m } (\circlearrowleft)$$
$$\Sigma F_X = 0 ; \quad H_A = 0$$

FBD of beam is as shown in Fig. 5.38 (b).

(ii) SF calculations :

$$SF_A = 12 \text{ kN}$$
$$SF_D = 0$$
$$SF_B \text{ (just to the right)} = 0$$
$$SF_B \text{ (just to the left)} = 0 - 48 = -48 \text{ kN}$$
$$SF_C \text{ (just to the left)} = 12 \text{ kN}$$
$$SF_C \text{ (just to the right)} = 12 - 20 = -8 \text{ kN}$$

SFD is as shown in Fig. 5.38 (c).

(iii) BM calculations :

$$BM_A = 0$$
$$BM_B = BM_D = -32 \text{ kN.m}$$
$$BM_C = 12 \times 2 = 24 \text{ kN.m}$$

To locate point of contraflexure, consider a section at a distance 'x' from A in zone CB.

$$BM_x = 12x - 20(x-2) - \frac{20(x-2)^2}{2} = 0$$
$$\therefore \quad x^2 - 3.2x = 0$$
$$\therefore \quad x = 3.2 \text{ m from A.}$$

BMD is as shown in Fig. 5.38 (d).

**Example 5.32 :** The beam is supported and loaded as shown in Fig. 5.39 (a). Draw SFD and BMD indicating all the important values.

**Data** : As shown in Fig. 5.39 (a).
**Required** : SFD, BMD.
**Solution** : (i) Reactions :

$$\Sigma M_A = 0 ; \quad \therefore \quad V_B \times 3.5 - 4 \times 2 \times 2.5 - 6 \times 4 - \frac{1}{2} \times 4 \times 1.5 \times \frac{1}{3} \times 1.5 = 0$$
$$\therefore \quad V_B = 13 \text{ kN } (\uparrow)$$
$$\Sigma F_y = 0 ; \quad \therefore \quad V_A + V_B - \frac{1}{2} \times 4 \times 1.5 - 4 \times 2 - 6 = 0$$
$$\therefore \quad V_A = 4 \text{ kN } (\uparrow)$$

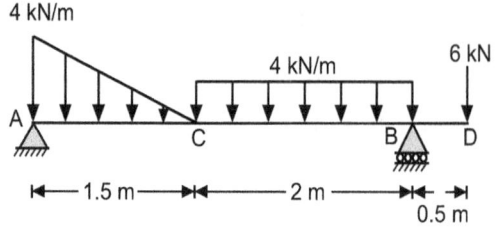

(a) Given structure

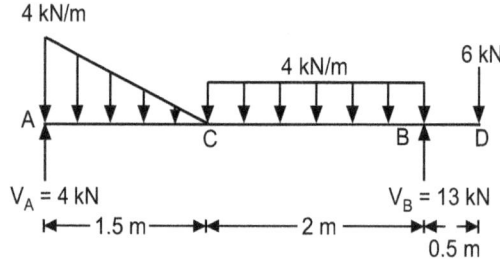

(b) FBD

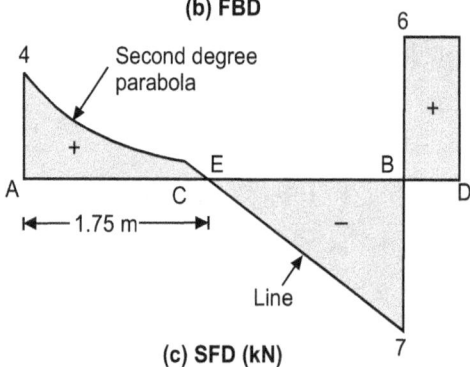

(c) SFD (kN)

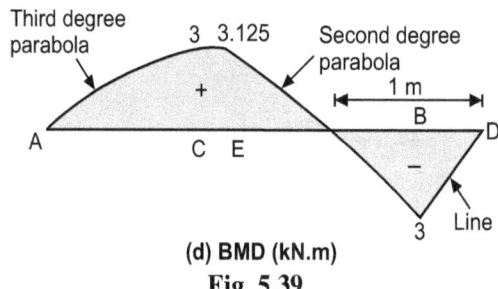

(d) BMD (kN.m)
Fig. 5.39

$\Sigma F_x = 0$;  $H_A = 0$

FBD of beam is as shown in Fig. 5.39 (b).

(ii) SF calculations :

$$SF_A = 4 \text{ kN}$$

$$SF_C = 4 - \frac{1}{2} \times 4 \times 1.5 = 1 \text{ kN}$$

$$SF_D = 6 \text{ kN}$$

$SF_B$ (just to the right) $= 6$ kN

$SF_B$ (just to the left) $= 6 - 13 = -7$ kN

To locate point of zero SF, consider a section at a distance x from A in zone CB.

$$SF_x = 4 - \frac{1}{2} \times 4 \times 1.5 - 4 \times (x - 1.5) = 0$$

∴ $x = 1.75$ m from A

SFD is as shown in Fig. 5.39 (c).

(iii) BM calculations :

$$BM_A = BM_D = 0$$

$$BM_C = 4 \times 1.5 - \frac{1}{2} \times 4 \times 1.5 \times \frac{2}{3} \times 1.5 = 3 \text{ kN.m}$$

BM at point of zero SF = $BM_E = 4 \times 1.75 - \frac{1}{2} \times 4 \times 1.5 \times \left(\frac{2}{3} \times 1.5 + 0.25\right) - 4 \times \frac{(0.25)^2}{2}$

$$= 3.125 \text{ kN.m}$$

$$BM_B = -6 \times 0.5 = -3 \text{ kN.m}$$

To locate point of contraflexure, consider a section at a distance x from D in zone BC.

$$BM_x = -6x + 13(x - 0.5) - 4 \frac{(x - 0.5)^2}{2} = 0$$

∴ $x^2 - 4.5x + 3.5 = 0$

Solving, $x = 1$ m > 0.5 m and < 2.5 m, OK

or $x = 3.5$ m > 2.5 m, hence neglected.

---

**Example 5.33** : The beam is supported and loaded as shown in Fig. 5.40 (a). Find the magnitude of force P such that reactions at A and B are equal. Also draw SFD and BMD.

**Data** : As shown in Fig. 5.40 (a).

**Required** : Magnitude of P and SFD, BMD.

**Solution** : (i) Reactions and magnitude of force 'P' :

Let $V_A = V_B = V$ (say)

$\sum M_A = 0$ ; $V \times 3 - P \times 4 - \frac{1}{2} \times 3 \times 6 \times \frac{1}{3} \times 3 = 0$

$$V = \frac{4}{3} P + 3 \qquad \ldots \text{(i)}$$

$\sum F_y = 0$ ; $2V - \frac{1}{2} \times 3 \times 6 - P = 0$

$$V = \frac{P}{2} + 4.5 \qquad \ldots \text{(ii)}$$

Equating (i) and (ii),

$$\frac{4}{3} P + 3 = \frac{P}{2} + 4.5$$

∴ $P = 1.8$ kN

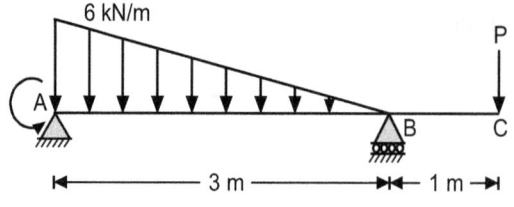

**(a) Given structure**

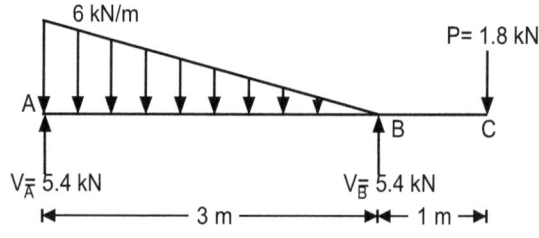

**(b) FBD**

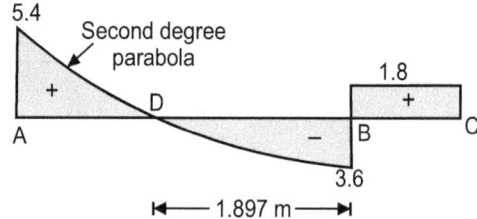

**(c) SFD (kN)**

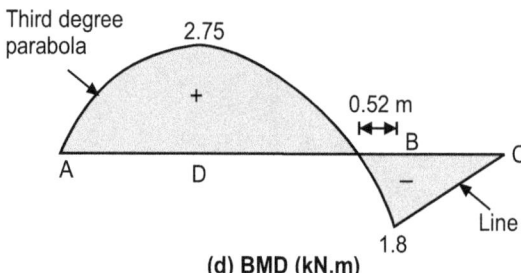

**(d) BMD (kN.m)**

**Fig. 5.40**

$$\therefore \quad V_A = V_B = \frac{P}{2} + 4.5 = \frac{1.8}{2} + 4.5 = 5.4 \text{ kN } (\uparrow)$$

(ii) SF calculations :

$$SF_A = 5.4 \text{ kN}$$

$$SF_B \text{ (just to the left)} = 5.4 - \frac{1}{2} \times 3 \times 6 = -3.6 \text{ kN}$$

$$SF_B \text{ (just to the right)} = -3.6 + 5.4 = 1.8 \text{ kN}$$

$$SF_C = 1.8 \text{ kN}$$

To locate point of zero SF, consider a section at a distance x from B in zone BA.

$$SF_x = -3.6 + \frac{1}{2} \times x \times 2x = 0$$

∴  $x = 1.897$ m from B.

(iii) BM calculations :

$$BM_A = BM_C = 0$$
$$BM_B = -1.8 \times 1 = -1.8 \text{ kN.m}$$

BM at point of zero SF = $BM_D = -1.8 \times 2.897 + 5.4 \times 1.897 - \frac{1}{2} \times 1.897 \times 2 \times 1.897 \times \frac{1.897}{3}$

$$= 2.75 \text{ kN.m}$$

To locate point of contraflexure, consider a section at a distance x from 'B' in zone BA.

$$BM_x = -1.8(x+1) - \frac{1}{2} \times x \times 2x \times \frac{x}{3} + 5.4 x = 0$$

∴  $3.6 x - \frac{x^3}{3} - 1.8 = 0$

Solving by trial and error,

$x = 0.52$ m from B.

**Example 5.34 :** The beam is supported and loaded as shown in Fig. 5.41 (a). Draw SFD and BMD indicating all the important values.

**Data :**   As shown in Fig. 5.41 (a).

**Required :** SFD, BMD.

**Solution :** (i) Reactions :

For member DE :  $V_D = V_E = \frac{40}{2} = 20$ kN (↑) by symmetry.

For member ABC :

$\Sigma M_A = 0$ ;   $V_B \times 4 - 20 \times 5 - 20 \times \frac{4^2}{2} = 0$

$V_B = 65$ kN (↑)

$\Sigma F_y = 0$ ;   $V_A + V_B - 20 \times 4 - 20 = 0$

∴   $V_A = 35$ kN (↑)

FBD of members is as shown in Fig. 5.41 (b).

(ii) SF calculations :

$SF_A = 35$ kN

$SF_B$ (just to the left) $= 35 - 20 \times 4 = -45$ kN

$SF_B$ (just to the right) $= -45 + 65 = 20$ kN

$SF_E = -20$ kN

$SF_F$ (just to the right) = – 20 kN

$SF_F$ (just to the left) = – 20 + 40 = 20 kN

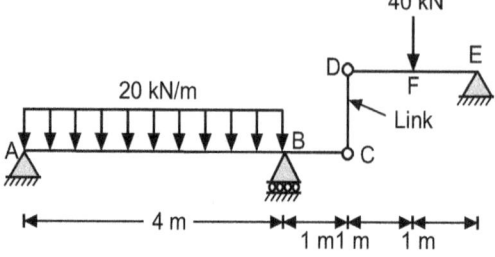

(a) Given beam

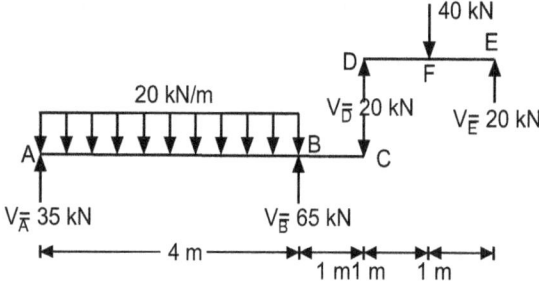

(b) FBD of members

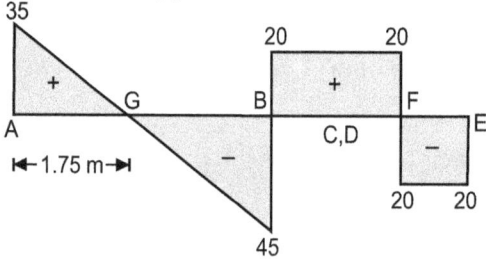

(c) SFD (kN)

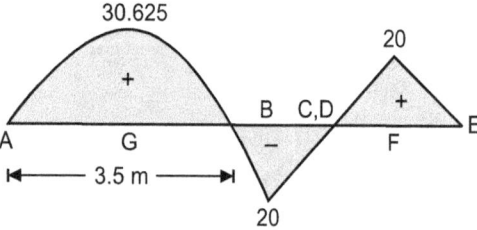

(d) BMD (kN.m)

Fig. 5.41

To locate point of zero SF, consider a section at a distance 'x' from A in zone AB.

$$SF_x = 35 - 20x = 0 \quad \therefore \quad x = 1.75 \text{ m from A}$$

SFD is as shown in Fig. 5.41 (c).

(iii) BM calculations :

$$BM_A = BM_C = BM_D = BM_E = 0$$

BM at point of zero SF $= BM_G$

$$= 35 \times 1.75 - 20 \times \frac{(1.75)^2}{2}$$

$$= 30.625 \text{ kN.m}$$

$$BM_B = -20 \times 1 = -20 \text{ kN.m}$$

$$BM_F = 20 \times 1 = 20 \text{ kN.m}$$

To locate point of contraflexure, consider a section at a distance 'x' from A in zone AB.

$$BM_x = 35x - 20\frac{x^2}{2} = 0$$

∴ $\quad x = 3.5$ m from A.

BMD is as shown in Fig. 5.41 (d)

**Example 5.35 :** The beam is supported and loaded as shown in Fig. 5.42 (a). Draw AFD, SFD and BMD indicating all the important values.

**Data** : As shown in Fig. 5.42 (a).

**Required** : AFD, SFD and BMD.

**Solution** : (i) Reactions :

Total vertical load due to UDL $= 10 \times 3 = 30$ kN (↓)

Component of load normal to AB $= 30 \cos 30 = 26$ kN (↘)

Component of load parallel to AB $= 30 \sin 30 = 15$ kN (↙)

By symmetry, reactions at A and B normal to AB

$$= \frac{26}{2} = 13 \text{ kN } (↖)$$

Reaction at A along AB $= 15$ kN (↗)

FBD of beam is as shown in Fig. 5.42 (b).

Length of beam AB $= \dfrac{3}{\cos 30} = 3.464$ m.

Intensity of UDL normal to AB $= \dfrac{26}{3.464} = 7.5$ kN/m.

Intensity of UDL tangential to AB $= \dfrac{15}{3.464} = 4.33$ kN/m.

(ii) Axial force, SF and BM equations :

Consider a section at a distance 'x' from 'A' along AB.

| Zone | Origin | Limits (m) | $AF_x$ (kN) | $SF_x$ (kN) | $BM_x$ (kN.m) |
|---|---|---|---|---|---|
| AB | A | 0 – 3.464 | $-15 + 4.33x$ | $13 - 7.5x$ | $13x - 7.5\dfrac{x^2}{2}$ |

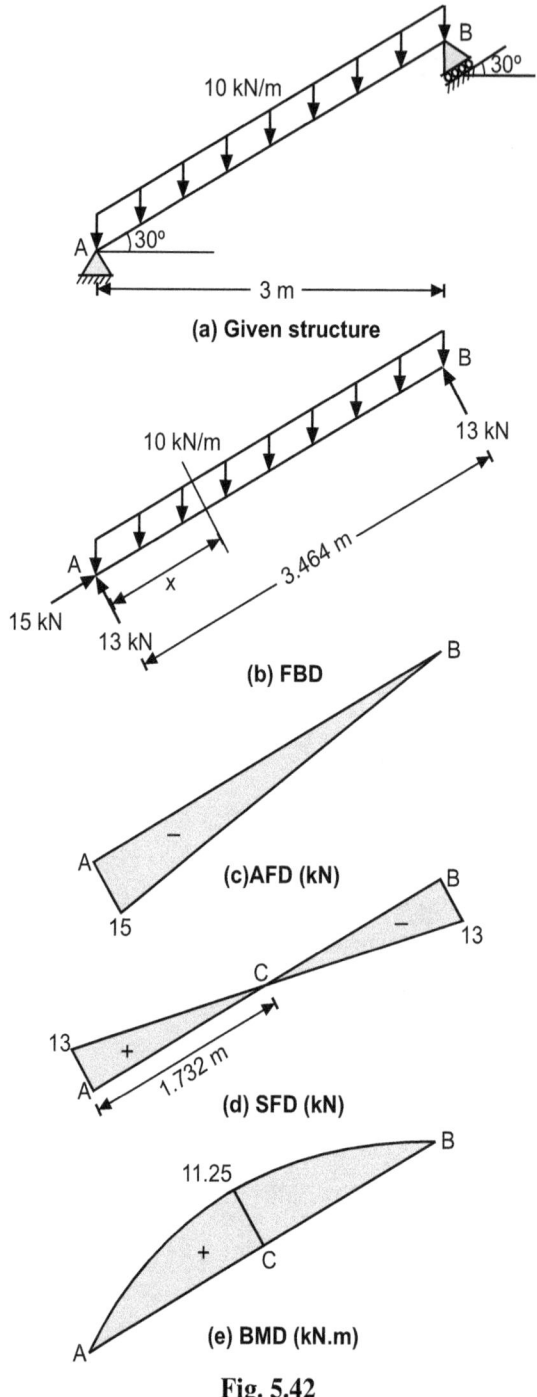

Fig. 5.42

(iii) Axial force :
 put x = 0 ;  $AF_A = -15 + 4.33 \times 0 = -15$ kN
 put x = 3.464 m ;  $AF_B = -15 + 4.33 \times 3.464 = 0$
 AFD is as shown in Fig. 5.42 (c).

(iv) Shear force :

put x = 0 ;   $SF_A = 13 - 7.5 \times 0 = 13$ kN

put x = 3.464 m ;   $SF_B = 13 - 7.5 \times 3.464 = -13$ kN

To locate point of zero SF ; equate SF equation to zero.
$$SF_X = 13 - 7.5 x = 0$$
$$\therefore \quad x = 1.733 \text{ m from A.}$$

SFD is as shown in Fig. 5.42 (d).

(v) Bending moment :

put x = 0 ;   $BM_A = 13 \times 0 - \frac{7.5}{2} (0) = 0$

put x = 1.732 m ;   $BM_C = 13 \times 1.733 - \frac{7.5}{2} (1.733)^2 = 11.25$ kN.m

put x = 3.464 m ;   $BM_B = 13 \times 3.464 - \frac{7.5}{2} (3.464)^2 = 0$

BMD is as shown in Fig. 5.42 (e).

**Example 5.36 :** The beam is supported and loaded as shown in Fig. 5.43 (a). Draw SFD and BMD, indicating all the important values.

**Data** : As shown in Fig. 5.43 (a).

**Required** : SFD, BMD.

**Solution** : (i) Reactions :

$\Sigma M_C = 0$ (LHS) ;   $-V_B \times 4 + 20 \times \frac{6^2}{2} = 0$

$\therefore \quad V_B = 90$ kN (↑)

$\Sigma F_y = 0$ ;   $V_B + V_D - 20 \times 8 = 0$

$\therefore \quad V_D = 70$ kN (↑)

$\Sigma M_C = 0$ (RHS) ;   $70 \times 2 - M_D - 20 \times \frac{2^2}{2} = 0$

$\therefore \quad M_D = 100$ kN.m (↻)

FBD of beam is as shown in Fig. 5.43 (b).

(ii) SF calculations :

$$SF_A = 0$$
$$SF_B \text{ (just to the left)} = -20 \times 2 = -40 \text{ kN}$$
$$SF_B \text{ (just to the right)} = -40 + 90 = 50 \text{ kN}$$
$$SF_D = -70 \text{ kN}$$

To locate point of zero SF, shear force at a distance x from D in zone DB is,
$$= SF_X = -70 + 20 x = 0$$
$$\therefore \quad x = 3.5 \text{ m from D.}$$

SFD of beam is as shown in Fig. 5.43 (c).

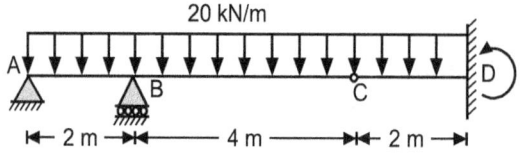
(a) Given beam

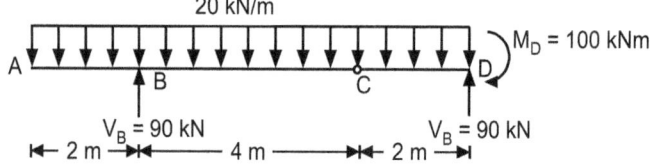
(b) FBD of beam

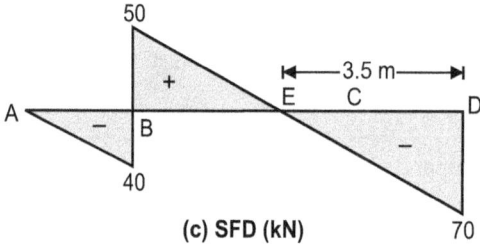
(c) SFD (kN)

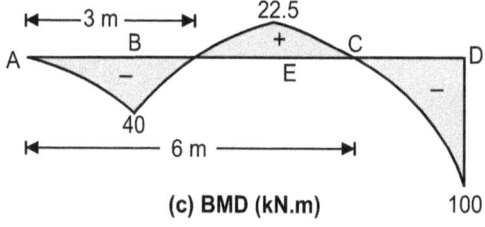
(c) BMD (kN.m)

**Fig. 5.43**

(iii) BM calculations :

$$BM_A = BM_C = 0$$

$$BM_B = \frac{-20 \times 2^2}{2} = -40 \text{ kN.m}$$

BM at point of zero SF $= BM_E = 90 \times 2.5 - 20 \times \frac{(4.5)^2}{2} = 22.5$ kN.m

$$BM_D = -100 \text{ kN.m}$$

To locate point of contraflexure, consider a section at a distance 'x' from A in the zone BC.

$$BM_x = 90(x-2) - 20\frac{x^2}{2} = 0$$

∴ $\quad 90x - 180 - 10x^2 = 0$

∴ $\quad x^2 - 9x + 18 = 0$

Solving, $\quad$ x = 3 m and 6 m

BMD is as shown in Fig. 5.43 (d).

**Example 5.37 :** The beam is supported and loaded as shown in Fig. 5.44 (a). Draw SFD and BMD indicating all the important values.

**Data** : As shown in Fig. 5.44 (a).

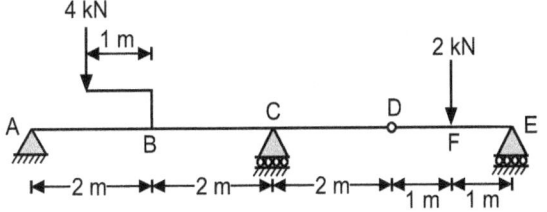

(a) Given structure

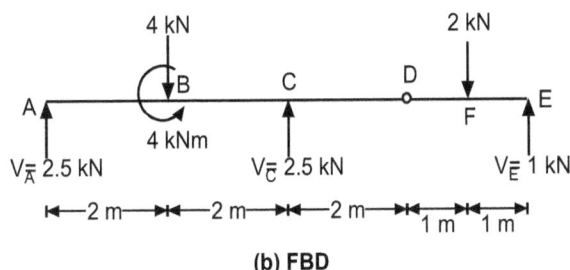

(b) FBD

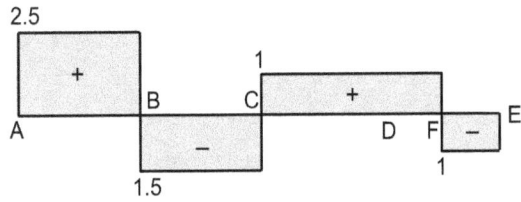

(c) SFD (kN)

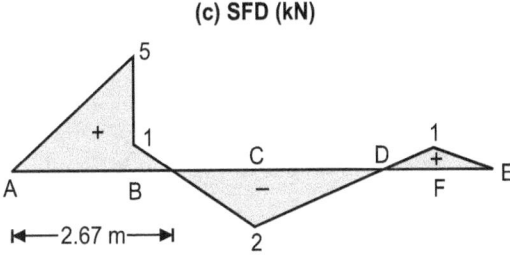

(d) BMD (kN.m)

Fig. 5.44

**Required :** SFD, BMD.

**Solution :** (i) Reactions :

At D, internal hinge is provided, hence,

$\Sigma M_{D\,(LHS)} = \Sigma M_{D\,(RHS)} = 0$

$\Sigma M_D = 0_{(RHS)};\quad V_E \times 2 - 2 \times 1 = 0$

∴   $V_E = 1$ kN (↑)

$\Sigma M_A = 0$ ;   $V_C \times 4 + V_E \times 8 - 2 \times 7 - 4 \times 2 + 4 = 0$

∴   $V_C = 2.5$ kN (↑)

$\Sigma F_y = 0$ ;   $V_A + V_C + V_E - 4 - 2 = 0$

∴   $V_A = 2.5$ kN (↑)

$\Sigma F_x = 0$ ;   $H_A = 0$

FBD of beam is as shown in Fig. 5.44 (b).

(ii) SF calculations :

$SF_A = 2.5$ kN

$SF_B$ (just to the left) = 2.5 kN

$SF_B$ (just to the right) = 2.5 − 4 = − 1.5 kN

$SF_C$ (just to the left) = − 1.5 kN

$SF_C$ (just to the right) = − 1.5 + 2.5 = 1 kN

$SF_E = -1$ kN

$SF_F$ (just to the right) = − 1 kN

$SF_F$ (just to the left) = − 1 + 2 = 1 kN

SFD is as shown in Fig. 5.44 (c).

(iii) BM calculations :

$BM_A = BM_D = BM_E = 0$

$BM_B$ (just to the left) = 2.5 × 2 = 5 kN.m

$BM_B$ (just to the right) = 5 − 4 = 1 kN.m

$BM_C = 1 \times 4 - 2 \times 3 = -2$ kN.m

$BM_F = 1 \times 1 = 1$ kN.m

To locate point of contraflexure, consider a section at a distance x from A in zone BC.

$BM_x = 2.5x - 4 - 4(x - 2) = 0$

x = 2.67 m from A.

BMD is as shown in Fig. 5.44 (d).

**Example 5.38 :** The beam is supported and loaded as shown in Fig. 5.45 (a). Draw SFD and BMD indicating all the important values.

**Data :**   As shown in Fig. 5.45 (a).

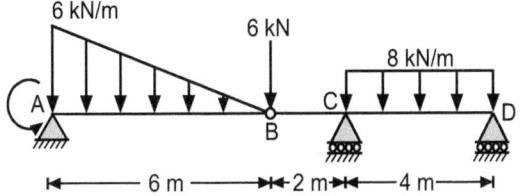
**(a) Given structure**

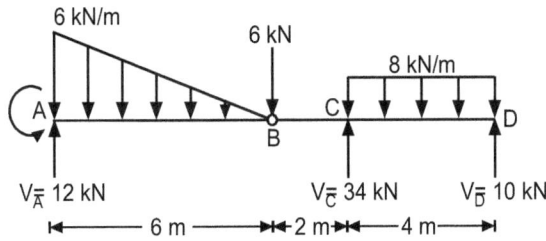
**(b) FBD**

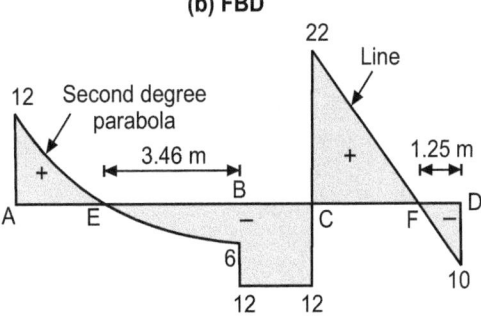
**(c) SFD (kN)**

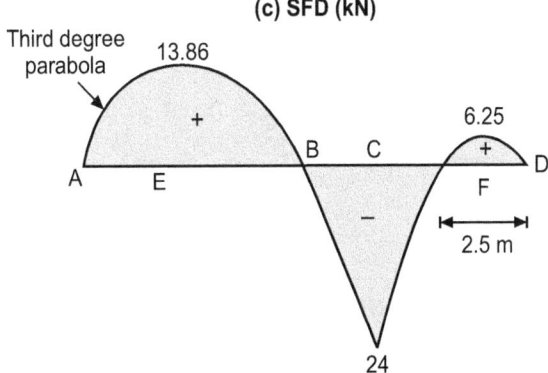
**(d) BMD (kN.m)**
Fig. 5.45

**Required :** SFD, BMD.

**Solution :** (i) Reactions :

At B, there is an internal hinge, hence ;

$\Sigma M_{B\,(LHS)} = \Sigma M_{B\,(RHS)} = 0$

$\Sigma M_{B\,(LHS)} = 0$ ;     $-V_A \times 6 + \frac{1}{2} \times 6 \times 6 \times \frac{2}{3} \times 6 = 0$

∴     $V_A = 12$ kN (↑)

$\Sigma M_D = 0$ ;     $-V_A \times 12 - V_C \times 4 + \frac{1}{2} \times 6 \times 6 \times (6+4) + 6 \times 6 + 8 \times \frac{4^2}{2} = 0$

∴     $V_C = 34$ kN (↑)

$\Sigma F_y = 0$ ;     $V_A + V_C + V_D - \frac{1}{2} \times 6 \times 6 - 6 - 8 \times 4 = 0$

∴     $V_A = 10$ kN (↑)

FBD of beam is as shown in Fig. 5.45 (b).

(ii)  SF calculations :

$SF_A = 12$ kN

$SF_B$ (just to the left) $= 12 - \frac{1}{2} \times 6 \times 6 = -6$ kN

$SF_B$ (just to the right) $= -6 - 6 = -12$ kN

$SF_D = -10$ kN

$SF_C$ (just to the right) $= -10 + 8 \times 4 = 22$ kN

$SF_C$ (just to the left) $= 22 - 34 = -12$ kN.

To locate point of zero SF in zone AB, consider a section at a distance x from B,

$SF_x = -6 + \frac{1}{2} \times x \times \frac{6}{6} \, x = 0$

∴     $-6 + \frac{x^2}{2} = 0$    ∴  $x = 3.46$ m from B.

To locate point of zero SF in zone DC, consider a section at a distance 'x' from D.

$SF_x = -10 + 8x = 0$   ∴  $x = 1.25$ m from D.

SFD is as shown in Fig. 5.45 (c).

(iii) BM calculations :

$BM_A = BM_B = BM_D = 0$

$BM_E = 6 \times 3.46 - \frac{1}{2} \times 3.46 \times 3.46 \times \frac{1}{3} \times 3.46 = 13.85$ kN.m

$BM_C = 10 \times 4 - 8 \times \frac{4^2}{2} = -24$ kN.m

$BM_F = 10 \times 1.25 - \frac{8 \times (1.25)^2}{2} = 6.25$ kN.m

To locate point of contraflexure, consider a section at a distance x from D in zone DC.

$BM_x = 10x - \frac{8x^2}{2} = 0$

∴     $x = 2.5$ m from D.

BMD is as shown in Fig. 5.45 (d).

**Example 5.39 :** The beam is supported and loaded as shown in Fig. 5.46 (a). Draw SFD and BMD indicating all the important values.

**Data**    :   As shown in Fig. 5.46 (a).

**Required :** SFD, BMD.

**Solution :** (i) Reactions :

Consider FBD of member as shown in Fig. 5.46 (b).

For member BC ;

$\Sigma M_B = 0$ ;   $V_C \times 4 - 4 \times 2 \times 3 - 10 \times 2 = 0$

$\therefore$   $V_C = 11$ kN ($\uparrow$)

$\Sigma F_y = 0$ ;   $V_B + V_C - 10 - 4 \times 2 = 0$

$V_B = 7$ kN ($\uparrow$)

For member AB ;

$\Sigma F_y = 0$ ;   $V_A - 7 = 0$   $\therefore$   $V_A = 7$ kN ($\uparrow$)

$\Sigma M_A = 0$ ;   $M_A - 7 \times 3 = 0$   $\therefore$   $M_A = 21$ kN.m ($\circlearrowleft$)

$\Sigma F_x = 0$ ;   $H_A = 0$

For member CD :

$\Sigma F_y = 0$ ;   $V_D - 11 - \frac{1}{2} \times 5 \times 4 = 0$   $\therefore$   $V_D = 21$ kN ($\uparrow$)

$\Sigma M_D = 0$ ;   $- M_D + 11 \times 4 + \frac{1}{2} \times 5 \times 4 \times \frac{4}{3} = 0$

$\therefore$   $M_D = 57.33$ kN.m ($\circlearrowleft$)

$\Sigma F_x = 0$ ;   $H_D = 0$

FBD of beam is as shown in Fig. 5.46 (c).

(ii) SF calculations :   $SF_A = 7$ kN

$SF_E$ (just to the left) = 7 kN

$SF_E$ (just to the right) = 7 − 10 = − 3 kN

$SF_C = 7 - 10 - 4 \times 2 = -11$ kN

$SF_D = -21$ kN

SFD is as shown in Fig. 5.46 (d).

(iii) BM calculations :

$BM_B = BM_C = 0$

$BM_A = -21$ kN.m

$BM_E = 7 \times 2 = 14$ kN.m

$BM_D = -57.33$ kN.m

BMD is as shown in Fig. 5.46 (e).

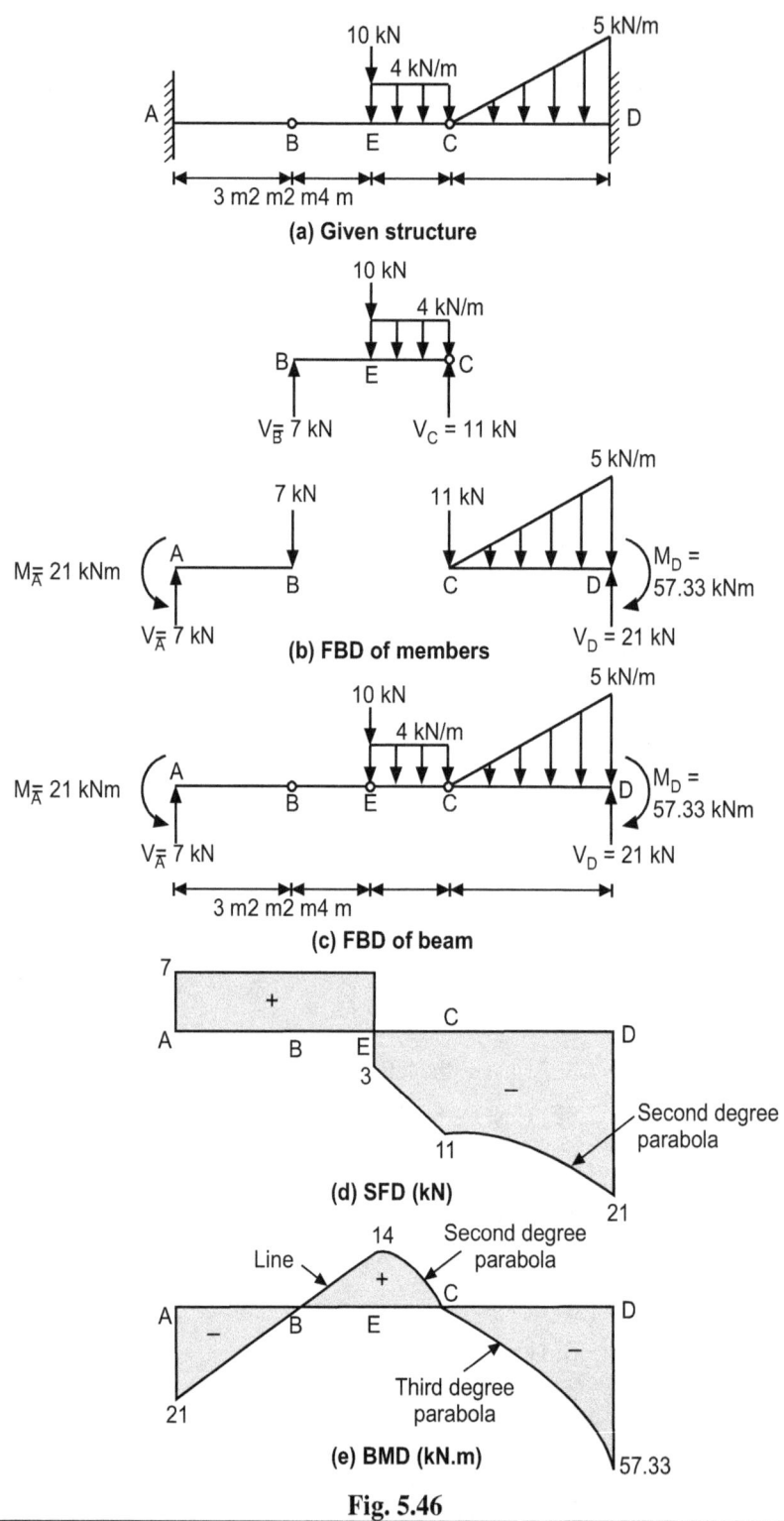

Fig. 5.46

**Example 5.40 :** Draw SFD and BMD for the beam shown in Fig. 5.47. A is a hinged support. Reaction offered by soil is uniformly distributed over length CD of the beam. Locate point of contraflexure and point of maximum B.M.

**Data :** As shown in Fig. 5.47.

**Required :** BMD.

**Solution :**

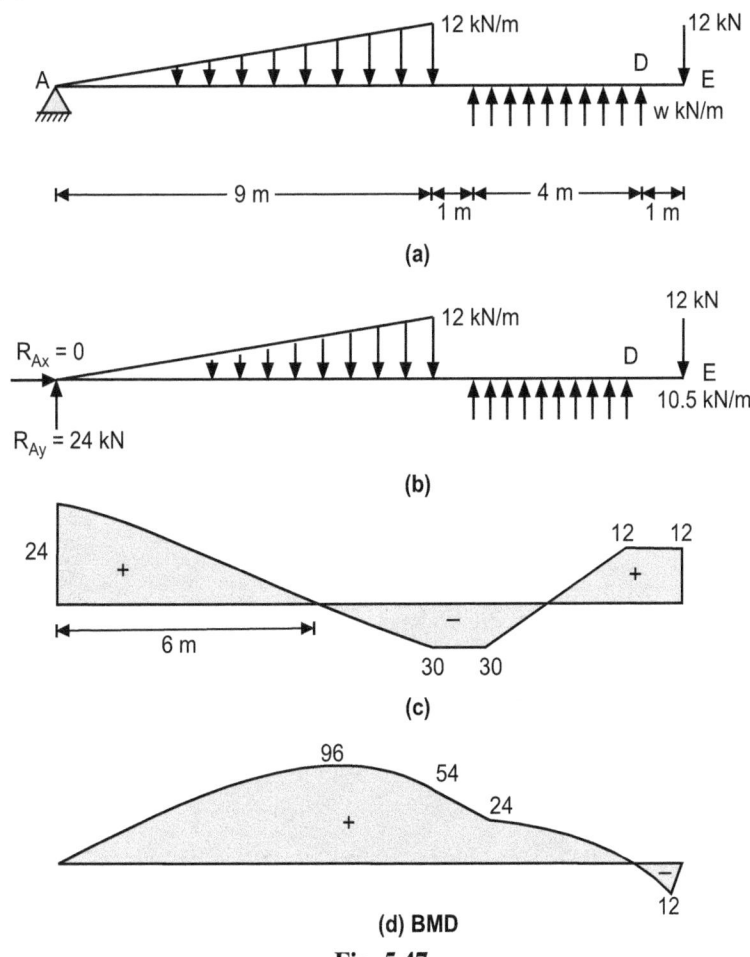

(d) BMD
Fig. 5.47

(i) Reactions :

$$\Sigma M @ A = 0; \quad -\frac{1}{2} \times 12 \times 9 \times 6.0 + w \times 4 \times 12 - 12 \times 15 = 0$$

∴  $w = 10.5$ kN/m

$$\Sigma F_y = 0; \quad R_{Ay} - \frac{1}{2} \times 12 \times 9 + 10.5 \times 4 - 12 = 0$$

∴  $R_{Ay} = 24$ kN (↑)

$\Sigma F_x = 0; \quad R_{Ax} = 0$

(ii) SF calculations :

$SF_A = 24$ kN

$$SF_B = 24 - \frac{1}{2} \times 12 \times 9 = -30 \text{ kN}$$

$$SF_C = -30 \text{ kN}$$

$$SF_D = -30 + 10.5 \times 4 = 12 \text{ kN}$$

$$SF_E = 12 \text{ kN}$$

To locate point of zero SF, consider a section at a distance x from A in zone AB.

$$\therefore \quad \frac{12}{9} = \frac{y}{x} \qquad \therefore y = \frac{4}{3} x$$

$$\therefore \quad SF_x = 24 - \frac{1}{2} \times x \times y = 0$$

$$24 - \frac{1}{2} \times x \times \frac{4}{3} x = 0$$

$$\therefore \quad x = 6 \text{ m from A.}$$

SFD is as shown in Fig. 5.47 (c).

(iii) BM calculations :

$$BM_A = BM_E = 0$$

BM at a point of zero SF $= BM_F$

$$= 24 \times 6 - \frac{1}{2} \times 6 \times \frac{4}{3} \times 6 \times \frac{6}{3}$$

$$= 96 \text{ kN-m}$$

$$BM_B = 24 \times 9 - \frac{1}{2} \times 12 \times 9 \times 3 = 54 \text{ kN.m}$$

$$BM_C = 24 \times 10 - \frac{1}{2} \times 12 \times 9 \times 4 = 24 \text{ kN.m}$$

$$BM_D = 24 \times 14 - \frac{1}{2} \times 12 \times 9 \times 8 + 10.5 \times 4 \times 2$$

$$= -12 \text{ kN.m}$$

To locate point of contraflexure, consider a section at a distance x from E in zone CD.

$$BM_x = -12 \times (x + 1) + 10.5 \frac{x^2}{2} = 0$$

$$= -2.286 x - 2.286 + x^2 = 0$$

$$\therefore \quad x = \frac{2.286 \pm \sqrt{(-2.286)^2 - 4 \times 1 \times (-2.286)}}{2}$$

$$= 3.04 \text{ m from E}$$

BMD is shown in Fig. 5.47 (d).

**Example 5.41 :** A simply supported beam ABC is loaded as shown in Fig. 5.48. Determine the location at which a concentrated load 5 kN must act from end A to make the reactions at A and B equal. Draw SFD and BMD.

**Data :** As shown in Fig. 5.48.
**Required :** x, SFD, BMD.

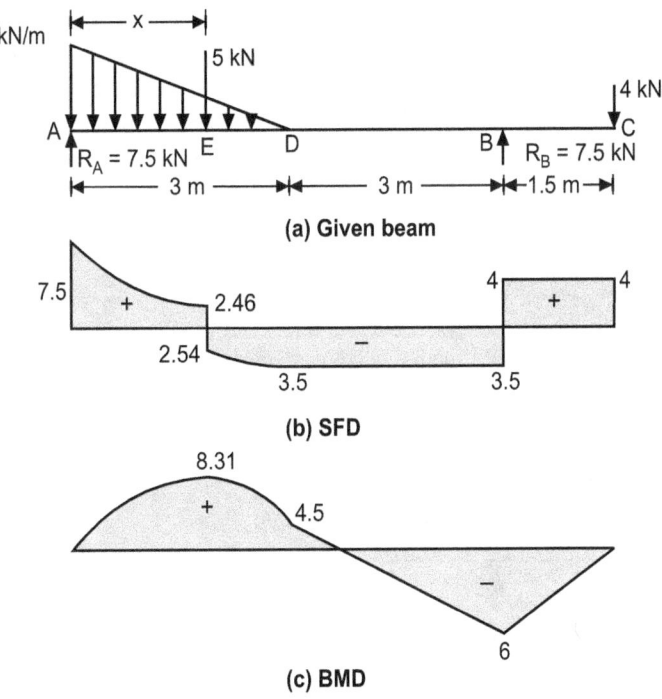

Fig. 5.48

**Solution :** (i) Reactions :

$$R_A = R_B$$

$$\therefore \quad R_A = R_B = \frac{\text{Total load}}{2} = \frac{\frac{1}{2} \times 4 \times 3 + 5 + 4}{2} = 7.5 \text{ kN}$$

(ii) Position of x :

$$\Sigma M @ A = 0; \quad -\frac{1}{2} \times 4 \times 3 \times \frac{3}{3} - 5 \times x + 7.5 \times 6 - 4 \times 7.5 = 0$$

$$\therefore \quad x = 1.8 \text{ m from A}$$

(iii) SF calculations :

$$SF_A = 7.5 \text{ kN}$$

$$SF_E \text{ (just to the left)} = 7.5 - \frac{(4 + 1.6)}{2} \times 1.8 = 2.46 \text{ kN}$$

$$SF_E \text{ (just to the right)} = 2.46 - 5 = -2.54 \text{ kN}$$

$$SF_D = -2.54 - \frac{1}{2} \times 1.6 \times 1.2 = -3.5 \text{ kN}$$

SF$_B$ (just to the left) = $-3.5$ kN
SF$_B$ (just to the right) = $-3.5 + 7.5 = 4.0$ kN
SF$_C$ = 4 kN

SFD is as shown in Fig. 5.48 (b).

(iv) BM calculations :

$$BM_A = 0$$

$$BM_E = 7.5 \times 1.8 - \left[\frac{1}{2} \times (4 + 1.6) \times 1.8 \left(\frac{2 \times 4 + 1.6}{4 + 1.6}\right) \times \frac{1.8}{3}\right]$$
$$= 8.316 \text{ kN.m}$$

$$BM_D = 7.5 \times 3 - \frac{1}{2} \times 4 \times 3 \times 2 - 5 \times 1.2 = 4.5 \text{ kN.m}$$

$$BM_B = 7.5 \times 6 - \frac{1}{2} \times 4 \times 3 \times 5 - 5 \times 4.2 = -6 \text{ kN.m}$$

$$BM_C = 0$$

BMD is as shown in Fig. 5.48 (c).

**Example 5.42 :** For a beam loaded as shown in Fig. 5.49, draw SFD and BMD, indicating all the important values.

**Data :** As shown in Fig. 5.49.

**Required :** SFD and BMD.

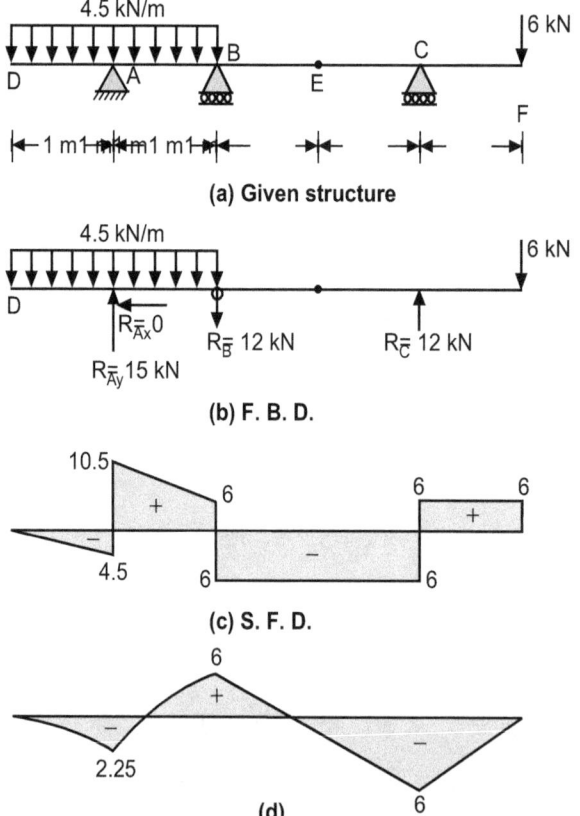

Fig. 5.49

**Solution :** (i) Reactions :

$\Sigma M @ E = 0$ (Right part of hinge)

∴ $\quad R_C \times 1 - 6 \times 2 = 0 \qquad\qquad \therefore R_C = 12$ kN

$\Sigma M @ E = 0$ (Left part of hinge)

$\quad -R_{Ay} \times 2 - R_B \times 1 + 4.5 \times 2 \times 2 = 0$

∴ $\qquad\qquad 2 R_{Ay} + R_B = 18$

$\qquad\qquad\qquad \Sigma F_y = 0$

∴ $\quad R_{Ay} + R_B + R_C - 4.5 \times 2 - 6 = 0$

∴ $\quad R_{Ay} + 18 - 2 R_{Ay} + 12 - 15 = 0$

∴ $\qquad\qquad\qquad R_{Ay} = +15$ kN (↑)

$\qquad\qquad 2 R_{Ay} + R_B = 18$

∴ $\qquad\qquad\qquad R_B = -12$ kN

$\qquad\qquad\qquad\quad = 12$ kN (↓)

(ii) SF calculations :

$\quad SF_A$ (just to the left) $= -4.5 \times 1 = -4.5$ kN

$\quad SF_A$ (just to the right) $= -4.5 + 15 = 10.5$ kN

$\quad SF_B$ (just to the left) $= 10.5 - 4.5 \times 1 = 6.0$ kN

$\quad SF_B$ (just to the right) $= 6 - 12 = -6$ kN

$\quad SF_C$ (just to the left) $= -6$ kN

$\quad SF_C$ (just to the right) $= -6 + 12 = 6$ kN

$\qquad\qquad\quad SF_F = 6$ kN

SFD is as shown in Fig. 5.49 (c).

(iii) BM calculations :

$\qquad BM_D = 0$

$\qquad BM_A = -4.5 \times 1 \times 0.5 = -2.25$ kN.m

$\qquad BM_B = -4.5 \times 2 \times 1 + 15 \times 1 = 6$ kN.m

$\qquad BM_E = -4.5 \times 2 \times 2 + 15 \times 2 - 12 \times 1 = 0$

$\qquad BM_C = -4.5 \times 2 \times 3 + 15 \times 3 - 12 \times 2$

$\qquad\qquad = -6$ kN-m

BMD is as shown in Fig. 5.49 (d).

**Example 5.43 :** Draw SFD and BMD for the beam loaded as shown in Fig. 5.50.

**Data :** As shown in Fig. 5.50.

**Required :** SFD, BMD.

**Solution :** (i) Reactions :

$\quad \Sigma M @ A = 0; \quad V_B \times 6 - 10 - 10 \times 2 - 3 \times 4 \times 6 = 0$

∴ $\qquad\qquad V_B = 17$ kN (↑)

$\quad \Sigma F_y = 0; \qquad V_A + V_B - 10 - 3 \times 4 = 0$

∴ $\qquad\qquad V_A = 5$ kN (↑)

(ii) SF calculations :

$$SF_A = 5 \text{ kN}$$
$$SF_C = 5 - 10 = -5 \text{ kN}$$
$$SF_D = -5 \text{ kN}$$
$$SF_B \text{ (just to the left)} = -5 - 3 \times 2 = -11 \text{ kN}$$
$$SF_B \text{ (just to the right)} = -11 + 17 = 6 \text{ kN}$$
$$SF_E = 6 - 6 = 0$$

SFD is as shown in Fig. 5.50 (c).

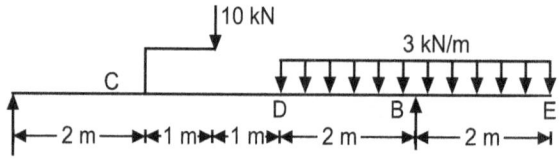

(a) Given structure

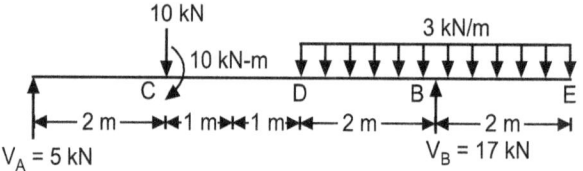

(b) F. B. D.

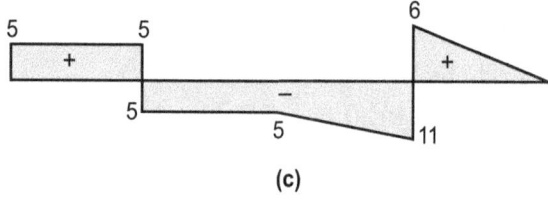

(c)

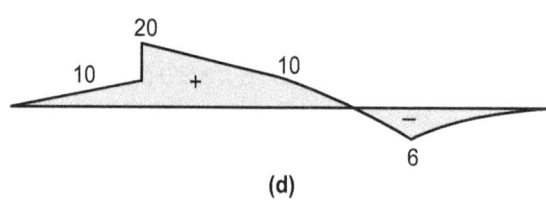

(d)

Fig. 5.50

(iii) BM calculations :

$$BM_A = 0$$
$$BM_C \text{ (just to the left)} = 5 \times 2 = 10 \text{ kN.m}$$
$$BM_C \text{ (just to the right)} = 5 \times 2 + 10 = 20 \text{ kN.m}$$
$$BM_D = 5 \times 4 + 10 - 10 \times 2 = 10 \text{ kN.m}$$
$$BM_B = 5 \times 6 + 10 - 10 \times 4 - 3 \times 2 \times 1 = -6 \text{ kN.m}$$
$$BM_E = 5 \times 8 + 10 - 10 \times 6 - 3 \times 4 \times 2 + 17 \times 2$$
$$= 0$$

BMD is as shown in Fig. 5.50 (d).

**Example 5.44 :** The beam ABC is supported and loaded as shown in Fig. 5.51 (a). Draw AFD, SFD and BMD, indicating all the important values.

**Data** : As shown in Fig. 5.51 (a).

**Required** : AFD, SFD and BMD.

**Solution** : (i) Reactions :

Let T be the tension in wire.

Horizontal and vertical components of tension in wire = 0.7 T as shown in Fig. 5.51 (b).

$\Sigma M_A = 0$ ;  $0.7\,T \times 4 - 40 \times 5 - 30 \times \dfrac{5^2}{2} = 0$

$\qquad\qquad 0.7\,T = 143.75$ kN

$\Sigma F_y = 0$ ;  $V_A + 0.7\,T - 30 \times 5 - 40 = 0$

$\qquad\qquad V_A = 46.25$ kN ($\uparrow$)

$\Sigma F_x = 0$ ;  $H_A - 143.75 = 0$

$\qquad\qquad H_A = 143.75$ kN ($\rightarrow$)

FBD of beam is as shown in Fig. 5.51 (b).

(ii) Axial force :

Beam is subjected to axial compressive force of 143.75 kN from A to B. AFD is as shown in Fig. 5.51 (c).

(iii) SF calculations :  $SF_A = 46.25$ kN

$\qquad\qquad SF_B$ (just to the left) $= 46.25 - 30 \times 4 = -73.75$ kN

$\qquad\qquad SF_B$ (just to the right) $= -73.75 + 143.75 = 70$ kN

$\qquad\qquad SF_C = 40$ kN.

To locate point of zero SF, consider a section at a distance x from A in zone AB.

$\qquad\qquad SF_x = 46.25 - 30\,x = 0$

$\therefore \qquad\qquad x = 1.54$ m from A.

SFD is as shown in Fig. 5.51 (c).

(iv) BM calculations :

$\qquad\qquad BM_A = BM_C = 0$

$\qquad\qquad BM_B = -40 \times 1 - 30 \times \dfrac{1^2}{2} = -55$ kN.m

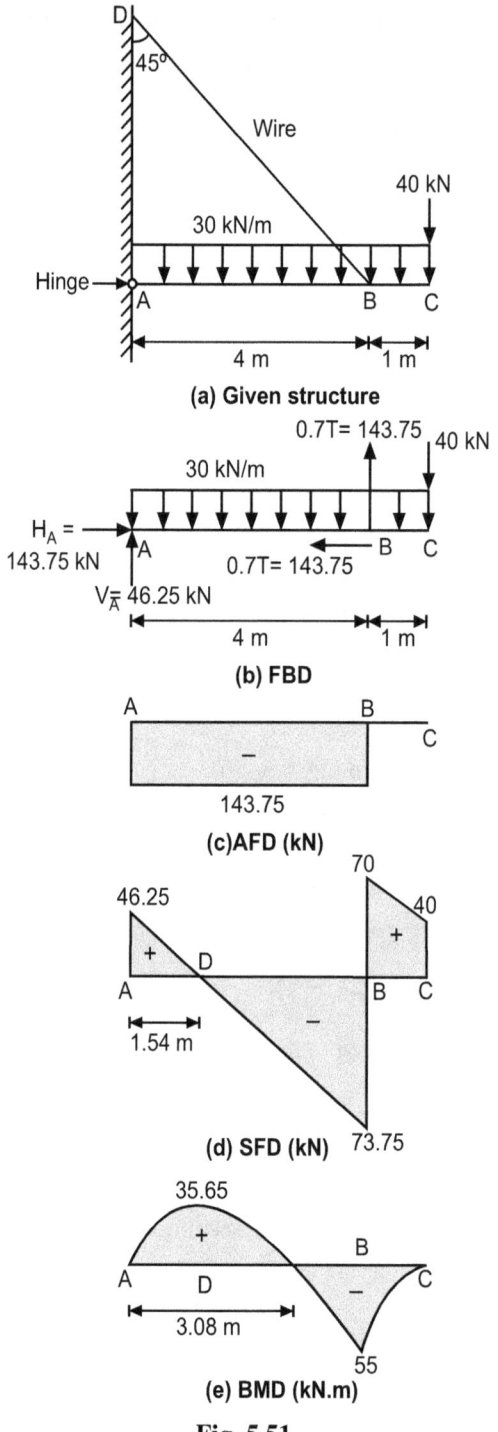

Fig. 5.51

BM at point of zero SF = $BM_D$ = 46.25 × 1.54 − 30 × $\frac{(1.54)^2}{2}$ = 35.65 kN.m

To locate point of contraflexure, consider a section at a distance 'x' from A in zone AB.

$$BM_x = 46.25x - 30\frac{x^2}{2} = 0$$

∴  $x = 3.08$ m from 'A'.

BMD is as shown in Fig. 5.51 (d).

**Example 5.45 :** For a bent up beam ABC shown in Fig. 5.52 (a), draw AFD, SFD and BMD.

**Data :**   As shown in Fig. 5.52 (a).

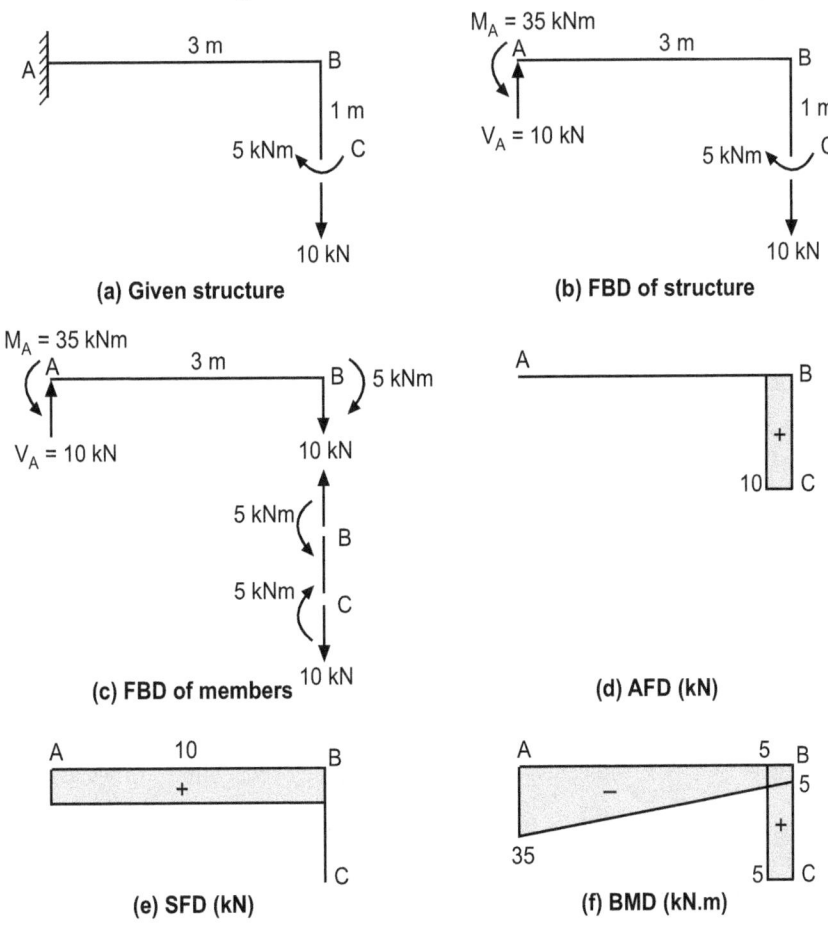

Fig. 5.52

**Required :** AFD, SFD, BMD.

**Solution :** (i) Reactions :

$\Sigma F_y = 0$ ;    $V_A - 10 = 0$    ∴   $V_A = 10$ kN (↑)

$\Sigma F_x = 0$ ;    $H_A = 0$

$\Sigma M_A = 0$ ;   $M_A - 5 - 10 \times 3 = 0$   ∴   $M_A = 35$ kN.m (↺)

FBD of structure is as shown in Fig. 5.52 (b).

Also considering equilibrium of individual members,

FBD of members is as shown in Fig. 5.52 (c).

(ii) Axial force : Member BC is subjected to axial tensile force of 10 kN.

AFD is as shown in Fig. 5.52 (d).

(iii) SFD is as shown in Fig. 5.52 (e).

(iv) BM calculations :

For member AB,

$$BM_A = -35 \text{ kN.m}$$
$$BM_B = -5 \text{ kN.m}$$

For member BC,

$$BM_B = 5 \text{ kN.m}$$
$$BM_C = 5 \text{ kN.m}$$

BMD is as shown in Fig. 5.52 (f).

**Example 5.46 :** A beam ABCD is simply supported at A and fixed at D. Shear force diagram for the beam is as shown in Fig. 5.53 (a). Obtain the load diagram and hence construct BMD.

**Data** : Given SFD as shown in Fig. 5.53 (a).

**Required** : Load diagram and BMD.

**Solution** : (i) Load diagram :

Rise in SFD at A indicates upward point force of magnitude 40 kN at A.

Drop in SFD at B indicates downward point force of magnitude 20 kN at B.

Drop in SFD at C indicates downward point force of magnitude 15 kN at C.

Rise in SFD at D indicates upward point force of magnitude 35 kN at D.

Zone AB ; intensity of udl $= \dfrac{dV}{dx} = \dfrac{35-40}{2} = -2.5$ kN/m.

Zone BC ; intensity of udl $= \dfrac{dV}{dx} = \dfrac{-5-15}{8} = -2.5$ kN/m.

Zone CD ; intensity of udl $= \dfrac{dV}{dx} = \dfrac{-35-(-20)}{6} = -2.5$ kN/m.

Thus, there is downward udl of intensity 2.5 kN/m throughout the length of beam.

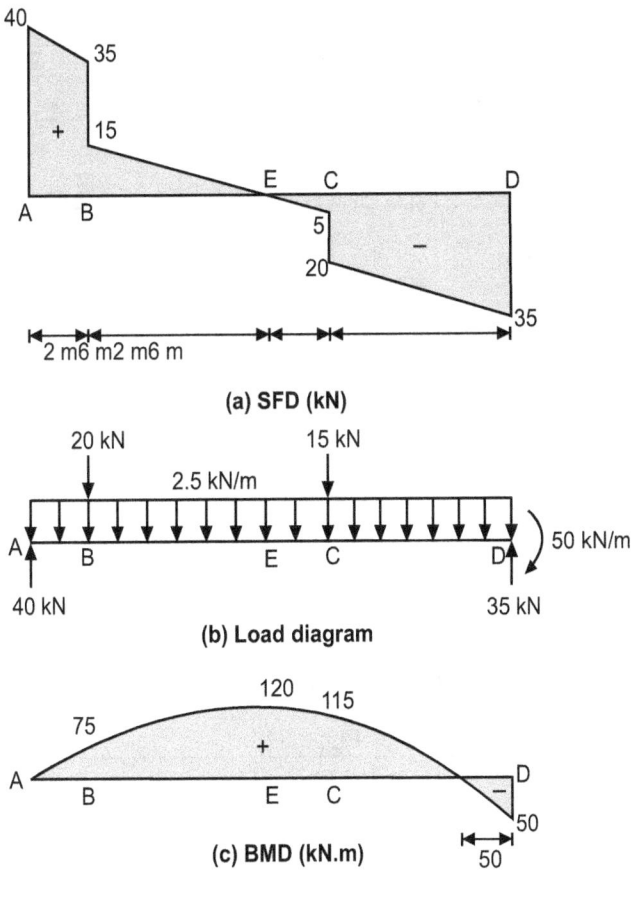

Fig. 5.53

(ii) Equilibrium of beam from load diagram :

$\Sigma F_y = 40 + 35 - 20 - 15 - 2.5 \times 16 = 0$

$\Sigma M_A = 35 \times 16 - 2.5 \times \dfrac{(16)^2}{2} - 15 \times 10 - 20 \times 2 = 50$ kN.m

Moment equilibrium is not satisfied.

Hence, moment at fixed end $D = -50$ kN.m $= 50$ kN.m

Load diagram is as shown in Fig. 5.53 (b).

(iii) BMD is as shown in Fig. 5.53 (c).

**Example 5.47 :** Draw the S.F.D. and B.M.D. for the beam shown in Fig. 5.54. Indicate the numerical values at all the important sections. Find the position of contraflexure, magnitude and position of maximum BM.

**Solution :**

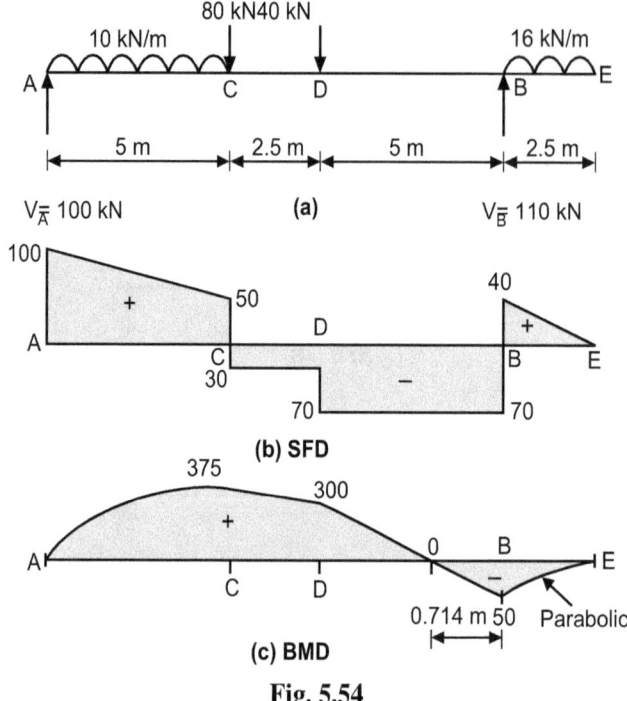

(c) BMD
Fig. 5.54

**Example 5.48 :** Draw the S.F.D. and B.M.D. for a simply supported beam of span 4 m, carrying a uniformly varying load, varying from zero at one end to 10 kN/m at the other end.

**Solution :**

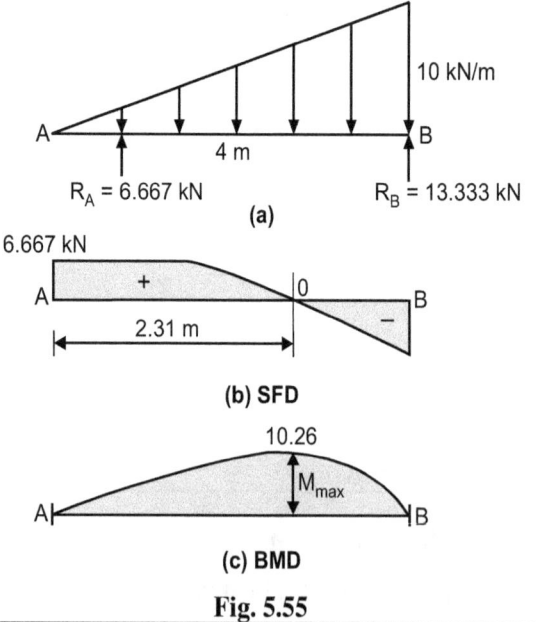

(c) BMD
Fig. 5.55

**Example 5.49 :** A horizontal beam AD 10 m long carries a uniformly distributed load of 20 kN/m along with a concentrated load of 60 kN at the left hand end 'A'. The beam is supported at 'B' 1 m from 'A' and at 'C' 'x' m from D. Determine the value of 'x' if the mid-section of the beam is a point of contraflexure. Locate any other point of inflection and plot S.F.D. and B.M.D.

**Solution :**

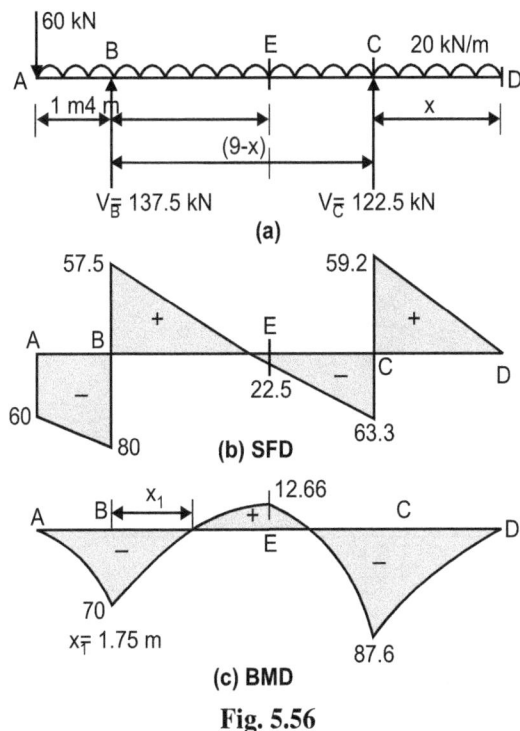

Fig. 5.56

**Example 5.50 :** A simply supported beam with overhanging ends, carries transverse load as shown in Fig. 5.57. If $wL = P$, what is the ratio $a/L$ for which the bending moment at middle of the beam will be zero ?

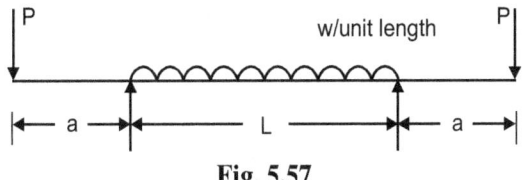

Fig. 5.57

**Solution :** Due to symmetry,

$$\text{Reactions} = P + \frac{wL}{2} = 1.5\, wL$$

B.M. at centre $= -P(a + 0.5 L) + 1.5\, wL\, (0.5 L) - (w/2)(0.5 L)^2 = 0$

∴ $\quad -wLa - 0.5\, wL^2 + 0.75\, wL^2 - 0.125\, wL^2 = 0$

∴ $\quad\quad\quad\quad\quad a = 0.125\, L$

∴ $\quad\quad\quad\quad\quad \dfrac{a}{L} = \dfrac{1}{8}$

**Example 5.51 :** Draw shear force and bending moment diagrams for the beam loaded as shown in Fig. 5.58. Find maximum bending moment on the beam.

**Solution :**

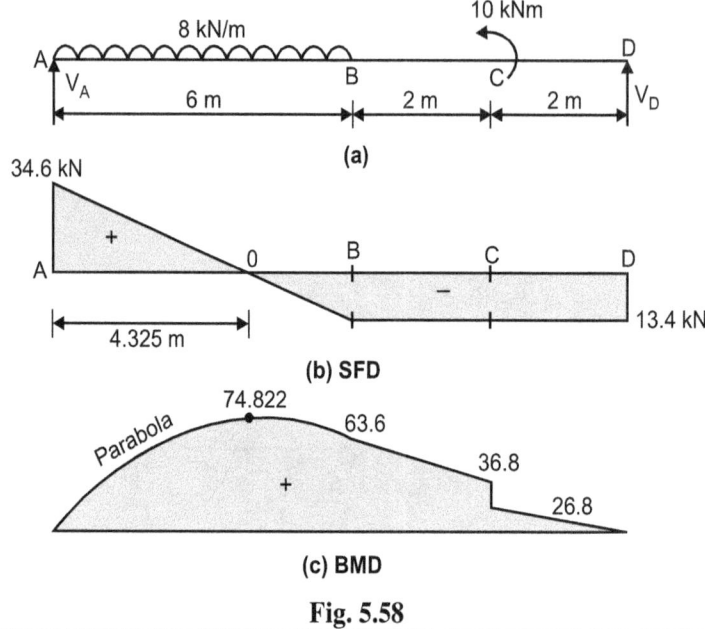

Fig. 5.58

### EXERCISE

Draw shear force and bending moment diagrams for the following beams indicating all the important values :

1.

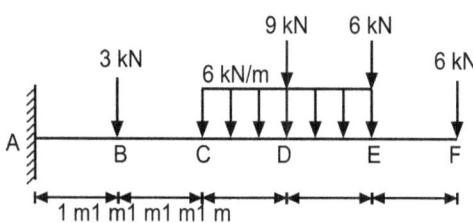

Fig. 5.59

$(BM_A = -120 \text{ kNm}, BM_B = -84 \text{ kNm}, BM_C = -51 \text{ kNm},$
$BM_D = -21 \text{ kNm}, BM_E = -6 \text{ kNm}, BM_F = 0)$

2.

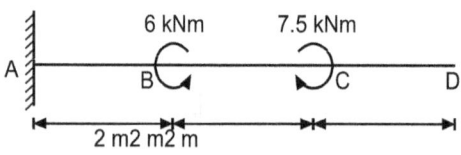

Fig. 5.60

$(BM_A = -1.5 \text{ kNm}, BM_{B(L)} = -1.5 \text{ kNm}, BM_{B(R)} = -7.5 \text{ kNm},$
$BM_{C(L)} = -7.5 \text{ kNm}, BM_{C(R)} = 0, BM_D = 0)$

3.

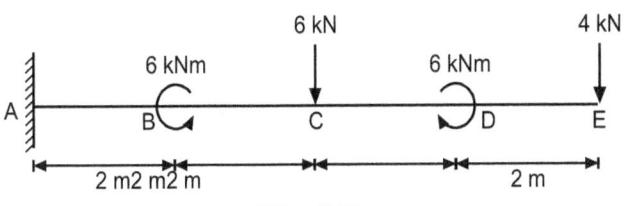

**Fig. 5.61**

$(BM_A = -58 \text{ kNm}, BM_{B(L)} = -38 \text{ kNm}, BM_{B(R)} = -42 \text{ kNm}, BM_C = -22 \text{ kNm},$
$BM_{D(L)} = -14 \text{ kNm}, BM_{D(R)} = -8 \text{ kNm}, BM_E = 0)$

4.

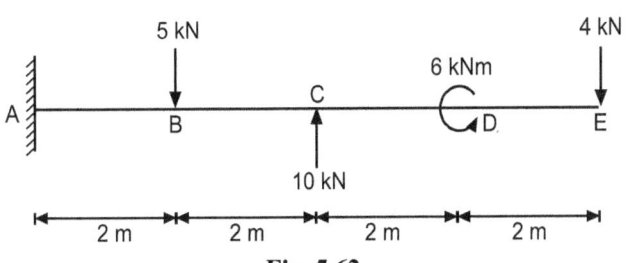

**Fig. 5.62**

$(BM_A = 10 \text{ kNm}, BM_B = 20 \text{ kNm}, BM_C = 20 \text{ kNm}, BM_{D(L)} = 40 \text{ kNm},$
$BM_{D(R)} = -20 \text{ kNm}, BM_E = 0)$

5.

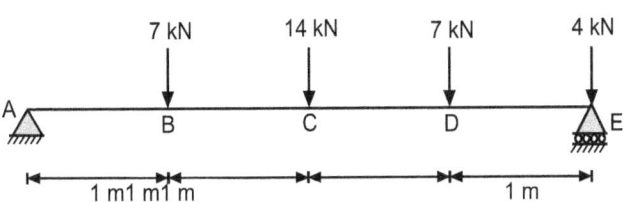

**Fig. 5.63**

$(BM_A = BM_E = 0, BM_B = 14 \text{ kNm}, BM_C = 21 \text{ kNm}, BM_D = 14 \text{ kNm})$

6.

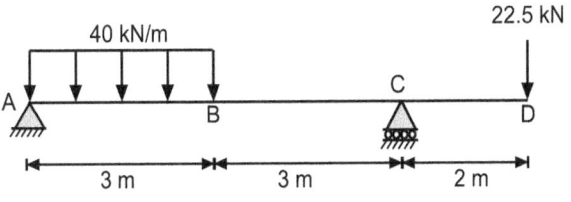

**Fig. 5.64**

$(BM_A = BM_D = 0, BM_B = 67.5 \text{ kNm}, BM_C = -45 \text{ kNm}, BM_{max} = 84.93 \text{ m at } 2.06 \text{ m}$
from A)

7.

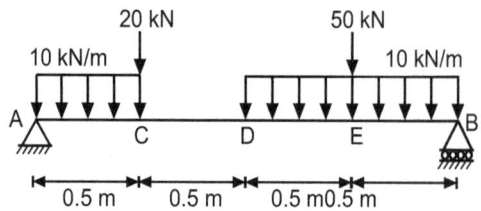

Fig. 5.65

$(BM_A = BM_B = 0,\ BM_C = 16.5\ kNm,\ BM_D = 21\ kNm,\ BM_E = 24.25\ kNm)$

8.

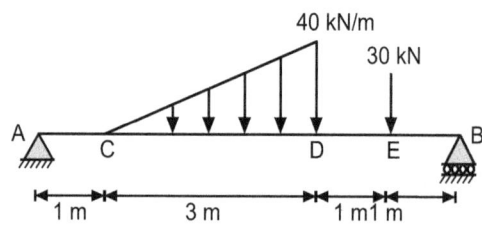

Fig. 5.66

$(BM_A = BM_B = 0,\ BM_C = 35\ kNm,\ BM_D = 80\ kNm,\ BM_E = 55\ kNm,$

$BM_{max} = 88.46\ kNm\ at\ 3.29\ m\ from\ A)$

9.

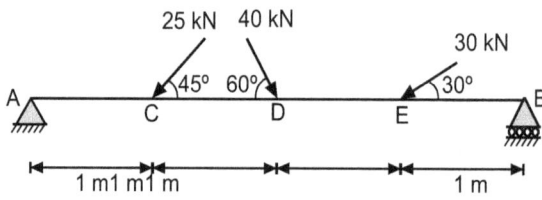

Fig. 5.67

$(BM_A = BM_B = 0,\ BM_C = 34.33\ kNm,\ BM_D = 50.985\ kNm,\ BM_E = 32.995\ kNm)$

10.

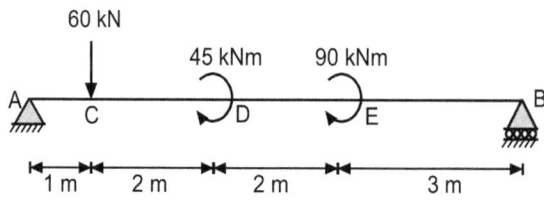

Fig. 5.68

$(BM_A = BM_B = 0,\ BM_C = 35.625\ kNm,\ BM_{D\,(L)} = -13.125\ kNm,$

$BM_{D\,(R)} = 31.875\ kNm,\ BM_{E\,(L)} = -16.875\ kNm,\ BM_{E\,(R)} = 73.125\ kNm)$

11.

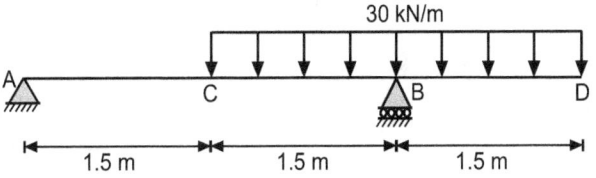

**Fig. 5.69**

$(BM_A = BM_D = BM_C = 0, \ BM_B = -33.75 \text{ kNm})$

12.

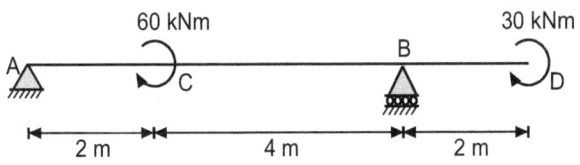

**Fig. 5.70**

$(BM_A = 0, \ BM_{C(L)} = -30 \text{ kNm}, \ BM_{C(R)} = 30 \text{ kNm}, \ BM_B = BM_D = -30 \text{ kNm})$

13.

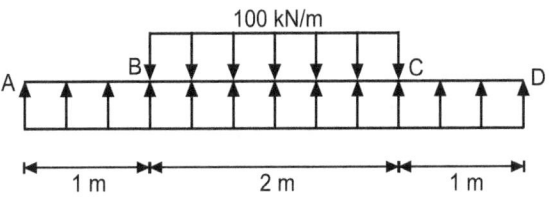

**Fig. 5.71**

$(BM_A = BM_D = 0, \ BM_B = BM_C = 25 \text{ kNm}, \ BM_{max} \text{ at centre} = 50 \text{ kNm})$

14.

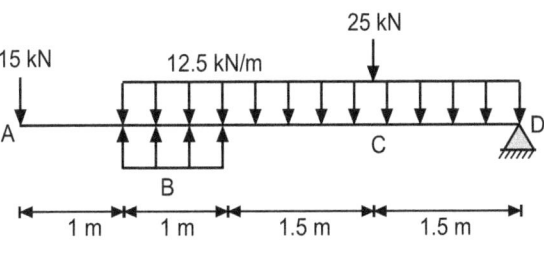

**Fig. 5.72**

**Hint :** Reaction at B is uniformly distributed over 1 m length.

$(BM_A = BM_D = 0, \ BM_B = -15 \text{ kNm}, \ BM_C = 29.875 \text{ kNm})$

15.

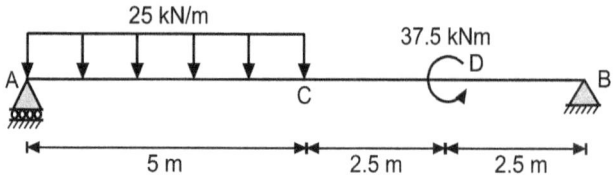

Fig. 5.73

(BM$_A$ = BM$_B$ = 0, BM$_C$ = 343.75 kNm, BM$_{D(L)}$ = 359.375 kNm,

BM$_{D(R)}$ = – 15.625 kNm)

16.

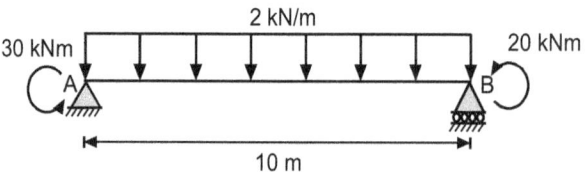

Fig. 5.74

(BM$_A$ = – 30 kNm, BM$_B$ = 20 kNm, BM$_{max}$ = 26.25 kNm at 7.5 m from A)

17.

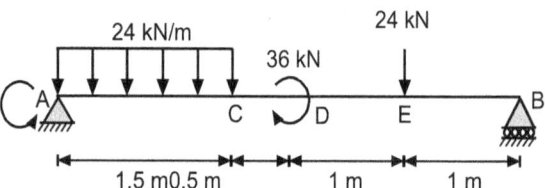

Fig. 5.75

(BM$_A$ = BM$_B$ = 0, BM$_C$ = 12.38 kNm, BM at zero SF in zone AC = 14.34 kNm,

BM$_{D(L)}$ = 7.48 kNm, BM$_{D(R)}$ = 43.48 kNm, BM$_E$ = 33.74 kNm)

18.

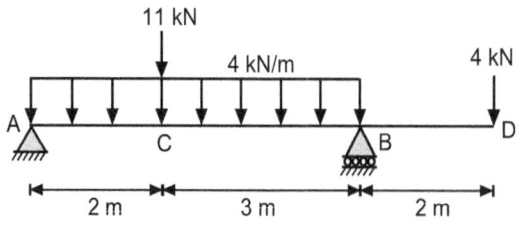

Fig. 5.76

(BM$_A$ = 0, BM$_C$ = 22 kNm, BM$_B$ = – 8 kNm)

19.

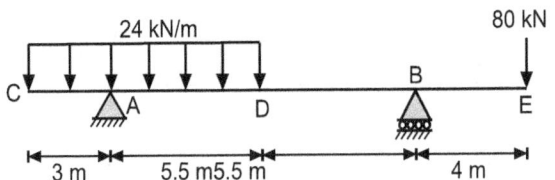

**Fig. 5.77**

($BM_C = BM_E = 0$; $BM_A = -108$ kNm, $BM_B = -32.68$ kNm, $BM_B = -320$ kNm;

BM at zero SF in zone AD = 24.16 kNm, at 6.32 m from C)

20.

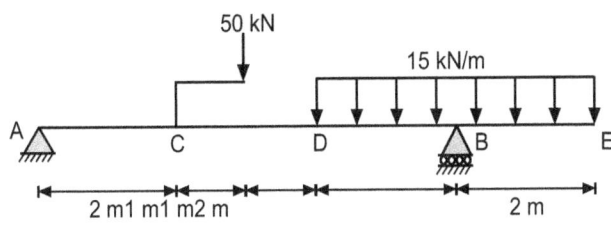

**Fig. 5.78**

($BM_A = BM_E = 0$, $BM_{C(L)} = 50$ kNm, $BM_{C(R)} = 100$ kNm, $BM_D = 50$ kNm,

$BM_B = -30$ kNm)

21.

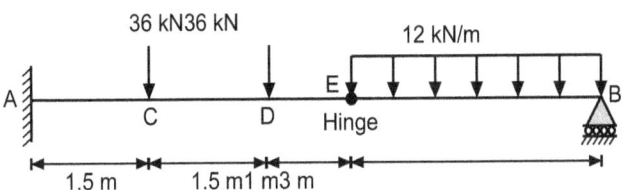

**Fig. 5.79**

($BM_E = BM_B = 0$; $BM_A = -234$ kNm, $BM_C = -99$ kNm, $BM_D = -18$ kNm, BM at zero SF in zone BE = 13.5 kNm)

22.

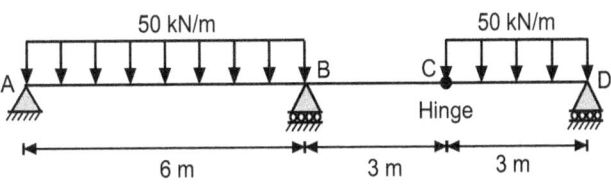

**Fig. 5.80**

($BM_A = BM_C = BM_D = 0$; $BM_B = -225$ kNm, BM at zero SF in zone AB = 126.56 kNm at 2.25 m from A; BM at zero SF in zone CD = 56.25 kNm 1.5 m from D)

23.

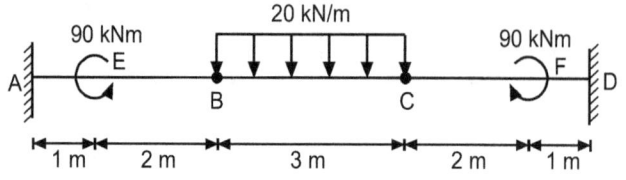

**Fig. 5.81**

$(BM_A = BM_B = BM_C = BM_D = 0; \ BM_{E(L)} = 30 \text{ kNm} = BM_{F(R)};$

$BM_{E(R)} = -60 \text{ kNm} = BM_{F(L)};$ BM at zero SF in zone BC = 22.5 kNm)

□□□

# CHAPTER SIX

# SHEAR FORCE AND BENDING MOMENT
## (PART-B)

## 6.1 RELATIONSHIP BETWEEN LOAD, SHEAR AND BENDING MOMENT

The relationship between load, shear and bending moment can be derived as under. Consider a beam supported and loaded as shown in Fig. 6.1 (a).

Let $V_x$ and $M_x$ be the shear and bending moment on a section at a distance 'x' from A. Likewise $V_x + dV_x$ and $M_x$ and $dM_x$ are the shear and bending moment at a section at a distance $x + dx$ from A. The free body diagram of the segment of the beam which is dx in length is shown in Fig. 6.1 (b).

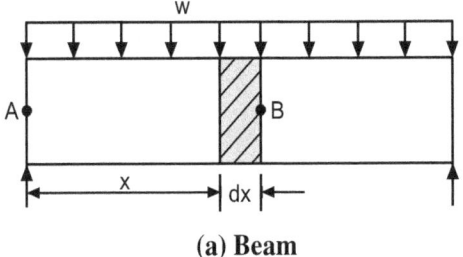
(a) Beam

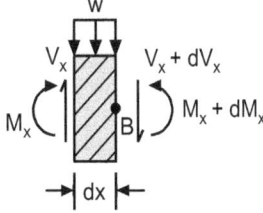
(b) FBD of beam segment

Fig. 6.1

Applying equations of equilibrium to FBD of segment as under :

$\sum F_y = 0 \Rightarrow \quad V_x - (V_x + dV_x) - w \cdot dx = 0$

$$dV_x = -w \cdot dx$$

$\therefore \quad \dfrac{dV_x}{dx} = -w \qquad \ldots (6.1)$

Thus, the rate of decrease of shear force with respect to x, on any section at a distance 'x' from left end of the beam is equal to the intensity of load at the section.

$\sum M_B = 0 \Rightarrow \quad V_x \cdot dx + M_x = M_x + dM_x + w\dfrac{dx^2}{2}$

The term $w\dfrac{dx^2}{2}$ being very small, can be neglected.

$$dM_x = V_x \cdot dx$$

$\dfrac{dM_x}{dx} = V_x \qquad \ldots (6.2)$

Thus, the rate of increase of bending moment with respect to 'x', on any section at a distance 'x' from left end of the beam, is equal to shear at the section.

(6.1)

## SOLVED EXAMPLES

**Example 6.1 :** A beam ABCD is simply supported at A and fixed at D. Shear force diagram for the beam is as shown in Fig. 6.2 (a). Obtain the load diagram and hence construct BMD.

**Data** : Given SFD as shown in Fig. 6.2 (a).
**Required** : Load diagram and BMD.
**Solution** : (i) Load diagram :

Rise in SFD at A indicates upward point force of magnitude 40 kN at A.
Drop in SFD at B indicates downward point force of magnitude 20 kN at B.
Drop in SFD at C indicates downward point force of magnitude 15 kN at C.
Rise in SFD at D indicates upward point force of magnitude 35 kN at D.

Zone AB : Intensity of UDL $= \dfrac{dV}{dx} = \dfrac{35-40}{2} = -2.5$ kN/m.

Zone BC : Intensity of UDL $= \dfrac{dV}{dx} = \dfrac{-5-15}{8} = -2.5$ kN/m.

Zone CD : Intensity of UDL $= \dfrac{dV}{dx} = \dfrac{-35-(-20)}{6} = -2.5$ kN/m.

Thus, there is downward udl of intensity 2.5 kN/m throughout the length of beam.

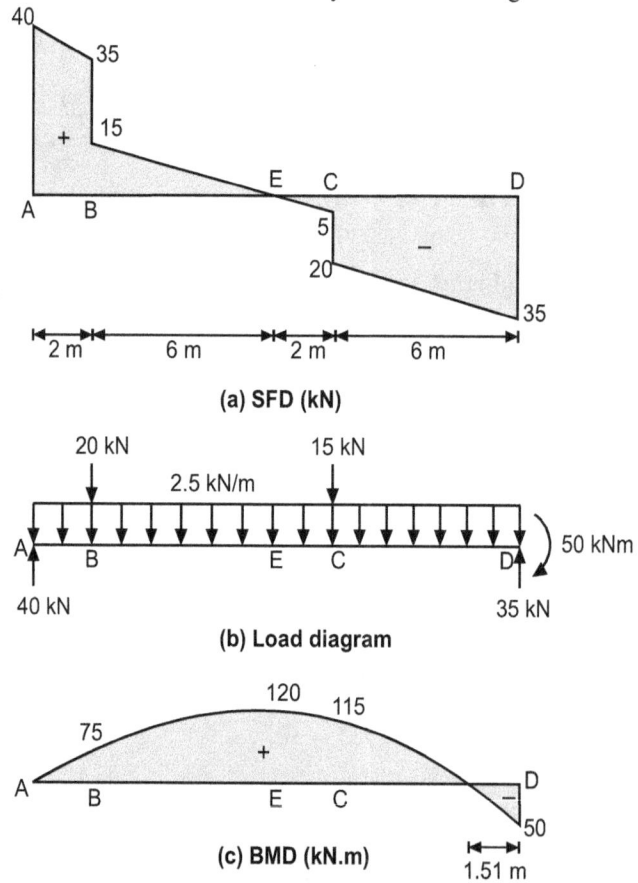

Fig. 6.2

(ii) Equilibrium of beam from load diagram :

$$\Sigma F_y = 40 + 35 - 20 - 15 - 2.5 \times 16 = 0$$

$$\Sigma M_A = 35 \times 16 - 2.5 \times \frac{(16)^2}{2} - 15 \times 10 - 20 \times 2 = 50 \text{ kN.m}$$

Moment equilibrium is not satisfied.

Hence, moment at fixed end D = – 50 kN.m = 50 kN.m (↺)

Load diagram is as shown in Fig. 6.2 (b).

(iii) BMD is as shown in Fig. 6.2 (c).

**Example 6.2 :** A beam ABC is simply supported at A and B. Supports at A and B are 3 m apart and overhang BC = 1 m. The shear force diagram for the beam is as shown in Fig. 6.3 (a). Obtain the load diagram and hence construct BMD. Assume that there is no couple acting on the beam.

**Data :**  Given SFD as shown in Fig. 6.3 (a).

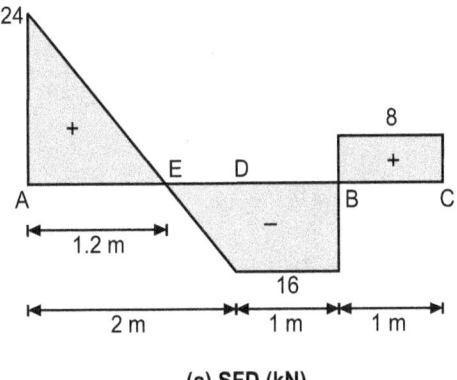

(a) SFD (kN)

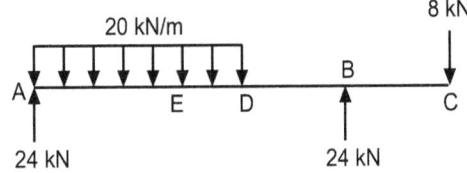

(b) Load diagram

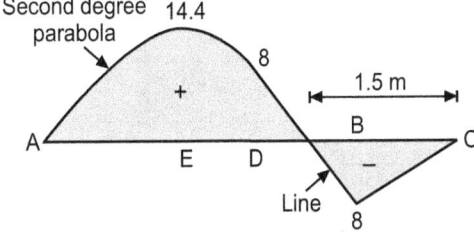

(c) BMD (kN.m)

**Fig. 6.3**

**Required** : Load diagram and BMD.

**Solution** : (i) Load diagram :

Rise in SFD at A indicates upward point force of 24 kN at A.

Zone AD, intensity of udl $= \dfrac{dV}{dx} = \dfrac{-16-(24)}{2} = -20$ kN/m

Thus, there is a downward udl from A to D of intensity 20 kN/m.
Rise in SFD at B indicates upward point force of 24 kN at B.
Drop in SFD at C indicates downward point force of 8 kN at C.
Load diagram is as shown in Fig. 6.3 (b).

(ii) Equilibrium of beam from load diagram :

$$\Sigma F_y = 24 + 24 - 20 \times 2 - 8 = 0$$

$$\Sigma M_A = -8 \times 4 + 24 \times 3 - 20 \times \dfrac{2^2}{2} = 0$$

Thus the load diagram obtained is justified.

(iii) BMD as shown in Fig. 6.3 (c).

**Example 6.3 :** A beam ABC is simply supported at A and B. Supports at A and B are 6 m apart and overhang BC = 1 m. The bending moment diagram for the beam is as shown in Fig. 6.4 (a). Construct SFD and load diagram.

**Data :** Given BMD as shown in Fig. 6.4 (a).

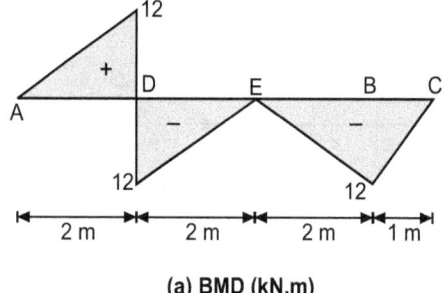

(a) BMD (kN.m)

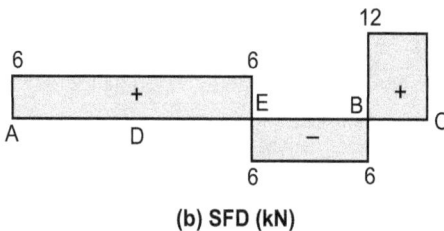

(b) SFD (kN)

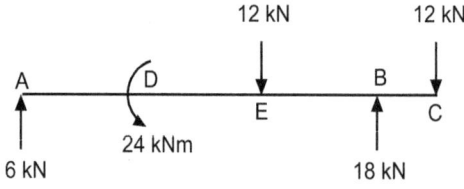

(c) Load diagram

**Fig. 6.4**

**Required :** SFD and load diagram.

**Solution :** (i) SFD :

Zone AD : $\quad SF = \dfrac{dM}{dx} = \dfrac{12-0}{2} = 6 \text{ kN}$

Zone DE : $\quad SF = \dfrac{dM}{dx} = \dfrac{0-(-12)}{2} = 6 \text{ kN}$

Zone EB : $\quad SF = \dfrac{dM}{dx} = \dfrac{-12-0}{2} = -6 \text{ kN}$

Zone BC : $\quad SF = \dfrac{dM}{dx} = \dfrac{0-(-12)}{1} = 12 \text{ kN}$

SFD is as shown in Fig. 6.4 (b).

(ii) Load diagram :

Rise in SFD at A indicates upward point force of magnitude 6 kN at A.

Drop in SFD at E indicates downward point force of magnitude 12 kN at E.

Rise in SFD at B indicates upward point force of magnitude 18 kN at B.

Drop in SFD at C indicates downward point force of magnitude 12 kN at C.

Also, at D, drop in BM diagram = 24 kN.m and BM changes from sagging to hogging from left of D to right of D, hence there must be an anticlockwise couple of magnitude 24 kN.m at D.

The load diagram for the beam is as shown in Fig. 6.4 (c).

**Note :** Having obtained the load diagram, check the equilibrium of beam to justify the results.

**Example 6.4 :** A beam ABC is supported on roller at A and hinged at C. The bending moment diagram for the beam ABC is as shown in Fig. 6.5 (a). Construct SFD and load diagram.

**Data :** Given BMD as shown in Fig. 6.5 (a).

**Required :** SFD and load diagram.

**Solution :** (i) SFD :

Zone AB : $\quad SF = \dfrac{dM}{dx} = \dfrac{5-(-10)}{1} = 15 \text{ kN}$

Zone BC : $\quad SF = \dfrac{dM}{dx} = \dfrac{10-(-5)}{1} = 15 \text{ kN}$

SFD is as shown in Fig. 6.5 (b).

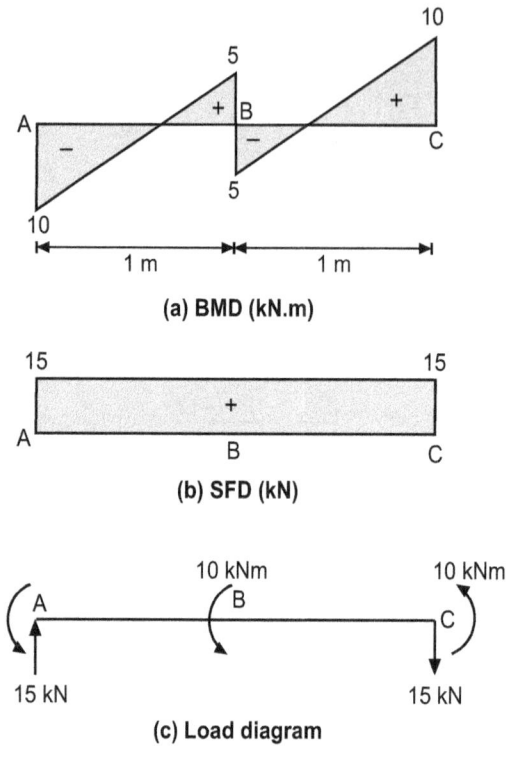

(a) BMD (kN.m)

(b) SFD (kN)

(c) Load diagram

Fig. 6.5

(ii) Load diagram :

In zone AC, constant SF = 15 kN.

∴ Upward reaction at A = 15 kN and downward reaction at C = 15 kN.

At A, BM = – 10 kN.m which indicates anticlockwise couple of magnitude 10 kN.m at A.

At B, drop in BM diagram = 10 kN.m and BM changes from sagging to hogging from left of B to right of B, hence there must be an anticlockwise couple of magnitude 10 kN.m at B.

At C, BM = 10 kN.m which indicates anticlockwise couple of magnitude 10 kN.m at C.

The load diagram for the beam is as shown in Fig. 6.5 (c).

**Note :** Having obtained the load diagram, check the equilibrium of beam to justify the results.

**Example 6.5 :** Fig. 6.6 shows SFD for a simply supported beam AB. Draw BMD for the beam.

**Data :** Given SFD as shown in Fig. 6.6.

**Required :** BMD.

**Solution :** (i) Load diagram : Rise in SFD at A indicates upward point force 12.5 kN at A.

Horizontal line between A to C shows no load between A to C.

Rise in SFD at B indicates upward point force of 7.5 kN at B.

**Zone CD :** Intensity of UDL $= \dfrac{dV}{dx} = \dfrac{-7.5 - 12.5}{4} = -5$ kN.m.

Load diagram is as shown in Fig. 6.6 (b).

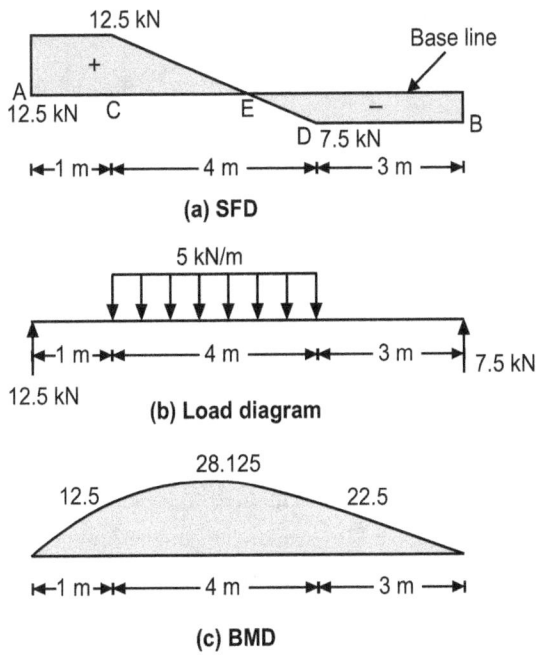

Fig. 6.6

(ii)  BMD : Bending moment, maximum at SF is zero.

$$\therefore \quad x = \dfrac{12.5}{5} = 2.5 \text{ m (from starting point of UDL)}$$

BMD is as shown in Fig. 6.6 (c).

**Example 6.6 :** The SFD of a 4 m long beam is a second degree curve as shown in Fig. 6.7 (a), with the maximum –ve SF of 3 kN at the beam centre. Assuming that no couples act on the beam, draw the loading and BMD. Locate the position of maximum BM and their magnitudes. Points of contraflexure if any, too, should be located.

**Data :** SFD as shown in Fig. 6.7 (a).

**Required :** Loading diagram and BMD.

**Solution :**

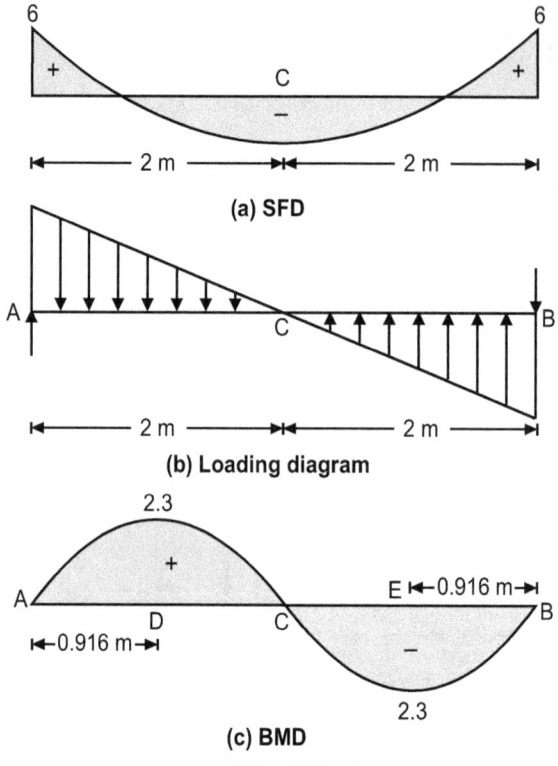

**Fig. 6.7**

(i) **Loading diagram :** Rise in SFD at A indicates upward point force of 6 kN at A. Drop in SFD at B indicates downward point force of 6 kN at B.

**Zone A to C :** Intensity of UVL $= (-3 - 6) = \frac{1}{2} w \times l$

$$-9 = \frac{1}{2} \times w \times 2$$

∴ $\qquad w = -9$ kN.m

**Zone C to B :** Intensity of UVL $= 6 - (-3) = \frac{1}{2} w \times l$

∴ $\qquad w = 9$ kN.m

To locate point of zero SF, consider a section at a distance x from A in zone AC.

$$SF_x = 6 - (\text{Area of trapezoidal load diagram}) = 0$$

$$\frac{9}{2} = \frac{y}{x} \qquad ∴ y = 4.5 x$$

∴ $\qquad 6 - \frac{(9 + 4.5 x)}{2} \times x = 0$

$$9x + 4.5x^2 - 12 = 0$$

∴ $\qquad x^2 + 2x - 2.67 = 0$

$$x = -2 \pm \frac{\sqrt{(2)^2 - 4 \times 1 \times (-2.67)}}{2}$$

$$= 0.916 \text{ m from A and B.}$$

(As beam is symmetrical, so points of zero SF are at same distance from both ends.)
Loading diagram is as shown in Fig. 6.7 (b).

(ii) BM calculations :

$$BM_A = BM_B = 0$$

BM at zero SF : $BM_D = 6 \times 0.916$ – Moment due to trapezoidal loading diagram

$$= 6 \times 0.916 - \frac{(9 + 4.5 \times 1.084)}{2} \times 0.916 \times \left(\frac{4.878 + 9 \times 2}{4.878 + 9}\right) \times \frac{0.916}{3}$$

$$= 2.3 \text{ kN.m}$$

$$BM_C = 6 \times 2 - \frac{1}{2} \times 9 \times 2 \times \frac{2}{3} \times 2$$

$$= 0$$

$$BM_E = -2.3 \text{ kN.m}$$

BMD is as shown in Fig. 6.7 (c).

**Example 6.7 :** The BMD of a simply supported beam is linear in the 1.5 m long portion AC and parabolic in the 3 m long portion CDEB. There is no slope discontinuity anywhere in the BMD. The moments of D and E are 28.125 kN.m and 22.5 kN.m respectively. Draw the SFD and loading diagrams for the beam and highlight all the significant values.

**Data :** BMD as shown in Fig. 6.8 (a).

**Required :** Loading diagram and SFD.

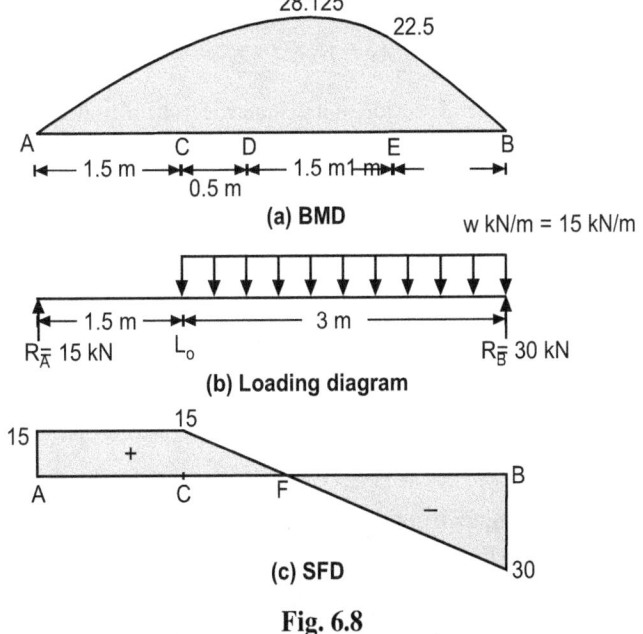

Fig. 6.8

(i) w and reactions :

$$M_E = R_B \times 1 - \frac{w \times 1^2}{2}$$

$$= 22.5$$

$$R_B - 0.5\,w = 22.5 \quad \ldots \text{(i)}$$

$$M_D = R_B \times 2.5 - \frac{w \times (2.5)^2}{2}$$

$$= 28.125$$

$$\therefore \quad R_B - 1.25\,w = 11.25 \quad \ldots \text{(ii)}$$

Solving equations (i) and (ii),

$$w = 15 \text{ kN/m}, \quad R_B = 30 \text{ kN } (\uparrow)$$

$$\Sigma F_y = 0; \quad R_A + R_B - w \times 3 = 0$$

$$R_A = 15 \text{ kN } (\uparrow)$$

(ii) Loading diagram as shown in Fig. 6.8 (b).

(iii) SF calculations :

$$SF_A = 15 \text{ kN}$$

$$SF_C = 15 \text{ kN}$$

$$SF_B = 15 - 15 \times 3 = -30 \text{ kN}$$

To locate point of SF, consider a section at a distance x from B in portion BC.

$$\therefore \quad SF_x = 30 - 15 \times x = 0$$

$$\therefore \quad x = 2 \text{ m from B.}$$

(iv) Maximum BM is at 2 m from B.

$$\therefore \quad BM_F = 30 \times 2 - 15 \times 2 \times 1$$

$$= 30 \text{ kN.m}$$

SFD is as shown in Fig. 6.8 (c).

**Example 6.8 :** The bending moment diagram for a beam ABCDE is as shown in Fig. 6.9 (a). Portions AB, CD and DE have linear curves whereas portion BC has a second degree curve with a peak located at 1.8 m from B and enjoys slope continuity at C. Draw the shear force and loading diagrams for the beam. Hence or otherwise locate the points of contraflexure.

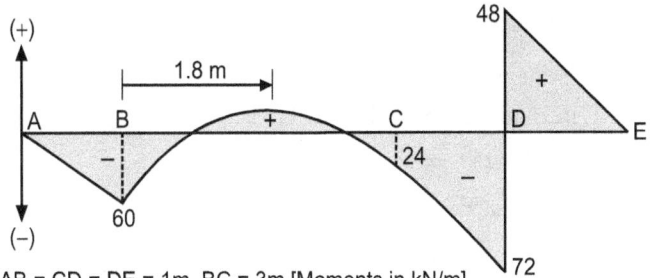

AB = CD = DE = 1m, BC = 3m [Moments in kN/m]

**(a) BMD**

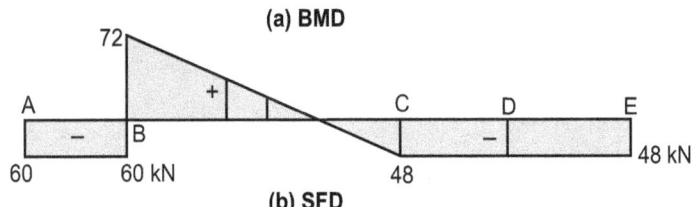

**(b) SFD**

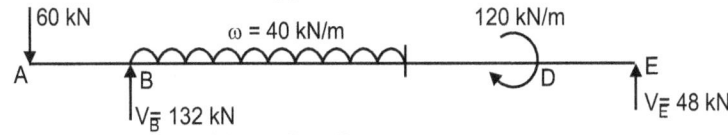

**(c) Loading diagram**

**Fig. 6.9**

**Solution :** (i) $\quad SF_{(AB)} = \dfrac{(-60 - 0)}{1} = -60$ kN

Let BM equation in zone BC be,

$M_X = Ax^2 + Bx + C \qquad$ (B as origin)

When x = 0, $\quad$ BM = $-60$ kN-m

∴ $\quad$ C = $-60$

When x = 3 m, $\quad$ BM = $-24$

∴ $\quad -24 = 9A + 3B - 60 \qquad$ ... (i)

$36 = 9A + 3B$

Also $\quad SF_X = 2Ax + B$

$SF_{(CD)} = \dfrac{[-72 - (-24)]}{1} = -48$ kN

When x = 3 m, $\quad SF_C = -48$ kN  Put in SF equation

$-48 = 6A + B \qquad$ ... (ii)

Solving (i) and (ii), $\quad A = -20, \ B = 72$

∴ $\quad M_X = -20x^2 + 72x - 60$

$SF_X = -40x + 72$

$w_X = -40$

At x = 0, $\quad SF_B = 72$ kN

At x = 3 m, $\quad SF_C = -48$ kN

$SF_{(DE)} = \dfrac{(0 - 48)}{1} = -48$ kN

SFD is as shown in Fig. 6.9 (b).

(ii)  Point load at A = 60 kN (↓)
Point load at B = 60 + 72 = 132 kN (↑)
UDL in zone BC = 40 kN/m (↑)
Couple at D = 120 kN/m (↻)
Point load at E = 48 kN (↑)

Load diagram is shown in Fig. 6.9 (c).

**Example 6.9 :** Fig. 6.10 shows the shear force for beam ABCD. Draw the loading diagram and bending moment diagram.

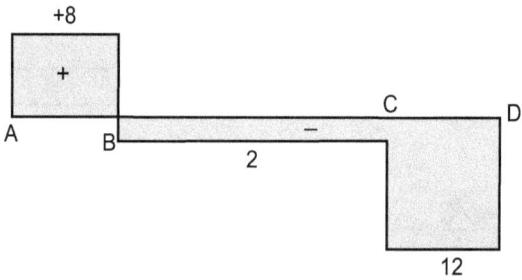

**Fig. 6.10**

**Data :** As shown in Fig. 6.10.
**Required :** Loading diagram and bending moment diagram.
**Solution :**

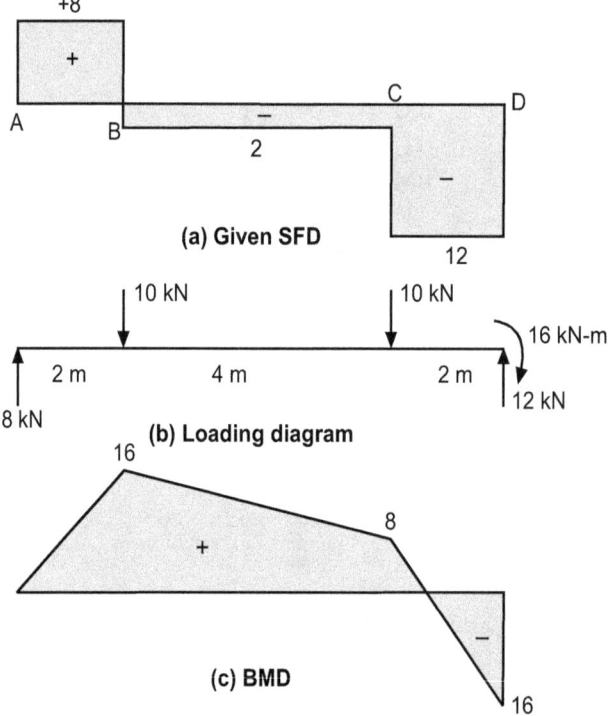

**Fig. 6.11**

**Example 6.10 :** Shown in Fig. 6.12 is the shear force diagram of a beam. The curve in portion AB is a second-degree curve that has zero slope at 'A'. Draw completely the loading diagram of the beam.

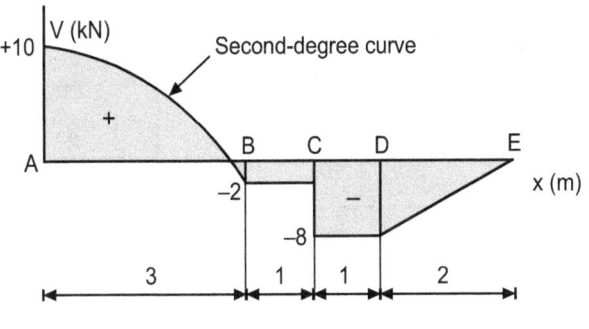

**Fig. 6.12 (a) S.F.D.**

**Solution :**

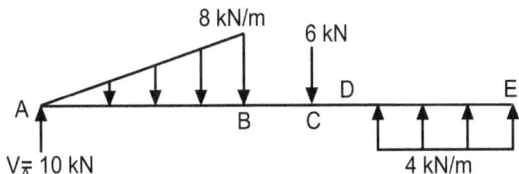

**Fig. 6.12 (b) : Load diagram**

At 'A' upward point load of 10 kN.

SF equation in zone AB = $Ax^2 + B$

When x = 0,    SF = 10 kN,    ∴ B = 10

When x = 3 m,  SF = − 2 kN    ∴ A = − 1.33

∴ $SF_{(x)} = -1.33 x^2 + 10$ ... (i)

∴ $w_{(x)} = -2.67 x$ ... (ii)

When x = 0,    w = 0

When x = 3 m,  w = 8 kN/m

Thus in zone AB, we have triangular load with zero intensity at A and 8 kN/m at B.

At 'C' downward point load of 6 kN is present.

Intensity of UDL from D to E = $\dfrac{0-(-8)}{2}$ = 4 kN/m (↑)

Load diagram is as shown in Fig. 6.12 (b).

## EXERCISE

1. Draw the bending moment diagram and loading diagram from the given shear force diagram. (Refer Fig. 6.13)

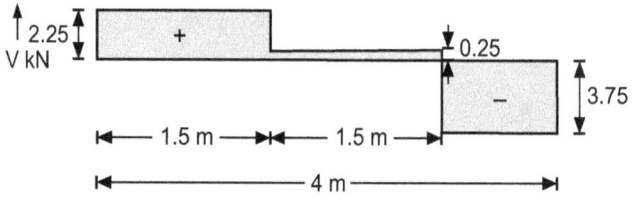

Fig. 6.13 : Shear force diagram

2. The shear force diagram for a simple beam is shown in Fig. 6.14. Determine the loading on the beam and draw the bending moment diagram, assuming that no couples act as loads on the beam.

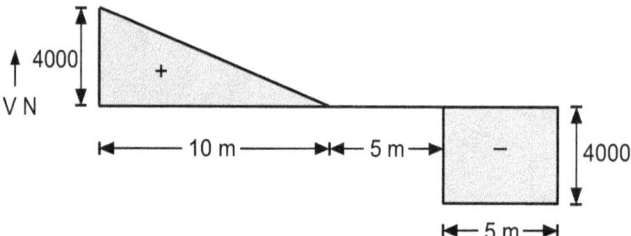

Fig. 6.14 : Shear force diagram

3. The shear force diagram for a beam is as shown in Fig. 6.15. Assuming that no couples act as load on the beam, draw the bending moment diagram and also show the loading diagram.

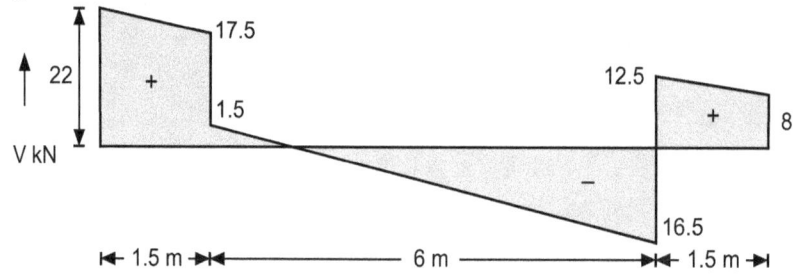

Fig. 6.15 : Shear force diagram

4. Construct the loading and shear force diagram for the beam with an overhang as shown in Fig. 6.16.

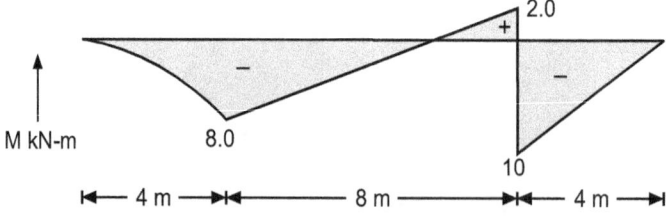

Fig. 6.16 : Bending moment diagram

5. Construct the shear force diagram and loading diagram for the cantilever beam shown in Fig. 6.17.

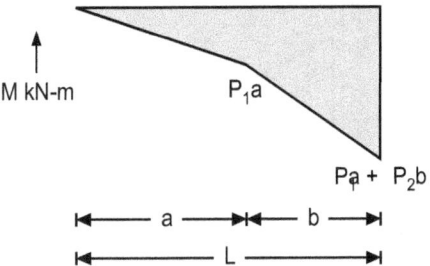

Fig. 6.17 : Bending moment diagram

6. Construct the bending moment diagram and loading diagram for the simply supported beam as shown in Fig. 6.18.

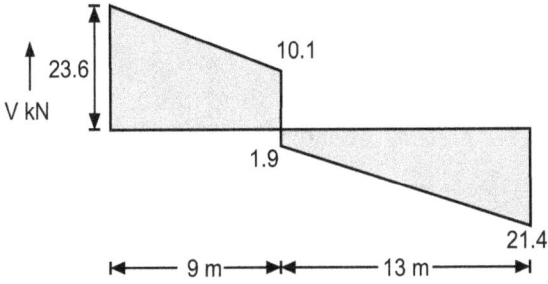

Fig. 6.18 : Shear force diagram

7. Draw the bending moment diagram and loading diagram from shear for the simply supported beam as shown in Fig. 6.19.

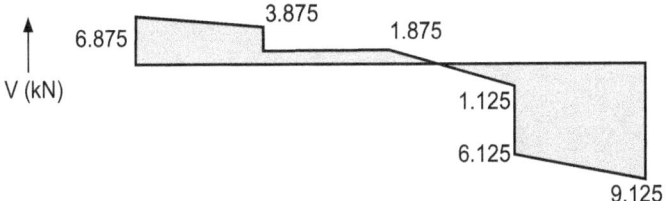

Fig. 6.19 : Shear force diagram

8. Draw bending moment diagram and loading diagram from shear force diagram for simply supported beam as shown in Fig. 6.20.

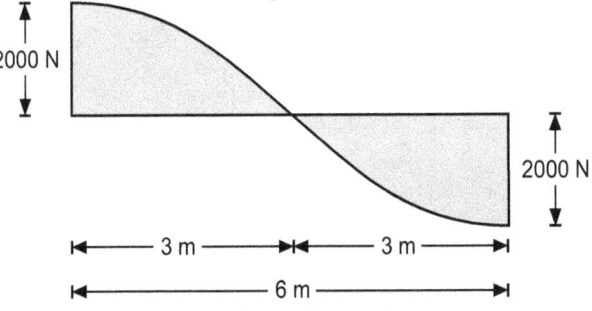

Fig. 6.20 : Shear force diagram

9. Construct bending moment diagram and loading diagram for the overhanging beam shown in Fig. 6.21.

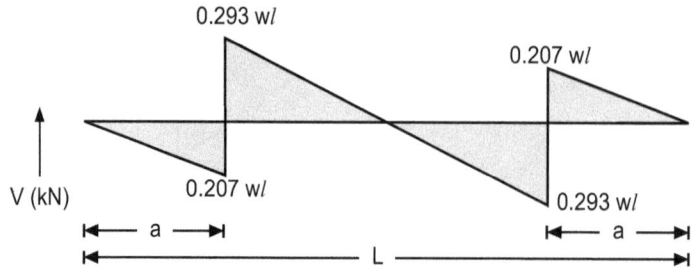

Fig. 6.21 : Shear force diagram

10. Construct the shear force diagram and loading diagram for the beam shown in Fig. 6.22.

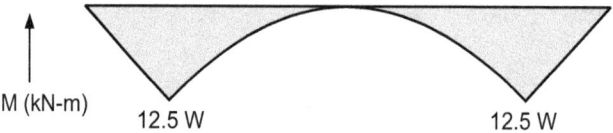

Fig. 6.22 : Bending moment diagram

❐❐❐

# Unit – IV

## CHAPTER SEVEN

# BENDING STRESSES IN BEAMS

## 7.1 INTRODUCTION

The stresses caused by bending moment are called as bending or flexural stresses. In this chapter, we shall study the relation between bending moment and flexural stress. In deriving these relations, following assumptions are made :

(i) A transverse section of the beam, which is plane before bending will remain plane after bending.

(ii) The material of the beam is homogeneous, isotropic (same elastic properties in all the directions), and it obeys Hooke's law.

(iii) The value of the Young's modulus is the same for the beam material in tension as well as compression.

(iv) The beam is initially straight and of constant cross-section.

(v) The plane of loading must contain a principal axis of the beam cross-section and the loads must be perpendicular to the longitudinal axis of the beam.

## 7.2 CENTRE OF GRAVITY

Every body consists of particles and these particles are attracted towards the centre of earth. All these weights form a system of parallel forces. The point, through which the resultant of all these parallel forces pass, is called the centre of gravity of a body.

## 7.3 CENTROID

Lines, curves or geometrical figures having lengths or areas do not have any effect due to earth's attraction as they do not possess mass. These figures have a point similar to the centre of gravity of the solids. This point is called the **centroid** of the line, curve or area.

The centroid is applicable to area, lines or curves and the centre of gravity is applicable to volumes.

## 7.4 CENTROIDS AND CENTRE OF GRAVITIES OF BASIC FIGURES

| | Shape | Length /Area / Volume | $\bar{x}$ | $\bar{y}$ |
|---|---|---|---|---|
| 1. | Line | $l = \sqrt{a^2 + b^2}$ | $\dfrac{a}{2}$ | $\dfrac{b}{2}$ |
| 2. | Rectangle | $A = bd$ | $\dfrac{b}{2}$ | $\dfrac{d}{2}$ |
| 3. | Isosceles triangle | $A = \dfrac{1}{2} bh$ | $\dfrac{b}{2}$ | $\dfrac{h}{3}$ |
| 4. | Right angled triangle | $A = \dfrac{1}{2} bh$ | $\dfrac{b}{3}$ | $\dfrac{h}{3}$ |
| 5. | Circle | $A = \pi r^2$ | $r$ | $r$ |
| 6. | Semicircle | $A = \dfrac{\pi r^2}{2}$ | $r$ | $\dfrac{4r}{3\pi}$ |
| 7. | Quarter circle | $A = \dfrac{\pi r^2}{4}$ | $\dfrac{4r}{3\pi}$ | $\dfrac{4r}{3\pi}$ |

| 8. | Circular sector : | | $A = r^2\alpha$ | $\dfrac{2r \sin \alpha}{3\alpha}$ | 0 |
|---|---|---|---|---|---|
| 9. | Semicircular arc : | | $l = \pi r$ | $r$ | $\dfrac{2r}{\pi}$ |

## 7.5 MOMENT OF INERTIA

**Definition of Moment of inertia :** In the region bounded by two principle axes OX and OY, consider any shaped area A. It consists of a number of elemental areas such that sum of these elemental areas is equal to the area A.

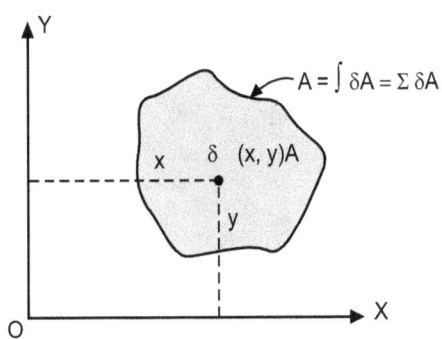

Fig. 7.1

$$\therefore \qquad A = \int \delta A = \Sigma \, \delta A$$

Let such an elemental area $\delta A$ be situated at (x, y) as shown in Fig. 7.1. The moment of inertia of the area A about OY is defined as *the sum of second moment of area*. Thus,

$$I_{YY} = \int \delta A \cdot x^2 \qquad \ldots (7.1)$$

where $I_{YY}$ = Moment of inertia of area A about the axis OY.

Similarly,
$$I_{XX} = \int \delta A \cdot y^2 \qquad \ldots (7.2)$$

where $I_{XX}$ = Moment of inertia of area A about the axis OX.

Obviously, the unit of moment of inertia is $mm^4$, $cm^4$, $m^4$ etc.

Instead of considering elemental area δA and area A, we consider elemental mass δm and mass M, and define,

$$I_{YY} = \int \delta m \cdot x^2 \qquad \ldots (7.3)$$

$$\text{and } I_{XX} = \int \delta m \cdot y^2 \qquad \ldots (7.4)$$

The moments of inertia given in equations (7.3) and (7.4) are called mass moment of inertia.

The moments of inertia given in equations (7.1) and (7.2) are called area moment of inertia. We will be calling it henceforth simply by moment of inertia.

In this text book, we will be requiring only moment of inertia and not mass moment of inertia.

### 7.5.1 Radius of Gyration

As the moment of inertia is the sum of second moment of area, it can be expressed in the form:

$$I = Ak^2 \qquad \ldots (7.5)$$

where k is called radius of gyration.

$$\therefore \quad k = \sqrt{\frac{I}{A}} \qquad \ldots (7.6)$$

Obviously, the unit of radius of gyration will be mm, cm, m etc.

Particular expressions for radius of gyration are:

$$k_{xx} = \sqrt{\frac{I_{xx}}{A}} \qquad \ldots (7.7)$$

$$\text{and} \quad k_{yy} = \sqrt{\frac{I_{yy}}{A}} \qquad \ldots (7.8)$$

### 7.5.2 Basic Theorems

The values of moment of inertia will change if we change reference axes OX and OY. This is not desirable. Therefore, the moments of inertia are calculated about centroidal xx and yy axes. These values are unique as centroidal axes can not vary. We must establish a relation between $I_{XX}$ and $I_{xx}$.

**(i) Theorem of Parallel axes :**

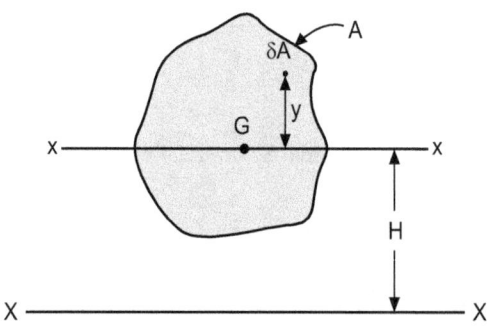

**Fig. 7.2**

Consider an area A as shown in Fig. 7.2. Let xx be the centroidal horizontal axes. Let an elemental area $\delta A$ be at y for xx. Let XX be a non-centroidal horizontal axis at a vertical distance H from xx.

$$I_{xx} = \int \delta A\, y^2$$

$$I_{XX} = \int \delta A\, (y + H)^2$$

$\therefore \quad I_{XX} = \int \delta A\, (y^2 + 2yH + H^2)$

$\therefore \quad I_{XX} = \int \delta A\, y^2 + 2H \int \delta A \cdot y + H^2 \int \delta A$

but $\quad \int \delta A\, y^2 = I_{xx}$

and $\quad \int \delta A \cdot y = A\, \bar{y}$, where $\bar{y}$ = vertical distance of centroid G from xx which happens to be zero in this case.

$\therefore \quad I_{XX} = I_{xx} + AH^2 \quad\quad\quad …(7.9)$

The above equation (7.9) represents mathematically the theorem of parallel axes, as XX is parallel to xx. Knowing the moment of inertia about the centroidal axis, we can find the moment of inertia about a non-centroidal axis parallel to the centroidal axis by using the equation (7.9).

Also, $\quad I_{YY} = I_{yy} + AH'^2 \quad\quad\quad …(7.10)$

Equations (7.9) and (7.10) represent the theorem of parallel axes.

**(ii) Theorem of Perpendicular axes :** In Fig. 7.3, axis OZ which is perpendicular to axes OX and OY is not seen, as it is at right angles to the plane of the paper. The elemental area $\delta A$ is at x from OY, y from OX and r from OZ.

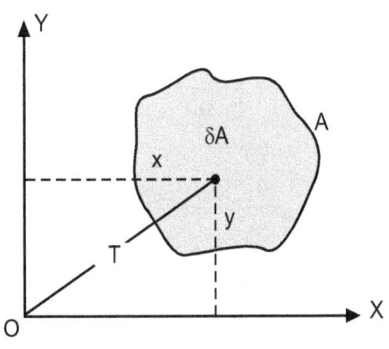

**Fig. 7.3**

$$I_{ZZ} = \int \delta A \, r^2$$

∴ $$I_{ZZ} = \int \delta A \, (y^2 + x^2) = \int \delta A \, y^2 + \int \delta A \, x^2$$

∴ $$I_{ZZ} = I_{XX} + I_{YY} \qquad \ldots (7.11)$$

If we consider centroidal axes mutually perpendicular to each other,

$$I_{ZZ} = I_{xx} + I_{yy} \qquad \ldots (7.12)$$

As the three axes are perpendicular to each other, equations (7.11) and (7.12) represent theorem of perpendicular axes. $I_{ZZ}$ is also denoted by J.

### 7.5.3 Standard Cases

We will derive the expressions for moment of inertia for standard areas such as rectangle, circle and triangle. The moment of inertia for other areas can be found by using theorem of parallel axes.

**(i) A rectangle :** (a) Consider a rectangular area of width b and depth d as shown in Fig. 7.4.

Consider an elemental strip parallel to xx at y from it and of thickness dy, so that the elemental area dA will be (bdy).

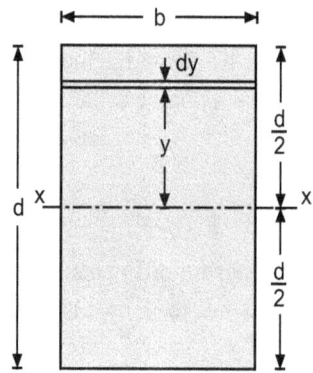

**Fig. 7.4**

By definition, $$I_{xx} = \int_{-d/2}^{+d/2} dA \cdot y^2 = \int_{-d/2}^{+d/2} b \, y^2 \, dy$$

∴ $$I_{xx} = \frac{b}{3}\left[\left(\frac{d}{2}\right)^3 - \left(-\frac{d}{2}\right)^3\right]$$

∴ $$I_{xx} = \frac{bd^3}{12} \qquad \ldots (7.13)$$

(b) It is obvious that $$I_{yy} = \frac{db^3}{12} \qquad \ldots (7.14)$$

(c) If we want the moment of inertia about the base, y should be measured from the base, as it is the reference line.

$$\therefore \quad I_{base} = \int_0^d by^2 \, dy$$

$$= \frac{bd^3}{3} \qquad \ldots (7.15)$$

The above result can also be found by using the theorem of parallel axes. Thus,

$$I_{base} = I_{xx} + AH^2$$

$$\therefore \quad I_{base} = \frac{bd^3}{12} + bd \left(\frac{d}{2}\right)^2 = \frac{bd^3}{12} + \frac{bd^3}{4}$$

$$= \frac{bd^3}{3} \qquad \ldots \text{(as before)}$$

**(ii) A triangle : (a) $I_{BC}$ :** Consider a triangular area of base b and height h as shown in Fig. 7.5. The centroidal axis parallel to the base is at $\frac{h}{3}$ from it.

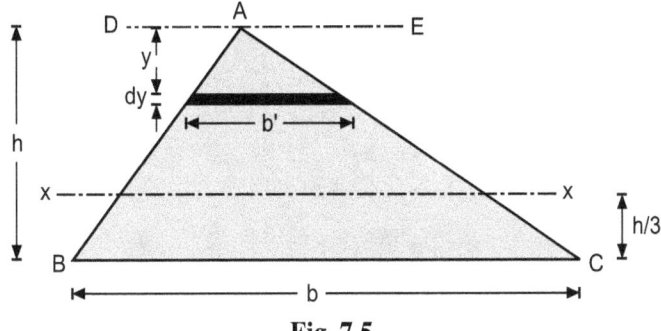

**Fig. 7.5**

Consider an elemental strip parallel to xx axis at y from apex A and of thickness dy, so that the elemental area will be bdy. From the similarity of triangles,

$$\frac{b'}{y} = \frac{b}{h}$$

$$\therefore \quad b' = \frac{b}{h} \cdot y$$

$$I_{BC} = \int_0^h \left(\frac{b}{h} \cdot y \, dy\right) (h-y)^2$$

$$\therefore \quad I_{BC} = \frac{b}{h} \int_0^h y \, (h^2 - 2yh + y^2) \, dy$$

$$= \frac{b}{h} \int_0^h (yh^2 - 2y^2h + y^3) \, dy$$

$$\therefore \quad I_{BC} = \frac{b}{h}\left[\frac{y^2}{2}h^2 - 2h\frac{y^3}{3} + \frac{y^4}{4}\right]_0^h$$

$$= \frac{b}{h}\left[\frac{h^4}{2} - \frac{2}{3}h^4 + \frac{h^4}{4}\right]$$

$$\therefore \quad I_{BC} = \frac{bh^3}{12} \qquad \ldots (7.16)$$

**(b) $I_{xx}$** : Using theorem of parallel axes,

$$I_{BC} = I_{xx} + AH^2$$

$$\therefore \quad I_{xx} = \frac{bh^3}{12} - \frac{bh}{2}\left(\frac{h}{3}\right)^2$$

$$= \frac{bh^3}{12} - \frac{bh^3}{18}$$

$$= \frac{bh^3}{36} \qquad \ldots (7.17)$$

**(c) $I_{DE}$** : DE is a line passing through apex A and is parallel to xx.

$$I_{DE} = I_{xx} + AH^2$$

$$= \frac{bh^3}{36} + \frac{bh}{2}\left(\frac{2}{3}h\right)^2$$

$$= \frac{bh^3}{36} + \frac{2}{9}bh^3$$

$$= \frac{bh^3(1+8)}{36}$$

$$= \frac{bh^3}{4} \qquad \ldots (7.18)$$

**(iii) A circle : (a) $I_{zz}$** :

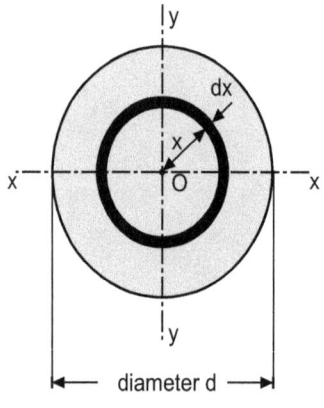

diameter d

**Fig. 7.6**

Consider a circle of diameter d as shown in Fig. 7.6. Consider an elemental ring at x from $O_z$ axis and of thickness dx.

$$dA = \text{Area of elemental ring} = (2\pi x)\,dx$$

$$\therefore \quad I_{zz} = \int_0^{d/2} (2\pi x\,dx)\,x^2$$

$$\therefore \quad I_{zz} = 2\pi \left(\frac{x^4}{4}\right)_0^{d/2} = \frac{\pi}{2}\left(\frac{d^4}{16}\right) = \frac{\pi}{32}\,d^4 \qquad \ldots (7.19)$$

This can be expressed in terms of radius, r also,

$$\therefore \quad I_{zz} = \frac{\pi}{32}(2r)^4 = \frac{\pi}{2}\,r^4 \qquad \ldots (7.20)$$

**(b) $I_{xx}$ and $I_{yy}$ :** As a circular section is symmetrical with respect to all axes, $I_{xx}$ will be equal to $I_{yy}$. Using theorem of perpendicular axes,

$$I_{zz} = I_{xx} + I_{yy} = 2\,I_{xx} = 2\,I_{yy}$$

$$\therefore \quad I_{xx} = I_{yy} = \frac{1}{2}\,I_{zz} = \frac{\pi}{64}\,d^4 \qquad \ldots (7.21)$$

$$= \frac{\pi}{4}\,r^4 \qquad \ldots (7.22)$$

**(iv) A semicircle :**

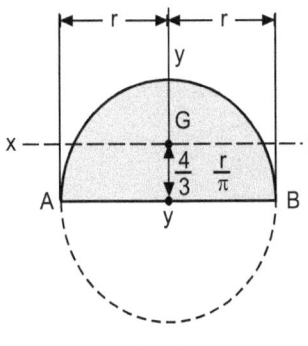

Fig. 7.7

(a) $I_{AB}$ : Consider a semicircle of radius r as shown in Fig. 7.7. The semicircle is symmetrical about the centroidal yy-axis but asymmetrical about the centroidal xx-axis.

The moment of inertia of complete circle about AB is equal to the sum of moments of inertia of two semicircles about AB.

$$\therefore \quad I_{AB} \text{ of the semicircle} = \frac{1}{2}\,I_{AB} \text{ of the circle}$$

$$= \frac{1}{2}\,\frac{\pi}{64}\,d^4$$

$$= \frac{\pi}{128}\,d^4 \qquad \ldots (7.23)$$

$$= \frac{\pi}{8}\,r^4 \qquad \ldots (7.24)$$

**(b) $I_{xx}$ :**

$$I_{AB} = I_{xx} + AH^2$$

$$\therefore \quad \frac{\pi}{8} r^4 = I_{xx} + \frac{1}{2} \pi r^2 \left(\frac{4}{3} \frac{r}{\pi}\right)^2$$

$$\therefore \quad I_{xx} = \frac{\pi}{8} r^4 - \frac{1}{2} \frac{16}{9} \frac{r^4}{\pi}$$

$$= r^4 \left[\frac{\pi}{8} - \frac{8}{9\pi}\right]$$

$$= 0.1098 \, r^4, \quad \text{say } 0.11 \, r^4 \qquad \ldots (7.25)$$

Thus, for a semicircle of radius r, I about the symmetrical axis is $\frac{\pi}{8}$ $r^4$ (i.e. 0.3927 $r^4$) and about the asymmetrical axis is 0.11 $r^4$.

## 7.6 DERIVATION OF FLEXURE FORMULA

Fig. 7.8 (a) shows a beam AB subjected to couple M at each end. It is easily seen that, between A and B, BM is constant and there is no shear force at all between A and B. This condition of the beam between A and B is called *pure bending or simple bending*.

Consider two adjacent sections ab and cd, separated by small distance dx as shown in Fig. 7.8 (a). Because of the bending, sections ab and cd rotate relative to each other by an amount dθ as shown in Fig. 7.8 (b) but remains straight and undistorted in accordance with the assumption (i) in article 7.1.

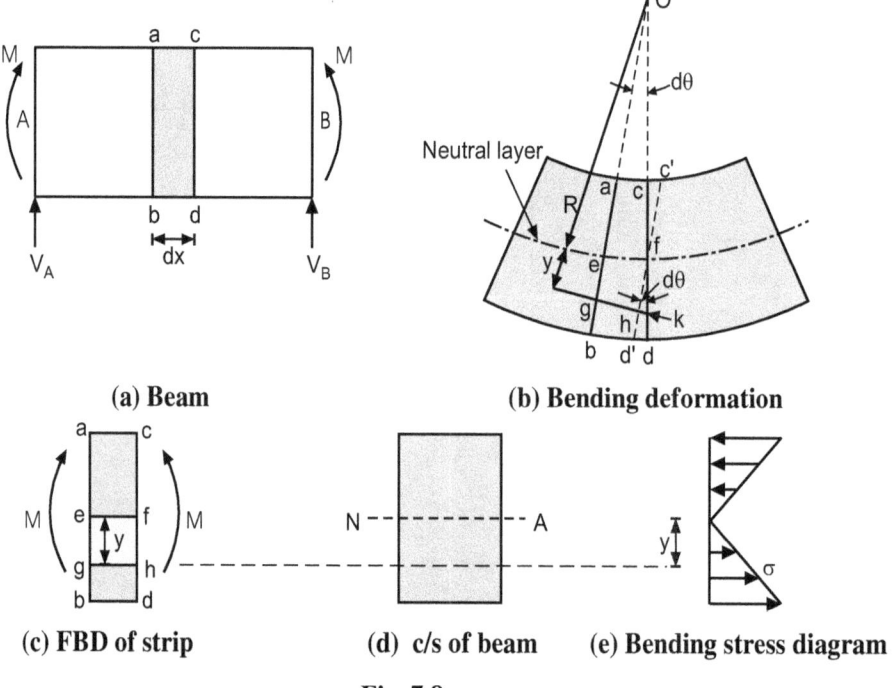

(a) Beam  (b) Bending deformation

(c) FBD of strip  (d) c/s of beam  (e) Bending stress diagram

Fig. 7.8

Fibre ac at the top gets shortened while fibre bd at the bottom gets elongated. Somewhere between them is fibre ef whose length is unchanged. Drawing a line c'd' through f parallel to ab shows that fibre ac gets shortened by an amount cc' and is in compression, while fibre bd gets elongated by an amount d'd and is in tension.

The plane containing fibres like ef is called as *neutral layer* because these fibres will remain unchanged in length and hence carry no stress. The line of intersection of neutral layer and cross-section of the beam is called as *neutral axis* abbreviated as NA.

Now consider deformation of typical fibre gh located at a distance 'y' from neutral layer. Its elongation hk is the arc of a circle of radius y subtended by an angle dθ and is given by

$$\delta L = hk = y \, d\theta$$

$$\therefore \quad \text{Longitudinal strain} = \varepsilon = \frac{dL}{L} = \frac{y \, d\theta}{ef} = \frac{y \, d\theta}{R \, d\theta} = \frac{y}{R}$$

where, R = Radius of curvature of neutral layer.

Because the material is homogeneous and obeys Hook's law; stress (σ) in the fibre gh is given by

$$\sigma = E \cdot \varepsilon = E \cdot \left(\frac{y}{R}\right) \quad \ldots (7.26)$$

where, E = Young's modulus of elasticity

Equation (7.26) indicates that; stress in any fibre varies directly with respect to its location y from neutral layer and therefore variation of bending stress over the cross-section of member is linear within elastic limit with zero stress at neutral layer and maximum at extreme fibres. Bending stress diagram is as shown in Fig. 7.8 (e). It should be noted that, bending stress diagram is irrespective of shape of cross-section.

Now, consider any beam subjected to transverse loading as shown in Fig. 7.9 (a). Consider a section at a distance x from support A.

Fig. 7.9 (b) shows free body diagram of beam element AC. The external loads that act on one side of the section are balanced by resisting shear V and bending moment M. For this equilibrium, consider an elementary area dA of cross-section. The state of forces on this elementary area for the beam element is as shown in Fig. 7.9 (c).

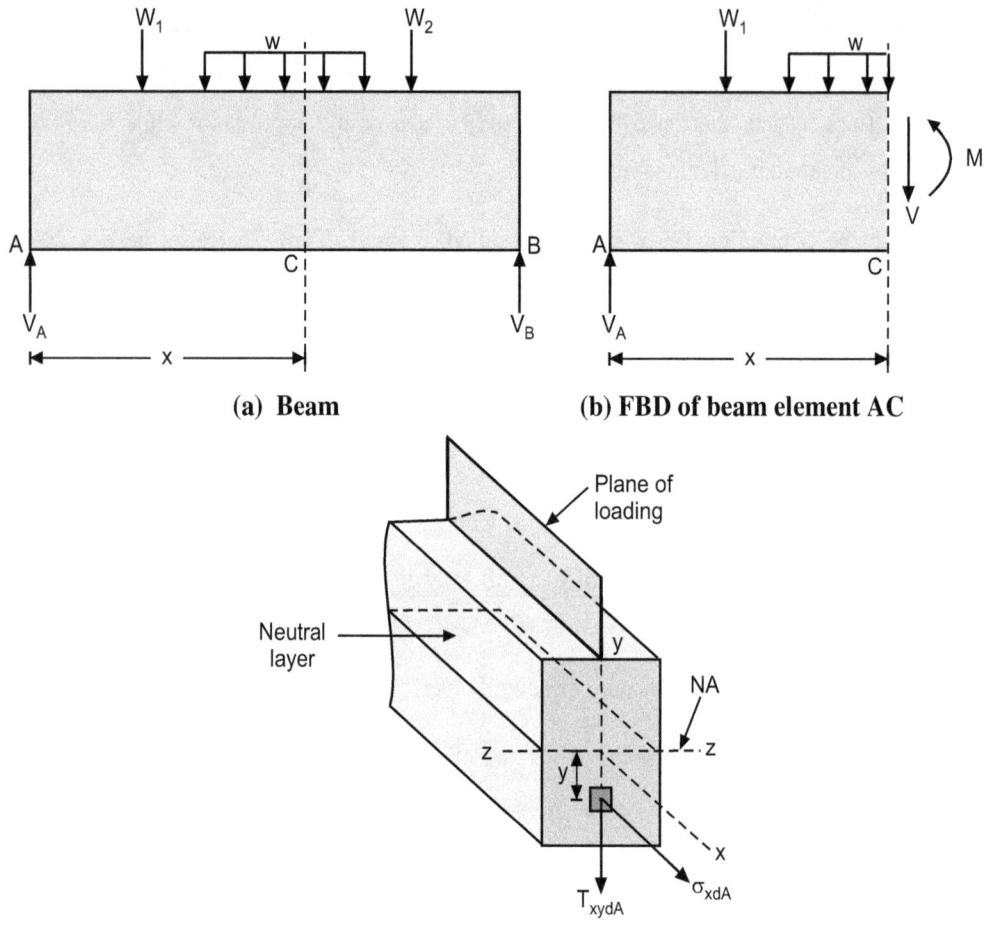

(a) Beam

(b) FBD of beam element AC

(c) Forces on typical element of beam cross-section

Fig. 7.9

As per assumption (v) of article (7.1), there is no external force normal to the cross-section, hence

$$\Sigma F_x = 0 \quad \therefore \quad \int \sigma_x \cdot dA = 0 \quad \ldots (7.27)$$

$$[\because \sigma_x = \sigma \text{ of equation (7.26)}]$$

Put equation (7.26) in equation (7.27)

$$\therefore \quad \int \frac{E}{R} (y) \, dA = 0$$

$$\therefore \quad \frac{E}{R} \int y \, dA = 0$$

$$\therefore \quad \frac{E}{R} A \bar{y} = 0 \quad \ldots (7.28)$$

where, $\frac{E}{R}$ is constant and $A \bar{y}$ = Total moment of area.

To satisfy equation (7.28), only $\bar{y}$ in that equation can be zero which means distance from neutral axis to the centroid of cross-section is zero. *Thus, the neutral axis is a centroidal axis.*

Applying second condition of equilibrium; because the external bending moment must be balanced by resisting moment;

$\sum M_z = 0$ we get,

$$M = \int y(\sigma_x \, dA) = \int y \cdot \left(\frac{E}{R} \cdot y\right) dA$$

$$= \frac{E}{R} \int y^2 \, dA$$

$\therefore$ 
$$M = \frac{E}{R} I \qquad \ldots (7.29)$$

where;
$$I = \int y^2 \, dA = \text{Moment of inertia @ neutral axis.}$$

From equation (7.26), $\dfrac{\sigma}{y} = \dfrac{E}{R}$ and from equation (7.29), $\dfrac{M}{I} = \dfrac{E}{R}$

$\therefore$
$$\frac{M}{I} = \frac{\sigma}{y} = \frac{E}{R} \qquad \ldots (7.30)$$

This is called **flexure formula**.

## 7.7 IMPORTANT DEFINITIONS

**Section Modulus (Z)** : It is defined as *the ratio of moment of inertia of cross-section to the distance of farthest fibre from NA.*

Thus,
$$Z = \frac{I}{y_{max}} \qquad \ldots (7.31)$$

Unit of section modulus is $mm^3$.

**Moment of Resistance (MR)** : It is defined as *capacity of section to resist bending moment and is given by the product of section modulus and allowable bending stress.*

Let; $\sigma_{bc}$ and $\sigma_{bt}$ = Allowable stress in bending compression and tension respectively.

If $\sigma_{bc} = \sigma_{bt}$; we shall indicate allowable stress in bending as '$\sigma_b$'.

Thus, in general, $\quad MR = Z \cdot \sigma_b \qquad \ldots (7.32)$

Following are the different possibilities, we may come across while finding MR of given section.

(i) Symmetric or unsymmetric section with $\sigma_{bc} = \sigma_{bt} = \sigma_b$ (say)

$$MR = Z \cdot \sigma_b$$

(ii) Symmetric section with $\sigma_{bc} \neq \sigma_{bt}$

$$MR_c = Z \cdot \sigma_{bc} \quad \text{and} \quad MR_t = Z \cdot \sigma_{bt}$$

where, $MR_c$ and $MR_t$ = Moment of resistance with reference to compression and tension side respectively.

Governing safe MR = Least of $MR_c$ and $MR_t$.

(iii) Unsymmetric section with $\sigma_{bc} \neq \sigma_{bt}$

$$\therefore \quad MR_c = \frac{I}{y_{c,\,max}} \sigma_{bc} = Z_c \cdot \sigma_{bc}$$

and

$$MR_t = \frac{I}{y_{t,\,max}} \sigma_{bt} = Z_t \cdot \sigma_{bt}$$

where, $Z_c$ and $Z_t$ = section modulus with respect to compression and tension side respectively.

Governing safe MR = least of $MR_c$ and $MR_t$.

Following points must be noted while calculating geometric properties of cross-section.

(i) Moment of inertia of section shall be calculated about the axis of bending (NA) and distance of extreme fibre is to be measured perpendicular to NA.

(ii) Sagging BM produces compression above NA and tension below NA, while hogging BM produces tension above NA and compression below NA, hence depending on the nature of bending moment, position of extreme compressive or tensile fibre shall be decided and accordingly distances $y_{c,\,max}$ or $y_{t,\,max}$ shall be written.

**Note :** In all the examples, x and y axes are considered as the axes of the cross-section since it is convenient for two dimensional study. But actual reference axes are as shown in Fig. 7.9.

## SOLVED EXAMPLES

**Example 7.1 :** Find moment of resistance of the beam section shown in Fig. 7.10 in following cases :

(i) Permissible stress in bending $\sigma_b$ = 100 MPa.
(ii) Permissible stress in bending compression and tension is 80 MPa and 100 MPa respectively.

**Data :** Cross-section as shown in Fig. 7.10.

Case (i)    $\sigma_b$ = 100 MPa

Case (ii)    $\sigma_{bc}$ = 80 MPa; $\sigma_{bt}$ = 100 MPa

**Required :** Moment of resistance.

**Concept :** (i) For symmetric sections with same allowable stress in bending compression and tension,

$$MR = Z_{xx} \times \sigma_b$$

(ii) For symmetric sections with different allowable stresses in bending compression and tension,

$$MR = (Z_{xx}) \cdot (\text{Least of } \sigma_{bc} \text{ and } \sigma_{bt})$$

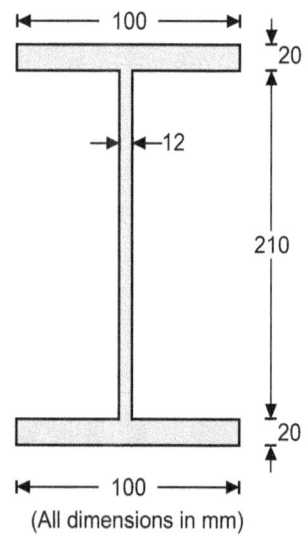

(All dimensions in mm)

**Fig. 7.10 : c/s of beam**

**Solution:** (i) Geometric properties:

$$I_{xx} = \frac{100 \times (250)^3}{12} - \frac{88 \times (210)^3}{12} = 62.29 \times 10^6 \text{ mm}^4$$

$$y_{max} = \frac{250}{2} = 125 \text{ mm}$$

$$Z_{xx} = \frac{I_{xx}}{y_{max}} = \frac{62.29 \times 10^6}{125} = 498.35 \times 10^3 \text{ mm}^3$$

(ii) Moment of resistance:

Case (i): When $\sigma_b = 100$ MPa

$$MR = Z_{xx} \cdot \sigma_b$$
$$= 498.35 \times 10^3 \times 100 \times 10^{-6} \text{ kNm} = \mathbf{49.835 \text{ kNm}}$$

Case (ii): When $\sigma_{bc} = 80$ MPa and $\sigma_{bt} = 100$ MPa

$$MR = Z_{xx} \times \sigma_{bc} \qquad (\because \sigma_{bc} < \sigma_{bt})$$
$$= 498.35 \times 10^3 \times 80 \times 10^{-6} \text{ kNm}$$
$$= \mathbf{39.868 \text{ kNm}}$$

**Example 7.2:** Find moment of resistance of the beam section shown in Fig. 7.11. @ xx axis in following cases:

(i) Permissible stress in bending is 100 MPa.

(ii) Permissible stress in bending compression and tension is 80 MPa and 100 MPa respectively. Assume sagging BM for cross-section.

**Data:** Cross-section as shown in Fig. 7.11.

Case (i)    $\sigma_b = 100$ MPa

Case (ii)   $\sigma_{bc} = 80$ MPa;

           $\sigma_{bt} = 100$ MPa

**Required:** Moment of resistance.

**Concept:** (i) For unsymmetric sections with same allowable stress in bending compression and tension,

$$MR = Z_{xx} \cdot \sigma_b$$

(ii) For unsymmetric sections with different allowable stresses in bending compression and tension,

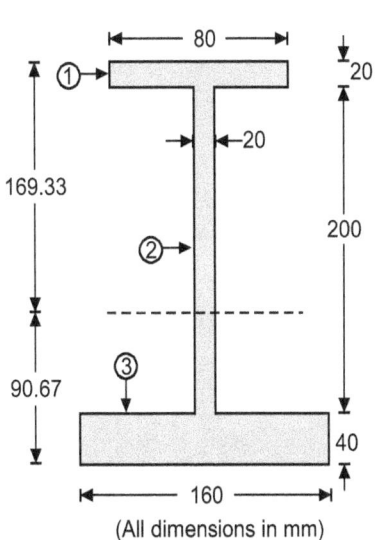

Fig. 7.11 : c/s of beam

$(MR)_c = (Z_{xx})_c \, (\sigma_{bc})$

$(MR)_t = (Z_{xx})_t \, (\sigma_{bt})$

Governing MR = least of $(MR)_c$ and $(MR)_t$

**Solution :** (i) Geometric properties :

Considering bottom fibre as reference for CG,

$a_1 = 80 \times 20 = 1600 \text{ mm}^2 \,; \quad y_1 = 250 \text{ mm}$

$a_2 = 200 \times 20 = 4000 \text{ mm}^2; \quad y_2 = 140 \text{ mm}$

$a_3 = 160 \times 40 = 6400 \text{ mm}^2; \quad y_3 = 20 \text{ mm}$

$$\bar{y} = \frac{1600 \times 250 + 4000 \times 140 + 6400 \times 20}{1600 + 4000 + 6400}$$

= 90.67 mm from bottom

= 169.33 mm from top

$I_{xx} = I_{xx_1} + I_{xx_2} + I_{xx_3}$

$I_{xx_1} = \dfrac{80 \times (20)^3}{12} + (1600)(250 - 90.67)^2 = 40.67 \times 10^6 \text{ mm}^4$

$I_{xx_2} = \dfrac{20 \times (200)^3}{12} + (4000)(140 - 90.67)^2 = 23.06 \times 10^6 \text{ mm}^4$

$I_{xx_3} = \dfrac{160 \times (40)^3}{12} + (6400)(90.67 - 20)^2 = 32.82 \times 10^6 \text{ mm}^4$

$\therefore \quad I_{xx} = (40.67 + 23.06 + 32.82) \times 10^6$

$= \mathbf{96.55 \times 10^6 \text{ mm}^4}$

(ii) Moment of resistance :

Case (i) : When $\sigma_b = 100$ MPa

$MR = Z_{xx} \cdot \sigma_b$

$= \dfrac{I_{xx}}{y_{max}} \cdot \sigma_b = \dfrac{96.55 \times 10^6}{169.33} \times 100 \times 10^{-6}$ kNm

= 57.02 kNm

Case (ii) : When $\sigma_{bc} = 80$ MPa and $\sigma_{bt} = 100$ MPa.

As the cross-section is subjected to sagging bending moment,

$y_c = 169.33$ mm and $y_t = 90.67$ mm, as sagging BM causes compression above neutral axis and tension below neutral axis.

$\therefore \quad (Z_{xx})_c = \dfrac{I_{xx}}{y_c} = \dfrac{96.55 \times 10^6}{169.33} = 570.19 \times 10^3 \text{ mm}^3$

$(Z_{xx})_t = \dfrac{I_{xx}}{y_t} = \dfrac{96.55 \times 10^6}{90.67} = 1064.85 \times 10^3 \text{ mm}^3$

Now, $(MR)_c = (Z_{xx})_c \cdot (\sigma_{bc})$

$= 570.19 \times 10^3 \times 80 \times 10^{-6}$ kNm $= 45.62$ kNm

and $(MR)_t = (Z_{xx})_t \cdot (\sigma_{bt})$

$= 1064.85 \times 10^3 \times 100 \times 10^{-6}$ kNm

$= 106.485$ kNm

∴ Governing MR = least of $(MR)_c$ and $(MR)_t$

$= \mathbf{45.62 \text{ kNm}}$

**Example 7.3 :** A beam has the cross-sectional dimensions as shown in Fig. 7.12 (a). If the allowable stress in bending is 50 MPa, find the intensity of UDL the beam can carry over simply supported span of 4 m.

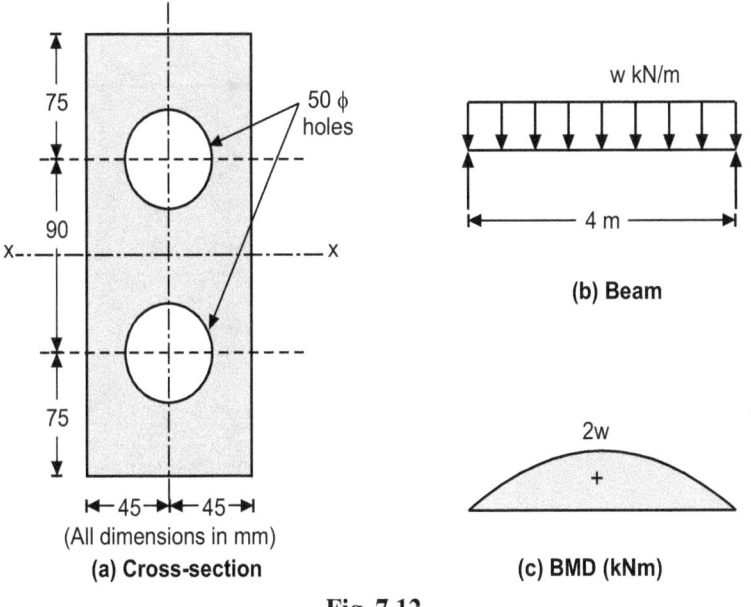

Fig. 7.12

**Data** : $\sigma_b = 50$ MPa

**Required** : Safe UDL on beam.

**Concept** : Equate maximum BM and MR.

**Solution** : (i) Geometric properties :

$$I_{xx} = \frac{90 \times (240)^3}{12} - 2\left[\frac{\pi}{64}(50)^4 + \frac{\pi}{4}(50)^2 \times (45)^2\right]$$

$= 95.11 \times 10^6$ mm$^4$

$y_{max} = \frac{240}{2} = 120$ mm

$Z_{xx} = \frac{I_{xx}}{y_{max}} = \frac{95.11 \times 10^6}{120} = 792.58 \times 10^3$ mm$^3$

(ii) Analysis of beam :

Let; w = Intensity of UDL in kN/m.

∴ Maximum BM at centre = $\dfrac{wl^2}{8} = \dfrac{w(4)^2}{8}$

= 2w kNm

(iii) Safe value of 'w' :

Equating maximum BM and MR,

$2w = Z_{xx} \cdot \sigma_b$

$= 792.58 \times 10^3 \times 50 \times 10^{-6}$

∴ w = **19.8 kN/m**

**Example 7.4 :** A groove in the form of a triangle is cut symmetrically from a beam section as shown in Fig. 7.13. If the stress in bending is not to exceed 25 MPa, find safe UDL which the beam can carry on a simply supported span of 4 m.

Data : Cross-section of beam as shown in Fig 7.13.

$\sigma_b = 25$ MPa

Required : Safe UDL the beam can carry over a simply supported span of 4 m.

Concept : Equate maximum BM to MR.

Solution : (i) Geometric properties :

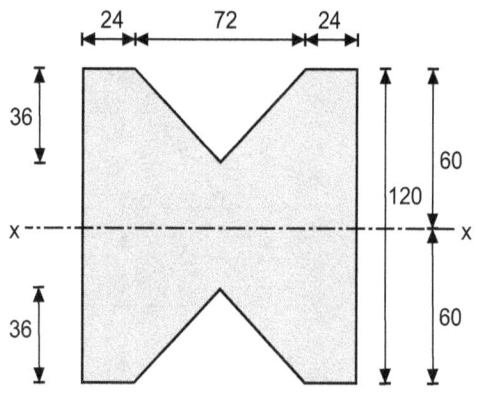

(All dimensions in mm)

**Fig. 7.13 : c/s of beam**

$$I_{xx} = \dfrac{120 \times (120)^3}{12} - 2\left[\dfrac{72 \times (36)^3}{36} + \dfrac{1}{2} \times 72 \times (36)\left(60 - \dfrac{1}{3} \times 36\right)^2\right]$$

$= 17.28 \times 10^6 - 6.16 \times 10^6$

$= 11.12 \times 10^6$ mm$^4$

$y_{max} = 60$ mm

$Z_{xx} = \dfrac{I_{xx}}{y_{max}} = \dfrac{11.12 \times 10^6}{60} = 185.36 \times 10^3$ mm$^3$

(ii) Safe UDL for the beam :

MR = $Z_{xx} \cdot \sigma_b = 185.36 \times 10^3 \times 25 \times 10^{-6} = 4.634$ kNm

Maximum BM = $\dfrac{wl^2}{8} = \dfrac{w(4)^2}{8} = 2w$ kNm

where, w = UDL in kN/m

Equating MR and maximum BM,

$$4.634 = 2w$$
$$w = \mathbf{2.317\ kN/m}\ \ \textbf{(Inclusive of self weight)}$$

**Example 7.5 :** The cross-section shown in Fig. 7.14 is used as a simply supported beam on a span of 4 m. If allowable stress in bending compression and tension is 100 MPa and 165 MPa respectively, find the safe UDL the beam can carry.

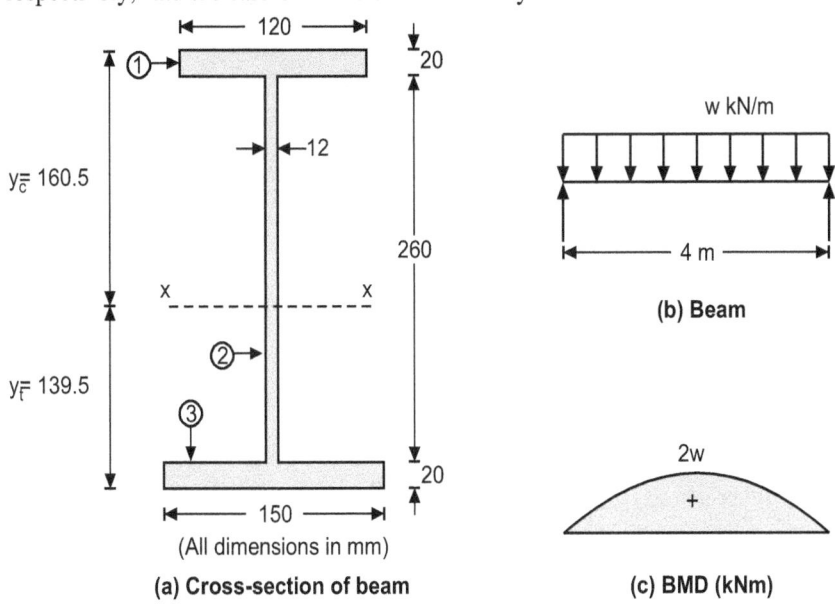

Fig. 7.14

**Data** : As shown in Fig. 7.14 (a) ; $\sigma_{bc}$ = 100 MPa ; $\sigma_{bt}$ = 165 MPa

**Required :** Safe UDL on beam.

**Concept :** Find MR w.r.t. tension and compression side.
Governing MR = Least of the two; then equate maximum BM = MR.

**Solution :** (i) Geometric properties :

Taking bottom most fibre as reference for C.G.,

$$a_1 = 120 \times 20 = 2400\ mm^2;\quad y_1 = 290\ mm$$
$$a_2 = 260 \times 10 = 2600\ mm^2;\quad y_2 = 150\ mm$$
$$a_3 = 150 \times 20 = 3000\ mm^2;\quad y_3 = 10\ mm$$

$$\bar{y} = \frac{2400 \times 290 + 2600 \times 150 + 3000 \times 10}{2400 + 2600 + 3000}$$

$$= 139.5\ mm\ \text{from bottom}.$$

∴ $\quad y_c = 160.5\ mm\ $ and $\ y_t = 139.5\ mm \quad$ (∵ sagging BM)

$$I_{xx} = I_{xx_1} + I_{xx_2} + I_{xx_3}$$

$$I_{xx_1} = \frac{120 \times (20)^3}{12} + 2400\,(290 - 139.5)^2 = 54.44 \times 10^6 \text{ mm}^4$$

$$I_{xx_2} = \frac{10 \times (260)^3}{12} + 2600\,(150 - 139.5)^2 = 14.93 \times 10^6 \text{ mm}^4$$

$$I_{xx_3} = \frac{150 \times (20)^3}{12} + 3000\,(139.5 - 10)^2 = 50.41 \times 10^6 \text{ mm}^4$$

$$\therefore \quad I_{xx} = (54.44 + 14.93 + 50.41) \times 10^6 = 119.78 \times 10^6 \text{ mm}^4$$

$$(Z_{xx})_c = \frac{I_{xx}}{y_c} = \frac{119.78 \times 10^6}{160.5} = 746.29 \times 10^3 \text{ mm}^3$$

$$(Z_{xx})_t = \frac{I_{xx}}{y_t} = \frac{119.78 \times 10^6}{139.5} = 858.63 \times 10^3 \text{ mm}^3$$

(ii) Moment of resistance (MR):

$$(MR)_c = (Z_{xx})\,\sigma_{bc} = 746.29 \times 10^3 \times 100 \times 10^{-6} \text{ kNm}$$

$$= 74.629 \text{ kNm}$$

$$(MR)_t = (Z_{xx})\,\sigma_{bt} = 858.63 \times 10^3 \times 165 \times 10^{-6} \text{ kNm}$$

$$= 141.67 \text{ kNm}$$

Governing MR = Least of $(MR)_c$ and $(MR)_t$

$$= 74.629 \text{ kNm}$$

(iii) Safe UDL on beam:

$$\text{Maximum BM} = \frac{wL^2}{8} = \frac{w\,(4)^2}{8} = 2w \text{ kNm}$$

where; w = UDL in kN/m

Equating maximum BM and MR,

$$2w = 74.629$$

$$\therefore \quad w = \mathbf{37.32 \text{ kN/m} \text{ (Inclusive of self weight)}}$$

**Example 7.6 :** A cast iron test beam 30 mm square in cross-section and 500 mm long is simply supported at ends. It fails at central point load at 4.32 kN. What load at free end will cause the failure of cantilever beam of 1 m span made of same material 30 mm × 60 mm in cross-section ?

**Data** : For simply supported beam : cross-section = 30 mm × 30 mm ;

span = L = 0.5 m ; failure load = 4.32 kN applied at centre of span.

For cantilever beam : cross-section = 30 mm × 60 mm ; span = 1 m

**Required :** Failure load for cantilever beam (P); applied at free end.

**Concept :** From the case of simply supported beam, obtain permissible stress in bending and then for cantilever beam equating Maximum BM to MR, obtain the failure load (P).

**Solution :** (i) Case of simply supported beam :

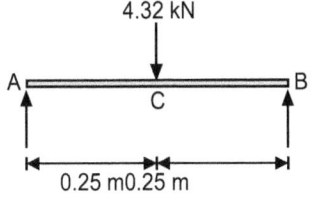

(a) Beam

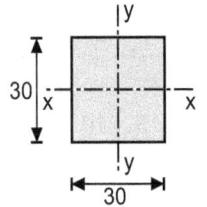

(All dimensions in mm)

(b) c/s of beam

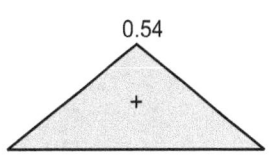

(c) BMD (kNm)

Fig. 7.15

$$I_{xx} = \frac{30 \times (30)^3}{12} = 67.5 \times 10^3 \text{ mm}^4$$

$$y_{max} = \frac{30}{2} = 15 \text{ mm}$$

$$Z_{xx} = \frac{I_{xx}}{y_{max}} = \frac{67.5 \times 10^3}{15} = 4.5 \times 10^3 \text{ mm}^3$$

Let $\sigma_b$ = Permissible stress in bending for cast iron

∴ $MR = Z_{xx} \cdot \sigma_b$

$= 4.5 \times 10^3 \times \sigma_b$ Nmm

Maximum BM $= \dfrac{4.32 \times 0.5}{4} = 0.54$ kNm

Equating maximum BM and MR,

$$0.54 = 4.5 \times 10^3 \times \sigma_b \times 10^{-6}$$

$$\sigma_b = \mathbf{120 \text{ MPa}}$$

(ii) Case of cantilever beam :

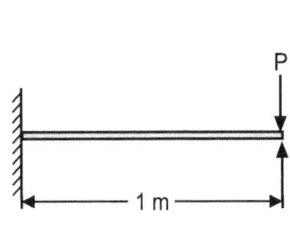

(a) Beam

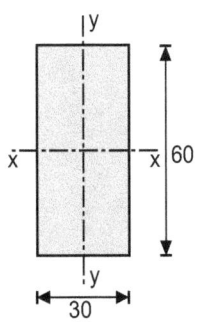

(All dimensions in mm)

(b) c/s of beam

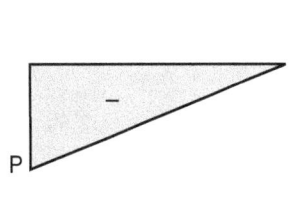

(c) BMD (kNm)

Fig. 7.16

$$I_{xx} = \frac{30 \times (60)^3}{12} = 540 \times 10^3 \text{ mm}^4$$

$$y_{max} = \frac{60}{2} = 30 \text{ mm}$$

$$Z_{xx} = \frac{I_{xx}}{y_{max}} = \frac{540 \times 10^3}{30}$$

$$= 18 \times 10^3 \text{ mm}^3$$

$$MR = Z_{xx} \cdot \sigma_b = 18 \times 10^3 \times 120 \times 10^{-6} \text{ kNm}$$

$$= 2.16 \text{ kNm}$$

Maximum BM = 'P' kNm ;   where  P = Failure load in kN
Equating maximum BM and MR,

$$P = \mathbf{2.16 \text{ kN}}$$

**Example 7.7** : A water main 600 mm external diameter and 10 mm thickness is made of mild steel plate and is running full. If the allowable bending stress is 60 MPa, find the maximum span for simply supported condition that the water main can be used. Assume density of steel as 78.5 kN/m³ and that of water as 9.81 kN/m³.

**Data**   : D = 600 mm ; d = 580 mm ; $\sigma_b$ = 60 MPa ;

Density of steel and water = 78.5 kN/m³ and 9.81 kN/m³ respectively.

**Required** : Simply supported span (L).

**Concept** : From cross-section dimensions and permissible stress, find moment of resistance (MR) and obtain maximum BM in terms of span. Equating MR and max. BM, span can be found out.

**Solution** : (i) Geometric properties :

$$I_{xx} = \frac{\pi}{64}(D^4 - d^4)$$

$$= \frac{\pi}{64}[(600)^4 - (580)^4]$$

$$= 806.75 \times 10^6 \text{ mm}^4$$

$$y_{max} = \frac{600}{2} = 300 \text{ mm}$$

$$Z_{xx} = \frac{I_{xx}}{y_{max}} = \frac{806.75 \times 10^6}{300}$$

$$= 2.69 \times 10^6 \text{ mm}^3$$

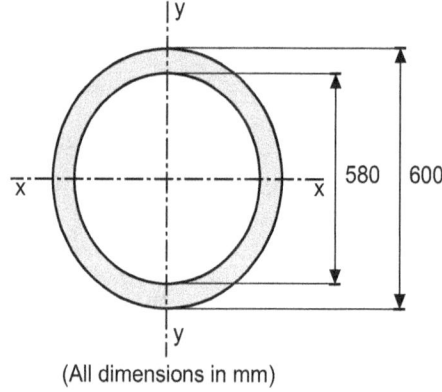

(All dimensions in mm)

**Fig. 7.17 : c/s of water main**

(ii)  Analysis :

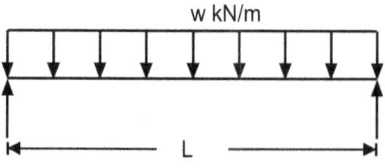

**Fig. 7.18**

Let  L = Span in metres

w = Total UDL due to self weight of pipe and water.

$$= \left(\frac{\pi}{4}[(600)^2 - (580)^2]\times 78.5 + \frac{\pi}{4}(580)^2 \times 9.81\right)\times 10^{-6}$$

$$= 4.05 \text{ kN/m}$$

∴ Maximum BM $= \dfrac{wL^2}{8} = 4.05 \times \dfrac{L^2}{8} = (0.50625)\, L^2$ kNm

(iii) Moment of Resistance (MR):

$$MR = Z_{xx} \cdot \sigma_b$$
$$= 2.69 \times 10^6 \times 60 \times 10^{-6} \text{ kNm}$$
$$= 161.4 \text{ kNm}$$

(iv) Span of water main (L):

Equating maximum BM and MR,

$$(0.50625)\, L^2 = 161.4$$

∴ **L = 17.85 m**

**Example 7.8 :** Fig. 7.19 shows the cross-section of a beam. What is the ratio of moment of resistance @ yy axis to that @ xx axis, if permissible bending stress is same in either directions?

**Data** : As shown in Fig. 7.19.

**Required** : $\dfrac{(MR)_y}{(MR)_x}$

**Concept** : Since permissible, stress in either direction is same.

$$\dfrac{(MR)_y}{(MR)_x} = \dfrac{Z_{yy}}{Z_{xx}}$$

**Solution** : (i) To find $Z_{yy}$ :

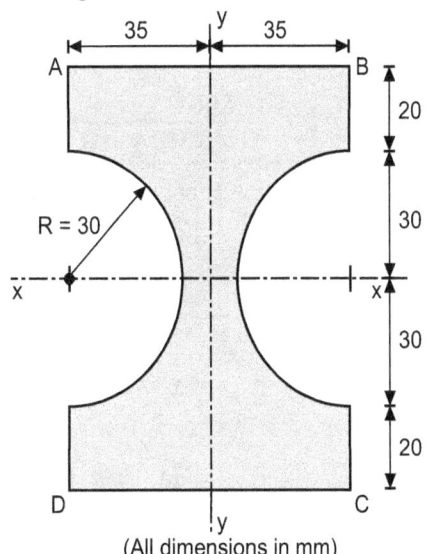

**Fig. 7.19 : c/s of beam**

$I_{yy} = I_{yy}$ of rectangle ABCD $-$ 2 ($I_{yy}$ of semicircle).

$I_{yy}$ of rectangle ABCD $= \dfrac{100 \times (70)^3}{12} = 2.86 \times 10^6$ mm$^4$.

$I_{yy}$ of semicircle @ vertical axis passing through its C.G.

$$I_{GG} = \frac{\pi}{8} r^4 - \frac{\pi r^2}{2} \left(\frac{4r}{3\pi}\right)^2$$

$$= \frac{\pi}{8} (30)^4 - \frac{\pi (30)^2}{2} \left(\frac{4 \times 30}{3\pi}\right)^2$$

∴ $I_{GG} = 88.9 \times 10^3$ mm⁴

$I_{yy}$ of semicircle $= I_{GG} + Ak^2$

$$= I_{GG} + \frac{\pi r^2}{2} \left(35 - \frac{4r}{3\pi}\right)^2$$

$$= 88.9 \times 10^3 + \frac{\pi \times (30)^2}{2} \left(35 - \frac{4 \times 30}{3\pi}\right)^2$$

$$= 789.89 \times 10^3 \text{ mm}^4$$

∴ $I_{yy}$ of cross-section of beam $= 2.86 \times 10^6 - 2(789.89 \times 10^3)$

$$= 1.28 \times 10^6 \text{ mm}^4$$

$y_{max} = 35$ mm

∴ $Z_{yy} = \dfrac{I_{yy}}{y_{max}} = \dfrac{1.28 \times 10^6}{35} = 36.58 \times 10^3$ mm³

(ii) To find $Z_{xx}$:  $I_{xx} = I_{xx}$ of rectangle ABCD $- I_{xx}$ of circle with r = 30 mm

$$= 70 \times \frac{(100)^3}{12} - \frac{\pi}{4} (30)^4 = 5.197 \times 10^6 \text{ mm}^4$$

$y_{max} = 50$ mm

$$Z_{xx} = \frac{I_{xx}}{y_{max}} = \frac{5.197 \times 10^6}{50} = 103.94 \times 10^3 \text{ mm}^3$$

(iii) $\dfrac{\text{MR @ yy axis}}{\text{MR @ xx axis}} = \dfrac{Z_{yy}}{Z_{xx}} = \dfrac{36.58 \times 10^3}{103.94 \times 10^3} = 0.35$

**Example 7.9 :** A simply supported beam has square cross-section throughout its length.

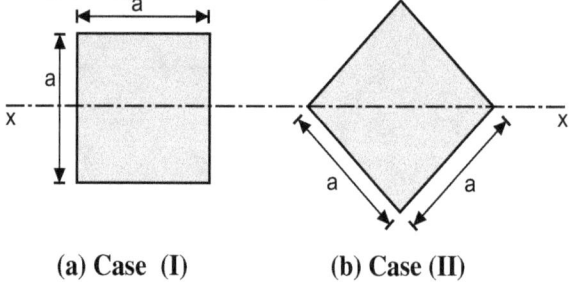

(a) Case (I)  (b) Case (II)

**Fig. 7.20 : c/s of beams**

The side of square is 'a'. The section carries BM = M. Calculate maximum bending stresses developed in beam when;

(i) side of square is kept vertical and

(ii) diagonal of square is kept horizontal; as shown in Fig. 7.20.

**Data :** As shown in Fig. 7.20.

**Required :** Bending stresses.

**Concept :** $\sigma_b = \dfrac{M}{Z_{xx}}$

**Solution :** (i) Analysis of case I :

$$I_{xx} = \dfrac{a^4}{12} \; ; \quad y_{max} = \dfrac{a}{2}$$

$$\therefore \quad Z_{xx} = \dfrac{I_{xx}}{y_{max}} = \dfrac{a^4}{12} \times \dfrac{2}{a} = \dfrac{a^3}{6}$$

$$\therefore \quad \text{Bending stresses } \sigma_b = \pm \dfrac{M}{Z_{xx}} = \pm \dfrac{M}{a^3/6} = \pm \dfrac{6M}{a^3}$$

(ii) Analysis of case II :

$$I_{xx} = 2\left(\dfrac{b\,h^3}{12}\right) = \dfrac{b\,h^3}{6} = \dfrac{(\sqrt{2}\,a)(a/\sqrt{2})^3}{6} = \dfrac{a^4}{12}$$

$$y_{max} = \dfrac{a}{\sqrt{2}}$$

$$\therefore \quad Z_{xx} = \dfrac{I_{xx}}{y_{max}} = \dfrac{a^4}{12} \times \dfrac{\sqrt{2}}{a} = \dfrac{a^3}{6\sqrt{2}}$$

$$\therefore \quad \text{Bending stresses} = \sigma_b = \pm \dfrac{M}{Z_{xx}} = \pm \dfrac{M}{a^3/6\sqrt{2}} = \pm \dfrac{(6\sqrt{2})\,M}{a^3}$$

**Note :** Bending stresses for case II are higher than that of case I.

**Example 7.10 :** A hollow rectangular beam is formed by joining four wooden pieces together as shown in Fig. 7.21. The Young's modulus of elasticity is same for all pieces. However, the permissible stress in bending is 10 MPa and 6 MPa for horizontal and vertical pieces respectively. Determine the moment of resistance of beam section.

**Data :** Cross-section of beam as shown in Fig. 7.21.

$\sigma_b$ = 10 MPa and 6 MPa for horizontal and vertical pieces.

**Required :** Moment of resistance of beam section.

**Concept :** Moment of resistance will be governed by allowable stress in bending for horizontal pieces or for vertical pieces, whichever gives the least value.

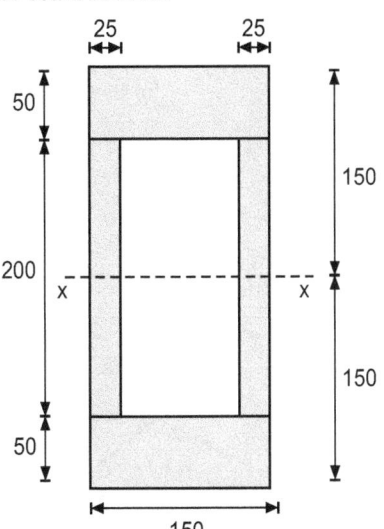

**Fig. 7.21 : c/s of beam**

**Solution :** (i) Geometric properties of cross-section :

$$I_{xx} = \frac{150 \times (300)^3}{12} - \frac{100 \times (200)^3}{12} = 270.83 \times 10^6 \text{ mm}^4$$

(ii) MR based on allowable stress of horizontal pieces :

$$(MR)_1 = (I_{xx}) \left(\frac{\sigma_b}{y_{max}}\right) \text{ for horizontal pieces.}$$

$$= 270.83 \times 10^6 \times \left(\frac{10}{150}\right) \times 10^{-6} \text{ kNm}$$

$$= 18.05 \text{ kNm} \qquad \ldots (i)$$

(iii) MR based on allowable stress of vertical pieces,

$$(MR)_2 = (I_{xx}) \left(\frac{\sigma_b}{y_{max}}\right) \text{ for vertical pieces.}$$

$$= 270.83 \times 10^6 \times \left(\frac{6}{100}\right) \times 10^{-6} \text{ kNm}$$

$$= 16.25 \text{ kNm} \qquad \ldots (ii)$$

∴ Governing MR = Least of $(MR)_1$ and $(MR)_2$

$$= 16.25 \text{ kNm}$$

**Example 7.11** : For the beam shown in Fig. 7.22, find bending stresses at cross-sections C and B.

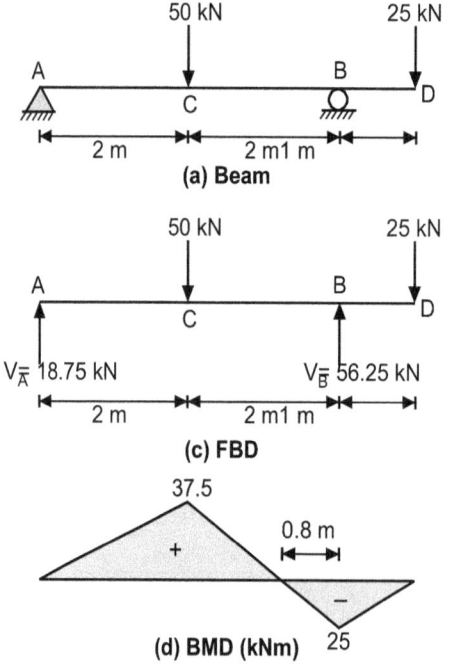

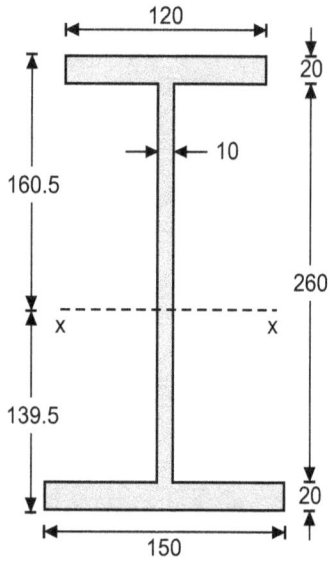

(b) Cross-section of beam
(All dimensions in mm)

**Fig. 7.22**

**Data** : As shown in Fig. 7.22 (a), (b).

**Required :** Bending stresses at 'C' and 'B'.

**Concept :** $\sigma_b = \dfrac{M}{I} \times y$; Note the nature of BM at cross-sections C and B.

**Solution :** (i) Geometric properties :

Distance of CG = 139.5 mm from bottom.

$$I_{xx} = 119.78 \times 10^6 \text{ mm}^4$$

(ii) Analysis of beam :

For reactions :

$\Sigma M_A = 0;$   $V_B \times 4 - 50 \times 2 - 25 \times 5 = 0$

$\therefore$   $V_B = 56.25 \text{ kN } (\uparrow)$

$\Sigma F_y = 0;$   $V_A + V_B - 50 - 25 = 0$

$\therefore$   $V_A = 18.75 \text{ kN } (\uparrow)$

$\Sigma F_x = 0;$   $H_A = 0$

$BM_C = 18.75 \times 2 = 37.5 \text{ kNm (Sagging)}$

$BM_B = -25 \times 1 = -25 \text{ kNm} = 25 \text{ kNm (Hogging)}$

BMD is shown in Fig. 7.22 (d).

(iii) Bending stresses at 'C' :

$$(\sigma_b)_{top} = \dfrac{BM_C}{I_{xx}} (y)_{top}$$

$$= \dfrac{37.5 \times 10^6}{119.78 \times 10^6} \times 160.5 = 50.24 \text{ MPa (Compressive)}$$

$$(\sigma_b)_{bottom} = \dfrac{BM_C}{I_{xx}} (y)_{bottom} = \dfrac{37.5 \times 10^6}{119.78 \times 10^6} \times 139.5 = 43.67 \text{ MPa (Tensile)}$$

(iv) Bending stresses at 'B' :

$$(\sigma_b)_{top} = \dfrac{BM_B}{I_{xx}} \cdot (y)_{top} = \dfrac{25 \times 10^6}{119.78 \times 10^6} \times 160.5 = 33.49 \text{ MPa (Tensile)}$$

$$(\sigma_b)_{bottom} = \dfrac{BM_B}{I_{xx}} (y)_{bottom} = \dfrac{25 \times 10^6}{119.78 \times 10^6} \times 139.5 = 29.11 \text{ MPa (Compressive)}$$

(v) Bending stress diagram is as shown in Fig. 7.23.

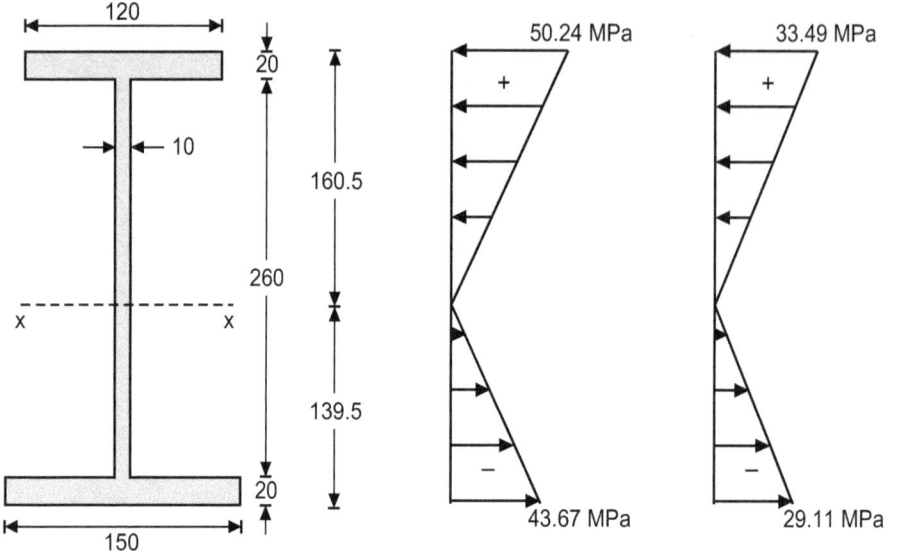

| (a) Cross-section of beam | (b) Bending stresses at 'C' | (c) Bending stresses at 'B' |

Fig. 7.23

**Example 7.12 :** A beam of constant section and symmetrical about the neutral axis is simply supported over a span of 8 m. The beam has to carry a concentrated load of 40 kN at midspan and a UDL of 15 kN/m on the entire span. If the central deflection is limited to $\frac{1}{480}$ th of span and maximum fibre stress due to bending is not to exceed 118 MPa, determine the required depth of beam and its moment of inertia. Assume E = 200 GPa.

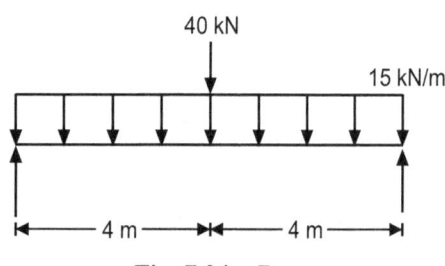

Fig. 7.24 : Beam

**Data** : $\Delta_{max} = \left(\frac{1}{480}\right)$ span;

$\sigma_b$ = 118 MPa; E = 200 GPa. Loading as shown in Fig. 7.24.

**Required** : Depth of beam and M.I.

**Concept** : Find the value of moment of inertia knowing central deflection and then find depth of beam from bending stress criteria.

**Solution** : (i) M.I. from deflection criteria :

Maximum deflection for given beam will occur at centre. By principle of superposition,

$$\Delta_{max} = \frac{5}{384}\frac{wL^4}{EI} + \frac{PL^3}{48\,EI} = \frac{5}{384} \cdot \frac{15 \times (8000)^4}{EI} + \frac{40 \times 10^3 \times (8000)^3}{48\,EI}$$

$$\therefore \quad \Delta_{max} = \frac{1.226 \times 10^{15}}{EI} \text{ mm;}$$

where EI = Flexural rigidity in Nmm²

$$\text{Allowable deflection} = \left(\frac{1}{480}\right) \text{span}$$

$$= \frac{8000}{480}$$

$$= 16.67 \text{ mm}$$

Equating $\Delta_{max}$ and allowable deflection, we get,

$$\frac{1.226 \times 10^{15}}{EI} = 16.67$$

$$\therefore \quad EI = 7.356 \times 10^{13} \text{ Nmm}^2$$

We have, $\quad E = 200$ GPa

$$\therefore \quad I = \frac{7.356 \times 10^{13}}{200 \times 10^3}$$

$$= 367.8 \times 10^6 \text{ mm}^4$$

(ii) Depth of beam from bending stress criteria :

$$\text{Maximum BM at midspan} = M = \frac{wL^2}{8} + \frac{PL}{4}$$

$$= \frac{15 \times 8^2}{8} + \frac{40 \times 8}{4}$$

$$\therefore \quad M = 200 \text{ kNm}$$

$$\text{Bending stress} = \frac{M}{I} \times y_{max}$$

$$118 = \frac{200 \times 10^6}{367.8 \times 10^6} \cdot y_{max}$$

$$\therefore \quad y_{max} = 217 \text{ mm}$$

$$\therefore \quad \text{Depth of beam} = 2 \, y_{max} = \mathbf{434 \text{ mm}} \quad (\because \text{symmetry @ N.A.})$$

**Example 7.13 :** The cross-section of beam shown in Fig. 7.25 (a) is to be used as a cantilever beam to carry a UDL over a span of 2 m. If permissible bending stress is 160 MPa, find the intensity of UDL that the beam can carry. Also find the shear stresses at neutral axis. The section is placed such that web of the channel forms tension flange for the beam.

**Data**   : As shown in Fig. 7.25 (a) and 7.25 (b).

**Required** : Safe UDL 'w'.

**Concept** : Equate maximum BM = MR.

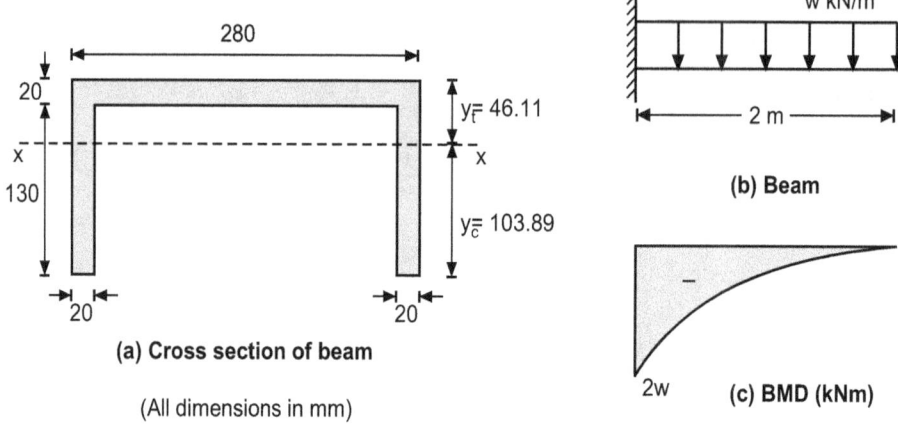

**(a) Cross section of beam**

(All dimensions in mm)

**(b) Beam**

**(c) BMD (kNm)**

**Fig. 7.25**

**Solution :** (i) Geometric properties :

Taking bottom most fibre as reference for CG of cross-section,

$$a_1 = 280 \times 20 = 5600 \text{ mm}^2; \quad y_1 = 140 \text{ mm}$$

$$a_2 = a_3 = 130 \times 20 = 2600 \text{ mm}^2; \quad y_2 = y_3 = 65 \text{ mm}$$

$$\bar{y} = \frac{5600 \times 140 + 2 \times 2600 \times 65}{5600 + 2 \times 2600} = 103.89 \text{ mm from bottom}$$

$$I_{xx} = I_{xx_1} + I_{xx_2} + I_{xx_3}$$

$$I_{xx_1} = \frac{280 \times (20)^3}{12} + (5600)\,(140 - 103.89)^2 = 7.49 \times 10^6 \text{ mm}^4$$

$$I_{xx_2} = I_{xx_3} = \frac{20 \times (130)^3}{12} + (2600)\,(103.89 - 65)^2 = 7.59 \times 10^6 \text{ mm}^4$$

$$I_{xx} = (7.49 + 2 \times 7.59) \times 10^6 = 22.67 \times 10^6 \text{ mm}^4$$

$$y_{max} = 103.89 \text{ mm}$$

$$Z_{xx} = \frac{I_{xx}}{y_{max}} = \frac{22.67 \times 10^6}{103.89} = \mathbf{218.21 \times 10^3 \text{ mm}^3}$$

(ii) Moment of resistance :

$$MR = Z_{xx} \cdot \sigma_b$$

$$= 218.21 \times 10^3 \times 160 \times 10^{-6} \text{ kNm}$$

$$= 34.91 \text{ kNm}$$

(iii) Safe UDL :

Let  w = Intensity of UDL in 'kN/m'

$$\text{Max. BM} = \frac{wL^2}{2} = w \times \frac{(2)^2}{2} = 2w \text{ kNm}$$

Equating maximum BM and MR,

$$2w = 34.91$$

$$\therefore \quad w = \mathbf{17.4\ kN/m}$$

**Example 7.14 :** A simply supported beam 6 m long carrying UDL throughout has cross-section shown in Fig. 7.26 (b). If permissible stresses in bending compression and tension are 100 MPa and 120 MPa respectively, determine the safe intensity of UDL.

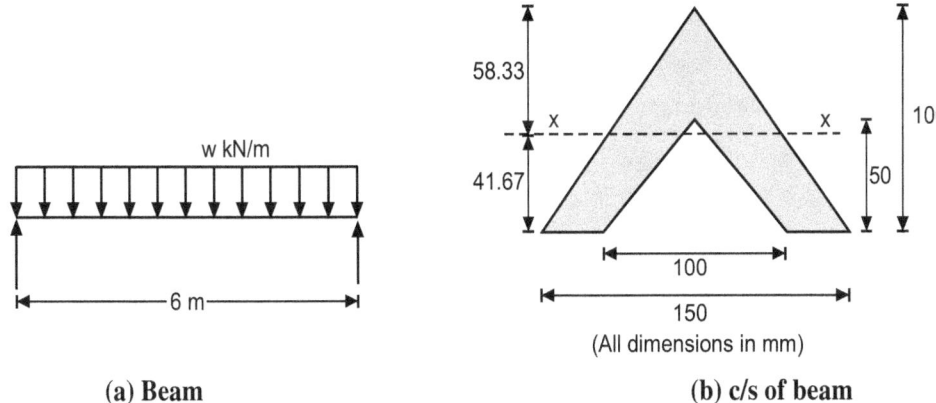

(a) Beam          (b) c/s of beam

Fig. 7.26

**Data** : $\sigma_{bc} = 100$ MPa; $\sigma_{bt} = 120$ MPa.

**Required** : Intensity of UDL.

**Concept** : Equate maximum BM and MR.

**Solution** : (i) Geometric properties :

Consider bottom most fibre as reference for locating C.G.

$$a_1 = \frac{1}{2} \times 150 \times 100 = 7500\ \text{mm}^2; \quad y_1 = \frac{100}{3}\ \text{mm}$$

$$a_2 = \frac{1}{2} \times 100 \times 50 = 2500\ \text{mm}^2; \quad y_2 = \frac{50}{3}\ \text{mm}$$

$$\bar{y} = \frac{a_1 y_1 - a_2 y_2}{a_1 - a_2} = \frac{7500 \times 100/3 - 2500 \times 50/3}{7500 - 2500}$$

$$= 41.67\ \text{mm from bottom}$$

$\therefore \quad y_c = 58.33$ mm and $y_t = 41.67$ mm ($\because$ sagging BM)

$$I_{xx} = I_{xx_1} - I_{xx_2}$$

$$I_{xx_1} = \frac{150 \times (100)^3}{36} + 7500\left(41.67 - \frac{100}{3}\right)^2 = 4.69 \times 10^6\ \text{mm}^4$$

$$I_{xx_2} = \frac{100 \times (50)^3}{36} + 2500\left(41.67 - \frac{50}{3}\right)^2 = 1.91 \times 10^6 \text{ mm}^4$$

$$\therefore \quad I_{xx} = (4.69 - 1.91) \times 10^6 = 2.78 \times 10^6 \text{ mm}^4$$

$$(Z_{xx})_c = \frac{I_{xx}}{y_c} = \frac{2.78 \times 10^6}{58.33} = \mathbf{47.66 \times 10^3 \text{ mm}^3}$$

$$(Z_{xx})_t = \frac{I_{xx}}{y_t} = \frac{2.78 \times 10^6}{41.67} = \mathbf{66.71 \times 10^3 \text{ mm}^3}$$

(ii) Moment of resistance of cross-section :

$$(MR)_c = (Z_{xx})_c \cdot \sigma_{bc}$$

$$= 47.66 \times 10^3 \times 100 \times 10^{-6} \text{ kNm}$$

$$= \mathbf{4.766 \text{ kNm}} \quad \quad \ldots (i)$$

$$(MR)_t = (Z_{xx})_t \cdot \sigma_{bt}$$

$$= 66.71 \times 10^3 \times 120 \times 10^{-6} \text{ kNm}$$

$$= \mathbf{8 \text{ kNm}} \quad \quad \ldots (ii)$$

Governing MR = **4.766 kNm**  ($\because$ Least of (i) and (ii))

(iii) Safe UDL on beam :

Let  $w$ = Intensity of safe UDL in kN/m

$$\therefore \quad \text{Maximum BM at midspan} = \frac{wl^2}{8} = \frac{w \times 6^2}{8} = 4.5w \text{ kNm}$$

Equating maximum BM and MR,

$$4.5w = 4.766$$

$$\therefore \quad w = \mathbf{1.059 \text{ kN/m}}$$

**Example 7.15 :** An unequal ISA 125 × 75 × 8 is used as a simply supported beam over a span of 3 m; with longer leg placed vertical. Find the safe UDL the beam can carry if allowable bending stress in tension = 120 MPa. Also find the maximum compressive stress induced, assuming bending @ xx axis.

**Data** : ISA 125 × 75 × 8 ; L = 3 m simply supported ; $\sigma_{bt}$ = 120 MPa.

**Required** : Safe UDL and stress in bending compression.

**Concept** : Using MR of tension side, find safe UDL and then evaluate stress in bending compression $(\sigma_{bc})_{cal}$.

**Solution :**

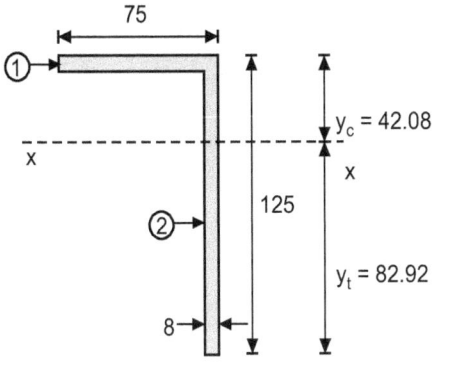
(a) Cross-section

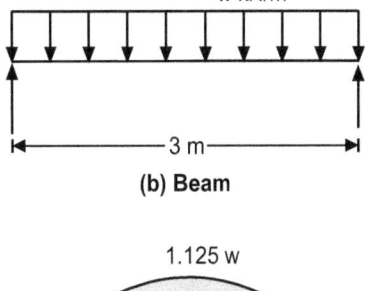
(b) Beam

(c) BMD (kNm)

Fig. 7.27

(i) Geometric properties :

Taking top most fibre as a reference for CG.

$$a_1 = 75 \times 8 = 600 \text{ mm}^2 \quad ; \quad y_1 = 4 \text{ mm}$$

$$a_2 = (125 - 8)\,8 = 936 \text{ mm}^2 \quad ; \quad y_2 = 8 + \left(\frac{125-8}{2}\right) = 66.5 \text{ mm}$$

∴ $$\bar{y} = \frac{600 \times 4 + 936 \times 66.5}{600 + 936} = 42.08 \text{ mm from AB}$$

$$I_{xx} = 75 \times \frac{8^3}{12} + (600)(42.08 - 4)^2 + \frac{8 \times (125-8)^3}{12} + 936\,(66.5 - 42.08)^2$$

$$= 2.5 \times 10^6 \text{ mm}^4$$

$$y_c = 42.08 \text{ mm} \quad \text{and} \quad y_t = 82.92 \text{ mm}$$

$$(Z_{xx})_c = \frac{I_{xx}}{y_c} = \frac{2.5 \times 10^6}{42.08} = 59.41 \times 10^3 \text{ mm}^3$$

$$(Z_{xx})_t = \frac{I_{xx}}{y_t} = \frac{2.5 \times 10^6}{82.92} = 30.15 \times 10^3 \text{ mm}^3$$

(ii) Safe UDL (w) :

$$(MR)_t = (Z_{xx})_t \times \sigma_{bt}$$

$$= 30.15 \times 10^3 \times 120 \times 10^{-6} \text{ kNm} = 3.618 \text{ kNm}$$

$$\text{Maximum BM} = \frac{wL^2}{8} = \frac{w\,(3)^2}{8} = (1.125\,w) \text{ kNm}$$

where; w = UDL in kN/m

Equating maximum BM and MR,

$$(1.125)\,w = 3.618$$

∴ w = **3.216 kN/m (inclusive of self weight)**

(iii) Stress in bending compression :

$$(\sigma_{bc})_{cal} = \frac{BM}{(Z_{xx})_c} = \frac{(1.125) \, w \times 10^6}{59.41 \times 10^3} = 60.9 \text{ MPa}$$

**Example 7.16 :** A uniform beam in pure bending has trapezoidal cross-section as shown in Fig. 7.28 (a). If allowable working stress in tension and compression is 40 MPa and 60 MPa respectively, calculate the ratio of $b_1$ to $b_2$ for maximum economy. Assume the cross-section to carry sagging bending moment.

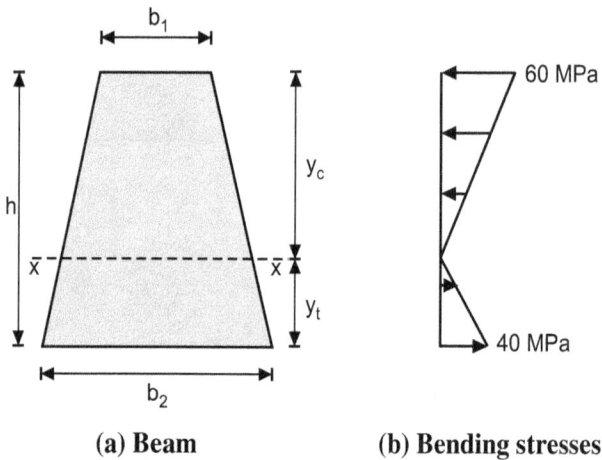

(a) Beam          (b) Bending stresses

Fig. 7.28

**Data**     : $\sigma_{bt} = 40$ MPa ; $\sigma_{bc} = 60$ MPa

**Required :** Ratio $\dfrac{b_1}{b_2}$

**Concept** : For maximum economy, stresses in tension and compression should reach to the permissible limits simultaneously.

**Solution** : (i) Geometric properties.

C.G. of cross-section from bottom $= \left[\dfrac{b_2 + 2b_1}{b_2 + b_1}\right] \dfrac{h}{3}$.

Due to sagging BM,

$$y_t = \left[\dfrac{b_2 + 2b_1}{b_2 + b_1}\right] \dfrac{h}{3} \qquad \ldots \text{(i)}$$

(ii) Relation between $y_c$ and $y_t$ :

From bending stress diagram, $\dfrac{60}{y_c} = \dfrac{40}{y_t}$

$\therefore \qquad y_t = \dfrac{2}{3} y_c \qquad \ldots \text{(ii)}$

Also; $\qquad y_t + y_c = h \qquad \ldots \text{(iii)}$

Putting equation (ii) in equation (iii),

$$\left(\frac{2}{3}\right) y_c + y_c = h$$

∴ $y_c = \mathbf{0.6\ h}$                    ∴ $y_t = \mathbf{0.4\ h}$     ... (iv)

(iii) Ratio of $b_1$ and $b_2$ :

Equating equation (i) and equation (iv),

$$\left[\frac{b_2 + 2 b_1}{b_2 + b_1}\right] \frac{h}{3} = 0.4\ h$$

$$\frac{b_2 + 2 b_1}{b_2 + b_1} = 1.2$$

∴ $b_2 + 2 b_1 = 1.2\ (b_2 + b_1)$

$0.8\ b_1 = 0.2\ b_2$

∴ $$\frac{b_1}{b_2} = \mathbf{0.25}$$

---

**Example 7.17** : A simply supported timber beam of 5 m span carries UDL of 12 kN/m and a point load of 12 kN at 2 m from left support. If the permissible bending stress in timber is 10 MPa, design suitable cross-section of beam if b = 0.4 D.

**Data** : Loading on beam as shown in Fig. 7.29 (a).

**Required** : Design of cross-section of beam.

**Concept** : Maximum bending moment shall be obtained from analysis and equate maximum BM to MR.

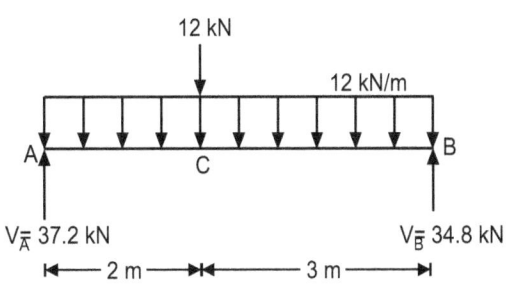

(a) FBD

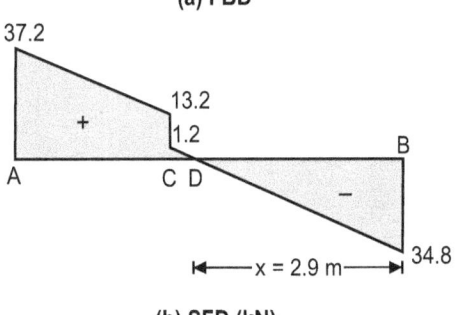

(b) SFD (kN)

Fig. 7.29

**Solution :** (i) Analysis of beam :

$\Sigma M_A = 0; V_B \times 5 - 12 \times \dfrac{5^2}{2} - 12 \times 2 = 0$

∴ $V_B = 34.8$ kN (↑)

$\Sigma F_y = 0$;    $V_A + V_B - 12 - 12 \times 5 = 0$

$\therefore$    $V_A = 37.2$ kN ($\uparrow$)

SFD is as shown in Fig. 7.22 (b).

$$x = \left[\frac{34.8}{34.8 + 1.2}\right] 3 = 2.9 \text{ m}$$

$$BM_{max} = BM_D = 34.8 \times 2.9 - 12 \times \frac{(2.9)^2}{2} = 50.46 \text{ kNm}$$

(ii) Design of cross-section :

$MR = Z_{xx} \cdot \sigma_b$

$= \frac{1}{6} bD^2 \times \sigma_b$

$= \frac{1}{6} (0.4 D) D^2 \times 10$

$= \frac{2}{3} D^3$

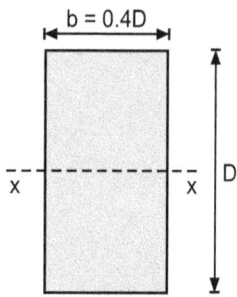

Fig. 7.30 : c/s of beam

Equating $BM_{max}$ to MR,

$$50.46 \times 10^6 = \frac{2}{3} D^3$$

$\therefore$    $D = 423$ mm; say 425 mm, $b = 0.4$, $D = 170$ mm

$\therefore$ Use    $b = 170$ mm    and    $D = 425$ mm

**Example 7.18 :** A hollow circular beam having outside diameter twice the inside diameter is subjected to a BM of 50 kN-m. If the permissible bending stress in the beam is 105 MN/m², find the diameters of the beam.

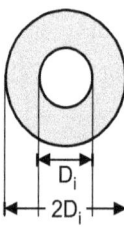

Fig. 7.31

**Data :** As shown in Fig. 7.31, M = 50 kN-m, $\sigma_b$ = 105 MN/m².

**Required :** $D_i$, $D_o$.

**Concept :** Equate maximum BM to MR.

**Solution :** Geometric properties :

$$I_{xx} = \frac{\pi}{64} \times (D_o^4 - D_i^4) = \frac{\pi}{64} \times ((2D_i)^4 - D_i^4)$$

$$= \frac{\pi}{64} \times 15 D_i^4$$

$$y_{max} = \frac{D_o}{2} = \frac{2D_i}{2} = D_i$$

$$\therefore \quad Z_{xx} = \frac{I_{xx}}{Y_{xx}} = \frac{\frac{15\pi}{64} D_i^4}{D_i} = \frac{15\pi}{64} D_i^3$$

$$\therefore \quad BM = MR = \sigma_b \times Z_{xx}$$

$$\therefore \quad 50 \times 10^6 = 105 \times \frac{15\pi}{64} D_i^3$$

$$\therefore \quad D_i = \mathbf{86.48 \ mm}$$

$$D_o = \mathbf{172.96 \ mm}$$

**Example 7.19 :** A square beam 20 mm × 20 mm in section and 2 m long is supported at the ends. The beam fails when a point load of 400 N is applied at the centre of the beam. What UDL will break a cantilever of the same material 40 mm wide, 60 mm deep and 3 m long ?

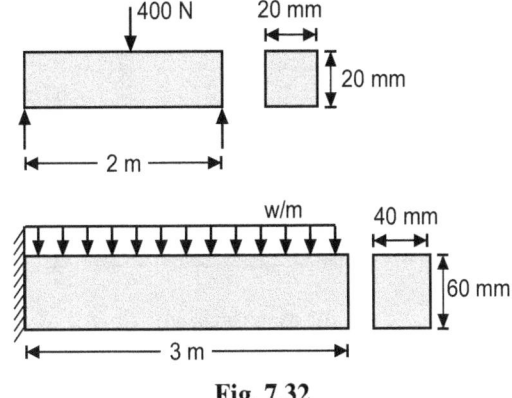

**Fig. 7.32**

**Data :** As shown in Fig. 7.32.

**Required :** w/m run.

**Concept :** (i) BM = MR

$$\therefore \quad BM = \frac{wl}{4} = \frac{400 \times 2}{4} = 200 \text{ N-m}$$

$$I_{xx} = \frac{bd^3}{12} = \frac{20 \times (20)^3}{12} \text{ mm}^4, \quad y_{max} = \frac{20}{2} = 10 \text{ mm}$$

$$Z_{xx} = \frac{I_{xx}}{y_{max}} = \frac{(20)^4 \times 10}{12} = 13333.33 \text{ mm}^3$$

$$\therefore \quad 200 \times 10^3 = \sigma_b \times 13333.33$$

$$\therefore \quad \sigma_b = 15 \text{ MPa}$$

(ii) Calculations for UDL :

$$MR = BM$$
$$MR = \sigma_b \times Z_{xx}$$
$$I_{xx} = \frac{bd^3}{12} = \frac{40 \times 60^3}{12} = 720 \times 10^3$$
$$Z_{xx} = \frac{I_{xx}}{y_{max}} = 24 \times 10^3 \text{ mm}^3$$
∴
$$BM = MR$$
$$\frac{wl^2}{2} = 15 \times 24 \times 10^3$$
$$w = \mathbf{80 \text{ N/m}}$$

**Example 7.20 :** The cross-section of the steel girder is as shown in Fig. 7.33. If the allowable bending compressive and bending tensile stress is 125 N/mm² and 165 N/mm² respectively, then determine the moment carrying capacity of the section under gravity loads.

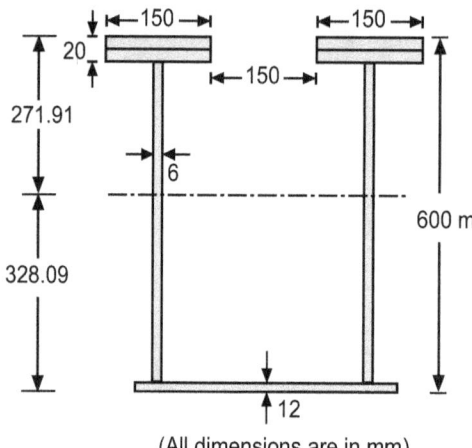

(All dimensions are in mm)

**Fig. 7.33**

**Data :** As shown in Fig. 7.33.
**Required :** MR
**Concept :** Standard formulae.
**Solution :** Geometric properties : Consider bottom most fibre as reference for locating C.G.

$$a_1 = 20 \times 150 = 3000 \text{ mm}^2, \quad y_1 = 590 \text{ mm}$$
$$a_2 = 6 \times 568 = 3408 \text{ mm}^2, \quad y_2 = 296 \text{ mm}$$
$$a_3 = 12 \times 350 = 4200 \text{ mm}^2, \quad y_3 = 6 \text{ mm}$$

∴
$$\bar{y} = \frac{2(a_1 \, y_1) + 2(a_2 \, y_2) + a_3 \, y_3}{2a_1 + 2a_2 + a_3}$$

$$\bar{y} = \frac{2(3000 \times 590) + 2(3408 \times 296) + (4200 \times 6)}{(2 \times 3000) + (2 \times 3408) + 4200}$$

$$\bar{y} = 328.09 \text{ mm}$$

$$I_{xx} = 2I_{xx_1} + 2I_{xx_2} + I_{xx_3}$$

$$= 2 \times \left(\frac{150 \times (20)^3}{12}\right) + 2(150 \times 20)(261.91)^2$$

$$+ 2\left(\frac{6 \times (568)^3}{12}\right) + 2(6 \times 568)(32.09)^2$$

$$+ \left(\frac{350 \times (12)^3}{12}\right) + (350 \times 12)(322.09)^2$$

$$= 200 \times 10^3 + 205.79 \times 10^6 + 183.25 \times 10^6$$

$$+ 7.02 \times 10^6 + 50.4 \times 10^3 + 435.72 \times 10^6$$

$$= 832.03 \times 10^6 \text{ mm}^4$$

$$Z_{xx_t} = \frac{I}{y_t} = \frac{832.03 \times 10^6}{271.91} = 3.06 \times 10^6 \text{ mm}^3$$

$$Z_{xx_b} = \frac{I}{y_b} = \frac{832.03 \times 10^6}{328.09} = 2.54 \times 10^6 \text{ mm}^3$$

∴ $MR_c = \sigma_{bc} \times Z_{xx_t}$

$= 125 \times 3.06 \times 10^6 = 382.5 \times 10^6$ N-mm

and $MR_t = \sigma_{bt} \times Z_{xx_b}$

$= 165 \times 2.54 \times 10^6 = 419.1 \times 10^6$ N-mm

∴ MR of section = **382.5 kN-m**

**Example 7.21 :** A rail road sleeper is subjected to two concentrated loads P acting as shown in Fig. 7.34. The reaction q of the ballast may be assumed to be uniformly distributed over the length of the sleeper. Calculate the maximum bending stress in the sleeper assuming P = 200 kN, L = 1676 mm, a = 500 mm, b = 300 mm and h = 250 mm.

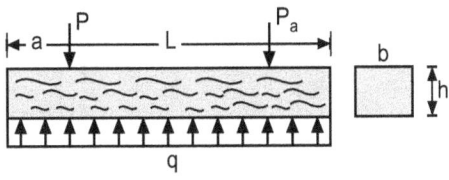

**Fig. 7.34**

**Data :** As shown in Fig. 7.34.
**Required :** Maximum bending stress and q.
**Concept :** Equilibrium and BM = MR
**Solution :** (i) Calculation for q :
$\Sigma F_y = 0$; $2P - q \times (L + 2a) = 0$

∴ $q = \dfrac{2 \times 200}{(1.676 + 0.5 \times 2)} = 149.48$ kN/m

(ii) **Bending stress** : Maximum BM will be at the centre, as beam is symmetrical with centre.

$$\therefore \quad BM = 200 \times \frac{L}{2} - \frac{149.48 \times \left(\frac{L}{2} + a\right)^2}{2}$$

$$= 200 \times \frac{1.676}{2} - \frac{149.48 \left(\frac{1.676}{2} + 0.5\right)^2}{2} = 33.79 \text{ kN-m}$$

$$MR = \sigma \times Z_{xx}$$

$$I_{xx} = \frac{bd^3}{12} = \frac{300 \times (250)^3}{12} = 3.91 \times 10^8 \text{ mm}^4$$

$$Z_{xx} = \frac{I_{xx}}{\frac{b}{2}} = 3.128 \times 10^6 \text{ mm}^3$$

Equating, $\quad BM = MR$

$$33.79 \times 10^6 = \sigma_b \times 3.128 \times 10^6$$

$$\therefore \quad \sigma_b = 10.8 \text{ MPa}$$

∴ Maximum bending stress is 10.8 MPa.

**Example 7.22** : Fig. 7.35 shows a cast iron beam section, which is subjected to sagging bending moment causing maximum tensile stress of 30 MPa. Determine a magnitude of bending moment and maximum compressive stress.

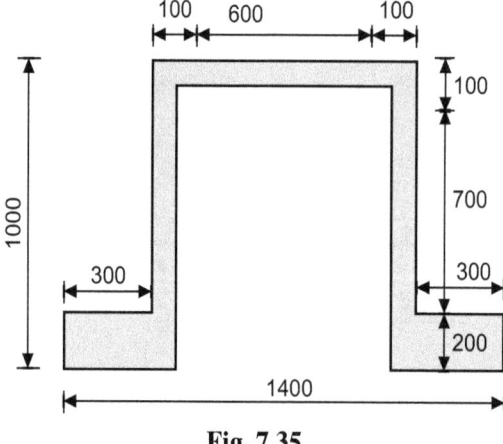

Fig. 7.35

**Solution :** (i) CG and MI

$$a_1 = 800 \times 100 = 8 \times 10^4 \text{ mm}^2, \quad y_1 = 950 \text{ mm}$$

$$a_2 = 2 \times 100 \times 700 = 14 \times 10^4 \text{ mm}^2, \quad y_2 = 550 \text{ mm}$$

$$a_3 = 2 \times 400 \times 200 = 16 \times 10^4 \text{ mm}^2, \quad y_3 = 100 \text{ mm}$$

$$\therefore \quad \bar{y} = y_t = 447.73 \text{ mm} \quad \therefore \ y_c = 555.27 \text{ mm}$$

$$I_x = \frac{800 \times (100)^3}{12} + 8 \times 10^4 \, (950 - 447.73)^2$$

$$+ \frac{200 \times (700)^3}{12} + 14 \times 10^4 \, (550 - 447.73)^2$$

$$+ \frac{800 \times (200)^3}{12} + 16 \times 10^4 \, (447.73 - 100)^2$$

$$= 47.3 \times 10^9 \text{ mm}^4$$

(ii) $\quad \dfrac{M}{I} = \dfrac{\sigma_c}{y_c} = \dfrac{\sigma_t}{y_t}$

$$\frac{M \times 10^6}{47.3 \times 10^9} = \frac{\sigma_x}{555.27} = \frac{30}{447.73}$$

∴ $\quad M = 3169.96 \text{ kN.m}$

and $\quad \sigma_c = 37.2 \text{ MPa}$

**Example 7.23 :** A beam with the cross-section shown in Fig. 7.36 is to be subjected to a constant bending moment. Due to practical limitations, it is decided to keep the beam width B and angle $\alpha$ as constant. Determine the optimum value of h in order to minimize the stresses in the outer fibres.

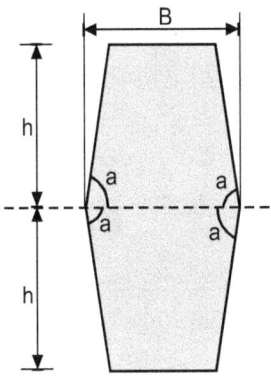

**Fig. 7.36**

**Solution :**

$$I = I_{\text{rectangle}} + 4 \, (I)_{\text{triangle @ base}}$$

$$= \frac{(B - 2h \cot (\alpha)) \, (2h)^3}{12} + 4 \left\{ \frac{h \cdot \cot (\alpha) \, h^3}{12} \right\}$$

$$= \frac{h^3}{12} \{8B - 16 h \cdot \cot (\alpha) + 4h \cdot \cot (\alpha)\} = \frac{2}{3} \, Bh^3 - h^4 \cot (\alpha)$$

$$z = \frac{I}{y_{\max}} = \frac{2}{3} \, Bh^2 - h^3 \cot (\alpha)$$

For optimum value of h (i.e. $z_{\max}$)

$$\frac{d}{dh} (z) = \frac{4}{3} \, Bh - 3h^2 \cot (\alpha) = 0$$

∴ $\quad h = \dfrac{4}{9} \, B \cdot \tan (\alpha)$

**Example 7.24 :** A beam in pure bending has a trapezoidal cross-section as shown in Fig. 7.37 with the top of the beam in compression. The allowable stresses in tension and compression are in the ratio $\sigma_t/\sigma_c = \alpha$. Determine the ratio $b_1/b_2$ of the base dimensions (in terms of $\alpha$) in order that the stresses at both the top and bottom of the beam have the maximum allowable values. What is the permissible range of values of $\alpha$ for the trapezoidal cross-section?

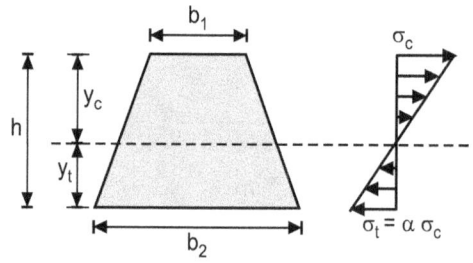

Fig. 7.37

**Solution :**         $\sigma_t/y_t = \sigma_c/y_c$

∴               $y_t/y_c = \sigma_t/\sigma_c = \alpha$         ... (i)

               $y_t = \{(b_2 + 2b_1)/(b_2 + b_1)\} h/3$         ... (ii)

Also,          $y_c + y_t = h$         ... (iii)

From (i) and (iii),     $y_c = h/(1 + \alpha)$ and $y_t = (\alpha/1 + \alpha) h$         ... (iv)

Equating $y_t$ from (ii) and (iv),

$$\alpha/(1 + \alpha) = [(b_2 + 2b_1)/(b_2 + b_1)] 1/3$$

$$3\alpha (b_2 + b_1) = (b_2 + 2b_1)(1 + \alpha)$$

$$2\alpha b_2 + \alpha b_1 = b_2 + 2b_1$$

$$b_1/b_2 = \frac{(2\alpha - 1)}{(2 - \alpha)}$$

For trapezoidal section, value of $b_1/b_2$ can vary from 0 to 1.

For $b_1/b_2 = 0$, $\alpha = \frac{1}{2}$ (Triangular section)

For $b_1/b_2 = 1$, $\alpha = 1$ (Rectangular section).

**Example 7.25 :** A wooden beam ABC of square cross-section is supported at A and B and carries a uniform load on BC as shown in Fig. 7.38. Calculate the required dimensions of the cross-section if the allowable stress in bending is 12 MPa. Include the weight of the beam assuming the specific weight of wood to be 5.5 kN/m³.

**Solution :**

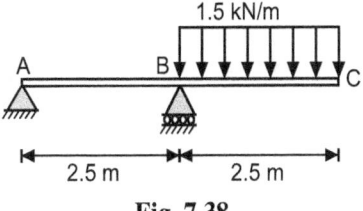

Fig. 7.38

**(i) Analysis of beam :** Line of action of self weight of beam passes through support B, hence does not affect BM.

$$\text{Max. BM at B} = \frac{-1.5 \times (2.5)^2}{2} = -4.6875 \text{ kN-m}$$

$$= 4.6875 \text{ kN-m (hogging)}$$

**(ii) Design of beam :** $M/I = \sigma/y$ ∴ $M/\sigma = I/y$

$$\therefore \quad \frac{4.6875 \times 10^6}{12} = \frac{b^3}{6}$$

$$\therefore \quad b = 132.82 \text{ mm}$$

Use 133 mm × 133 mm sq. beam.

**Example 7.26 :** The cantilever beam AB, loaded as shown in Fig. 7.39, is constructed of a channel section. Find the maximum tensile and compressive stresses due to bending if $I = 1.2 \times 10^6$ mm⁴ about the neutral axis.

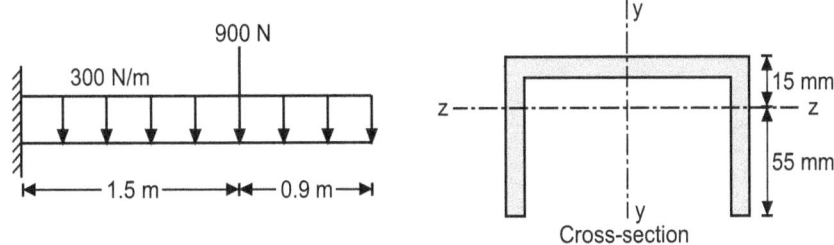

Fig. 7.39 : Given beam

**Data :** As shown in Fig. 7.39.
**Required :** Bending stresses.
**Solution :** (i) Reactions :

$\Sigma F_y = 0,$ ∴ $R_A = 300 \times 2.7 + 900$

$= 1710 \text{ N}$

$\Sigma M @ A = 0,$ ∴ $M_A = 300 \times 2.7 \times \frac{2.7}{2} + 900 \times 1.5$

$= 2443.5 \text{ N-m}$

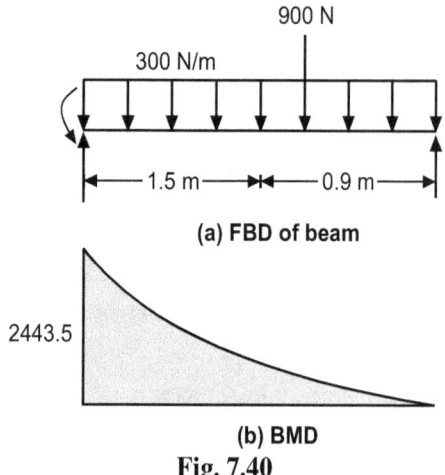

(a) FBD of beam

(b) BMD

Fig. 7.40

(ii) Bending stresses :
Maximum compressive (bottom) stresses :

$$\therefore \quad \sigma_{bc} = \frac{M}{I} \times y_b = \frac{2443.5 \times 10^3}{1.2 \times 10^6} \times 55$$
$$= 111.99 \text{ N/mm}^2$$

Maximum tensile stresses (top) :

$$\sigma_{bt} = \frac{M}{I} \times y_t = \frac{2443.5 \times 10^3}{1.2 \times 10^6} \times 15 = 30.54 \text{ N/mm}^2$$

**Example 7.27** : A wood beam 100 mm × 250 mm is supported as shown in Fig. 7.41. Determine the maximum permissible P if the allowable bending stress is 10 MPa. Consider the self weight of the beam which has a specific weight 5.5 kN/m³, a = 0.6 m and L = 2.5 m.

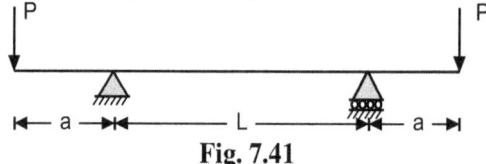

Fig. 7.41

**Data :** a = 0.6 m, L = 2.5 m, w = 5.5 kN/m³, $\sigma_{bc}$ = 10 MPa, beam 100 mm × 250 mm.
**Required :** Value of P.
**Solution :** Geometric properties :

$$A = 100 \times 250 = 25 \times 10^3 \text{ mm}^2$$
$$I = \frac{bd^3}{12} = \frac{100 \times (250)^3}{12} = 130.21 \times 10^6 \text{ mm}^4$$

S.W. = Specific weight × Area = 5.5 × 0.1 × 0.25 = 0.14 kN/m

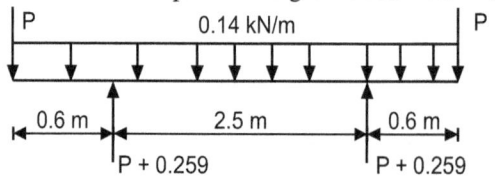

(a) Given beam

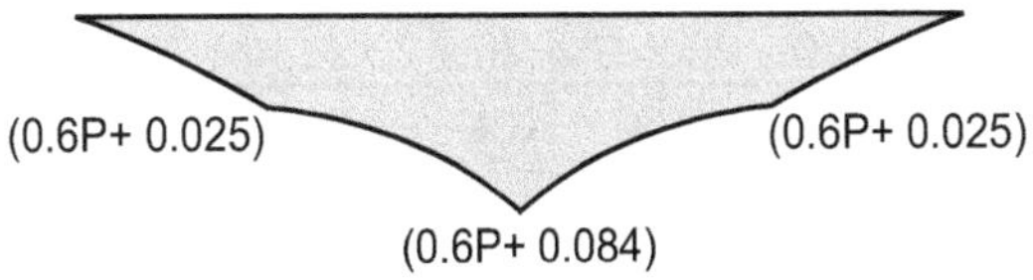

(0.6P+ 0.025)  (0.6P+ 0.025)

(0.6P+ 0.084)

**(b) BMD**

**Fig. 7.42**

$$\sigma = \frac{M}{I} \times y$$

$$10 = \frac{(0.6P + 0.084) \times 10^6}{130.21 \times 10^6} \times 125$$

$$10.42 = 0.6P + 0.084$$

∴ $P = 17.22$ kN

**Example 7.28 :** A cast iron beam 2.75 m long has one support at left end A and other support at B which is at 0.75 m from end C as shown in Fig. 7.43. The beam is of 'T' section consisting of a top flange 150 mm × 20 mm and a web of 20 mm wide and 80 mm deep. If tensile and compressive stresses are not to exceed 40 N/mm² and 70 N/mm² respectively, find the safe concentrated load W that can be applied.

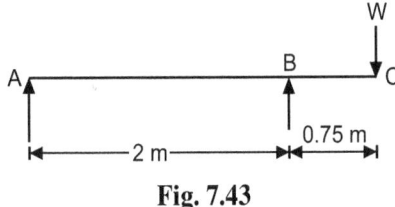

**Fig. 7.43**

**Data**       : As shown in Fig. 7.43
**Required**   : Value of W.
**Concept**    : Standard formulae.
**Solution**   :

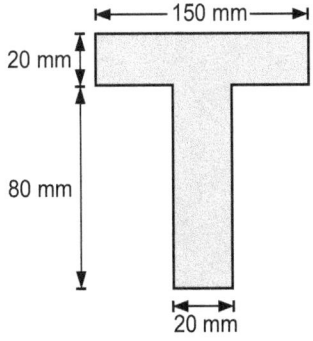

**Fig. 7.44**

$$\bar{y} = \frac{150 \times 20 \times 10 + 80 \times 20 \times (40 + 20)}{150 \times 20 + 80 \times 20}$$

$$= 27.39 \text{ mm from top}$$

$$\bar{y} = 72.61 \text{ mm from bottom}$$

$$I = \frac{150 \times 20^3}{12} + 150 \times 20 \times (27.39 - 10)^2$$

$$+ \frac{20 \times 80^3}{12} + 20 \times 80 \times (60 - 27.39)^2$$

$$= 100 \times 10^3 + 907.24 \times 10^3 + 853.33 \times 10^3 + 1.70 \times 10^6$$

$$= 3.56 \times 10^6 \text{ mm}^4$$

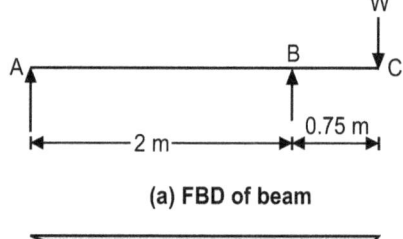

(a) FBD of beam

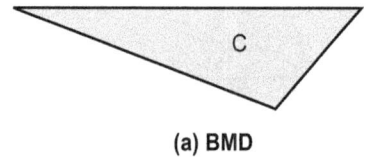

(a) BMD

**Fig. 7.45**

$$R_B \times 2 - W \times 2.75 = 0$$

∴ $\quad R_B = 1.375 \text{ W } (\uparrow)$

∴ $\quad R_A = 0.375 \text{ W } (\downarrow)$

Tension = Upward

Compression = Downward

$$\frac{M}{I} = \frac{\sigma}{y}$$

Tension side :
$$M = \frac{\sigma}{y} \times I$$

$$= \frac{40}{27.39} \times 3.56 \times 10^6$$

$$= 5.2 \text{ kN-m}$$

Compressive side :
$$M = \frac{70}{72.61} \times 3.56 \times 10^6$$

$$= 3.43 \text{ kN-m}$$

∴   Allowable bending moment = 3.43 kN-m
∴              Maximum B.M. = 0.75 W = 3.43
∴                         W = 4.57 kN
∴   Safe concentrated load = **4.57 kN**

**Example 7.29 :** A simply supported beam of 5 m span carries a uniformly distributed load of 2 kN/m over entire span. The cross-section of beam is shown in Fig. 7.46. Find out the maximum bending stress induced in the beam.

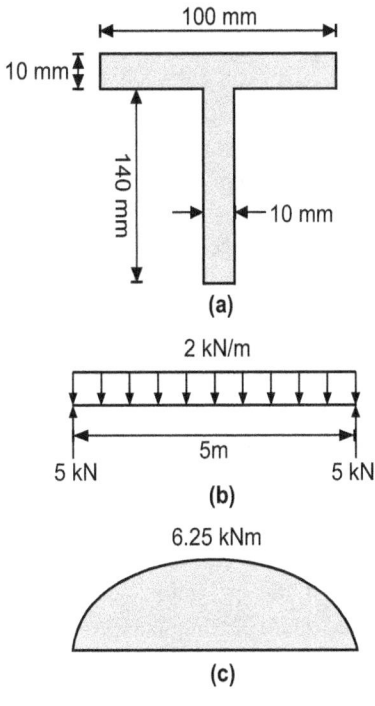

Fig. 7.46

**Data**      : UDL = 2 kN/m, span = 5 m, cross-section as shown in Fig. 7.46 (a).
**Required** : Maximum bending stress induced in the beam.
**Concept**  : Standard formula.
**Solution** :

$$\bar{y} = \frac{100 \times 10 \times 5 + 140 \times 10 \times (70 + 10)}{100 \times 10 + 140 \times 10}$$

$$= 48.75 \text{ mm}$$

$$I_{xx} = \frac{100 \times 10^3}{12} + 100 \times 10 \times (48.75 - 5)^2$$

$$+ \frac{10 \times 140^3}{12} + 140 \times 10 \times (80 - 48.75)^2$$

$$= 8333.33 + 1.91 \times 10^6 + 2.29 \times 10^6 + 1.37 \times 10^6$$

$$= 5.58 \times 10^6 \text{ mm}^4$$

$$\sigma = \frac{My}{I}$$

$$\sigma_{max} = \frac{6.25 \times 10^6 \times (150 - 48.75)}{27.12 \times 10^6}$$

$$\sigma_{max} = 23.33 \text{ N/mm}^2$$

## EXERCISE

1. A steel rod of 16 mm diameter is to be bent to a circular arc. Find the minimum radius of curvature to which it should be bent, so that stress in steel may not exceed 120 MPa. Assume E = 200 GPa. (13.33 m)

2. A rectangular beam 300 mm deep is simply supported over a span of 5 m. Find the intensity of safe UDL the beam can carry if bending stress is not to exceed 120 MPa. Assume $I = 8 \times 10^7$ mm$^4$. (20.48 kN/m)

3. A 4 m long simply supported beam is loaded as shown in Fig. 7.47. The beam is rectangular in cross-section, 100 mm wide and 200 mm deep. Determine the maximum bending stress in the beam. (210.93 MPa)

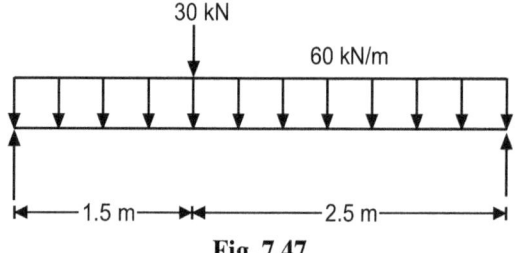

Fig. 7.47

4. An unequal angle bar 150 mm × 75 mm, thickness of metal 8 mm is used as a joist, simply supported over a span of 4 m with its longer leg placed vertically. Find the safe UDL the beam can carry if the maximum permissible bending stress is 130 MPa in tension. Also calculate maximum bending compressive stress induced.
(W = 23.91 kN/m; $\sigma_{bc; cal}$ = 71.23 MPa)

5. A rectangular section of beam 40 mm × 200 mm is simply supported and carries UDL of 8 kN/m. If the bending stress is not to exceed 125 MPa, determine the longest span over which beam can be supported. (5.77 m)

6. Determine the dimensions of timber beam rectangular in section, simply supported over 8 m span to carry a brick masonry wall 230 mm thick, 4 m high. Assume density of brick masonry as 20 kN/m³, allowable bending stress = 8 MPa and $b = \frac{d}{2}$ for the cross-section.
(b = 302.2 mm, d = 604.4 mm)

7. The floor is supported on rectangular timber beams 100 mm × 300 mm, 4 m long. If the total floor load is 10 kN/m², calculate the spacing of beams such that the bending stress in beams does not exceed 10 MPa. (0.75 m)

8. A hollow circular bar having outside diameter twice the inside diameter is subjected to bending moment of 50 kNm. If allowable bending stress is 120 MPa, find outside and inside diameters of bar. (D = 165.42 mm; d = 82.71 mm)

9. Find the width of flange 'b' for the cross-section of beam shown in Fig. 7.48 such that, bending compressive stress is three times the bending tensile stress, when subjected to sagging bending moment. (b = 200 mm)

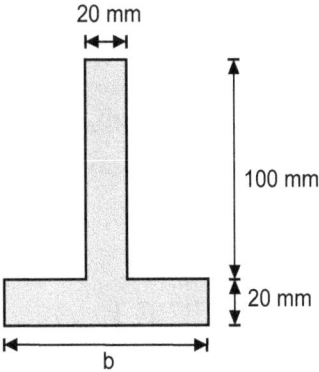

**Fig. 7.48**

10. The cross-section of a simply supported beam of 5 m span is as shown in Fig. 7.49. If permissible stresses are 100 MPa in compression and 40 MPa in tension, find the safe UDL the beam can carry. (42.26 kN/m)

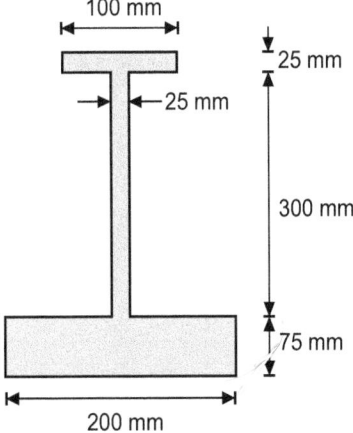

**Fig. 7.49**

11. The cross-section of cantilever bracket is as shown in Fig. 7.50. If allowable bending stresses are 90 MPa and 140 MPa in tension and compression respectively, find the maximum value of vertical point load it can support at free end. Assume span of bracket as 1.2 m. (127 kN)

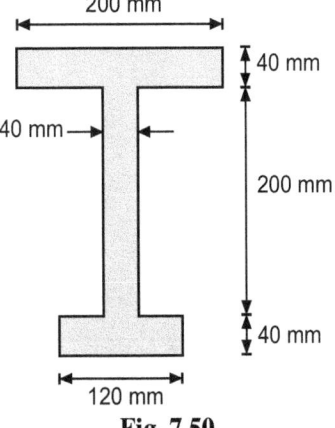

**Fig. 7.50**

12. A simply supported beam with an overhang is loaded as shown in Fig. 7.51. The cross-section of the beam is also shown in Fig. 7.51. Determine the bending stresses induced in the section at C and B.

(At C : BM = 9.18 kNm, $\sigma_{bc, cal}$ = 70.59 MPa, $\sigma_{bt, (a)}$ = 187.12 MPa.
At B : BM = – 8.64 kNm, $\sigma_{bc, cal}$ = 176.11 MPa; $\sigma_{bt, cal}$ = 66.43 MPa)

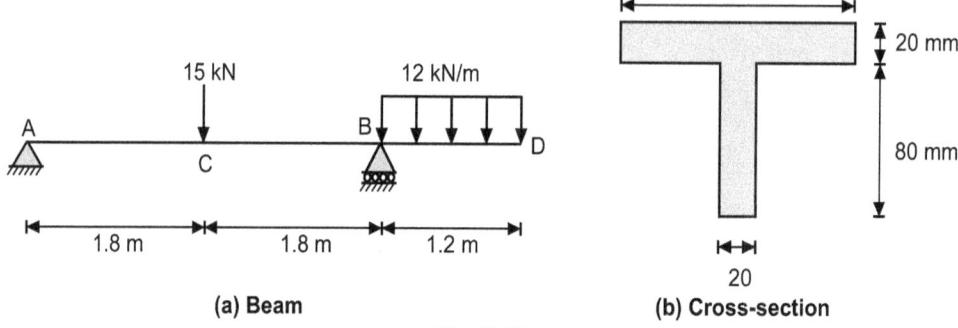

(a) Beam
(b) Cross-section

Fig. 7.51

13. A beam having cross-section in the form of a channel is as shown in Fig. 7.52. It is subjected to bending moment about x-x-axis. Calculate the thickness 't' of the channel in order that the bending stresses at the top and at the bottom of the section will be in the ratio 7 : 3. (50 mm)

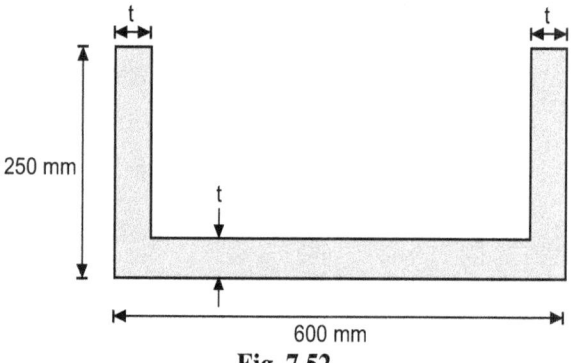

Fig. 7.52

14. A simply supported beam, 4 m span of cross-section shown in Fig. 7.53 is to carry UDL throughout the span. Calculate the intensity of UDL if the tensile and compressive stresses must not exceed 25 MPa and 45 MPa respectively. (3.07 kN/m)

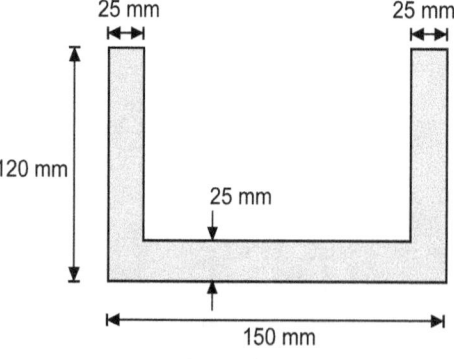

Fig. 7.53

15. Fig. 7.54 shows the cross-section of beam. When this section is subjected to bending moment, the tensile stress at the bottom is 40 MPa. Calculate : (i) the value of bending moment, (ii) stress induced at the top edge.

(BM = 40 kNm; $\sigma_{b,\,top}$ = 53.32 MPa compressive)

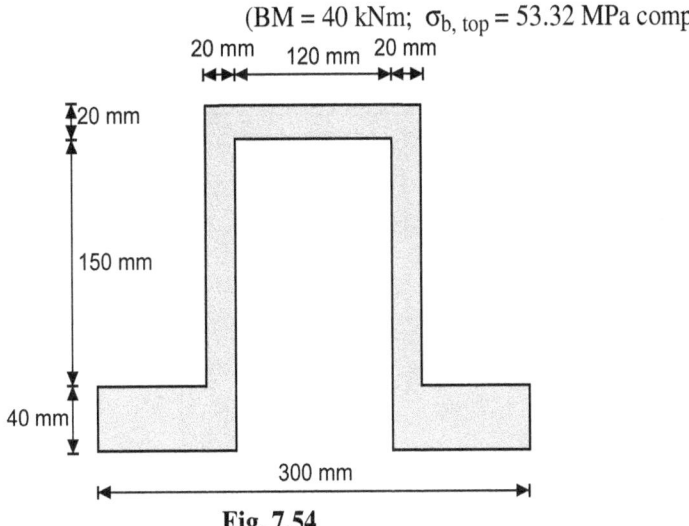

Fig. 7.54

16. A horizontal cantilever 2.5 m long is of rectangular cross-section 50 mm wide throughout its length and depth varying uniformly from 50 mm at the free end to 150 mm at the fixed end. A load of 5 kN acts at free end. Find the position of highest stressed section and the value of maximum bending stress induced. Neglect the self weight of cantilever.

(x = 1.25 m; $\sigma_{b,\,max}$ = 75 MPa)

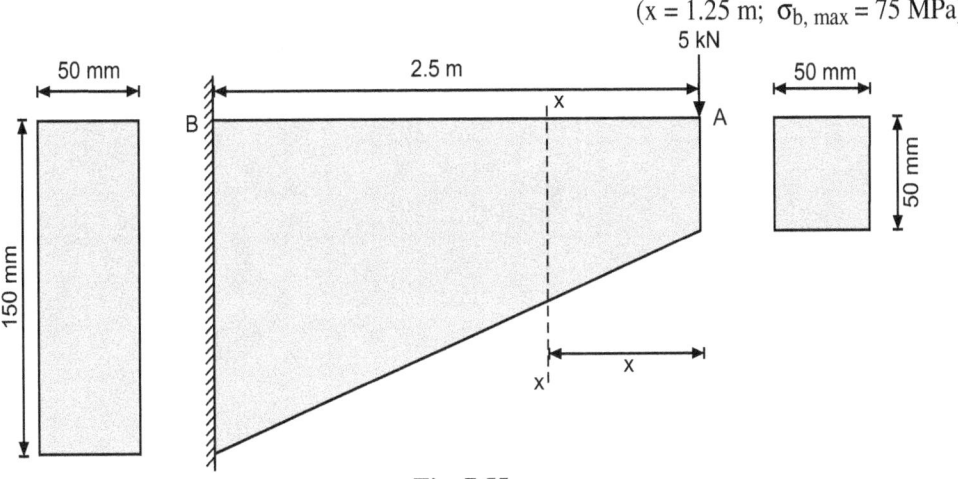

Fig. 7.55

17. Fig. 7.56 shows the cross-section of a simply supported beam. The permissible stresses in bending compression and tension are 90 MPa and 30 MPa respectively. It is desired to achieve a balanced design so that the largest possible bending stresses are reached simultaneously. Find (i) the width of the flange, (ii) the magnitude of concentrated load that can be applied to the beam at its centre if the span is 6 m.

(b = 270 mm, P = 7.776 kN)

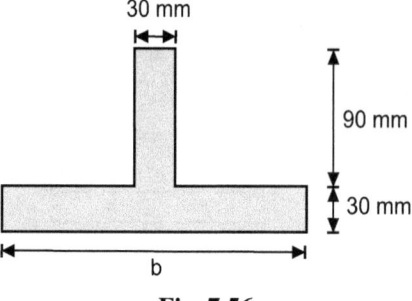

Fig. 7.56

# CHAPTER EIGHT

# DIRECT AND BENDING STRESSES

## 8.1 INTRODUCTION

In this chapter, we shall study the combination of axial and flexural loadings. Stresses due to axial forces are uniform over the cross-section while flexural stresses vary linearly within elastic limit, over the section with no stress at neutral axis and maximum at extreme fibres. However, both these stresses are normal to the cross-section, hence this combination of axial and flexural loading is simplest to understand. Resultant stresses over the cross-section can be obtained by algebraic addition of stresses due to axial force and bending moment.

## 8.2 STRESS ANALYSIS

Stresses corresponding to axial loading and flexure can be summarized as follows :

Direct stresses due to axial loading = $\sigma_d = \dfrac{P}{A}$.

Bending stresses due to bending moment = $\sigma_b = \pm \dfrac{M}{I} \cdot y$.

Fig. 8.1 (a) shows the prismatic view of a member subjected to axial load P, bending moment @ x axis $M_x$ and bending moment @ y axis $M_y$. Figs. 8.1 (b), 8.1 (c) and 8.1 (d) respectively show corresponding stresses.

It should be noted that, while evaluating bending stresses due to bending moment (Mx) @ x axis, $\sigma_{bx} = \left(\dfrac{M_y}{I}\right)_x$ indicates that, moment of inertia of cross-section @ x axis shall be taken and distance 'y' shall be measured perpendicular to 'x' axis.

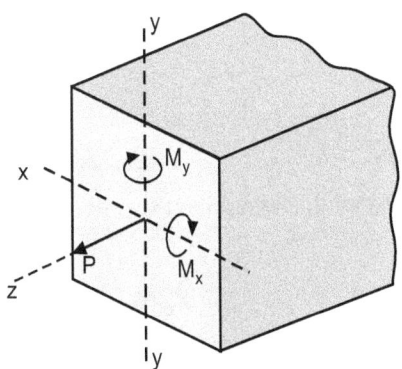

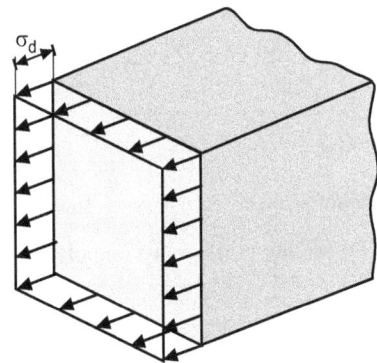

(a) Member with axial load & BM @ x and y axes        (b) Direct stresses $\sigma_d = \dfrac{P}{A}$

(8.1)

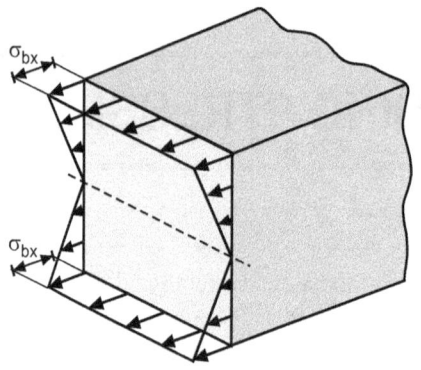 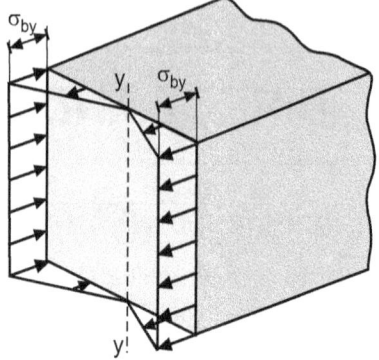

(c) Bending stresses due to BM @ x-axis $\sigma_{bx} = \left(\dfrac{M_y}{I}\right)_x$

(d) Bending stresses due to BM @ y-axis $\sigma_{by} = \left(\dfrac{M_y}{I}\right)_y$

**Fig. 8.1 : Direct and Bending Stresses**

Similarly, while evaluating $\sigma_{by} = \left(\dfrac{M_y}{I}\right)_y$ indicates that moment of inertia of cross-section @ y axis shall be taken and distance 'y' shall be measured perpendicular to 'y' axis.

## 8.3 SIGN CONVENTION

Compressive stresses are considered +ve while tensile stresses are considered –ve. Nature of the direct stresses due to axial force is same as that of applied force while the nature of bending stresses depends on nature of bending moment which may be sagging or hogging. From the above discussion, it must be clear that, nature of direct stresses is same over the entire cross-section, while nature of bending stresses depends on position of elementary area where the stress is to be evaluated with respect to axis of bending.

## 8.4 RESULTANT STRESSES

For the cross-section subjected to axial load and biaxial moment, general equation of resultant stresses can be written as under :

$$\sigma_{max} \,;\, \sigma_{min} = \sigma_d \pm \sigma_{bx} \pm \sigma_{by}$$

$$= \dfrac{P}{A} \pm \left(\dfrac{M_y}{I}\right)_x \pm \left(\dfrac{M_y}{I}\right)_y \qquad \ldots (8.1)$$

where, $\sigma_{max} \,;\, \sigma_{min}$ = Maximum and minimum resultant stresses.

Following points must be noted :

(i) From the analysis or design point of view, we are interested in maximum and minimum values of resultant stresses which can be obtained by equation (8.1) taking due care of signs.

(ii) If the cross-section is subjected to axial load and uniaxial moment, only corresponding terms from equation (8.1) need to be considered.

## 8.5 ECCENTRIC LOADING

When the applied load does not pass through centroid of cross-section, it is called as eccentric loading. Eccentricity (e) is defined as *perpendicular distance from centroid of cross-section to the line of action of force*. Eccentricity may be zero or only with respect to x axis or only with respect to y axis or with respect to both x and y axes as illustrated in Fig. 8.2.

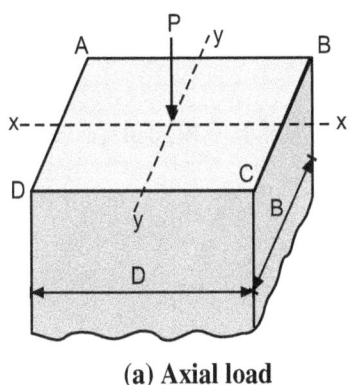

(a) Axial load

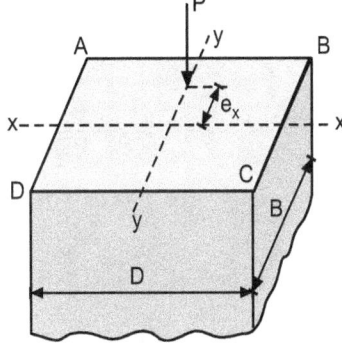

(b) Eccentric load with respect to x axis

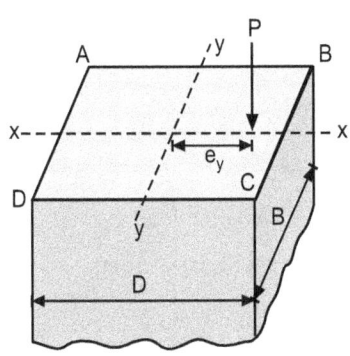

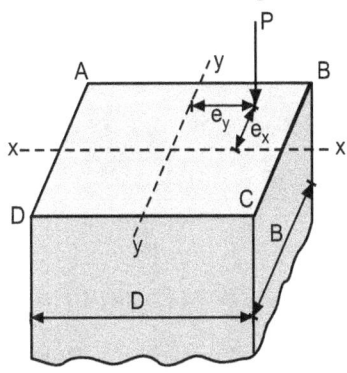

(c) Eccentric load with respect to y axis  (d) Eccentric load with respect to x and y axes

Fig. 8.2 : Eccentric loading

Fig. 8.2 (a) shows column subjected to axial load P which causes only direct stresses

$$\sigma_d = \frac{P}{A} \qquad \text{... (Compressive)}$$

Fig. 8.2 (b) shows column with load P eccentric to x axis for which stresses are,

$$\sigma_d = \frac{P}{A} \qquad \text{... (Compressive)}$$

$$\sigma_{bx} = \pm \left(\frac{M_y}{I}\right)_x = \pm \frac{P \cdot e_x}{DB^3/12}\left(\frac{B}{2}\right)$$

$$= \pm \frac{6 P \cdot e_x}{DB^2}$$

... (Compressive on face AB and tensile on face CD).

∴ Resultant stresses :

$$\sigma_{max}; \sigma_{min} = \sigma_d \pm \sigma_{bx}$$

Fig. 8.2 (c) shows column with load P eccentric to y axis for which stresses can be similarly written as,

$$\sigma_d = \frac{P}{A} \quad \text{... (Compressive)}$$

$$\sigma_{by} = \pm \frac{6P \cdot e_y}{BD^2} \quad \text{... (Compressive on face BC and tensile on face AD)}$$

Resultant stresses :

$$\sigma_{max}; \sigma_{min} = \sigma_d \pm \sigma_{by}$$

Fig. 8.2 (d) shows column load P eccentric to both x and y axes. Resultant stresses for this case can be obtained as ;

$$\sigma_{max}; \sigma_{min} = \sigma_d \pm \sigma_{bx} \pm \sigma_{by}$$

where $\sigma_d$, $\sigma_{bx}$ and $\sigma_{by}$ are as illustrated above.

## 8.6 CORE OF A SECTION

It is defined as *the partial area of cross-section within which the load may be placed so as not to produce resultant tensile stresses*. It is also called as kernel of the section.

### 8.6.1 Core of a Rectangular Section

Fig. 8.3 shows a rectangular column with load P eccentric to y axis.

Let e be the eccentricity.

$$\text{Direct stresses} = \sigma_d = \frac{P}{A} = \frac{P}{B \times D}$$

$$\text{Bending stresses} = \sigma_b = \pm \frac{M_y}{I}$$

$$= \pm \frac{P \cdot e}{BD^3/12} \left(\frac{D}{2}\right)$$

$$= \pm \frac{6 P \cdot e}{BD^2}$$

Depending on magnitude of direct and bending stresses, the possible resultant stress diagrams are shown in Figs. 8.3 (c), 8.3 (d) and 8.3 (e).

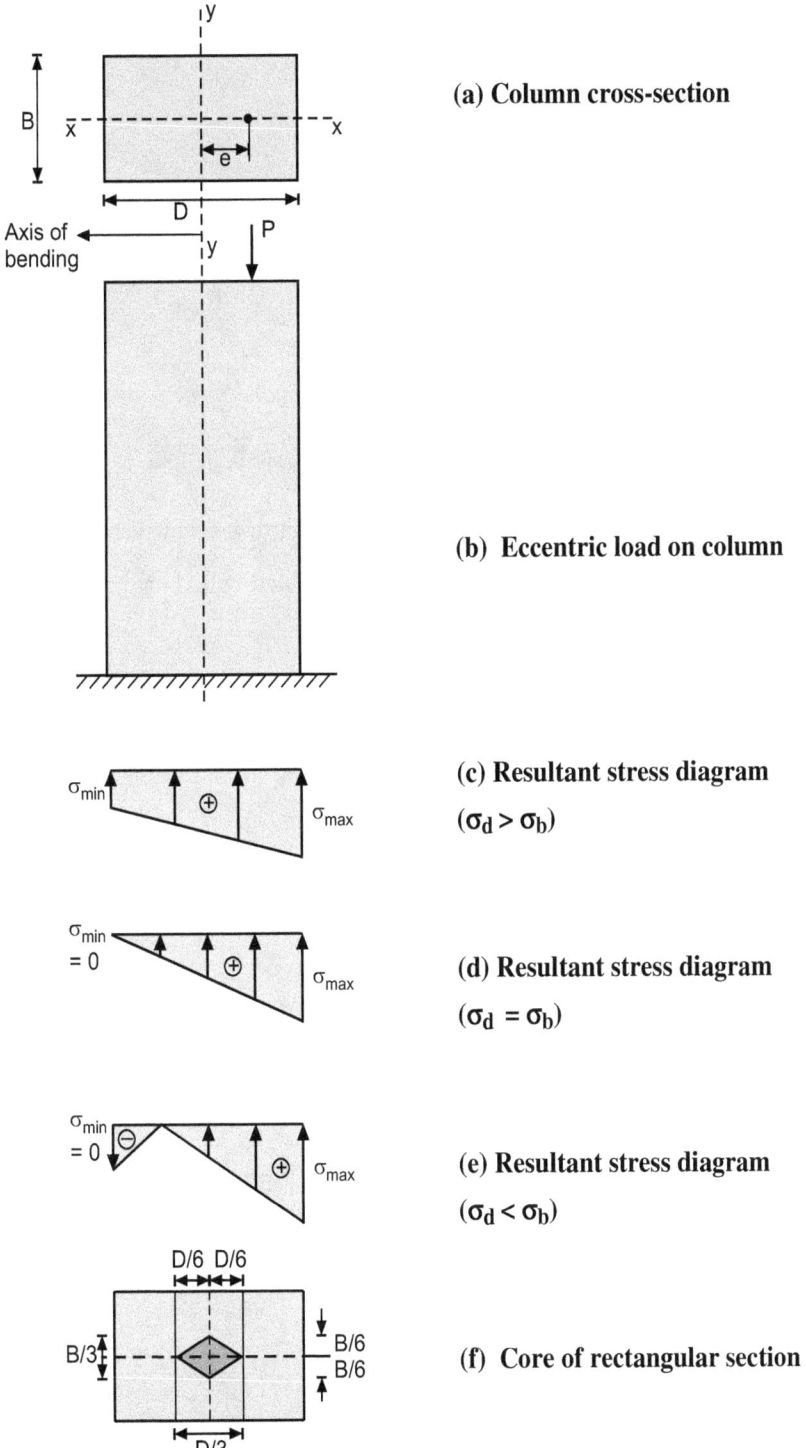

Fig. 8.3 : Resultant stresses and core of a section

Limiting condition for the whole cross-section to have resultant compressive stress i.e. no tension is (See Fig. 8.3 (d)),

$$\sigma_d = \sigma_b$$

i.e.
$$\frac{P}{BD} = \pm \frac{6 P \cdot e}{BD^2}$$

∴
$$1 = \pm \frac{6e}{D}$$

∴
$$e = \pm \frac{D}{6}$$

Thus, limiting value of eccentricity with respect to y axis is $e_{max} = \pm \frac{D}{6}$ for no tension condition. Similarly, limiting value of eccentricity with respect to x axis will be $e_{max} = \pm \frac{B}{6}$ as shown in Fig. 8.4 (a) and 8.4 (b). This is called as **middle third rule**. For rectangular section, core or kernel of the section is therefore as shown in Fig. 8.3 (f).

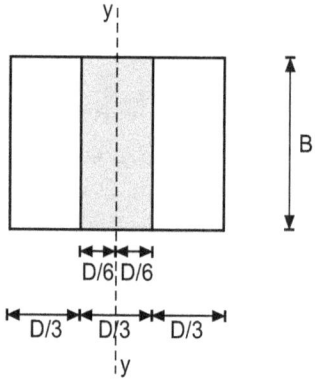

**(a) Limiting eccentricity with respect to y-axis**

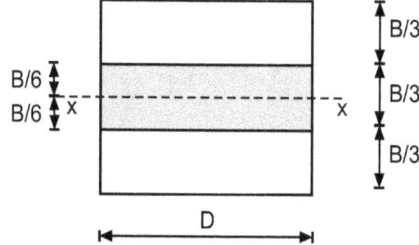

**(b) Limiting eccentricity with respect to x-axis**

**Fig. 8.4 : Middle third rule**

## 8.6.2 Core of a Solid Circular Section

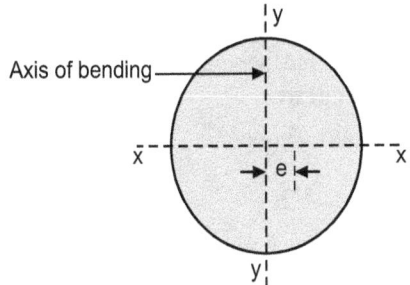

(a) Column cross-section

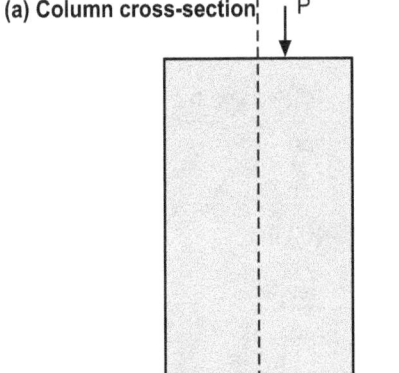

(b) Eccentric load on column

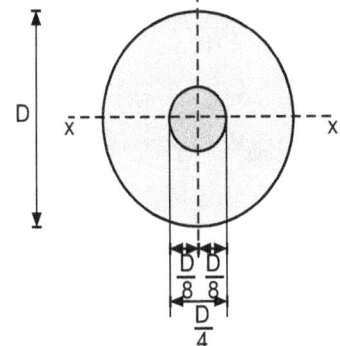

(c) Core of solid circular section

**Fig. 8.5**

Fig. 8.5 shows a solid circular column with load eccentric about y axis.

Let, e be the eccentricity.

$$\text{Direct stress} = \sigma_d = \frac{P}{A} = \frac{P}{\frac{\pi}{4} D^2}$$

$$\text{Bending stresses} = \sigma_b = \pm \frac{M_y}{I}$$

$$= \pm \frac{P \cdot e}{\frac{\pi}{64}(D)^4} \left(\frac{D}{2}\right)$$

$$= \pm \frac{32 Pe}{\pi D^3}$$

Limiting condition for the whole cross-section to have resultant compressive stresses i.e. no tension is

$$\sigma_d = \sigma_b$$

$$\therefore \quad \frac{P}{\frac{\pi}{4} D^2} = \pm \frac{32 Pe}{\pi D^3}$$

$$e = \pm \frac{D}{8}$$

∴ Core or kernel of solid circular section will be circle with radius $= \frac{D}{8}$ as shown in Fig. 8.5 (c).

---

### SOLVED EXAMPLES

**Example 8.1 :** A rectangular column 200 mm × 150 mm is carrying a compressive load of 50 kN at an eccentricity of 50 mm in a plane bisecting 150 mm side. Neglecting self weight, determine maximum and minimum stresses across the cross-section and maximum permissible eccentricity so as to develop no tension across the cross-section.

**Data** : Cross-section – 200 mm × 150 mm ; P = 50 kN ; e = 50 mm.

**Required** : Maximum and minimum stresses and $e_{max}$ for no tension.

**Concept** : Axis of bending yy; see Fig. 8.6; Direct and bending stresses ; for no tension condition ; use direct stress = bending stress.

**Solution** :

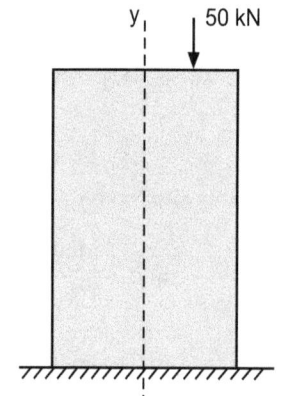

(a) Eccentric load on column

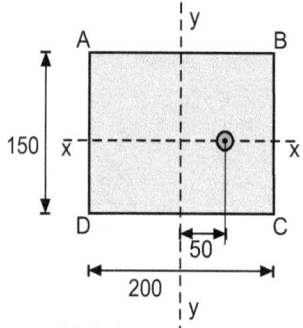

(b) Column cross-section

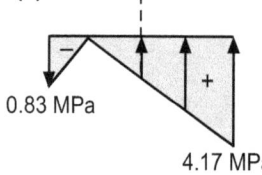

(c) Resultant stress

Fig. 8.6

(i) Geometric properties :

$$A = 200 \times 150$$
$$= 30 \times 10^3 \, mm^2$$

$$I_{yy} = \frac{150 \times (200)^3}{12}$$
$$= 100 \times 10^6 \, mm^4$$

$$y_{max} = \frac{200}{2}$$
$$= 100 \, mm$$

$$Z_{yy} = \frac{I_{yy}}{y_{max}}$$
$$= \frac{100 \times 10^6}{100}$$
$$= 1 \times 10^6 \, mm^3$$

(ii) Direct and bending stresses :

$$\text{Direct stress} = \sigma_d$$
$$= \frac{P}{A}$$
$$= \frac{50 \times 10^3}{30 \times 10^3}$$
$$= 1.67 \, MPa$$
... (Compressive)

$$\text{Bending stress} = \sigma_b = \pm\frac{P \cdot e}{Z_{yy}} = \pm\frac{50 \times 10^3 \times 50}{1 \times 10^6} = \pm 2.5 \, MPa$$

= 2.5 MPa compressive at B, C and tensile at A, D.

(iii) Resultant stresses :

$$\sigma_{max} = \sigma_d + \sigma_b = 1.67 + 2.5 = \mathbf{4.17 \, MPa} \text{ (Compressive at B and C)}$$

$$\sigma_{min} = \sigma_d - \sigma_b = 1.67 - 2.5 = -0.83 \, MPa$$

$$= \mathbf{0.83 \, MPa} \text{ (Tensile at A and D)}$$

(iv) $e_{max}$ for no tension :

Equating direct and bending stresses,

$$\sigma_d = \sigma_b$$

$$1.67 = \frac{50 \times 10^3 \times e_{max}}{1 \times 10^6}$$

∴             $e_{max}$ = **33.4 mm**

∴             $e \leq$ 33.4 mm for no tension

**Example 8.2 :** A hollow rectangular pier is 500 mm × 800 mm externally with uniform thickness of 150 mm. It carries a compressive load of 1200 kN in a vertical plane bisecting 800 mm side at an eccentricity of 100 mm.

(i)   Calculate maximum and minimum stresses over the cross-section neglecting self weight.

(ii)  If maximum compressive stress is limited to 5 MPa, find the permissible load at an eccentricity of 100 mm.

(iii) If maximum compressive stress is limited to 5 MPa, find the permissible eccentricity for 1200 kN load.

**Data**    : Cross-section :     800 × 500   Externally
                                        500 × 200   Internally

         P = 1200 kN ;      e = 100 mm

**Required** : (i)  Maximum and minimum stresses for P = 1200 kN and e = 100 mm

               (ii)  For $\sigma_{max}$ = 5 MPa, permissible load at e = 100 mm

               (iii) For $\sigma_{max}$ = 5 MPa, permissible eccentricity for P = 1200 kN.

**Concept**  : Axis of bending is yy axis ; See Fig. 8.7.

**Solution**  : (i)  Geometric properties :

$$A = 800 \times 500 - 500 \times 200 = 300 \times 10^3 \text{ mm}^2$$

$$I_{yy} = \frac{800 \times (500)^3}{12} - \frac{500 \times (200)^3}{12}$$

$$= 8 \times 10^9 \text{ mm}^4$$

$$y_{max} = \frac{500}{2} = 250 \text{ mm}$$

$$Z_{yy} = \frac{I_{yy}}{y_{max}} = \frac{8 \times 10^9}{250} = 32 \times 10^6 \text{ mm}^3$$

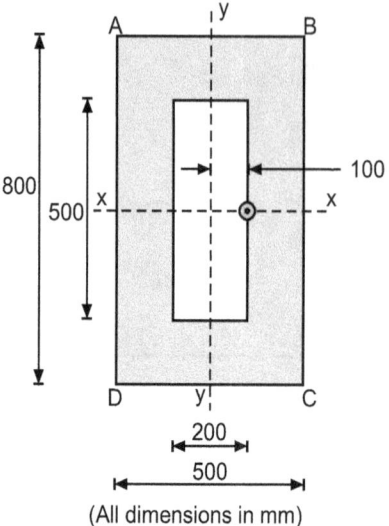

(a) c/s of pier

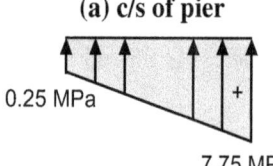

7.75 MPa

(b) Resultant stresses

Fig. 8.7

(ii) Maximum and minimum stresses for P = 1200 kN and e = 100 mm.

$$\text{Direct stress} = \sigma_d = \frac{P}{A} = \frac{1200 \times 10^3}{300 \times 10^3} = 4 \text{ MPa (Compressive)}$$

$$\text{Bending stress} = \sigma_b = \pm \frac{M}{Z_{yy}} = \pm \frac{Pe}{Z_{yy}} = \pm \frac{1200 \times 10^3 \times 100}{32 \times 10^6}$$

$$= \pm 3.75 \text{ MPa}$$

$$= 3.75 \text{ MPa (Compressive at B, C \& tensile at A, D)}$$

Resultant stresses :

$$\sigma_{max} = \sigma_d + \sigma_b = 4 + 3.75 = 7.75 \text{ MPa (Compressive at B and C)}$$

$$\sigma_{min} = \sigma_d - \sigma_b = 4 - 3.75 = 0.25 \text{ MPa (Compressive at A and D)}$$

(iii) Permissible load at e = 100 mm for $\sigma_{max}$ = 5 MPa.

Let P = load in kN

$$\sigma_{max} = 5 = \frac{P}{A} + \frac{Pe}{Z_{yy}} = \frac{P \times 10^3}{300 \times 10^3} + \frac{P \times 10^3 \times 100}{32 \times 10^6}$$

∴ P = 774.19 kN

(iv) Permissible eccentricity (e) for P = 1200 kN such that

$$\sigma_{max} = 5 \text{ MPa}$$

Let e = Eccentricity in mm

$$\sigma_{max} = 5 = \frac{P}{A} + \frac{Pe}{Z_{yy}} = \frac{1200 \times 10^3}{300 \times 10^3} + \frac{1200 \times 10^3 \times e}{32 \times 10^6}$$

∴ e = **26.67 mm**

**Example 8.3** : A hollow circular column having external diameter 300 mm and internal diameter 200 mm carries a compressive load of 100 kN at outer edge of column. Calculate maximum and minimum stresses over the cross-section.

**Data** : D = 300 mm ; d = 200 mm ; P = 100 kN ; e = 150 mm = $\left(\frac{D}{2}\right)$.

**Required** : Maximum and minimum stresses.

**Concept** : Direct and bending stresses ; axis of bending = diameter normal to the diameter on which load acts.

**Solution** :

(i) Geometric properties :

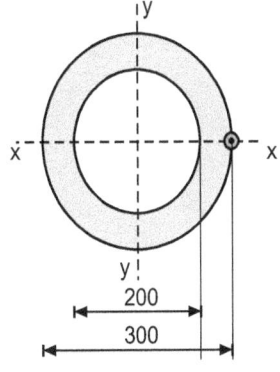

(a) Cross-section of column

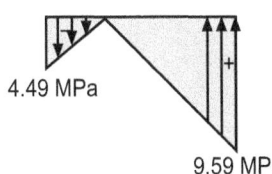

(b) Resultant stresses

Fig. 8.8

$$A = \frac{\pi}{4}(D^2 - d^2)$$

$$= \frac{\pi}{4}[(300)^2 - (200)^2]$$

$$= 39.27 \times 10^3 \text{ mm}^2$$

$$I_{yy} = \frac{\pi}{64}(D^4 - d^4)$$

$$= \frac{\pi}{64}[(300)^4 - (200)^4]$$

$$= 319.07 \times 10^6 \text{ mm}^4$$

$$y_{max} = \frac{D}{2} = \frac{300}{2} = 150 \text{ mm}$$

$$Z_{yy} = \frac{I_{yy}}{y_{max}} = \frac{319.07 \times 10^6}{150}$$

$$= 2.13 \times 10^6 \text{ mm}^3$$

(ii) Maximum and minimum stresses :

$$\text{Direct strain} = \sigma_d = \frac{P}{A} = \frac{100 \times 10^3}{39.27 \times 10^3} = 2.55 \text{ MPa (Compressive)}$$

$$\text{Bending stresses} = \sigma_b = \pm \frac{M}{Z_{yy}} = \pm \frac{Pe}{Z_{yy}} = \pm \frac{100 \times 10^3 \times 150}{2.13 \times 10^6}$$

$$= \pm 7.04 \text{ MPa}$$

Resultant stresses :

$$\sigma_{max} = \sigma_d + \sigma_b$$
$$= 2.55 + 7.04 = \mathbf{9.59 \text{ MPa (Compressive)}}$$
$$\sigma_{min} = \sigma_d - \sigma_b$$
$$= 2.55 - 7.04 = -4.49 \text{ MPa}$$
$$= \mathbf{4.49 \text{ MPa (Tensile)}}$$

**Example 8.4 :** In a tension specimen 12 mm diameter, the line of pull is parallel to the axis of specimen but is displaced from it. Determine the distance of line of pull from the axis such that maximum stress is 15% greater than the direct stress.

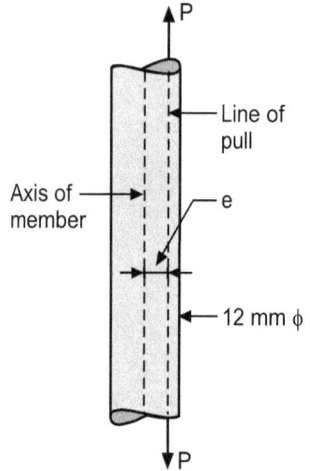

**Data :** $D = 12$ mm ; $\sigma_{max} = 1.15\ \sigma_d$

**Required :** Eccentricity (e)

**Concept :** Direct and bending stresses

**Fig. 8.9 : Eccentric pull on specimen**

**Solution :** (i) Geometric properties :

$$A = \frac{\pi}{4}(12)^2 = 113.1 \text{ mm}^2$$

$$I = \frac{\pi}{64}(12)^4 = 1017.87 \text{ mm}^4$$

$$y_{max} = \frac{D}{2} = \frac{12}{2} = 6 \text{ mm}$$

$$Z = \frac{I}{y_{max}} = \frac{1017.87}{6} = 169.65 \text{ mm}^3$$

(ii) To find eccentricity such that $\sigma_{max} = 1.15\ \sigma_d$

We have, $\sigma_{max} = 1.15\ \sigma_d$

$$\sigma_d + \sigma_b = 1.15\ \sigma_d$$
$$\sigma_b = 0.15\ \sigma_d$$

$$\therefore \quad \frac{P \cdot e}{169.65} = 0.15 \times \frac{P}{113.1}$$

$$\therefore \quad e = \mathbf{0.225 \text{ mm}}$$

**Example 8.5 :** A cantilever has a profile as shown in Fig. 8.10. It supports a load of 25 kN at free end as shown. Determine the stresses at A and B.

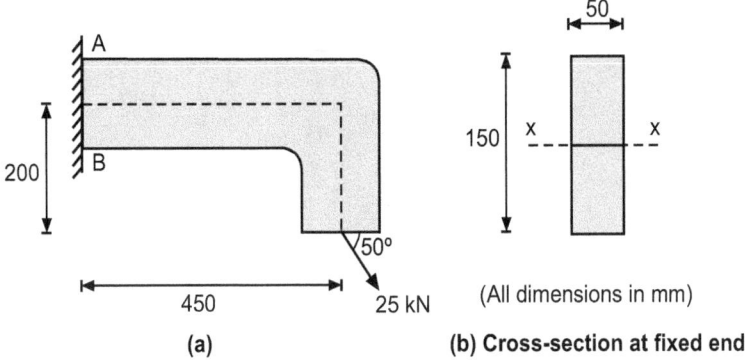

(a)  (b) Cross-section at fixed end

**Fig. 8.10 : Cantilever bracket**

**Data** : As shown in Fig. 8.10.

**Required** : Stresses at A and B (top and bottom of fixed end).

**Concept** : Analyse the cantilever bracket by laws of statics and get reactions at fixed end; then analyse the cross-section at fixed end for direct and bending stresses.

**Solution** : (i) Analysis :

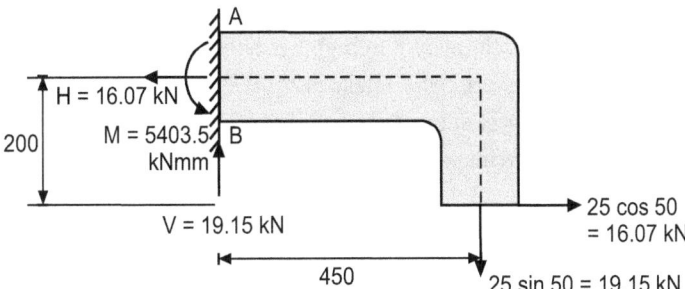

**Fig. 8.11 : F.B.D. of cantilever bracket**

Reactions for equilibrium :

$\Sigma F_x = 0$;

$\quad\quad\quad\quad H + 16.07 = 0 \quad \therefore H = 16.07$ kN ($\leftarrow$)

$\Sigma F_y = 0$; $\quad V - 19.15 = 0 \quad \therefore V_A = 19.15$ kN ($\uparrow$)

$\Sigma M = 0$; $\quad M - 19.15 \times 450 + 16.07 \times 200 = 0$

$\therefore \quad\quad\quad\quad\quad M = 5403.5$ kNmm ($\circlearrowleft$)

$\therefore$ For cross-section at fixed end,

$\quad\quad\quad\quad$ Axial force = 16.07 kN (Tensile)

$\quad\quad\quad\quad$ Shear force = 19.15 kN

$\quad\quad\quad\quad$ Bending moment = 5403.5 kNmm (Hogging)

(ii) Geometric properties :

$$A = 50 \times 150 = 7500 \text{ mm}^2$$

$$I_{xx} = \frac{50 \times (150)^3}{12} = 14.0625 \times 10^6 \text{ mm}^4$$

$$y_{max} = \frac{150}{2} = 75 \text{ mm}$$

$$Z_{xx} = \frac{I_{xx}}{y_{max}} = \frac{14.0625 \times 10^6}{75} = 187.5 \times 10^3 \text{ mm}^3$$

(iii) Direct and bending stresses :

$$\text{Direct stress} = \sigma_d = \frac{-16.07 \times 10^3}{7500} = -2.14 \text{ MPa}$$

$$\text{Bending stress} = \sigma_b = \pm \frac{M}{Z} = \pm \frac{5403.5 \times 10^3}{187.5 \times 10^3}$$

$$= \pm 28.82 \text{ MPa (Tensile at A and Compressive at B)}$$

Resultant stresses :

$$\sigma_A = -2.14 - 28.82 = -30.96 \text{ MPa} = \mathbf{30.96 \text{ MPa (Tensile)}}$$

$$\sigma_B = -2.14 + 28.82 = \mathbf{26.68 \text{ MPa (Compressive)}}$$

**Example 8.6 :** A masonry chimney 8 m high has hollow rectangular cross-section of outer dimensions 1.5 m × 1 m with uniform wall thickness of 0.25 m. Density of masonry is 25 kN/m³. The longer face of the chimney is subjected to uniform wind pressure of 1 kN/m². Determine maximum and minimum pressure intensities at the base of chimney.

**Data :** As shown in Fig. 8.12.

**Required :** Maximum and minimum pressure at base.

**Concept :** Self weight of chimney will cause direct pressure while, wind pressure will cause bending pressure. Axis of bending is yy axis.

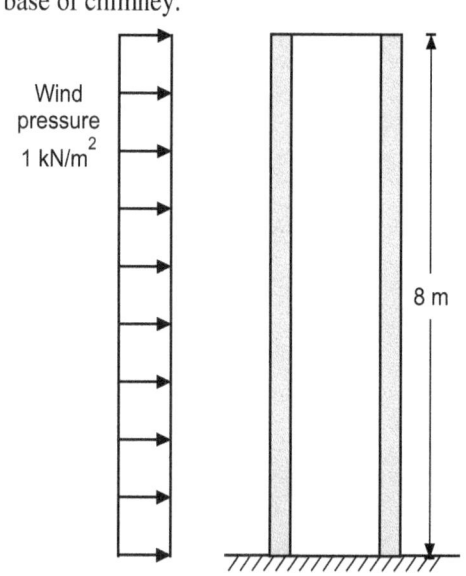

**(a) Chimney with wind load**

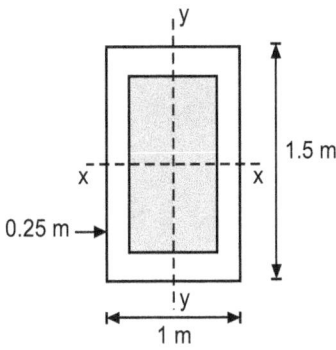

**(b) c/s of chimney**
**Fig. 8.12**

**Solution :** (i) Geometric properties :

$$A = 1.5 \times 1 - 1 \times 0.5$$
$$= 1 \text{ m}^2$$

$$I_{yy} = \frac{1.5 \times (1)^3}{12} - \frac{1 \times (0.5)^3}{12}$$
$$= 0.115 \text{ m}^4$$

$$y_{max} = \frac{1}{2} = 0.5 \text{ m}$$

$$Z_{yy} = \frac{I_{yy}}{y_{max}} = \frac{0.115}{0.5} = 0.23 \text{ m}^3$$

(ii) Direct and bending stresses :

Self weight of chimney = Volume × Density

$$P = 1 \times 8 \times 25 = 200 \text{ kN}$$

Bending moment @ yy axis due to wind pressure is

$$M = (1 \times 1.5 \times 8) \times \frac{8}{2}$$
$$= 48 \text{ kNm}$$

$$\text{Direct pressure} = \sigma_d = \frac{P}{A} = \frac{200}{1} = 200 \text{ kN/m}^2 \text{ (Compressive)}$$

$$\text{Bending pressure} = \sigma_b = \pm \frac{M}{Z_{yy}} = \pm \frac{48}{0.23} = \pm 208.69 \text{ kN/m}^2$$

Resultant stresses :

$$\sigma_{max} = \sigma_d + \sigma_b = 200 + 208.69 = \mathbf{408.69 \text{ kN/m}^2 \text{ (Compressive)}}$$

$$\sigma_{min} = \sigma_d - \sigma_b = 200 - 208.69 = -8.69 \text{ kN/m}^2$$
$$= \mathbf{8.69 \text{ kN/m}^2 \text{ (Tensile)}}$$

**Example 8.7 :** A square cross-section of column of side 400 mm carries a load of 900 kN with the maximum eccentricity about one principal axis; but there is no tension in the column. Compute the eccentricity and draw the resulting stress distribution diagram.

**Data** : For square column b = 400 mm ; eccentricity = $e_{max}$ for no tension ;
P = 900 kN.

**Required** : Maximum eccentricity for no tension and resulting stresses.

**Concept** : $e_{max} = \frac{b}{6}$ for no tension.

**Solution** : (i) Geometric properties :

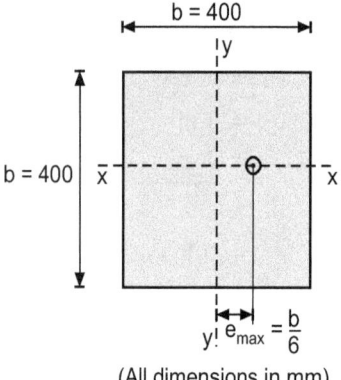

$A = (400)^2 = 160 \times 10^3 \text{ mm}^2$

$I = 400 \times \dfrac{(400)^3}{12} = 2.13 \times 10^9 \text{ mm}^4$

$y_{max} = \dfrac{400}{2} = 200 \text{ mm}$

(a) Cross-section of column

Section modulus $= Z = \dfrac{I}{y_{max}}$

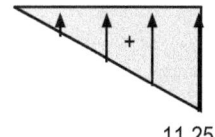

$= \dfrac{2.13 \times 10^9}{200}$

$= 10.67 \times 10^6 \text{ mm}^3$

11.25 MPa

(b) Resultant stresses

Fig. 8.13

(ii) Direct and bending stresses :

$$\text{Direct stress} = \sigma_d = \dfrac{P}{A} = \dfrac{900 \times 10^3}{160 \times 10^3} = 5.625 \text{ MPa (Compressive)}$$

$$\text{Bending stress} = \sigma_b = \pm \dfrac{M}{Z} = \pm \dfrac{P \cdot e}{Z} = \pm \dfrac{900 \times 10^3 \times 400/6}{10.67 \times 10^6} = \pm 5.625 \text{ MPa}$$

Resultant stresses :

$$\sigma_{max} = \sigma_d + \sigma_b = 5.625 + 5.625 = \mathbf{11.25 \text{ MPa (Compressive)}}$$

$$\sigma_{min} = \sigma_d - \sigma_b = 5.625 - 5.625 = 0$$

**Example 8.8** : A hollow circular steel pipe has 100 mm external diameter and 10 mm wall thickness. The supporting cable AB is pretensioned at 4 kN. Determine the resultant stresses at points 1, 2, 3 and 4 of cross-section at base as shown in Fig. 8.14. Assume unit weight of steel = 78 kN/m³.

**Data** : As shown in Fig. 8.14.

**Required** : Stresses at points 1, 2, 3 and 4 of bottom cross-section of pipe.

**Concept** : Self weight will produce only direct stresses while tension in cable will produce direct as well as bending stresses for cross-section at the base of a pipe.

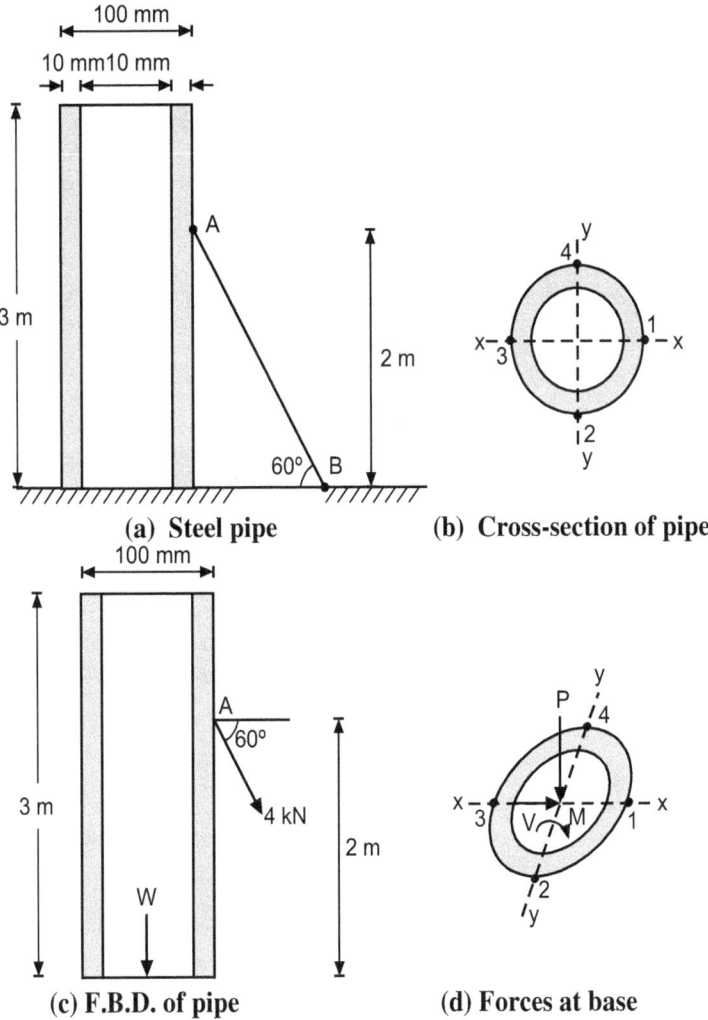

**Fig. 8.14**

**Solution :** (i) Geometric properties of cross-section at base :

$$A = \frac{\pi}{4}[(100)^2 - (80)^2] = 2827.43 \text{ mm}^2$$

$$I = \frac{\pi}{64}[(100)^4 - (80)^4] = 2.89 \times 10^6 \text{ mm}^4$$

$$y_{max} = \frac{100}{2} = 50 \text{ mm}$$

$$\text{Section modulus} = Z = \frac{I}{y_{max}} = \frac{2.89 \times 10^6}{50} = 57.8 \times 10^3 \text{ mm}^3$$

Horizontal component of 4 kN force at A
$= 4 \times \cos 60 = 2 \text{ kN } (\rightarrow)$

Vertical component of 4 kN force at A $= 4 \times \sin 60 = 3.464 \text{ kN } (\downarrow)$

Self weight of pipe $= W = \text{Volume} \times \text{Density}$
$= (2827.43 \times 10^{-6} \times 3) \times 78 = 0.66 \text{ kN } (\downarrow)$

Bending moment at base of the pipe $= M = 2 \times 2 + 3.464 \times \dfrac{0.1}{2} = 4.173$ kNm

Total axial compressive force at the base of the pipe is
$$P = 3.464 + 0.66 = 4.124 \text{ kN } (\downarrow)$$
Shear force at base of the pipe $= V = 2$ kN.

**Note :** For evaluation of minimum and maximum normal stresses, shear force is not considered.

(iii) Direct and bending stresses :

Direct stress $= \sigma_d = \dfrac{P}{A} = \dfrac{4.124 \times 10^3}{2827.43} = 1.46$ MPa (Compressive)

Bending stress $= \sigma_b = \pm \dfrac{M}{Z} = \pm \dfrac{4.173 \times 10^6}{57.8 \times 10^3} = \pm 72.2$ MPa

**Note :** Bending stress is compressive at 1; tensile at 3; while zero at 2 and 4.

∴ Resultant stresses : $\sigma_1 = 1.46 + 72.2 = $ **73.66 MPa (Compressive)**

$\sigma_2 = $ **1.46 MPa (Compressive)**

$\sigma_3 = 1.46 - 72.2 = -70.74$ MPa $= $ **70.74 MPa (Tensile)**

$\sigma_4 = $ **1.46 MPa (Compressive)**

---

**Example 8.9 :** The cross-section of plain concrete pier is as shown in Fig. 8.15 (b). It is required to support an axial load of 300 kN acting at top. Find the maximum horizontal force 'H' acting parallel to the direction of longer side so that no tension is induced in pier. Neglect self weight of pier.

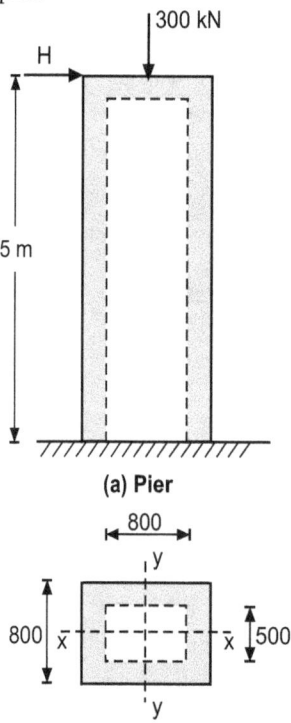

(a) Pier

(b) Cross-section of pier

**Fig. 8.15**

**Data :** As shown in Fig. 8.15.

**Required :** Magnitude of 'H' such that no tension is developed.

**Concept :** For no tension condition, direct stress is equal to bending stress. Axis of bending is yy-axis.

**Solution :** (i) Geometric properties :

$A = 1200 \times 800 - 800 \times 500$

$= 560 \times 10^3$ mm²

$I_{yy} = \dfrac{800 \times (1200)^3}{12} - \dfrac{500 \times (800)^3}{12}$

$= 9.386 \times 10^{10}$ mm⁴

$y_{max} = \dfrac{1200}{2} = 600$ mm

$Z_{yy} = \dfrac{I_{yy}}{y_{max}} = \dfrac{9.386 \times 10^{10}}{600}$

$= 156.44 \times 10^6$ mm³

**(ii) Magnitude of 'H' for no tension condition :**

Direct stress due to axial force of 300 kN = $\sigma_d = \dfrac{P}{A}$

$$= \dfrac{300 \times 10^3}{560 \times 10^3} = 0.5357 \text{ MPa}$$

Let 'H' be the magnitude of force in kN.

Bending stress due to 'H' $= \pm \dfrac{M}{Z_{yy}}$

$$= \pm \dfrac{H \times 5 \times 10^6}{156.44 \times 10^6} \text{ MPa}$$

$$= \pm \, 0.03196 \, (H) \text{ MPa}$$

Equating direct and bending stresses,

$$0.5357 = 0.03196 \, (H)$$

∴ **H = 16.76 kN**

**Example 8.10 :** A short 100 mm square steel bar with a 50 mm diameter axial hole is built in at the base and is loaded at the top as shown in Fig. 8.16. Neglecting the weight of the bar, determine the value of the force 'P' so that maximum compressive stress at built in end does not exceed 140 MPa.

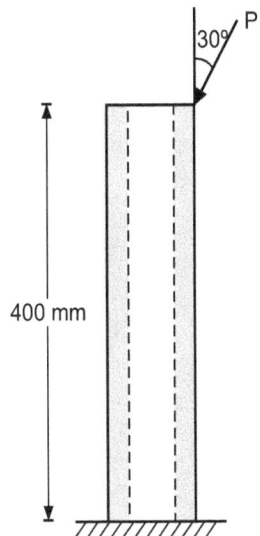

(a) Steel bar with eccentric load

(b) Cross-section of bar

(All dimensions in mm)

**Fig. 8.16**

**Data** : As shown in Fig. 8.16.

**Required** : Magnitude of 'P' so that maximum compressive stress = 140 MPa.

**Concept** : Maximum stress = Direct stress + Bending stress;

Axis of bending is yy axis.

**Solution** : (i) Geometric properties :

$$A = 100 \times 100 - \frac{\pi}{4}(50)^2 = 8036.5 \text{ mm}^2$$

$$I_{yy} = \frac{100 \times (100)^3}{12} - \frac{\pi}{64}(50)^4$$

$$= 8.026 \times 10^6 \text{ mm}^4$$

$$y_{max} = 50 \text{ mm}$$

$$Z_{yy} = \frac{I_{yy}}{y_{max}} = \frac{8.026 \times 10^6}{50} = 160.53 \times 10^3 \text{ mm}^3$$

(ii) Analysis :

Vertical component of 'P' = P cos 30 (↓) having eccentricity of 50 mm w.r.t. bottom most cross-section of bar.

Horizontal component of 'P' = P sin 30 (←) having eccentricity of 400 mm w.r.t. bottom most cross-section of bar.

**Note** : Component P cos 30 is normal while component P sin 30 is tangential to the cross-section.

Forces acting at the bottom most cross-section of bar are as shown in Fig. 8.17.

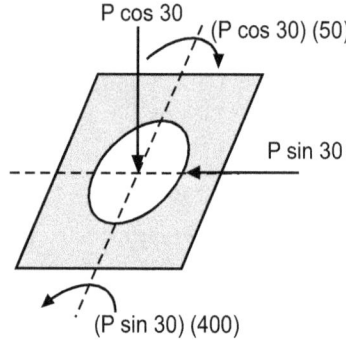

**Fig. 8.17 : Forces on bottom most cross-section**

(iii) Magnitude of 'P' so that maximum compressive stress is 140 MPa.

$$\text{Direct stress due to axial force} = \sigma_d = \frac{P \cos 30}{A}$$

$$= \frac{P \cos 30}{8036.5} = 107.76 \times 10^{-6} \text{ (P) MPa (Compressive)}$$

Net bending moment at base of bar = M

$$= P \sin 30 \times 400 - P \cos 30 \times 50$$

$$\therefore \quad M = 156.69 \, (P) \, \text{Nmm}$$

**Note :** Net moment obtained above, causes compression on left face while tension on right face.

$$\therefore \quad \text{Bending stresses} = \sigma_b = \pm \frac{M}{Z_{yy}} = \pm \frac{156.69 \, P}{160.53 \times 10^3}$$

$$= \pm 976.08 \times 10^{-6} \, (P) \, \text{MPa}$$

Maximum compressive stress $= 140 \, \text{MPa} = \sigma_d + \sigma_b$

$$\therefore \quad 140 = (107.76 + 976.08) \times 10^{-6} \, (P) \, \text{MPa}$$

$$\therefore \quad P = 129.17 \times 10^3 \, \text{N}$$

$$= \mathbf{129.17 \, kN}$$

**Example 8.11 :** A chain hook made out of 40 mm diameter steel rod is bent in a circular arc of radius 40 mm as shown in Fig. 8.18. If maximum permissible tensile stress in a material is 150 MPa, what maximum load 'W' can be applied to the hook ?

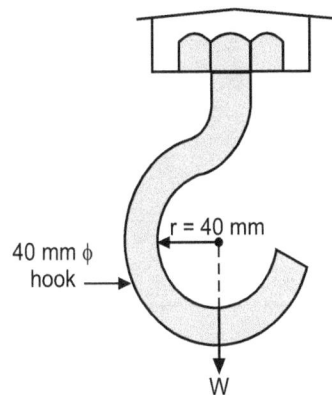

40 mm φ hook
r = 40 mm
W

**Fig. 8.18 : Chain hook**

**Data :** Maximum permissible tensile stress = 150 MPa

**Required :** Safe value of 'W'.

**Concept :** Cross-section of hook farthest from line of action of force is subjected to maximum resultant stress.

**Solution :** (i) Geometric properties of cross-section :

$$A = \frac{\pi}{4} (D)^2 = \frac{\pi}{4} (40)^2 = 1256.63 \, \text{mm}^2$$

$$I = \frac{\pi}{64} (D)^4 = \frac{\pi}{64} (40)^4 = 125.66 \times 10^3 \, \text{mm}^4$$

$$y_{max} = \frac{D}{2} = \frac{40}{2} = 20 \, \text{mm}$$

$$\text{Section modulus} = Z = \frac{I}{y_{max}} = \frac{125.66 \times 10^3}{20} = 6.28 \times 10^3 \, \text{mm}^3$$

(ii) Analysis :

Cross-section of hook on horizontal radius is subjected to maximum stresses.

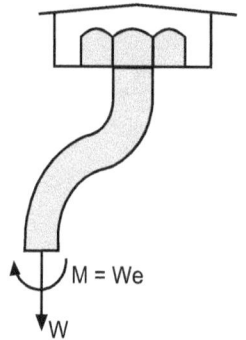

Fig. 8.19 : Forces on c/s of hook

Forces at this cross-section are as shown in Fig. 8.19.

Eccentricity 'e' of 'W' w.r.t. C.G. of cross-section on horizontal radius of hook

$$= 40 + \frac{40}{2} = 60 \text{ mm}$$

∴  Let W = Safe force in newton

(iii) Magnitude of 'W' so that maximum stress = 150 MPa.

$$\text{Direct stress} = \sigma_d = \frac{W}{A} = \frac{W}{1256.63} \text{ MPa (Tensile)}$$

$$\text{Bending stress} = \sigma_b = \pm \frac{M}{Z} = \pm \frac{We}{Z}$$

$$= \pm \frac{W \times 60}{6.28 \times 10^3} \text{ MPa}$$

$$\text{Maximum stress} = 150 = \sigma_d + \sigma_b$$

$$= \frac{W}{1256.63} + \frac{60 W}{6.28 \times 10^3}$$

∴  W = 14492.86 N

   = **14.49 kN**

**Example 8.12 :** Fig. 8.20 shows plan of a short column having dimensions b × d. External vertical compressive force 'P' is applied at a distance 'd' from yy-axis. Additional axial vertical compressive force 'Q' is acting on a column. Find the relation between magnitudes of 'P' and 'Q' such that no tension is developed for the column.

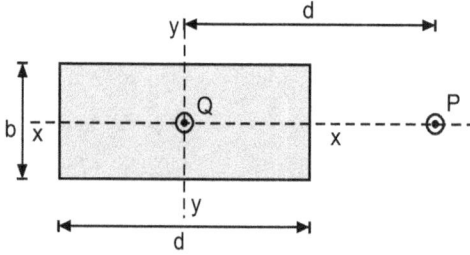

**Fig. 8.20 : Cross-section of column**

**Data**  : No tension for the column.

**Required** : Relation between 'P' and 'Q'.

**Concept** : For no tension, direct stress = bending stress.

**Solution** : (i) Geometric properties :

$$A = b \cdot d$$

$$I_{yy} = \frac{bd^3}{12}$$

$$y_{max} = \frac{d}{2}$$

$$Z_{yy} = \frac{I_{yy}}{y_{max}} = \frac{bd^3}{12} \times \frac{2}{d} = \frac{bd^2}{6}$$

(ii) Relation between 'P' and 'Q' :

$$\text{Direct stress} = \sigma_d = \frac{P+Q}{A} = \frac{P+Q}{bd}$$

$$\text{Bending stress} = \sigma_b = \pm \frac{M}{Z_{yy}} = \pm \frac{P \times d}{bd^2/6} = \pm \frac{6P}{bd}$$

Equating $\sigma_d$ and $\sigma_b$,

$$\frac{P+Q}{bd} = \frac{6P}{bd}$$

∴  $Q = 5P$

**Example 8.13 :** A horizontal wooden cantilever 3 m long is 50 mm wide and 100 mm deep. The beam is supported and loaded as shown in Fig. 8.21. Evaluate maximum normal compressive stress on the cross-section of beam and state the position of cross-section where it occurs.

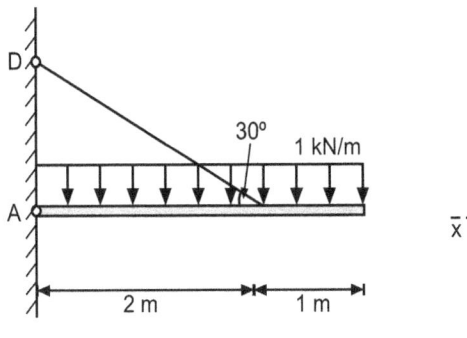
(a) Beam

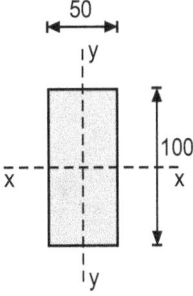
(b) Cross-section of beam

(All dimensions in mm)

Fig. 8.21

**Data** : As shown in Fig. 8.21.
**Required** : Maximum normal compressive stress.
**Concept** : Maximum normal stress will depend on axial force and bending moment.
**Solution** : (i) Geometric properties of cross-section of beam :

$$A = 50 \times 100 = 5 \times 10^3 \text{ mm}^2$$

$$I_{xx} = 50 \times \frac{(100)^3}{12} = 4.167 \times 10^6 \text{ mm}^4$$

$$y_{max} = \frac{100}{2} = 50 \text{ mm}$$

$$Z_{xx} = \frac{I_{xx}}{y_{max}} = \frac{4.167 \times 10^6}{50} = 83.33 \times 10^3 \text{ mm}^3$$

(ii) Analysis of beam :

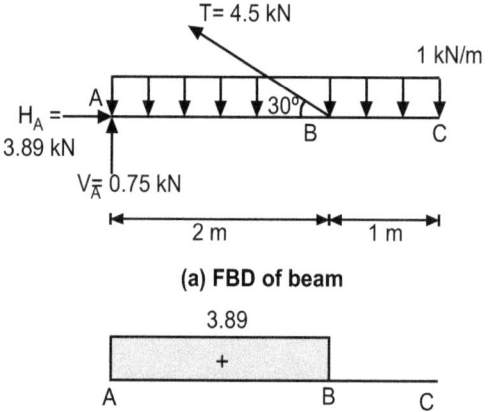

(a) FBD of beam

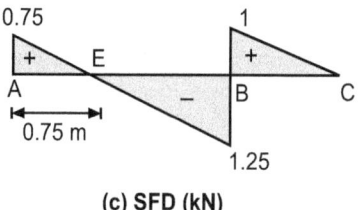

(b) Axial force diagram (kN) (+ ve sign indicates compression)

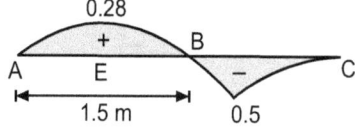

(c) SFD (kN)

(d) BMD (kNm)

Fig. 8.22

$\sum M_A = 0$ ;    $T \sin 30 \times 2 - 1 \times \frac{3^2}{2} = 0$    ∴    $T = 4.5$ kN

$\sum F_x = 0$ ;    $H_A - T \cos 30 = 0$    ∴    $H_A = 3.89$ kN (→)

$\sum F_y = 0$ ;    $V_A + T \sin 30 - 1 \times 3 = 0$    ∴    $V_A = 0.75$ kN (↑)

Axial force and shear force diagram are as shown in Fig. 8.22 (a) and 8.22 (b).

$$\text{B.M. at B} = -1 \times \frac{1^2}{2} = -0.5 \text{ kNm}$$

$$\text{B.M. at E} = 0.75 \times 0.75 - 1 \times \frac{(0.75)^2}{2} = 0.28 \text{ kNm}$$

B.M.D. is as shown in Fig. 8.22 (d).

(iii) Stress analysis :

**Note :** (i) Cross-sections of beam from A to B are subjected to direct as well as bending stresses while cross-sections in zone BC are subjected to only bending stresses.

(ii) BM at B is greater than BM at E, hence the cross-section just to the left of 'B' is subjected to maximum normal stresses.

$$\text{Direct stress} = \sigma_d = \frac{P}{A} = \frac{3.89 \times 10^3}{5 \times 10^3} = 0.78 \text{ MPa (Compressive)}$$

$$\text{Bending stress} = \sigma_b = \pm \frac{M}{Z_{yy}} = \pm \frac{0.5 \times 10^6}{83.33 \times 10^3} = \pm 6 \text{ MPa}$$

∴ Maximum normal stress = $\sigma_{max}$ = $\sigma_d + \sigma_b$

$$= 0.78 + 6$$

$$= \mathbf{6.78 \text{ MPa}}$$

**Example 8.14 :** A masonry pillar having diameter 'D' is subjected to horizontal intensity of wind pressure 'p'. If coefficient of wind resistance is 'c', prove that the maximum permissible height for pillar so that no tension is induced at the base is given by $h = \frac{\rho \pi D^2}{16 cp}$; where $\rho$ = specific weight of masonry.

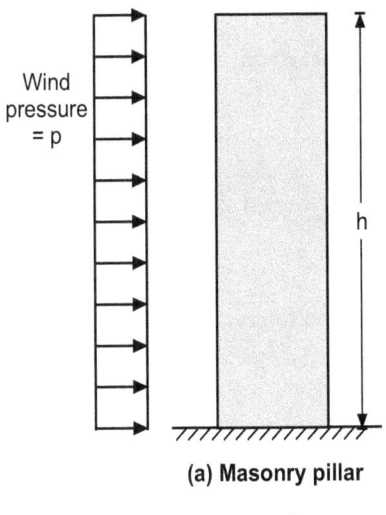

(a) Masonry pillar

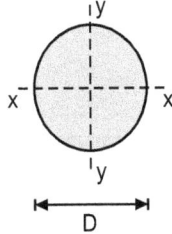

(b) Cross-section of pillar

**Fig. 8.23**

**Data** : As shown in Fig. 8.23.
**Required** : Height of pillar.
**Concept** : For no tension condition; direct stress = bending stress.
**Solution** : (i) Geometric properties :

$$A = \frac{\pi}{4} D^2$$

$$I = \frac{\pi}{64} (D)^4$$

$$y_{max} = \frac{D}{2}$$

$$Z = \frac{I}{y_{max}} = \frac{\pi}{32} D^3$$

(ii) Height of pillar for no tension :

$$\text{Self weight of pillar} = \left(\frac{\pi}{4} D^2 h\right) \rho$$

$$\text{Wind force} = (p)(D \times h)$$

$$\text{Effective wind force} = c(p D h)$$

$$\text{Bending moment due to wind force} = M = c(p D h) \frac{h}{2}$$

$$= c p D \frac{h^2}{2}$$

$$\text{Direct stress due to self weight} = \sigma_d = \frac{\pi}{4} D^2 h \rho \times \frac{4}{\pi D^2}$$

$$= h \rho$$

$$\text{Bending stress due to wind force} = \sigma_b = \pm \frac{M}{Z}$$

$$= \pm c p D \frac{h^2}{2} \times \frac{32}{\pi D^3}$$

$$= \pm \frac{16 c p h^2}{\pi D^2}$$

Equating $\sigma_d$ and $\sigma_b$,

$$h \rho = \frac{16 c p h^2}{\pi D^2}$$

$$\therefore \quad h = \frac{\rho \pi D^2}{16 c p}$$

**Example 8.15** : A cylindrical chimney of hollow circular section 2 m external diameter, 1 m internal diameter is 30 m high. If lateral wind pressure intensity varies directly as $y^{2/3}$ where, y = vertical height from ground level, calculate overturning moment at the base of chimney taking wind pressure coefficient = 0.6. Given that the lateral wind pressure at a height of 20 m is 1 kN/m², density of masonry = 24 kN/m³. Calculate normal stresses at base.

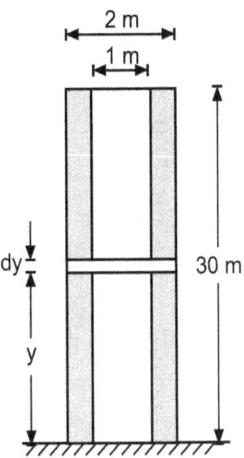

**(a) Chimney with wind pressure**

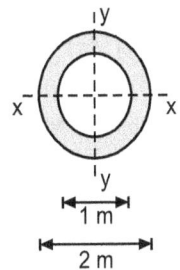

**(a) Cross-section of chimney**

**Fig. 8.24**

**Data** : As shown in Fig. 8.24, wind pressure coefficient = 0.6 ;
Density of masonry = 24 kN/m³.

**Required** : Overturning moment and normal stresses at the base of chimney.

**Concept** : Wind pressure intensity varies directly as $y^{2/3}$, hence overturning moment due to wind is to be obtained by integration.

**Solution** : (i) Geometric properties :

$$A = \frac{\pi}{4}(D^2 - d^2) = \frac{\pi}{4}(2^2 - 1^2) = 2.356 \text{ m}^2$$

$$I = \frac{\pi}{64}(D^4 - d^4) = \frac{\pi}{64}(2^4 - 1^4) = 0.736 \text{ m}^4$$

$$y_{max} = \frac{D}{2} = \frac{2}{2} = 1 \text{ m}$$

$$\text{Section modulus} = Z = \frac{I}{y_{max}} = \frac{0.736}{1} = 0.736 \text{ m}^3$$

(ii) Analysis for overturning moment :

Consider an elementary strip of thickness 'dy' at 'y' from bottom.

We have, wind pressure $p \propto y^{2/3}$

$\therefore \qquad p = k y^{2/3}$ ... (i)

Also at $y = 20$ m; $p = 1$ kN/m² put in (A)

$\therefore \qquad 1 = k \cdot (2)^{2/3} \Rightarrow k = 0.136$

Thus $\qquad p = 0.136 \, y^{2/3}$

Effective wind pressure $= P = 0.6 \times 0.136 \times y^{2/3}$

$\qquad p = 0.082 \, y^{2/3}$ ... (ii)

Wind force on elementary strip $= dF = p \times dA$

where $\qquad dA =$ Projected area of elementary strip $= D \, dy = 2 \cdot dy$

$\therefore \qquad dF = (0.082 \, y^{2/3})(2 \cdot dy)$

$\qquad = (0.164 \, y^{2/3}) \, dy$ ... (iii)

Moment at the base due to force 'dF' $= dM = dF \cdot y$

$\therefore \qquad dM = (0.164 \, y^{2/3})(dy) \cdot y$

$\qquad = (0.164 \, y^{5/3}) \, dy$ ... (iv)

$\therefore$ Total overturning moment at base $= M = \int_0^{30} dM$

$$= \int_0^{30} 0.164 \, y^{5/3} \cdot dy$$

$$= \frac{0.164}{8/3} (y^{8/3})_0^{30}$$

$M = 534.4$ kNm

Self weight of chimney $=$ Volume $\times$ Density
$= 2.356 \times 30 \times 24$
$= 1696.32$ kN

(iii) Stress analysis :

Direct stress due to self weight $= \sigma_d = \dfrac{1696.32}{2.356}$

$= 720$ kN/m² (Compressive)

Bending pressure $= \sigma_b = \pm \dfrac{M}{Z}$

$= \pm \dfrac{534.4}{0.736}$

$= \pm 726.08$ kN/m²

$\therefore$ Resultant stresses :

$\sigma_{max} = \sigma_d + \sigma_b = 720 + 726.08 =$ **1446.08 kN/m² (Compressive)**

$\sigma_{min} = \sigma_d - \sigma_b = 720 - 726.08 = -6.08$ kN/m²

$=$ **6.08 kN/m² (Tensile)**

**Example 8.16 :** A tapering chimney of hollow circular cross-section is 40 m high. External diameter is 3.5 m and 2 m at base and top respectively. It is subjected to uniform wind pressure of 0.8 kN/m² of projected area. Calculate the overturning moment at base. If total weight of chimney is 5000 kN and internal diameter at base is 1.5 m, calculate the normal stress intensities at base.

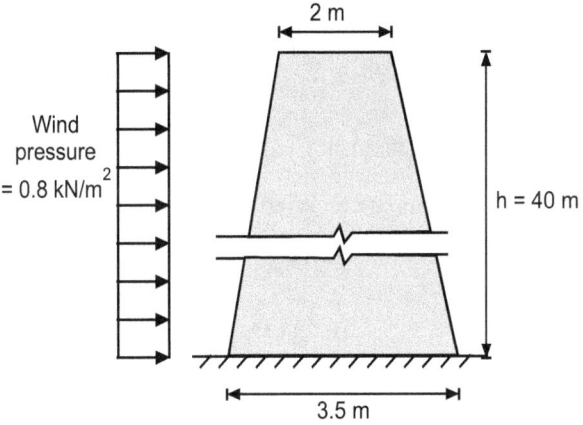

(a) Chimney with wind pressure

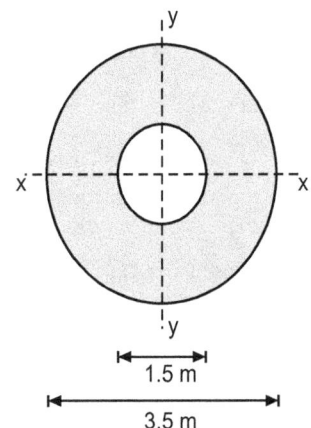

1.5 m

3.5 m

(b) Cross-section of chimney at base

Fig. 8.25

**Data** : As shown in Fig. 8.25.
**Required** : Overturning moment ; pressure at the base.
**Concept** : Uniform wind pressure acting on trapezoidal area of chimney causes overturning moment.
**Solution** : (i) Geometric properties :

At base, $\quad A = \dfrac{\pi}{4}(D^2 - d^2)$

$\qquad\qquad\quad = \dfrac{\pi}{4}[(3.5)^2 - (1.5)^2]$

$\qquad\qquad\quad = 7.86\ m^2$

$$I = \frac{\pi}{64}(D^4 - d^4) = \frac{\pi}{64}[(3.5)^4 - (1.5)^4]$$

$$= 7.12 \text{ m}^4$$

$$y_{max} = \frac{3.5}{2} = 1.75 \text{ m}$$

$$Z = \frac{I}{y_{max}} = \frac{7.12}{1.75} = 4.07 \text{ m}^3$$

(ii) Analysis for overturning moment:

$$\text{Wind force} = \text{Wind pressure} \times \text{Projected area}$$

$$= 0.8 \times \left(\frac{3.5+2}{2} \times 40\right)$$

$$= 88 \text{ kN}$$

$$\text{Point of application of wind force} = \text{CG of projected area.}$$

$$= \left(\frac{3.5 + 2\times 2}{3.5 + 2}\right) \times \frac{40}{3}$$

$$= 18.18 \text{ m from bottom}$$

$$\therefore \quad \text{Overturning moment} = M = 88 \times 18.18$$

$$= 1600 \text{ kNm}$$

(iii) Stress analysis:

$$\text{Direct stress due to self weight} = \sigma_d$$

$$= \frac{5000}{7.86} = 636.13 \text{ kN/m}^2 \text{ (Compressive)}$$

$$\text{Bending stress} = \sigma_b = \pm\frac{M}{Z} = \pm\frac{1600}{4.07}$$

$$= \pm 393.12 \text{ kN/m}^2$$

Resultant stresses:

$$\sigma_{max} = \sigma_d + \sigma_b = 636.13 + 393.12 = \mathbf{1029.25 \text{ kN/m}^2} \text{ (Compressive)}$$

$$\sigma_{min} = \sigma_d - \sigma_b = 636.13 - 393.12 = \mathbf{243.01 \text{ kN/m}^2} \text{ (Compressive)}$$

**Example 8.17 :** A wooden mast 15 m high tapers linearly from 250 mm diameter at base to 100 mm at top. At what point will the mast break under a horizontal load applied as shown in Fig. 8.26. Take maximum permissible stress in bending in wood as 35 MPa. Also calculate the magnitude of load 'P' which causes failure. Neglect the effect of self weight and shear.

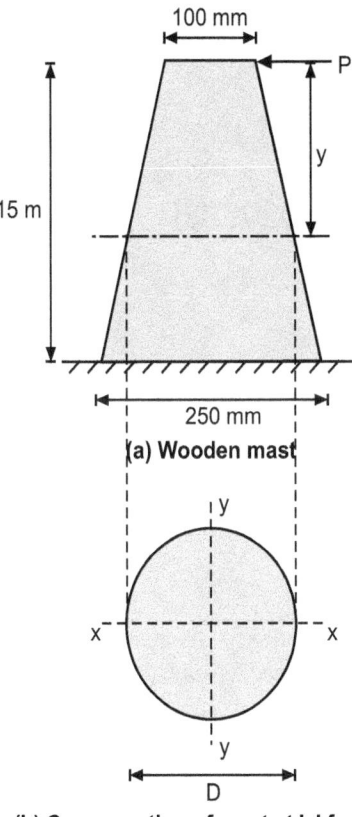

(a) Wooden mast

(b) Cross-section of mast at 'y' from top

Fig. 8.26

**Data :** Permissible stress in bending = 35 MPa.

**Required :** Magnitude of 'P' at failure and position of cross-section where failure occurs.

**Concept :** Bending moment due to 'P' and cross-sectional dimensions, both are varying as a function of position of cross-section.

**Solution :** (i) Geometric properties of cross-section at 'y' from top :

Consider a cross-section at 'y' from top.

Let D = Diameter of section at 'y' from top.

$$\therefore \quad I = \frac{\pi}{64}(D)^4 \quad (\because \text{yy axis is the axis of bending})$$

$$y_{max} = \frac{D}{2}$$

$$\text{Section modulus} = Z = \frac{I}{y_{max}} = \frac{\pi}{32}D^3 \quad \ldots \text{(i)}$$

Also, from geometry, $\quad \dfrac{250-100}{15} = \dfrac{D-100}{y}$

$$\therefore \quad D = 100 + 10y \quad \ldots \text{(ii)}$$

Put equation (ii) in equation (i)

$$\therefore \quad Z = \frac{\pi}{32}(100+10y)^3$$

where y is in metres and Z is in mm³.

(ii) Stress analysis :

$$M = \text{BM at 'y' from top} = Py \text{ kNm} \quad (\because \text{Assuming force 'P' in kN})$$

$$\therefore \text{ Bending stress at 'y' from top, } \sigma_b = \pm\frac{M}{Z}$$

$$\sigma_b = \pm\frac{32 \, P\cdot y \times 10^6}{\pi(100+10y)^3} \text{ MPa} \quad \ldots \text{(iii)}$$

For bending stress $\sigma_b$ to be maximum,

$$\frac{d}{dy}(\sigma_b) = 0$$

∴ $\dfrac{d}{dy}\left[\dfrac{32\,Py \times 10^6}{\pi\,(100+10y)^3}\right] = \dfrac{32\,P \times 10^6}{\pi}\left[\dfrac{d}{dy}\left(\dfrac{y}{(100+10y)^3}\right)\right] = 0$

∴ $\dfrac{32\,P \times 10^6}{\pi}\left[\dfrac{(100+10y)^3(1) - y(3)(100+10y)^2(10)}{(100+10y)^6}\right] = 0$

∴ $(100+10y)^3 - 30y\,(100+10y)^2 = 0$

∴ $100 + 10y - 30y = 0$

∴ $y = 5\,m$

Thus at 5 m from top, bending stress will be maximum.
Substituting y = 5 m in equation (C),

$$\text{Maximum bending stress} = \pm \frac{32\,P \times 5 \times 10^6}{\pi\,(100+10\times 5)^3} = \pm\,15.09\,(P)\ \text{MPa}$$

But maximum allowable bending stress = 35 MPa (Given)
Hence     15.09 (P) = 35

∴     **P = 2.32 kN**

**Example 8.18 :** A masonry dam of trapezoidal cross-section is 10 m high as shown in Fig. 8.27 (a). Find maximum and minimum normal stresses at base. Assume density of masonry 22 kN/m³ and that of water = 9.81 kN/m³.

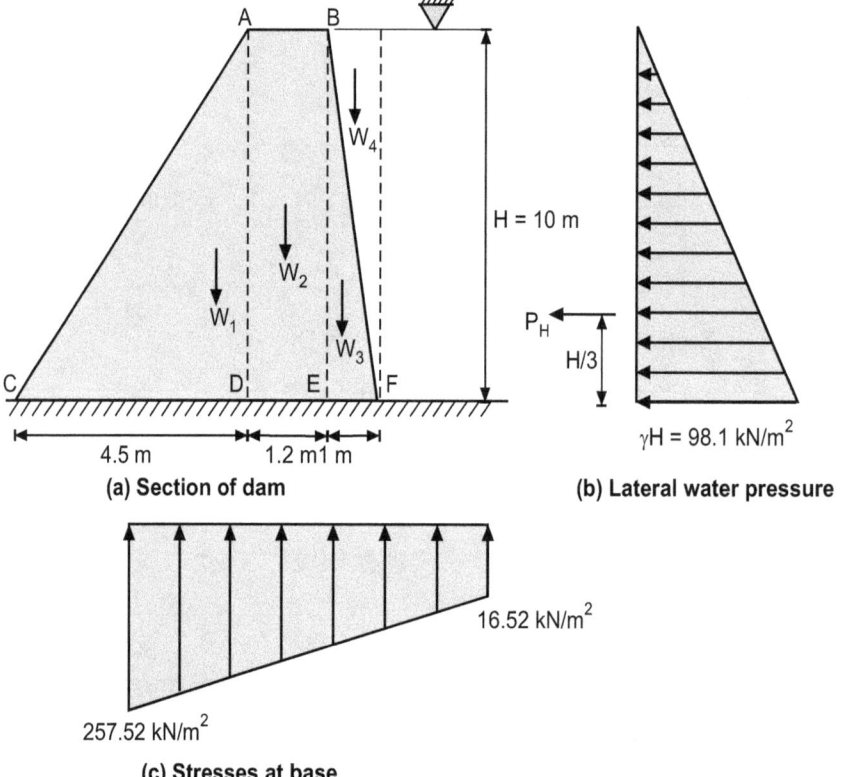

(a) Section of dam

(b) Lateral water pressure

(c) Stresses at base

Fig. 8.27

**Data** : As shown in Fig. 8.27 (a) ; Density of masonry and water are 22 kN/m³ and 8.81 kN/m³.

**Required** : Stresses at base.

**Concept** : Considering 1 m run of dam ; the cross-section at bottom is analysed for direct and bending stresses.

**Solution** : (i) Geometric properties at base for 1 m run :

$$A = B \times 1$$

$$I_{yy} = \frac{B^3}{12}$$

$$y_{max} = \frac{B}{2}$$

$$Z_{yy} = \frac{I_{yy}}{y_{max}} = \frac{B^2}{6}$$

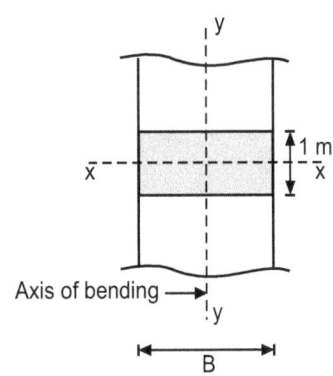

Fig. 8.28 : Base plan

(ii) Force analysis :

| Sr. No. | Force due to | Magnitude of force (kN) | Lever arm w.r.t. 'C' (m) | Moment @ 'C' (kNm) |
|---|---|---|---|---|
| 1. | Self weight of dam | | | |
| | $W_1 = \frac{1}{2} \times 4.5 \times 10 \times 1 \times 22$ | 495 (↓) | $\frac{2}{3} \times 4.5 = 3$ | 1485 (↻) |
| | $W_2 = 1.2 \times 10 \times 1 \times 22$ | 264 (↓) | $4.5 + \frac{1.2}{2} = 5.1$ | 1346.4 (↻) |
| | $W_3 = \frac{1}{2} \times 1 \times 10 \times 1 \times 22$ | 110 (↓) | $4.5 + 1.2 + \frac{1}{3} \times 1 = 6.034$ | 663.74 (↻) |
| 2. | Self weight of water | | | |
| | $W_4 = \frac{1}{2} \times 1 \times 10 \times 1 \times 9.81$ | 49.05 (↓) | $4.5 + 1.2 + \frac{2}{3} \times 1 = 6.37$ | 312.45 (↻) |
| 3. | Lateral water pressure | | | |
| | $P_H = \frac{1}{2} \times 98.1 \times 10 \times 1$ | 490.5 (←) | $\frac{10}{3} = 3.33$ | 1633.36 (↻) |
| | | $\Sigma W = 918.05$ | | $\Sigma M = 2174.22$ (↻) |

Let the resultant of horizontal and vertical forces strike the base slab at '$\bar{x}$' from 'C'.

$$\therefore \quad \bar{x} = \frac{\Sigma M}{\Sigma W} = \frac{2174.22}{918.05} = 2.368 \text{ m}$$

$$\therefore \quad \text{Eccentricity} = e = \frac{B}{2} - \bar{x} = \frac{6.7}{2} - 2.368 = 0.982 \text{ m}$$

$0.982 < \frac{6.7}{6}$ i.e. $e < \frac{B}{6}$, hence no tension is developed.

(iii) **Stress analysis :**

$$\text{Direct stress} = \sigma_d = \frac{\Sigma W}{A} = \frac{\Sigma W}{B \times 1} \quad \text{(Compressive)}$$

$$\text{Bending stress} = \sigma_b = \pm \frac{M}{Z_{yy}} = \pm \frac{\Sigma We}{Z_{yy}} = \pm \frac{6 \Sigma We}{B^2}$$

Resultant stresses :

$$\sigma_{max} \,;\, \sigma_{min} = \sigma_d \pm \sigma_b$$

$$= \frac{\Sigma W}{B} \left(1 \pm \frac{6e}{B}\right)$$

$$= \frac{918.05}{6.7} \left(1 \pm \frac{6 \times 0.982}{6.7}\right)$$

$$\therefore \quad \sigma_{max} = \mathbf{257.52 \text{ kN/m}^2}$$

$$\sigma_{min} = \mathbf{16.52 \text{ kN/m}^2}$$

**Note :** Stability of dam against overturning and sliding can be checked as under.

(a) Stability against overturning :

Overturning moment = $M_o$ = Moment due to lateral water pressure
 = 1633.36 kNm

Stabilising moment = $M_s$ = Moment due to vertical forces
 = 1485 + 1346.4 + 663.74 + 312.45
 = 3807.59 kNm

$$\therefore \quad \text{Factor of safety against overturning} = \frac{M_s}{M_o}$$

$$= \frac{3807.59}{1633.36} = 2.33$$

(b) Stability against sliding :

Force responsible for sliding = Lateral force due to water pressure
 = 490.5 kN

Resistance to sliding = Frictional force = $\mu \Sigma W$
where $\mu$ = coefficient of friction = 0.6 (say)

$$\therefore \quad \text{Resistance} = 0.6 \times 918.05 = 550.83 \text{ kN}$$

$$\therefore \quad \text{Factor of safety against sliding} = \frac{550.83}{490.5} = \mathbf{1.123}$$

**Example 8.19 :** A masonry retaining wall is supporting soil as shown in Fig. 8.29 (a). Density of masonry = 22 kN/m³ and that of soil = 16 kN/m³. Find maximum and minimum stresses at base of wall.

Assume angle of repose $\phi = 30°$.

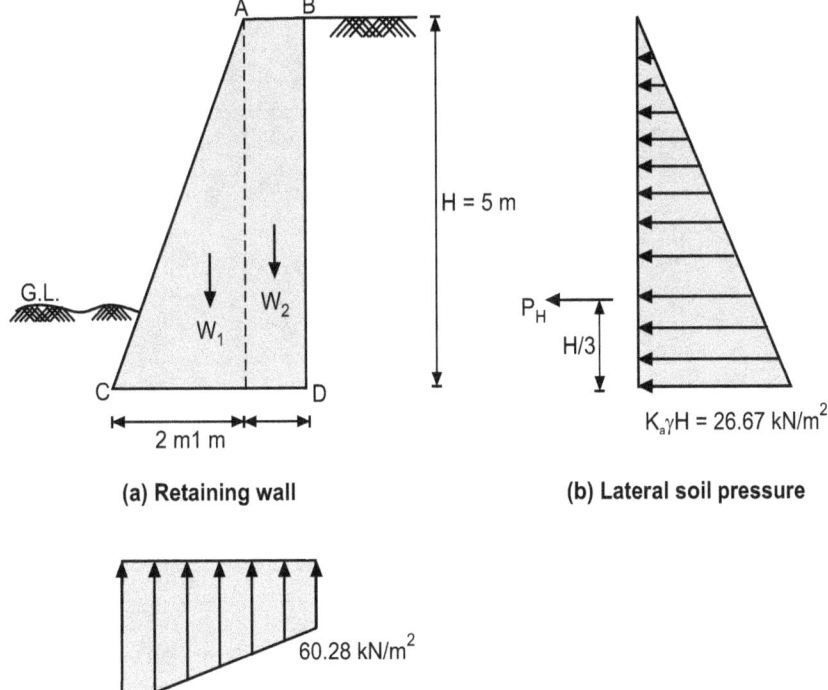

(a) Retaining wall

(b) Lateral soil pressure

(c) Stresses at base

Fig. 8.29

**Data** : As shown in Fig. 8.29, density of masonry and soil as 22 kN/m³ and 16 kN/m³.

**Required** : Stresses at base.

**Concept** : Considering 1 m run of retaining wall; the cross-section at bottom is analysed for direct and bending stresses.

**Solution** : (i) Geometric properties at base for 1 m run :

$$A = B \times 1$$

$$I_{yy} = \frac{B^2}{12}$$

$$y_{max} = \frac{B}{2}$$

$$Z_{yy} = \frac{I_{yy}}{y_{max}} = \frac{B^2}{6}$$

(ii) Force analysis :

$$\text{Coefficient of active earth pressure} = K_a = \frac{1 - \sin \phi}{1 + \sin \phi}$$

$$= \frac{1 - \sin 30}{1 + \sin 30} = \frac{1}{3}$$

$$K_a \cdot \gamma \cdot H = \frac{1}{3} \times 16 \times 5 = 26.67 \text{ kN/m}^2$$

| Sr. No. | Force due to | Magnitude of force (kN) | Lever arm w.r.t. 'C' (m) | Moment @ 'C' (kNm) |
|---|---|---|---|---|
| 1. | Self weight of wall $W_1 = \frac{1}{2} \times 2 \times 5 \times 1 \times 22$ | 110 (↓) | $\frac{2}{3} \times 2 = \frac{4}{3}$ | 146.67 (↻) |
|  | $W_2 = 1 \times 5 \times 1 \times 22$ | 110 (↓) | $2 + \frac{1}{2} = 2.5$ | 275 (↻) |
| 2. | Lateral earth pressure $P_H = \frac{1}{2} \times 26.67 \times 5 \times 1$ | 66.675 (←) | $\frac{5}{3}$ | 111.125 (↺) |
|  |  | $\Sigma W = 220$ |  | $\Sigma M = 310.54$ (↺) |

Let the resultant of horizontal and vertical forces strike the base slab of $\bar{x}$ ' from 'C'.

$$\therefore \quad \bar{x} = \frac{\Sigma M}{\Sigma W} = \frac{310.54}{220} = 1.411 \text{ m}$$

$$\therefore \quad \text{Eccentricity} = e = \frac{B}{2} - \bar{x} = \frac{3}{2} - 1.411 = 0.089 \text{ m}$$

$0.089 < \frac{3}{6}$ i.e. $e < \frac{B}{6}$ hence no tension is developed.

(iii) Stress analysis :

Resultant stresses :

$$\sigma_{max} ; \sigma_{min} = \sigma_d \pm \sigma_b$$

$$= \frac{\Sigma W}{B} \left( 1 \pm \frac{6e}{B} \right)$$

$$= \frac{220}{3} \left( 1 \pm \frac{6 \times 0.089}{3} \right)$$

$$\therefore \quad \sigma_{max} = 86.39 \text{ kN/m}^2 \text{ (Compressive)}$$

$$\sigma_{min} = 60.28 \text{ kN/m}^2 \text{ (Compressive)}$$

**Example 8.20 :** A tie bar 250 mm wide × 20 mm thick, transmits an axial pull of 400 kN. A 40 mm φ hole is drilled through bar such that its centre is 50 mm above the axis of member. Find the maximum and minimum stresses over the cross-section.

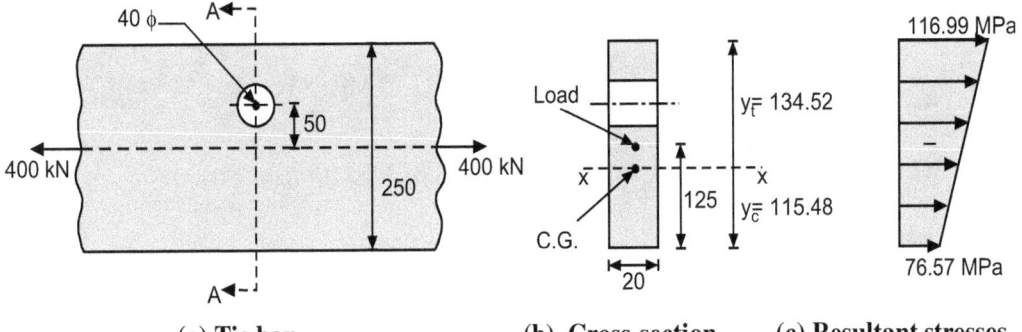

(a) Tie bar  (b) Cross-section  (c) Resultant stresses

Fig. 8.30

**Data** : As shown in Fig. 8.30 (a).
**Required** : Maximum and minimum stresses.
**Concept** : Axial load of member becomes eccentric to the cross-section through hole. Section is unsymmetric with uniaxial bending.
**Solution** : (i) Geometric properties :
To locate CG, consider bottom most fibre as reference.

$$a_1 = 250 \times 20 = 5000 \text{ mm}^2 \quad ; \quad y_1 = 125 \text{ mm}$$
$$a_2 = 20 \times 40 = 800 \text{ mm}^2 \quad ; \quad y_2 = 125 + 50 = 175 \text{ mm}$$

∴ Cross-sectional area $= A = a_1 - a_2 = 5000 - 800 = 4200 \text{ mm}^2$

$$\bar{y} = \frac{a_1 y_1 - a_2 y_2}{a_1 - a_2} = \frac{5000 \times 125 - 800 \times 175}{4200}$$

$$= 115.48 \text{ mm from bottom.}$$

∴ Eccentricity $= e = 125 - 115.48 = 9.52 \text{ mm}$

M.I. @ axis of bending $= I_{xx} = I_{xx_1} - I_{xx_2}$

$$= \left[\frac{20 \times (250)^3}{12} + (5000)(125 - 115.48)^2\right] - \left[\frac{20 \times (40)^3}{12} + (800)(175 - 115.48)^2\right]$$

$$= 23.55 \times 10^6 \text{ mm}^4$$

$y_c = 115.48 \text{ mm and } y_t = 134.52 \text{ mm}$

$$Z_c = \frac{I_{xx}}{y_c} = \frac{23.55 \times 10^6}{115.48} = 203.93 \times 10^3 \text{ mm}^3$$

$$Z_t = \frac{I_{xx}}{y_t} = \frac{23.55 \times 10^6}{134.52} = 175.07 \times 10^3 \text{ mm}^3$$

(ii) Maximum and minimum stresses :

$$\text{Direct stress} = \sigma_d = \frac{P}{A} = \frac{-400 \times 10^3}{4200} = -95.24 \text{ MPa}$$

$$= 95.24 \text{ MPa (Tensile)}$$

Bending stresses :

At top, $\sigma_b = -\dfrac{Pe}{Z_t} = \dfrac{-400 \times 10^3 \times 9.52}{175.07 \times 10^3} = 21.75$ MPa (Tensile)

At bottom, $\sigma_b = \dfrac{P \cdot e}{Z_c} = \dfrac{400 \times 10^3 \times 9.52}{203.93 \times 10^3} = 18.67$ MPa (Compressive)

Resultant stresses :

At top, $\sigma_{top} = -95.24 - 21.75 = -116.99$ MPa

$= 116.99$ **MPa (Tensile)**

At bottom, $\sigma_{bottom} = -95.24 + 18.67 = -76.57$ MPa

$= 76.57$ **MPa (Tensile)**

**Example 8.21 :** A tension member consists of a T-section symmetrical about the vertical centre line having the following dimensions.

Top flange : 100 mm wide and 15 mm thick.

Web : 80 mm deep and 10 mm thick.

The member transmits a longitudinal pull 'P' which acts on the section at a point on the centre line and 40 mm from the bottom edge of the web. Find :

(i) the magnitude of 'P' if the greatest tensile stress on the section is 150 MPa.

(ii) the minimum stress on the section when 'P' is being transmitted.

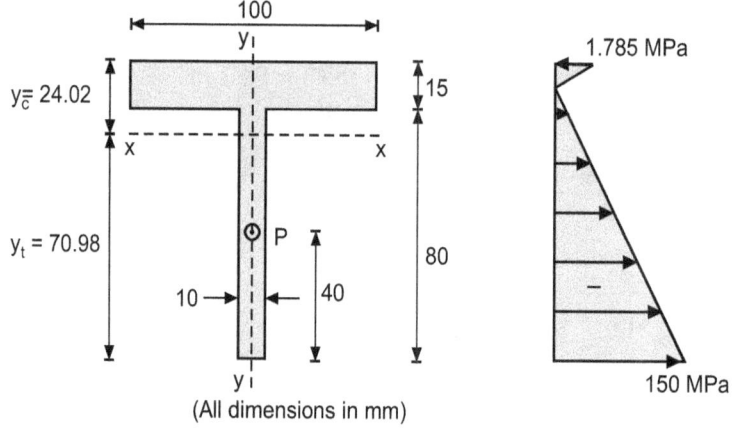

(a) **Cross-section of tension member** (b) **Resultant stresses**

**Fig. 8.31**

**Data** : As shown in Fig. 8.31 (a).

**Required** : (i) Magnitude of P for maximum tensile stress = 150 MPa

(ii) Minimum stress when P is being transmitted.

**Concept** : Unsymmetric section with uniaxial bending.

**Solution** : (i) Geometric properties :

To locate CG, consider bottom most fibre as reference.

$$a_1 = 100 \times 15 = 1500 \text{ mm}^2 \ ; \quad y_1 = 87.5 \text{ mm}$$
$$a_2 = 80 \times 10 = 800 \text{ mm}^2 \ ; \quad y_2 = 40 \text{ mm}$$

∴ Cross-sectional area $= A = a_1 + a_2 = 1500 + 800 = 2300 \text{ mm}^2$

$$\bar{y} = \frac{a_1 y_1 + a_2 y_2}{a_1 + a_2} = \frac{1500 \times 87.5 + 800 \times 40}{1500 + 800}$$

$$= 70.98 \text{ mm from bottom.}$$

∴ Eccentricity $= e = 70.98 - 40 = 30.98 \text{ mm}$

M.I. @ axis of bending $= I_{xx} = I_{xx_1} + I_{xx_2}$

$$I_{xx} = \left[\frac{100 \times (15)^3}{12} + 1500 \,(87.5 - 70.98)^2\right] + \left[\frac{10 \times (80)^3}{12} + 800 \,(70.98 - 40)^2\right]$$

$$= 1.632 \times 10^6 \text{ mm}^4$$

$$y_t = 70.98 \text{ mm} \ ; \quad y_c = 24.02 \text{ mm}$$

$$Z_t = \frac{I_{xx}}{y_t} = \frac{1.632 \times 10^6}{70.98} = 23 \times 10^3 \text{ mm}^3$$

$$Z_c = \frac{I_{xx}}{y_c} = \frac{1.632 \times 10^6}{24.02} = 67.94 \times 10^3 \text{ mm}^3$$

(ii) Magnitude of P for maximum tensile stress = 150 MPa.

∴ $\sigma_{bottom} = \sigma_{max} \text{ (tensile)} = \sigma_d + \sigma_b$

$$150 = \frac{P}{A} + \frac{M}{Z_t} = \frac{P}{A} + \frac{P \cdot e}{Z_t}$$

$$150 = \frac{P}{2300} + \frac{P \times 30.98}{23 \times 10^3}$$

$$P = 84187 \text{ N}$$
$$P = 84.187 \text{ kN}$$

(iii) Minimum stress, $\sigma_{top} = -\frac{P}{A} + \frac{P \cdot e}{Z_c}$

$$= -\frac{84187}{2300} + \frac{84187 \times 30.98}{67.94 \times 10^3}$$

$$= \mathbf{1.785 \text{ MPa}}$$

**Example 8.22** : Fig. 8.32 shows the cross-section of a short hollow column. Outside diameter of column is 200 mm and diameter of core is 125 mm. The centre line of core is displaced by 25 mm from centre line of column as shown. Calculate maximum and minimum stresses resulting from 1000 kN compressive load acting through centre of outer circle.

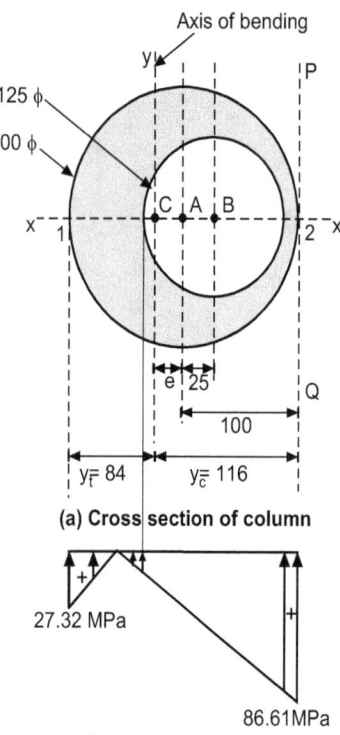

(a) Cross section of column

27.32 MPa

86.61 MPa
(b) Resultant stresses
(All dimensions in mm)

**Fig. 8.32**

**Data** : As shown in Fig. 8.32 (a).
**Required** : Maximum and minimum stresses.
**Concept** : Direct and bending stresses for unsymmetric section with uniaxial bending.
**Solution** : (i) Geometric properties :
To locate CG – xx is axis of symmetry, let PQ be reference axis.

$$a_1 = \frac{\pi}{4} (200)^2 = 31.42 \times 10^3 \text{ mm}^2 \; ; \quad x_1 = 100 \text{ mm}$$

$$a_2 = \frac{\pi}{4} (125)^2 = 12.27 \times 10^3 \text{ mm}^2 \; ; \quad x_2 = 100 - 25 = 75 \text{ mm}$$

∴  Cross-sectional area $= A = a_1 - a_2 = (31.42 - 12.27) \times 10^3 = 19.15 \times 10^3 \text{ mm}^2$

$$\bar{x} = \frac{a_1 x_1 - a_2 x_2}{a_1 - a_2} = \frac{(31.42 \times 100 - 12.27 \times 75) \times 10^3}{19.15 \times 10^3}$$

$$= 116 \text{ mm from PQ}$$

∴  Eccentricity $= e = 116 - 100 = 16$ mm
Moment of inertia @ axis of bending $= I = I_1 - I_2$

$$= \left[ \frac{\pi}{64} (200)^4 + 31.42 \times 10^3 (116 - 100)^2 \right] - \left[ \frac{\pi}{64} (125)^4 + 12.27 \times 10^3 (116 - 75)^2 \right]$$

$$= 53.97 \times 10^6 \text{ mm}^4$$

$y_t = 84$ mm ;   $y_c = 116$ mm ;   see Fig. 8.32.

$$Z_c = \frac{53.97 \times 10^6}{116} = 465.26 \times 10^3 \text{ mm}^3$$

$$Z_t = \frac{53.97 \times 10^6}{84} = 642.5 \times 10^3 \text{ mm}^3$$

(ii) Maximum and minimum stresses :

$$\text{Direct stress} = \sigma_d = \frac{P}{A} = \frac{1000 \times 10^3}{19.15 \times 10^3}$$
$$= 52.22 \text{ MPa (Compressive)}$$

Bending stresses : at 1; $\sigma_{b_1} = \frac{-P \cdot e}{Z_t} = \frac{-1000 \times 10^3 \times 16}{642.5 \times 10^3}$
$$= 24.9 \text{ MPa (Tensile)}$$

at 2 ; $\sigma_{b_2} = + \frac{P \cdot e}{Z_c} = \frac{1000 \times 10^3 \times 16}{465.26 \times 10^3}$
$$= 34.39 \text{ MPa (Compressive)}$$

Resultant stresses :

At 1 ; $\sigma_1 = 52.22 - 24.9 = $ **27.32 MPa (Compressive)**

At 2 ; $\sigma_2 = 52.22 + 34.39 = $ **86.61 MPa (Compressive)**

**Example 8.23 :** A rectangular column is subjected to a compressive load of 500 kN as shown in Fig. 8.33 (a). Find resultant stresses at all the four corners.

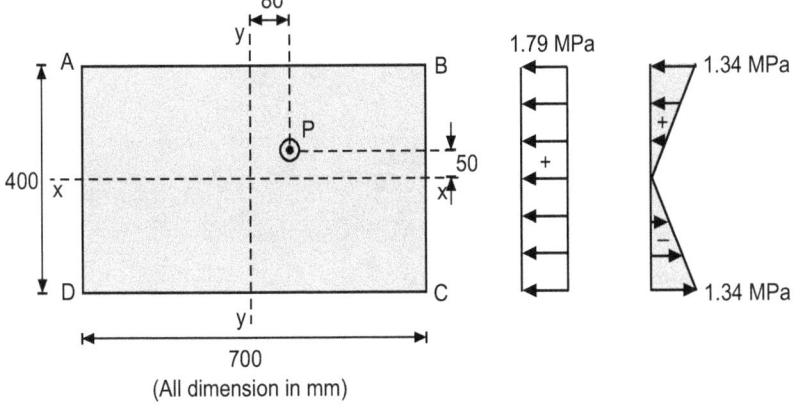

(a) Cross-section of column  (b) Direct stress  (c) Stresses due to $M_x$

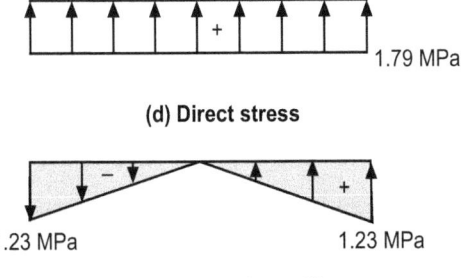

(d) Direct stress

(e) Stresses due to $M_y$

**Fig. 8.33**

**Data**      : As shown in Fig. 8.33 (a).

**Required**  : Resultant stresses at all the four corners.

**Concept**   : Biaxial bending; 50 mm eccentricity causes bending @ x-x axis and 80 mm eccentricity causes bending @ y-y axis.

**Solution**  : (i) Geometric properties :

$$A = 400 \times 700 = 280 \times 10^3 \text{ mm}^2$$

$$I_{xx} = \frac{700 \times (400)^3}{12} = 3.73 \times 10^9 \text{ mm}^4$$

$$I_{yy} = \frac{400 \times (700)^3}{12} = 1.14 \times 10^{10} \text{ mm}^4$$

$$(y_{max}) \text{ from x} - \text{axis} = \frac{400}{2} = 200 \text{ mm}$$

$$(y_{max}) \text{ from y-axis} = \frac{700}{2} = 350 \text{ mm}$$

$$Z_{xx} = \frac{I_{xx}}{y_{max}} = \frac{3.73 \times 10^9}{200} = 18.65 \times 10^6 \text{ mm}^3$$

$$Z_{yy} = \frac{I_{yy}}{y_{max}} = \frac{1.14 \times 10^{10}}{350} = 32.57 \times 10^6 \text{ mm}^3$$

(ii) Direct and bending stresses :

(a)     Direct stress $= \sigma_d = \dfrac{P}{A} = \dfrac{500 \times 10^3}{280 \times 10^3}$

$$= 1.79 \text{ MPa (Compressive)}$$

(b) Bending stresses due to moment @ x-axis

$$(\sigma_b)_x = \pm \frac{M_x}{Z_{xx}} = \pm \frac{500 \times 10^3 \times 50}{18.65 \times 10^6} = \pm 1.34 \text{ MPa}$$

**Note :** Moment about x-axis causes compression at A, B and tension at C, D.

(c) Bending stresses due to moment @ y-axis

$$(\sigma_b)_y = \pm \frac{M_y}{Z_{yy}} = \pm \frac{500 \times 10^3 \times 80}{32.57 \times 10^6} = \pm 1.23 \text{ MPa}$$

**Note :** Moment @ y-axis causes compression at B, C and tension at A and D.

Resultant stresses :

Corner 'A' :    $\sigma_A = 1.79 + 1.34 - 1.23 =$ **1.9 MPa (Compressive)**

Corner 'B' :    $\sigma_B = 1.79 + 1.34 + 1.23 =$ **4.36 MPa (Compressive)**

Corner 'C' :    $\sigma_C = 1.79 - 1.34 + 1.23 =$ **1.68 MPa (Compressive)**

Corner 'D' :    $\sigma_D = 1.79 - 1.34 - 1.23 =$ **– 0.78 MPa = 0.78 MPa (Tensile)**

**Example 8.24 :** A short column has a cross-section as shown in Fig. 8.34 (a). An external compressive load of 315 kN acts at 'P'. Calculate the resultant stresses at all the four corners. Also find what additional axial load is required for no tension condition.

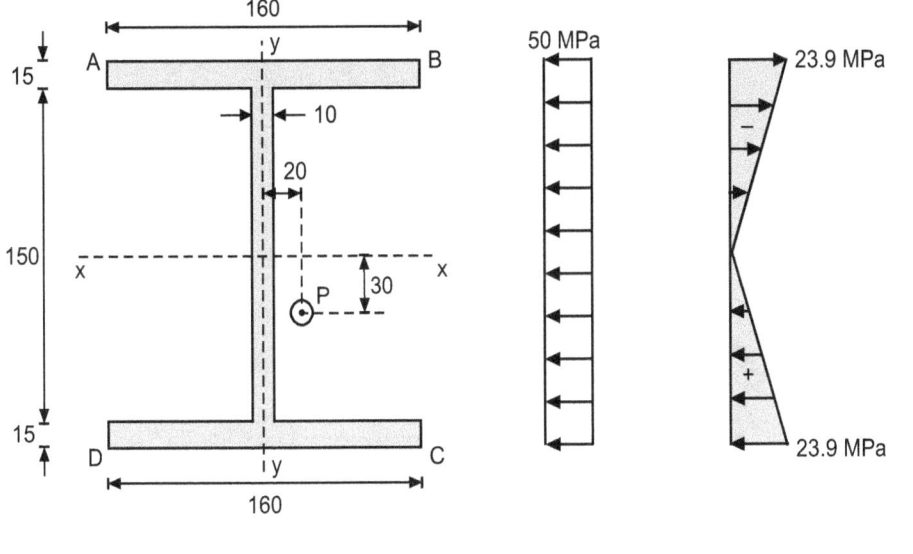

(a) Cross-section of column  (b) Direct stress  (c) Bending stress due to $M_x$

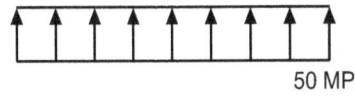

(d) Direct stress

(e) Bending stress due to $M_y$

**Fig. 8.34**

**Data** : As shown in Fig. 8.34 (a).
**Required** : Stresses at all four corners, additional axial load for no tension conditions.
**Concept** : Biaxial bending, Eccentricity of 30 mm causes moment @ x-axis, while that of 20 mm causes moment @ y-axis.
**Solution** : (i) Geometric properties :

$$A = 2 \times 160 \times 15 + 150 \times 10 = 6300 \text{ mm}^2$$

$$I_{xx} = \frac{160 \times (180)^3}{12} - \frac{150 \times (150)^3}{12} = 35.57 \times 10^6 \text{ mm}^4$$

$$I_{yy} = 2 \times \left(\frac{15 \times (160)^3}{12}\right) + \frac{150 \times 10^3}{12} = 10.25 \times 10^6 \text{ mm}^4$$

$y_{max}$ for x-axis $= \dfrac{150}{2} + 15 = 90$ mm

$y_{max}$ for y-axis $= \dfrac{160}{2} = 80$ mm

$$Z_{xx} = \dfrac{I_{xx}}{y_{max}} = \dfrac{35.57 \times 10^6}{90} = 395.22 \times 10^3 \text{ mm}^3$$

$$Z_{yy} = \dfrac{I_{yy}}{y_{max}} = \dfrac{10.25 \times 10^6}{80} = 128.125 \times 10^3 \text{ mm}^3$$

(ii) Direct and bending stresses :

(a) Direct stress $= \sigma_d = \dfrac{P}{A} = \dfrac{315 \times 10^3}{6300} = 50$ MPa (Compressive)

(b) Bending stresses due to moment @ x axis

$$\sigma_{b(x)} = \pm \dfrac{M_x}{Z_{xx}} = \pm \dfrac{315 \times 10^3 \times 30}{395.22 \times 10^3} = \pm 23.9 \text{ MPa}$$

**Note :** Moment @ x-axis causes compression at C, D and tension at A, B.

(c) Bending stresses due to moment @ y axis :

$$\sigma_{b(y)} = \pm \dfrac{M_y}{Z_{yy}} = \pm \dfrac{315 \times 10^3 \times 20}{128.125 \times 10^3} = \pm 49.16 \text{ MPa}$$

**Note :** Moment @ y axis causes compression at B, C and tension at A and D.

Resultant stresses :

Corner 'A' : $\sigma_A = 50 - 23.9 - 49.16 = -23.06$ MPa $=$ **23.06 MPa (Tensile)**

Corner 'B' : $\sigma_B = 50 - 23.9 + 49.16 =$ **75.26 MPa (Compressive)**

Corner 'C' : $\sigma_C = 50 + 23.9 + 49.16 =$ **123.06 MPa (Compressive)**

Corner 'D' : $\sigma_D = 50 + 23.9 - 49.16 =$ **24.74 MPa (Compressive)**

(iii) Axial load for no tension :

Let $P_1 =$ Additional force required at C.G. of cross-section

∴ $\dfrac{P_1}{A} - 23.06 = 0$

∴ $P_1 = 23.06 \times 6300 = 145.278 \times 10^3 =$ **145.278 kN**

**Example 8.25 :** An R.C.C. footing rectangular in plan 1.5 m × 2 m carries three vertical compressive loads of 75 kN ; 90 kN ; 120 kN as shown in Fig. 8.35. Neglecting self weight of the footing,

(i) Calculate stresses at all the four corners.

(ii) Determine the location of additional 100 kN load to make stresses at all the four corners equal.

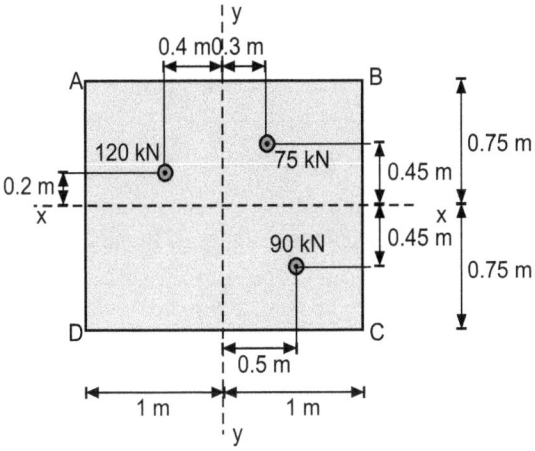

**Fig. 8.35 : c/s of column**

**Data** : As shown in Fig. 8.35.

**Required** : Stresses at all the four corners and location of additional load of 100 kN to have uniform stress at all the four corners.

**Concept** : (i) Biaxial bending, (ii) Position of additional 100 kN load should be such that there is no moment @ any of the axis, then stresses at all the four corners will be uniform.

**Solution** : (i) Geometric properties :

$$A = 2 \times 1.5 = 3 \text{ m}^2$$

$$I_{xx} = 2 \times \frac{(1.5)^3}{12} = 0.5625 \text{ m}^4$$

$$I_{yy} = 1.5 \times \frac{(2)^3}{12} = 1 \text{ m}^4$$

$y_{max}$ from 'x' axis = 0.75 m

$y_{max}$ from 'y' axis = 1 m

$$Z_{xx} = \frac{I_{xx}}{y_{max}} = \frac{0.5625}{0.75} = 0.75 \text{ m}^3$$

$$Z_{yy} = \frac{I_{yy}}{y_{max}} = \frac{1}{1} = 1 \text{ m}^3$$

(ii) Axial force and moments :

Total axial compressive force = P = 75 + 90 + 120 = 285 kN

Total bending moment @ x-axis = $M_x$ = 120 × 0.2 + 75 × 0.45 − 90 × 0.45

= 17.25 kNm

Total bending moment @ y-axis = $M_y$ = 75 × 0.3 + 90 × 0.5 − 120 × 0.4

= 19.5 kNm

(iii) Direct and bending stresses :

$$\sigma_d = \frac{P}{A} = \frac{285}{3} = 95 \text{ kN/m}^2$$

$$\sigma_{bx} = \pm \frac{M_x}{Z_{xx}} = \pm \frac{17.25}{0.75} = \pm 23 \text{ kN/m}^2$$

**Note :** Moment @ x-axis causes compression at A, B and tension at C, D.

$$\sigma_{by} = \pm \frac{M_y}{Z_{yy}} = \pm \frac{19.5}{1} = \pm 19.5 \text{ kN/m}^2$$

**Note :** Moment @ y-axis causes compression at B, C and tension at A, D.

Resultant stresses :

    Corner 'A' :    $\sigma_A = 95 + 23 - 19.5 = \mathbf{98.5 \text{ kN/m}^2}$

    Corner 'B' :    $\sigma_B = 95 + 23 + 19.5 = \mathbf{137.5 \text{ kN/m}^2}$

    Corner 'C' :    $\sigma_C = 95 - 23 + 19.5 = \mathbf{91.5 \text{ kN/m}^2}$

    Corner 'D' :    $\sigma_D = 95 - 23 - 19.5 = \mathbf{52.5 \text{ kN/m}^2}$

(iv) Position of 100 kN load for uniform stresses :

Stresses at all the four corners will be uniform when there is no resultant moment about x or y axis.

Let x and y be the distances of 100 kN load from yy and xx axes respectively.

$\sum$ Moment @ x-x axis = 0

$\therefore$                     $100(y) + M_x = 0$

$\therefore$                     $100(y) + 17.25 = 0$

$\therefore$                             $y = \mathbf{-0.1725 \text{ m}}$

Similarly, $\sum$ Moment @ y-y axis = 0

                        $100(x) + M_y = 0$

$\therefore$                     $100(x) + 19.5 = 0$

$\therefore$                             $x = \mathbf{-0.195 \text{ m}}$

Position of 100 kN load is as shown in Fig. 8.36.

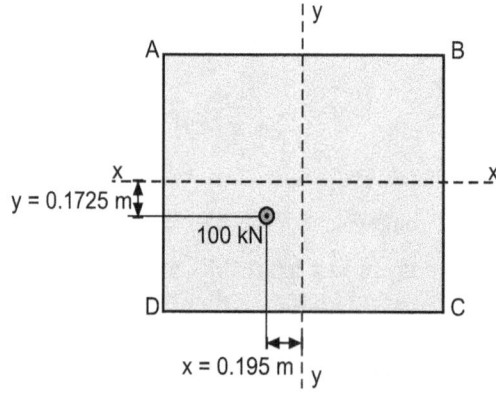

**Fig. 8.36 : Location of additional 100 kN load**

**Example 8.26 :** A mild steel specimen is subjected to 50 kN compressive force at 'B' as shown in Fig. 8.37. Find stresses at all the three corners.

**Data :** As shown in Fig. 8.37.

**Required :** Stresses at all the three corners.

**Concept :** Unsymmetric section with biaxial bending.

**Solution :** (i) Geometric properties :

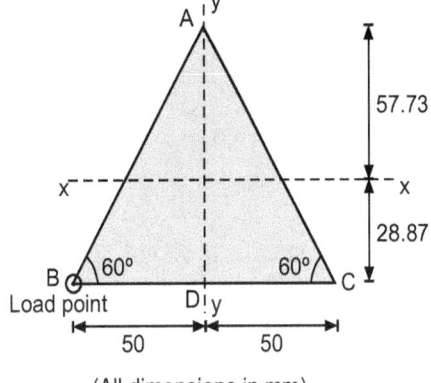

Fig. 8.37 : c/s of specimen

$$A = \frac{1}{2} \times 100 \times 50 \times \tan 60$$

$$A = 4330.13 \text{ mm}^2$$

yy is axis of symmetry.

CG at $\frac{h}{3}$ from base.

$$\therefore \quad \frac{h}{3} = \frac{50 \times \tan 60}{3} = 28.87 \text{ from base.}$$

$$I_{xx} = \frac{bh^3}{36} = \frac{100 \times (50 \times \tan 60)^3}{36} = 1.8 \times 10^6 \text{ mm}^4$$

$$I_{yy} = 2 \left( \frac{1}{12} (AD) \times (DC)^3 \right)$$

$$= 2 \left( \frac{50 \tan 60}{12} \times (50)^3 \right) = 1.8 \times 10^6 \text{ mm}^4$$

(ii) Force analysis :

Eccentricity for moment @ x-axis = $e_x$ = 28.87 mm
Eccentricity for moment @ y-axis = $e_y$ = 50 mm
Bending moment @ x-axis, $M_x = P \cdot e_x$ = 50 × 28.87
= 1443.5 kNmm
Bending moment @ y-axis, $M_y = P \cdot e_y$ = 50 × 50
= 2500 kNmm

**Note :** $M_x$ will cause compression at B and C while tension at A. $M_y$ will cause compression at B, tension at C and no stress at A.

(iii) Stress analysis :

$$\text{Direct stress} = \sigma_d = \frac{P}{A} = \frac{50 \times 10^3}{4330.13} = 11.55 \text{ MPa (Compressive)}$$

Bending stresses due to $M_X$ :

$$\sigma_{Ax} = \frac{-M_X}{I_{xx}} \times y_A = \frac{-1443.5 \times 10^3}{1.8 \times 10^6} \times 57.73 = -46.29 \text{ MPa}$$

$$= 46.29 \text{ MPa (Tensile)}$$

$$\sigma_{Bx} = \frac{M_X}{I_{xx}} \times y_B = \frac{1443.5 \times 10^3}{1.8 \times 10^6} \times 28.87 = 23.15 \text{ MPa (Compressive)}$$

$$\sigma_{Cx} = \sigma_{Bx} = 23.15 \text{ MPa (Compressive)}$$

Bending stresses due to $M_y$ :

$$\sigma_{Ay} = 0$$

$$\sigma_{By} = \frac{M_y}{I_{yy}} \cdot y_B = \frac{2500 \times 10^3}{1.8 \times 10^6} \times 50 = 69.44 \text{ MPa (Compressive)}$$

$$\sigma_{Cy} = -69.44 \text{ MPa} = 69.44 \text{ MPa (Tensile)}$$

∴   Resultant stresses :

$$\sigma_A = 11.55 - 46.29 + 0 = -34.74 \text{ MPa} = \mathbf{34.74 \text{ MPa (Tensile)}}$$

$$\sigma_B = 11.55 + 23.15 + 69.44 = \mathbf{104.14 \text{ MPa (Compressive)}}$$

$$\sigma_C = 11.55 + 23.15 - 69.44 = -34.74 \text{ MPa} = \mathbf{34.74 \text{ MPa (Tensile)}}$$

**Example 8.27 :** Knowing that the allowable stress is 150 MPa in section a-a of the hanger shown in Fig. 8.38, determine the largest force P which may be applied at D.

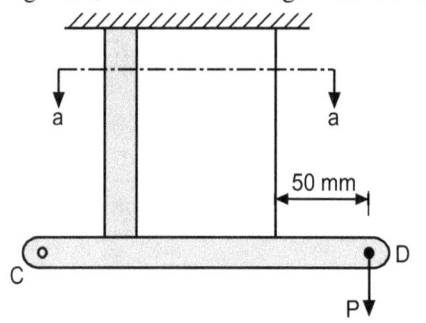
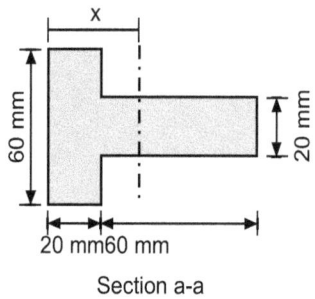

Section a-a

**Fig. 8.38**

**Solution :** (i)   $\bar{x} = 30$ mm,  $e = 50 + 50 = 100$ mm

$$I = 1.36 \times 10^6 \text{ mm}^4, \quad A = 2400 \text{ mm}^2$$

(ii)   $$\sigma_{max} = \frac{P}{A} + \frac{Pe}{I} \cdot y_{max}$$

$$150 = \frac{P \times 10^3}{2400} + \frac{P \times 10^3 \times 100 \times 50}{1.36 \times 10^6}$$

∴   $P = \mathbf{36.64 \text{ kN}}$

**Example 8.28 :** A column supports a load of 600 kN as shown in Fig. 8.39. Find the stresses at the corners of the column at its base.

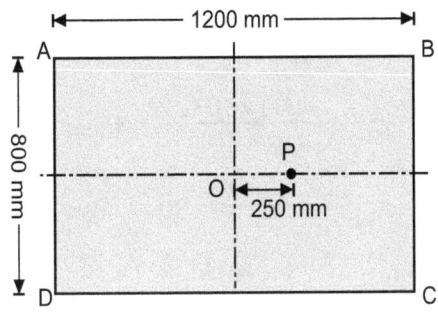

Fig. 8.39

Data : P = 600 kN, As shown in Fig. 8.39.
Required : Stresses at the corners of the column at its base.
Concept : Standard formula.
Solution : $\sigma_a = \dfrac{P}{A}$

$$\sigma_z = \dfrac{600 \times 10^3}{1200 \times 800} = 0.6225 \text{ N/mm}^2$$

$$\sigma_{bx} = \dfrac{(P \times e_x) \, y}{I_{xx}}$$

$$= \dfrac{600 \times 10^3 \times 250 \times (1200/2)}{\dfrac{800 \times 1200^3}{12}} = 0.78 \text{ N/mm}^2$$

$\sigma_A = \sigma_B = \sigma_a + \sigma_{bx} = 0.625 + 0.78 = $ **1.405 N/mm² (Compression)**
$\sigma_C = \sigma_D = \sigma_a - \sigma_{bz} = 0.625 - 0.78 = $ **− 0.155 N/mm² (Tension)**

**Example 8.29 :** A tapering chimney of hollow circular section is 30 m high. Its external diameter at base is 24 m and at the top it is 1.6 m. It is subjected to a wind pressure of 2.2 kN/m² of the projected area. If the weight of chimney is 4000 kN and the internal diameter at base is 0.8 m, determine the maximum and minimum stress intensities at the base.

Data : $D_{top} = 1.6$ m, $D_{bottom} = 2.4$ m, $d_{bottom} = 0.8$ m, wind pressure = 2.2 kN/m²,
$l = 30$ m, W = 4000 kN

Required : Maximum and minimum stress intensity at the base.
Concept : Standard formula.
Solution : Area of cross-section at the base,

$$A = \dfrac{\pi}{4} (2.4^2 - 0.8^2) = 4.02 \text{ m}^2$$

Moment of inertia at base, $I = \dfrac{\pi}{64}(2.4^4 - 0.8^4) = 1.61 \text{ m}^4$

$$\sigma_a = \dfrac{W}{A}$$

$$\sigma_a = \dfrac{4000 \times 10^3}{4.02 \times 10^6} = 1 \text{ N/mm}^2$$

Project area, $A_p = \dfrac{2.4 + 1.6}{2} \times 30 = 60 \text{ m}^2$

Total wind force $= 2.2 \times 60 = 132 \text{ kN}$

C.G. of projected area from bottom $= \dfrac{2.4 + 2 \times 1.6}{2.4 + 1.6} \times \dfrac{30}{3} = 14 \text{ m}$

Bending moment at base $= 132 \times 14 = \mathbf{184 \text{ kNm}}$

Bending stress at base $= \dfrac{1848 \times 10^6 \times (2400/2)}{1.61 \times 10^{12}} = \mathbf{1.38 \text{ N/mm}^2}$

**Example 8.30** : A concrete trapezoidal dam 4 m high, 1 m wide at its top and 3 m wide at its bottom retains water on its vertical face. Determine the intensity of maximum and minimum stresses at the base when reservoir is full of water, i.e. water level coincides with top of dam. Assume unit weight of concrete as 24 kN/m³ and that of water as 9.81 kN/m³.

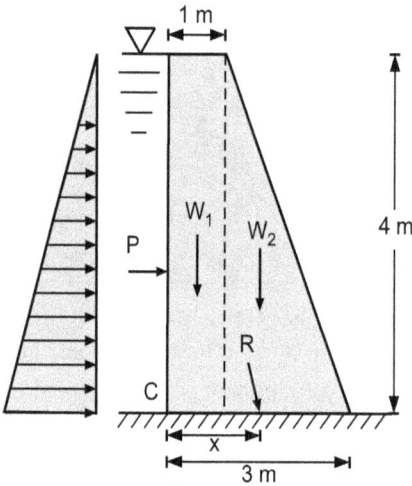

Fig. 8.40

**Data** : As shown in Fig. 8.40, $\gamma_w = 9.81 \text{ kN/m}^3$, $\gamma_c = 24 \text{ kN/m}^3$

**Required** : Maximum and minimum stresses at base.

**Concept** : Standard formulae.

**Solution** : Consider 1 m length of wall.

Area of cross-section, $A = \dfrac{1}{2}(1+3) \times 1 = 2 \text{ m}^2$

Total pressure on wall, $P = \dfrac{Wh^2}{2}$

$= \dfrac{9.81}{2} \times 4^2 = 78.48 \text{ kN}$

Pressure acts at (4/3) from bottom $= \dfrac{4}{3} = 1.33 \text{ m}$

Weight of rectangular portion of wall,

$W_1 = 24 \times 4 \times 1 = 96 \text{ kN}$ acts at 0.5 m from C

Weight of triangular portion of wall,

$W_2 = \left(24 \times 4 \times \dfrac{2}{2}\right) = 96 \text{ kN}$ acts at 1.67 m from C

Total weight, $W = W_1 + W_2 = 192 \text{ kN}$

Let the resultant R of P and W intersects the base at D at a distance x from C. The reactive forces given by foundation will be equal and opposite to R and will have components W and P acting at D as shown in figure.

Taking moment of forces about C,

$W_x = P \times \dfrac{h}{3} + W_1 \times X_1 + W_2 \times X_2$

$192 \, X = 78.48 \times 1.33 + 96 \times 0.5 + 96 \times 1.67$

∴ $X = 1.63 \text{ m}$

Eccentricity, $e = X - \dfrac{b}{2} = 1.63 - 1.5 = 0.13 \text{ m}$

$\sigma_{max} = \dfrac{W}{A}\left(1 + \dfrac{\sigma e}{b}\right) = \dfrac{192}{2}\left(1 + \dfrac{6 \times 0.13}{3}\right)$

$= 120.96 \text{ kN/m}^2 \text{ (Compression)}$

$\sigma_{min} = \dfrac{W}{A}\left(1 - \dfrac{\sigma e}{b}\right) = \dfrac{192}{2}\left(1 - \dfrac{6 \times 0.13}{3}\right)$

$= 71.04 \text{ kN/m}^2 \text{ (Compression)}$

## EXERCISE

1. A short cast iron column of hollow circular section 200 mm external diameter and 120 mm internal diameter is subjected to a vertical compressive load whose line of action is 50 mm from the axis of the column. If the maximum compressive stress is not to exceed 100 MPa and the maximum tensile stress is not to exceed 25 MPa, determine the magnitude of load that can be carried. (812 kN)

2. A short column of 200 mm external diameter and 160 mm internal diameter when subjected to eccentric compressive load, the stress measurements indicate that the stress varies from 150 MPa compressive at one end to 25 MPa tensile at the other end. Estimate the load and corresponding eccentricity.  (P = 706.8 kN; e = 57.4 mm)

3. A locomotive coupling rod is of rectangular cross-section 40 mm wide and 80 mm deep. The maximum axial thrust on the rod is 60 kN and the maximum lateral load at 2 kN/m. The length of the rod between the centres of end pins is 3 m. Neglecting the friction at the pins, estimate the maximum and minimum stress intensities in the rod.

$$(\sigma_{max} = 71.4 \text{ MPa (compressive)}, \quad \sigma_{min} = 33.9 \text{ MPa (tensile)})$$

4. A rectangular strut 200 mm wide and 150 mm thick carries a load of 50 kN at an eccentricity of 20 mm in a plane bisecting the thickness. Find the maximum and minimum intensities of stress in the section.

$$(\sigma_{max} = 2.67 \text{ MPa (compressive)}, \quad \sigma_{min} = 0.67 \text{ MPa (compressive)})$$

5. A hollow rectangular masonry pier is 1.2 m × 0.8 m overall, the wall thickness being 0.15 m. A vertical load of 1000 kN is transmitted in the vertical plane bisecting 1.2 m side at an eccentricity of 0.1 m from the geometric axis of the section. Calculate the maximum and minimum stress intensities in the section.

$$(\sigma_{max} = 2.92 \text{ MPa (compressive)}, \quad \sigma_{min} = 1.0 \text{ MPa (compressive)})$$

6. A horizontal wooden cantilever, 3 m long, 40 mm wide and 100 mm deep is hinged at the wall end. A wire is connected to it at 1 m from the free end and the other end is attached to the wall. The wire makes an angle of 30° with the cantilever which carries a UDL of 2 kN/m over the entire length. Find the maximum compressive stress in it and the position of section where it occurs.  (0.75 m from hinge, 10.38 MPa)

7. A cast iron vertical pillar is 150 mm in diameter. It has a hole of 50 mm diameter drilled along its axis. The centre of the hole is 40 mm from centre of the pillar. Find the values of maximum and minimum stresses on the section if a load of 1000 kN is applied at the centre of the pillar.

$$(\sigma_{max} = 82.7 \text{ MPa (compressive)}, \quad \sigma_{min} = 47 \text{ MPa (compressive)})$$

8. A tie member has a square cross-section 60 mm × 60 mm. It carries an axial tensile force F = 12 kN. From this member a rectangular piece 60 mm × 60 mm × 20 mm is then removed as shown in Fig. 8.41. Find maximum value of normal stress in a member.

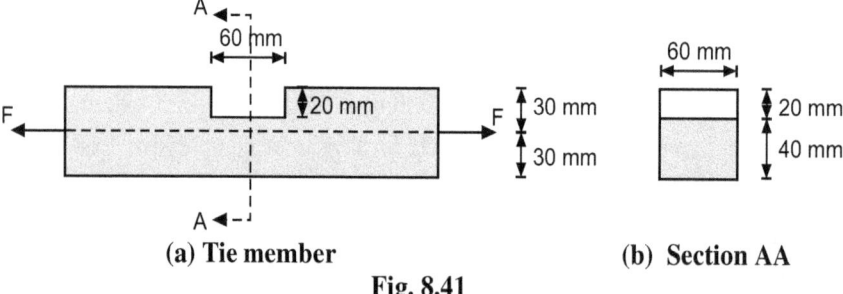

(a) Tie member  (b) Section AA

Fig. 8.41

9. A circular cylindrical tower having height 'h', inside diameter '$d_1$' and outside diameter '$d_2$' begins to lean slightly. What is the maximum permissible angle of inclination '$\theta$' of tower with vertical in order that no tension is produced in the base section of the tower? Consider only self weight of tower.

$$\left(\theta = \frac{d_1^2 + d_2^2}{4 d_2 h}\right)$$

10. A short length of tube 100 mm external diameter and 80 mm internal diameter is subjected to longitudinal eccentric compressive force of 150 kN. The force acts along the line parallel to the axis of the tube. If the maximum compressive stress produced is 90 MPa, find (i) the minimum stress in the section, (ii) the eccentricity of the load.

$$(\sigma_{min} = 16.1 \text{ MPa (compressive) and } e = 14.278 \text{ mm})$$

11. A column of an industrial building is loaded as shown in Fig. 8.42. The geometric properties of I section used as a column are as under :

$A = 9000$ mm², $I_{xx} = 1.35 \times 10^8$ mm⁴, $I_{yy} = 1.12 \times 10^7$ mm⁴. Analyse the cross-section at A and B for the resultant normal stresses and draw stress distribution diagrams over the cross-section. Also find the value of axial force at cross-section A so as to develop no tension at cross-section B.

(For cross-section A, $\sigma = 11.11$ MPa uniform compressive,

For cross-section B, $\sigma_{max} = 100$ MPa (compressive), $\sigma_{min} = 33.34$ MPa (tensile),

Additional load at A = 300 kN)

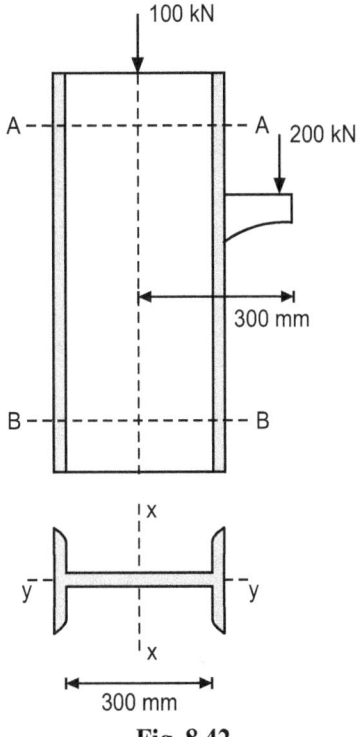

Fig. 8.42

12. A short hollow pier 1.5 m square outside and 1m square inside supports a vertical compressive load of 10 kN located on a diagonal 0.8 m from the vertical axis of the pier. Calculate the normal stresses at the four outside corners of the pier neglecting self weight.

   ($\sigma_1 = 33.07$ kN/m² (compressive), $\sigma_2 = \sigma_4 = 8$ kN/m² (compressive), $\sigma_3 = 17.07$ kN/m² (tensile))

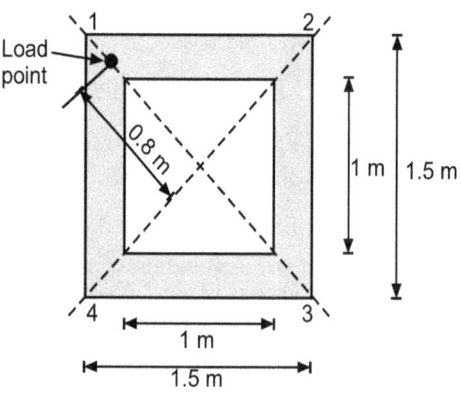

**Fig. 8.43**

13. A masonry pier 3 m × 4 m supports a load of 60 kN as shown in Fig. 8.44.

   (i) Find the stresses developed at each corner of the pier. (ii) What additional load shall be placed at the centre of the pier, so that there is no tension anywhere in the pier section ? (iii) What are the stresses at the corners with additional load ?

   (i) $\sigma_1 = 2.5$ kN/m² (compressive), $\sigma_2 = 17.49$ kN/m² (compressive), $\sigma_3 = 7.5$ kN/m² (compressive), $\sigma_4 = 7.5$ kN/m² (tensile).

   (ii) Additional load = 90 kN.

   (iii) Final stresses : $\sigma_1 = 10$ kN/m² (compressive), $\sigma_2 = 24.99$ kN/m² (compressive), $\sigma_3 = 15$ kN/m² (compressive), $\sigma_4 = 0$.

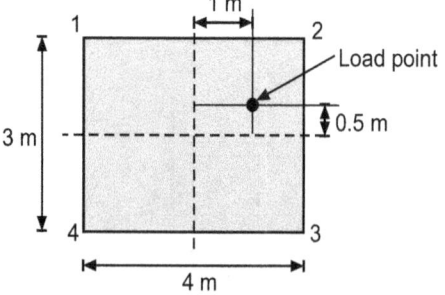

**Fig. 8.44**

14. A cylindrical chimney 22 m high of uniform circular section is having 4 m external diameter and 2 m internal diameter. The intensity of horizontal wind pressure is 1.5 kN/m². Find the maximum and minimum normal stress intensities at the section, if the specific weight of the masonry is 22 kN/m³. Assume coefficient of wind pressure = 2/3.

$$(\sigma_{max} = 648.34 \text{ kN/m}^2 \text{ (compressive)}, \sigma_{min} = 319.65 \text{ kN/m}^2 \text{ (tensile)})$$

15. A long rectangular wall is 2.5 m wide. If the maximum wind pressure on the face of the wall is 1 kN/m², find the maximum height of the wall so that there is no tension in the base of the wall. The specific weight of the masonry is 22 kN/m³.  (45.83 m)

16. A cylindrical steel chimney of 30 m height and 2 m external diameter is exposed to a horizontal wind pressure whose intensity varies as the square root of the height above the ground. At a height of 25 m, the intensity of wind pressure on a flat surface is 2.5 kN/m² and the coefficient of wind resistance is 0.6. Calculate the overturning moment at the base of the chimney.  (1183 kNm)

17. A tapering chimney of hollow circular section is 45 m high. Its external diameter at the base is 3.6 m and at the top it is 2.4 m. It is subjected to wind pressure of 2.2 kN/m² of the projected area. If the total weight of the chimney is 6000 kN and internal diameter at the base is 1.2 m, determine the maximum and minimum stress intensities at the base.

$$(\sigma_{max} = 2041.7 \text{ MPa (compressive)}, \quad \sigma_{min} = 715.5 \text{ MPa (tensile)})$$

18. Knowing that the clamp shown in Fig. 8.45 is tightened until P = 400 N, determine the stresses at points A and B. ($\sigma_A$ = 46.25 MPa (tensile), $\sigma_B$ = 64.40 MPa (compressive))

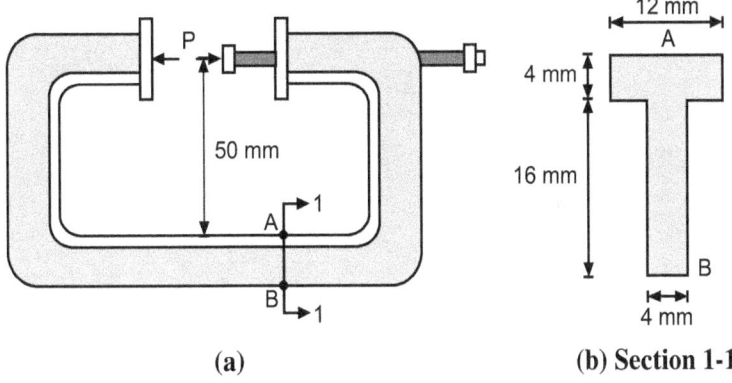

(a)          (b) Section 1-1

Fig. 8.45

19. The horizontal cross-section of a hollow rectangular pier is 1500 mm long and 1000 mm wide, overall, the wall thickness being 250 mm. A vertical load of 300 kN is eccentric from the geometric centre of the section by 'e' mm, measured along the centre line parallel to the long side. Evaluate e' so that the maximum compressive stress on the section is twice the minimum and state their values.

(e = 106.5 mm, $\sigma_{max}$ = 400 kN/m² (compressive), $\sigma_{min}$ = 200 kN/m² (compressive))

20. A vertical flag staff standing 10 m above the ground is of square section throughout, the dimensions being 80 mm × 80 mm at the top tapering uniformly to 160 mm × 160 mm at the ground. A horizontal pull of 500 N is applied at the top, the direction of the load being along a diagonal of the section. Find the maximum stress due to bending.

(12.275 MPa at 5 m from top)

21. A tie rod of solid circular section is subjected to a tensile force of 94.25 kN at an eccentricity of 5 mm from the longitudinal axis. If the maximum tensile stress is limited to 150 MPa, find the minimum diameter of the rod. (40 mm)

# CHAPTER NINE

# SHEAR STRESS DISTRIBUTION IN BEAMS

## 9.1 INTRODUCTION

The shearing force at any cross-section of a beam will set up a shear stress on transverse sections which in general will vary across the section. Following two assumptions are made in the analysis of shearing stress :

(i) The shearing stress is uniform along the width i.e. parallel to neutral axis of the beam.

(ii) The shearing stress does not affect the distribution of bending stress.

Second assumption cannot be strictly true because of distortion of the transverse plane due to shearing stress.

## 9.2 DERIVATION OF FORMULA FOR HORIZONTAL SHEARING STRESS

Consider two adjacent sections in a beam seperated by a small distance 'dx' as shown in Fig. 9.1 (a). Fig. 9.1 (b) shows bending stresses on two cross-sections. Assuming bending moment at cross-section 'cd' to be greater than that at cross-section 'ab', therefore the resulting horizontal force at cross-section 'cd', $F_{cd}$ will be greater than that at 'ab', $F_{ab}$.

Let it be required to find the shear stress intensity at '$y_1$' from NA. Consider free body diagram of elementary length 'dx' as shown in Fig. 9.1 (c) and Fig. 9.1 (e). Above this layer, difference in horizontal forces at two cross-sections will be resisted by shear force 'dF' acting on the bottom face of the free body since no external force acts on the section in this direction.

Thus, for equilibrium,

$$\sum F_x = 0; \qquad dF = F_{cd} - F_{ab}$$

$$= \int_{y_1}^{y_{max}} \sigma_{cd} \cdot dA - \int_{y_1}^{y_{max}} \sigma_{ab} \cdot dA$$

$$= \frac{M_{cd}}{I} \int_{y_1}^{y_{max}} y \cdot dA - \frac{M_{ab}}{I} \int_{y_1}^{y_{max}} y \cdot dA$$

$$= \frac{M_{cd} - M_{ab}}{I} \int_{y_1}^{y_{max}} y \cdot dA \qquad \ldots (9.1)$$

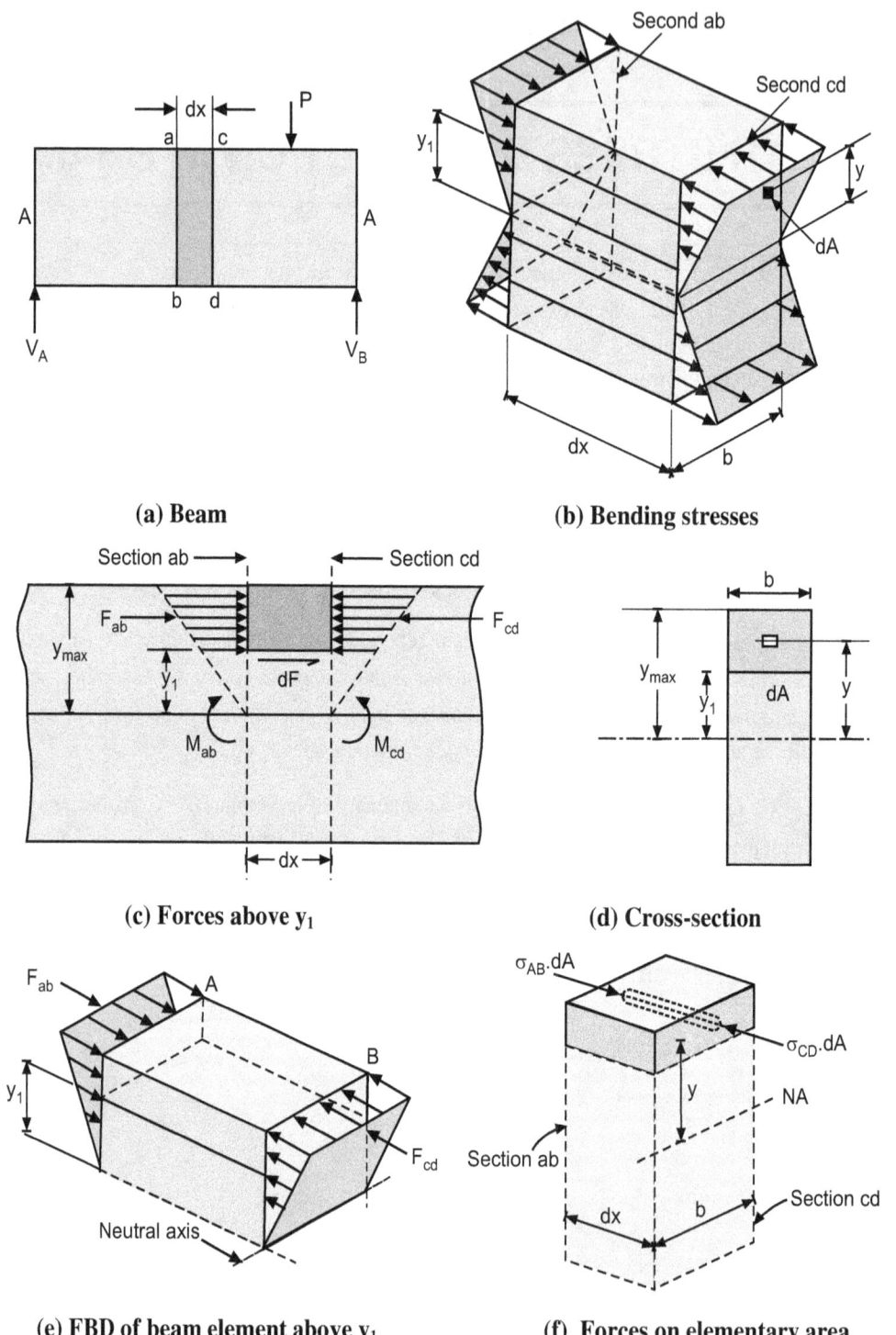

**Fig. 9.1 : Derivation of horizontal shearing stress**

where $M_{ab}$ and $M_{cd}$ = Bending moments at cross-sections 'ab' and 'cd' respectively.

From Fig. 9.1 (c),
$$dF = \tau \cdot b \cdot dx \qquad \ldots (9.2)$$
where $\tau$ = Average shear stress on area of length 'dx' and width 'b'.
Equating equations (9.1) and (9.2),
$$\tau \cdot b \cdot dx = \frac{M_{cd} - M_{ab}}{I} \int_{y_1}^{y_{max}} y \cdot dA$$

$$\therefore \quad \tau = \frac{M_{cd} - M_{ab}}{dx} \cdot \frac{1}{bI} \int_{y_1}^{y_{max}} y \cdot dA = \frac{S}{bI} \int_{y_1}^{y_{max}} y \cdot dA$$

where  S = Vertical shear force at a section
$$= \frac{M_{cd} - M_{ab}}{dx} = \text{Rate of change of bending moment}$$

$$\therefore \quad \tau = \frac{SA\bar{y}}{bI} \qquad \ldots (9.3)$$

where $A\bar{y} = \int_{y_1}^{y_{max}} y \cdot dA$

= Moment of area above or below the level at which shear stress is required about the neutral axis.

**Note** : It is the vertical shear force which comes in the equation (9.3) of calculating horizontal shear stress. However, horizontal shear stress is always accompanied by equal vertical shear stress as shown in Fig. 9.2.

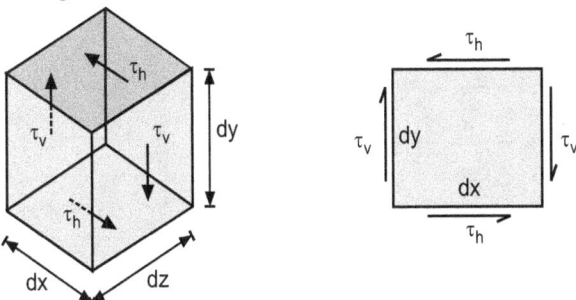

Fig. 9.2 : State of shear stress on typical beam element

## 9.3 DESIGN OF SHEAR CONNECTORS

Consider a wooden plank placed on top of another as shown in Fig. 9.3. If these planks act as a beam and are not interconnected, they will slide over each other at their contact surface. The interconnection of these components is necessary so that, they act as one unit.

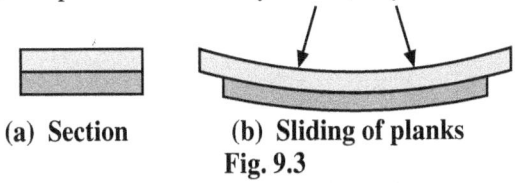

(a) Section     (b) Sliding of planks
Fig. 9.3

If the shear stress is multiplied by the width of cross-section, we get longitudinal force per unit length transmitted across the section (q) at the respective level. This quantity (q) is called as shear flow.

Thus, horizontal shear per unit length is

$$q = \tau \cdot b = \frac{SA\bar{y}}{I} \qquad \ldots (9.4)$$

Let, p = Pitch of rivets or nails along the length of member.
Then, to avoid shear failure and to make components behave as one unit,

$$q \cdot p = \text{Strength of rivet or nail} \qquad \ldots (9.5)$$

From equation (9.5), pitch of the shear connectors can be obtained.

## SOLVED EXAMPLES

**Example 9.1 :** Derive the relation between $\tau_{max}$ and $\tau_{avg}$ for
(i) Rectangular section.
(ii) Circular section.

**Data** : Shear stresses for rectangular section and circular section as shown in Fig. 9.4 (a) and Fig. 9.5 (a).

**Required** : Relation between $\tau_{max}$ and $\tau_{avg}$ for rectangular and circular section.

**Concept** : Actual shear stress $= \tau = \dfrac{SA\bar{y}}{bI}$ and $\tau_{avg} = \dfrac{\text{Shear force}}{\text{Cross-sectional area}}$.

**Solution** : (I) Rectangular section :
(i) Geometric properties of cross-section :

$$I_{xx} = \frac{bd^3}{12}$$

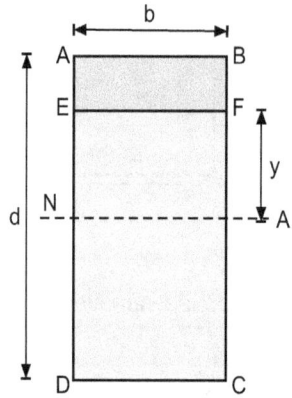
(a) Cross-section of beam

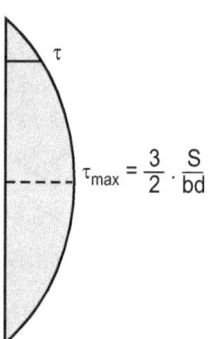
(b) Shear stress distribution diagram

$$\tau_{max} = \frac{3}{2} \cdot \frac{S}{bd}$$

Fig. 9.4

(ii) Stress analysis :
Intensity of shear stress at level EF,

$$\tau = \frac{Sa\bar{y}}{bI}$$

where $\quad a\bar{y}$ = Moment of the area above EF

$$\therefore \quad a\bar{y} = b\left(\frac{d}{2} - y\right) \cdot \frac{1}{2}\left(\frac{d}{2} + y\right) = \frac{b}{2}\left(\frac{d^2}{4} - y^2\right)$$

$$\therefore \quad \tau = \frac{S}{bI} \cdot \frac{b}{2}\left(\frac{d^2}{4} - y^2\right) = \frac{12}{bd^3} \cdot \frac{S}{b} \cdot \frac{b}{2}\left(\frac{d^2}{4} - y^2\right)$$

$$= \frac{6S}{bd^3}\left(\frac{d^2}{4} - y^2\right)$$

At the top edge i.e. at $\quad y = \frac{d}{2}; \quad \tau = 0$

At the neutral axis, i.e. at $\quad y = 0$

$$\tau = \frac{6S}{bd^3} \cdot \frac{d^2}{4} = \frac{3}{2} \cdot \frac{S}{bd}$$

Average shear stress $\quad \tau_{avg} = \frac{S}{bd}$

$$\tau_{max} = \frac{3}{2}\tau_{avg}.$$

Hence, the maximum shear stress intensity for a rectangular section is 1.5 times the average shear stress.

(II) Circular section :

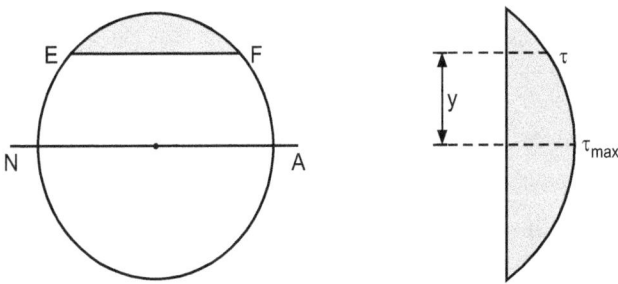

(a) Cross-section of beam  (b) Shear stress distribution diagram

Fig. 9.5

(i) Geometric properties of cross-section :

$$I_{xx} = \frac{\pi r^4}{4}$$

(ii) Stress analysis :

Consider any level EF at a distance "y" from the neutral axis.

Width of the section at the level EF :

$$= 2\sqrt{r^2 - y^2}$$

Moment of the area above EF @ the NA,

$$a\bar{y} = \int_{y}^{r} 2y\sqrt{r^2 - y^2}\, dy$$

Let
$$2\sqrt{r^2 - y^2} = u$$
$$4(r^2 - y^2) = u^2$$
$$-8y \cdot dy = 2u \cdot du$$
$$y \cdot dy = -\frac{1}{4} u \cdot du$$

$$a\bar{y} = \int_u^0 -\frac{1}{4} u \cdot du = \frac{1}{4} \int_0^u u^2 \cdot du = \frac{u^3}{12}$$

Shear stress at level EF,

$$\tau = \frac{Sa\bar{y}}{bI}$$

where
$b$ = Width of the section at level EF
$= EF = 2\sqrt{r^2 - y^2} = u$

∴
$$\tau = \frac{S}{I} \cdot \frac{u^3}{12u} = \frac{S}{12I} u^2$$

$$\tau = \frac{S}{12I} \cdot 4(r^2 - y^2)$$

$$= \frac{S}{3I} \cdot (r^2 - y^2)$$

$$= \frac{S \times 4}{3\pi r^4} \cdot (r^2 - y^2)$$

$$= \frac{4}{3} \frac{S}{\pi r^4} \cdot (r^2 - y^2)$$

Hence, the shear stress distribution is according to a parabolic law.

At $y = r$; i.e. at the extreme distance from the neutral axis,

$$\tau = 0$$

At $y = 0$; i.e. at the neutral axis, the shear stress

$$\tau_{max} = \frac{4}{3} \cdot \frac{S}{\pi r^2}$$

But the average shear stress $= \tau_{avg} = \frac{S}{\pi r^2}$

∴
$$\tau_{max} = \frac{4}{3} \tau_{avg}$$

**Example 9.2** : Two cross-sections of timber beam, square and solid circular, are subjected to shear force of 53 kN. If maximum allowable shear stress for timber is 8 MPa, design the cross-sectional dimensions.

**Data** : SF = 53 kN ; $\tau_{max} = 8$ MPa
**Required** : Cross-sectional dimensions.
**Concept** : $\tau_{max} = 1.5 \tau_{avg}$ for rectangular or square cross-section and

$\tau_{max} = \frac{4}{3} \tau_{avg}$ for solid circular cross-section.

**Solution** : (i) Design of square cross-section :
Let
$a$ = side of square in mm

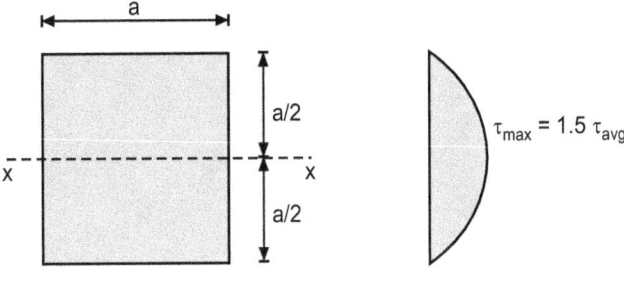

**(a) Cross-section**   **(b) Shear stresses**

**Fig. 9.6**

$$\therefore \quad \tau_{avg} = \frac{SF}{c/s\ area} = \frac{53 \times 10^3}{a^2}$$

$$\therefore \quad \tau_{max} = \frac{1.5 \times 53 \times 10^3}{a^2} = 8\ MPa \quad (\because Given)$$

$$\therefore \quad a = 99.68\ mm$$

$$\cong 100\ mm\ (say)$$

∴ Use **100 mm × 100 mm beam**.

(ii) Design of solid circular cross-section :

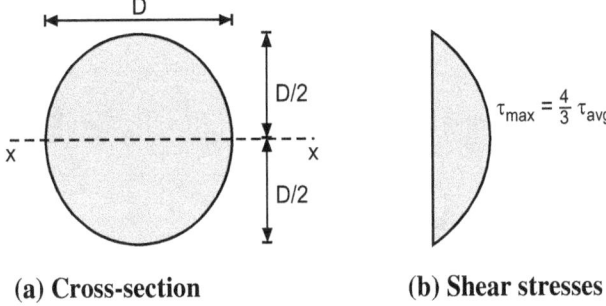

**(a) Cross-section**   **(b) Shear stresses**

**Fig. 9.7**

Let  D = Diameter of section in mm

$$\therefore \quad \tau_{avg} = \frac{SF}{c/s\ area} = \frac{53 \times 10^3}{\frac{\pi}{4} \cdot D^2}$$

$$\tau_{max} = \frac{4}{3} \times \frac{53 \times 10^3}{\left(\frac{\pi}{4}\right) D^2} = 8\ MPa \quad (\because given)$$

$$\therefore \quad D = 106.05\ mm$$

∴ Use  D = **107 mm**

**Example 9.3 :** A beam is triangular in section having a base "b" and an altitude "h". It is placed with its base horizontal. If at a certain section of the beam, the shear force is "S", find the maximum shear stress and the shear stress at the neutral axis.

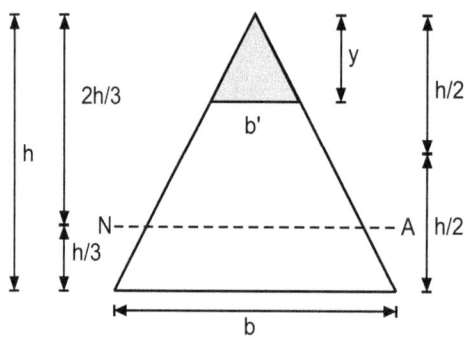
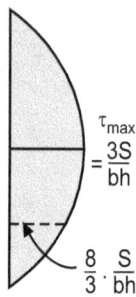

(a) Cross-section of beam    (b) Shear stress distribution diagram

Fig. 9.8

**Data** : As shown in Fig. 9.8.

**Required** : Maximum shear stress and shear stress at the neutral axis.

**Concept** : $\tau = \dfrac{SA\bar{y}}{bI}$

**Solution** : (i) Geometric properties of cross-section :

$$I_{xx} = \dfrac{bh^3}{36}$$

(ii) Stress analysis :

Let the shear stress intensity be "$\tau$" at a depth "y" from top. Width of the beam at a depth "y" from the top is say b'.

$$b' = \dfrac{b}{h} \cdot y$$

$$\tau = \dfrac{Sa\bar{y}}{Ib'} = \dfrac{S\left(\dfrac{y}{2} \cdot \dfrac{by}{h}\right)\left(\dfrac{2}{3}h - \dfrac{2}{3}y\right)}{\left(\dfrac{bh^3}{36}\right)\left(\dfrac{by}{h}\right)}$$

$$\tau = \dfrac{12S}{bh^3} y(h - y)$$

For $\tau$ to be maximum,

$$\dfrac{d\tau}{dy} = \dfrac{12S}{bh^3}(h - 2y) = 0$$

$$\therefore \quad y = \dfrac{h}{2}$$

$$\tau_{max} = \dfrac{12S}{bh^3} \cdot \dfrac{h}{2} \cdot \dfrac{h}{2} = \dfrac{3S}{bh}$$

To find shear stress at the neutral axis, put $y = \frac{2}{3}h$

$$\tau = \frac{12S}{bh^3} \cdot \frac{2}{3}h \cdot \frac{h}{3} = \frac{8}{3} \cdot \frac{S}{bh}$$

**Example 9.4 :** A beam of square section is placed with one diagonal horizontal. If the shear force at a section of the beam is S, draw the shear stress distribution diagram for the section.

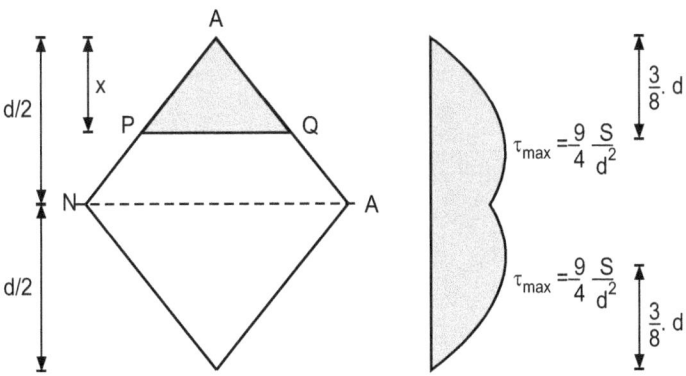

(a) Cross-section of beam   (b) Shear stress distribution diagram

Fig. 9.9

**Data** : As shown in Fig. 9.9 (a).

**Required** : Shear stress distribution diagram for the section :

**Concept** : $\tau = \dfrac{SA\bar{y}}{bI}$

**Solution** : (i) Geometric properties of cross-section.

$$I_{xx} = 2 \; \frac{d\left(\frac{d}{2}\right)^3}{12} = \frac{d^4}{48}$$

(ii) Stress analysis :

Consider a point in the section at a depth x from A. Shear stress at this point is given by

$$\tau = \frac{Sa\bar{y}}{bI}$$

where  $a$ = Area above the level PQ

$\bar{y}$ = Centroidal distance of the shaded area from the neutral axis.

$b$ = Width of the beam at a depth x from A

$$\therefore \quad a = x^2 \text{ and } \bar{y} = \left(\frac{d}{2} - \frac{2}{3}x\right) = \frac{1}{6}(3d - 4x)$$

$$b = 2x$$

$$\tau = Sx^2 \cdot \frac{\frac{1}{6}(3d - 4x)}{\left(\frac{d^4}{48}\right) \times 2x}$$

$$\therefore \quad \tau = \frac{4S}{d^4} \, x \, (3d - 4x)$$

At $x = 0$, i.e. at A, $\tau = 0$

At $x = \frac{d}{2}$, i.e. at the neutral axis,

$$\tau_{na} = \frac{4S}{d^4} \cdot \frac{d}{2}\left(3d - \frac{4d}{2}\right) = \frac{2S}{d^2}$$

Average shear stress, $\tau_{avg} = \dfrac{S}{\text{Area of beam section}}$

$$= \frac{S}{\left(\frac{d^2}{2}\right)} = \frac{2S}{d^2}$$

$$\therefore \quad \tau_{avg} = \tau_{na}$$

For shear stress to be maximum,

$$\frac{d\tau}{dx} = \frac{4S}{d^4}(3d - 8x) = 0$$

i.e. $\quad x = \dfrac{3}{8} \cdot d$

Hence, at a distance of $\dfrac{3}{8} \cdot d$ from 'A', maximum shear stress occurs.

Putting $x = \dfrac{3}{8} d$ in the general expression for the shear stress, the maximum shear stress is given by

$$\tau_{max} = \frac{4S}{d^4} \cdot \frac{3}{8} \cdot d \left(3d - 4 \times \frac{3}{8} \cdot d\right)$$

$$= \frac{9}{4} \cdot \frac{S}{d^2} = \frac{9}{8} \cdot \left(\frac{2S}{d^2}\right)$$

$$\therefore \quad \tau_{max} = \frac{9}{8} \tau_{avg}$$

**Example 9.5 :** Draw shear stress distribution diagram for the cross-section of beam shown in Fig. 9.10 (a) if SF = 100 kN.

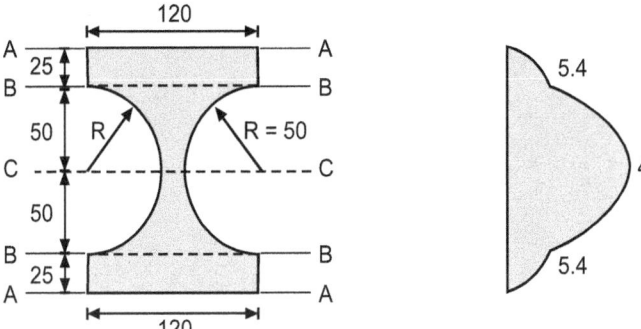

(a) Cross-section of beam    (b) Shear stress distribution diagram (MPa)

Fig. 9.10

**Data**       : SF = 100 kN ; Cross-section as shown in Fig. 9.10 (a).
**Required**   : Shear stress distribution diagram.

**Concept**    : Shear stress = $\tau = \dfrac{SA\bar{y}}{bI}$.

**Solution**   : (i) Geometric properties of cross-section :

$$I_{xx} = \dfrac{120 \times (150)^3}{12} - \dfrac{\pi}{4}(50)^4 = 28.84 \times 10^6 \text{ mm}^4$$

(ii) Shear stress analysis :

$$\tau_{AA} = 0$$

$$\tau_{BB} = \dfrac{SA\bar{y}}{bI}$$

Refer Fig. 9.11.

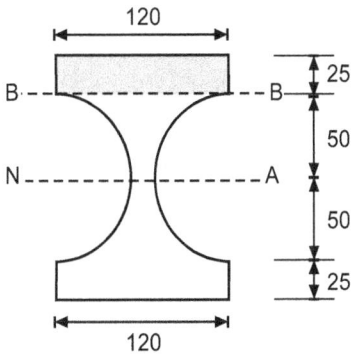

(All dimensions in mm)

Fig. 9.11

where    S = 100 kN
         A = 120 × 25 = 3000 mm²
         $\bar{y}$ = 50 + $\frac{25}{2}$ = 62.5 mm
         b = 120 mm
         I = 28.84 × 10⁶ mm⁴

∴        $\tau_{BB} = \frac{100 \times 10^3 \times 3000 \times 62.5}{120 \times 28.84 \times 10^6}$

         = 5.4 MPa

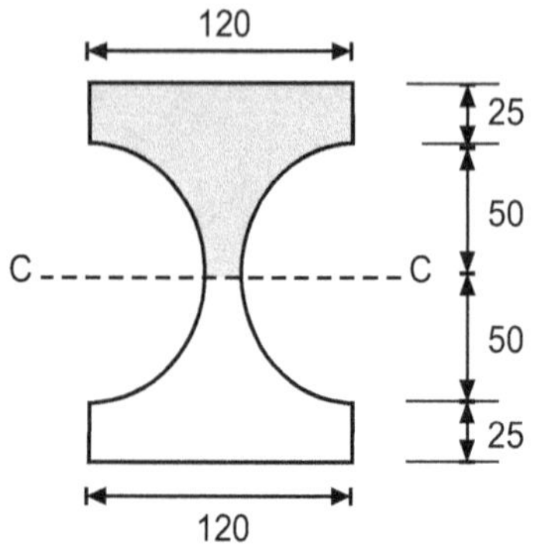

         $\tau_{CC} = \frac{SA\bar{y}}{bI}$    Refer Fig. 9.12

where    $A\bar{y} = 120 \times 75 \times \frac{75}{2} - \frac{\pi}{2}(50)^2 \times \frac{4 \times 50}{3\pi}$

         = 254.16 × 10³ mm³

∴        b = 120 − 2 × 50 = 20 mm

∴        $\tau_{CC} = \frac{100 \times 10^3 \times 254.16 \times 10^3}{20 \times 28.84 \times 10^6}$ = **44 MPa**

Fig. 9.12
(All dimensions in mm)

∴    Shear stress distribution diagram is as shown in Fig. 9.10 (b).

**Example 9.6 :** A simply supported beam of span 4 m carries UDL of 6 kN/m throughout the span. The cross-section of the beam is as shown in Fig. 9.13 (c). Draw shear stress distribution diagram for cross-section at 1 m from support. Also find average shear stress.

**Data**     : Span = 4 m ; simply supported ; UDL = 6 kN/m ; cross-section as shown in Fig. 9.13 (c).

**Required** : Shear stress distribution diagram for c/s at 1 m from left support.

**Concept**  : $\tau = \frac{SA\bar{y}}{bI}$

**Solution** : (i) Geometric properties of cross-section :
Consider bottom most fibre as a reference for locating CG.

    $a_1$ = 100 × 10 = 1000 mm² ;   $y_1$ = 105 mm
    $a_2$ = 100 × 10 = 1000 mm² ;   $y_2$ = 50 mm

    $\bar{y} = \frac{a_1 y_1 + a_2 y_2}{a_1 + a_2}$

    $= \frac{1000 \times 105 + 1000 \times 50}{1000 + 1000}$

    = 77.5 mm from bottom

Now,     $I_{xx} = I_{xx_1} + I_{xx_2}$

$$I_{xx_1} = \frac{100 \times 10^3}{12} + (1000)(105 - 77.5)^2$$

$$= 764.58 \times 10^3 \text{ mm}^4$$

$$I_{xx_2} = \frac{10 \times (100)^3}{12} + (1000)(77.5 - 50)^2$$

$$= 1.589 \times 10^6 \text{ mm}^4$$

$$\therefore \quad I_{xx} = (764.58 + 1.589) \times 10^3 = \mathbf{2.354 \times 10^6 \text{ mm}^4}$$

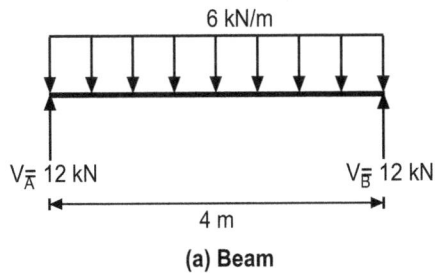

(a) Beam

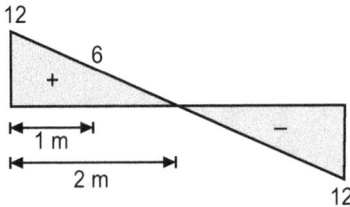

(b) SFD (kN)

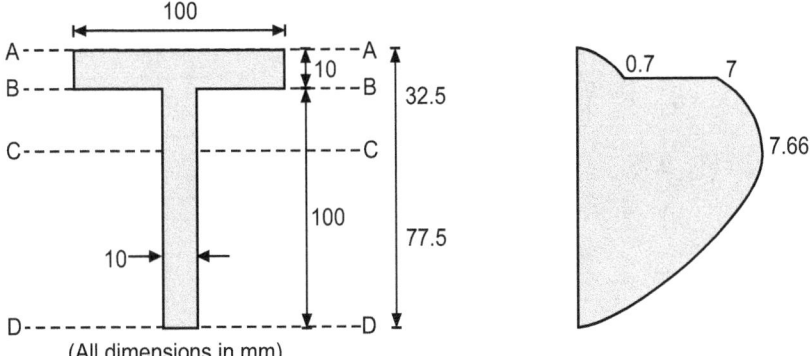

(c) Cross-section  (d) Shear stresses (MPa) at c/s 1m from LHS

Fig. 9.13

(ii) Analysis of beam :

Reactions :   $V_A = V_B = \dfrac{6 \times 4}{2} = 12 \text{ kN } (\uparrow)$

SF at 1 m from LHS = **6 kN**

(iii) Shear stress analysis :

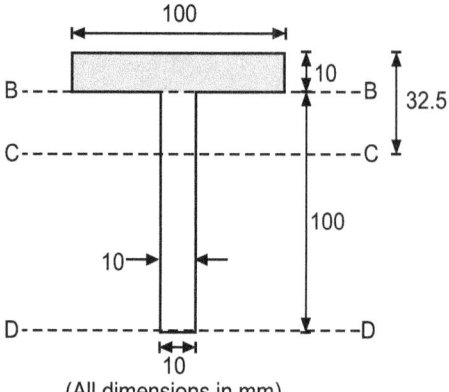

Fig. 9.14

$$\tau_{AA} = \tau_{DD} = 0$$

$$\tau_{BB} = \frac{SA\bar{y}}{bI}, \text{ Refer Fig. 9.14.}$$

where $A = 100 \times 10 = 1000 \text{ mm}^2$

$\bar{y} = 32.5 - 5 = 27.5 \text{ mm}$

Substituting, $\tau_{BB} = \dfrac{6 \times 10^3 \times 1000 \times 27.5}{100 \times 2.354 \times 10^6} = 0.7 \text{ MPa}$

$$\tau_{BB}' = \frac{\tau_{BB} \times b, \text{ just below "BB"}}{b, \text{ just above "BB"}} = \frac{0.7}{10} \times 100 = 7 \text{ MPa}$$

**Note :** Sudden change in width of cross-section at BB.

$$\tau_{CC} = \frac{SA\bar{y}}{bI}$$

Refer Fig. 9.15.

where $A = 77.5 \times 10 = 775 \text{ mm}^2$

$\bar{y} = \dfrac{77.5}{2} = 38.75 \text{ mm}$

$\tau_{CC} = \dfrac{6 \times 10^3 \times 775 \times 38.75}{10 \times 2.354 \times 10^6}$

$= 7.66 \text{ MPa}$

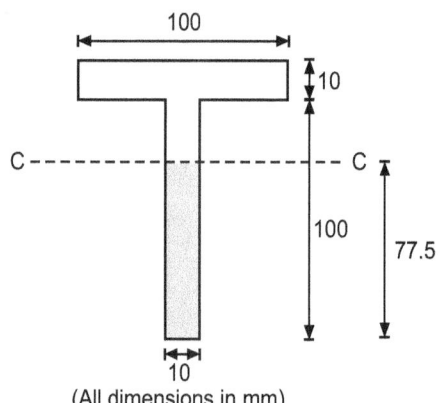

Fig. 9.15

Shear stress distribution diagram is as shown in Fig. 9.13 (d).

(iv) Average shear stress :

$$\tau_{avg} = \frac{SF}{c/s \text{ area}} = \frac{6 \times 10^3}{2000} = 3 \text{ MPa}$$

**Example 9.7 :** A wooden beam consists of three horizontal pieces each 50 mm × 100 mm giving on overall size of beam as 100 mm wide and 150 mm deep. The joints are glued together. The maximum permissible shear stress for the glued joint is 0.8 MPa. If the beam is 2 m long simply supported at ends, find what safe load can be applied at midspan.

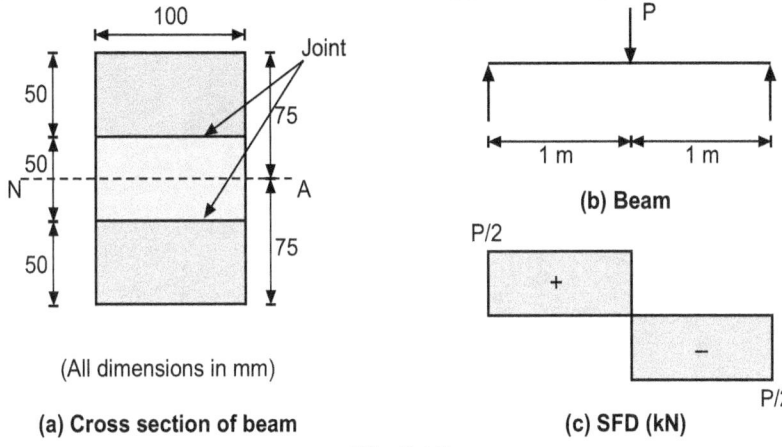

**Fig. 9.16**

**Data** : $\tau_{joint}$ = 0.8 MPa, as shown in Fig. 9.16 (a) and (b).

**Required** : Safe value of 'P'.

**Concept** : Shear stress at joint in terms of 'P' shall be equated to allowable shear stress.

**Solution** : (i) Geometric properties :

$$I_{xx} = \frac{100 \times (150)^3}{12} = 28.125 \times 10^6 \text{ mm}^4$$

(ii) Shear stress at the level of joint and magnitude of (P) :

$$\tau = \frac{SA\bar{y}}{bI}$$

where  $S$ = SF at support = $\frac{P}{2}$ (kN)

$A\bar{y}$ = Moment of area above or below the joint @ NA
= 100 × 50 × 50 = 250 × 10³ mm³

$b$ = Width of cross-section at joint = 100 mm

$I$ = 28.125 × 10⁶ mm⁴

Substituting  $\tau = \dfrac{\left(\dfrac{P}{2}\right) \times 10^3 \times 250 \times 10^3}{100 \times 28.125 \times 10^6}$ = 0.044 P  MPa

= 0.8 MPa  (∵ Allowable shear stress)

∴  P = **18 kN**

**Example 9.8 :** A wooden beam is prepared by connecting three pieces; as shown in Fig. 9.17. If the cross-section of the beam is subjected to maximum shear force of 25 kN, determine the spacing of the connectors assuming their shear strength to be 7.5 kN.

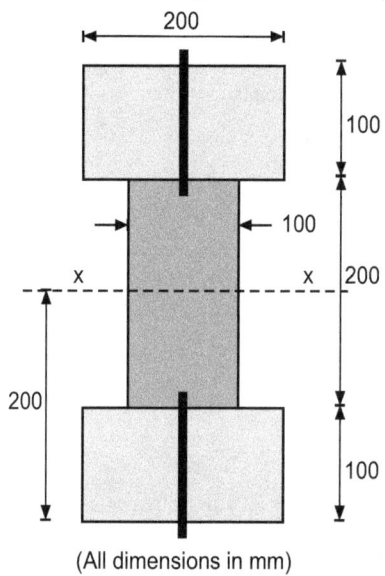

(All dimensions in mm)

**Fig. 9.17 : Cross-section of beam**

**Data** : SF = 25 kN ; shear strength of connectors = 7.5 kN; cross-section of beam as shown in Fig. 9.17.

**Required** : Spacing of shear connectors.

**Concept** : This connection is to be designed for horizontal shear between flange and web.

**Solution** : (i) Horizontal shear / mm run between flange and web :

$$q = \tau b = \frac{SA\bar{y}}{I}$$

where;
- $S$ = Shear force = 25 kN
- $A$ = Area above or below the level considered
  = $200 \times 100 = 2 \times 10^4$ mm²
- $\bar{y}$ = Distance of CG of area 'A' from NA
  = $100 + 50 = 150$ mm
- $I$ = MI of section @ NA = $I_{xx}$
  = $\frac{200 \times (400)^3}{12} - \frac{100 \times (200)^3}{12} = 1 \times 10^9$ mm⁴

Substituting, $q = \frac{25 \times 2 \times 10^4 \times 150}{1 \times 10^9}$ = **0.075 kN/mm**

(ii) Spacing of shear connectors :

Let $p$ = Pitch of shear connectors in 'mm'

∴ $0.075\, p = 7.5$

∴ $p$ = **100 mm c/c.**

**Example 9.9 :** The cross-section shown in Fig. 9.18 (a) is used as a simply supported beam over an effective span of 3 m. If the permissible stress in bending compression and tension is 100 MPa and 150 MPa respectively, find the safe value of 'P'. Neglect weakening of tension flange due to rivet holes. Also find pitch of rivets at supports assuming diameter of rivets as 16 mm and allowable shear stress for rivets is 100 MPa.

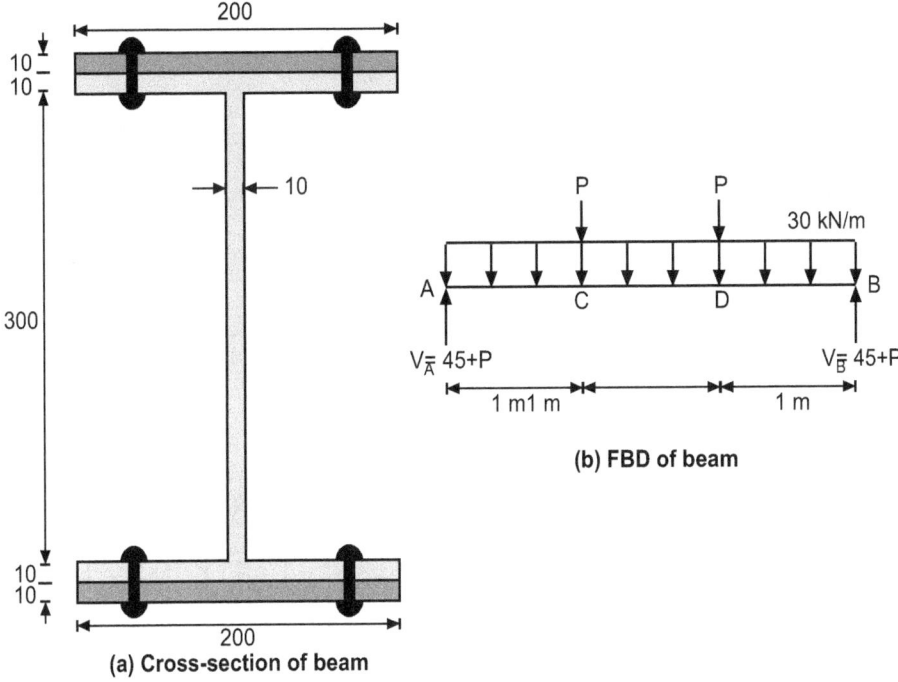

Fig. 9.18

**Data** : $\sigma_{bc} = 100$ MPa ; $\sigma_{bt} = 150$ MPa ; $\phi$ for rivets = 16 mm ;

$\tau$ for rivets = 100 MPa.

**Required** : Magnitude of 'P' and pitch of rivets.

**Concept** : Magnitude of 'P' will be governed by flexure criteria while pitch of rivets is to be designed for horizontal shear between flange plate and flange of 'T' section.

**Solution** : (i) Geometric properties.

$$I_{xx} = \frac{200 \times (340)^3}{12} - \frac{190 \times (300)^3}{12} = 227.57 \times 10^6 \text{ mm}^4$$

$$y_{max} = 170 \text{ mm}$$

$$Z_{xx} = \frac{I_{xx}}{y_{max}} = \frac{227.57 \times 10^6}{170} = 1.34 \times 10^6 \text{ mm}^3$$

(ii) Moment of resistance :

MR will be governed by allowable stress in bending compression.

$$MR = Z_{xx} \cdot \sigma_{bc} = 1.34 \times 10^6 \times 100 \times 10^{-6}$$

$$= \mathbf{133.86 \text{ kN-m}}$$

(iii) **Magnitude of 'P' :**

Let 'P' be the magnitude in kN.

Due to symmetry ; $V_A = V_B = \dfrac{30 \times 3}{2} + P = 45 + P\ (\uparrow)$

$\therefore$ Maximum BM at centre $= (45 + P)\ 1.5 - 30 \times \dfrac{(1.5)^2}{2} - P \times 0.5$

$\qquad\qquad\qquad\qquad\qquad = 33.75 + P$

Equating maximum BM and MR,

$\qquad\qquad 33.75 + P = 133.86$

$\qquad\qquad\qquad P = \mathbf{100.11\ kN}$

(iv) **Design of connection between flange plate and flange of 'T' section :**

Horizontal shear/mm run $= \tau = \dfrac{SA\bar{y}}{I}$

where, $A\bar{y} = (200 \times 10)(150 + 10 + 5) = 330 \times 10^3\ mm^3$

$\qquad S =$ Shear force $= 45 + P = 45 + 100.11 = 145.11\ kN$

$\qquad I = I_{xx} = 227.57 \times 10^6\ mm^4$

Substituting, $q = \dfrac{145.11 \times 330 \times 10^3}{227.57 \times 10^6} = 0.21\ kN/mm$

Let $p =$ Pitch of rivets in mm

$q \times p = 2 \times$ (Strength of rivet) $\quad (\because\ 2$ rivets for each flange)

$0.21 \times p = 2 \times \dfrac{\pi}{4} \times (16)^2 \times 100 \times 10^{-3}$

$\therefore \qquad\qquad p = \mathbf{191.4\ mm\ say\ 190\ mm\ c/c}$

**Example 9.10 :** A simply supported beam of span 4 m is loaded with concentrated load 'P' acting at centre. Determine the magnitude of load 'P', if the maximum bending stress allowed is 165 MPa and the section used for the beam is as shown in Fig. 9.19 (a). Also determine the maximum shear stress in the section.

**Data** : As shown in Fig. 9.19 (a); $\sigma_b = 165$ MPa.

**Required :** Safe value of 'P' and maximum shear stress induced.

**Concept :** Equating MR and maximum BM, find magnitude of 'P'. Maximum shear stress occurs at neutral axis of support section.

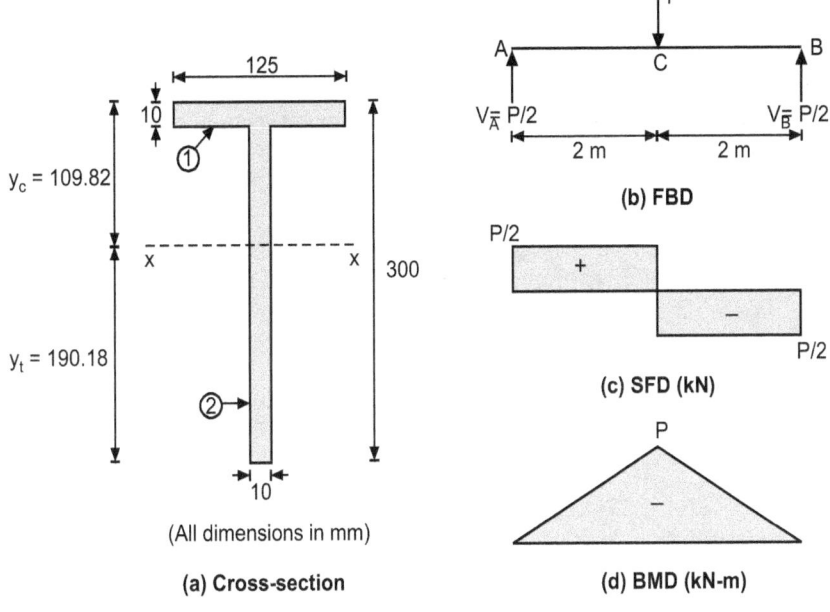

(a) Cross-section  (b) FBD  (c) SFD (kN)  (d) BMD (kN-m)

**Fig. 9.19**

**Solution :** (i) Geometric properties :
To locate CG, consider bottom most fibre as a reference.

$$a_1 = 125 \times 10 = 1250 \text{ mm}^2; \quad y_1 = 295 \text{ mm}$$
$$a_2 = 290 \times 10 = 2900 \text{ mm}^2; \quad y_2 = 145 \text{ mm}$$
$$\bar{y} = \frac{1250 \times 295 + 2900 \times 145}{1250 + 2900} = 190.18 \text{ mm from bottom}$$

∴  $y_c = 109.82$ mm ; $y_t = 190.18$ mm as shown in Fig. 9.19 (a)

$$I_{xx} = I_{xx_1} + I_{xx_2}$$

$$I_{xx_1} = \frac{125 \times 10^3}{12} + (1250)(295 - 190.18)^2 = 13.74 \times 10^6 \text{ mm}^4$$

$$I_{xx_2} = \frac{10 \times (290)^3}{12} + (2900)(190.18 - 145)^2 = 26.24 \times 10^6 \text{ mm}^4$$

∴  $I_{xx} = (13.74 + 26.24) \times 10^6 = \mathbf{39.98 \times 10^6 \text{ mm}^4}$

$y_{max} = 190.18$ mm

$$Z_{xx} = \frac{I_{xx}}{y_{max}} = \frac{39.98 \times 10^6}{190.18} = \mathbf{210.22 \times 10^3 \text{ mm}^3}$$

(ii) Analysis of beam :

$$\text{Maximum BM} = \frac{PL}{4} = \frac{P(4)}{4} = P \text{ kN-m}$$

where  $P$ = Magnitude of point load in kN
SF and BM diagrams are drawn as shown in Fig. 9.19 (c) and (d).

(iii) Magnitude of (P) :

Moment of resistance = MR = $Z_{xx} \cdot \sigma_b$ = $210.22 \times 10^3 \times 165 \times 10^{-6}$ kN/m
= 34.68 kN-m

Equating maximum BM and MR,
$$P = 34.68 \text{ kN}$$

(iv) **Maximum shear stresses ($\tau_{max}$):**

Maximum shear stress will occur at neutral axis of support section.

$$\tau_{max} = \tau_{NA} = \frac{SA\bar{y}}{bI}$$

where; $S$ = Shear force = $\frac{P}{2} = \frac{34.68}{2} = 17.34$ kN

$A$ = Area above or below the NA = $10 \times 190.18 = 1901.8$ mm²

$\bar{y}$ = Distance of CG of area 'A' from NA = $\frac{190.18}{2}$

= 95.09 mm

$b$ = Width of cross-section at NA = 10 mm

$I = I_{xx} = 39.98 \times 10^6$ mm⁴

Substituting, $\tau_{NA} = \dfrac{17.34 \times 10^3 \times 1901.8 \times 95.09}{10 \times 39.98 \times 10^6} = \mathbf{7.84 \text{ MPa}}$

**Example 9.11 :** A symmetrical I section with flanges 120 mm × 20 mm and web 20 mm × 180 mm ; is used as a simply supported beam and carries UDL of 60 kN/m over a span of 3 m. Evaluate maximum bending and shear stresses and draw the stress diagrams.

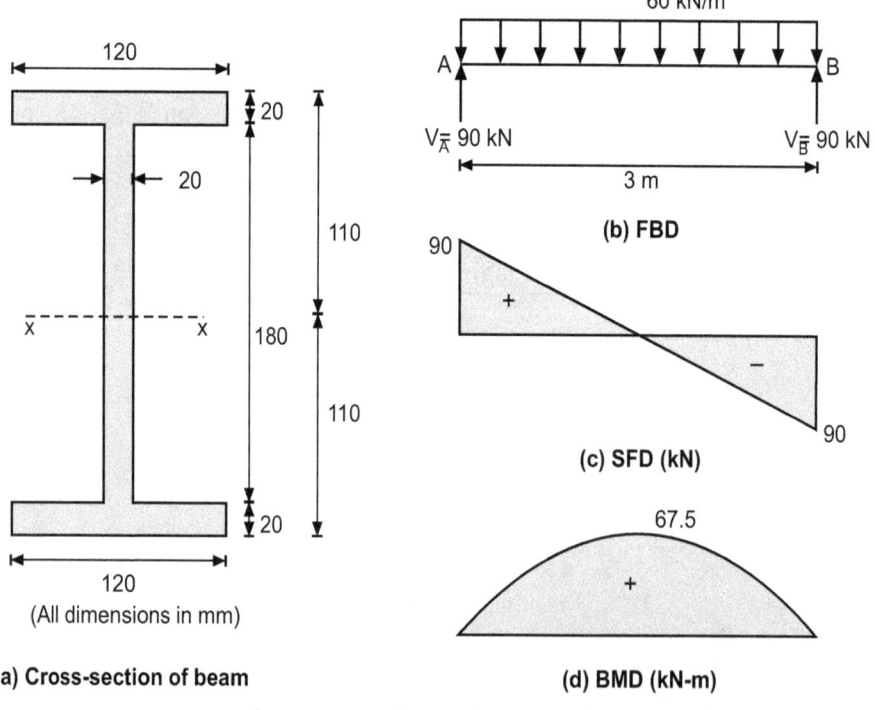

Fig. 9.20

**Data** : As shown in Fig. 9.20 (a) and (b).

**Required** : Bending and shear stresses.

**Concept** : Bending stress = $\sigma_b = \dfrac{M}{I_{xx}} \cdot y$. Shear stresses = $\tau = \dfrac{S A \bar{y}}{b I}$.

**Solution** : (i) Geometric properties :

C.G. by symmetry :

$$I_{xx} = \frac{120 \times (220)^3}{12} - \frac{100 \times (180)^3}{12} = 57.88 \times 10^6 \text{ mm}^4$$

$$y_{max} = 110 \text{ mm}$$

$$Z_{xx} = \frac{I_{xx}}{y_{max}} = \frac{57.88 \times 10^6}{110} = 526.18 \times 10^3 \text{ mm}^3$$

(ii) Analysis of beam :

Reactions = 90 kN (↑) by symmetry.

$$\text{Central BM} = \frac{wL^2}{8} = \frac{60 \times 3^2}{8} = 67.5 \text{ kN-m (sagging)}$$

SF and BM diagrams are as shown in Fig. 9.20 (c) and (d).

(iii) Bending stresses at midspan :

$$\sigma_b = \pm \frac{BM}{Z_{xx}} = \pm \frac{67.5 \times 10^6}{526.18 \times 10^3} = \pm 128.28 \text{ MPa}$$

(iv) Shear stresses at support section :

$$\tau_{AA} = 0$$

$$\tau_{BB} = \frac{S A \bar{y}}{b I} = \frac{90 \times 10^3 \times (120 \times 20)(90 + 10)}{120 \times 57.88 \times 10^6}$$

$$= 3.1 \text{ MPa} \quad (\because \text{ shear stress at a section within the flange,}$$

is very close to junction of flange and web)

$$\tau_{BB'} = \frac{S A \bar{y}}{b I} = \frac{3.1 \times 120}{20} = 18.6 \text{ MPa}$$

($\because$ shear stress at a section within the web, is very close to junction of flange and web)

$$\tau_{NA} = \frac{S A \bar{y}}{b I}$$

where $A \bar{y} = 120 \times 20 \times 100 + 90 \times 20 \times 45 = 321 \times 10^3 \text{ mm}^3$

Substituting,

$$\tau_{NA} = \frac{90 \times 10^3 \times 321 \times 10^3}{20 \times 57.88 \times 10^6} = 24.96 \text{ MPa}$$

Bending and shear stress diagrams are as shown in Fig. 9.21 (b) and (c).

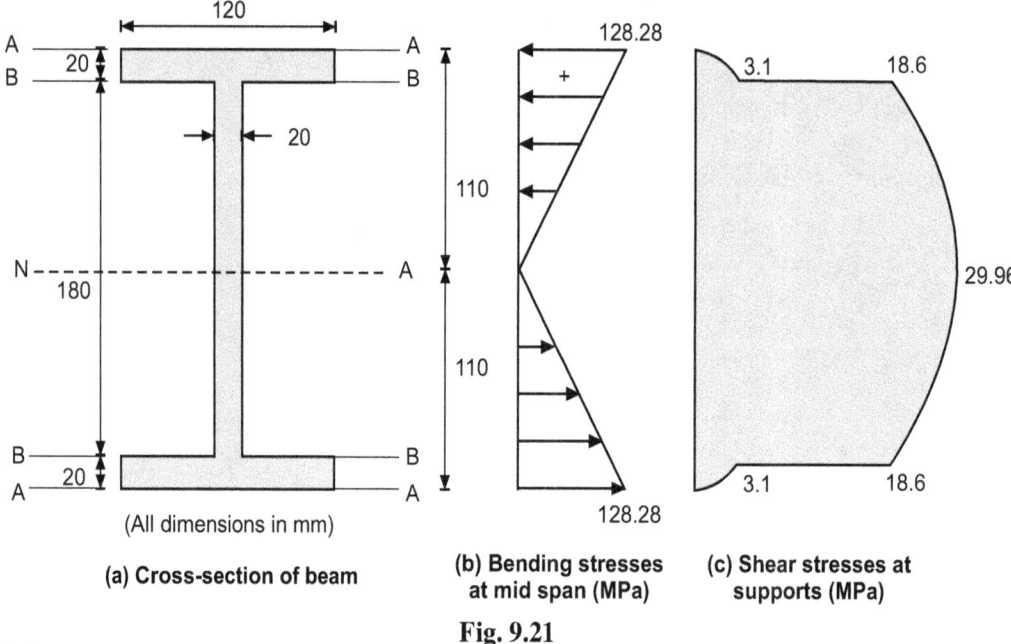

(a) Cross-section of beam
(b) Bending stresses at mid span (MPa)
(c) Shear stresses at supports (MPa)

Fig. 9.21

**Example 9.12**: A simply supported beam of cross-section in Fig. 9.22 (a) having 6 m span carries UDL of 30 kN/m throughout the span. Draw bending stress distribution diagram at midspan and shear stress distribution diagram at support section.

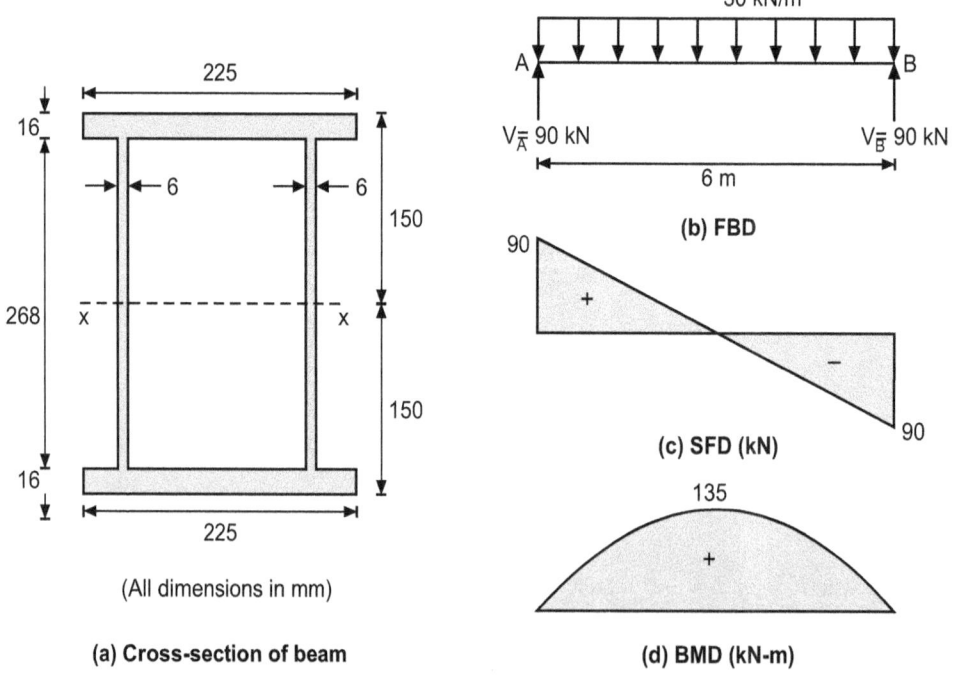

(a) Cross-section of beam
(b) FBD
(c) SFD (kN)
(d) BMD (kN-m)

Fig. 9.22

**Data** : As shown in Fig. 9.22 (a) and 9.22 (b).

**Required** : Bending and shear stresses.

**Concept** : Bending stresses = $\sigma_b = \dfrac{M}{Z_{xx}}$ ; Shear stresses = $\tau = \dfrac{SA\bar{y}}{bI}$.

**Solution** : (i) Geometric properties :

$$I_{xx} = \frac{225 \times (300)^3}{12} + \frac{213 \times (268)^3}{12} = 164.58 \times 10^6 \text{ mm}^4$$

$$y_{max} = \frac{300}{2} = 150 \text{ mm}$$

$$Z_{xx} = \frac{I_{xx}}{y_{max}} = \frac{164.58 \times 10^6}{150} = 1.097 \times 10^6 \text{ mm}^3$$

(ii) Analysis of beam :

Due to symmetry, $V_A = V_B = 30 \times \dfrac{6}{2} = 90$ kN ($\uparrow$)

Maximum BM at centre = $\dfrac{wL^2}{8} = 30 \times \dfrac{6^2}{8} = 135$ kN-m (sagging)

SF and BM diagrams are as shown in Fig. 9.22 (c) and 9.22 (d).

(iii) Bending stresses at midspan section :

$$\sigma_{bc;\,cal} = \sigma_{bt,\,cal} = \frac{M}{Z_{xx}} = \frac{135 \times 10^6}{1.097 \times 10^6} = 123.04 \text{ MPa}$$

(iv) Shear stresses at support section :

$$\tau_{AA} = 0$$

$$\tau_{BB} = \frac{SA\bar{y}}{bI}$$

where $A\bar{y} = (225 \times 16) \times 142 = 511.2 \times 10^3 \text{ mm}^3$

$$\therefore \quad \tau_{BB} = \frac{90 \times 10^3 \times 511.2 \times 10^3}{225 \times 164.58 \times 10^6} = 1.24 \text{ MPa}$$

$$\tau_{BB'} = \frac{1.24 \times 225}{2 \times 6} = 23.29 \text{ MPa}$$

$$\tau_{max} = \tau_{NA} = \frac{SA\bar{y}}{bI}$$

where $A\bar{y} = (225 \times 16 \times 142) + 2 \times (134 \times 6 \times 67)$

$= 618.936 \times 10^3 \text{ mm}^3$

$$\therefore \quad \tau_{NA} = \frac{90 \times 10^3 \times 618.936 \times 10^3}{2 \times 6 \times 164.58 \times 10^6}$$

$= \mathbf{28.2 \text{ MPa}}$

(v) Bending and shear stress distribution diagrams are as shown in Fig. 9.23 (b) and 9.23 (c).

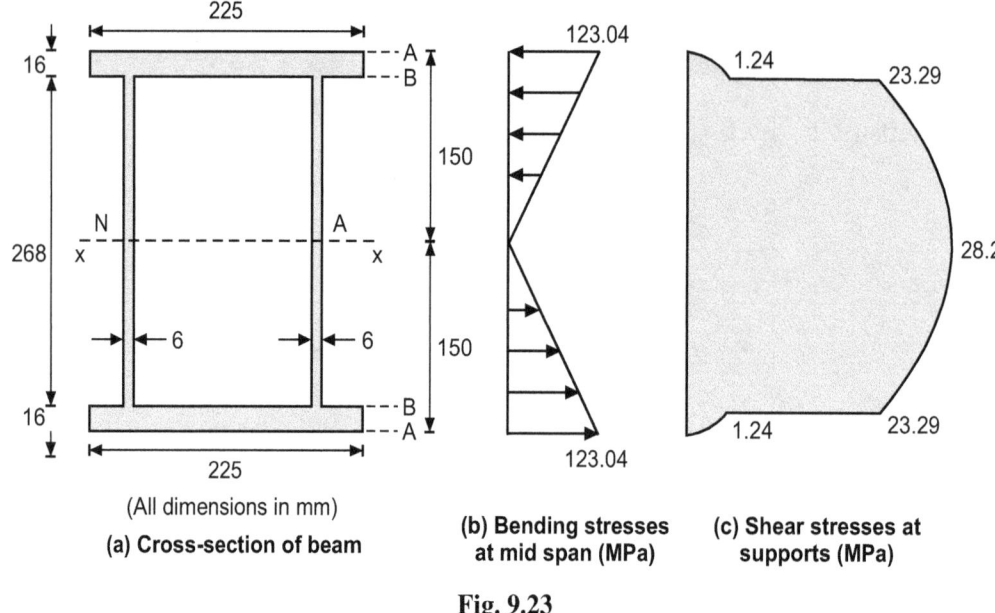

(a) Cross-section of beam
(All dimensions in mm)

(b) Bending stresses at mid span (MPa)

(c) Shear stresses at supports (MPa)

**Fig. 9.23**

**Example 9.13 :** Fig. 9.24 (a) and 9.24 (b) show a simply supported beam and its cross-section. The maximum permissible stress in bending is 125 MPa and the shear stress is 84 MPa. Find the maximum allowable value of 'P' neglecting self weight of the beam.

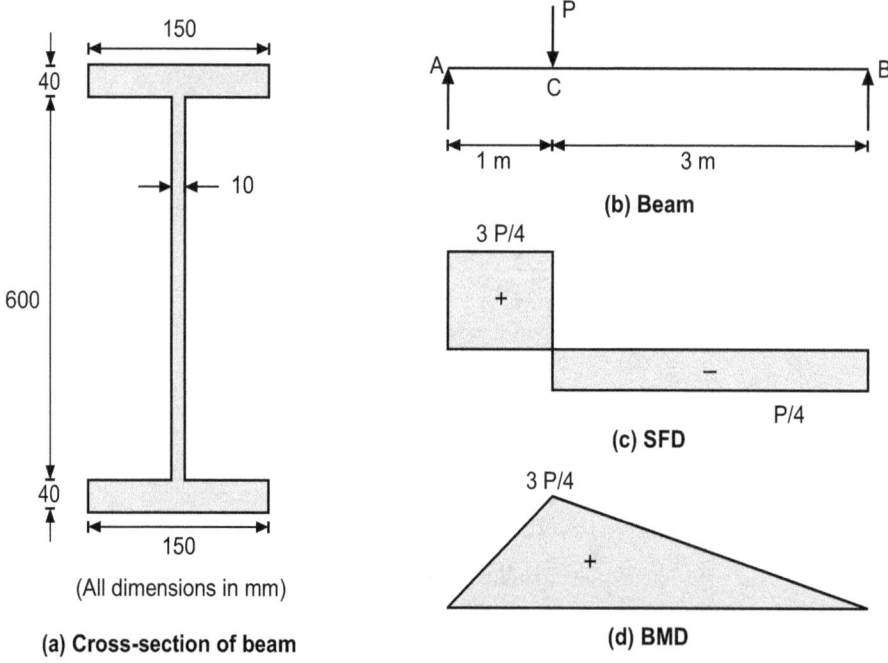

(a) Cross-section of beam
(All dimensions in mm)

(b) Beam

(c) SFD

(d) BMD

**Fig. 9.24**

**Data** : $\sigma_b = 125$ MPa ; $\tau_{max} = 84$ MPa; as shown in Fig. 9.24 (a) and 9.24 (b).

**Required** : Safe value of 'P'.

**Concept** : Find magnitude of 'P' from BM criteria and shear criteria. Least of the two is safe value of 'P'.

**Solution** : (i) Geometric properties :

$$I_{xx} = \frac{150 \times (680)^3}{12} - \frac{140 \times (600)^3}{12} = 1.41 \times 10^9 \text{ mm}^4$$

$$y_{max} = 340 \text{ mm}$$

$$Z_{xx} = \frac{I_{xx}}{y_{max}} = \frac{1.41 \times 10^9}{340} = 4.15 \times 10^6 \text{ mm}^3$$

(ii) Analysis of beam :

$$V_A = \frac{Pb}{L} = \frac{3P}{4} (\uparrow) \text{ and } V_B = \frac{Pa}{L} = \frac{P}{4} (\uparrow)$$

$$\text{BM at 'C'} = \frac{Pab}{L} = \frac{3P}{4}$$

SF and BM diagrams are drawn as shown in Fig. 9.24 (c) and 9.24 (d).

(iii) Magnitude of 'P' from BM criteria :

Let 'P' be the force in kN.

Maximum BM = MR

$$\frac{3P}{4} = 4.15 \times 10^6 \times 125 \times 10^{-6}$$

$\therefore \qquad P = 691.67$ kN  ... (i)

(iv) Magnitude of 'P' from shear criteria :

Maximum shear stress will occur at neutral axis of cross-section at support 'A'.

$$\tau_{NA} = \tau_{max} = \frac{SA\bar{y}}{bI}$$

where   S = Shear force at support A = $\frac{3P}{4}$ kN

$A\bar{y}$ = Moment of area above or below the NA @ NA

= $150 \times 40 \times 320 + 300 \times 10 \times 150$

= $2.37 \times 10^6$ mm³

b = Width of cross-section at NA = 10 mm

I = $I_{xx}$ of section = $1.41 \times 10^9$ mm⁴

Substituting,

$$\tau_{max} = \frac{\left(\frac{3P}{4}\right) \times 10^3 \times 2.37 \times 10^6}{10 \times 1.41 \times 10^9}$$

$$= 0.126 \, (P) \text{ MPa}$$

$$= 84 \text{ MPa} \qquad (\because \text{ Allowable stress})$$

$$\therefore \quad P = 666.67 \text{ kN} \qquad \ldots \text{(ii)}$$

$$\therefore \quad \text{Safe value of } P = \mathbf{666.67 \text{ kN}} \qquad (\because \text{ Least of (i) and (ii)})$$

**Example 9.14 :** A simply supported beam, 'L' m carries a UDL of 16 kN/m over the entire span. The cross-section of the beam is as shown in Fig. 9.25. If the maximum flexural stress is 40 MPa, find the span of the beam. Find the maximum shear stress developed. Draw the shear stress distribution diagram.

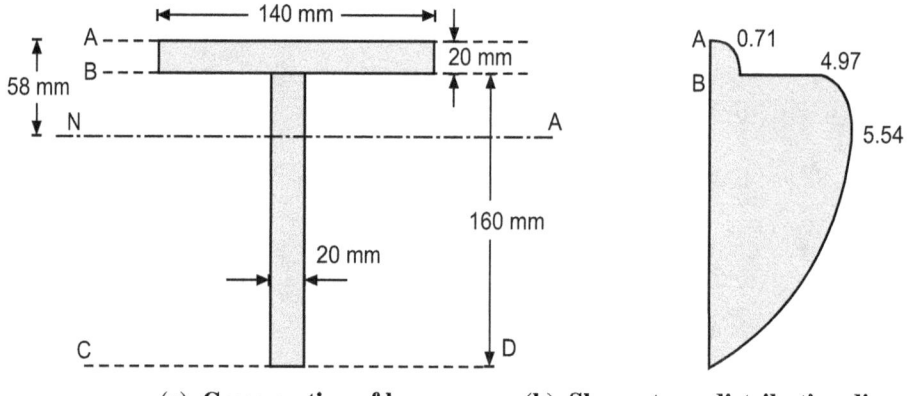

(a) Cross-section of beam  (b) Shear stress distribution diagram

Fig. 9.25

**Data :** As shown in Fig. 9.25 (a).
**Required :** Span, shear stress diagram.
**Concept :** B.M. = M.R., standard formulae.
**Solution :** (i) Geometric properties :

$$a_1 = 140 \times 20 = 2800 \text{ mm}^2, \quad y_1 = 160 + 10 = 170 \text{ mm}$$

$$a_2 = 160 \times 20 = 3200 \text{ mm}^2, \quad y_2 = \frac{160}{2} = 80 \text{ mm}$$

$$\bar{y} = \frac{a_1 y_1 + a_2 y_2}{a_1 + a_2} = \frac{2800 \times 170 + 3200 \times 80}{2800 + 3200}$$

$$= 122 \text{ mm}$$

$$y_c = 58 \text{ mm}, \quad y_t = 122 \text{ mm}$$

$$I_{xx_1} = \frac{140 \times (20)^3}{12} + 140 \times 20 \times (58 - 10)^2 = 6.45 \times 10^6 \text{ mm}^4$$

$$I_{xx_2} = \frac{20 \times (160)^3}{12} + 160 \times 20 \, (122 - 80)^2 = 12.47 \times 10^6 \text{ mm}^4$$

∴ $I_{xx} = I_{xx_1} + I_{xx_2} = 6.45 \times 10^6 + 12.47 \times 10^6 = 18.92 \times 10^6 \text{ mm}^4$

(ii) **Span calculation :**

$$\text{B.M.} = \text{M.R.}$$

$$Z_{xx} = \frac{I}{y_{max}} = \frac{18.92 \times 10^6}{122} = 155.08 \times 10^3 \text{ mm}^3$$

∴ Equating, $\dfrac{wl^2}{8} = \sigma_b \times Z_{xx}$

$$\frac{16 \times l^2}{8} = 40 \times 155.08 \times 10^3 \times 10^{-6}$$

∴ $l = \textbf{1.76 m}$

(iii) **Shear stress calculations :**

$$\tau = \frac{SA\bar{y}}{Ib}$$

$$SF = \frac{wl}{2} = \frac{16 \times 1.76}{2} = 14.08 \text{ kN}$$

$S = 14.08$ kN

$I = I_{xx} = 18.92 \times 10^6 \text{ mm}^4$

$$\tau_{AA} = \frac{SA\bar{y}}{Ib}$$

$A = $ Area above AA $= 0$

$\tau_{AA} = \tau_{CC} = 0$

$$\tau_{BB} = \frac{SA\bar{y}}{Ib}$$

$A = $ Area above BB $= 140 \times 20 = 2800 \text{ mm}^2$

$\bar{y} = $ C.G. of area from N.A. $= (58 - 10) = 48$ mm

$b = 140$ mm

∴ $\tau_{BB} = \dfrac{14.08 \times 10^3 \times 2800 \times 48}{18.92 \times 10^6 \times 140} = 0.71 \text{ MPa}$

$\tau_{B'B'} = \tau_{BB} \times \dfrac{140}{20} = 4.97 \text{ MPa}$

$$\tau_{NA} = \frac{SA\bar{y}}{Ib}$$

$A\bar{y} = (140 \times 20 \times 48) + (20 \times 38 \times 19)$
$= 148840 \text{ mm}^3$

∴ $\tau_{NA} = \dfrac{14.08 \times 10^3 \times 148840}{18.92 \times 10^6 \times 20} = \textbf{5.54 MPa}$

Shear stress distribution diagram is as shown in Fig. 9.25 (b).

**Example 9.15 :** A steel section shown in Fig. 9.26 is subjected to a shear force of 200 kN. Draw shear stress distribution diagram. Also find the ratio of maximum shear stress to average shear stress.

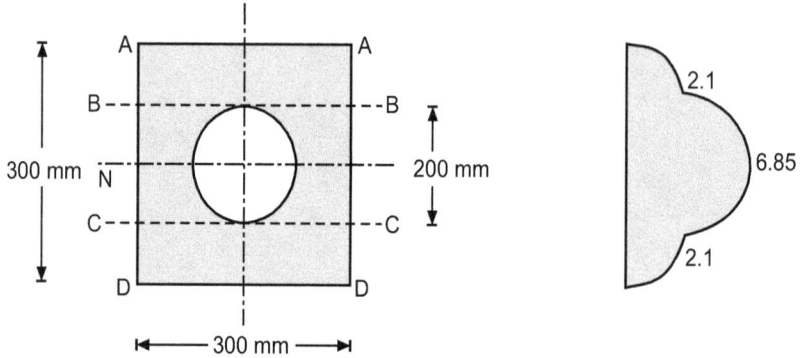

(a) Cross-section of beam   (b) Shear stress distribution diagram

Fig. 9.26

**Data :** As shown in Fig. 9.26 (a); S = 200 kN.

**Required :** $\dfrac{\text{Maximum shear stress}}{\text{Average shear stress}}$

**Concept :** $\tau = \dfrac{SA\bar{y}}{Ib}$

**Solution :** (i) Geometric properties :

$$\text{M.I.} = \dfrac{bd^3}{12} - \dfrac{\pi}{64} D^4$$

$$= \dfrac{300 \times (300)^3}{12} - \dfrac{\pi}{64} \times (200)^4 = 5.96 \times 10^8 \text{ mm}^4$$

(ii) Shear stress calculation :

Shear stress at A-A and D-D = 0.

Shear stress at B-B :

$$\tau_{BB} = \dfrac{SA\bar{y}}{Ib}$$

S = 200 kN = 200 × 10³ N
I = 5.96 × 10⁸ mm⁴
A = Area above B-B = 300 × 50 = 15000 mm²
$\bar{y}$ = 125 mm,  b = 300 mm

$$\tau_{BB} = \dfrac{200 \times 10^3 \times 15000 \times 125}{5.96 \times 10^8 \times 300} = 2.10 \text{ N/mm}^2$$

∴  $\tau_{BB} = \tau_{CC} = 2.10$ N/mm²

$$\tau_{NA} = \dfrac{SA\bar{y}}{Ib}$$

$$A\bar{y} = 300 \times 150 \times 75 - \frac{1}{2} \times \frac{\pi}{4} \times (200)^2 \times \frac{4 \times 200}{3 \times \pi}$$

$$= 2041666.7 \text{ mm}^3$$

$$\therefore \quad \tau_{NA} = \frac{200 \times 10^3 \times 2041666.7}{5.96 \times 10^8 \times 100}$$

$$= \mathbf{6.85 \text{ N/mm}^2}$$

**Example 9.16 :** A timber section as shown in Fig. 9.27 is subjected to a shearing force of 15 kN.

If the permissible shear stress for the material of section is 2 N/mm², determine the safety of section.

Further, the top flange is connected to vertical web by means of nails spaced at 200 K. Determine the minimum shear strength of the nail required to be provided for safety of joint.

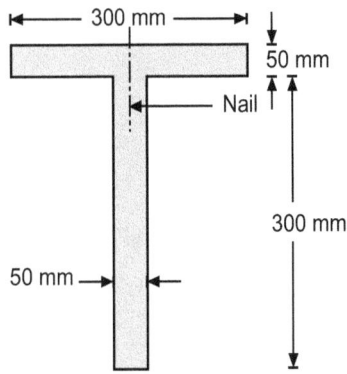

**Fig. 9.27 : Cross-section of beam**

**Data :** As shown in Fig. 9.27, $\tau_{max}$ = 2 N/mm², S.F. = 15 kN.

**Required :** Check for safety, minimum shear strength of web.

**Concept :** Standard formulae.

**Solution :** $$q = \frac{SA\bar{y}}{Ib}$$

$$S = S.F. = 15 \text{ kN}$$

(i) Geometric properties :

To locate CG, consider bottom most fibre as a reference.

$$a_1 = 300 \times 50 = 15000 \text{ mm}^2, \ y_1 = 325 \text{ mm}$$

$$a_2 = 50 \times 300 = 15000 \text{ mm}^2, \ y_2 = 150 \text{ mm}$$

$$\therefore \quad \bar{y} = \frac{a_1 y_1 + a_2 y_2}{a_1 + a_2} = \frac{15000 \times 325 + 15000 \times 150}{15000 + 15000}$$

$\bar{y}$ = 237.5 mm (from bottom)

$y_c$ = 112.5 mm, $y_t$ = 237.5 mm

$$I_{xx_1} = \frac{300 \times (50)^3}{12} + 300 \times 50 \left(112.5 - \frac{50}{2}\right)^2$$

$$= 117.97 \times 10^6 \text{ mm}^4$$

$$I_{xx_2} = \frac{50 \times (300)^3}{12} + 50 \times 300 (237.5 - 150)^2$$

$$= 2.27 \times 10^8 \text{ mm}^4$$

∴ $I_{xx}$ = 117.97 × 10$^6$ + 2.27 × 10$^8$ = 3.45 × 10$^8$ mm$^4$

$$Z_{xx} = \frac{I_{xx}}{y_{max}} = \frac{3.45 \times 10^8}{237.5} = 1.45 \times 10^6 \text{ mm}^3$$

(ii) Shear stress :

$$q = \frac{SA\bar{y}}{Ib}$$

S = 15 × 10$^3$ N

A = Area above or below N.A.

= (237.5 × 50) = 11875 mm$^2$

$\bar{y}$ = Distance of C.G. of area from N.A.

$$= \frac{237.5}{2} = 118.75 \text{ mm}$$

b = 50 mm

I = $I_{xx}$ = 3.45 × 10$^8$ mm$^4$

$$\tau_{NA} = \frac{15 \times 10^3 \times 11875 \times 118.75}{3.45 \times 10^8 \times 50}$$

$\tau_{NA}$ = 1.23 MPa < 2 MPa

∴ Section is safe.

(iii) Shear stress at the connection of flange and web.

$$\tau_j = \frac{SA\bar{y}}{Ib}$$

S = 15 kN = 15 × 10$^3$ N

A = Area above junction = 300 × 50 = 15000 mm$^2$

$\bar{y}$ = C.G. of area from N.A. = (112.5 – 25) = 87.5 mm

I = $I_{xx}$ = 3.45 × 10$^8$ mm$^4$

b = 300 mm

∴ $$\tau_j = \frac{15 \times 10^3 \times 15000 \times 87.5}{3.45 \times 10^8 \times 300} = \mathbf{0.19 \text{ MPa}}$$

Shear force developed due to S.F.

$$= \text{Required strength of nail}$$
$$= \tau_j \times b \times l = 0.19 \times 300 \times 200 = 11400 \text{ N}$$
$$= 11.4 \text{ kN}$$

Minimum shear strength of nail required = **11.4 kN.**

**Example 9.17 :** A circular hole is to be punched through a 5 mm thick aluminium plate. If the ultimate shear strength of aluminium is 120 MPa and safe compressive strength for the punch is 80 MPa, determine the maximum diameter of the hole that can be punched.

**Solution :** Normal force on punch = Shear force on portion removed

$$\left(\frac{\pi}{4} \phi^2\right) \sigma = (\pi \phi t) \tau$$

$$\frac{\pi}{4} (\phi^2) \, 80 = \pi \phi \times 5 \times 120$$

∴ $\phi = \textbf{30 mm}$

**Example 9.18 :** A section of beam is an isosceles triangle with base 260 mm and base angles 45°. It is used with base horizontal and carries a shear force of 62 kN at a particular section. Find the maximum intensity of shear stress and shear stress at neutral axis.

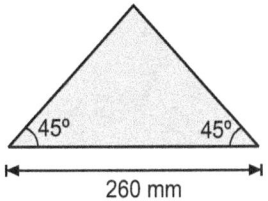

Fig. 9.28

**Solution :**

$$\tau_{max} = \frac{3S}{bh} = \frac{3 \times 62 \times 10^3}{260 \times 130} = 5.502 \text{ MPa}$$

$$\tau_{NA} = \frac{2.67 \, S}{bh} = 4.89 \text{ MPa}$$

**Example 9.19 :** A cylindrical tube of diameter 100 mm is to be anchored in a concrete block as shown in Fig. 9.29. If the maximum allowable shear stress in concrete is 0.5 MPa, find minimum length of cylindrical anchor tube, so that it will not be pulled out from concrete block under a force of 200 kN.

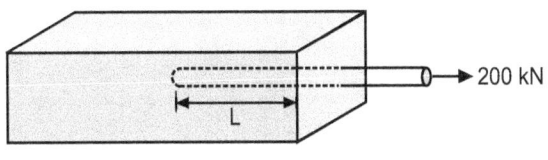

Fig. 9.29

**Solution:** Axial force on tube = Shear force on contact area

$$200 = (\pi dL) \tau$$
$$= (\pi \times 100 \times L) \times 0.5 \times 10^{-3}$$
$$\therefore \quad L = 1273.24 \text{ mm}$$

**Example 9.20 :** The cross-section and loading of a timber beam is as shown in Fig. 9.30. If the allowable stresses in bending and shear are respectively 12 MPa and 0.9 MPa, find the required dimensions of the beam (breadth and depth).

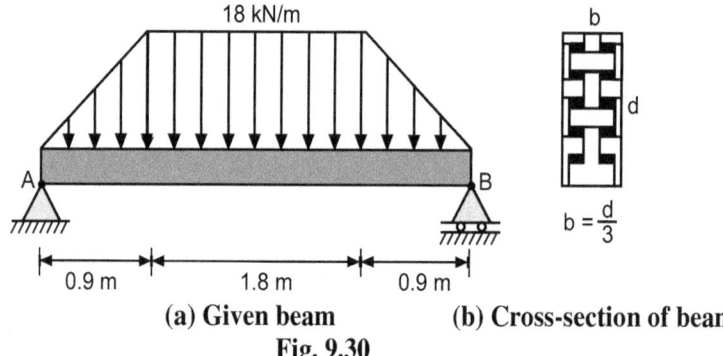

(a) Given beam  (b) Cross-section of beam
Fig. 9.30

**Solution :** (i) Analysis of beam :

$$V_A = V_B = \frac{1}{2} \text{ (Total load)}$$
$$= \frac{1}{2} \{(3.6 + 1.8)/2 \times 18\}$$
$$= 24.3 \text{ kN}$$
$$\therefore \quad SF_{max} = 24.3 \text{ kN}$$
$$BM_{max \text{ (at centre)}} = 24.3 \times 1.8 - (1/2 \times 0.9 \times 18)(0.9 + 0.9/3)$$
$$- (0.9 \times 18)(0.45)$$
$$= 26.73 \text{ kN-m}$$

(ii) For cross-section of beam :

$$I = bd^3/12 = d^4/36$$
$$y_{max} = d/2$$

(iii) Design for bending :

$$\frac{M}{I} = \frac{\sigma}{y}$$
$$\frac{26.73 \times 10^6}{d^4/36} = \frac{12}{d/2}$$
$$\therefore \quad d = 342.26 \text{ mm}$$

(iv) Design for shear :

$$\tau_{max} = 1.5\{S/bd\}$$
$$0.9 = 1.5\{(24.3 \times 10^3)/(d^2/3)\}$$
$$\therefore \quad d = 348.57 \text{ mm}$$
use, $\quad d = 349 \text{ mm and } b = 117 \text{ mm}$

**Example 9.21 :** A wooden beam of rectangular cross-section is simply supported and uniformly loaded. The height of the beam is 200 mm, and the allowable stresses in bending and shear are 8.2 MPa and 1.0 MPa respectively. Determine the span length L below which the shear stress governs the permissible load and above which the bending stress governs.

**Solution :** (i) Shear design :

$$\tau_{max} = 1.5\{S/bd\}$$
$$1 = 1.5\{(wL/2)\,10^3/200\,b\}$$
$$\therefore \quad wL/b = 0.267 \quad \ldots(i)$$

(ii) Flexure design :

$$\sigma = 6M/bd^2$$
$$8.2 = (6 \times wL^2/8)\,10^6/b \times (200)^2$$
$$wL^2/b = 0.437 \quad \ldots(ii)$$

Dividing equation (ii) by (i),

$$L = 1.636 \text{ m}$$

**Example 9.22 :** A beam is constructed of two beams 50 mm × 250 mm in cross-section that are attached by two 25 × 250 mm boards as shown in Fig. 9.31. The boards are nailed to the beams at a longitudinal spacing of 100 mm. If each nail has an allowable shear force of 1300 N, what is the maximum permissible shear force V ?

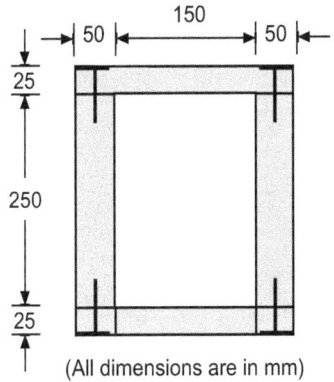

Fig. 9.31

**Solution :** (i) $\quad I = 250 \times 300^3/12 - 150 \times 250^3/12$
$$= 367.18 \times 10^6 \text{ mm}^4$$

(ii) $\quad (SA\,\bar{y}/I)\,p = 2 \text{ (Shear strength of nail)}$
$$S \times (250 \times 25)(137.5) \times 100/367.18 \times 10^6 = 2 \times 1.3$$
$$\therefore \quad S = 11.1 \text{ kN}$$

**Example 9.23 :** The beam section is as shown in Fig. 9.32 is subjected to the shear force of 35 kN. Determine the magnitude of shear stress at important points and plot the same. Also determine average stress.

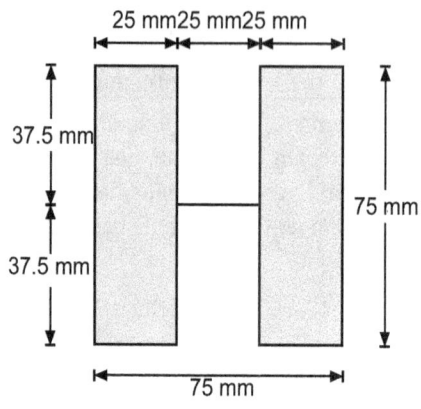

Fig. 9.32

**Data** : As shown in Fig. 9.32, S = 35 kN
**Required** : Shear stress distribution, average stress.
**Concept** : Standard formulae.

**Solution** :
$$\bar{y} = \frac{\left(75 \times 75 \times 37.5 - 25 \times 37.5 \times \frac{37.5}{2}\right)}{(75 \times 75 - 25 \times 37.5)}$$

= 41.25 mm from top

$$I = \frac{75 \times 75^3}{12} - \frac{25 \times 37.5^3}{12} - 25 \times 37.5 \times \left(41.25 - \frac{37.5}{2}\right)^2$$

= 2.05 × 10⁶ mm⁴

Shear stress analysis :

$$\tau_{A-A} = \tau_{D-D} = 0$$

$$\tau_{B-B} = \frac{SA\bar{y}}{IB}$$

$$A\bar{y} = 2 \times 25 \times 37.5 \times \left(41.25 - \frac{37.5}{2}\right)$$

= 42.19 × 10³ mm³

$$\tau_{B-B} = \frac{35 \times 10^3 \times 42.19 \times 10^3}{2.05 \times 10^6 \times b}$$

$$\tau_{B-B} = \frac{720.32}{b}$$

$$\tau_{B-B \text{ just above}} = \frac{720.32}{75} = 14.41 \text{ N/mm}^2$$

$$\tau_{B-B \text{ just below}} = \frac{720.32}{75} = 9.60 \text{ N/mm}^2$$

$$\tau_{C-C} = \frac{SA\bar{y}}{Ib}$$

$$A\bar{y} = 75 \times (75 - 41.25) \times \frac{(75 - 41.25)}{2}$$

$$= 42.71 \times 10^3 \text{ mm}^3$$

$$\therefore \quad \tau_{C-C} = \frac{35 \times 10^3 \times 42.71 \times 10^3}{2.05 \times 10^6 \times 75}$$

$$= \mathbf{9.72 \text{ N/mm}^2}$$

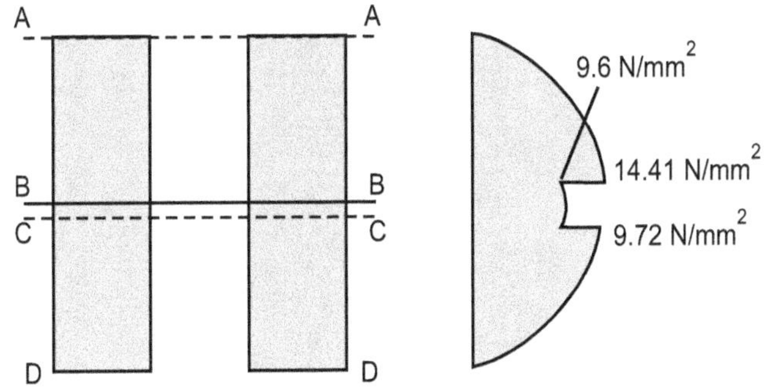

**Fig. 9.33 : Shear stress distribution diagram**

$$\text{Average stress} = \frac{\text{Force}}{\text{Area}}$$

$$= \frac{35 \times 10^3}{(75 \times 75 - 25 \times 37.5)} = \mathbf{7.47 \text{ N/mm}^2}$$

**Example 9.24 :** A steel beam of I section, 20 mm deep and 160 mm wide has 16 mm thick flanges and 10 mm thick web. The beam is subjected to a shear force of 200 kN. Determine the stress distribution over the beam section if the web of the beam is kept horizontal as shown in Fig. 9.34.

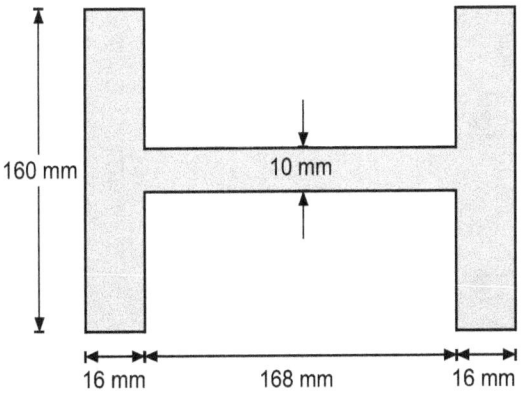

Fig. 9.34

**Data** : As shown in Fig. 9.34, S = 200 kN

**Required** : Stress distribution diagram.

**Concept** : Standard formula.

**Solution** :
$$I = \frac{2 \times 16 \times 160^3}{12} + \frac{168 \times 10^3}{12}$$
$$= 10.94 \times 10^6 \text{ mm}^4$$

**Shear stress analysis :**

$$\tau_{A-A} = \tau_{D-D} = 0$$

$$\tau_{B-B} = \frac{S A \bar{y}}{Ib}$$

$$A\bar{y} = 2 \times 75 \times 16 \times \left(80 - \frac{75}{2}\right) = 102 \times 10^3 \text{ mm}^3$$

$$\tau_{B-B} = \frac{200 \times 10^3 \times 102 \times 10^3}{10.94 \times 10^6 \, b}$$

$$= \frac{1864.72}{b}$$

$$\tau_{B-B \text{ just above}} = \frac{1864.72}{2 \times 16} = 58.27 \text{ N/mm}^2$$

$$\tau_{B-B \text{ just below}} = \frac{1864.72}{200} = 9.32 \text{ N/mm}^2$$

$$\tau_{C-C} = A\bar{y} = 2 \times 80 \times 16 \times 40 + 168 \times 5 \times (5/2)$$
$$= 104500 \text{ mm}^2$$

$$\tau_{C-C} = \frac{200 \times 10^3 \times 104.5 \times 10^3}{10.94 \times 10^6 \times 200} = \mathbf{9.55 \text{ N/mm}^2}$$

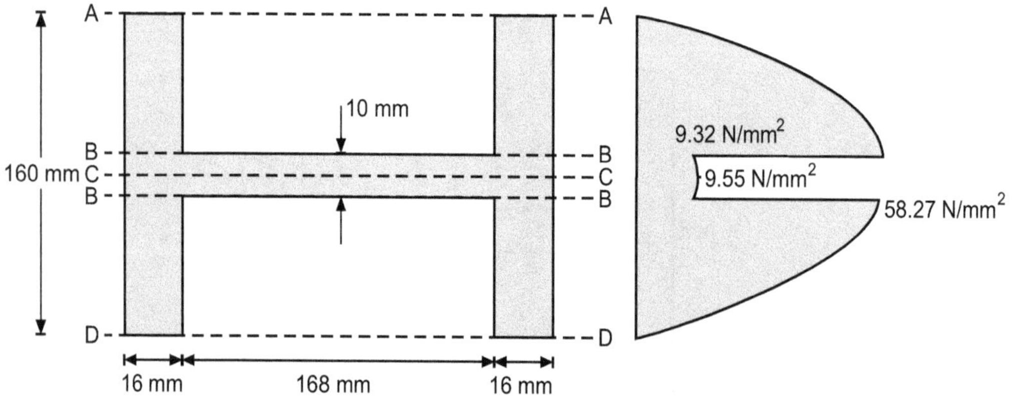

**Fig. 9.35 : Shear stress distribution diagram**

**Example 9.25 :** For beam and loading shown in Fig. 9.36, consider section n-n and determine :

(i) The largest shearing stress in that section.

(ii) The shearing stress at point a.

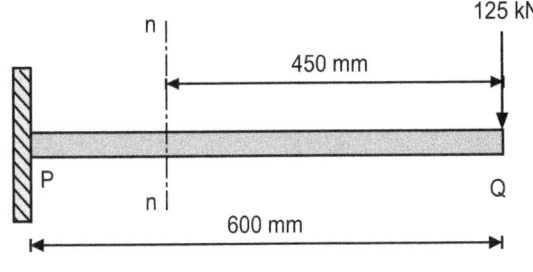
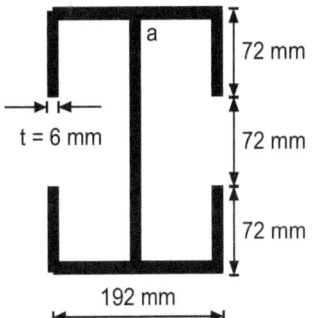

**Fig. 9.36**

**Data** : As shown in Fig. 9.36

**Required** : Largest shearing stress and shearing stress at point a.

**Concept** : Standard formula.

**Solution** :
$$I_{xx} = \frac{4 \times 6 \times (72)^3}{12} + 4 \times 6 \times 72 \times (108-36)^2 + \frac{2 \times 192 \times 6^3}{12}$$

$$+ 2 \times 192 \times 6 \times (108-3)^2 + \frac{6 \times 204^3}{12}$$

$$= 746.5 \times 10^3 + 8.96 \times 10^6 + 6912 + 25.4 \times 10^6 + 4.24 \times 10^6$$

$$= 39.35 \times 10^6$$

$$A\bar{y} = 2 \times 72 \times 6 \times (108-36) + 192 \times 6 \times (108-3) + 6 \times 102 \times (102/2)$$

$$= 214.38 \times 10^3$$

$$\tau_{max} = \frac{VA\bar{y}}{Ib} = \frac{125 \times 10^3 \times 214.38 \times 10^3}{39.35 \times 10^6 \times 6} = 113.5 \text{ N/mm}^2$$

$$A\bar{y}_a = 192 \times 6 \times (108-3) = 120.96 \times 10^3$$

$$\tau_a = \frac{VA\bar{y}}{Ib} = \frac{125 \times 10^3 \times 120.96 \times 10^3}{39.35 \times 10^6 \times 6} = 64 \text{ N/mm}^2$$

**Example 9.26 :** A timber box of span 3 m carries a concentrated vertical load at mid span of 4 kN. The cross-section of beam is shown in Fig. 9.37. Each screw can transmit a shear force of 600 kN. Find out the spacing of the screws along the span.

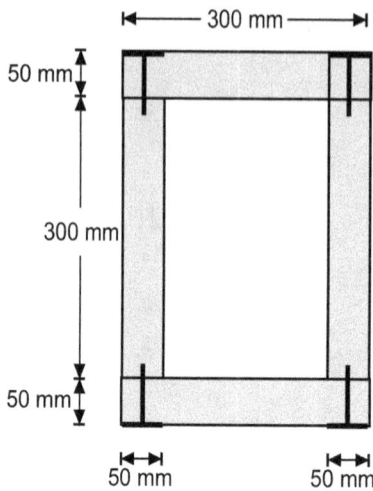

Fig. 9.37

**Data** : As shown in Fig. 9.37.

**Required** : Spacing of screws along span.

**Concept** : Standard formula.

**Solution** :
$$I_{xx} = \frac{300 \times (400)^3}{12} - \frac{200 \times (300)^3}{12} = 1.15 \times 10^9$$

$$\tau \times b = \frac{VA\bar{y}}{I} = \frac{2 \times 10^3 \times 300 \times 50 \times (200 - 25)}{1.15 \times 10^9}$$

$$= 4.57 \text{ N/mm}$$

Strength of nail = (Shear stress/mm) × Spacing of nail

$$2 \times F = \tau \times b \times s$$

$$s = \frac{2 \times 600}{4.57} = 262.58 \text{ mm}$$

Provided spacing of nail = **260 mm**

## EXERCISE

1. A circular pipe 80 mm external diameter and 60 mm internal diameter is subjected to a shear force of 30 kN at a certain section. Calculate the intensity of maximum shear stress. (26.92 MPa)

2. For a hollow circular section whose external diameter is twice the internal diameter, find the ratio of maximum shear stress to average shear stress. (1.866)

3. Fig. 9.38 shows the cross-section of beam. Draw shear stress distribution diagram if this cross-section is subjected to a shear force of 150 kN.

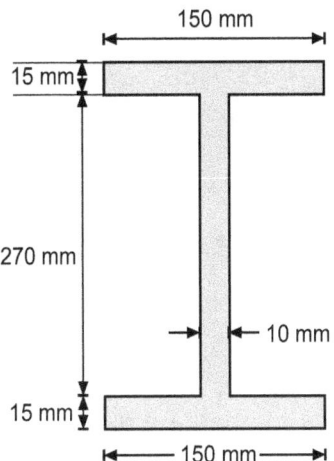

**Fig. 9.38**

(Shear stress at the junction of web and flange = 2.97 MPa, 44.58 MPa and $\tau_{max} = 57.25$ MPa)

4. For the cross-section of beam shown in Fig. 9.48, find the percentage of bending moment resisted by flanges and percentage of shear force resisted by web. (Bending moment resisted by flanges = 84.77%, shear force resisted by web = 95.48%)

5. Find the ratio of maximum shear stress to average shear stress for the cross-section of beam shown in Fig. 9.39.

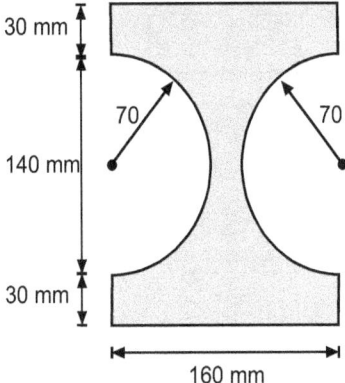

**Fig. 9.39**

6. Fig. 9.40 shows the cross-section of a beam. If this section is subjected to a shear force of 70 kN, draw the shear stress distribution diagram.

(Shear stress at the junction of web and flange = 6.67 MPa; 62.44 MPa; $\tau_{max} = 79.56$ MPa)

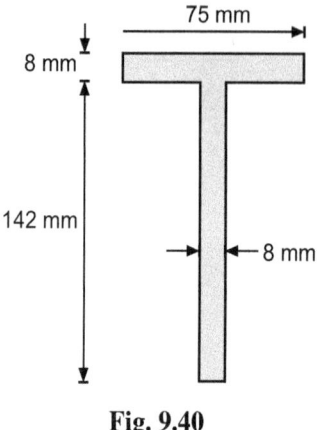

Fig. 9.40

7. Fig. 9.41 shows the cross-section of a beam. If this cross-section is subjected to a shear force of 15 kN, draw shear stress distribution diagram and find the ratio of maximum shear stress to minimum shear stress.

(Shear stress at the junction of web and flange = 2.75 MPa; 13.23 MPa;

$\tau_{max}$ = 13.78 MPa, $\dfrac{\tau_{max}}{\tau_{avg}}$ = 2.206)

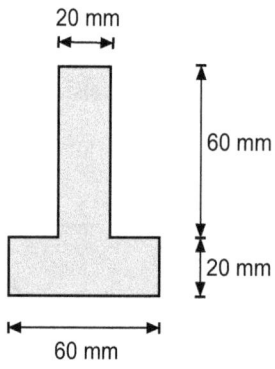

Fig. 9.41

8. Determine the shear stress distribution for the cross-section of a beam shown in Fig. 9.42 when subjected to shear force of 400 kN.

(Shear stress at the junction of flange and web = 4 MPa; 47.94 MPa; $\tau_{NA}$ = 4.168 MPa)

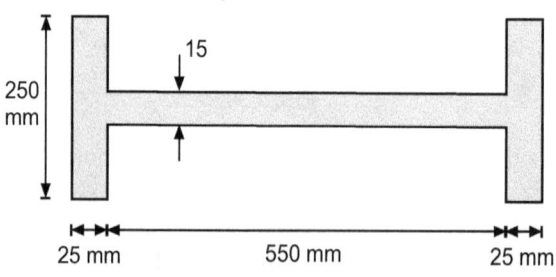

Fig. 9.42

9. A compound beam of cross-section 100 mm wide and 300 mm deep is made up from three uniform wooden sections 100 mm × 100 mm each glued together. Calculate the maximum intensity of UDL that a simply supported beam of 4 m span of above cross-section can carry if permissible horizontal shear per unit length of glued joint is 7 N/mm. (0.7876 kN/m)

10. Fig. 9.43 shows the cross-section of beam made out of five wooden planks glued together. A simply supported beam of the given cross-section is carrying UDL of 5 kN/m over 2 m span. (i) Find the maximum bending stress. (ii) What should be the strength of the glued joint ? (iii) What is the percentage contribution of the plank B towards the moment of resistance at 0.5 m from the support. (iv) What is their contribution in resisting shear at the same section ? (Maximum bending stress = 4.34 MPa; strength of glued joint = 38.88 N/mm; percentage contribution of B = 28.96% towards moment and 19.1% towards shear)

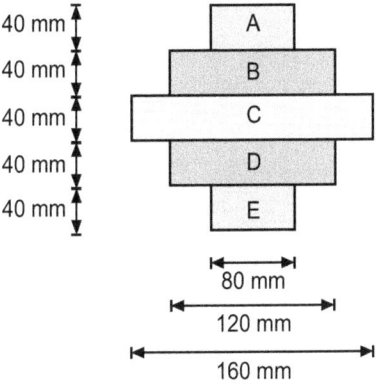

Fig. 9.43

11. A simply supported beam AB of span 8 m carries UDL of 25 kN/m over the entire span. The beam is also subjected to clockwise couple of 75 kNm at centre. Check the safety of section for flexure and shear with following data : (i) Maximum flexural stress in tension and compression = 150 MPa (ii) Maximum shear stress = 100 MPa.

$(I_{XX} = 8.71 \times 10^8$ mm$^4$, $SF_{max} = 109.375$ kN, $BM_{max} = 237.5$ kN.m

$\sigma_{b, max} = 93$ MPa $< 150$ MPa, $\tau_{max} = 17.81$ MPa $< 100$ MPa.

∴ Safe in flexure and shear).

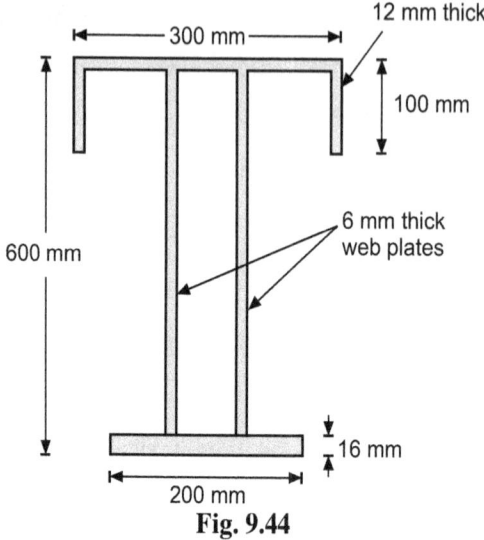

**Fig. 9.44**

# Unit – V

# CHAPTER TEN

# TORSION

## 10.1 INTRODUCTION

In this chapter, study is aimed at evaluation of stresses and deformation within elastic range due to torque applied on solid and hollow circular shafts. In practice, members that transmit torque, such as shafts of motors or power equipments etc. are predominantly circular or tubular in cross-section. Hence the scope is restricted to circular sections only. Various situations for statically determinate and indeterminate shafts subjected to pure torque are illustrated. But in practice, members are generally subjected to bending and torsion or bending, torsion and axial force which involve evaluation of stresses and strains due to each of these actions and then by using principle of superposition, resultant stresses are obtained. Evaluation of principal stresses and strains for such combined actions is of prime importance from practical design point of view.

## 10.2 BASICS OF TORSION

Torsion is defined as the *resultant moment on any one side of the section about longitudinal or polar axis of the member*. It is also called as torque or torsional moment or twisting moment.

Deformation corresponding to torque is rotation about polar axis called as twist. Thus, various cross-sections of shaft subjected to torque tend to rotate relatively with respect to each other; about polar axis which developes shear stresses normal to shaft within elastic limit, magnitude of angle of twist and shear stresses are proportional to the magnitude of torque section is subjected to.

## 10.3 METHOD OF SECTION

For analysis of members subjected to torques, the basic approach of method of section is used. First the system as a whole is examined for equilibrium. Section is considered perpendicular to the axis of the member and then equilibrium of any one side of the section is examined. Internal torque necessary for equilibrium of isolated part on any one side of the section is then evaluated by using equation of statics viz. $\sum M$ @ polar axis = 0. This is illustrated in following example :

**Note :** Sign convention

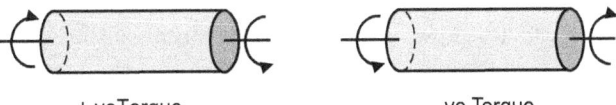

+ veTorque   − ve Torque

**Fig. 10.1 : Sign convention**

Consider a shaft ABC subjected to torques $T_A = 30$ kNm, $T_B = 80$ kNm and $T_C = 50$ kNm as shown in Fig. 10.2 (a). Let, it be required to find torque for portions AB and BC. Consider sections 1-1 and 2-2 in segments AB and BC respectively as shown.

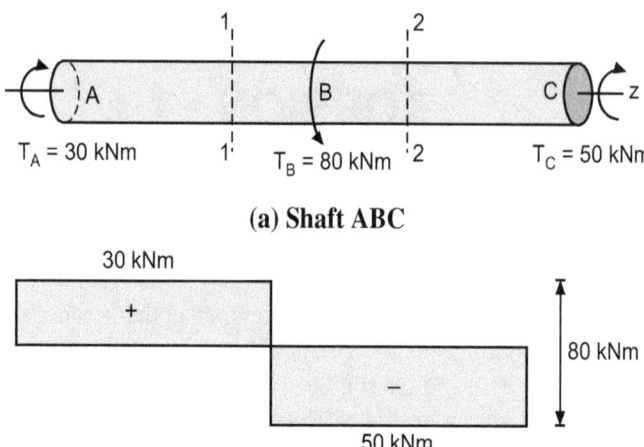

(a) Shaft ABC

(b) Torsional moment diagram

Fig. 10.2

$\sum M_z$ on LHS of section 1-1 = 30 kNm, OR

$\sum M_z$ on RHS of section 1-1 = $-50 + 80 = 30$ kNm

$\sum M_z$ on LHS of section 2-2 = $30 - 80 = -50$ kNm OR

$\sum M_z$ on RHS of section 2-2 = $-50$ kNm

Thus, the torque of 30 kNm is constant in portion AB and torque of – 50 kNm is constant in portion BC. It should be noted that, torque just to the left of cross-section B is + 30 kNm and just to the right of cross-section B is – 50 kNm.

### 10.3.1 Torsional Moment Diagram

It is the diagram which shows variation of torsional moment along the length of member. With above discussion, torsional moment diagram for the shaft ABC is drawn as shown in Fig. 10.2 (b).

**Note :** There is a vertical drop or rise in torsional moment diagram at a section of application of torque and magnitude of drop or rise in the diagram is equal to magnitude of torque acting at that section.

Above example illustrates drawing of torsional moment diagram for shaft subjected to concentrated torques. However, torque can be uniformly distributed over the length of a member as shown in Fig. 10.3 (a). Torsional moment diagram for such a shaft will vary linearly as shown in Fig. 10.3 (b).

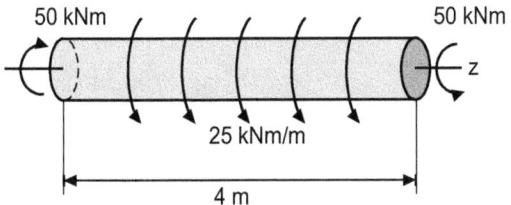

**(a) Uniformly distributed torque on a member**

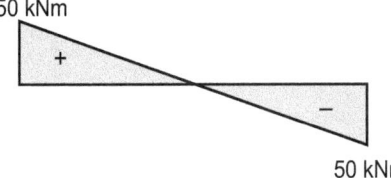

**(b) Torsional moment diagram**

**Fig. 10.3**

However, intensity of torque along the length of member can be varying. Such situations are not discussed in the present text.

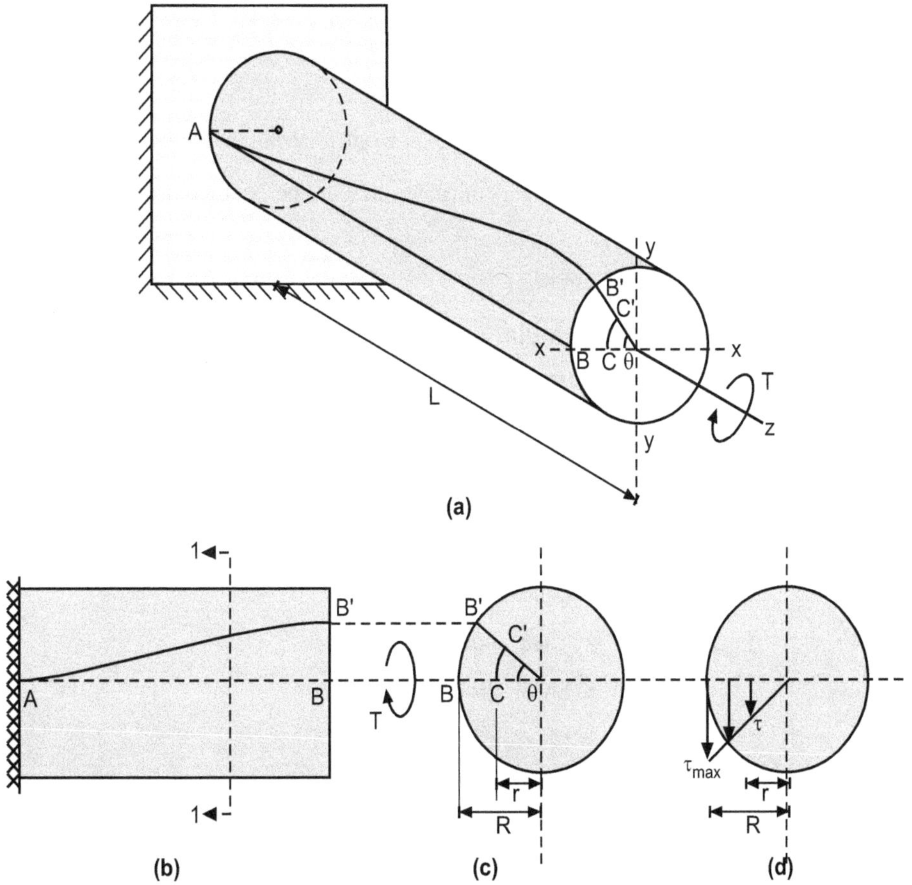

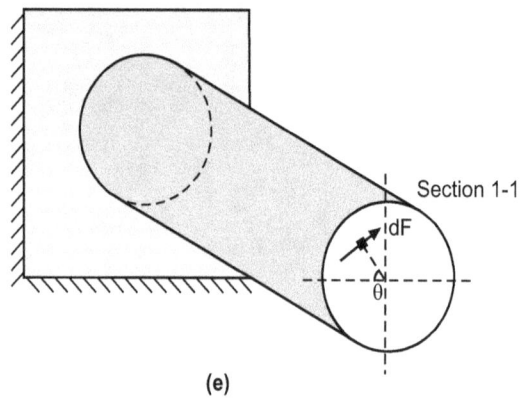

(a) Shaft subjected to torque
(b) Side view of shaft
(c) Angular deformation in cross-section
(d) Shear stress variation over the cross-section
(e) Section 1-1

**Fig. 10.4**

## 10.4 THEORY OF TORSION

### 10.4.1 Assumptions in Deriving the Torsion Formulae

(i) Plane sections remain plane and do not warp.

(ii) Stresses do not exceed the limit of proportionality.

(iii) Radial lines remain radial after twisting.

(iv) Material is elastic and obeys Hook's law.

i.e. Shear stress at any point is proportional to shear strain at that point.

(v) Shaft is loaded by twisting couples in planes that are perpendicular to the axis of the shaft.

(vi) Circular sections remain circular.

### 10.4.2 Derivation of Torsion Formula

Symbols :
$T$ = Torsional moment
$L$ = Length of shaft
$R$ = Radius of shaft
$r$ = Radial distance
$\theta$ = Angle of twist
$G$ = Shear modulus
$\tau$ = Shear stress
$\tau_{max}$ = Maximum shear stress
$J$ = Polar moment of inertia
$T_a$ = Average torque
$P$ = Power transmitted by shaft

Consider a circular shaft subjected to pure torque as shown in Fig. 10.4 (a). Imagine the shaft to consist of infinite number of circular laminas which individually are rigid and joined to each other by elastic fibres. Thus, due to the application of torque each lamina rotates with respect to each other.

Consider now any internal fibre located at radial distance 'r' from origin. The deformation of such a fibre is marked by CC' in the Fig. 10.4 (c). It should be noted that deformation is maximum at outermost periphery marked by BB' and zero at the centre of the shaft. Thus, axis passing through centre of the shaft and normal to the cross-section is neutral axis (polar axis). It is clearly seen from Fig. 10.4 that deformation of a fibre is directly proportional to its distance from polar axis and hence the stress. The shear stress variation over the cross-section when loaded within elastic limit is also shown in Fig. 10.4 (a).

Thus, $\qquad BB' = R\theta \quad \text{and} \quad CC' = r\theta \qquad$ ... (10.1)

Shear deformation per unit length of fibre at a distance 'r'

$$= \frac{CC'}{L} = \frac{r\theta}{L}$$

∴ $\qquad$ Shear strain $= \gamma = \dfrac{r\theta}{L}$

$\qquad$ Shear stress $= \tau = \dfrac{Gr\theta}{L} = \left(\dfrac{G\theta}{L}\right) r \qquad$ ... (10.2)

*"Thus, shear stress along any radius varies linearly with the radial distance of the shaft."*

∴ $\qquad \dfrac{\tau}{r} = \dfrac{\tau_{max}}{R} = \dfrac{G\theta}{L} \qquad$ ... (10.3)

**Torsional Resistance :**

Consider FBD of section 1-1 as shown in Fig. 10.4 (e). An elementary area dA is considered at a distance r from axis of the shaft on which shear stress is equal to $\tau$. By considering area to be infinitely small, we can assume stress to be uniform over area dA. Shear force acting on elementary area $= dF = dA \cdot \tau$. This force dF must be normal to the radius vector as it has to resist the applied torque as efficiently as possible so that energy is conserved.

Small twisting moment produced by dF about polar axis $= dT = dF \cdot r$

∴ $$T = \int_0^R dF \cdot r$$

$$= \int_0^R (dA \cdot \tau) \, r$$

$$= \int_0^R dA \cdot \dfrac{G\theta}{L} \cdot r^2$$

$$= \dfrac{G\theta}{L} \int_0^R dA \cdot r^2$$

∴ $$T = \frac{G\theta}{L} J \qquad \ldots (10.4)$$

Since $$J = \int_0^R dA \cdot r^2 = \text{polar moment of inertia of cross-section}$$

From equations (10.3) and (10.4),

$$\frac{T}{J} = \frac{\tau_{max}}{R} = \frac{G\theta}{L} \qquad \ldots (10.5)$$

## 10.5 IMPORTANT TERMS

### 10.5.1 Torsional Stiffness

*It is the torque required to produce unit angle of twist.*

Thus, Torsional stiffness $= \dfrac{GJ}{L}$

Unit of torsional stiffness is Nm/radian.

### 10.5.2 Torsional Flexibility

*It is the angle of twist produced by unit torque applied.*

Thus, Torsional flexibility $= \dfrac{L}{GJ}$

Unit of torsional flexibility is radian/Nm.

It should be noted that stiffness and flexibility coefficients are reciprocal of each other.

### 10.5.3 Torsional Rigidity

*Product of shear modulus and polar moment of inertia of cross-section is called as torsional rigidity (GJ).*

Unit of torsional rigidity is Nm².

### 10.5.4 Torsional Section Modulus

*Ratio of polar moment of inertia of cross-section to its radius is called as torsional section modulus (J/R).*

Unit of torsional section modulus is m³.

**Torsional section modulus for solid circular shaft :**

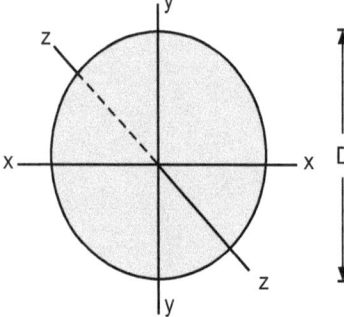

Fig. 10.5

$$I_{xx} = I_{yy} = \frac{\pi}{64} D^4$$

$$J = I_{zz} = I_{xx} + I_{yy}$$

$$= 2 \times \frac{\pi}{64} D^4$$

$$= \frac{\pi}{32} D^4$$

$$R = \frac{D}{2}$$

∴ $$\frac{J}{R} = \frac{\pi}{32} D^4 \times \frac{2}{D} = \frac{\pi}{16} D^3 \ldots (10.6)$$

## Torsional section modulus for hollow circular shaft :

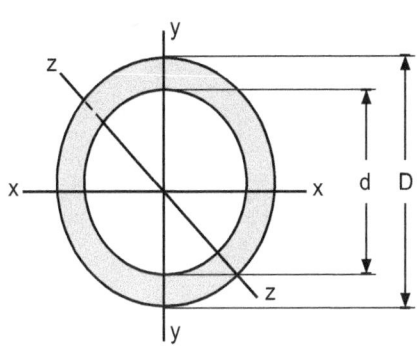

Fig. 10.6

$$I_{xx} = I_{yy} = \frac{\pi}{64}(D^4 - d^4)$$

$$J = I_{zz} = I_{xx} + I_{yy}$$

$$= 2 \times \frac{\pi}{64}(D^4 - d^4)$$

$$= \frac{\pi}{32}(D^4 - d^4)$$

$$R = \frac{D}{2}$$

$$\therefore \quad \frac{J}{R} = \frac{\pi}{32}(D^4 - d^4) \times \frac{2}{D}$$

$$= \frac{\pi}{16D}(D^4 - d^4) \quad \ldots (10.7)$$

### 10.5.5 Power Transmitted by Shaft

*It is the product of average torque and corresponding angle turned per unit duration of time.*

$$\text{Power} = \text{Average torque} \times \text{Angle of rotation/sec.}$$

$$= T_a \times \frac{2\pi N}{60}$$

$$\therefore \quad P = \text{Power} = \frac{2\pi N T_a}{60} \quad \ldots (10.8)$$

where N = No. of revolutions per minute (RPM). Unit of power is Nm/s or watts.

However, power can also be expressed in Horse power (H.P.) unit.

$$1 \text{ H.P.} = \frac{2\pi N T_a}{4500} \quad \ldots (10.9)$$

## SOLVED EXAMPLES

**Example 10.1 :** Find power transmitted by a shaft having 60 mm diameter rotating at 150 rpm, if maximum permissible shear stress = 80 MPa.

**Data :** D = 60 mm; N = 150 rpm; $\tau_{max}$ = 80 MPa

**Required :** Power transmitted.

**Concept :** Find the value of torque based on shear stress criteria and then use equation of power.

**Solution :** (i) Geometric properties :

$$J = \frac{\pi}{32} \cdot D^4 = \frac{\pi}{32}(60)^4 = 1.272 \times 10^6 \text{ mm}^3$$

$$R = \frac{D}{2} = \frac{60}{2} = 30 \text{ mm}$$

(ii) Torque corresponding to shear stress :

$$T = \frac{J}{R} \cdot \tau_{max}$$

$$= \frac{1.272 \times 10^6}{30} \times 80$$

$$= 3.392 \times 10^6 \text{ N.mm}$$

$$= 3.392 \times 10^3 \text{ N.m.}$$

(iii) Power transmitted :

$$P = \frac{2\pi N T_a}{60}$$

$$= \frac{2 \times \pi \times 150 \times 3.392 \times 10^3}{60}$$

$$= 53281.41 \text{ W}$$

$$= \mathbf{53.281 \text{ kW}}$$

**Example 10.2 :** A hollow circular shaft of 150 mm external diameter; thickness of metal 20 mm is rotating at 200 rpm. The angle of twist on 3 m length was found to be 0.7°. Calculate the power transmitted and maximum shear stress induced in the material. Assume G = 80 GPa.

**Data** : $D = 150$ mm ; $t = 20$ mm ; $N = 200$ rpm ; $\theta = 0.7° = 0.0122$ rad.; $G = 80$ GPa ; $L = 3000$ mm.

**Required** : Power transmitted (P) and maximum shear stress ($\tau_{max}$).

**Concept** : Find torque based on angle of twist criteria and then use equation of power.

**Solution** : (i) Geometric properties :

$$d = \text{Internal diameter of shaft}$$

$$= 150 - 2 \times 20$$

$$= 110 \text{ mm}$$

$$J = \frac{\pi}{32} (D^4 - d^4) = \frac{\pi}{32} [(150)^4 - (110)^4]$$

$$= 35.32 \times 10^6 \text{ mm}^4$$

$$R = \frac{150}{2} = 75 \text{ mm}$$

$$\therefore \quad \frac{J}{R} = \frac{35.32 \times 10^6}{75} = 471.03 \times 10^3 \text{ mm}^3$$

(ii) Torque corresponding to angle of twist :

$$T = \left(\frac{G \cdot \theta}{L}\right) \cdot J$$

$$= \frac{80 \times 10^3 \times 0.0122}{3000} \times 35.32 \times 10^6$$

$$= 11.49 \times 10^6 \text{ Nmm}$$

$$= 11.49 \times 10^3 \text{ Nm}$$

(iii) Power transmitted (P):

$$P = \frac{2\pi N T_a}{60} = \frac{2 \times \pi \times 200 \times 11.49 \times 10^3}{60}$$

$$= 240.66 \times 10^3 \text{ W}$$

$$= 240.66 \text{ kW}$$

(iv) Maximum shear stress ($\tau_{max}$):

$$\tau_{max} = \frac{T}{J/R} = \frac{11.49 \times 10^6}{471.03 \times 10^3}$$

$$= 24.39 \text{ MPa}$$

**Example 10.3**: A hollow circular shaft has external diameter of 100 mm and internal diameter of 80 mm. Find the safe power that can be transmitted if allowable shear stress is 100 MPa and maximum angle of twist is 3° for 2 m length. Take speed of shaft = 2.5 revolutions per second and maximum torque to exceed by mean torque by 20%. Take G = 80 GPa.

**Data**  : D = 100 mm ; d = 80 mm ; $\tau_{max}$ = 100 MPa ; $\theta$ = 3° = 0.0524 rad ; L = 2000 mm ; N = 2 r.p.s. ; G = 80 GPa ; T = 1.2 $T_a$

**Required** : Safe power.

**Concept** : Safe torque is the least of that obtained from shear stress and angle of twist criteria.

**Solution** : (i) Geometric properties:

$$J = \frac{\pi}{32} (D^4 - d^4)$$

$$= \frac{\pi}{32} [(100)^4 - (80)^4]$$

$$= 5.796 \times 10^6 \text{ mm}^4$$

$$R = \frac{100}{2} = 50 \text{ mm}$$

$$\therefore \quad \frac{J}{R} = \frac{5.796 \times 10^6}{50} = 115.93 \times 10^3 \text{ mm}^3$$

(ii) Torque based on strength criteria:

$$T = \left(\frac{J}{R}\right) \cdot \tau_{max}$$

$$= 115.93 \times 10^3 \times 100$$

$$= 11.59 \times 10^6 \text{ Nmm} \quad \ldots (A)$$

(iii) Torque based on stiffness criteria:

$$T = \left(\frac{G\theta}{L}\right) J$$

$$= \frac{80 \times 10^3 \times 0.0524}{2000} \times 5.796 \times 10^6$$

$$= 12.15 \times 10^6 \text{ Nmm} \quad \ldots (B)$$

(iv) Safe maximum torque (T) :

$$T = \text{Least of (A) and (B)}$$
$$= 11.59 \times 10^6 \text{ Nmm}$$
$$= 11.59 \times 10^3 \text{ Nm}$$

∴ Safe average torque, $T_a = \dfrac{T}{1.2}$

$$= \dfrac{11.59 \times 10^3}{1.2}$$
$$= 9.66 \times 10^3 \text{ Nm}$$

(v) Safe power (P) :

$$P = 2\pi N\, T_a \quad \ldots \text{(Note : N = 2.5 revolutions per second)}$$
$$= 2\pi \times 2.5 \times 9.66 \times 10^3$$
$$= 151.74 \times 10^3 \text{ W}$$
$$= \mathbf{151.74 \text{ kW}}$$

**Example 10.4 :** A steel bar 38 mm diameter and 450 mm long, when tested under an axial tensile load of 100 kN found to stretch by 0.2 mm. The same bar when subjected to a torque of 1.27 kNm is found to twist by 1.922°. Determine the values of four elastic constants.

**Data** : $D = 38$ mm; $L = 450$ mm; $P = 100$ kN; $\delta L = 0.2$ mm; $T = 1.27$ kNm; $\theta = 1.922°$.

**Required** : E; G; K and μ.

**Concept** : Standard formulae,

**Solution** : (i) Geometric properties :

$$A = \dfrac{\pi}{4}(D)^2 = \dfrac{\pi}{4}(38)^2 = 1134.12 \text{ mm}^2$$

$$J = \dfrac{\pi}{32}(D^4) = \dfrac{\pi}{32}(38)^4 = 204.7 \times 10^3 \text{ mm}^4$$

(ii) Modulus of elasticity (E)

$$\delta L = \dfrac{PL}{AE}$$

$$0.2 = \dfrac{100 \times 10^3 \times 450}{1134.12\, E}$$

∴ $$E = 198.39 \times 10^3$$
$$= \mathbf{198.39 \text{ GPa}}$$

(iii) Modulus of rigidity (G) :

$$\theta = \dfrac{TL}{GJ} \quad \therefore\quad 1.922 \times \dfrac{\pi}{180} = \dfrac{1.27 \times 10^6 \times 450}{G \times 204.7 \times 10^3}$$

∴ $$G = 83.23 \times 10^3 \text{ MPa} = \mathbf{83.23 \text{ GPa.}}$$

(iv) Poisson's ratio ($\mu$) :

$$E = 2G(1 + \mu)$$
$$198.39 = 2 \times 83.23 (1 + \mu)$$
$$\mu = \mathbf{0.19}$$

(v) Bulk modulus (K) :

$$E = 3K(1 - 2\mu)$$
$$198.39 = 3K(1 - 2 \times 0.19)$$
$$\therefore \quad K = \mathbf{106.66 \text{ GPa}}$$

**Example 10.5 :** A metal bar 16 mm $\phi$, subjected to a pull of 35 kN, elongates by 0.40 mm over a gauge length of 500 mm. In a torsion test on the same material, maximum shear stress of 45 MPa was measured on a bar of 40 mm $\phi$ and angle of twist over a length of 400 mm was measured to be 0.6°. Determine Poisson's ratio for the material.

**Data** : For axial pull : P = 35 kN ; $\delta L$ = 0.40 mm; D = 16 mm ; L = 500 mm
For torsion test : $\tau$ = 45 MPa; D = 40 mm; $\theta$ = 0.6° = 0.01047; L = 400 mm.

**Required** : Poisson's ratio ($\mu$)

**Concept** : Standard formulae.

**Solution** : (i) For axial pull :

$$\delta L = \frac{PL}{AE}$$

$$0.40 = \frac{35 \times 10^3 \times 500}{\frac{\pi}{4}(16)^2 \times E}$$

$$\therefore \quad E = 217.59 \times 10^3 \text{ MPa}$$
$$= \mathbf{217.59 \text{ GPa}}$$

(ii) For torsion test : $\dfrac{\tau}{R} = \dfrac{G\theta}{L}$

$$\therefore \quad G = \frac{\tau L}{R\theta}$$

$$= \frac{45 \times 400}{0.01047 \times 20}$$

$$= 85.96 \times 10^3 \text{ MPa}$$
$$= \mathbf{85.96 \text{ GPa}}$$

(iii) Poisson's ratio ($\mu$) : $E = 2G(1 + \mu)$

$$217.59 = 2 \times 85.96 (1 + \mu)$$
$$\mu = \mathbf{0.266}$$

## 10.6 DESIGN OF SHAFTS

For the design of circular shafts (solid or hollow), following are the two criteria :
(i) **Strength criteria :** It means, with the designed diameter, shear stress shall not exceed the allowable value.
(ii) **Stiffness criteria :** It means, with the designed diameter, angle of twist shall not exceed the allowable value.

Diameter of the shaft is obtained using above two conditions and greater of the two is to be used.

## 10.7 SOLID AND HOLLOW CIRCULAR SHAFTS FOR THE SAME TORQUE

When solid shaft is replaced by hollow shaft, there is saving in material. This is due to the fact that for solid shaft, material very near to the polar axis contributes very little for resisting the applied torque, while the same material placed away from polar axis provides greater polar moment of inertia and section modulus in case of hollow shaft $\left( \because J = \int_0^R dar^2 \right)$.

However, the hollow circular shaft requires more space to accommodate as compared to solid shaft.

**Example 10.6 :** Design the diameter of solid circular shaft to transmit 50 kW power rotating at 150 rpm. Maximum torque is likely to exceed mean torque by 25%. Permissible shear stress = 60 MPa. Also calculate angle of twist for 2 m length. Assume G = 85 GPa.

**Data** : $P = 50$ kW ; $N = 150$ r.p.m. ; $T = 1.25 \, T_a$ ;
$\tau_{max} = 60$ MPa ; $L = 2000$ mm ; $G = 85$ GPa.

**Required :** Diameter of shaft (D) and angle of twist ($\theta$).
**Concept :** Design based on strength criteria.
**Solution :** (i) Average torque ($T_a$) :

We have, $$P = \frac{2\pi N \, T_a}{60}$$

$$50 \times 10^3 = \frac{2\pi \times 150 \times T_a}{60}$$

$$T_a = 3183.1 \text{ Nm}$$
$$= 3183.1 \times 10^3 \text{ Nmm}$$

(ii) Maximum torque (T), $T = 1.25 \, T_a$
$$= 1.25 \times 3183.1 \times 10^3$$
$$= 3978.87 \times 10^3 \text{ Nmm}$$

(iii) Diameter based on strength criteria :
$$T = \frac{J}{R} \cdot \tau_{max}$$

$$3978.87 \times 10^3 = \frac{\pi}{16} (D)^3 \times 60$$

$\therefore$ $D = 69.64$ mm, say 70 mm.

(iv) Angle of twist ($\theta$) :

$$\frac{T}{J} = \frac{G\theta}{L} \quad \therefore \quad \theta = \frac{TL}{GJ}$$

where
$$J = \frac{\pi}{32}(70)^4 = 2.357 \times 10^6 \text{ mm}^4$$

$$\therefore \quad \theta = \frac{3978.87 \times 10^3 \times 2000}{85 \times 10^3 \times 2.357 \times 10^6}$$

$$= 0.0397 \text{ rad.}$$

$$\theta = \mathbf{2.27^o}$$

**Example 10.7 :** A steel shaft of solid circular cross-section has to transmit 200 kW at 180 r.p.m. The maximum shear stress is not to exceed 50 MPa and the angle of twist must not be more than 1.6° in a length of 2.6 m. Design suitable diameter of shaft. Take G = 80 GPa.

**Data** : P = 200 kW; N = 180 r.p.m.; $\tau_{max}$ = 50 MPa;
$\theta$ = 1.6° = 0.0279 rad; L = 2600 mm; G = 80 GPa.

**Required** : Design of cross-section of shaft.

**Concept** : Design based on strength and stiffness criteria. Diameter to be used is greater of that obtained from above two conditions.

**Solution** : (i) Average torque ($T_a$) :

We have,
$$P = \frac{2\pi N T_a}{60}$$

$$200 \times 10^3 = \frac{2\pi \times 180 \times T_a}{60}$$

$$T_a = 10.61 \times 10^3 \text{ Nm}$$

Assuming maximum torque, $T = T_a = 10.61 \times 10^3$ Nm
$$= 10.61 \times 10^6 \text{ Nmm}$$

(Note : Relation between maximum torque and average torque is not given.)

(ii) Diameter based on strength criteria :

$$T = \left(\frac{J}{R}\right) \cdot \tau_{max}$$

$$10.61 \times 10^6 = \left(\frac{\pi}{16} \cdot D^3\right) \cdot 50$$

$\therefore \quad D = 102.62$ mm ... (1)

(iii) Diameter based on stiffness criteria :

$$\frac{T}{J} = \frac{G\theta}{L} \quad \therefore \quad J = \frac{TL}{G\theta}$$

$$\frac{\pi}{32} \cdot D^4 = \frac{10.61 \times 10^6 \times 2600}{80 \times 10^3 \times 0.0279}$$

$\therefore \quad D = 105.92$ mm ... (2)

$\therefore \quad D = \mathbf{105.92}$ mm

**say 106 mm** (Greater of (1) and (2))

**Example 10.8 :** Design the cross-section of hollow shaft for which internal diameter is $\frac{3}{4}$ th of its external diameter to resist a torque of 1600 Nm, such that shear stress does not exceed 60 MPa and angle of twist does not exceed 2° for 1.8 m length. Assume G = 80 GPa.

**Data** : $d = \frac{3}{4} D$; T = 1600 Nm; $\tau_{max}$ = 60 MPa;

$\theta = 2° = 0.0349$ rad; L = 1800 mm; G = 80 GPa.

**Required** : Design of cross-section of shaft.

**Concept** : Same as Example (10.7).

**Solution** : (i) Diameter based on strength criteria :

$$T = \left(\frac{J}{R}\right) \tau_{max}$$

$$1600 \times 10^3 = \frac{\pi}{16 D} (D^4 - d^4) \, 60$$

$$1600 \times 10^3 = \frac{\pi}{16 D} \left[D^4 - \left(\frac{3}{4}D\right)^4\right] 60$$

$$D = 58.35 \text{ mm}$$

(ii) Diameter based on stiffness criteria :

$$\frac{T}{J} = \frac{G\theta}{L} \quad \therefore J = \frac{TL}{G\theta}$$

$$\frac{\pi}{32}(D^4 - d^4) = \frac{1600 \times 10^3 \times 1800}{80 \times 10^3 \times 0.0349}$$

$$\frac{\pi}{32}\left[D^4 - \left(\frac{3}{4}D\right)^4\right] = 1.031 \times 10^6$$

$$D = 62.61 \text{ mm}$$

$\therefore$ Use  D = 62.61 mm ≅ **63 mm**

and  $d = \frac{3}{4}(63) = 47.25$ mm ≅ **47 mm**

**Example 10.9 :** A hollow steel shaft 2.5 m long transmits a torque of 15 kNm. Total angle of twist is not to exceed 2.5° and permissible shear stress = 80 MPa. Determine inside and outside diameter of shaft. G = 82 GPa.

**Data** : L = 2500 mm; T = 15 kNm; $\theta = 2.5° = 0.0436$ rad; $\tau_{max}$ = 80 MPa; G = 82 GPa

**Required** : Design of cross-section of shaft.

**Concept** : Generally cross-section of shaft is designed for strength and stiffness criteria and dimensions to be provided are governed by greater of the requirement for above two conditions. For the design of hollow shaft, relation between external and internal diameter must be known to use the conventional procedure. In this example, this relation is not given.

**Solution :** (i) External diameter of shaft (D)

Using $\dfrac{\tau_{max}}{R} = \dfrac{G\theta}{L}$

$$\dfrac{80}{D/2} = \dfrac{82 \times 10^3 \times 0.0436}{2500}$$

∴ D = **111.9 mm say 112 mm.**

(ii) Polar M.I. of shaft :

$$\dfrac{T}{J} = \dfrac{G\theta}{L}$$

∴ $J = \dfrac{TL}{G\theta} = \dfrac{15 \times 10^6 \times 2500}{82 \times 10^3 \times 0.0436}$

$J = \mathbf{10.49 \times 10^6 \ mm^4}$

(iii) Internal diameter of shaft :

$$J = \dfrac{\pi}{32}(D^4 - d^4)$$

$10.49 \times 10^6 = \dfrac{\pi}{32}[(112)^4 - d^4]$ = **84.3 mm say 84 mm**

Thus; D = **112 mm and d = 84 mm**

(**Note :** Internal diameter shall be rounded off on lower side.)

**Example 10.10 :** A hollow shaft has 60 mm external diameter and 50 mm internal diameter. Determine the twisting moment it can resist if permissible shear stress is 100 MPa. Determine the diameter of solid circular shaft made of the same material which can transmit same twisting moment. Hence, compare their weights per metre length. Take G = 80 GPa.

**Data :** D = 60 mm; d = 50 mm for hollow shaft, $\tau_{max}$ = 100 MPa; G = 80 GPa.

**Required :** Twisting moment, Diameter of solid shaft; Comparison of weights.

**Concept :** Hollow shaft is economical as compared to solid shaft.

**Solution :** (i) Geometric properties :

For hollow shaft, $J = \dfrac{\pi}{32}(D^4 - d^4) = \dfrac{\pi}{32}[(60)^4 - (50)^4]$

$= 658.75 \times 10^3 \ mm^4$

$R = \dfrac{60}{2} = 30 \ mm$

∴ $\dfrac{J}{R} = \dfrac{658.75 \times 10^3}{30} = 21.96 \times 10^3 \ mm^3$

(ii) Torque based on shear stress (T) :

$T = \left(\dfrac{J}{R}\right)\tau_{max}$

$= 21.96 \times 10^3 \times 100$

$= \mathbf{2.196 \times 10^6 \ Nmm}$

(iii) Diameter of solid shaft ($D_1$) :

$$T = \left(\frac{J}{R}\right) \tau_{max}$$

$$2.196 \times 10^6 = \left(\frac{\pi}{16} D_1^3\right) 100$$

$$D_1 = 48.18 \text{ mm} \cong \mathbf{49 \text{ mm}}$$

(iv) Comparison of weights :

$$(A)_{solid} = \frac{\pi}{4} D_1^2 = \frac{\pi}{4} (49)^2 = \mathbf{1885.74 \text{ mm}^2}$$

$$(A)_{hollow} = \frac{\pi}{4}(D^2 - d^2) = \frac{\pi}{4}[(60)^2 - (50)^2] = \mathbf{863.94 \text{ mm}^2}$$

∴ $\dfrac{\text{Weight of solid shaft}}{\text{Weight of hollow shaft}} = \dfrac{(A)_{solid}}{(A)_{hollow}} = \dfrac{1885.74}{863.94} = \mathbf{2.18}$

**Example 10.11 :** Design diameter of solid shaft for resisting torque of 2500 Nm. Also design cross-section of hollow shaft made of same material assuming internal diameter as 0.7 times the external diameter for the same torque. Hence, comment on percentage saving in weight and shear stress for shaft. Assume allowable angle of twist 2° for 1 m length of both shafts. Take G = 80 GPa.

**Data** : T = 2500 Nm; d = 0.7 D for hollow shaft;
$\theta = 2° = 0.0349$ rad; L = 1000 mm; G = 80 GPa.
**Required** : Comparison of hollow and solid shaft.
**Concept** : Design of shafts based on stiffness criteria.
**Solution** : (i) Design of solid shaft :

Let $D_1$ = Diameter of solid shaft

$$\frac{T}{J} = \frac{G\theta}{L} \quad \therefore \quad J = \frac{TL}{G\theta}$$

∴ $\dfrac{\pi}{32} D_1^4 = \dfrac{2500 \times 10^3 \times 1000}{80 \times 10^3 \times 0.0349}$

$= 895.41 \times 10^3$ mm$^4$

∴ $D_1 = \mathbf{54.95 \text{ mm}}$

(ii) Design of hollow shaft :

$$J = \frac{TL}{G\theta}$$

∴ $\dfrac{\pi}{32}(D^4 - d^4) = 895.41 \times 10^3$ mm$^4$

$\dfrac{\pi}{32}[D^4 - (0.7 D)^4] = 895.41 \times 10^3$

D = **58.85 mm**

∴ d = **41.19 mm**

(iii) Comparison of weights :

$$A_s = \frac{\pi}{4}(D_1^2) = \frac{\pi}{4} \times (54.95)^2 = \mathbf{2.37 \times 10^3 \, mm^2}$$

$$A_h = \frac{\pi}{4}(D^2 - d^2) = \frac{\pi}{4}[(58.85)^2 - (41.19)^2]$$

$$= \mathbf{1.387 \times 10^3 \, mm^2}$$

∴ Percentage saving in weight $= \dfrac{A_s - A_h}{A_s} \times 100$

$$= \dfrac{(2.37 - 1.387) \times 10^3}{2.37 \times 10^3} \times 100$$

$$= \mathbf{41.47\,\%}$$

(iv) Comparison of shear stresses :

For solid shaft, $\dfrac{J}{R} = \dfrac{895.41 \times 10^3}{\frac{54.95}{2}} = 32.59 \times 10^3 \, mm^3$

$$\tau_s = \dfrac{T}{J/R} = \dfrac{2500 \times 10^3}{32.59 \times 10^3} = \mathbf{76.71 \, MPa}$$

For hollow shaft, $\dfrac{J}{R} = \dfrac{895.41 \times 10^3}{58.85/2}$

$$= 30.43 \times 10^3 \, mm^3$$

$$\tau_h = \dfrac{T}{J/R} = \dfrac{2500 \times 10^3}{30.43 \times 10^3} = \mathbf{82.15 \, MPa}$$

Thus; $\dfrac{\tau_s}{\tau_h} = \dfrac{76.71}{82.15} = 0.93$

∴ $\tau_s = 0.93\,\tau_h$

i.e. $\tau_h = 1.075\,\tau_s$

**Note :** For the same torque when solid and hollow shafts are designed from stiffness criteria, there is saving in weight when hollow shaft is used. However, shear stress developed for hollow shaft is of higher magnitude than that of solid shaft. If this stress of comparatively higher magnitude for hollow shaft is less than permissible stress, then only replacement of solid shaft by hollow shaft will be possible.

It should also be noted that for stress criteria of design, polar section modulii (J/R) of solid and hollow shafts are same; while for stiffness criteria of design, polar moment of inertia (J) of solid and hollow shafts are same.

**Example 10.12 :** Design diameter of solid shaft for resisting torque of 2500 Nm. Also design cross-section of hollow shaft made of same material assuming internal diameter as 0.7 times the external diameter for the same torque. Hence, comment on percentage saving in weight and angle of twist per unit length of shafts. Assume permissible shear stress = 60 MPa.

**Data** : $T = 2500$ Nm; $d = 0.7\,D$ for hollow shaft; $\tau_{max} = 60$ MPa.

**Required** : Comparison of hollow and solid shaft.

**Concept** : Design of shafts based on strength criteria.

**Solution** : (i) Design of solid shaft :

Let $D_1$ = Diameter of solid shaft

$$T = \left(\frac{J}{R}\right) \tau_{max}$$

$\therefore \quad 2500 \times 10^3 = \left[\frac{\pi}{16}(D_1^3)\right] 60$

$\therefore \quad D_1 = \textbf{59.64 mm}$

(ii) Design of hollow shaft :

$$T = \left(\frac{J}{R}\right) \tau_{max}$$

$2500 \times 10^3 = \dfrac{\pi}{16\,D}(D^4 - d^4) \times 60$

$\quad\quad\quad\quad\quad = \dfrac{\pi}{16\,D}(D^4 - (0.7\,D)^4) \times 60$

$\therefore \quad D = \textbf{65.36 mm}$

$\therefore \quad d = 0.7\,D$

$\quad\quad = 0.7 \times 65.36 = \textbf{45.75 mm}$

(iii) Comparison of weights :

$$A_{solid} = \frac{\pi}{4} D_1^2 = \frac{\pi}{4}(59.64)^2 = 2.79 \times 10^3 \text{ mm}^2$$

$$A_{hollow} = \frac{\pi}{4}(D^2 - d^2) = \frac{\pi}{4}[(65.36)^2 - (45.75)^2]$$

$$= 1.71 \times 10^3 \text{ mm}^2$$

Percentage saving in weight $= \dfrac{A_{solid} - A_{hollow}}{A_{solid}} \times 100$

$$= \dfrac{(2.79 - 1.71) \times 10^3}{2.79 \times 10^3} \times 100$$

$$= \textbf{38.7 \%}$$

(iv) Comparison of angle of twist :

For solid shaft, $J = \dfrac{\pi}{32} \cdot D_1^4 = \dfrac{\pi}{32}(59.64)^4$

$\quad\quad\quad\quad\quad\quad = 1.242 \times 10^6 \text{ mm}^4$

For hollow shaft, $J = \dfrac{\pi}{32}(D^4 - d^4) = \dfrac{\pi}{32}[(65.36)^4 - (45.75)^4]$

$\quad\quad\quad\quad\quad\quad\quad = 1.36 \times 10^6 \text{ mm}^4$

Angle of twist for solid shaft:

$$\theta_s = \frac{TL}{GJ_s}$$

$$= \frac{TL}{G \times 1.242 \times 10^6}$$

Angle of twist for hollow shaft $= \theta_h = \frac{TL}{GJ_h}$

$$\theta_h = \frac{TL}{G \times 1.36 \times 10^6}$$

$$\therefore \quad \frac{\theta_s}{\theta_h} = \frac{TL}{G \times 1.242 \times 10^6} \times \frac{G \times 1.36 \times 10^6}{TL}$$

$$\frac{\theta_s}{\theta_h} = 1.095$$

$$\therefore \quad \theta_s = 1.095\ \theta_h$$

i.e. $\quad \theta_h = 0.913\ \theta_s$

**Note :** For the same torque when solid and hollow shafts are designed from strength criteria, there is saving in weight if hollow shaft is used. Also angle of twist for hollow shaft is smaller than that of solid shaft. Hence, if stress is the criteria of design, hollow shaft has advantage over solid shaft.

**Example 10.13 :** Compare the weights of equal lengths of hollow and solid shaft to resist same torsional moment for same maximum shear stress. Assume internal diameter 0.8 times the external diameter for hollow shaft.

**Data** : $d = 0.8\ D$ for hollow shaft.
**Required** : Ratio of weights for hollow and solid shaft.
**Concept** : Design based on strength criteria and then comparison of weights.
**Solution** : (i) For solid shaft :
Let $\quad D_1 = $ Diameter of solid shaft

$$\tau_{max} = \left(\frac{T}{J}\right) \cdot R = \frac{T}{J/R}$$

$$= \frac{T}{\left(\frac{\pi}{16}\right) D_1^3} \quad \ldots (1)$$

(ii) For hollow shaft :
Let $\quad D = $ External diameter
$\quad d = 0.8\ D = $ Internal diameter

$$\therefore \quad \tau_{max} = \left(\frac{T}{J}\right) \cdot R = \frac{T}{(J/R)}$$

$$= \frac{T}{\left(\frac{\pi}{16\ D}\right)(D^4 - d^4)}$$

$$= \frac{T}{\left(\frac{\pi}{16\,D}\right)[D^4 - (0.8\,D)^4]}$$

$$= \frac{T}{\left(\frac{\pi}{16}\right) \cdot (0.59\,D^3)} \quad \ldots (2)$$

(iii) Relation between diameter of solid and hollow shaft :

Equating (1) and (2),

$$\frac{T}{\left(\frac{\pi}{16}\right)D_1^3} = \frac{T}{\left(\frac{\pi}{16}\right)(0.59\,D^3)}$$

we get, $\quad D_1 = 0.84\,D$

(iv) Comparison of weights :

Cross-sectional area of solid shaft $= A_s = \frac{\pi}{4} \cdot D_1^2$

$$= \frac{\pi}{4}(0.84\,D)^2$$

$$= (0.7056) \cdot \frac{\pi}{4} D^2$$

Cross-sectional area of hollow shaft $= A_h = \frac{\pi}{4}(D^2 - d^2)$

$$= \frac{\pi}{4}[D^2 - (0.8\,D)^2]$$

$$= (0.36) \cdot \frac{\pi}{4} \cdot D^2$$

$\therefore \quad \dfrac{\text{Weight of hollow shaft}}{\text{Weight of solid shaft}} = \dfrac{A_h}{A_s} = \dfrac{0.36}{0.7056} = \mathbf{0.51}$

**Example 10.14 :** A solid shaft of 200 mm diameter has the same cross-sectional area as that of hollow shaft of the same materials of inside diameter 150 mm.

(i) Find the ratio of power transmitted by the two shafts of same angular velocity.

(ii) Compare angle of twist in equal lengths of these shafts when stressed equally.

**Data :** $d = 150$ mm for hollow shaft, $D_1 = 20$ mm for solid shaft

**Required :** Comparison of hollow and solid shaft.

**Concept :** Design of shafts based on stiffness criteria.

**Solution :** (i) Outside diameter of hollow shaft :

$$\frac{\pi}{4}(D^2 - d^2) = \frac{\pi}{4} D_1^2$$

$$[D^2 - (150^2)] = (200)^2$$

$$D = 250 \text{ mm}$$

(ii) Ratio of power transmitted :

$$\frac{\text{Power transmitted by hollow shaft}}{\text{Power transmitted by solid shaft}} = \frac{\text{Torque transmitted by hollow shaft}}{\text{Torque transmitted by solid shaft}}$$

Torque transmitted by hollow shaft $= \left(\dfrac{J}{R}\right) \tau_{max}$.

$$\therefore \quad T = \pi \frac{[(250^4 - 150^4)]}{16 \times 250} \times \tau_{max}$$

$$= 2.67 \times 10^6 \, \tau_{max}$$

$$T_1 = \frac{\pi}{16} D^3 \, \tau_{max}$$

$$= \frac{\pi}{16} \times (200)^3 \times \tau_{max}$$

$$= 1.57 \times \tau_{max}$$

$$\therefore \quad \frac{T}{T_1} = \frac{2.67 \times 10^6 \times \tau_{max}}{1.57 \times \tau_{max}}$$

$$\therefore \quad \frac{P}{P_1} = \frac{T}{T_1} = 1.7$$

(iii) Comparison of angle of twist :

$$\frac{\tau_{max}}{R} = \frac{G\theta}{l}$$

$$\therefore \quad \theta_{hollow} = \frac{\tau_{max} \times l}{G \times 125}$$

$$\therefore \quad \theta_{solid} = \frac{\tau_{max} \times l}{G \times 100}$$

$$\therefore \quad \frac{\theta_{hollow}}{\theta_{solid}} = \frac{100}{125} = 0.8$$

$$\therefore \quad \theta_{hollow} = 0.8 \, \theta_{solid}$$

**Example 10.15 :** A hollow circular shaft having internal diameter 50% of its external diameter transmits 600 kW at 150 rpm. Determine the external diameter of the shaft if the shear stress is not to exceed 65 N/mm² and a twist in a length of 3 m should not exceed 1.4°. Assume $\tau_{max}$ = 1.2 times $T_{mean}$, G = 100 GPa.

**Data :** $d = \dfrac{D}{2}$, $\tau_{max}$ = 65 N/mm², $\theta$ = 1.4° = 0.0244 rad, $l$ = 3000 mm, G = 100 GPa, P = 600 kW, N = 150 rpm.

**Required :** External diameter.

**Concept :** Design based on strength and stiffness criteria.

**Solution :** (i) Torque calculation :

$$P = \frac{2\pi NT}{60}$$

$$T = \frac{P \times 60}{2\pi N} = \frac{600 \times 10^3 \times 60}{2\pi \times 150}$$

$$= 38.197 \times 10^3 \text{ N-m}$$

$$T_{max} = 1.2 \times T = 1.2 \times 38.197 \times 10^6 = 45.384 \times 10^6 \text{ N-mm}$$

(ii) Diameter based on strength criteria :

$$T = \frac{J}{R} \tau_{max}$$

Substituting,

$$45.384 \times 10^6 = \frac{\pi}{16D} (D^4 - d^4)\, 65$$

$$45.384 \times 10^6 = \frac{\pi}{16D} \left(D^4 - \frac{D^4}{16}\right) 65$$

$$D = 156.47 \text{ mm}$$

(iii) Diameter based on stiffness criteria :

$$\frac{T}{J} = \frac{G\theta}{l} \qquad \therefore J = \frac{TL}{G\theta}$$

$$\frac{\pi}{32}(D^4 - d^4) = \frac{45.384 \times 10^6 \times 3000}{100 \times 10^3 \times 0.0244}$$

$$D = 156.92 \text{ mm, say } 160 \text{ mm}$$

## 10.8 SHAFTS IN SERIES

When two or more shafts are connected length-wise, they are said to be in series. It is also called as compound shaft. For the analysis of shafts in series, following points are to be noted :

(i) All the component shafts are co-axially connected i.e. polar axis is common for all the shafts.

(ii) Joint between the components is rigid i.e. there is no relative rotation between the two adjacent shafts at a joint.

Consider a compound shaft ABC subjected to torque 'T' as shown in Fig. 10.7.

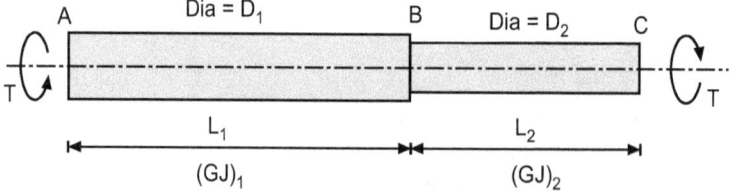

**Fig. 10.7 : Shafts in series**

Shear stress for portion AB $= \tau_1 = \dfrac{T}{J_1}\left(\dfrac{D_1}{2}\right)$

Shear stress for portion BC $= \tau_2 = \dfrac{T}{J_2}\left(\dfrac{D_2}{2}\right)$

Total angle of twist at C relative to A :

$$\begin{aligned}(\theta)_{AC} &= (\theta)_{AB} + (\theta)_{BC}\\ &= \left(\dfrac{TL}{GJ}\right)_{AB} + \left(\dfrac{TL}{GJ}\right)_{BC}\\ &= T\left[\dfrac{L_1}{(GJ)_1} + \dfrac{L_2}{(GJ)_2}\right] \quad \ldots (10.10\ a)\\ &= T\,[\text{Sum of flexibility coefficients for components}]\end{aligned}$$

If material for shafts AB and BC is same,

$$(\theta)_{AC} = \dfrac{T}{G}\left[\dfrac{L_1}{J_1} + \dfrac{L_2}{J_2}\right] \quad \ldots (10.10\ b)$$

**Example 10.16 :** A compound shaft ABCD has details as shown in Fig. 10.8. Determine inside diameter of portion AB such that shear stresses developed in portions AB and CD are equal. Also find total angle of twist if shaft is subjected to torque of 1.1 kNm. Assume G = 80 GPa.

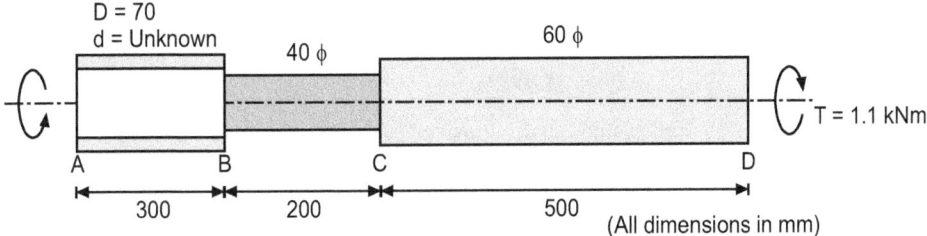

Fig. 10.8

**Data** : As shown in Fig. 10.8, T = 1.1 kNm; G = 80 GPa, $\tau_{AB} = \tau_{CD}$.

**Required** : Inside diameter (d) for AB and total angle of twist.

**Concept** : (i) Equating shear stress for portions AB and CD, get the diameter of portion AB.

(ii) Total angle of twist at D relative to A $= \theta_{AD} = \theta_{AB} + \theta_{BC} + \theta_{CD}$.

**Solution** : (i) Geometric properties :

| Component | J (mm⁴) | R (mm) | (J/R) (mm³) |
|---|---|---|---|
| AB | $\dfrac{\pi}{32}[(70)^4 - d^4]$ | $\dfrac{70}{2} = 35$ | $\dfrac{\pi}{1120}[(70)^4 - d^4]$ |
| BC | $\dfrac{\pi}{32}(40)^4 = 251.33 \times 10^3$ | $\dfrac{40}{2} = 20$ | $12.57 \times 10^3$ |
| CD | $\dfrac{\pi}{32}(60)^4 = 1272.35 \times 10^3$ | $\dfrac{60}{2} = 30$ | $42.41 \times 10^3$ |

(ii) Inside diameter for AB :

$$\tau_{AB} = \tau_{CD}$$

$$\left(\frac{T}{J/R}\right)_{AB} = \left(\frac{T}{J/R}\right)_{CD}$$

$$\therefore \quad \left(\frac{J}{R}\right)_{AB} = \left(\frac{J}{R}\right)_{CD}$$

Substituting, $\frac{\pi}{1120} [(70)^4 - d^4] = 42.41 \times 10^3$

$$\therefore \quad d = 54.605 \text{ mm}$$

$$\therefore \quad (J)_{AB} = \frac{\pi}{32} [(70)^4 - (54.605)^4]$$

$$= 1.484 \times 10^6 \text{ mm}^4$$

(iii) Total angle of twist : $\theta = \theta_{AB} + \theta_{BC} + \theta_{CD}$

$$= \left(\frac{T}{G}\right) \left[\left(\frac{L}{J}\right)_{AB} + \left(\frac{L}{J}\right)_{BC} + \left(\frac{L}{J}\right)_{CD}\right]$$

$$= \frac{1.1 \times 10^6}{80 \times 10^3} \left[\frac{300}{1.484 \times 10^6} + \frac{200}{251.33 \times 10^3} + \frac{500}{1272.35 \times 10^3}\right]$$

$$= 0.01912 \text{ rad.}$$

$$\theta = 1.095^\circ$$

**Example 10.17 :** A compound shaft consists of brass and steel components coaxially attached; fixed at one end and subjected to torque T at free end as shown in Fig. 10.9. Find the safe value of torque T at free end subjected to following conditions :

(i) $\tau_{brass} \leq 40$ MPa  (ii) $\tau_{steel} \leq 60$ MPa  (iii) $\theta \leq 2.5^\circ$.

Assume $G_s = 80$ GPa and $G_b = 35$ GPa.

Also find actual stresses developed in each part.

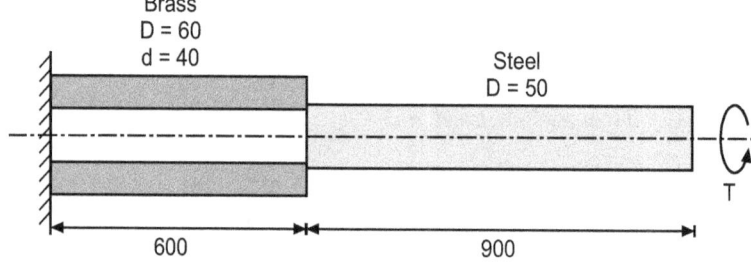

Fig. 10.9

**Data** : As shown in Fig. 10.9, $\tau_B \leq 40$ MPa, $\tau_s \leq 60$ MPa, $\theta \leq 2.5^\circ$, $G_s = 80$ GPa, $G_b = 35$ GPa.

**Required** : Safe torque (T) at free end and shear stresses.

**Concept** : Safe torque (T) is the least of that obtained from given conditions of strength and stiffness.

**Solution** : (i) Geometric properties :

| Component | J (mm⁴) | R (mm) | $\left(\dfrac{J}{R}\right)$ (mm³) |
|---|---|---|---|
| Brass | $\dfrac{\pi}{32}[(60)^4-(40)^4] = 1.021 \times 10^6$ | $\dfrac{60}{2}=30$ | $34.03 \times 10^3$ |
| Steel | $\dfrac{\pi}{32}(50)^4 = 613.59 \times 10^3$ | $\dfrac{50}{2}=25$ | $24.54 \times 10^3$ |

(ii) Torque based on strength criteria :

(a) $\tau_B \leq 40$ MPa.

$\therefore$
$$T = \left(\dfrac{J}{R}\right)_B \times \tau_B = 34.03 \times 10^3 \times 40$$
$$= 1361.2 \times 10^3 \text{ Nmm} \qquad \ldots (1)$$

(b) $\tau_S \leq 60$ MPa

$\therefore$
$$T = \left(\dfrac{J}{R}\right)_S \cdot \tau_S$$
$$= 24.54 \times 10^3 \times 60 = 1472.4 \times 10^3 \text{ Nmm} \qquad \ldots (2)$$

(iii) Torque based on stiffness criteria ($\theta \leq 2.5°$) :

Maximum angle of twist at free end = $\theta_B + \theta_S$

$$2.5 \times \dfrac{\pi}{180} = T\left[\left(\dfrac{L}{GJ}\right)_B + \left(\dfrac{L}{GJ}\right)_S\right]$$

$$= T\left[\dfrac{600}{35 \times 10^3 \times 1.021 \times 10^6} + \dfrac{900}{80 \times 10^3 \times 613.59 \times 10^3}\right]$$

$\therefore \qquad T = 1242.227 \times 10^3$ Nmm $\qquad \ldots (3)$

$\therefore$ Safe torque, $T = 1242.227 \times 10^3$ Nmm (Least of 1, 2, and 3)

(iv) Shear stresses : $\tau_B = \dfrac{T}{(J/R)_B} = \dfrac{1242.227 \times 10^3}{34.03 \times 10^3} = 36.50$ MPa

$\tau_S = \dfrac{T}{(J/R)_S} = \dfrac{1242.227 \times 10^3}{24.54 \times 10^3} = 50.62$ MPa

**Example 10.18** : A compound shaft consists of steel and aluminium segments acted upon by two torques as shown in Fig. 10.10. Determine maximum permissible value of 'T' subjected to following conditions.

(i) $\tau_s \leq 80$ MPa (ii) $\tau_a \leq 55$ MPa (iii) $\theta \leq 6°$

Assume $G_s = 83$ GPa and $G_a = 28$ GPa.

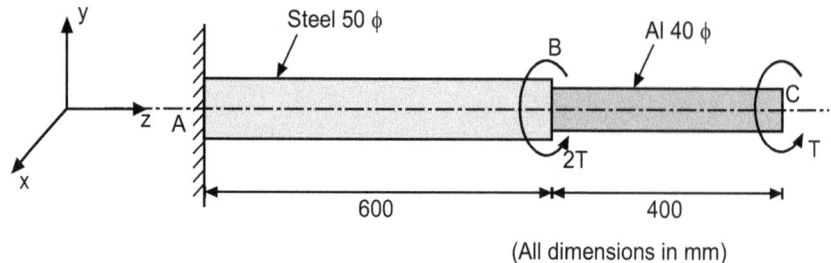

Fig. 10.10

**Data** : As shown in Fig. 10.10, $\tau_s \leq 80$ MPa, $\tau_a \leq 55$ MPa;

$\theta \leq 6°$, $G_s = 83$ GPa, $G_a = 28$ GPa.

**Required** : Safe value of torque 'T'.

**Concept** : Reactive torque at fixed end, torsional moment diagram, strength criteria, stiffness criteria.

**Solution** : (i) Analysis :

From statistics;

$\sum M_Z = 0$ gives reactive torque at fixed end A = 3 T (↻)

FBD of shaft and torsional moment diagram is as shown in Fig. 10.11.

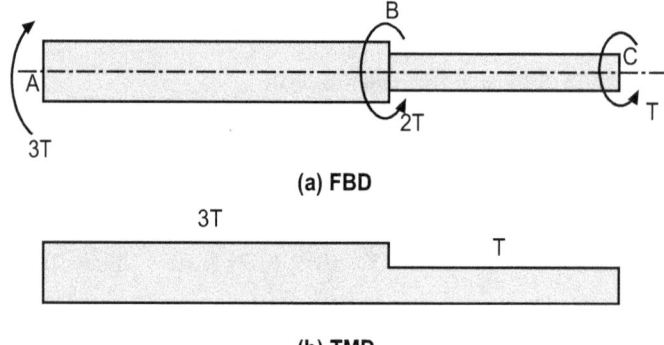

(a) FBD

(b) TMD

Fig. 10.11

(ii) Geometric properties :

| Component | J (mm⁴) | R (mm) | $\left(\dfrac{J}{R}\right)$ (mm³) |
|---|---|---|---|
| Steel | $\dfrac{\pi}{32}(50)^4 = 613.59 \times 10^3$ | $\dfrac{50}{2} = 25$ | $24.54 \times 10^3$ |
| Aluminium | $\dfrac{\pi}{32}(40)^4 = 251.33 \times 10^3$ | $\dfrac{40}{2} = 20$ | $12.57 \times 10^3$ |

(iii) Strength criteria :

(a) $\tau_s \leq 80$ MPa

$$3T = \left(\frac{J}{R}\right)_s \cdot \tau_s = 24.54 \times 10^3 \times 80$$

∴ $\quad T = 654.4 \times 10^3$ Nmm  ... (1)

(b) $\tau_a \leq 55$ MPa

$$T = \left(\frac{J}{R}\right)_a \cdot \tau_a = 12.57 \times 10^3 \times 55$$

∴ $\quad T = 691.35 \times 10^3$ Nmm  ... (2)

(iv) Stiffness criteria ($\theta \leq 6°$) :

$\theta_{max}$ at free end $= 6° = \theta_{AB} + \theta_{BC}$

$$6 \times \frac{\pi}{180} = \left(\frac{TL}{GJ}\right)_{AB} + \left(\frac{TL}{GJ}\right)_{BC}$$

$$= \frac{3T \times 600}{83 \times 10^3 \times 613.59 \times 10^3} + \frac{T \times 400}{28 \times 10^3 \times 251.33 \times 10^3}$$

$\quad T = 1135.98 \times 10^3$ Nmm  ... (3)

Safe value of $T = 654.4 \times 10^3$ Nmm  (Least of (1), (2) and (3))

**Example 10.19 :** The shaft shown in Fig. 10.12 below rotates at 200 rpm with 40 H.P. and 20 H.P. taken off at A and B respectively and 60 H.P. applied at C. Find the maximum shear stress developed in the shaft and angle of twist of gear 'A' relative to gear 'C'. G = 85 GPa.

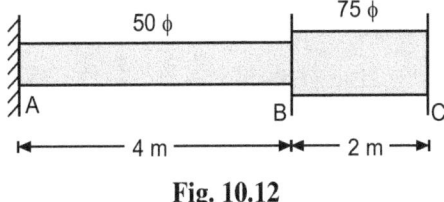

Fig. 10.12

**Data** : N = 200 r.p.m.; at A and B 40 H.P. and 20 H.P. taken off, while at C 60 HP applied; G = 85 GPa.

**Required** : Maximum shear stress and angle of twist at A w.r.t. C.

**Concept** : From the given power, find torques at A, B and C, draw torsional moment diagram and then analyse for stresses and angle of twist.

**Solution** : (i) Analysis and T.M.D. :

$$P_A = 40 \text{ H.P.} = \frac{2\pi NT_A}{4500} = \frac{2\pi \times 200 \times T_A}{4500}$$

∴ $\quad T_A = 143.24$ Nm (↻)

$$P_B = 20 \text{ H.P.} = \frac{2\pi NT_B}{4500} = \frac{2\pi \times 200 \times T_B}{4500}$$

∴ $T_B = 71.62$ Nm (↻)

$$P_C = 60 \text{ H.P.} = \frac{2\pi NT_C}{4500} = \frac{2\pi \times 200 \times T_C}{4500}$$

∴ $T_C = 214.86$ Nm (↻)

Fig. 10.13 (a) below shows FBD and Fig. 10.13 (b) shows torsional moment diagram for the shaft.

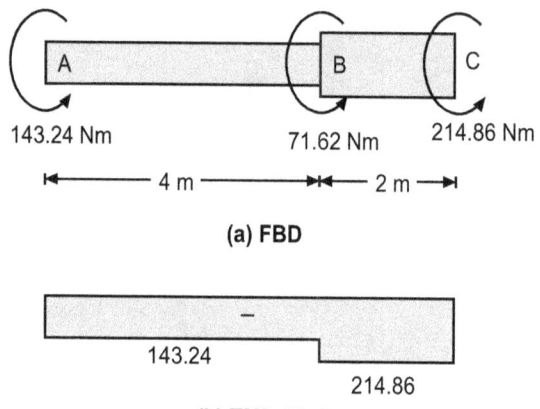

(a) FBD

(b) TMD (Nm)

Fig. 10.13

(ii) Geometric properties :

| Component | J (mm⁴) | R (mm) | $\left(\dfrac{J}{R}\right)$ (mm³) |
|---|---|---|---|
| AB | $\dfrac{\pi}{32}(50)^4 = 613.59 \times 10^3$ | $\dfrac{50}{2} = 25$ | $24.54 \times 10^3$ |
| BC | $\dfrac{\pi}{32}(75)^4 = 3106.31 \times 10^3$ | $\dfrac{75}{2} = 37.5$ | $82.83 \times 10^3$ |

(iii) Shear stresses :

$$\tau_{AB} = \frac{T_{AB}}{(J/R)_{AB}} = \frac{143.24 \times 10^3}{24.54 \times 10^3} = 5.83 \text{ MPa}$$

$$\tau_{BC} = \frac{T_{BC}}{(J/R)_{BC}} = \frac{214.86 \times 10^3}{82.83 \times 10^3} = 2.59 \text{ MPa}$$

∴ $\tau_{max} = 5.83$ MPa

(iv) Angle of twist of gear 'A' w.r.t. gear 'C' :

$$\theta_{AC} = \theta_{AB} + \theta_{BC} = \left(\frac{TL}{GJ}\right)_{AB} + \left(\frac{TL}{GJ}\right)_{BC}$$

$$= \frac{1}{85 \times 10^3}\left[\frac{143.24 \times 10^3 \times 4000}{613.59 \times 10^3} + \frac{214.86 \times 10^3 \times 2000}{3106.31 \times 10^3}\right]$$

$$= 0.0126 \text{ rad} = \mathbf{0.7219°}$$

**Example 10.20 :** An aluminium shaft of constant diameter 80 mm is loaded by torques applied to gears attached to it, as shown in Fig. 10.14. Determine the angle of twist of gear A relative to gear D. Take G = 30 GPa.

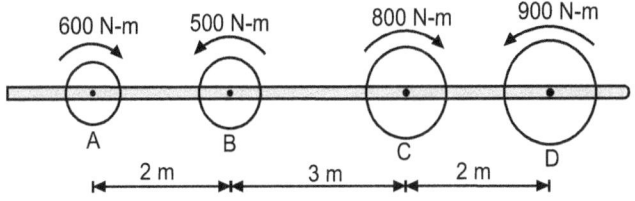

Fig. 10.14

**Data :** As shown in Fig. 10.14, D = 80 mm, G = 30 GPa.
**Required :** Twist at D w.r. to A.
**Concept :** $\theta_{A/D} = \theta_A + \theta_B + \theta_C + \theta_D$.
**Solution :** (i) Geometric properties :

$$J = \frac{\pi}{32} D^4 = \frac{\pi}{32} \times (80)^4 = 4.02 \times 10^6 \text{ mm}^4$$

(ii) Calculation for $\theta_{A/D}$ :

$$\theta_{A/D} = \theta_A + \theta_B + \theta_C + \theta_D = \left(\frac{TL}{JG}\right)_{AB} + \left(\frac{TL}{JG}\right)_{BC} + \left(\frac{TL}{JG}\right)_{CD}$$

$$= \frac{1}{JG} [(TL)_{AB} + (TL)_{BC} + (TL)_{CD}]$$

$$= \frac{[-600 \times 10^3 \times 2000 - 100 \times 10^3 \times 3000 - 900 \times 10^3 \times 2000]}{4.02 \times 10^6 \times 30 \times 10^3}$$

$$\theta_{A/D} = 0.027 \text{ radians} = 1.57°$$

**Example 10.21 :** A stepped shaft is subjected to the couples (in the same direction) at change in section at the free end as shown in Fig. 10.15 (a). The length of each section is 0.5 m and diameters are 80 mm, 60 mm and 40 mm. If G = 80 GPa, find the angle of twist θ in degrees at the free end.

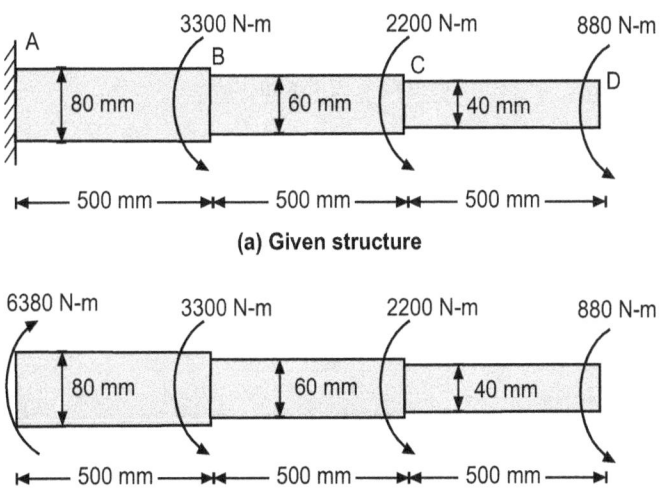

(a) Given structure

(b) FBD

Fig. 10.15

**Data :** As shown in Fig. 10.15 (a), G = 80 GPa.

**Required :** Angle of twist '$\theta$' at the free end.

**Concept :** $\theta = \theta_{AB} + \theta_{BC} + \theta_{CD}$.

**Solution :** (i) Geometric properties :

$$J_{AB} = \frac{\pi}{32} D^4 = \frac{\pi}{32} \times (80)^4$$

$$= 4.02 \times 10^6 \text{ mm}^4$$

$$J_{BC} = \frac{\pi}{32} D^4 = \frac{\pi}{32} \times (60)^4$$

$$= 1.27 \times 10^6 \text{ mm}^4$$

$$J_{CD} = \frac{\pi}{32} D^4 = \frac{\pi}{32} \times (40)^4$$

$$= 251.33 \times 10^3 \text{ mm}^4$$

(ii) Torsion in members :

$$T_{AB} = 3300 + 2200 + 880 = 6380 \text{ Nm}$$

$$= 6.38 \times 10^6 \text{ Nmm}$$

$$T_{BC} = 2200 + 880 = 3080 \text{ Nm}$$

$$= 3.08 \times 10^6 \text{ Nmm}$$

$$T_{CD} = 880 \text{ N-m}$$

$$= 880 \times 10^3 \text{ Nmm}$$

Now,
$$\theta = \theta_{AB} + \theta_{BC} + \theta_{CD}$$

$$= \left(\frac{TL}{GJ}\right)_{AB} + \left(\frac{TL}{GJ}\right)_{BC} + \left(\frac{TL}{GJ}\right)_{CD}$$

$$= \frac{L}{G}\left[\left(\frac{T}{J}\right)_{AB} + \left(\frac{T}{J}\right)_{BC} + \left(\frac{T}{J}\right)_{CD}\right]$$

$$= \frac{500}{80 \times 10^3}\left[\frac{6.38 \times 10^6}{4.02 \times 10^6} + \frac{3.08 \times 10^6}{1.27 \times 10^6} + \frac{880 \times 10^3}{251.33 \times 10^3}\right]$$

$$\theta = \mathbf{0.047 \text{ radians} = 2.69°}$$

## 10.9 STATICALLY INDETERMINATE PROBLEMS

### 10.9.1 Shafts Fixed at Both Ends

When equations of statics are not sufficient to evaluate the unknown forces, it is called as statically indeterminate problem. For example, consider a shaft fixed at two ends and subjected to torque T as shown in Fig. 10.16.

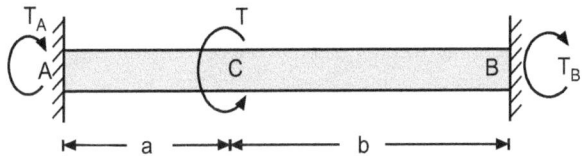

Fig. 10.16 : Shaft fixed at both ends

Unknown reactions = $T_A$ and $T_B$ i.e. resistive torques at A and B.

Equation of statics : $\sum M_Z = 0$ gives

$$T_A + T_B = T \qquad \ldots (10.11)$$

Second equation can be formulated using the fact that angle of twist of C ($\theta_{CA}$) due to torque '$T_A$' acting over length AC is equal to angle of twist at C ($\theta_{CB}$) due to torque '$T_B$' acting over length CB.

$$\theta_{CA} = \theta_{CB}$$

$$\left(\frac{TL}{GJ}\right)_{CA} = \left(\frac{TL}{GJ}\right)_{CB} \qquad \ldots (10.12)$$

Substituting geometric properties for portions CA and CB in equation (10.12), relation between $T_A$ and $T_B$ can be obtained. Then by using equation (10.11), $T_A$ and $T_B$ can be evaluated.

**Note :** Equation (10.12) is the condition of deformation called as equation of **compatibility** wherein member deformation is assumed continuous.

The above situation will be called as externally indeterminate because equations of statics are not sufficient enough to evaluate external reactive torques $T_A$ and $T_B$. However, member can be internally indeterminate also as discussed below.

### 10.9.2 Shafts in Parallel

When one shaft is surrounded by other shaft, the two shafts are said to be in parallel.

Consider two shafts placed in parallel as shown in Fig. 10.17.

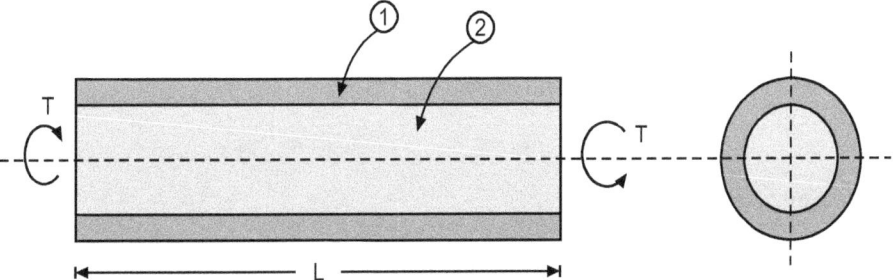

Fig. 10.17 : Shafts in parallel

Let,  T = Total torque acting on the shaft

$T_1, T_2$ = Torque resisted by individual components 1 and 2 respectively.

Unknown torques are $T_1$ and $T_2$, while the equation of statics available is only one i.e.

$$\sum M_z = 0 \Rightarrow T = T_1 + T_2 \qquad \ldots (10.13)$$

Second equation can be formulated using the fact that the angle of twist for both the shafts for a given length under the action of given torque, is constant. This is the equation of **compatibility** here.

Thus,  $\theta_1 = \theta_2$

$$\left(\frac{TL}{GJ}\right)_1 = \left(\frac{TL}{GJ}\right)_2 \qquad \ldots (10.14\ a)$$

Lengths of both components being same for the shaft considered in Fig. 10.17,

$$\left(\frac{T}{GJ}\right)_1 = \left(\frac{T}{GJ}\right)_2 \qquad \ldots (10.14\ b)$$

Solving equations (10.13) and (10.14), values of $T_1$ and $T_2$ can be obtained.

The above situation will be called as internally indeterminate because equations of statics are not sufficient enough to evaluate internal resistive torques $T_1$ and $T_2$.

**Note :** In the above analysis, it is assumed that the shafts are co-axially fitted and there is no relative rotation between the two components.

**Example 10.22 :** A uniform bar AB of length 'L' is fixed at A and B. It is subjected to torque 'T' at 'C' at a distance 'a' from left end and 'b' from right end. Derive expressions for reactive torques developed at A and B and draw torsional moment diagram.

**Data**        : As shown in Fig. 10.18 (a).

**Required** : Expressions for reactive torques.

**Concept**  : Statically indeterminate; equation of statics and compatibility.

**Solution**  : (i) Equation of statics :

$$\sum M_z = 0 ; \quad T_A + T_B = T \qquad \ldots (1)$$

(ii) Equation of compatibility :

$$\theta_{CA} = \theta_{CB}$$

$$\left(\frac{TL}{GJ}\right)_{CA} = \left(\frac{TL}{GJ}\right)_{CB}$$

$$T_A \cdot a = T_B \cdot b \quad \therefore \quad T_A = \frac{b}{a} T_B \qquad \ldots (2)$$

(iii) Solution of equations :

Solving (1) and (2),

$$T_A = \frac{Tb}{L} \; (\circlearrowleft) \text{ and } T_B = \frac{Ta}{L} \; (\circlearrowleft)$$

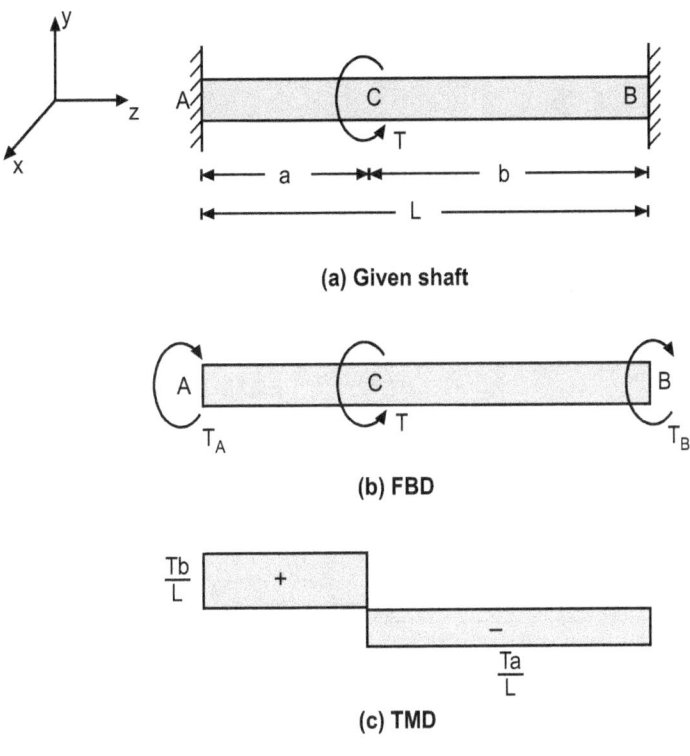

**(a) Given shaft**

**(b) FBD**

**(c) TMD**

**Fig. 10.18**

**Example 10.23 :** A steel shaft ABCD is subjected to torques as shown in Fig. 10.19. (i) Determine reactive torques at fixed ends, (ii) Draw torsional moment diagram, (iii) Find maximum shear stress and angle of twist. Assume $G = 80$ GPa.

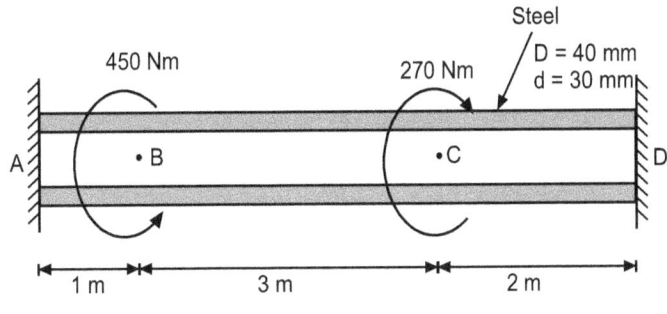

**Fig. 10.19**

**Data**      : As shown in Fig. 10.19, $G = 80$ GPa.

**Required** : Reactive torques at A and D, TMD, Maximum shear stress and angle of twist.

**Concept**  : Statically indeterminate problem, use of standard results and principle of superposition.

**Solution** : (i) Reactive torques :

Using standard result and principle of superposition.

Reactions due to 450 Nm (↻), $T_A = \dfrac{450 \times 5}{6} = 375$ **Nm** (↺)

$$T_D = \dfrac{450 \times 1}{6} = 75 \text{ Nm } (\circlearrowleft)$$

Reactions due to 270 Nm (↺), $T_A = \dfrac{270 \times 2}{6} = 90$ **Nm** (↻)

$$T_D = \dfrac{270 \times 4}{6} = 180 \text{ Nm } (\circlearrowleft)$$

Final reactions, $T_A = 375 - 90 = 285$ **Nm** (↺)

$T_B = 75 - 180 = -105$ Nm $= 105$ **Nm** (↻)

(ii) FBD and torsional moment diagram :

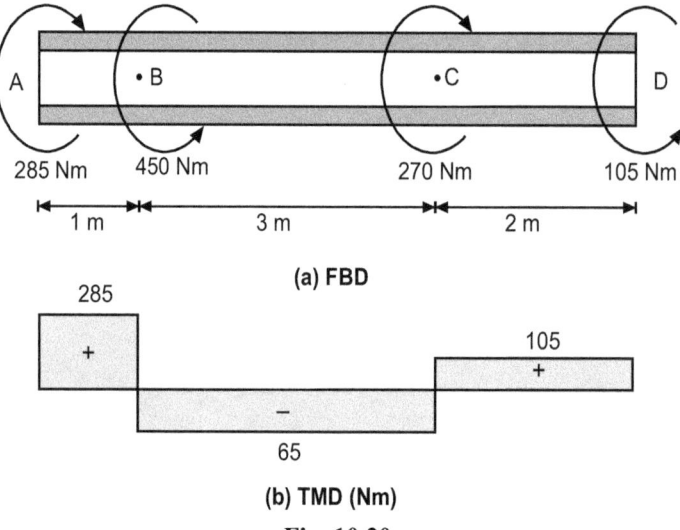

(a) FBD

(b) TMD (Nm)

**Fig. 10.20**

(iii) Geometric properties :

$$J = \dfrac{\pi}{32}[(40)^4 - (30)^4] = 171.8 \times 10^3 \text{ mm}^4$$

$$R = \dfrac{40}{2} = 20 \text{ mm}$$

$$\dfrac{J}{R} = \dfrac{171.8 \times 10^3}{20} = 8.59 \times 10^3 \text{ mm}^3$$

(iv) Maximum shear stress ($\tau_{max}$) :

Maximum shear stress will occur in portion AB.

$$\therefore \quad \tau_{max} = \dfrac{T_{AB}}{(J/R)} = \dfrac{285 \times 10^3}{8.59 \times 10^3} = \mathbf{33.18 \text{ MPa}}$$

(v) Maximum angle of twist :

$$\theta_{AB} = \left(\frac{TL}{GJ}\right)_{AB} = \frac{285 \times 10^3 \times 1000}{80 \times 10^3 \times 171.8 \times 10^3} = 0.0207 \text{ rad } (\circlearrowright)$$

$$\theta_{BC} = \left(\frac{TL}{GJ}\right)_{BC} = \frac{165 \times 10^3 \times 3000}{80 \times 10^3 \times 171.8 \times 10^3} = 0.036 \text{ rad } (\circlearrowleft)$$

$$\theta_{CD} = \left(\frac{TL}{GJ}\right)_{CD} = \frac{105 \times 10^3 \times 2000}{80 \times 10^3 \times 171.8 \times 10^3} = 0.0153 \text{ rad } (\circlearrowright)$$

∴ Maximum angle of twist = 0.036 rad = 2.063° which occurs in portion BC.

**Note :** Total angle of twist from A to D

$$= \theta_{AB} + \theta_{BC} + \theta_{CD}$$
$$= -0.0207 + 0.036 - 0.0153$$
$$= 0 \text{ (Ends A and D are fixed)}.$$

**Example 10.24 :** A compound shaft shown in Fig. 10.21 is attached to rigid supports. Determine the ratio of lengths 'b' to 'a' so that each material is stressed to its permissible limit. What torque T is applied ? Assume $G_b = 42$ GPa; $G_s = 84$ GPa; $\tau_b \leq 70$ MPa; $\tau_s \leq 100$ MPa.

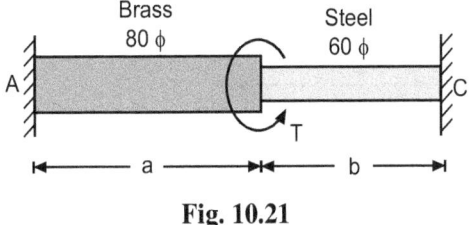

Fig. 10.21

**Data** : As shown in Fig. 10.21.

**Required** : Ratio $\frac{b}{a}$ and T.

**Concept** : Both materials brass and steel are stressed to their permissible limit, hence torques on portions AB and BC are known. Equation of equilibrium and compatibility.

**Solution** : (i) Geometric properties :

| Component | J (mm⁴) | R (mm) | $\left(\frac{J}{R}\right)$ (mm³) |
|---|---|---|---|
| Brass | $\frac{\pi}{32}(80)^4 = 4.02 \times 10^6$ | $\frac{80}{2} = 40$ | $100.5 \times 10^3$ |
| Steel | $\frac{\pi}{32}(60)^4 = 1.27 \times 10^6$ | $\frac{60}{2} = 30$ | $42.41 \times 10^3$ |

(ii) Torque for components :

$$T_{brass} = \text{Reactive torque at A} = T_A$$
$$= \left(\frac{J}{R}\right)_b \cdot \tau_b$$
$$= 100.5 \times 10^3 \times 70$$
$$= \mathbf{7.035 \times 10^6 \ Nmm}$$

$$T_{steel} = \text{Reactive torque at C} = T_C$$
$$= \left(\frac{J}{R}\right)_s \cdot \tau_s$$
$$= 42.41 \times 10^3 \times 100$$
$$= \mathbf{4.241 \times 10^6 \ Nmm}$$

(iii) FBD and torsional moment diagram :

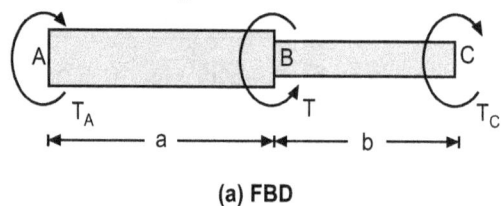

(a) FBD

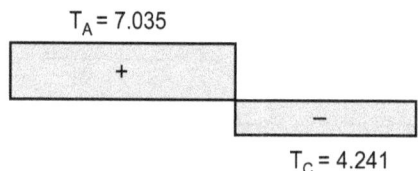

$T_C = 4.241$

(b) TMD (kNm)

Fig. 10.22

(iv) Compatibility :

$$\theta_{BA} = \theta_{BC}$$
$$\left(\frac{TL}{GJ}\right)_{BA} = \left(\frac{TL}{GJ}\right)_{BC}$$

Substituting, $\dfrac{7.035 \times 10^6 \times a}{42 \times 10^3 \times 4.02 \times 10^6} = \dfrac{4.241 \times 10^6 \times b}{84 \times 10^3 \times 1.27 \times 10^6}$

$$\therefore \quad \frac{b}{a} = 1.048$$

(v) Equilibrium :
$$T = T_A + T_C$$
$$= (7.035 + 4.241) \times 10^6$$
$$= \mathbf{11.276 \times 10^6 \ Nmm}$$

**Example 10.25 :** A shaft ABC fixed at 'A' and 'B' is subjected to torque of 42.5 Nm at 'C' as shown in Fig. 10.23. Calculate the end reactions and shear stresses in both components. Also find angle of twist at junction 'C'.

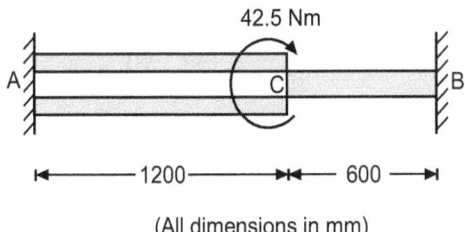

(All dimensions in mm)

Fig. 10.23

**Data :** As shown in Fig. 10.23.

**Required :** End reactions, shear stresses, and angle of twist at 'C'.

**Concept :** Equations of equilibrium and compatibility.

| AC | CB |
|---|---|
| Brass | Steel |
| D = 30 mm | D = 20 mm |
| d = 20 mm | |
| $G_b$ = 39 GPa | $G_s$ = 79 GPa |

**Solution :** (i) Geometric properties :

| Component | J (mm⁴) | R (mm) | $\left(\dfrac{J}{R}\right)$ (mm³) |
|---|---|---|---|
| Brass | $\dfrac{\pi}{32}[(30)^4 - (20)^4] = 63.81 \times 10^3$ | $\dfrac{30}{2} = 15$ | $4.254 \times 10^3$ |
| Steel | $\dfrac{\pi}{32}(20)^4 = 15.71 \times 10^3$ | $\dfrac{20}{2} = 10$ | $1.571 \times 10^3$ |

(ii) Equation of statics :

$$T = T_A + T_B$$
$$42.5 = T_A + T_B \quad \ldots (1)$$

(iii) Equation of compatibility :

$$\theta_{CA} = \theta_{CB}$$
$$\left(\dfrac{TL}{GJ}\right)_{CA} = \left(\dfrac{TL}{GJ}\right)_{CB}$$

Substituting, $\dfrac{T_A \times 1200}{39 \times 10^3 \times 63.81 \times 10^3} = \dfrac{T_B \times 600}{79 \times 10^3 \times 15.71 \times 10^3}$

$$T_A = T_B \quad \ldots (2)$$

(iv) Solution of equations :

Solving equations (1) and (2),

$$T_A = T_B = 21.25 \text{ Nm}$$

(v) Shear stresses :

$$\tau_{brass} = \left(\frac{T}{J/R}\right)_{brass} = \frac{21.25 \times 10^3}{4.254 \times 10^3} = 4.99 \text{ MPa}$$

$$\tau_{steel} = \left(\frac{T}{J/R}\right)_{steel} = \frac{21.25 \times 10^3}{1.571 \times 10^3} = 13.52 \text{ MPa}$$

(vi) Angle of twist at C :

$$\theta_{CA} = \theta_{CB} = \left(\frac{TL}{GJ}\right)_{brass} \text{ OR } \left(\frac{TL}{GJ}\right)_{steel}$$

$$= \frac{21.25 \times 10^3 \times 1200}{39 \times 10^3 \times 63.81 \times 10^3}$$

$$= 0.0102 \text{ rad.}$$

$$= 0.587°$$

**Example 10.26 :** For a compound shaft ABC shown in Fig. 10.24 if allowable shear stress is 70 MPa, find the safe value of torque T at C.

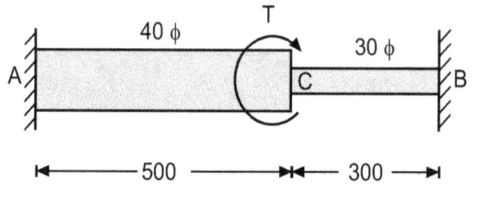

(All dimensions in mm)

**Fig. 10.24**

**Data**      : As shown in Fig. 10.24; $\tau_{max} = 70$ MPa.
**Required** : Safe value of torque T at C.
**Concept**  : Equations of statics and compatibility.
**Solution** : (i) Geometric properties :

| Component | J (mm⁴) | R (mm) | $\left(\frac{J}{R}\right)$ (mm³) |
|---|---|---|---|
| AC | $\frac{\pi}{32}(40)^4 = 251.33 \times 10^3$ | $\frac{40}{2} = 20$ | $12.57 \times 10^3$ |
| CB | $\frac{\pi}{32}(30)^4 = 79.52 \times 10^3$ | $\frac{30}{2} = 15$ | $5.3 \times 10^3$ |

(ii) Equation of compatibility :

$$\theta_{CA} = \theta_{CB}$$

$$\left(\frac{TL}{GJ}\right)_{CA} = \left(\frac{TL}{GJ}\right)_{CB}$$

$$\frac{T_A \times 500}{251.33 \times 10^3} = \frac{T_B \times 300}{79.52 \times 10^3} \qquad (\because G = \text{constant})$$

$$\therefore \quad T_A = 1.896 \; T_B \qquad \ldots (1)$$

(iii) Equation of equilibrium :

$$T = T_A + T_B$$

Let, stress in portion CB reaches to allowable value of 70 MPa.

$$\therefore \quad T_B = \left(\frac{J}{R}\right)_{CB} \tau_{CB} = 5.3 \times 10^3 \times 70$$

$$= 371 \times 10^3 \; \text{Nmm}$$

Put $T_B$ in equation (1)

$$T_A = 1.896 \times 371 \times 10^3 = \mathbf{703.416 \times 10^3 \; Nmm}$$

$$\therefore \quad \tau_{AC} = \frac{T_A}{(J/R)_{AC}} = \frac{703.416 \times 10^3}{12.57 \times 10^3} = 55.96 \; \text{MPa} < 70 \; \text{MPa} \;\; (OK)$$

$$\therefore \quad T = (703.416 + 371) \times 10^3$$

$$= 1074.416 \times 10^3 \; \text{Nmm}$$

$$= \mathbf{1074.416 \; Nm}$$

**Note :** If stress calculated for portion AC is greater than 70 MPa, allow portion AC to get stressed to 70 MPa and find corresponding stress in portion CB. Stress calculated for portion CB will then be less than 70 MPa.

**Example 10.27 :** A composite shaft consists of copper rod 40 mm $\phi$ enclosed in a steel tube of 50 mm external diameter and 5 mm thickness. There is no relative motion between the two and shafts are coaxially fixed. Determine shear stresses developed in copper and steel rods if both the shafts have equal lengths. Assume $G_c = 40$ GPa; $G_s = 80$ GPa and torque = 1400 Nm.

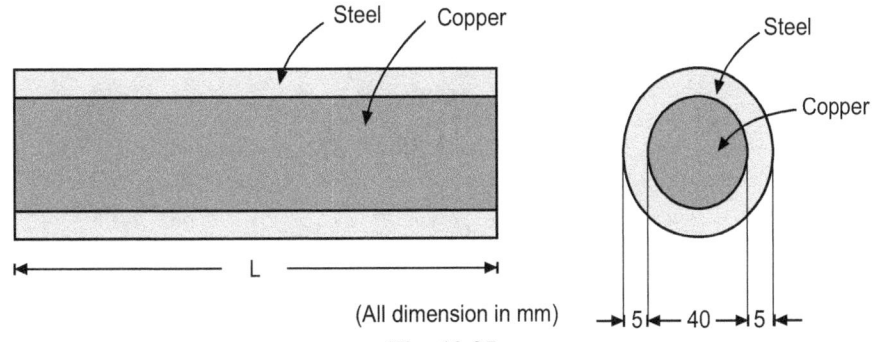

Fig. 10.25

**Data** : As shown in Fig. 10.25, $G_c = 40$ GPa, $G_s = 80$ GPa, T = 1400 Nm.

**Required** : Shear stresses for steel and copper.

**Concept** : Statically indeterminate problem; Equation of statics : $T_s + T_c = T$.

Equation of compatibility : $\theta_s = \theta_c$.

**Solution :** (i) Geometric properties :

For copper,    $J_c = \dfrac{\pi}{32}(40)^4 = 251.33 \times 10^3$ mm$^4$

$R = \dfrac{40}{2} = 20$ mm

$\therefore \left(\dfrac{J}{R}\right)_c = \dfrac{251.33 \times 10^3}{20} = 12.56 \times 10^3$ mm$^3$

For steel,    $J_s = \dfrac{\pi}{32}[(50)^4 - (40)^4] = 362.26 \times 10^3$ mm$^4$

$R = \dfrac{50}{2} = 25$

$\left(\dfrac{J}{R}\right)_s = \dfrac{362.26 \times 10^3}{25} = 14.49 \times 10^3$ mm$^3$

(ii) Equation of statics :

$$T = T_c + T_s$$
$$1400 = T_c + T_s \quad \ldots (1)$$

(iii) Equation of compatibility :

$$\theta_c = \theta_s$$
$$\left(\dfrac{TL}{GJ}\right)_c = \left(\dfrac{TL}{GJ}\right)_s \qquad [\because L_c = L_s]$$

$$\dfrac{T_c}{40 \times 10^3 \times 251.33 \times 10^3} = \dfrac{T_s}{80 \times 10^3 \times 362.26 \times 10^3}$$

$\therefore \quad T_c = 0.3469\ T_s \quad \ldots (2)$

(iv) Solution of equations :

Solving (1) and (2),    $T_c = 360.58$ Nm

$T_s = 1039.42$ Nm

(v) Shear stresses :

For copper,    $\tau_c = \dfrac{T_c}{(J/R)_c} = \dfrac{360.58 \times 10^3}{12.56 \times 10^3} = 28.7$ MPa

For steel,    $\tau_s = \dfrac{T_s}{(J/R)_s} = \dfrac{1039.42 \times 10^3}{14.49 \times 10^3} = 71.73$ MPa

**Example 10.28 :** A composite shaft is made of 40 mm $\phi$ steel core enclosed in alloy tube of 60 mm external diameter and 10 mm thickness. There is no relative motion between the two and shafts are coaxially fitted. Permissible shear stress for steel and alloy are 60 MPa and 40 MPa respectively. Find maximum power transmitted by composite shaft at 500 rpm. Assume $G_s = 80$ GPa and $G_a = 44$ GPa.

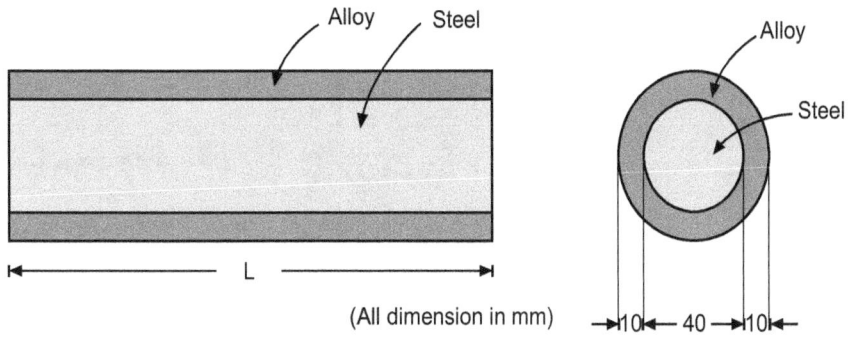

**Fig. 10.26**

**Data** : $\tau_s = 60$ MPa; $\tau_a = 40$ MPa; $G_s = 80$ GPa; $G_a = 44$ GPa; $N = 500$ rpm.
**Required** : Power transmitted by composite shaft.
**Concept** : Permissible shear stresses for the two materials are given. It does not mean that both the materials are subjected to given values of stresses. Hence governing stresses shall be found out from angle of twist which is constant for both the shafts.
**Solution** : (i) Geometric properties :

For steel, $\quad J_s = \dfrac{\pi}{32}(40)^4 = 251.33 \times 10^3$ mm$^4$

$$R = \dfrac{40}{2} = 20 \text{ mm}$$

$\therefore \quad \left(\dfrac{J}{R}\right)_s = \dfrac{251.33 \times 10^3}{20} = 12.57 \times 10^3 \text{ mm}^3$

For alloy, $\quad J_a = \dfrac{\pi}{32}[(60)^4 - (40)^4] = 1021.01 \times 10^3$

$$R = \dfrac{60}{2} = 30 \text{ mm}$$

$\therefore \quad \left(\dfrac{J}{R}\right)_a = \dfrac{1021.01 \times 10^3}{30} = 34.03 \times 10^3 \text{ mm}^3$

(ii) Governing stresses using compatibility :

$$\theta_s = \theta_a$$

$$\left(\dfrac{\tau L}{GR}\right)_s = \left(\dfrac{\tau L}{GR}\right)_a \qquad \left(\because \text{ using } \dfrac{\tau}{R} = \dfrac{G\theta}{L}\right)$$

$$\dfrac{\tau_s}{80 \times 10^3 \times 20} = \dfrac{\tau_a}{44 \times 10^3 \times 30}$$

$$\tau_s = 1.21 \, \tau_a \qquad \ldots (1)$$

Let stress in alloy is allowed to reach to 40 MPa.

$\qquad$ Stress in steel $= \tau_s = 1.21 \times 40 = $ **48.4 MPa $< 60$ MPa** ... (OK)

**Note** : If this condition is not satisfied, give second trial by allowing stress in steel to reach its permissible value and find stress in alloy using equation (1) and compare it with permissible stress.

Thus, in our case, $\tau_a = 40$ MPa and $\tau_s = 48.4$ MPa

(iii) Torque by composite shafts from statics :

$$T_a = \left(\frac{J}{R}\right)_a \times \tau_a = 34.03 \times 10^3 \times 40 = \mathbf{1.36 \times 10^6 \text{ Nmm}}$$

$$T_s = \left(\frac{J}{R}\right)_s \times \tau_s = 12.57 \times 10^3 \times 48.4 = \mathbf{0.608 \times 10^6 \text{ Nmm}}$$

$$\therefore \quad T = T_a + T_s = (1.36 + 0.608) \times 10^6 = \mathbf{1.968 \times 10^6 \text{ Nmm}}$$
$$= \mathbf{1.968 \times 10^3 \text{ Nm.}}$$

(iv) Power transmitted (P) :

$$P = \frac{2\pi NT}{60} = \frac{2\pi \times 500 \times 1.968 \times 10^3}{60}$$
$$= 103.04 \times 10^3 \text{ W}$$
$$= \mathbf{103.04 \text{ kW}}$$

**Example 10.29 :** A shaft of 80 mm diameter transmits 150 kN power at 180 r.p.m. A flanged coupling is keyed to the shaft by means of a key 100 mm long and 30 mm wide. The coupling has 6 bolts of 20 mm diameter symmetrically arranged along a bolt circle of 200 mm diameter. Calculate the shear stress in the shaft, the key and the bolts of the coupling.

**Solution :** (i) For shaft, $J = (\pi/32)(80)^4 = 4.02 \times 10^6 \text{ mm}^4$

$$P = \frac{(2\pi NT)}{60}$$

$$150 \times 10^3 = \frac{2\pi \times 180 \times T}{60} \qquad \therefore T = \mathbf{7957.74 \text{ Nm}}$$

$$\tau = (T/J) \times R = \frac{7957.74 \times 10^3}{4.02 \times 10^6} \times 40 = \mathbf{79.18 \text{ MPa}}$$

(ii) For key, Shear force $= \dfrac{T}{R} = \dfrac{7957.74 \times 10^3}{40} = \mathbf{198943.5 \text{ N}}$

Shear stress $= \dfrac{198943.5}{100 \times 30} = \mathbf{66.31 \text{ MPa}}$

(iii) For bolts, $\tau = (T/J) \times R'$

$$= \frac{7957.74 \times 10^3}{6 \times (\pi/4) \times (20)^2 \times (100)^2} (100) = \mathbf{42.21 \text{ MPa}}$$

**Example 10.30 :** A bar of steel is 40 mm in diameter and 450 mm long. A tensile load of 100 kN is found to stretch the bar by 0.25 mm. The same bar when subjected to a torque of 1.2 kNm, is found to twist through 2°. Find the values of four elastic constants.

**Solution :** (i) $A = 1256.63 \text{ mm}^2$

$J = 251.32 \times 10^3 \text{ mm}^4$

(ii) $\delta_L = \dfrac{PL}{AE}$

$\therefore \quad 0.25 = \dfrac{100 \times 450}{1256.63 \text{ E}}$

$\therefore \quad E = \mathbf{143.24 \text{ GPa}}$

(iii) $\theta = \dfrac{TL}{GJ}$

$\dfrac{2\pi}{180} = \dfrac{1.2 \times 10^3 \times 450}{G \times 251.32 \times 10^3}$ ∴ $G = 61.55$ GPa

(iv) $E = 2G(1+\upsilon) = 3K(1-2\upsilon)$

∴ $\upsilon = 0.163;\ K = 70.96$ GPa

**Example 10.31 :** A steel shaft (G = 80 GPa) of total length 4 m is encased over half its length by a brass tube (40 GPa) that is securely bonded to the steel as shown in Fig. 10.27. The diameters of the shaft and tube are 70 mm and 90 mm respectively.

(i) Determine the allowable torque $T_1$ if the angle of twist $\theta$ between ends A and C is limited to $\theta = 12°$.

(ii) Determine the allowable torque $T_2$ if the shear stress in brass is limited to $\tau_b = 100$ MPa.

(iii) Determine the allowable torque $T_3$ if the shear stress in steel is limited to $\tau_s = 80$ MPa.

(iv) What is the allowable torque T, if all three of the preceding conditions must be satisfied ?

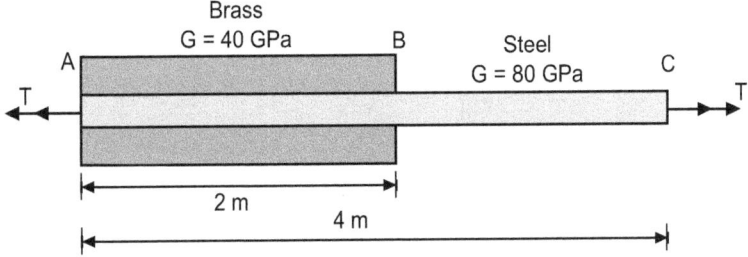

Fig. 10.27

**Solution :** (i) $J_{AB} = J_{Brass} = 4.084 \times 10^6$ mm$^4$

$J_{BC} = J_{steel} = 2.35 \times 10^6$ mm$^4$

Apparent shear modulus for portion AB

$G' = \dfrac{G_S J_S + G_B J_B}{J_S + J_B} = 54.609$ GPa

(ii) For $\theta \leq 12°$,

$\theta_{A/C} = \{TL/GJ\}_{AB + BC}$

$\dfrac{12\pi}{180} = (T \times 2000)\{(1/54.609 \times 10^3 \times 6.434 \times 10^6) + (1/80 \times 10^3 \times 2.35 \times 10^6)\}$

$T = 12.82 \times 10^6$ Nmm ... (i)

(iii) For $\tau_B \leq 100$ MPa,

∴ $\tau_s = 155.55$ MPa (equating angle of twist)

$$T = \{(J/R) \cdot \tau\}_B + \{(J/R) \cdot \tau\}_s = 19.51 \times 10^6$$

$$= 19.51 \times 10^6 \text{ Nmm} \qquad \ldots \text{(ii)}$$

(iv) For $\tau_s \leq 80$ MPa,

$$T = \{(J/R) \tau\}_s = 2.35 \times 10^6 \times 80/35$$

$$= 5.37 \times 10^6 \text{ Nmm} \qquad \ldots \text{(iii)}$$

If all above conditions are to be satisfied, safe torque = **5.37 kN/m**.

**Example 10.32 :** A 2.5 m long solid steel shaft of 30 mm diameter rotates at a frequency of 30 Hz. Determine the maximum power that the shaft may transmit, knowing that the allowable shearing stress is 50 MPa and that the angle of twist must not exceed 7.5°. Take G = 80 GPa.

**Solution :** (i) $\quad J = 79.52 \times 10^3 \text{ mm}^4$

(ii) Strength criteria :

$$\frac{T}{J} = \frac{\tau_{max}}{R}$$

$$T = 79.52 \times 10^3 \times \frac{50}{15} = 265.07 \times 10^3 \text{ Nmm} \qquad \ldots \text{(i)}$$

(iii) Stiffness criteria : $\dfrac{T}{J} = \dfrac{G\theta}{L}$

$$T = \frac{79.52 \times 10^3 \times 80 \times 10^3 \times 7.5\pi}{180 \times 2500} = 333.1 \times 10^3 \text{ Nmm} \qquad \ldots \text{(ii)}$$

Safe torque = $265.07 \times 10^3$ Nmm = **265.07 Nm**

(iv) $\quad$ Power = $2\pi$ NT

$$= 2\pi \times 30 \times 265.07 = 49.96 \times 10^3 \text{ watts}$$

**Example 10.33 :** A tube of 50 mm outside diameter and 2 mm thickness is attached to a solid shaft of 25 mm diameter as shown in Fig. 10.28. If both the tube and the shaft are of the same material, what percentage of applied torque T is carried by the tube ?

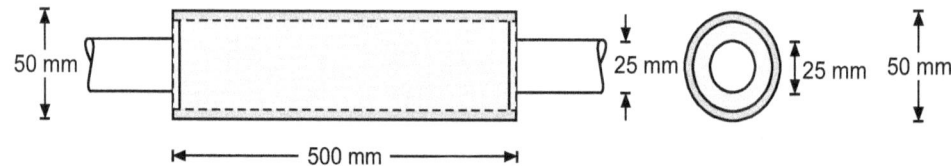

**Fig. 10.28**

**Data:** As shown in Fig. 10.28.

**Required:** Torque carried by the tube.

**Solution:**
$$T = T_t + T_s$$

$$J_t = \frac{\pi}{32}[(50)^4 - (46)^4]$$
$$= 174.02 \times 10^3 \text{ mm}^4$$

$$J_s = \frac{\pi}{32} D^4 = \frac{\pi}{32} \times (25)^4$$
$$= 38.35 \times 10^3 \text{ mm}^4$$

$$Q_t = Q_s$$

$$\therefore \left(\frac{TL}{GJ}\right)_t = \left(\frac{TL}{GJ}\right)_s$$

$$\frac{T_t \times 500}{G \times 174.02 \times 10^3} = \frac{T_s \times 500}{G \times 38.35 \times 10^3}$$

$$T_t = 4.54 \, T_s$$

$$\therefore T = T_t + 0.22 \, T_t$$

$$\therefore T_t = \frac{T}{1.22} = 0.820 \, T$$

∴ 82% torque is carried by the tube.

**Example 10.34 :** Modulus of rigidity of steel and brass are respectively $G_s$ = 80 GPa and $G_b$ = 36 GPa for the shaft shown in Fig. 10.29. If the allowable shear stresses in steel and brass are respectively $\tau_s$ = 82 MPa and $\tau_b$ = 50 MPa, determine the maximum permissible torque T that may be applied to the shaft.

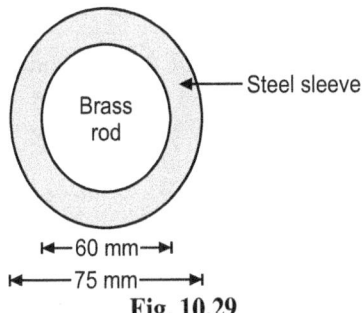

Fig. 10.29

**Data:** $G_s$ = 80 GPa, $G_b$ = 36 GPa, $\tau_s$ = 82 MPa, $\tau_b$ = 50 MPa.

**Required:** Torque.

**Solution:** (i) Geometric properties:

$$A_b = \frac{\pi}{4} \times (60)^2 = 2827.43 \text{ mm}^2$$

$$A_s = \frac{\pi}{4}[(75)^2 - (60)^2] = 1590.43 \text{ mm}^2$$

$$J_b = \frac{\pi}{32} \times (60)^4 = 1.27 \times 10^6 \text{ mm}^4$$

$$J_s = \frac{\pi}{32} [(75)^4 - (60)^4] = 18.68 \times 10^6 \text{ mm}^4$$

(ii) Governing stresses using compatibility :

$$\theta_b = \theta_s$$

$$\left(\frac{\tau L}{GR}\right)_b = \left(\frac{\tau L}{GR}\right)_s$$

$$\frac{\tau_b \times L}{36 \times 10^3 \times 30} = \frac{\tau_s \times L}{80 \times 10^3 \times \left(\frac{75}{2}\right)}$$

∴  $\tau_b = 0.36 \, \tau_s$

Let us assume stress in steel is 82 MPa.

∴ $\tau_b = 29.52$ MPa $< 50$ MPa

∴ $\tau_b = 29.52$ MPa and $\tau_s = 82$ MPa

We have $T = T_b + T_s$

$$= \left(\frac{J}{R}\right)_b \times \tau_b + \left(\frac{J}{R}\right)_s \times \tau_s$$

$$= \frac{1.27 \times 10^6}{30} \times 29.52 + \frac{1.83 \times 10^6}{37.5} \times 82$$

$$= 4.01 \times 10^6 \text{ Nmm}$$

$$= 4.01 \text{ kNm}$$

**Example 10.35 :** A hollow cylindrical shaft is 1.5 m long. It has inner and outer diameter respectively equal to 40 mm and 60 mm. What is the largest torque that can be applied to the shaft if the shearing stress is not to exceed 120 MPa ? What is corresponding minimum value of shearing stress in the shaft ?

**Data** : $l = 1.5$ m, $D = 60$ mm, $d = 40$ mm, $\tau_{max} = 120$ MPa

**Required** : Largest torque and corresponding minimum value of shearing stress.

**Concept** : Standard formula.

**Solution** :
$$T = \frac{\tau \times J}{R}$$

$$J = \frac{\pi}{32} (D^4 - d^4)$$

$$= \frac{\pi}{32} (60^4 - 40^4)$$

$$= 1.02 \times 10^6 \text{ mm}^4$$

$$T = \frac{120 \times 1.02 \times 10^6}{30} = 4.08 \times 10^6 \text{ N-mm}$$

$$T_{min} = \frac{4.08 \times 10^6 \times 20}{1.02 \times 10^6} = 80 \text{ N/mm}^2$$

**Example 10.36 :** A hollow circular steel shaft has external and internal diameters as 75 mm and 30 mm respectively, while the shaft rotates at 120 rpm, its twist was observed as 2 in 4 m length. Using G = 77 GPa, determine the power being transmitted.

**Data** : D = 75 mm, d = 30 mm, N = 120 rpm, $\theta = 2°$, $l = 4$ m, G = 77 GPa

**Required** : Transmitted power.

**Concept** : Standard formula.

**Solution** :
$$T = \frac{G \times \theta \times J}{L}$$

$$= \frac{77 \times 10^3 \times 0.0349 \times 3.027 \times 10^6}{4000}$$

$$= 2.034 \times 10^6 \text{ N-mm}$$

$$P = \frac{2\pi NT}{60}$$

$$= \frac{2\pi \times 120 \times 2.034 \times 10^3}{60}$$

$$P = \mathbf{25.56 \times 10^3 \text{ watt}}$$

**Example 10.37 :** A shaft transmits 75 kW power at 120 rpm. Determine the diameter of shaft if allowable shear stress is 50 N/mm². The twist in the shaft shall not exceed 1.5° in 5 m length. Take G = 85 kN/mm².

**Data** : Power transmitted = 75 kW = $75 \times 10^3$ W, Speed = 120 rpm,
$\tau_{allowable} = 50$ N/mm², $\theta = 1.5$, L = 5 m, G = $85 \times 10^3$ N/mm²

**Required** : Diameter of shaft.

**Concept** : Standard formula.

**Solution** :
$$P = \frac{2\pi NT}{60}$$

$$75 \times 10^3 = \frac{2\pi (120) \times T}{60}$$

$$T = 5968.31 \text{ N-m}$$

$$T = 5.97 \times 10^6 \text{ N-mm}$$

$$\frac{T}{J} = \frac{\tau_{max}}{R}$$

$$\frac{J}{R} = \frac{T}{\tau_{max}}$$

$$\frac{\pi}{32} \times \frac{D^4}{\frac{D}{2}} = \frac{5.97 \times 10^6}{50}$$

$$\frac{\pi}{18} D^3 = 119400$$

$$D^3 = 684111.61$$

$$D = 88.11 \text{ mm}$$

$$\frac{T}{J} = \frac{G\theta}{L}$$

$$\frac{5.97 \times 10^6}{J} = \frac{85 \times 10^3 \times 1.5}{5000}$$

$$J = \frac{5.97 \times 10^6 \times 5000}{85 \times 10^3 \times 1.5}$$

$$J = 234117.65$$

$$\frac{\pi}{32} D^4 = 234117.65$$

$$D^4 = 2384702.77$$

$$D = 39.30 \text{ mm}$$

**Example 10.38 :** A hollow shaft whose internal diameter is 0.55 times its external diameter and is to replace a solid shaft of the same material to transmit the same power at the same speed. Find the ratio of external diameter of hollow shaft to diameter of shaft. Find also the % saving in the weight.

**Data** : Let the external diameter be D.
∴ internal diameter = 0.55 D

**Required** : Ratio of external diameter of hollow shaft to diameter of solid shaft and % saving in the weight.

**Concept** : Standard formula.

**Solution** :

$$T_h = T_s$$

But,

$$\frac{T}{J} = \frac{\tau_{max}}{R}$$

∴

$$T = \frac{J\tau_{max}}{R}$$

∴

$$T_h = T_s$$

$$\left[\frac{J\tau_{max}}{R}\right]_h = \left[\frac{J\tau_{max}}{R}\right]_s$$

$$\frac{\pi}{32}\left[\frac{D^4 - (0.55D)^4}{0.5D}\right] = \frac{\pi}{32} \frac{D_s^4}{0.5D_s}$$

$$\frac{0.91 D^4}{0.5 D} = 2 D_s^3$$

$$1.82 D^3 = 2 D_s^3$$

$$0.91 D^3 = D_s^3$$

$$D_s = 0.97 D$$

Cross-sectional area of solid shaft, $A_s = \frac{\pi}{4}(D_s)^2$

$$= \frac{\pi}{4}(0.97D)^2$$

$$= \frac{\pi}{4} D^2 (0.94)$$

Cross-sectional area of hollow shaft, $A_h = \frac{\pi}{4}[D^2 - (0.55D)^2]$

$$= \frac{\pi}{4} D^2 (0.70)$$

$$\frac{D_h}{D_s} = \frac{D}{0.91D} = 1.098$$

$$\text{Saving in weight} = \frac{A_s - A_h}{A_s} \times 100$$

$$= \frac{\frac{\pi}{4} D^2 (0.97 - 0.70)}{\frac{\pi}{4} D^2 (0.94)} \times 100$$

$$= \mathbf{38.57\%}$$

**Example 10.39 :** A composite shaft consists of a steel rod 100 mm in diameter surrounded by a closely fitting tube of brass fixed to it. Find the outer diameter of the tube so that when a torque is applied to the composite shaft, it will be shared equally by both the materials. If the torque is 20 kNm, calculate maximum shear stress in each material and angle of twist in length of 4 m. Take $G_{ST} = 80$ GPa, $G_{BR} = 40$ GPa.

**Data** : Diameter of steel rod = 100 mm, $d_{tube} = 100$ mm, T = 20 kN-m,

$l = 4$ m, $G_{ST} = 80$ GPa, $G_{Br} = 40$ GPa

**Required** : Maximum shear stress and angle of twist.

**Concept** : Standard formula.

**Solution :**

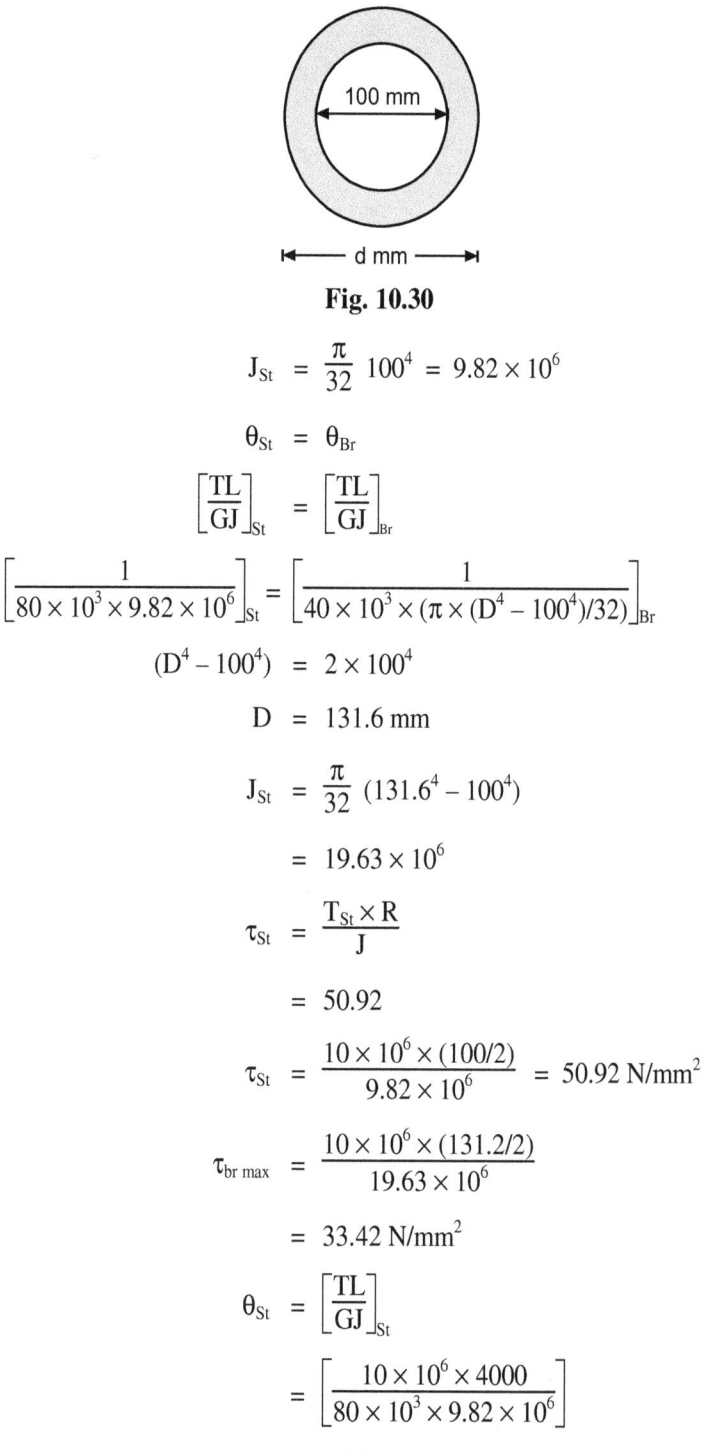

Fig. 10.30

$$J_{St} = \frac{\pi}{32} \, 100^4 = 9.82 \times 10^6$$

$$\theta_{St} = \theta_{Br}$$

$$\left[\frac{TL}{GJ}\right]_{St} = \left[\frac{TL}{GJ}\right]_{Br}$$

$$\left[\frac{1}{80 \times 10^3 \times 9.82 \times 10^6}\right]_{St} = \left[\frac{1}{40 \times 10^3 \times (\pi \times (D^4 - 100^4)/32)}\right]_{Br}$$

$$(D^4 - 100^4) = 2 \times 100^4$$

$$D = 131.6 \text{ mm}$$

$$J_{St} = \frac{\pi}{32} (131.6^4 - 100^4)$$

$$= 19.63 \times 10^6$$

$$\tau_{St} = \frac{T_{St} \times R}{J}$$

$$= 50.92$$

$$\tau_{St} = \frac{10 \times 10^6 \times (100/2)}{9.82 \times 10^6} = 50.92 \text{ N/mm}^2$$

$$\tau_{br \, max} = \frac{10 \times 10^6 \times (131.2/2)}{19.63 \times 10^6}$$

$$= 33.42 \text{ N/mm}^2$$

$$\theta_{St} = \left[\frac{TL}{GJ}\right]_{St}$$

$$= \left[\frac{10 \times 10^6 \times 4000}{80 \times 10^3 \times 9.82 \times 10^6}\right]$$

$$= 0.051 \text{ rad}$$

**Example 10.40 :** A solid steel rod, 6 m long is fixed at both ends. A torque of 12 kNm is applied at 2.4 m from left end. What are the fixing torques if diameter of shaft is 40 mm ? Find maximum shear stress in two portions. Also calculate angle of twist from the section where torque is applied. Assume G = 80 GPa.

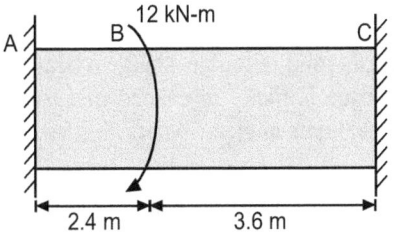

Fig. 10.31

**Data** : $l = 6$ m, T = 12 kN-m, D = 40 mm, G = 80 GPa

**Required** : Maximum shear stress and angle of twist.

**Concept** : Standard formula.

**Solution** :

$$\theta_{BA} = \theta_{BC}$$

$$\left[\frac{TL}{GJ}\right]_{BA} = \left[\frac{TL}{GJ}\right]_{BC}$$

$$T_{BA} \times 2400 = T_{BC} \times 3600$$

$$T_{BA} = 1.5\, T_{BC}$$

$$T_{BA} + T_{BC} = 12$$

$$T_{BC} = 4.8 \text{ kN-m}$$

$$T_{BA} = 7.2 \text{ kN-m}$$

$$\tau_B = \frac{T_{AB} \times R}{J}$$

$$\tau = \frac{4.8 \times 10^6 \times (40/2)}{\frac{\pi}{32} \times (40)^4} = 381.97 \text{ N/mm}^2$$

$$\tau_{BC} = \frac{T_{BC} \times R}{J} = \frac{7.2 \times 10^6 (40/2)}{\frac{\pi}{32} \times (40)^4} = 572.96 \text{ N/mm}^2$$

$$\theta_{BA} = \left[\frac{TL}{GJ}\right]_{BA}$$

$$\theta_{BA} = \left[\frac{4.8 \times 10^6 \times 2400}{80 \times 10^3 \times 251.33 \times 10^3}\right] = \textbf{0.57 rad}$$

## EXERCISE

1. Find the power transmitted by a shaft having 50 mm diameter at 150 rpm if maximum permissible shear stress is 80 MPa. (P = 30.834 kW)
2. A hollow circular shaft of 125 mm external diameter thickness of metal 25 mm is rotating at 150 rpm. The angle of twist on 5 m length was found to be 0.8°. Calculate the power transmitted and maximum shear stress induced in the material. Assume G = 80 GPa. (P = 73.19 kW, $\tau_{max}$ = 13.96 MPa)

3. A hollow circular shaft has external diameter of 125 mm and internal diameter of 100 mm. Find the safe power that can be transmitted if allowable shear stress is 100 MPa and maximum angle of twist is 4° for 3.5 m length. Take speed of shaft = 3 revolutions per second and maximum torque to exceed by mean torque by 25%. Take G = 80 MPa.
(P = 340.498 kW)

4. Design the diameter of solid circular shaft to transmit 40 kW power rotating at 120 rpm. Maximum torque is likely to exceed mean torque by 20%. Permissible shear stress = 60 MPa. Also calculate angle of twist for 2.5 m length, assume G = 85 GPa.
(D = 68.698 mm, θ = 2.9435°)

5. A steel shaft of solid circular cross-section has to transmit 220 kW at 200 rpm. The maximum shear stress is not to exceed 50 MPa and angle of twist must not be more than 1.5° in a length of 2.5 m. Design suitable diameter of shaft. Take G = 80 MPa.
(D (based on strength criteria) = 102.278 mm,
D (based on stiffness criteria) = 86.798 mm ∴ D = 102.278 mm)

6. Design the cross-section of hollow shaft for which internal diameter is 3/4th of its external diameter to resist a torque of 2000 Nm such that shear stress does not exceed 60 MPa and angle of twist does not exceed 2° for 2 m length. Assume G = 80 GPa.
(D (based on strength criteria) = 62.85 mm, D (based on stiffness criteria) = 67.96 mm
∴ D = 67.96 mm, d = 50.977 mm)

7. A hollow steel shaft 3 m long transmits a torque of 2 kNm. Total angle of twist is not to exceed 3° and permissible shear stress = 80 MPa. Determine inside and outside diameters of shaft, G = 85 MPa.
(D = 107.85 mm, d = 105.05 mm)

8. A hollow shaft has 75 mm external diameter and 50 mm internal diameter. Determine the twisting moment it can resist if permissible shear stress is 110 MPa. Determine the diameter of solid circular shaft made of same material which can transmit same twisting moment. Hence compare their weights per metre length. Take G = 80 GPa.
(T = 7.312 × $10^6$ N.mm, $D_{(solid\ shaft)}$ = 69.69 mm, $\frac{\text{Weight of solid shaft}}{\text{Weight of hollow shaft}}$ = 1.55)

9. Design diameter of solid shaft for resisting torque of 3000 Nm. Also design cross-section of hollow shaft made of same material assuming internal diameter as 0.75 times the external diameter for the same torque. Hence comment on percentage saving in weight and shear stress for shaft. Assume allowable angle of twist 2.5° for 2 m length of both shafts. Take G = 80 GPa.
($D_{solid}$ = 64.686 mm, $(D_{ext})_{hollow}$ = 71.139 mm, $(D_{int})_{hollow}$ = 53.354 mm
% saving in weight = 47.085%
$\tau_{solid}$ = 0.909 $\tau_{hollow}$ or $\tau_{hollow}$ = 1.099 $\tau_{solid}$)

10. Design diameter of solid shaft for resisting torque of 3000 Nm. Also design cross-section of hollow shaft made of same material assuming internal diameter 0.75 times the external diameter for the same torque. Hence comment on percentage saving in weight and angle of twist per unit length of shafts. Assume permissible shear stress as 60 MPa.
($D_{solid}$ = 63.384 mm, $(D_{ext})_{hollow}$ = 71.952 mm, $(D_{int})_{hollow}$ = 53.965 mm
% saving in wt. = 43.625%, $\theta_s$ = 1.135 $\theta_h$ or $\theta_h$ = 0.88 $\theta_s$)

11. Compare the weights of equal lengths of hollow and solid shaft to resist same torsional moment for same maximum shear stress. Assume internal diameter 0.75 times the external diameter for hollow shaft. $\left(\dfrac{\text{wt. of hollow shaft}}{\text{wt. of solid shaft}} = 0.564\right)$

12. The shaft shown in Fig. 10.32 below rotates at 250 rpm with 40 H.P. and 20 HP taken off at A and B respectively and 60 HP applied at C. Find the maximum shear stress developed in the shaft and angle of twist of gear A relative to gear C. Take G = 85 GPa.
    $(\tau_{max} = 11.399$ MPa, $\theta = 2.034°)$

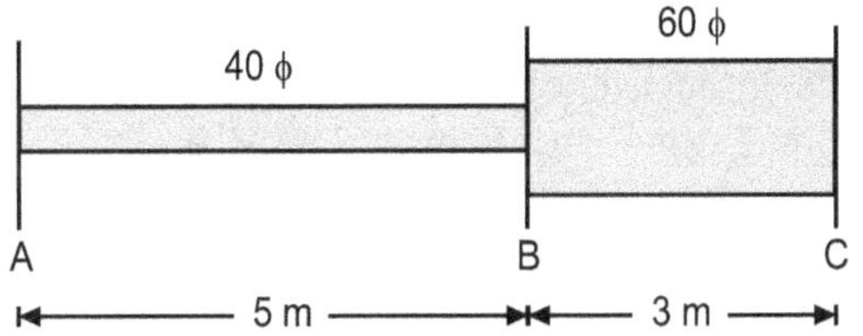

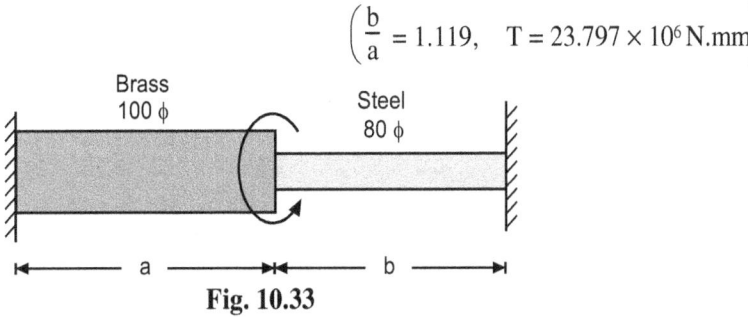

Fig. 10.32

13. A compound shaft as shown in Fig. 10.33 is attached to rigid supports. Determine the ratio of lengths 'b' to 'a' so that each material is stressed to its permissible limit. What torque T is applied ? Assume $G_b = 42$ GPa, $G_s = 84$ GPa, $\tau_b \le 70$ MPa, $\tau_s \le 100$ MPa.
    $\left(\dfrac{b}{a} = 1.119,\quad T = 23.797 \times 10^6 \text{ N.mm}\right)$

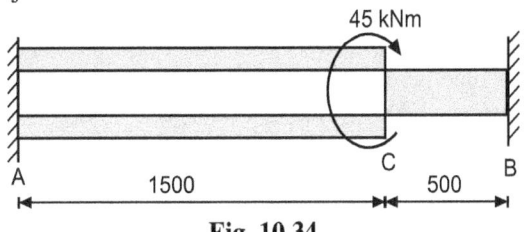

Fig. 10.33

14. A shaft ABC fixed at A and B is subjected to torque of 45 Nm at C as shown in Fig. 10.34. Calculate the end reactions and shear stresses in both components. Also find angle of twist at junction C.

Fig. 10.34

| AC | CB |
|---|---|
| Brass | Steel |
| D = 50 mm | D = 25 mm |
| d = 25 mm | |
| $G_b$ = 40 GPa | $G_s$ = 80 GPa |

$(T_A = 32.142$ kNm; $T_B = 12.857$ kNm; $\theta_C = 0.12°)$

15. A steel bar 40 mm diameter and 500 mm long when tested under an axial tensile load of 150 kN is found to stretch by 0.24 mm. The same bar when subjected to a torque of 1.5 kN.m is found to twist by 2°. Determine the values of four elastic constants.
(E = 248.67 GPa; G = 85.48 GPa; μ = 0.4545; K = 910.912 GPa)

16. A metal bar 15 mm φ subjected to a pull of 40 kN elongates by 0.5 mm over a gauge length of 500 mm. In a torsion test on the same material, maximum shear stress of 45 MPa was measured on a bar of 50 mm φ and angle of twist over a length of 300 mm was measured to be 0.4°. Determine Poisson's ratio for the material.   (μ = 0.463)

17. A circular shaft supported on bearings 5 m apart transmits 80 kW power at 130 rpm. A pulley provided at 2m from one bearing exerts a transverse load of 50 kN on the shaft. Determine the suitable diameter of shaft if
    (i)  Maximum normal stress is not to exceed 90 MPa.
    (ii) Maximum intensity of shear stress is not to exceed 40 MPa.
    ((i) D = 189.52 mm, D = 197.26 mm, Select D = 197.26 mm)

18. Fig. 10.35 shows a horizontal shaft AB subjected to torques at C and D. Determine (i) the end fixing couples in magnitude and direction, (ii) the diameter of the shaft if the maximum shear stress is not to exceed 80 MPa, (iii) the position of section where the shaft suffers no angular twist.
    ($T_A$ = 12.25 kNm; $T_B$ = 13.75 kNm; D = 95.7 mm; 1.182 m)

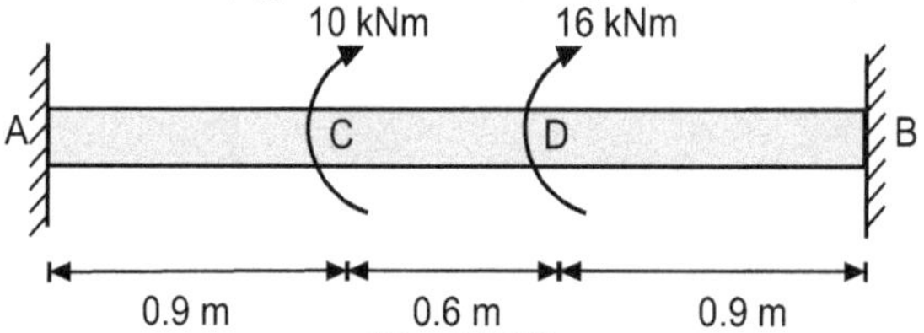

**Fig. 10.35**

19. A circular shaft supported on bearings 4 m apart transmits 75 kW power at 120 rpm. A pulley provided at 1.5 m from one bearing exerts a transverse load of 40 kN on the shaft. Determine the suitable diameter of shaft if (i) maximum normal stress is not to exceed 90 MPa, (ii) maximum shear stress is not to exceed 40 MPa.
    ((i) D = 162 mm, (ii) D = 169 mm  ∴ use D = 169 mm)

20. A solid alloy shaft of 50 mm diameter is to be coupled in series with a hollow steel shaft of the same external diameter. If the angle of twist per unit length of the steel shaft is to be 70% of that of alloy shaft, find the diameter of the steel shaft. Also find the speed at which the shaft should be driven to transmit 20 kW if allowable shear stresses in alloy and steel are 56 MPa and 80 MPa respectively. Assume $G_{steel}$ = 2.25 $G_{alloy}$.
    (38.87 mm; 153.3 rpm)

21. Two shafts are of length 'L' and outside diameter D. The first one is solid while the second one is hollow with inside diameter D/2. What is the ratio of strain energies that two steel shafts can absorb without exceeding the allowable shear stress ?
    $$\left(\frac{\mu_S}{\mu_H} = \frac{16}{15}\right).$$

22. A hollow circular shaft 20 mm thick transmits 294 kW at 200 rpm. Determine the diameters of the shaft if shear strain due to torsion is not to exceed 8 × 10⁻⁴. Assume G = 80 GPa.   (D = 110 mm; d = 70 mm)

# CHAPTER ELEVEN

# COMBINED LOADING

## 11.1 INTRODUCTION

In chapter 10, we have studied the stresses and strains set up by the cross-section of circular shaft to resist the action of torsional moment. But sometimes shaft has to resist bending moment and or axial thrust along with the torsional moment, also called as combined actions. In this chapter, we are going to discuss the combined action on the shaft.

## 11.2 COMBINED ACTIONS

### 11.2.1 Bending and Torsion

In practice, members are generally subjected to combined bending and torsion. In this article, we shall discuss the evaluation of principal stresses and maximum shear stress for such combined action.

Consider a solid circular shaft subjected to bending moment and torsion as shown in Fig. 11.1.

Let,  M = Bending moment (sagging)

T = Torsional moment

D = Diameter of shaft

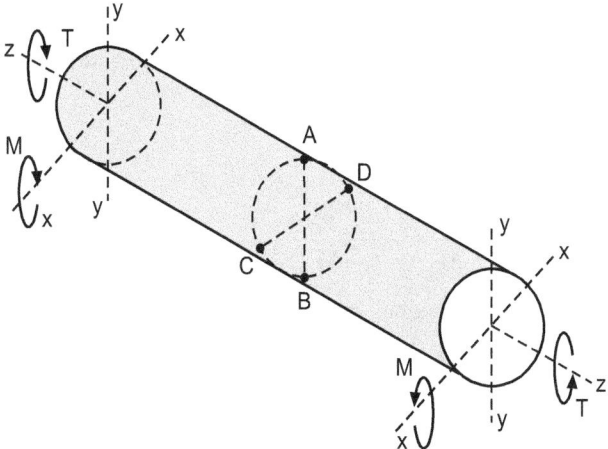

**Fig. 11.1 : Combined bending and torsion**

Consider an intermediate cross-section of shaft as shown in Fig. 11.1.

Shear stress due to torque $T = \tau = \dfrac{16\,T}{\pi D^3}$  ... (11.1)

Bending stress due to $M = \sigma = \dfrac{32\,M}{\pi D^3}$  ... (11.2)

It should be noted that shear stress $\tau$ is uniform at all elements A, B, C and D while bending stress $\sigma$ is compressive in nature at A, tensile in nature at B while zero at elements C and D. Hence, elements C and D are subjected to state of pure shear while principal stresses will occur at elements A and B. Principal stresses $\sigma_1$ and $\sigma_2$ at any of these two points are given by

$$\sigma_1\,;\,\sigma_2 = \dfrac{\sigma}{2} \pm \sqrt{\left(\dfrac{\sigma}{2}\right)^2 + \tau^2}$$  ... (11.3)

Substituting equations (11.1) and (11.2) in equation (11.3), we get

$$\sigma_1\,;\,\sigma_2 = \dfrac{32M}{2\pi D^3} \pm \sqrt{\left(\dfrac{32M}{2\pi D^3}\right)^2 + \left(\dfrac{16T}{\pi D^3}\right)^2}$$

$$= \dfrac{16M}{\pi D^3} \pm \sqrt{\left(\dfrac{16M}{\pi D^3}\right)^2 + \left(\dfrac{16T}{\pi D^3}\right)^2}$$

$$\sigma_1\,;\,\sigma_2 = \dfrac{16}{\pi D^3}\left[M \pm \sqrt{M^2 + T^2}\right]$$  ... (11.4)

Principal planes can be located by using

$$\tan(2\theta_1) = \dfrac{2\tau}{\sigma} = \dfrac{T}{M}$$  ... (11.5)

and $\quad \theta_2 = \theta_1 + 90°$

Maximum shear stress is given by,

$$\tau_{max} = \dfrac{\sigma_1 - \sigma_2}{2} = \dfrac{16}{\pi D^3}\sqrt{M^2 + T^2}$$  ... (11.6)

**Equivalent Bending and Torsional Moment :**

Let $\quad M_e$ = Equivalent bending moment which acting alone produces the same maximum normal stress.

Bending stress due to $M_e = \sigma = \dfrac{32\,M_e}{\pi D^3}$  ... (11.7)

Equating equations (11.4) and (11.7), we get

$$M_e = \dfrac{1}{2}\left[M + \sqrt{M^2 + T^2}\right]$$  ... (11.8)

Let $\quad T_e$ = Equivalent torsional moment which acting alone produces the same maximum shear stress.

Shear stress due to $T_e = \tau = \dfrac{16\,T_e}{\pi D^3}$  ... (11.9)

Equating equations (11.6) and (11.9), we get

$$T_e = \sqrt{M^2 + T^2}$$  ... (11.10)

## 11.2.2 Axial Force and Torsion

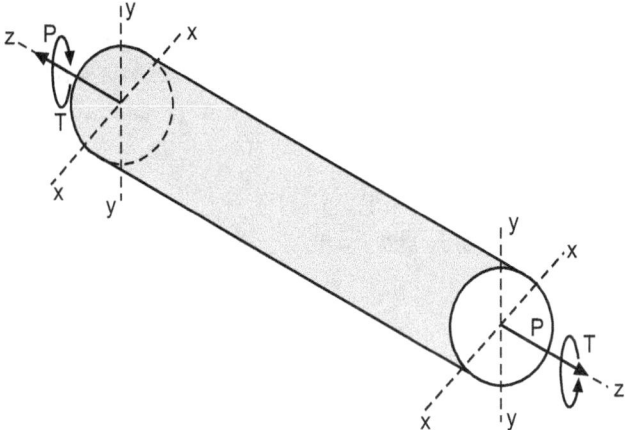

**Fig. 11.2 : Combined axial force and torsion**

Consider a solid circular shaft subjected to axial force and torsional moment as shown in Fig. 11.2.

Let  P  =  Axial force (tensile)

T  =  Torsional moment

D  =  Diameter of shaft

**Normal stress due to axial force** $P = \sigma = \dfrac{4P}{\pi D^2}$ ... (11.11)

Shear stress due to torque T is obtained from equation (11.1).

It should be noted that normal stress '$\sigma$' due to axial force is uniform over the entire cross-section, while shear stress $\tau$ due to torque is same at any point on the surface of the shaft.

Principal stresses can be evaluated by equation (11.3) and principal planes can be located by

$$\tan 2\theta_1 = \dfrac{2\tau}{\sigma} \quad \text{and} \quad \theta_2 = \theta_1 + 90°$$

## 11.2.3 Axial Force, Bending and Torsion

When a shaft is subjected to all these three actions, for elements farthest from neutral axis of bending; normal stresses due to bending and axial force will get added algebraically and shear stress due to torque is same on all the elements at surface of the shaft. Nature of normal stresses on various elements will depend on nature of axial force and bending moment. Algebraic addition of normal stresses is possible within elastic behaviour of the material, since principle of superpositions is valid till then. Principal stresses can then be obtained by using same equations discussed earlier.

## SOLVED EXAMPLES

**Example 11.1**: A shaft section 80 mm in diameter is subjected to bending moment of 3 kNm and torque of 8 kNm. Find the maximum normal stresses induced on section and locate the plane on which it acts. Find also what stress acting alone can produce the same maximum strain. Take $\mu = 0.3$.

**Data** : $D = 80$ mm; $M = 3$ kNm; $T = 8$ kNm; $\mu = 0.3$

**Required** : Principal stresses and single normal stress to produce equivalent principal strain.

**Concept** : Principal stresses for combined bending and torsion using equations (11.4), and (11.5).

**Solution** : (i) Principal stresses :

$$\sigma_1 ; \sigma_2 = \frac{16}{\pi D^3}\left(M \pm \sqrt{M^2 + T^2}\right)$$

$$= \frac{16}{\pi \times (80)^3}\left(3 \pm \sqrt{3^2 + 8^2}\right) \times 10^6$$

$$= 9.95\,(3 \pm 8.54)$$

$$\sigma_1 = 114.82 \text{ MPa}$$

and $\sigma_2 = -55.12$ MPa

(ii) Principal planes :

$$\tan(2\theta_1) = \frac{T}{M} = \frac{8}{3}$$

∴ $\theta_1 = 34.72°$ and $\theta_2 = \theta_1 + 90° = 34.72 + 90 = 124.72°$

(iii) Major principal strain :

$$\varepsilon_1 = \frac{1}{E}(\sigma_1 - \mu\sigma_2) = \frac{1}{E}(114.82 - 0.3(-55.12))$$

$$= \frac{131.36}{E}$$

(iv) Single normal stress to produce major principal strain :

Let $\sigma$ = Normal stress to produce major principal strain

∴ $\dfrac{\sigma}{E} = \dfrac{131.36}{E}$

∴ $\sigma = 131.36$ MPa

**Example 11.2** : A steel shaft is subjected to torque of 15 kNm and bending moment of 12 kNm. Calculate the principal stresses and maximum shear stress if diameter of shaft is 100 mm.

**Data** : $T = 15$ kNm; $M = 12$ kNm; $D = 100$ mm

**Required** : Principal stresses, maximum shear stress.

**Concept** : Same as Example (11.1).

**Solution** : (i) Principal stresses :

$$\sigma_1 ; \sigma_2 = \frac{16}{\pi D^3} (M \pm \sqrt{M^2 + T^2})$$

$$= \frac{16}{\pi \times (100)^3} (12 \pm \sqrt{(12)^2 + (15)^2}) \times 10^6$$

$$= 5.09 (12 \pm 19.2)$$

$$\sigma_1 = 158.8 \text{ MPa}$$

and $\sigma_2 = -36.65$ **MPa**

(ii) Position of principal planes :

$$\tan (2\theta_1) = \frac{T}{M} = \frac{15}{12}$$

∴ $\theta_1 = 25.67°$ and $\theta_2 = \theta_1 + 90° = 25.67 + 90° = 115.67°$

(iii) Maximum shear stress :

$$\tau_{max} = \frac{16}{\pi D^3} \sqrt{M^2 + T^2}$$

$$= \frac{16}{\pi \times (100)^3} (\sqrt{(12)^2 + (15)^2}) \times 10^6$$

$$\tau_{max} = 97.83 \text{ MPa}$$

**Example 11.3** : A hollow shaft is subjected to torque of 400 kNm and bending moment of 200 kNm. Internal diameter of shaft is 0.6 times the external diameter. If maximum normal stress is not to exceed 150 MPa and shear stress is not to exceed 80 MPa, design the cross-section of shaft.

**Data** : $T = 400$ kNm; $M = 200$ kNm; $d = 0.6$ D; $\sigma_{max} \leq 150$ MPa; $\tau_{max} \leq 80$ MPa.

**Required** : Design of cross-section of shaft.

**Concept** : Design of shaft based on maximum normal stress and maximum shear stress criteria. Governing dimensions will be greater of that obtained for above two conditions.

**Solution** : (i) Cross-section based on maximum normal stress :

Principal stresses : $\sigma_1 ; \sigma_2 = \dfrac{16D}{\pi (D^4 - d^4)} (M \pm \sqrt{M^2 + T^2})$

Major principal stress : $\sigma_1 = 150$ MPa

$$\sigma_1 = \frac{16D}{\pi [D^4 - (0.6 D)^4]} (200 + \sqrt{(200)^2 + (400)^2}) \times 10^6$$

$$= \frac{3.296 \times 10^9 \, D}{0.8704 \, D^4}$$

∴ $D = $ **293.36 mm** and $d = $ **176.02 mm** ... (1)

(ii) Cross-section based on maximum shear stress :

$$\tau_{max} = \frac{16 D}{\pi (D^4 - d^4)} \cdot \sqrt{M^2 + T^2}$$

Substituting, $\quad 80 = \dfrac{16 D}{\pi [D^4 - (0.6 D)^4]} \cdot \left(\sqrt{(200)^2 + (400)^2}\right) \times 10^6$

$$= \frac{2.278 \times 10^9}{0.8704 D^3}$$

∴ $\qquad$ D = 319.8 mm and d = 191.89 mm ... (2)

∴ Use $\qquad$ D = 320 mm and d = 0.6 × 320 = 192 mm

(Greater of (1) and (2))

**Example 11.4** : A flywheel weighing 4 kN is mounted on a shaft 50 mm ϕ; 600 mm long. Shaft is free to rotate at ends and flywheel is mounted on centre of shaft. If shaft is transmitting 44 kW at 300 rpm, calculate the principal stresses and maximum shear stresses in the shaft at the ends of horizontal and vertical diameter of cross-section close to that of flywheel.

**Data** : Weight of flywheel = W = 4 kN; diameter of shaft = D = 50 mm; L = 600 mm; Power = 44 kW; N = 300 r.p.m.

**Required** : Principal stresses and maximum shear stresses in the shaft at the ends of horizontal and vertical diameter of cross-section close to flywheel.

**Concept** : (i) Self weight of flywheel will produce bending moment and shear force for shaft and knowing power and speed of shaft, torque can be obtained.

(ii) Stresses at the ends of horizontal diameter (AB) :

(a) Shear stresses due to shear force.

(b) Shear stresses due to torque.

Normal stresses due to bending moment are zero at horizontal diameter.

(iii) Stresses at the ends of vertical diameter (CD) :

(a) Shear stresses due to torque.

(b) Normal stresses due to bending moment.

Shear stresses due to shear force are zero at the ends of vertical diameter.

**Solution** : (i) Analysis of forces :

Reactions at supports due to self weight of flywheel = 2 kN (↑)

Maximum BM at centre = $\dfrac{WL}{4} = \dfrac{4 \times 0.6}{4}$ = 0.6 kNm.

SF and BM diagrams are drawn as shown in Fig. 11.3.

Also $\quad P = \dfrac{2\pi NT}{60} \quad$ ∴ $\quad 44 \times 10^3 = \dfrac{2\pi \times 300 \times T}{60}$

∴ $\qquad$ T = 1400.56 Nm

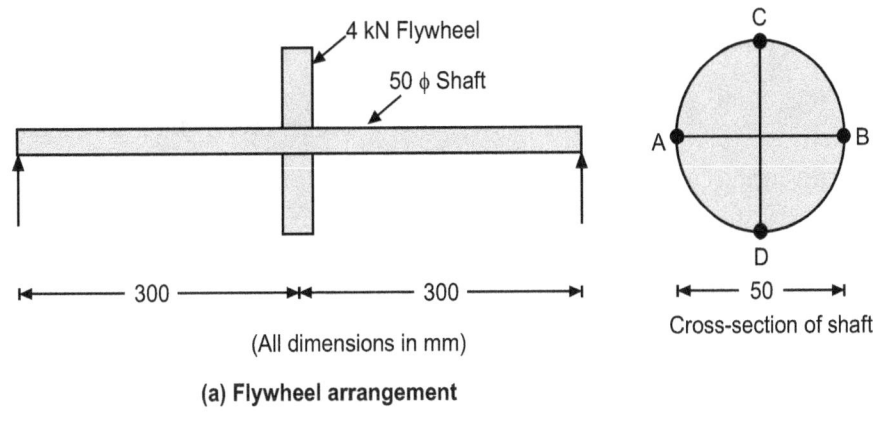

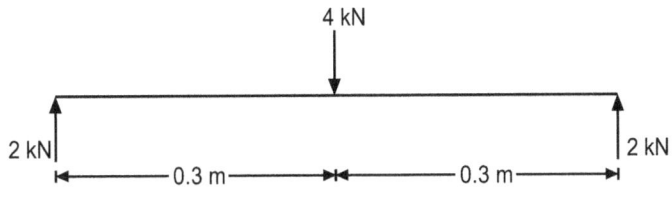

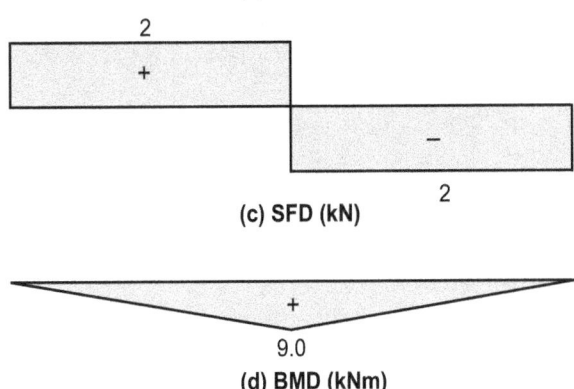

**Fig. 11.3**

(ii) Geometric properties of shaft :

$$I_x = \frac{\pi}{64} \cdot D^4 = \frac{\pi}{64} (50)^4 = 306.796 \times 10^3 \text{ mm}^4$$

$$J = \frac{\pi}{32} \cdot D^4 = \frac{\pi}{32} (50)^4 = 613.592 \times 10^3 \text{ mm}^4$$

Section modulus @ x axis = $Z_x = \dfrac{I_x}{y_{max}}$

$$= \frac{306.796 \times 10^3}{50/2} = \mathbf{12.27 \times 10^3 \text{ mm}^3}$$

$$\text{Polar section modulus} = \frac{J}{R} = \frac{613.592 \times 10^3}{50/2} = 24.54 \times 10^3 \text{ mm}^3$$

$$A = \frac{\pi}{4} \cdot D^2 = \frac{\pi}{4}(50)^2 = 1963.49 \text{ mm}^2$$

(iii) Evaluation of different stresses :

Shear stresses due to torque,

$$\tau_1 = \frac{T}{J/R} = \frac{1400.56 \times 10^3}{24.54 \times 10^3}$$

$$= 57.07 \text{ MPa}$$

[**Note :** $\tau_1 = 57.07$ MPa is same at all elements A, B, C and D.]

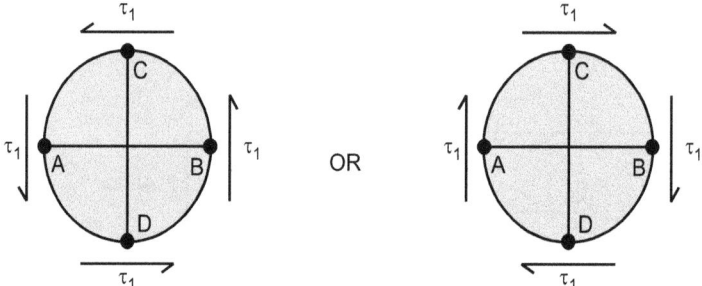

**Fig. 11.4 : Shear stresses due to torque**

Shear stresses due to shear force :

$$\tau_2 = \frac{4}{3}\tau_a$$

where $\tau_a$ = Average shear stress = $\dfrac{\text{Shear force}}{\text{Cross-sectional area}}$

$$= \frac{2 \times 10^3}{1963.49} = 1.02 \text{ MPa}$$

$$\therefore \quad \tau_2 = \frac{4}{3} \times 1.02 = 1.36 \text{ MPa}$$

[**Note :** $\tau_2 = 1.36$ MPa is at A and B only]

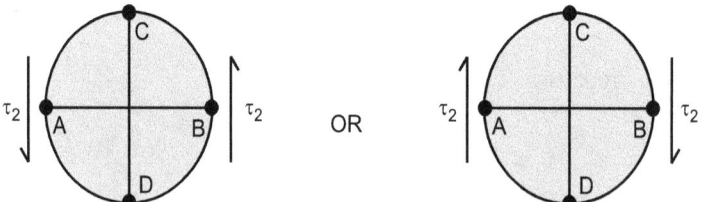

**Fig. 11.5 : Shear stresses due to shear force**

Bending stresses, $\quad \sigma = \dfrac{\text{B.M.}}{Z_x}$

$$= \frac{0.6 \times 10^6}{12.27 \times 10^3} = 48.9 \text{ MPa}$$

[**Note :** $\sigma = 48.9$ MPa is at C and D only]

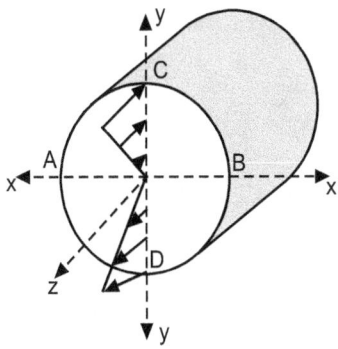

Bending compression at C.

Bending tension at D.

**Fig. 11.6 : Bending stresses**

(iv) Analysis of stresses at elements A and B :

Out of A and B, one element will have resultant shear stress

$$= \tau_1 + \tau_2$$
$$= 57.07 + 1.36$$
$$= \mathbf{58.43 \text{ MPa}}$$

While other elements will have resultant shear stress

$$= \tau = -\tau_1 + \tau_2$$
$$= -57.07 + 1.36$$
$$= \mathbf{-55.71 \text{ MPa}}$$

**Note :** Because the direction of torque is not specified and position of cross-section of shaft whether on left or on right of flywheel is not defined, no comment can be made about whether the maximum shear stress is at element A or B. However, both these elements are subjected to state of pure shear.

Selecting maximum shear stress

$$\tau_{max} = \mathbf{58.43 \text{ MPa}}$$

∴ Principal stresses $\sigma_1 = \sigma_2 = \pm \mathbf{58.43 \text{ MPa}}$

**Note :** For element subjected to state of pure shear stress '$\tau$', principal stresses $\sigma_1 = \sigma_2 = \tau$. Out of the two, one principal stress is tensile in nature while other is compressive.

(v) Analysis of stresses C and D :

$$\sigma_1 \, ; \, \sigma_2 = \frac{\sigma}{2} \pm \sqrt{\left(\frac{\sigma}{2}\right)^2 + \tau_1^2}$$

$$= \frac{48.9}{2} \pm \sqrt{\left(\frac{48.9}{2}\right)^2 + (57.07)^2}$$

$$= 24.45 \pm 62.08$$

$$\sigma_1 = \mathbf{86.53 \text{ MPa}} \text{ and } \sigma_2 = \mathbf{-37.63 \text{ MPa}}$$

Maximum shear stress $= \tau_{max} = \dfrac{\sigma_1 - \sigma_2}{2} = \dfrac{86.53 + 37.63}{2} = \mathbf{62.08 \text{ MPa}}$

However, principal stresses at elements C and D subjected to stresses due to bending and torsion can be worked out by standard expression as ;

$$\sigma_1 ; \sigma_2 = \frac{16}{\pi D^3} \left( M \pm \sqrt{M^2 + T^2} \right)$$

$$= \frac{16}{\pi \times (50)^3} \left( 0.6 \pm \sqrt{(0.6)^2 + (1.4)^2} \right) \times 10^6$$

$$\sigma_1 = 86.5 \text{ MPa} \text{ and } \sigma_2 = -37.6 \text{ MPa}$$

**Note :** + ve sign of $\sigma_1$ OR $\sigma_2$ indicates that it is of the same nature as that of normal stress produced by B.M. Thus, normal stress of 86.53 MPa is compressive at 'C' and tensile at 'D' while normal stress of 37.63 MPa is tensile at 'C' and compressive at 'D' because bending moment produces compression at 'C' and tension at 'D'.

**Example 11.5 :** A cantilever steel rod 25 mm diameter is supporting force 'F' as shown in Fig. 11.7. Determine the maximum force 'F' that can be applied if (a) the bending stress is not to exceed 125 MPa and (b) resultant shear stress due to bending and torsion is not to exceed 100 MPa.

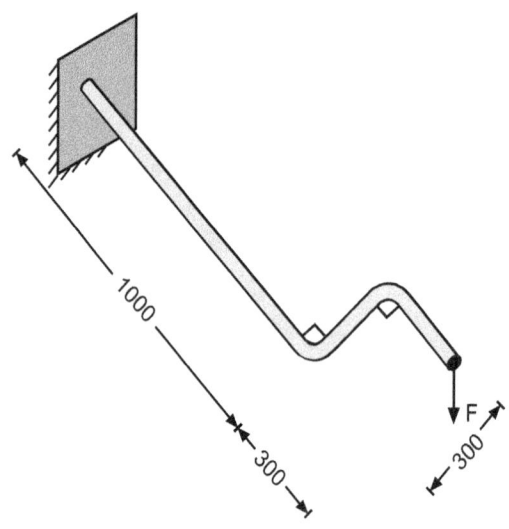

**Fig. 11.7**

**Data** : As shown in Fig. 11.7; bending stress ≤ 125 MPa and maximum shear stress ≤ 100 MPa.

**Required** : Safe value of F.

**Concept** : Maximum bending moment is at fixed end; Bending stresses; Shear stresses due to bending and torsion.

**Solution** : (i) Analysis :

Let 'F' be the force in newtons.

Maximum bending moment at fixed end = **1300 F Nmm**

Maximum torque at fixed end = **300 F Nmm**

(ii) From bending stress criteria,

$$I_x = \frac{\pi}{64} D^4 = \frac{\pi}{64} \times (25)^4 = 19.17 \times 10^3 \text{ mm}^4$$

$$y_{max} = \frac{25}{2} = 12.5 \text{ mm}$$

∴ Section modulus $= Z_x = \dfrac{I_x}{y_{max}} = \dfrac{19.17 \times 10^3}{12.5} = 1533.98 \text{ mm}^3$

Bending stress $= \sigma = 125 = \dfrac{BM}{Z_x}$

$$= \frac{1300 \, F}{1533.98}$$

∴ $F = \mathbf{147.49 \text{ N}}$ ... (1)

(iii) From resultant shear stress due to bending and torsion,

$$\tau_{max} = \frac{16}{\pi D^3} \sqrt{M^2 + T^2}$$

$$100 = \frac{16}{\pi \times (25)^3} \left( \sqrt{(1300 \, F)^2 + (300 \, F)^2} \right)$$

∴ $F = \mathbf{229.95 \text{ N}}$ ... (2)

∴ Safe value of $F$ = Least of (1) and (2)

$$= \mathbf{147.49 \text{ N}}$$

**Example 11.6 :** A solid circular shaft 20 mm ϕ is loaded as shown in Fig. 11.8.

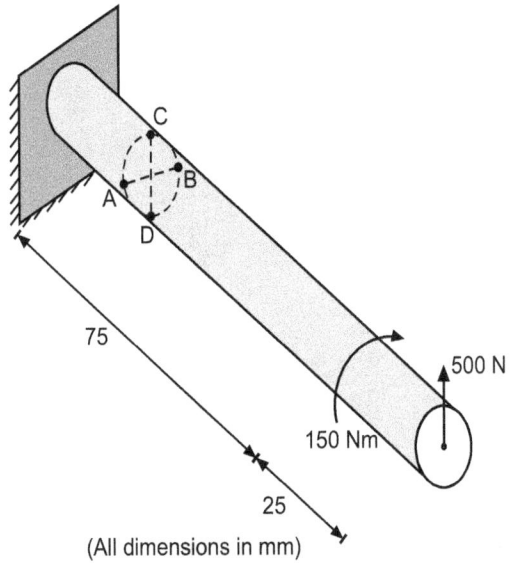

(All dimensions in mm)

**Fig. 11.8**

Determine (i) maximum shear stress on horizontal diameter AB and (ii) principal stresses at element C of vertical diameter.

**Data** : As shown in Fig. 11.8.

**Required** : Maximum shear stress on AB and principal stresses at element C.

**Concept** : Combined stresses : Normal stresses due to bending moment and shear stresses due to torque and shear force.

**Solution** : (i) Geometric properties.

$$A = \frac{\pi}{4} (20)^2 = 314.16 \text{ mm}^2$$

$$I_x = \frac{\pi}{64} (20)^4 = 7853.98 \text{ mm}^4$$

$$y_{max} = \frac{20}{2} = 10 \text{ mm}$$

$$\therefore \quad \text{Section modulus} = Z_x = \frac{I_x}{y_{max}}$$

$$= \frac{7853.98}{10} = 785.39 \text{ mm}^3$$

$$J = \frac{\pi}{32} (20)^4 = 15.71 \times 10^3 \text{ mm}^4$$

$$\frac{J}{R} = \frac{15.71 \times 10^3}{10} = 1.57 \times 10^3 \text{ mm}^3$$

(ii) Evaluation of different stresses :

$$\text{Shear stress due to torque} = \tau_1 = \frac{T}{J/R}$$

$$= \frac{150 \times 10^3}{1.57 \times 10^3}$$

$$= 95.54 \text{ MPa}$$

$$\text{Shear stress due to shear force} = \tau_2 = \frac{4}{3} \left(\frac{SF}{A}\right)$$

$$\therefore \quad \tau_2 = \frac{4}{3} \times \frac{500}{314.16} = 2.14 \text{ MPa}$$

Bending stresses due to B.M. ($\sigma$)

$$\sigma = \frac{B.M.}{Z_x} \quad \text{where} \quad BM = 500 \times 100 \text{ Nmm}$$

$$\therefore \quad \sigma = \frac{500 \times 100}{785.39} = 63.66 \text{ MPa}$$

Compressive at C and tensile at D.

(iii) Maximum shear stress on horizontal diameter :

$$\tau_{max} = \tau_1 + \tau_2 = 95.54 + 2.14$$

$$= \mathbf{97.68 \text{ MPa}}$$

(iv) Principal stresses at C :

$$\sigma_1 ; \sigma_2 = \frac{\sigma}{2} \pm \sqrt{\left(\frac{\sigma}{2}\right)^2 + \tau_i^2}$$

$$= \frac{63.66}{2} \pm \sqrt{\left(\frac{63.66}{2}\right)^2 + (95.54)^2}$$

$$= 31.83 \pm 100.7$$

$\sigma_1 = 132.53$ MPa i.e. compressive at C.

$\sigma_2 = -68.87$ MPa i.e. tensile at C.

**Note :** + ve sign of $\sigma_1$ or $\sigma_2$ indicates that principal stress is of same nature as that of $\sigma$.

Principal planes :

$$\tan(2\theta_1) = \frac{2\tau_1}{\sigma} = \frac{2 \times 95.54}{63.66}$$

$$\theta_1 = 35.78°$$

and $\theta_2 = \theta_1 + 90°$

$$= 35.78 + 90$$

$$= 125.78°$$

**Example 11.7 :** A solid shaft of 100 mm diameter transmits 500 kW at 500 r.p.m. and is also subjected to an axial thrust of 200 kN. If the maximum principal stress is not to exceed 100 MPa, find what additional bending moment may safely be carried ?

**Data** : D = 100 mm; Power = 500 kW; N = 500 rpm;
P = 200 kN; Maximum principal stress = 100 MPa.

**Required :** Additional bending moment carrying capacity.

**Concept :** Combined stresses : Normal stresses due to bending moment and axial force and shear stresses due to torsion.

**Solution :** (i) Geometric properties :

$$A = \frac{\pi}{4} D^2 = \frac{\pi}{4} (100)^2 = 7.85 \times 10^3 \text{ mm}^2$$

$$I_x = \frac{\pi}{64} (D)^4 = \frac{\pi}{64} (100)^4 = 4.91 \times 10^6 \text{ mm}^4$$

$$y_{max} = \frac{100}{2} = 50 \text{ mm}$$

$$Z_x = \frac{I_x}{y_{max}} = \frac{4.91 \times 10^6}{50} = 98.17 \times 10^3 \text{ mm}^3$$

$$J = \frac{\pi}{32} (D)^4 = \frac{\pi}{32} (100)^4 = 9.82 \times 10^6 \text{ mm}^4$$

$$\frac{J}{R} = \frac{9.82 \times 10^6}{50} = 196.4 \times 10^3 \text{ mm}^3$$

(ii) Evaluation of different stresses :

Normal stress due to axial force :

$$\sigma_a = \frac{P}{A} = \frac{200 \times 10^3}{7.85 \times 10^3} = 25.48 \text{ MPa}$$

$$\text{Power} = \frac{2\pi NT}{60}$$

$$500 \times 10^3 = \frac{2\pi \times 500 \times T}{60}$$

$$\therefore \quad T = 9.55 \times 10^3 \text{ Nm}$$
$$= 9.55 \times 10^6 \text{ Nmm}$$

$\therefore$ Shear stresses due to torque $= \dfrac{T}{J/R}$

$$= \frac{9.55 \times 10^6}{196.4 \times 10^3} = 48.62 \text{ MPa}$$

(iii) Additional maximum bending moment :

For an element subjected to normal stress in one direction and shear stress,

Principal stresses $\quad \sigma_1 ; \sigma_2 = \dfrac{\sigma}{2} \pm \sqrt{\left(\dfrac{\sigma}{2}\right)^2 + \tau^2}$

$\therefore$ Maximum principal stress $= \sigma_1 = \dfrac{\sigma}{2} + \sqrt{\left(\dfrac{\sigma}{2}\right)^2 + \tau^2}$

$$100 = \frac{\sigma}{2} + \sqrt{\left(\frac{\sigma}{2}\right)^2 + (48.62)^2}$$

$\therefore \quad \sigma = 76.36 \text{ MPa}$
$\quad = $ Stress due to axial force +
$\quad \quad$ Stress due to bending moment
$\quad = \sigma_a + \sigma_b$
$\quad = 25.48 + \sigma_b$

$\therefore \quad \sigma_b = 50.88 \text{ MPa} = $ Maximum additional normal stress.

$\therefore \quad$ Additional maximum BM $= \sigma_b \times Z_x$
$$= 50.88 \times 98.17 \times 10^3$$
$$= 4.99 \times 10^6 \text{ Nmm}$$
$$= \mathbf{4.99 \text{ kNm}}$$

**Example 11.8 :** A solid shaft in a small hydraulic turbine is 100 mm in diameter. It supports an axial compressive load of 440 kN. Determine the maximum power that will be developed at a speed of 240 r.p.m. without exceeding maximum shear stress of 70 MPa and maximum normal stress of 90 MPa.

**Data** : $D = 100$ mm; Axial compressive load $= P = 440$ kN; $N = 240$ r.p.m.; $\tau_{max} = 70$ MPa and Maximum normal stress $= 90$ MPa.

**Required** : Safe power P.

**Concept** : Combined stresses : Normal stress due to axial force and shear stress due to torsion.

**Solution** : (i) Geometric properties :

$$A = \frac{\pi}{4} D^2 = \frac{\pi}{4} (100)^2 = 7853.98 \text{ mm}^2$$

$$J = \frac{\pi}{32} (D)^4 = \frac{\pi}{32} (100)^4 = 9.82 \times 10^6 \text{ mm}^4$$

$$R = \frac{100}{2} = 50 \text{ mm}$$

$$\frac{J}{R} = \frac{9.82 \times 10^6}{50} = 196.35 \times 10^3 \text{ mm}^3$$

(ii) Normal stress due to axial force ($\sigma$) :

$$\sigma = \frac{P}{A} = \frac{440 \times 10^3}{7853.98} = 56.02 \text{ MPa}$$

(iii) From maximum normal stress criteria,

$$\sigma_1 = \frac{\sigma}{2} + \sqrt{\left(\frac{\sigma}{2}\right)^2 + \tau^2}$$

$$90 = \frac{56.02}{2} + \sqrt{\left(\frac{56.02}{2}\right)^2 + \tau^2}$$

∴ $\tau = 55.3$ MPa ... (1)

(iv) From maximum shear stress criteria,

$$\tau_{max} = \sqrt{\left(\frac{\sigma}{2}\right)^2 + \tau^2}$$

$$70 = \sqrt{\left(\frac{56.02}{2}\right)^2 + \tau^2}$$

$\tau = 64.15$ MPa ... (2)

(v) Safe torque :

Shear stress due to torque to be allowed for safety = 55.3 MPa.

(Least of (1) and (2))

∴ $$\tau = \frac{T}{(J/R)}$$

$$55.3 = \frac{T}{196.35 \times 10^3}$$

∴ T = $10.86 \times 10^6$ Nmm = **10.86 × 10³ Nm**

(vi) Safe power, $$P = \frac{2\pi NT}{60}$$

$$= \frac{2\pi \times 240 \times 10.86 \times 10^3}{60}$$

$$= 272.94 \times 10^3 \text{ W} = \mathbf{272.94 \text{ kW}}$$

## 11.3 STRAIN ENERGY DUE TO TORSION

Refer to Fig. 11.9. Total strain energy of a shaft of length L, under the action of torque T is the work done in twisting i.e. for gradually applied torque,

$$U = \frac{1}{2} T\theta \qquad \ldots (11.12)$$

Expressed in terms of maximum shear stress,

$$U = \frac{1}{2}\left(\frac{J}{R}\tau_{max}\right)\left(\frac{\tau_{max}}{R} \cdot \frac{L}{G}\right) \qquad \ldots (11.13)$$

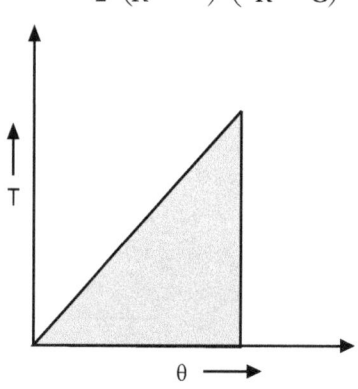

Fig. 11.9

(a) For solid circular shaft,

$$U = \frac{1}{2}\left[\frac{\pi D^3}{16} \times \tau_{max}\right]\left[\frac{\tau_{max}}{D/2} \times \frac{L}{G}\right] = \frac{\tau_{max}^2}{4G} \times \frac{\pi}{4} D^2 L$$

$$= \frac{\tau_{max}^2}{4G} \times (\text{Volume}) \qquad \ldots (11.14)$$

(b) For hollow circular shaft,

$$U = \frac{1}{2} \cdot \left[\frac{\pi}{16 D} \cdot (D^4 - d^4) \times \tau_{max}\right]\left[\frac{\tau_{max}}{D/2} \times \frac{L}{G}\right]$$

$$= \frac{\tau_{max}^2}{4G} \cdot \left[\frac{D^2 + d^2}{D^2}\right] \times (\text{Volume}) \qquad \ldots (11.15)$$

**Example 11.9 :** A hollow shaft subjected to a pure torque, attains maximum shear stress $\tau$. Given that strain energy per unit volume is $\tau^2/3G$.

(i) Calculate the ratio of shaft diameters.

(ii) Determine the actual diameters of such a shaft to transmit 4 MW at 100 r.p.m. when energy stored is 25 kN.m/m³ and G = 80 GPa.

**Data** : Power = 4 MW, N = 100 r.p.m.; U = 25 kNm/m³, G = 80 GPa.

**Required** : (i) Ratio of shaft diameters, (ii) Diameter of shaft.

**Concept** : Strain energy due to torsion.

**Solution :** (i) Let, 'D' and 'd' be the external and internal diameters respectively.

From equation (11.15),

$$\frac{U}{Volume} = \frac{\tau^2}{4G}\left(\frac{D^2}{D^2 + d^2}\right)$$

$$= \frac{\tau^2}{3G}$$

∴ $\frac{D^2 + d^2}{D^2} = \frac{4}{3}$

∴ $1 + \frac{d^2}{D^2} = \frac{4}{3}$

$\frac{d}{D} = \sqrt{\frac{1}{3}}$

∴ $\frac{D}{d} = 1.732$

(ii) Diameters of shaft, $P = 4$ MW $= 4 \times 10^6$ N.m/sec.

$N = 100$ r.p.m.

$$P = \frac{2\pi N T_a}{60}$$

$$4 \times 10^6 = \frac{2\pi \times 100 \times T_a}{60}$$

$T_a = 381971.86$ Nm $= 381971.86 \times 10^3$ N.mm

Also, it is given that, $G = 80 \times 10^3$ MPa

Energy stored $= 25$ kN.m/m³ $= 25 \times 10^{-3}$ N.mm/mm³

i.e. $\frac{\tau^2}{3G} = 25 \times 10^{-3}$

$$\frac{\tau^2}{3 \times 80 \times 10^3} = 25 \times 10^{-3}$$

$\tau = $ **77.46 MPa**

Using $\frac{T}{J} = \frac{\tau}{R}$

$\frac{J}{R} = \frac{T}{\tau} = \frac{381971.86 \times 10^3}{77.46} = $ **4931214.3 mm³**

∴ $\frac{J}{R} = \frac{\pi}{16 D}(D^4 - d^4) = 4931214.3$

$\frac{\pi}{16 \times 1.732\,d}[(1.732\,d)^4 - d^4] = 4931214.3$

$d = $ **175.85 mm**

$D = $ **304.57 mm**

**Example 11.10 :** A solid shaft 60 mm diameter has to resist a B.M. of 450 kN-mm accompanied by torque 360 kN-mm. Calculate maximum principal stress induced in the shaft. Also calculate maximum shear stress produced.

**Data** : $T = 360 \times 10^3$ N-mm, $M = 450 \times 10^3$ N-mm, $D = 60$ mm

**Required** : Principal stresses.

**Concept** : Using equations of combined bending and torsion.

**Solution** : Principal stresses.

$$\sigma_{max} = \frac{16}{\pi D^3}(M + \sqrt{M^2 + T^2})$$

$$= \frac{16}{\pi \times 60^3}\left[450 \times 10^3 + \sqrt{(450 \times 10^3)^2 + (360 \times 10^3)^2}\right]$$

$$= 24.2 \text{ MPa}$$

$\tau_{max}$ = Maximum shear stress induced

$$= \frac{16}{\pi D^3}\sqrt{M^2 + T^2}$$

$$= \frac{16}{\pi (60)^3}\sqrt{(450 \times 10^3)^2 + (360 \times 10^3)^2}$$

$$= 13.6 \text{ MPa}$$

**Example 11.11 :** A solid circular shaft is required to transmit 120 kW at 400 RPM. It is also subjected to B.M. of 4 kN-m. Find the suitable minimum diameter of the shaft if the maximum principal stress is limited to 100 MPa. What will be the maximum shear stress produced in the shaft.

**Data** : Power = 120 kW = $120 \times 10^3$ watt, N = 400 RPM

$M = 4 \times 10^6$ N-mm, maximum principal stress = 100 MPa

**Required** : Diameter of the shift.

**Concept** : Using equations of combined bending and torsion.

**Solution** : Evaluation of different stresses :

$$P = \frac{2\pi NT}{60}$$

$\therefore$
$$T = \frac{120 \times 10^3 \times 60}{2\pi \times 400} = 2864.79 \text{ N-m}$$

$$= 2864.79 \times 10^3 \text{ N-mm}$$

$$\sigma_{max} = \frac{16}{\pi D^3}\left[M + \sqrt{M^2 + T^2}\right]$$

$$100 = \frac{16}{\pi D^3}\left[4 \times 10^6 + \sqrt{(4 \times 10^6)^2 + (2864.79 \times 10^3)^2}\right]$$

∴          D = 76.87 mm

Maximum shear stress $= \dfrac{16}{\pi D^3} \sqrt{M^2 + T^2}$

$= \dfrac{16}{\pi \times (76.87)^3} \times \sqrt{(4 \times 10^6)^2 + (2864.7 \times 10^3)^2}$

$= 55.16 \text{ N/mm}^2$

**Example 11.12 :** A solid shaft 100 mm in diameter is subjected to a B.M. M and twisting moment T. The maximum principal stress produced in the shaft is 120 MPa. If the maximum bending stress due to M is equal to maximum shear stress due to T, find the values of M and T.

**Data** : Maximum principal stress = 120 MPa, Bending stress = shear stress.

**Required** : Bending moment (M), twisting moment (T).

**Concept** : Using equations of combined loading.

**Solution** :

$$\sigma_b = \tau$$

$$\dfrac{M}{Z} = \dfrac{T}{J}$$

∴ $\dfrac{M}{\dfrac{\pi}{32}D^3} = \dfrac{T}{\dfrac{\pi}{16}D^3}$

∴ Maximum shear stress $= \dfrac{16}{\pi D^3}\left[(M) + \sqrt{M^2 + T^2}\right]$

∴ $120 = \dfrac{16}{\pi \times 100^3}\left[M + \sqrt{M^2 + 4M^2}\right]$

$120 = \dfrac{16}{\pi \times 100^3}\left[M(1 + \sqrt{5})\right]$

M $= 7.28 \times 10^6$ N-mm $= $ **7.28 kN-m**

T $= 2M$

∴    T $= $ **14.56 kN-m**

**Example 11.13 :** A solid shaft 200 m in diameter is subjected to a bending moment M and a twisting moment 0.8 m. Find the value of M if the maximum shear stress is limited to 60 MPa. What is then maximum principal stress ?

**Data** : T = 0.8 M, maximum shear stress = 60 MPa

**Required** : Maximum principal stress.

**Concept** : Using equation of combined loading.

**Solution** : Geometric properties :

$$Z = \dfrac{\pi}{16}D^3 = \dfrac{\pi}{16} \times 200^3$$

$= 1.57 \times 10^6 \text{ mm}^3$

$$\tau_{max} = \frac{16}{\pi D^3}\left[\sqrt{M^2 + T^2}\right]$$

$$60 = \frac{1}{1.57 \times 10^6}\left[\sqrt{M^2 + (0.8M)^2}\right]$$

$$60 = \frac{1}{1.57 \times 10^6} \times 1.28\,M$$

$$\therefore \quad M = 7.36 \times 10^7 \text{ N-mm}$$

$$\therefore \quad M = 73.6 \text{ kN-m}$$

∴ Maximum principal stress

$$= \frac{16}{\pi D^3}\left[M + \sqrt{M^2 + T^2}\right]$$

$$= \frac{16}{\pi \times 200^3}\left[73.6 + \sqrt{(73.6)^2 + (0.8 \times 73.6)^2}\right]$$

$$= \mathbf{106.88 \text{ MPa}}$$

**Example 11.14 :** A hollow circular shaft of the external diameter 240 mm and internal diameter 180 mm is subjected to a torque of $2.8 \times 10^7$ N-mm and a bending moment of $1.4 \times 10^7$ N-mm. Find the maximum principal and shear stress produced.

**Data** : D = 240 mm, d = 180 mm, T = $2.8 \times 10^7$ N-mm, M = $1.4 \times 10^7$ N-mm.

**Required** : Maximum principal and shear stress.

**Concept** : Using equations of combined loading.

**Solution** : Geometric properties :

$$\text{Polar section modulus, } Z_p = \frac{\pi}{16}\frac{(D^4 - d^4)}{D}$$

$$= \frac{\pi}{16}\left(\frac{240^4 - 180^4}{240}\right) = 18.56 \times 10^5 \text{ mm}^3$$

$$\text{Maximum principal stress} = \frac{\left(M + \sqrt{M^2 + T^2}\right)}{Z_p}$$

$$= \frac{1.4 \times 10^7 + \left(\sqrt{1.4 \times 10^7 + 2.8 \times 10^7}\right)}{18.56 \times 10^5}$$

$$= 244.41 \text{ N/mm}^2$$

$$\text{Maximum shear stress} = \frac{\sqrt{M^2 + T^2}}{Z_s}$$

$$= \frac{\sqrt{1.4 \times 10^7 + 2.8 \times 10^7}}{18.56 \times 10^5}$$

$$= \mathbf{16.86 \text{ MPa}}$$

**Example 11.15 :** In a circular shaft subjected to twisting moment 'T' and bending moment 'M', show that when M = 1.2 T, the ratio of maximum shear stress to the greater principal stress is nearly 0.566.

**Solution :**

$$\sigma_1; \sigma_2 = \frac{16}{\pi D^3}\left[M \pm \sqrt{M^2 + T^2}\right]$$

$$\sigma_1 = \frac{16}{\pi D^3}\left[M + \sqrt{M^2 + T^2}\right]$$

$$\sigma_1 = \frac{16}{\pi D^3}\left[1.2T + \sqrt{(1.2T)^2 + T^2}\right]$$

$$\sigma_1 = \frac{16T}{\pi D^3}\left[1.2 + \sqrt{(1.2)^2 + 1}\right]$$

$$\sigma_1 = \frac{44.19\, T}{\pi D^3}$$

$$\sigma_2 = \frac{16}{\pi D^3}\left[M - \sqrt{M^2 + T^2}\right]$$

$$\tau_{max} = \frac{\sigma_1 - \sigma_2}{2} = \frac{25\, M}{\pi D^3} = \frac{25T}{\pi D^3}$$

$$\frac{\tau_{max}}{\sigma_1} = \frac{\frac{25T}{\pi D^3}}{\frac{44.19T}{\pi D^3}} = \mathbf{0.566}$$

---

**Example 11.16 :** A shaft of hollow circular section with outside diameter 200 mm and inside diameter 160 mm is subjected to simultaneously a torque of 12 kNm and a axial compressive load of 300 kN. Determine the maximum tensile stress, maximum compressive stress and maximum shear stress in the shaft.(8)

**Data** : D = 200 mm, d = 160 mm, T = 12 × 10$^6$ N-mm, P = 300 × 10$^3$ N

**Required** : Maximum tensile stress, maximum compressive stress, shear stress.

**Concept** : Standard formula.

**Solution :**

$$A = \frac{\pi}{4}(200^2 - 160^2) = 11309.73 \text{ mm}^2$$

$$J = \frac{\pi}{32}(200^4 - 160^4) = 92.7 \times 10^6 \text{ mm}^4$$

$$\sigma = \frac{P}{A} = \frac{300000}{11309.73} = 26.53 \text{ N/mm}^2$$

$$\tau = \frac{T}{J} \times R = \frac{12 \times 10^6}{92.74 \times 10^6} \times 100$$

$$= 12.94 \text{ N/mm}^2$$

$$\sigma_1; \sigma_2 = \frac{\sigma}{2} \pm \sqrt{\left(\frac{\sigma}{2}\right)^2 + \tau^2}$$

$$\sigma_1; \sigma_2 = \frac{26.53}{2} \pm \left[\left(\frac{26.53}{2}\right)^2 + 12.94^2\right]$$

$$\sigma_1 = 31.8 \text{ N/mm}^2 \text{ (T)}$$
$$\sigma_2 = -5.27 \text{ N/mm}^2 \text{ (C)}$$

Maximum shear stress $= \dfrac{\sigma_1 - \sigma_2}{2} = \dfrac{31.8 - (-5.27)}{2} = \dfrac{37.07}{2} = 18.53 \text{ N/mm}^2$

**Example 11.17 :** A solid shaft of 60 mm diameter has to resist a bending moment of 450 kN-mm accompanied by a torque of 360 kN-mm. Calculate the maximum principal stress induced in the shaft, also calculate the maximum shear stress induced.

**Data** : $D = 60$ mm, $M = 450 \times 10^3$ N-mm, $T = 360 \times 10^3$ N-mm
**Required** : Maximum principal stress, maximum shear stress.
**Concept** : Standard formula.
**Solution** :

$$P = \frac{2\pi NT}{60}$$

$$\sigma_1; \sigma_2 = \frac{16}{\pi D^3}[M \pm \sqrt{M^2 + T^2}]$$

$$\sigma_1; \sigma_2 = \frac{16 \times 10^6}{\pi (60)^3}[450 \pm \sqrt{450^2 + 360^2}]$$

$$\sigma_1; \sigma_2 = \frac{16 \times 10^3}{\pi (60)^3}[450 \pm \sqrt{332100}]$$

$$\sigma_1 = 24.20 \text{ N/mm}^2$$
$$\sigma_2 = -2.98 \text{ N/mm}^2$$

$$\tau_{max} = \frac{24.20 - (-2.98)}{2} = 13.55 \text{ N/mm}^2$$

**Example 11.18 :** A shaft of a hollow circular section of internal and external diameters 150 mm and 200 mm respectively is subjected to a bending moment M and twisting moment M/Z. Find the value of M if the normal maximum stress is limited to 100 MPa. What is then the maximum shear stress ?

**Solution :**  $Z_s$ = Polar section modulus

$$= \frac{\pi}{16}\left[\frac{D^4 - d^4}{D}\right] = \frac{\pi}{16}\left[\frac{200^4 - 150^4}{200}\right] = 3.42 \times 10^5 \text{ mm}^3$$

$$T_e = M + \sqrt{M^2 + T^2} = M + \sqrt{M^2 + \frac{M^2}{4}}$$

$$= M + 1.118 M = 2.118 M$$

$\sigma_{p_1}$ = Maximum normal stress = Major principal stress

$$= \frac{1}{Z_s} T_e$$

∴  $T_e = \sigma_{p_1} Z_s = 100 \times 3.42 \times 10^5 = 3.42 \times 10^7$ N-mm

∴ $2.118\, M = 3.42 \times 10^7$

∴ $M = 1.61 \times 10^7$ N-mm

$(\tau)_{max}$ = Maximum shear stress

$$= \frac{1}{Z_s} \sqrt{M^2 + T^2} = \frac{1}{Z_s}\, 1.118\, M$$

$$= \frac{1.118 \times 1.61 \times 10^7}{3.42 \times 10^5} = 52.63 \text{ MPa}$$

**Example 11.19**: Find the external diameter of a hollow shaft of diameter ratio 0.50, if it is subjected to a bending moment of $2 \times 10^7$ N-mm and a torque of $4 \times 10^7$ N-mm. The permissible shear stress is limited to 100 N/mm². What then will be the magnitude of the major principal stress?

**Solution**: $Z_s$ = Polar section modulus

$$= \frac{\pi}{16} \left( \frac{D^4 - d^4}{D} \right) = \frac{\pi}{16} \left( \frac{D^4 - \frac{D^4}{16}}{D} \right)$$

$$= \frac{\pi}{16} \times \frac{15}{16} \times D^3 = 0.184\, D^3$$

$T_e$ = Equivalent torque due to M and T

$$= M + \sqrt{M^2 + T^2} = \left[2 + \sqrt{4 + 16}\right] \times 10^7$$

$$= (2 + 4.47) \times 10^7 = 6.47 \times 10^7 \text{ N-mm}$$

$(\tau)_{max}$ = Permissible shear stress = $\frac{1}{Z_s} \sqrt{M^2 + T^2}$

∴ $100 = \dfrac{4.47 \times 10^7}{0.184\, D^3}$

∴ $D = \left[\dfrac{4.47}{0.184} \times 10^5\right]^{1/3} = 134.43$ mm

and $d = 67.22$ mm

$\sigma_{P_1}$ = Major principal stress

$$= \frac{1}{Z_s} T_e = \frac{6.47 \times 10^7}{0.184 \times (134.43)^3}$$

$\sigma_{P_1} = 144.47$ MPa

**Example 11.20**: A solid circular shaft of 100 mm diameter transmits 60 kW at 150 R.P.M. The bearings are spread at 5000 mm apart. The shaft supports a central point load of 5 kN. Find the maximum and minimum stresses at the centre of the shaft and bearings.

**Solution**: $60 \text{ kW} = 60,000 \text{ W} = \dfrac{2\pi N}{60} T$

∴ $T = \dfrac{60,000 \times 60}{2\pi \times 150} = 3819.72$ N-mm $= 3.82 \times 10^6$ N-mm

The torque acts throughout the entire length of the shaft. Bending moment at the centre of the shaft = M

$$= \frac{Wl}{4} = \frac{5 \times 5000}{4} = 6250 \text{ kN-mm} = 6.25 \times 10^6 \text{ N-mm}$$

The bending moment is zero at bearings.

Consider the section of the shaft at bearings. Here M = 0 and T = $3.82 \times 10^5$ N-mm

$$T = \frac{\pi}{16} d^3 \cdot \tau$$

∴ $$\tau = \frac{3.82 \times 10^6 \times 16}{\pi \, 10^6} = 19.46 \text{ MPa}$$

This creates a state of simple shear at the section. Hence at diagonal planes, normal stresses are produced having the same magnitude but difference in nature, i.e. one diagonal stress is 19.46 N/mm² (tensile) and the other diagonal stress is 19.46 N/mm² (compressive).

Now, consider the section of the shaft at the centre of the span.

Here,  M = Bending moment = $6.25 \times 10^6$ N-mm and

T = Twisting moment = $3.82 \times 10^6$ N-mm is acting.

∴ $T_e$ = Equivalent torque = $M \pm \sqrt{M^2 + T^2}$

$$= \left[6.25 \pm \sqrt{6.25^2 + 3.82^2}\right] \times 10^6 = [6.25 \pm 7.32] \times 10^6$$

$$Z_s = \frac{\pi}{16} d^3 = \frac{\pi}{16} \times 10^6 = 19.63 \times 10^4 \text{ mm}^3$$

∴ $\sigma_p$ = Principal stress = $\frac{1}{Z_s} T_e$

$$= \frac{1}{19.63 \times 10^4} [6.25 \pm 7.32] \times 10^6$$

∴ $\sigma_{p_1}$ = Major principal stress = $\frac{13.57 \times 10^6}{19.63 \times 10^4}$

= **+ 69.13 MPa (tensile)**

$\sigma_{p_2}$ = Minor principal stress

$$= \frac{-1.07 \times 10^6}{19.63 \times 10^4}$$

= **– 5.54 MPa (compressive)**

$\sigma_{p_1}$ and $\sigma_{p_2}$ are both normal stresses having opposite sense.

---

**Example 11.21** : A hollow shaft of the external diameter 200 mm and the internal diameter 100 mm transmits 500 kW at 100 rev/min. At the same time, it is acted upon by a bending moment of $3 \times 10^7$ N-mm and by an end thrust of 250 kN. Find the maximum principal stress and the maximum shear stress.

**Solution :**    A = Area of cross-section of the shaft

$$= \frac{\pi}{4}(D^2 - d^2) = \frac{\pi}{4}(200^2 - 100^2) = 23561.95 \text{ mm}^2$$

$Z_s$ = Polar section modulus of the shaft

$$= \frac{\pi}{16}\left[\frac{D^4 - d^4}{D}\right] = \frac{\pi}{16}\left[\frac{200^4 - 100^4}{200}\right] = 14.72 \times 10^5 \text{ mm}^3$$

$Z$ = Modulus of section (for bending)

$$= \frac{\pi}{32}\left[\frac{D^4 - d^4}{D}\right] = 7.36 \times 10^5 \text{ mm}^3$$

$\sigma_o$ = Direct stress due to the thrust = $\frac{P}{A}$

$$= \frac{250 \times 1000}{23561.95} = 10.61 \text{ MPa}$$

$\sigma_b$ = Bending stress = $\frac{M}{Z} = \frac{3 \times 10^7}{7.36 \times 10^5} = 40.76 \text{ MPa}$

$\sigma$ = Maximum direct stress = $\sigma_o + \sigma_b$

$$= 10.61 + 40.76 = 51.37 \text{ MPa}$$

$P$ = Power transmitted = $500 \text{ kW} = 500000 \text{ W} = \frac{2\pi N}{60}T$

∴   $T = \frac{500000 \times 60}{2\pi \times 100} = 47746.48 \text{ N-m} = 4.77 \times 10^7 \text{ N-mm}$

$\tau$ = Shear stress produced by the torque T

$$= \frac{T}{Z_s} = \frac{4.77 \times 10^7}{14.72 \times 10^5} = 32.40 \text{ MPa}$$

$\sigma_{p_1}$ = Maximum principal stress

$$= \frac{\sigma}{2} + \sqrt{\left(\frac{\sigma}{2}\right)^2 + (\tau)^2} = 25.69 + \sqrt{25.69^2 + 32.40^2}$$

$$= 25.69 + 41.34 = \mathbf{67.04 \text{ MPa}}$$

$(\tau)_{max}$ = Maximum shear stress

$$= \sqrt{\left(\frac{\sigma}{2}\right)^2 + (\tau)^2} = \mathbf{41.34 \text{ MPa}}$$

## EXERCISE

1. A propeller shaft of 240 mm external diameter and 180 mm internal diameter has to transmit 1000 kW at 100 rpm. It is additionally subjected to bending moment of 10 kN/m and an end thrust of 200 kN. Determine : (i) principal stresses and their planes, (ii) maximum shear stress.   ($\sigma_1$ = 62.94 MPa (compressive), $\sigma_2$ = 42.05 MPa (tensile), $\theta_1$ = 39.26°, $\theta_2$ = 129.26°, $Z_{max}$ = 52.49 MPa)

2. A propeller shaft 200 mm in diameter transmits 2250 kW at 240 rev/min. The propeller weighing 50 kN is carried by the shaft overhanging the support by 400 mm. If the propeller thrust is 150 kN, calculate the maximum direct stress induced in the cross-section of the propeller shaft.  ($\tau = $ 74 N/mm²)

3. A solid shaft 127 mm diameter transmits 600 kW at 300 r.p.m. It is also subjected to a bending moment of 9.1 kN/m and an end thrust. If the maximum principal stress is limited to 77 N/mm², find the end thrust.  (End thrust = 39 kN)

4. In a shaft subjected to bending moment and twisting moment, the greater principal stress is numerically 5 times the lesser one. Find the ratio of M : T and the angle which the plane of greater principal stresses makes with plane of bending stress.

$(2/\sqrt{5}, 24°5')$

5. At a certain section of a shaft of 80 mm diameter, there is a bending moment of 35 kN-m and a twisting moment of 50 kN-m. Determine the principal stresses and the plane where they act.  ($\sigma_1 = $ 95.5 N/mm² (compression),

$\sigma_2 = $ 26.0 N/mm² (tension), $\theta_1 = 27°30'$ and $\theta_2 = 117° 30'$)

6. A shaft section 75 mm in diameter is subjected to bending moment of 5 kNm and torque of 10 kNm. Find the maximum normal stresses induced on section and locate the plane on which it acts. Find also what stress acting along can produce the same maximum strain ? Take $\mu = 0.3$.

(Max. normal stresses $\sigma_1 = $ 195.33 MPa; $\sigma_2 = - $74.61 MPa;

$\theta_1 = 31.717°$, $\theta_2 = 121.717°$, $\sigma = 217.713$ MPa)

7. A steel shaft is subjected to torque of 20 kNm and bending moment 15 kNm. Calculate the principal stresses and maximum shear stress if diameter of shaft is 115 mm.

($\sigma_1 = $ 133.948 MPa; $\sigma_2 = -$ 33.487 MPa; $\theta_1 = 26.56°$, $\theta_2 = 116.56°$, $\tau_{max} = 83.717$ MPa)

8. A hollow shaft is subjected to torque of 500 kNm and bending moment of 250 kNm. Internal diameter of shaft is 0.75 times the external diameter. If maximum normal stress is not to exceed 150 MPa and shear stress is not to exceed 80 MPa, design the cross-section of shaft.  (D = 373.395 mm, d = 280 mm)

9. A solid shaft in a small hydraulic turbine is 125 mm in diameters, it supports an axial compressive load of 500 kN. Determine the maximum power that will be developed at a speed of 250 rpm without exceeding maximum shear stress of 70 MPa and maximum normal stress of 90 MPa.

($\sigma = 40.74$ MPa, $\tau = 66.58$ MPa, T = $25.53 \times 10^3$ Nm, Safe power = 668.455 kW)

# CHAPTER TWELVE

# PRESSURE VESSELS

## 12.1 INTRODUCTION

Vessels of cylindrical and spherical shapes are used to store fluids under pressure. For example, boilers, compressed air receivers etc. A shell is considered thin if its thickness is less than $\frac{1}{20}$ of its diameter. If thickness is more than the above limit, it is called as a thick shell. For thick shells, the stress variation over the thickness is not uniform. Thick shells are discussed at the end of the chapter.

## 12.2 THIN CYLINDRICAL SHELLS

On account of internal fluid pressure, cylindrical shell is subjected to two types of stresses at the surface.

(i) **Hoop stress** ($\sigma_h$) : Stress acting along circumference of a cylinder is called as hoop stress.

(ii) **Longitudinal stress** ($\sigma_L$) : Stress acting along the length of a cylinder is called as longitudinal stress.

## 12.3 DERIVATIONS OF IMPORTANT FORMULAE FOR THIN CYLINDRICAL SHELL

Symbols :
- $p$ = Internal fluid pressure,
- $d$ = Internal diameter of shell,
- $t$ = Thickness of shell,
- $L$ = Length of shell,
- $E$ = Young's modulus of Elasticity,
- $\mu$ = Poisson's ratio,
- $\sigma_h, \sigma_L$ = Hoop and longitudinal stresses respectively,
- $\varepsilon_h, \varepsilon_L$ = Hoop and longitudinal strains respectively,
- $\delta d, \delta t, \delta L$ = Change in diameter, thickness and length of shell respectively,
- $\varepsilon_v$ = Volumetric strain,
- $\delta V$ = Change in volume, and
- $V$ = Original volume

### 12.3.1 Hoop and Longitudinal Stresses

Fig. 12.1 shows a thin cylindrical shell subjected to internal fluid pressure. Consider a longitudinal section 1-1 through the axis dividing the shell in two halves (I) and (II). Now, let us consider two elementary strips subtending an angle $d\theta$ at the centre, at an angle $\theta$ on either side of vertical diameter as shown.

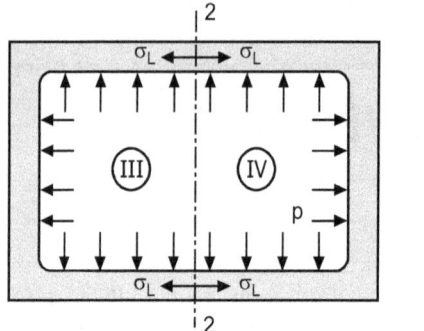 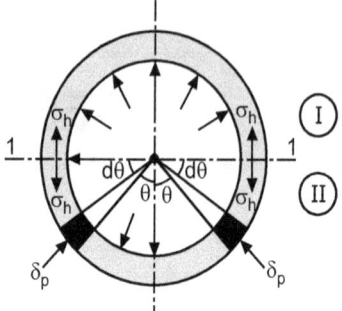

**Fig. 12.1**

Normal force on each strip = $\delta p = p \cdot r \cdot d\theta \cdot L$

where,  $r$ = radius of the shell

Vertical components of these two normal forces are getting added.

Total vertical force = $2\, p \cdot r \cdot d\theta \cos \theta$

Total force normal to 1-1 acting vertically on any one side of section.

$$= \text{Total bursting force}$$

$$= \int_0^{\pi/2} 2\, p \cdot r \cdot d\theta \cdot \cos \theta$$

$$= p\,(dL) \qquad \ldots (12.1)$$

= Intensity of radial pressure × Projected area on horizontal plane.

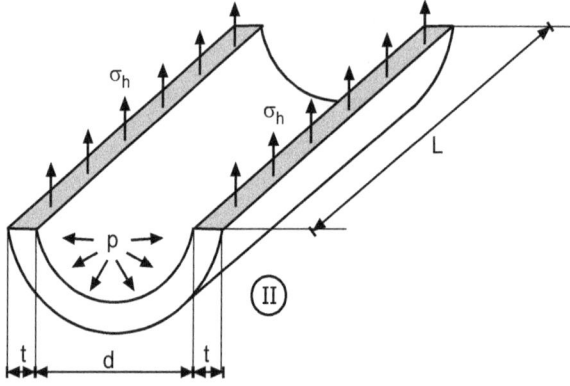

**Fig. 12.2 : Failure due to hoop stress**

Let, $\sigma_h$ = Intensity of tensile stress induced in the material across section 1-1.

Resistance normal to section 1.1

$$= 2\, \sigma_h\,(Lt) \qquad \ldots (12.2)$$

Equating equations (12.1) and (12.2);

$$p\,(dL) = 2\, \sigma_h \cdot (Lt)$$

$$\sigma_h = \frac{p\,d}{2\,t} \qquad \ldots (12.3)$$

Let us now consider section 2-2 normal to the axis of the shell dividing the shell into two parts (III) and (IV).

Force acting on the end of the shell = $p \left( \dfrac{\pi}{4} d^2 \right)$ ... (12.4)

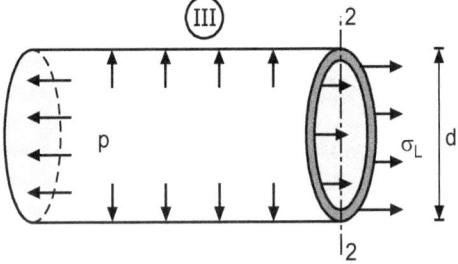

**Fig. 12.3 : Failure due to longitudinal stress**

Resistance normal to section 2-2 = $\sigma_L \cdot (\pi d t)$ ... (12.5)

Considering equilibrium along length and equating equations (12.4) and (12.5),

$$p \left( \dfrac{\pi}{4} d^2 \right) = \sigma_L (\pi d t)$$

$$\sigma_L = \dfrac{pd}{4t}$$ ... (12.6)

Thus, state of stress on the surface of the shell is as shown in Fig. 12.4.

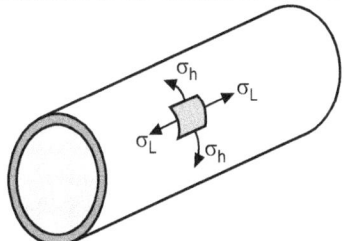

**Fig. 12.4 : State of stress on the surface of cylindrical shell**

Hoop stress is acting along circumference while longitudinal stress is acting along length of the shell. These two normal stresses, which are not accompanied by shear stresses are called as *principal stresses*. $\sigma_h$ is a major principal stress while $\sigma_L$ is a minor principal stress. Maximum shear stress is therefore given by,

$$\tau_{max} = \dfrac{\sigma_1 - \sigma_2}{2} = \dfrac{pd}{8t}$$ ... (12.7)

**Note :** State of stress for an element of thin walled pressure vessel is as shown in Fig. 12.5. It is a triaxial state of stress. Internal pressure causes local compressive stress as shown, which, being very small compared to $\sigma_1$ and $\sigma_2$, is neglected and only biaxial state of stress is considered.

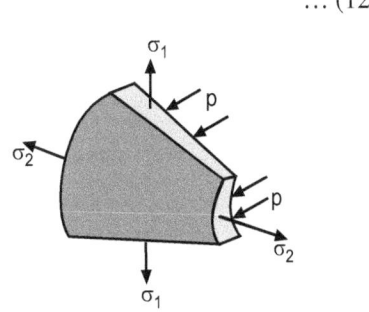

**Fig. 12.5**

## 12.3.2 Change in Dimensions of Shell

$$\varepsilon_h = \frac{\delta d}{d} = \frac{1}{E}(\sigma_h - \mu\sigma_L)$$

$$= \frac{1}{E}\left(\frac{pd}{2t} - \mu\frac{pd}{4t}\right)$$

$$= \frac{pd}{4tE}(2-\mu) \qquad \ldots (12.8)$$

$$\delta d = \frac{pd^2}{4tE}(2-\mu) \qquad \ldots (12.9)$$

$$\varepsilon_L = \frac{\delta L}{L} = \frac{1}{E}(\sigma_L - \mu\sigma_h)$$

$$= \frac{1}{E}\left(\frac{pd}{4t} - \mu\frac{pd}{2t}\right)$$

$$= \frac{pd}{4tE}(1-2\mu) \qquad \ldots (12.10)$$

$$\delta L = \frac{pdL}{4tE}(1-2\mu) \qquad \ldots (12.11)$$

$$\frac{\delta t}{t} = -\frac{\mu}{E}(\sigma_h + \sigma_L)$$

$$= -\frac{\mu}{E}\left(\frac{pd}{2t} + \frac{pd}{4t}\right) = \frac{-3\mu pd}{4tE}$$

$$\therefore \quad \delta t = \frac{-3\mu pd}{4E} \qquad \ldots (12.12)$$

**Note :** Positive sign for $\delta d$ and $\delta L$ indicates increase in diameter and length while negative sign for $\delta t$ indicates reduction in thickness.

## 12.3.3 Change in Volume

Volume of cylindrical shell $= V = \frac{\pi}{4}d^2 L$

Change in volume $= \delta V = \frac{\pi}{4}[2d\,\delta d + d^2\,\delta L]$

Volumetric strain $= \varepsilon_v = \frac{\delta V}{V} = \frac{2\delta d}{d} + \frac{\delta L}{L}$

$$= 2\varepsilon_h + \varepsilon_L$$

$$\therefore \quad \varepsilon_v = 2\left[\frac{pd}{4tE}(2-\mu)\right] + \frac{pd}{4tE}(1-2\mu)$$

$$\varepsilon_v = \frac{pd}{4tE}(5-4\mu) \qquad \ldots (12.13)$$

$$\delta V = \frac{pd}{4tE}(5-4\mu)\frac{\pi}{4}d^2 L \qquad \ldots (12.14)$$

## 12.4 THIN SPHERICAL SHELL

On account of internal fluid pressure, spherical shell is subjected to hoop stress only.

## 12.5 DERIVATIONS OF IMPORTANT FORMULAE FOR THIN SPHERICAL SHELL

### 12.5.1 Hoop Stress

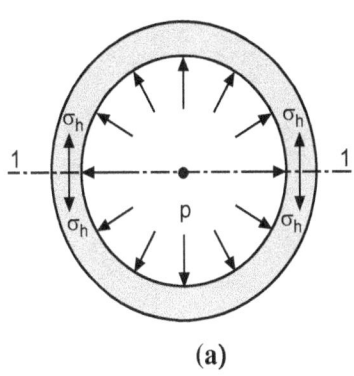
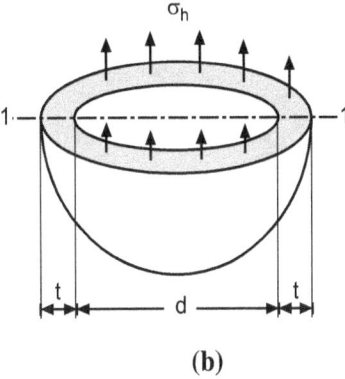

(a)                        (b)

**Fig. 12.6**

Bursting force = p × projected area

$$= p \times \left(\frac{\pi}{4} d^2\right) \quad \ldots (12.15)$$

Let, $\sigma_h$ be the stress induced on section normal to 1-1.

$$\text{Resisting force} = \sigma_h \,(\pi\, d\, t) \quad \ldots (12.16)$$

Considering equilibrium and equating equations (12.15) and (12.16),

$$p \left(\frac{\pi}{4} d^2\right) = \sigma_h \,(\pi\, d\, t)$$

$$\sigma_h = \frac{p\,d}{4\,t} \quad \ldots (12.17)$$

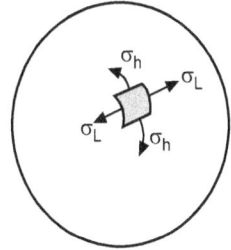

Thus, state of stress on the surface of spherical shell is as shown in Fig. 12.7. It should be noted that, both principal stresses $\sigma_1 = \sigma_2 = \frac{pd}{4t}$. Shear stress therefore is equal to zero.

**Fig. 12.7 : State of stress on the surface of thin spherical shell**

### 12.5.2 Change in dimensions of shell

$$\varepsilon_h = \frac{\delta d}{d} = \frac{1}{E}(\sigma_h - \mu\, \sigma_h)$$

$$= \frac{1}{E}\left(\frac{pd}{4t} - \frac{\mu pd}{4t}\right) = \frac{pd}{4tE}(1-\mu) \quad \ldots (12.18)$$

$$\delta d = \frac{p d^2}{4 t E}(1-\mu) \qquad \ldots (12.19)$$

$$\frac{\delta t}{t} = \frac{-\mu}{E}(\sigma_h + \sigma_h)$$

$$= \frac{-\mu}{E}\left(2 \cdot \frac{pd}{4t}\right) = \frac{-\mu}{E}\left(\frac{pd}{2t}\right)$$

$$\therefore \quad \delta t = \frac{-\mu\, pd}{2 E} \qquad \ldots (12.20)$$

**Note :** + ve sign for $\delta d$ indicates increase in diameter while – ve sign for $\delta t$ indicates reduction in thickness.

### 12.5.3 Change in Volume

$$\text{Volume of spherical shell} = V = \frac{\pi}{6} d^3$$

$$\text{Change in volume} = \delta V = \frac{\pi}{6}(3d^2\, \delta d)$$

$$\text{Volumetric strain} = \varepsilon_v = \frac{\delta V}{V} = 3 \cdot \frac{\delta d}{d} = 3\varepsilon_h$$

$$\varepsilon_v = 3\left[\frac{pd}{4 t E}(1-\mu)\right] \qquad \ldots (12.21)$$

$$\delta V = \frac{3 pd}{4 t E}(1-\mu)\,\frac{\pi}{6} d^3 \qquad \ldots (12.22)$$

## SOLVED EXAMPLES

**Example 12.1 :** A 750 mm diameter penstoke has 12 mm wall thickness. It connects reservoir at A with generating station at B. B is 120 m below water level at A. Determine maximum normal stress and maximum shear stress under static conditions. Take weight density of water as 10 kN/m³.

**Data :** $d = 750$ mm; $t = 12$ mm; $h = 120$ m; $\gamma = 10$ kN/m³

**Required :** Maximum normal and shear stress

**Concept :** Water pressure at depth h is $p = \gamma h$; Standard formulae.

**Solution :** (i) Water pressure : $p = \gamma h$
$$= 10 \times 120 = 1200 \text{ kN/m}^2 = 1.2 \text{ MPa}$$

(ii) Maximum normal stresses :
$$\sigma_h = \frac{pd}{2t} = \frac{1.2 \times 750}{2 \times 12} = 37.5 \text{ MPa (tensile)}$$

$$\sigma_L = \frac{pd}{4t} = 18.75 \text{ MPa (tensile)}$$

(iii) Maximum shear stresses :
$$\tau_{max} = \frac{pd}{8t} = \frac{1.2 \times 750}{8 \times 12} = 9.375 \text{ MPa}$$

**Example 12.2 :** The change in volume of thin walled cylinder 1200 mm long, 150 mm internal diameter, and 5 mm thickness of metal is 15000 mm³. If E = 200 GPa and γ = 0.28, find the internal fluid pressure and the principal stresses.

**Data :** $\delta v$ = 15000 mm³; L = 1200 mm ; d = 150 mm ; t = 5 mm ; E = 200 × 10³ MPa ; $\mu$ = 0.28.

**Required :** Internal fluid pressure (p) and principal stresses.

**Concept :** From the given change in volume, obtain the internal fluid pressure and then evaluate principal stress.

**Solution :** (i) Internal fluid pressure :

$$\delta v = \frac{pd}{4tE}(5-4\mu) \cdot \frac{\pi}{4} d^2 L$$

$$15000 = \frac{p \times 150\,(5 - 4 \times 0.28)}{4 \times 5 \times 200 \times 10^3} \times \frac{\pi}{4} \times 150^2 \times 1200$$

$$p = 4.86 \text{ MPa}$$

(ii) Principal stresses :

$$\sigma_1 = \sigma_h = \frac{pd}{2t} = \frac{4.86 \times 150}{2 \times 5}$$

$$\sigma_h = 72.9 \text{ MPa}$$

$$\sigma_2 = \sigma_L = \frac{pd}{4t} = \frac{72.9}{2}$$

$$\sigma_L = 36.45 \text{ MPa}$$

**Example 12.3 :** A thin cylindrical shell has 1.5 m diameter and 4 m long. It is subjected to internal pressure of 3 MPa. If the maximum shear stress is not to exceed 37.5 MPa, find

(i) The thickness of the shell. (ii) Change in diameter. (iii) Change in length.

(iv) Change in volume.

E = 200 GPa, $\mu$ = 0.25

**Data :** $\tau_{max}$ = 37.5 MPa; d = 1.5 m = 1500 mm; L = 4000 mm; p = 3 MPa; E = 200 GPa

∴ E = 200 × 10³ MPa; $\mu$ = 0.25.

**Required :** Thickness of the shell (t) ; Change in diameter ($\delta d$) ; Change in length ($\delta L$); Change in volume ($\delta V$).

**Concept :** From the given allowable shear stress, obtain the thickness of shell and then using standard formulae get the required unknowns.

**Solution :** (i) Thickness of shell (t) :

$$\tau_{max} = \frac{pd}{8t}$$

∴ $$37.5 = \frac{3 \times 1500}{8 \times t}$$

∴ $$t = 15 \text{ mm}$$

∴ Corresponding hoop and longitudinal stresses are ;

$$\sigma_h = \frac{pd}{2t} = \frac{2250}{15} = 150 \text{ MPa}$$

$$\sigma_L = \frac{pd}{4t} = \frac{1125}{15} = 75 \text{ MPa}$$

(ii) Change in diameter ($\delta d$) :

$$\frac{\delta d}{d} = \frac{1}{E} [\sigma_h - \mu \sigma_L]$$

$$\frac{\delta d}{d} = \frac{1}{200 \times 10^3} [150 - 0.25 \times 75]$$

$$\frac{\delta d}{d} = 6.56 \times 10^{-4}$$

∴ $\delta d = 6.56 \times 10^{-4} \times 1500$

$\delta d = \mathbf{0.98 \text{ mm}}$ **(increase)**

(iii) Change in length ($\delta L$) :

$$\frac{\delta L}{L} = \frac{1}{E} [\sigma_L - \mu \sigma_h]$$

$$\frac{\delta L}{L} = \frac{1}{200 \times 10^3} [75 - 0.25 \times 150]$$

$$\frac{\delta L}{L} = 1.875 \times 10^{-4}$$

$\delta L = 1.875 \times 10^{-4} \times 4000$

$\delta L = \mathbf{0.75 \text{ mm}}$ **(increase)**

(iv) Change in volume ($\delta V$) :

$$\frac{\delta V}{V} = 2 \left(\frac{\delta d}{d}\right) + \frac{\delta L}{L}$$

$$\frac{\delta V}{V} = 2 [6.56 \times 10^{-4}] + [1.875 \times 10^{-4}]$$

$$\frac{\delta V}{V} = 14.995 \times 10^{-4}$$

$\delta V = 14.995 \times 10^{-4} \times \frac{\pi}{4} (1500)^2 \times 4000$

$\delta V = \mathbf{10.6 \times 10^6 \text{ mm}^3}$ **(increase)**

**Example 12.4 :** A cylindrical pressure vessel is 20 mm thick. The diameter of the vessel is 500 mm and length is 3 m. If the normal stress in plate is limited to 140 MPa, determine the internal pressure and change in length of the vessel. E = 210 GPa, $\mu$ = 0.28.

**Data :** t = 20 mm ; d = 500 mm ; L = 3 m ; $\sigma_h$ = 140 MPa ; E = 210 GPa ; $\mu$ = 0.28.

**Required :** Internal pressure and change in length of the vessel.

**Concept :** Maximum normal stress is nothing but hoop stress. From the given maximum normal stress, obtain internal fluid pressure and then get the required unknowns.

**Solution :** (i) Internal fluid pressure (p) :

Maximum normal stress = Hoop stress = 140 MPa

$$\therefore \quad \sigma_h = \frac{pd}{2t}$$

$$140 = \frac{p \times 500}{2 \times 20}$$

$$\therefore \quad p = \mathbf{11.2 \ MPa}$$

(ii) Change in length ($\delta L$) :

$$\sigma_h = 140 \ MPa$$

$$\therefore \quad \sigma_L = 70 \ MPa$$

$$\therefore \quad \varepsilon_L = \frac{1}{E}(\sigma_L - \mu \sigma_h) = \frac{1}{E}(70 - 0.28 \times 140) = \frac{30.8}{E}$$

Change in length, $\quad \delta L = \varepsilon_L \times L$

$$= \frac{30.8}{210 \times 10^3} \times 3000$$

$$= \mathbf{0.44 \ mm} \quad \textbf{(increase)}$$

**Example 12.5 :** A thin cylindrical shell of length 2 m and internal volume 2.26 m³ is subjected to an internal fluid pressure of 3 MPa. If maximum permissible tensile stress is 180 MPa, find change in volume. Assume E = 210 GPa, µ = 0.25.

**Data :** L = 2 m; V = 2.26 m³; p = 3 MPa ; $\sigma_h$ = 180 MPa ; E = 210 GPa = 210 × 10³ MPa ;

$$\mu = 0.25.$$

**Required :** Change in volume ($\delta V$).
**Concept :** Maximum allowable tensile stress shall be equated to hoop stress.
**Solution :** (i) Diameter of shell (d) :

$$\left(\frac{\pi}{4} d^2\right) L = V$$

$$\frac{\pi}{4} d^2 \times 2000 = 2.26 \times 10^9$$

$$\therefore \quad d = \mathbf{1200 \ mm}$$

(ii) Thickness of shell (t) :

$$\text{Maximum stress} = \text{hoop stress} = \sigma_h = \frac{pd}{2t}$$

$$\therefore \quad 180 = \frac{3 \times 1200}{2 \times t}$$

$$\therefore \quad t = 10 \ mm$$

$$\therefore \quad \text{Longitudinal stress} = \sigma_L = \frac{pd}{4t} = \mathbf{90 \ MPa}$$

(iii) Change in volume ($\delta V$):

$$\varepsilon_h = \frac{1}{E}(\sigma_h - \mu \sigma_L)$$

$$= \frac{1}{E}(180 - 0.25 \times 90)$$

$$= \frac{157.5}{E}$$

$$\varepsilon_L = \frac{1}{E}(\sigma_L - \mu \sigma_h)$$

$$= \frac{1}{E}(90 - 0.25 \times 180)$$

$$= \frac{45}{E}$$

$$\frac{\delta V}{V} = 2\varepsilon_h + \varepsilon_L$$

$$= 2 \times \frac{157.5}{E} + \frac{45}{E} = \frac{360}{E}$$

$$\therefore \quad \delta V = \frac{360}{E} \times V = \frac{360}{2.1 \times 10^5} \times 2.26 \times 10^9$$

$$\delta V = 3.87 \times 10^6 \text{ mm}^3 \text{ (increase)}$$

**Example 12.6 :** A thin cylindrical shell 3 m long ; 1 m diameter is subjected to an internal fluid pressure of 2 MPa. If the thickness of shell is 10 mm, find circumferential and longitudinal stresses. Also find maximum shear stress and changes in dimension of shell. Take $E = 200$ GPa; $\mu = 0.3$.

**Data :** $L = 3$ m; $d = 1$ m; $p = 2$ MPa; $t = 10$ mm; $E = 200$ GPa; $\mu = 0.3$.

**Required :** Circumferential and longitudinal stresses. Maximum shear stress and changes in dimension.

**Concept :** Standard formulae.

**Solution :** (i) Stresses :

$$\text{Circumferential stress} = \sigma_h = \frac{pd}{2t}$$

$$= \frac{2 \times 1000}{2 \times 10} = 100 \text{ MPa}$$

$$\text{Longitudinal stress} = \sigma_L = \frac{pd}{4t} = 50 \text{ MPa}$$

$$\text{Maximum shear stress} = \frac{\sigma_h - \sigma_L}{2}$$

$$= \frac{100 - 50}{2} = 25 \text{ MPa}$$

(ii) **Change in dimensions :**

$$\text{Circumferential strain } \varepsilon_h = \frac{1}{E}(\sigma_h - \mu\,\sigma_L)$$

$$= \frac{1}{E}(100 - 0.3 \times 50)$$

$$= \frac{85}{E}$$

∴  $\delta d$ = change in diameter = $\varepsilon_h \times d$

$$= \frac{85}{E} \times 1000$$

$$= \frac{85}{200 \times 10^3} \times 1000$$

$$= \mathbf{0.425\ mm\ (increase)}$$

$$\text{Longitudinal strain, } \varepsilon_L = \frac{1}{E}(\sigma_L - \mu\,\sigma_h)$$

$$= \frac{1}{E}(50 - 0.3 \times 100)$$

$$= \frac{20}{E}$$

∴  Change in length, $\delta L = \varepsilon_L \times L$

$$= \frac{20}{E} \times L$$

$$= \frac{20}{200 \times 10^3} \times 3000$$

$$= \mathbf{0.3\ mm\ (increase)}$$

$$\text{Change in thickness, } \delta t = \frac{-3}{4}\mu\,\frac{pd}{E}$$

$$= \frac{-3 \times 0.3 \times 2 \times 1000}{4 \times 200 \times 10^3}$$

$$= \mathbf{2.25 \times 10^{-3}\ mm\ (decrease)}$$

$$\text{Volumetric strain, } \varepsilon_v = 2\varepsilon_h + \varepsilon_L$$

$$= 2\left(\frac{85}{E}\right) + \frac{20}{E}$$

$$= \frac{190}{E}$$

Change in volume, $\delta V = \varepsilon_v \times V$

$$= \frac{190}{E}\left(\frac{\pi}{4}d^2 L\right)$$

$$= \frac{190}{200 \times 10^3} \times \frac{\pi}{4}(1000)^2 \times 3000$$

$$= \mathbf{2.238 \times 10^6\ mm^3\ (increase)}$$

**Example 12.7 :** A thin spherical shell of 1.5 m diameter is 10 mm thick. It is filled with liquid at internal pressure of 3 MPa. Find hoop stress, change in diameter, change in thickness and change in volume. Assume E = 200 GPa and $\mu$ = 0.3.

**Data :** d = 1.5 m ; t = 10 mm ; p = 3 MPa ; E = 200 MPa ; $\mu$ = 0.3.

**Required :** Hoop stress ; change in diameter ; change in thickness ; change in volume.

**Concept :** Standard formulae.

**Solution :** (i) Hoop stress :

$$\sigma_h = \frac{pd}{4t} = \frac{3 \times 1500}{4 \times 10} = 112.5 \text{ MPa}$$

(ii) Change in diameter ($\delta d$) :

$$\text{Hoop strain} = \varepsilon_h = \frac{1}{E}(\sigma_h - \mu\sigma_h)$$

$$= \frac{1}{E}(112.5 - 0.3 \times 112.5)$$

$$= \frac{78.75}{E}$$

Change in diameter ($\delta d$) = $\varepsilon_h \times d$

$$= \frac{78.75}{E} \times d$$

$$= \frac{78.75}{200 \times 10^3} \times 1500$$

$$= \mathbf{0.59 \text{ mm (increase)}}$$

(iii) Change in thickness ($\delta t$) :

$$\delta t = -\frac{\mu pd}{2E}$$

$$= \frac{-0.3 \times 3 \times 1500}{2 \times 200 \times 10^3}$$

$$= \mathbf{3.375 \times 10^{-3} \text{ mm (decrease)}}$$

(iv) Change in volume ($\delta V$) :

Volumetric strain = $3\varepsilon_h$

$$= \frac{3 \times 78.75}{E}$$

$$= \frac{236.25}{E}$$

Change in volume, $\delta V = \varepsilon_v \times V = \frac{236.25}{E}\left(\frac{\pi}{6}d^3\right)$

$$= \frac{236.25}{200 \times 10^3}\left(\frac{\pi}{6} \times (1500)^3\right)$$

$$= \mathbf{2.08 \times 10^6 \text{ mm}^3 \text{ (increase)}}$$

**Example 12.8 :** A thin spherical shell of internal diameter 500 mm and thickness 10 mm is subjected to an internal pressure of 10 MPa. Determine the principal stresses and principal strains. Also find change in diameter, change in volume. Assume E = 200 GPa and $\mu$ = 0.3.

**Data :** d = 500 mm ; t = 10 mm ; p = 10 MPa ; E = 200 GPa ; $\mu$ = 0.3
**Required :** Principal stresses ; principal strains ; $\delta d$ ; $\delta V$.
**Concept :** Standard formulae.
**Solution :** (i) Principal stresses :

$$\sigma_1 = \sigma_2 = \frac{pd}{4t} = \frac{10 \times 500}{4 \times 10} = 125 \text{ MPa (tensile)}$$

**Note :** Hoop stress itself is a principal stress.

(ii) Principal strains :

$$\varepsilon_1 = \varepsilon_2 = \frac{1}{E}(\sigma_1 - \mu\sigma_2)$$

$$= \frac{1}{200 \times 10^3}(125 - 0.3 \times 125)$$

$$= 4.37 \times 10^{-4} \text{ (tensile)}$$

**Note :** Hoop strain itself is a principal strain.

(iii) Change in diameter :

$$\varepsilon_h = \text{Hoop strain} = \frac{\delta d}{d} = 4.37 \times 10^{-4}$$

$\therefore \quad \delta d = 4.37 \times 10^{-4} \times 500$

$= \mathbf{0.2185 \text{ mm (increase)}}$

(iv) Change in volume :

$$\frac{\delta V}{V} = 3\varepsilon_h$$

$\therefore \quad \delta V = 3 \cdot \varepsilon_h \times V$

$$= 3 \times 4.37 \times 10^{-4} \times \frac{\pi}{6}(500)^3$$

$= \mathbf{85804.7 \text{ mm}^3 \text{ (increase)}}$

**Example 12.9 :** A thin cylindrical shell with hemispherical ends is subjected to internal fluid pressure of 2 MPa. The length of the cylindrical portion is 1 m and the internal diameter of cylindrical as well as spherical portion is 500 mm. Thickness of the metal is 16 mm. If E = 210 GPa and $\mu$ = 0.3, find change in volume of the shell.

**Data :** d = 500 mm; t = 16 mm; p = 2 MPa; E = 210 GPa = $210 \times 10^3$ MPa; $\mu$ = 0.3; L = 1 m

**Required :** Change in volume of the shell.

**Concept :** Cylindrical shell with hemispherical ends can be considered as one cylindrical shell + one spherical shell.

**Solution :** (i) To find $\delta V_1$ (change in volume for cylindrical portion) :

$$\delta V_1 = \frac{pd}{4tE}(5-4\mu) \cdot \frac{\pi}{4} d^2 L$$

$$= \frac{2 \times 500 (5 - 4 \times 0.3)}{4 \times 16 \times 210 \times 10^3} \left(\frac{\pi}{4} \times 500^2 \times 1000\right)$$

$$\delta V_1 = 55515.5 \text{ mm}^3$$

(ii) To find $\delta V_2$ (change in volume for spherical portion) :

$$\delta V_2 = \frac{3 pd}{4tE}(1-\mu) \cdot \frac{\pi}{6} d^3$$

$$= \frac{3 \times 2 \times 500 (1 - 0.3)}{4 \times 16 \times 210 \times 10^3} \times \frac{\pi}{6} (500)^3$$

$$\delta V_2 = 10226.5 \text{ mm}^3$$

(iii) Change in volume ($\delta V$) :

$$\delta V = \delta V_1 + \delta V_2 = 55515.5 + 10226.5$$

$$\delta V = 65742 \text{ mm}^3 \text{ (increase)}$$

## 12.6 EFFECT OF NON-COMPRESSIBLE AND COMPRESSIBLE FLUID

When non-compressible fluid is injected or released to cause change in internal fluid pressure, the volume of fluid put in or let out is equal to change in volume of shell only.

However, when compressible fluid is injected or released to cause change in internal fluid pressure, the volume of fluid put in or let out is equal to sum of change in volume of shell and change in volume of fluid.

**Example 12.10 :** A cylindrical shell 120 mm diameter, 840 mm long, 5 mm thickness is filled with an incompressible fluid at atmospheric pressure. If an additional quantity of fluid equal to 10 cm³ is pumped in, calculate

(i) the pressure developed within the cylinder,
(ii) the stresses induced.

Take $E = 200$ GPa, $\mu = 0.3$.

**Data :** $d = 120$ mm; $L = 840$ mm; $\delta V = 10 \times 10^3$ mm³; $t = 5$ mm; $E = 200$ GPa; $\mu = 0.3$.

**Required :** Pressure developed within the cylinder and stresses induced.

**Concept :** Fluid being incompressible, the quantity of fluid pumped in is equal to change in volume of shell only.

**Solution :** (i) Compatibility of strains :

$$\varepsilon_V = \varepsilon_{V_1} + \varepsilon_{V_2}$$

$\therefore \qquad \varepsilon_V = \varepsilon_{V_1} \qquad (\because \varepsilon_{V_2} = \text{volumetric strain for fluid} = 0)$

$$\frac{\delta V}{V} = \frac{pd}{4tE}(5-4\mu)$$

$$\frac{10 \times 10^3}{\frac{\pi}{4}(120)^2 \times 840} = \frac{p \times 120 (5 - 4 \times 0.3)}{4 \times 5 \times 200 \times 10^3}$$

$\therefore \qquad p = 9.23$ MPa

(ii) Stresses induced :

$$\sigma_h = \frac{pd}{2t} = \frac{9.23 \times 120}{2 \times 5} = 110.8 \text{ MPa}$$

$$\sigma_L = \frac{pd}{4t} = \frac{9.23 \times 120}{4 \times 5} = 55.4 \text{ MPa}$$

**Example 12.11 :** A steel cylinder 2 m long, 1 m diameter and 10 mm thickness is filled with water at atmospheric pressure. The additional quantity of water is pumped in so as to have the internal pressure of 2 MPa. On releasing the pressure, the water, let out measured $3 \times 10^6$ mm³. If for the shell material E = 200 GPa and $\mu = 0.3$, estimate the bulk modulus of water.

**Data :** d = 1000 mm ; L = 2000 mm ; t = 10 mm ; p = 2 MPa ; E = 200 GPa ; $\mu = 0.3$ ; $\delta V = 3 \times 10^6$ mm³.

**Required :** Bulk modulus of water 'K'.

**Concept :** Water being compressible fluid, the volume of water let out will be equal to sum of change in volume of shell and that of fluid.

**Solution :** (i) Volumetric strain for shell ($\varepsilon_{V_1}$) :

$$\varepsilon_{V_1} = \frac{pd}{4tE}(5-4\mu)$$

$$= \frac{2 \times 1000 (5 - 4 \times 0.3)}{4 \times 10 \times 200 \times 10^3}$$

$$\varepsilon_{V_1} = 9.5 \times 10^{-4}$$

(ii) Volumetric strain for fluid ($\varepsilon_{V_2}$) :

$$\varepsilon_{V_2} = \frac{p}{K}$$

$$= \frac{2}{K}$$

(iii) Compatibility of strains :

$$\frac{\delta V}{V} = \frac{\delta V_1}{V_1} + \frac{\delta V_2}{V_2}$$

$$\varepsilon_V = \varepsilon_{V_1} + \varepsilon_{V_2}$$

$$\frac{3 \times 10^6}{\frac{\pi}{4}(1000)^2 \times 2000} = 9.5 \times 10^{-4} + \frac{2}{K}$$

$\therefore \qquad K = 2083$ MPa
i.e. $\qquad K = 2.08$ GPa

**Example 12.12 :** A spherical shell of 500 mm internal diameter and 10 mm wall thickness is filled with water under a pressure of 5 MPa. The pressure is gradually reduced by letting out some water. To reduce the pressure to atmospheric, the volume of water let out was $2.05 \times 10^5$ mm³. If bulk modulus for water is 2 GPa and E for steel is 210 GPa, estimate Poisson's ratio for the material of vessel.

**Data :** $d = 500$ mm ; $t = 10$ mm; $p = 5$ MPa; $\delta V = 2.05 \times 10^5$ mm³;
$K = 2$ GPa; $E = 210$ GPa.

**Required :** Poisson's ratio.

**Concept :** Same as Example (12.11).

**Solution :** (i) Volumetric strain for shell $(\varepsilon_{v_1})$ :

$$\varepsilon_{v_1} = \frac{3\,pd}{4\,tE}(1-\mu)$$

$$= \frac{3 \times 5 \times 500}{4 \times 10 \times 210 \times 10^3}(1-\mu)$$

$$= 8.928 \times 10^{-4}\,(1-\mu)$$

(ii) Volumetric strain for fluid $(\varepsilon_{v_2})$ :

$$\varepsilon_{v_2} = \frac{p}{K} = \frac{5}{2 \times 10^3} = 2.5 \times 10^{-3}$$

(iii) Compatibility of strains :

$$\varepsilon_v = \varepsilon_{v_1} + \varepsilon_{v_2}$$

$$\frac{\delta V}{V} = 8.928 \times 10^{-4}(1-\mu) + 2.5 \times 10^{-3}$$

$$\frac{2.05 \times 10^5}{\frac{\pi}{6}(500)^3} = 8.928 \times 10^{-4}(1-\mu) + 2.5 \times 10^{-3}$$

$$\therefore \quad \mu = \mathbf{0.29}$$

**Example 12.13 :** A spherical vessel of 0.75 m diameter is made from 11 mm thick steel plate and is just filled with water at atmospheric pressure. When an additional 0.000885 m³ water is pumped in, the pressure rises to 5.8 MPa. Find the bulk modulus of water. Take $E = 200$ GPa; $\mu = 0.28$.

**Data :** $d = 0.75$ m $= 750$ mm ; $\delta V = 0.000885$ m³ $= 885 \times 10^3$ mm³ ;
$p = 5.8$ MPa ; $E = 200$ GPa ; $\mu = 0.28$; $t = 11$ mm.

**Required :** Bulk modulus of water.

**Concept :** Same as Example (12.11).

**Solution :** (i) Volumetric strain for shell $(\varepsilon_{v_1})$ :

$$\varepsilon_{v_1} = \frac{3\,pd}{4\,tE}(1-\mu) = \frac{3 \times 5.8 \times 750}{4 \times 11 \times 200 \times 10^3}(1-0.28)$$

$$\varepsilon_{v_1} = 1.067 \times 10^{-3}$$

(ii) Volumetric strain for fluid ($\varepsilon_{v_2}$):

$$\varepsilon_{v_2} = \frac{p}{K} = \frac{5.8}{K}$$

(iii) Compatibility of strains.

$$\varepsilon_v = \varepsilon_{v_1} + \varepsilon_{v_2}$$

$$\frac{\delta V}{V} = \varepsilon_{v_1} + \varepsilon_{v_2}$$

$$\frac{885 \times 10^3}{\frac{\pi}{6}(750)^3} = 1.067 \times 10^{-3} + \frac{5.8}{K}$$

∴ $\quad K = 1973.6$ MPa

i.e. $\quad K = 1.97$ GPa

**Example 12.14 :** A thin spherical copper shell of diameter 300 mm and thickness 1.6 mm is just full of water at atmospheric pressure. Find how much the internal pressure will be increased by pumping in 25000 m³ of water. Take E = 100 GPa; $\mu$ = 0.28 and K = 2.2 GPa.

**Data :** d = 300 mm; t = 1.6 mm; $\delta V$ = 25000 mm³; E = 100 GPa; $\mu$ = 0.28; K = 2.2 GPa.

**Required :** Internal pressure

**Concept :** Same as Example (12.11).

**Solution :** (i) Volumetric strain for shell ($\varepsilon_{v_1}$) let; "p" be the rise in internal pressure in MPa.

$$\varepsilon_{v_1} = \frac{3 pd}{4 t E}(1 - \mu) = \frac{3 \times p \times 300}{4 \times 1.6 \times 100 \times 10^{+3}}(1 - 0.28)$$

$$\varepsilon_{v_1} = 1.0125 \times 10^{-3} p$$

(ii) Volumetric strain for fluid ($\varepsilon_{v_2}$) :

$$\varepsilon_{v_2} = \frac{p}{K} = \frac{p}{2.2 \times 10^3}$$

(iii) Compatibility of strains :

$$\varepsilon_v = \varepsilon_{v_1} + \varepsilon_{v_2}$$

$$\frac{\delta V}{V} = 1.0125 \times 10^{-3}(p) + \frac{p}{2.2 \times 10^3}$$

$$\frac{25000}{\frac{\pi}{6}(300)^3} = (1.0125 \times 10^{-3}) p + \frac{p}{2.2 \times 10^3}$$

∴ $\quad p = 1.2$ MPa

## 12.7 EFFECT OF EXTERNAL FORCE

External axial force, either push or pull has effect on longitudinal stress only. Considering equilibrium of part of the shell on any one side of the section, normal to the length, stress in longitudinal direction shall be worked out. However, hoop stress is not affected by external axial force. Volumetric strain for shell and that of compressible fluid must be equal but opposite in nature. This is the compatibility of strain to be used for finding required unknowns.

**Example 12.15 :** A thin cylinder of 150 mm internal diameter and 2.5 mm thickness has its ends closed by rigid plates and is then filled with water. When an axial pull of 40 kN is applied to the ends, the water pressure is observed to fall by 0.1 MPa. If E = 200 GPa for the material of cylinder and Bulk modulus = 2.2 GPa for water, find Poisson's ratio for the material of cylinder assuming its behaviour to be elastic.

**Data :** d = 150 mm; t = 2.5 mm; Axial pull = F = 40 kN;

Change in internal pressure = 0.1 MPa (fall), E = 200 GPa; K = 2.2 GPa.

**Required :** Poisson's ratio $\mu$.

**Concept :** Application of axial force will change longitudinal stress for the shell which should be worked out from equilibrium of forces and then use compatibility of strains to find required unknowns.

**Solution :** (i) Hoop and longitudinal stresses :

$$\sigma_h = \frac{pd}{2t} = \frac{0.1 \times 150}{2 \times 2.5} = 3 \text{ MPa}$$

... Compressive due to pressure fall

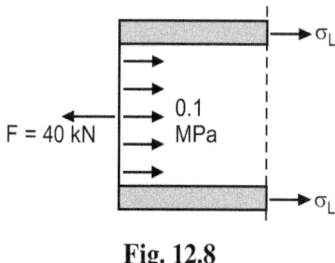

Fig. 12.8

For equilibrium;

$$\Sigma F_x = 0;$$

$$40 \times 10^3 =$$

$$= 0.1 \times \frac{\pi}{4} (150)^2 + \sigma_L (\pi \times 150 \times 2.5)$$

$$\sigma_L = 32.45 \text{ MPa}$$

(+ve sign indicates tensile nature of longitudinal stress)

Thus; $\sigma_h = -3$ MPa and

$\sigma_L = 32.45$ MPa

(ii) Volumetric strain for shell ($\varepsilon_{v_1}$) :

$$\varepsilon_{v_1} = 2\varepsilon_h + \varepsilon_L \text{ where;}$$

$$\varepsilon_h = \frac{1}{E}(\sigma_h - \mu \sigma_L)$$

$$= \frac{1}{E}(-3 - 32.45 \mu)$$

$$\varepsilon_L = \frac{1}{E}(\sigma_L - \mu\,\sigma_h) = \frac{1}{E}(32.45 - \mu(-3))$$

$$= \frac{1}{E}(32.45 + 3\mu)$$

$$\therefore \quad \varepsilon_{v_1} = \frac{2}{E}(-3 - 32.45\,\mu) + \frac{1}{E}(32.45 + 3\mu)$$

$$= \frac{1}{E}(26.45 - 61.9\,\mu)$$

(iii) Volumetric strain for fluid ($\varepsilon_{v_2}$) :

$$\varepsilon_{v_2} = \frac{p}{K} = \frac{0.1}{K} \text{ Compressive due to pressure fall} = \frac{-0.1}{K}$$

(iv) Compatibility of strains :

$$\varepsilon_{v_1} + \varepsilon_{v_2} = 0$$

$$\therefore \quad \frac{1}{E}(26.45 - 61.9\,\mu) - \frac{0.1}{K} = 0$$

$$26.45 - 61.9\,\mu = 0.1\,\frac{E}{K}$$

$$\therefore \quad 26.45 - 61.9\,\mu = 0.1 \times \frac{200 \times 10^3}{2.2 \times 10^3}$$

$$\therefore \quad \mu = \mathbf{0.28}$$

**Example 12.16 :** A thin cylinder 150 mm internal diameter, 2.5 mm thickness has its ends closed rigidly. It is filled with water. When an external pull is applied to the cylinder axially; the internal water pressure drops by 0.1 MPa. If E = 140 GPa; μ = 0.3 and K = 2.1 GPa, find the value of pull.

**Data :** d = 150 mm; t = 2.5 mm; p = 0.1 MPa; E = 140 GPa; μ = 0.3; K = 2.1 GPa
**Required :** Value of pull.
**Concept :** Same as Example (12.15).
**Solution :** (i) Hoop and longitudinal stresses :

$$\sigma_h = \frac{pd}{2t} = \frac{0.1 \times 150}{2 \times 2.5} = 3 \text{ MPa}\ldots \text{ Compressive due to pressure fall}$$

$$\therefore \quad \sigma_h = -3 \text{ MPa}$$

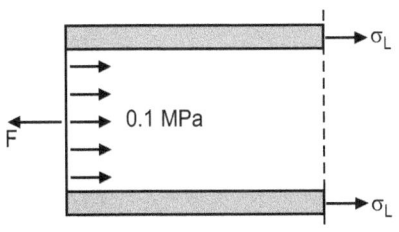

Fig. 12.9

For equilibrium ;

$$\Sigma F_x = 0$$

$$F = 0.1 \times \frac{\pi}{4}\,d^2 + \sigma_L\,(\pi dt)$$

$$F = 0.1 \times \frac{\pi}{4}(150)^2 + \sigma_L(\pi \times 150 \times 2.5)$$

$$\therefore \quad \sigma_L = -1.5 + \frac{F}{1178}$$

(ii) Volumetric strain for shell ($\varepsilon_{v_1}$):

$$\varepsilon_{v_1} = 2\varepsilon_h + \varepsilon_L$$

where
$$\varepsilon_h = \frac{1}{E}(\sigma_h - \mu\sigma_L)$$

$$= \frac{1}{E}\left[-3 - 0.3 \times \left(-1.5 + \frac{F}{1178}\right)\right]$$

$$= \frac{1}{E}\left[-2.55 - \frac{F}{3926.67}\right]$$

$$\varepsilon_L = \frac{1}{E}(\sigma_L - \mu\sigma_h)$$

$$= \frac{1}{E}\left[\left(-1.5 + \frac{F}{1178}\right) - 0.3 \times (-3)\right]$$

$$= \frac{1}{E}\left[-0.6 + \frac{F}{1178}\right]$$

$$\therefore \quad \varepsilon_{v_1} = \frac{2}{E}\left[-2.55 - \frac{F}{3926.67}\right] + \frac{1}{E}\left[-0.6 + \frac{F}{1128}\right]$$

$$= \frac{1}{E}[-5.7 + 3.3955 \times 10^{-4}(F)]$$

(iii) Volumetric strain for fluid ($\varepsilon_{v_2}$):

$$\varepsilon_{v_2} = \frac{p}{K} = \frac{0.1}{K} \quad \text{... Compressive due to pressure fall}$$

$$= \frac{-0.1}{K}$$

(iv) Compatibility of strains:

$$\varepsilon_{v_1} + \varepsilon_{v_2} = 0$$

$$\frac{1}{E}(-5.7 + 3.3955 \times 10^{-4}(F)) - \frac{0.1}{K} = 0$$

$$-5.7 + 3.3955 \times 10^{-4}(F) = \frac{0.1(E)}{K}$$

$$= \frac{0.1 \times 140 \times 10^3}{2.1 \times 10^3}$$

$$\therefore \quad F = 36419.78 \text{ N}$$

$$= \mathbf{36.41 \text{ kN}}$$

**Example 12.17 :** A copper tube having 50 mm internal diameter and 2 mm thick wall thickness is closed at its ends by plugs which are 450 mm apart. The tube subjected to an internal fluid pressure of 3 MPa and at the same time pulled in axial direction with a force of 5 kN. Compute :

(i) the change in the length between the plugs and

(ii) change in internal diameter of the tube.

Assume $E = 100$ GPa and $\mu = 0.3$

**Data :** $d = 50$ mm; $t = 2$ mm; $L = 450$ mm; $P = 3$ MPa; $F = 5$ kN; $E = 100$ GPa; $\mu = 0.3$.

**Required :** Change in length between the plugs and change in internal diameter of the tube.

**Concept :** Change in dimensions due to internal fluid pressure and axial force are obtained separately and then added algebraically by principle of superposition to get the final result. Also, change in internal fluid pressure due to external force applied is neglected.

**Solution :** (i) Effect of fluid pressure :

$$\sigma_h = \frac{pd}{2t} = \frac{3 \times 50}{2 \times 2} = 37.5 \text{ MPa}$$

$$\sigma_L = \frac{pd}{4t} = 18.75 \text{ MPa}$$

$$\varepsilon_h = \frac{\delta d}{d} = \frac{1}{E}(\sigma_h - \mu\,\sigma_L)$$

$$= \frac{1}{100 \times 10^3}(37.5 - 0.3 \times 18.75)$$

$$= 3.1875 \times 10^{-4}$$

∴ $\delta d = 3.1875 \times 10^{-4} \times 50$

$$= \mathbf{0.0159 \text{ mm (increase)}}$$

$$\varepsilon_L = \frac{\delta L}{L} = \frac{1}{E}(\sigma_L - \mu\,\sigma_h) = \frac{1}{100 \times 10^3}(18.75 - 0.3 \times 37.5)$$

$$= 7.5 \times 10^{-5}$$

∴ $\delta L = 7.5 \times 10^{-5} \times 450$

$$= \mathbf{0.03375 \text{ mm (increase)}}$$

(ii) Effect of axial pull :

Area of cross-section $= A = \pi\,d\,t$

$$= \pi \times 50 \times 2 = 314.15 \text{ mm}^2$$

$$\sigma = \frac{F}{A} = \frac{5000}{314.15} = 15.91 \text{ MPa}$$

$$\varepsilon_L = \frac{\sigma}{E} = \frac{15.91}{100 \times 10^3} = 1.59 \times 10^{-4}$$

$$\varepsilon_h = -\mu\,\varepsilon_L = -0.3 \times 1.59 \times 10^{-4}$$
$$\varepsilon_h = -4.77 \times 10^{-5}$$

∴
$$\delta L = \varepsilon_L \cdot L = 1.59 \times 10^{-4} \times 450$$
$$\delta L = \mathbf{0.07155 \text{ mm (increase)}}$$
$$\delta d = \varepsilon_h \cdot d = -4.77 \times 10^{-5} \times 50 = -0.00238 \text{ mm}$$
$$= \mathbf{0.00238 \text{ mm (decrease)}}$$

(iii) Combined effect = We will add these results in (i) and (ii) to get the combined effect.

∴
$$\delta L = 0.03375 + 0.07155 = \mathbf{0.105 \text{ mm (increase)}}$$
$$\delta d = 0.0159 - 0.00238 = \mathbf{0.0135 \text{ mm (increase)}}$$

## 12.8 EFFECT OF JOINT EFFICIENCY

A shell of required size and shape is generally made by bending plates to the required diameter and connecting them usually by butt joint. In case of this shell, the surface stresses are of higher magnitude than what we have discussed.

Let, $\eta_h$ and $\eta_L$ be the joint efficiencies for circumferential and longitudinal joints respectively.

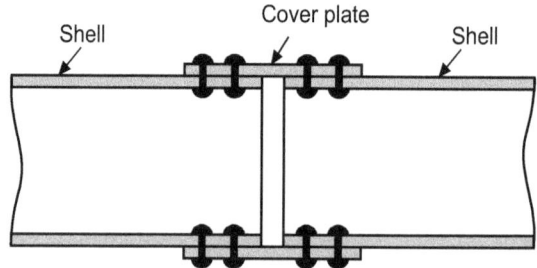

Fig. 12.10 : Longitudinal joint

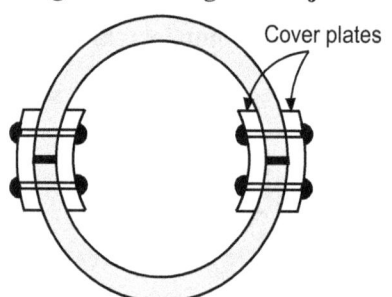

Fig. 12.11 : Circumferential joint

Hoop stress is given by, $\sigma_h = \dfrac{pd}{2\,t\,\eta_L}$ ... (12.23)

Longitudinal stress is given by, $\sigma_L = \dfrac{pd}{4\,t\,\eta_h}$ ... (12.24)

**Example 12.18 :** A cylindrical shell 100 mm diameter, 10 mm thick, 1 m long is subjected to internal fluid pressure of 10 MPa. If the efficiency of circumferential joint is 80% and that of longitudinal joint is 90%, find

(i) the stresses induced.

(ii) change in volume.

Assume E = 200 GPa, $\mu$ = 0.3.

**Data :** d = 100 mm, t = 10 mm, L = 1 m = 1000 mm, p = 10 MPa, $\eta_L$ = 0.9, $\eta_h$ = 0.8, E = 200 GPa, $\mu$ = 0.3.

**Required :** Stresses induced and change in volume.

**Concept :** Standard formulae.

**Solution :** (i) 
$$\sigma_h = \frac{pd}{2 t \eta_L} = \frac{10 \times 100}{2 \times 10 \times 0.9}$$

$$\sigma_h = 55.55 \text{ MPa}$$

$$\sigma_L = \frac{pd}{4 t \eta_h} = \frac{10 \times 100}{4 \times 10 \times 0.8} = \mathbf{31.25 \text{ MPa}}$$

(ii) Change in volume :

$$\varepsilon_h = \frac{1}{E}(\sigma_h - \mu \sigma_L)$$

$$\varepsilon_h = \frac{1}{200 \times 10^3}[55.55 - 0.3 \times 31.25]$$

$$\varepsilon_h = 2.30 \times 10^{-4}$$

$$\varepsilon_L = \frac{1}{E}[\sigma_L - \mu \sigma_h]$$

$$= \frac{1}{200 \times 10^3}[31.25 - 0.3 \times 55.55]$$

$$\varepsilon_L = 7.29 \times 10^{-5}$$

$$\varepsilon_v = 2 \varepsilon_h + \varepsilon_L$$

$$= 2(2.30 \times 10^{-4}) + 7.29 \times 10^{-5}$$

$$\varepsilon_v = 5.34 \times 10^{-4}$$

$$\therefore \quad \delta V = \varepsilon_v \cdot V$$

$$= 5.34 \times 10^{-4} \times \frac{\pi}{4}(100)^2 \times 1000$$

$$\delta V = \mathbf{4.18 \times 10^3 \text{ mm}^3}$$

**Example 12.19 :** A boiler is subjected to an internal pressure of 2 MPa. The thickness of the boiler is 10 mm and maximum permissible stress is 150 MPa. Find maximum permissible diameter when the efficiency of longitudinal joint is 90% and that of circumferential joint is 60%.

**Data :** $p = 2$ MPa; $t = 10$ mm; $\sigma_h = 150$ MPa; $\eta_L = 0.9$; $\eta_h = 0.6$.

**Required :** Maximum permissible diameter.

**Concept :** Standard formulae.

**Solution :** (i) Let, Maximum stress = Hoop stress

$$\sigma_h = 150 \text{ MPa}$$

$$\sigma_h = \frac{pd}{2\,t\,\eta_L}$$

$$150 = \frac{2 \times d}{2 \times 10 \times 0.9}$$

$\therefore \quad d = \mathbf{1350\ mm}$

(ii) Check for longitudinal stress

$$\sigma_L = \frac{pd}{4\,t\,\eta_h} = \frac{2 \times 1350}{4 \times 10 \times 0.6} = 112.5 \text{ MPa} < 150 \text{ MPa} \quad \ldots \text{(OK)}$$

$\therefore$ Use $\quad d = \mathbf{1350\ mm}$

**Note :** If longitudinal stress exceeds maximum allowable stress then diameter shall be found out by equating longitudinal stress to allowable stress and hoop stress shall be checked.

**Example 12.20 :** A riveted boiler 2m in diameter is subjected to internal fluid pressure of 1 MPa. The efficiency of longitudinal riveted joints is 80% and maximum allowable stress for the material is 100 MPa. Find the thickness of shell and pitch of rivets assuming 20 mm diameter rivets and rivets to be in single shear.

**Data :** $d = 2$ m $= 2000$ mm; $p = 1$ MPa; $\eta_L = 0.8$; $\sigma_h = 100$ MPa;

Diameter of rivets = 20 mm; Rivets in single shear.

**Required :** Thickness of shell and pitch of rivets.

**Concept :** From given maximum stress, obtain the thickness of shell. Centre to centre distance between rivets in a line of rivets is called as pitch.

**Solution :** (i) Thickness of shell :

$$\text{Maximum stress} = \sigma_h = \frac{pd}{2\,t\,\eta_L}$$

$$100 = \frac{1 \times 2000}{2 \times t \times 0.8}$$

$\therefore \quad t = \mathbf{12.5\ mm}$

(ii) Pitch of rivets :

$$\text{Joint efficiency} = \frac{\text{pitch} - \text{diameter of rivets}}{\text{pitch}}$$

$$0.80 = \frac{\text{pitch} - 20}{\text{pitch}}$$

$\therefore \quad \text{pitch} = \mathbf{100\ mm}$

## 12.9 EFFECT OF CORROSION ON THIN SHELLS

Due to corrosion, thickness of the shell reduces which results in increase in surface stresses.

**Example 12.21 :** A cylindrical shell when put in service is subjected to internal fluid pressure p which causes hoop stress $\sigma_h$. It is found that over the period of time, the thickness of shell reduces by 3 mm due to corrosion which causes hoop stress to increase by 12%. Find the original thickness of shell.

**Data :** Reduction in thickness by 3 mm causes increase in hoop stress by 12%.
**Required :** Original thickness of shell (t).
**Concept :** Standard formulae.
**Solution :** (i) Initial stage :

$$\sigma_h = \frac{pd}{2t} \quad \ldots \text{(i)}$$

(ii) Final stage :

$$1.12\, \sigma_h = \frac{pd}{2(t-3)} \quad \ldots \text{(ii)}$$

Divide equation (ii) by (i),

$$1.12 = \frac{t}{t-3}$$

$$\therefore \quad t = 28 \text{ mm}$$

**Example 12.22 :** A spherical vessel with a diameter of 6 m contains a corrosive gas at pressure of 1.4 MN/m². The vessel can withstand a maximum tensile stress of 85 MN/m². Due to corrosion, metal wall is rotten at the rate of 0.3 mm per year. If thickness of metal used initially is 28 mm, determine the life of spherical shell.

**Data :** d = 6 m; p = 1.4 MN/m²; $\sigma_h$ = 85 MN/m²; Rate of reduction in thickness = 0.3 mm per year; t = 28 mm.
**Required :** Life of spherical shell.
**Concept :** From the given maximum stress, minimum required thickness of the shell can be obtained. Knowing original thickness and minimum thickness required to prevent the failure, life of shell can be obtained.
**Solution :** (i) Minimum thickness of shell for safety ($t_{min}$) :

$$\text{Maximum stress} = \text{hoop stress} = \sigma_h = \frac{pd}{4\, t_{min}}$$

$$\sigma_h = \frac{pd}{4\, t_{min}}$$

$$\therefore \quad 85 = \frac{1.4 \times 6000}{4 \times t_{min}}$$

$$\therefore \quad t_{min} = 24.7 \text{ mm}$$

If thickness of shell reduces further, it will cause bursting of shell.

(ii) Life of shell :

Original thickness = 28 mm

Minimum thickness required for safety = 24.7 mm

Rate of reduction in thickness = 0.3 mm per year.

$$\therefore \quad \text{Life of shell} = \frac{28 - 24.7}{0.3} = \textbf{11 years}$$

**Example 12.23 :** A thin spherical vessel of steel has internal diameter of 650 mm and metal thickness 5 mm. It is filled with water under pressure intensity of 3 MN/m². Find the volume of water to be let out to reduce the pressure inside the shell gradually to zero. Take E = 200 GPa. Poisson's ratio = 0.3, Bulk modulus of water = 2 GN/m².

**Solution :**

$$\varepsilon_V = \varepsilon_{V\,\text{shell}} + \varepsilon_{V\,\text{fluid}}$$

$$\frac{\delta V}{V} = \frac{3pd}{4tE}(1-\mu) + \frac{p}{K}$$

$$\frac{\delta V}{(\pi/6)(650)^3} = \frac{3 \times 3 \times 650\,(1-0.3)}{4 \times 5 \times 200 \times 10^3} + \frac{3}{2 \times 10^3}$$

$$\therefore \quad \delta V = \textbf{362.89} \times \textbf{10}^3 \textbf{ mm}^3$$

**Example 12.24 :** A thin cylindrical water pipe of 600 mm diameter contains water pressure head of 100 m. If the weight of water is 9810 N/cu.m., find the thickness of metal required, if the permissible stress is 30 MPa.

**Solution :** (i) Water pressure = $\gamma h$

$$p = 9810 \times 100$$
$$= 981 \times 10^3 \text{ N/m}^2 = 0.981 \text{ MPa}$$

(ii) 
$$\sigma_h = (pd/2t)$$
$$30 = (0.981 \times 600)/2t$$

$$\therefore \quad t = \textbf{9.81 mm}$$

**Example 12.25 :** A pipe carrying steam at 3.5 MPa has an outside diameter of 450 mm and a wall thickness of 10 mm. A gasket is inserted between flange at one end of the pipe and a flat plate used to cap the end. How many 40 mm diameter bolts are required to hold the cap in position if the allowable stress in the bolts is 25 MPa ? Find the circumferential stress developed in the pipe. **(Dec. 2000)**

**Solution :** (i)

$$d = D - 2t = 430 \text{ mm}$$

$$\sigma_h = \frac{pd}{2t} = 75.25 \text{ MPa}$$

$$\sigma_L = \frac{pd}{4t} = 37.625 \text{ MPa}$$

(ii) Longitudinal force due to $\sigma_L$ = $\sigma_L \pi dt$

$$= 37.625 \times \pi \times 430 \times 10^3$$
$$= \textbf{508.27} \times \textbf{10}^3 \textbf{ N}$$

(iii)  Strength of each bolt $= (\pi/4) \phi^2 \times \tau = (\pi/4)(40)^2 \times 25$

$\qquad\qquad\qquad\qquad\qquad = 31.42 \times 10^3$ N

$\therefore \qquad$ No. of bolts $= \dfrac{508.27 \times 10^3}{31.42 \times 10^3} \approx $ **17 Nos.**

**Example 12.26 :** A cylindrical steel pressure vessel 400 mm in diameter with a wall thickness of 20 mm is subjected to an internal pressure of 4.5 MPa.

(i) Calculate the tangential and longitudinal stresses in the steel.

(ii) To what value may the internal pressure be increased, if the stress in the steel is limited to 120 MPa.

(iii) If the internal pressure were increased until the vessel bursts, sketch the type of fracture that would occur.

**Solution :** (i) $\qquad \sigma_h = \dfrac{pd}{2t} = \dfrac{(4.5 \times 400)}{(2 \times 20)} = $ **45 MPa**

$\qquad\qquad\qquad \sigma_L = \dfrac{pd}{4t} = \dfrac{4.5 \times 400}{4 \times 20} = $ **22.5 MPa**

(ii) $\qquad\qquad \sigma_{max} = \dfrac{pd}{2t}$

$\qquad\qquad\qquad 120 = \dfrac{(p \times 400)}{(2 \times 20)}$

$\therefore \qquad\qquad\qquad p = $ **12 MPa**

(iii) The type of fracture is as shown in Fig. 12.12.

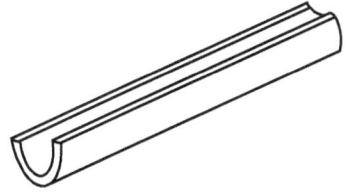

**Fig. 12.12**

## 12.10 THICK CYLINDRICAL AND SPHERICAL VESSELS

As discussed earlier, if ratio d/t is less than 20, shell is considered as thick. The stress variation across the thickness of shell is *not uniform* for thick shells. The hoop stress will vary from maximum value at inner surface to minimum value at outer surface.

**Lame's Theorem :** The complete theory of thick shells was given by Lame. Following are the assumptions made;

(i) The cylinder is made of homogeneous and isotropic material.

(ii) Plane sections perpendicular to the longitudinal axis remain plane i.e. the longitudinal strain is constant and is independent of radius.

**Symbols :** $\qquad r_1 ; r_2 = $ External and internal radii of the shell.

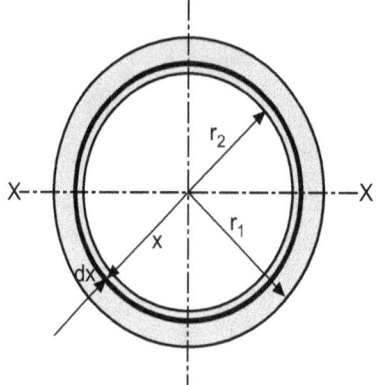 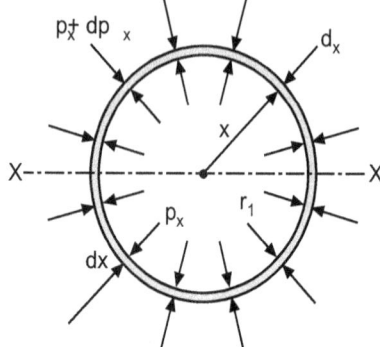

**Fig. 12.13 : Thick shell**    **Fig. 12.14 : FBD of elementary strip**

Consider an elementary ring of radius x and thickness dx. Let the radial pressure intensities be $p_x$ and $(p_x + dp_x)$ at the inner and outer surface of elementary ring as shown in Fig. 12.14.

Consider section xx

$$\text{Bursting force} = p_x (2xL) - (p_x + dp_x) 2 (x + dx) L$$
$$\text{Resisting force} = \sigma_x (2dx\, L)$$

Considering equilibrium, we have

$$\sigma_x (2 dx \cdot L) = p_x (2xL) - (p_x + dp_x) 2 (x + dx) L$$
$$\sigma_x\, dx = - p_x\, dx - x\, dp_x - dp_x\, dx$$

Neglecting $dp_x$, dx being very small

$$\sigma_x = - p_x - x \frac{dp_x}{dx} \qquad \ldots (12.25)$$

Also, longitudinal stress $\sigma_L = \dfrac{p\, \pi\, r_2^2}{\pi\, (r_1^2 - r_2^2)}$

$$= \frac{p\, r_2^2}{r_1^2 - r_2^2} \qquad \ldots (12.26)$$

Thus, at any point on the elementary strip, following are the three stresses :
(i) The radial pressure $p_x$  (ii) The hoop stress $\sigma_x$
(iii) The longitudinal stress $\sigma_L$.

As the longitudinal strain is constant, we have,

$$\frac{1}{E} [\sigma_L - \mu\, \sigma_x - \mu\, p_x] = \text{constant} \qquad \ldots (12.27)$$

In the above equation, $\sigma_L$; $\mu$ and t are constants.

$$\sigma_x - p_x = \text{constant}$$
$$\sigma_x - p_x = 2A \qquad \ldots (12.28)$$

∴ $\qquad \sigma_x = p_x + 2A$

Putting in equation (12.25),

$$p_x + 2A = -p_x - x\frac{dp_x}{dx}$$

$$\therefore \quad \frac{dp_x}{dx} = -\frac{2(p_x + A)}{x}$$

$$\frac{dp_x}{p_x + A} = -\frac{2dx}{x}$$

Integrating, $\quad \log_e(p_x + A) = -2\log_e x + \log_e(B)$

where $\quad \log_e(B) = $ constant

$$\therefore \quad \log_e(p_x + A) = \log_e\left(\frac{B}{x^2}\right)$$

$$p_x + A = \frac{B}{x^2}$$

$$p_x = \frac{B}{x^2} - A$$

Substituting in equation (12.28),

$$\sigma_x = \frac{B}{x^2} + A$$

Thus, the radial pressure $p_x$ and hoop stress $\sigma_x$ at any radius x is given by,

$$p_x = \frac{B}{x^2} - A \qquad \ldots (12.29)$$

$$\sigma_x = \frac{B}{x^2} + A \qquad \ldots (12.30)$$

*The above two equations are called as Lame's equations.*

Knowing boundary conditions i.e. at $x = r_2$; $p_x = p$ and at $x = r_1$; $p_x = 0$, the constants A and B can be evaluated.

The variation of radial pressure and hoop stress across the thickness of the shell is as shown in Fig. 12.15.

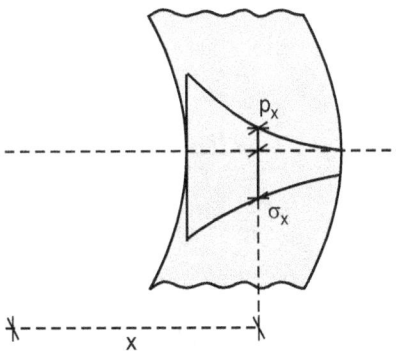

**Fig. 12.15 : Variation of hoop stress and pressure across the thickness of thick shell**

**Example 12.27**: A pipe of 500 mm internal diameter and 80 mm thickness contains a fluid at a pressure of 10 MPa. Find the maximum and minimum hoop stress across the section, also draw radial pressure and hoop stress variation over the thickness of shell.

**Data**: $r_1 = 330$ mm; $r_2 = 250$ mm; $p = 10$ MPa

**Required**: Maximum and minimum hoop stress.

**Concept**: Lame's equations.

**Solution**: (i) Lame's equations are,

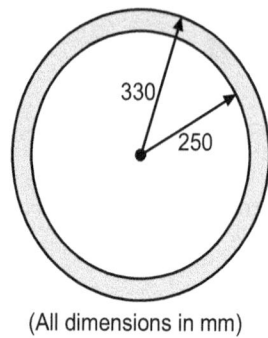

(All dimensions in mm)

**Fig. 12.16**

$$p_x = \frac{B}{x^2} - A \quad \ldots(i)$$

$$\sigma_x = \frac{B}{x^2} + A \quad \ldots(ii)$$

Boundary conditions

At $x = 250$ mm; $\quad p_x = 10$ MPa

At $x = 330$ mm; $\quad p_x = 0$

Substituting in equation (i),

$$10 = \frac{B}{250^2} - A \quad \ldots(iii)$$

$$0 = \frac{B}{330^2} - A \quad \ldots(iv)$$

Solving equations (iii) and (iv)

$$A = 13.47$$
$$B = 1466883$$

(ii) Hoop stresses:

$$\sigma_x = \frac{B}{x^2} + A$$

$$\sigma_x = \frac{1466883}{x^2} + 13.47$$

$$\sigma_{250} = \frac{1466883}{250^2} + 13.47$$

$$= 36.94 \text{ MPa}$$

$$\sigma_{330} = \frac{1466883}{330^2} + 13.47$$

$$= 26.94 \text{ MPa}$$

(iii) Variation of pressure and hoop stress is as shown in Fig. 12.17.

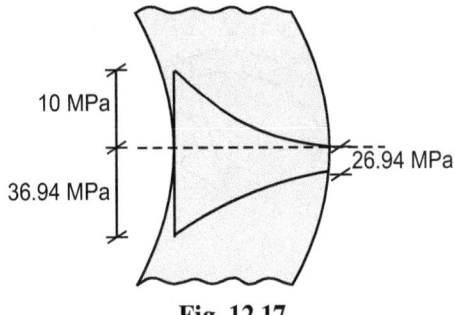

**Fig. 12.17**

**Example 12.28 :** A cylindrical shell of internal diameter 200 mm is to withstand an internal fluid pressure of 60 MPa. The maximum hoop stress in the section is not to exceed 150 MPa. Find the necessary metal thickness.

**Data :** d = 200 mm, p = 60 MPa, $\sigma_{h,\,max}$ = 150 MPa.

**Required :** thickness of shell.

**Concept :** Lame's equations.

**Solution :** (i) Lame's equations,

$$p_x = \frac{B}{x^2} - A \qquad \ldots (i)$$

$$\sigma_x = \frac{B}{x^2} + A \qquad \ldots (ii)$$

Boundary conditions
At  x = 100 mm,    $p_x$ = 60 MPa and
At  x = 100 mm,    $\sigma_x$ = 150 MPa

Putting in equations (i) and (ii) respectively,

$$60 = \frac{B}{100^2} - A \qquad \ldots (iii)$$

$$150 = \frac{B}{100^2} + A \qquad \ldots (iv)$$

Solving equations (iii) and (iv),

$$A = 45$$
$$B = 1050000$$

(ii) Thickness of the shell :
We have,
At  x = $r_1$;  $p_x$ = 0

$$p_x = \frac{1050000}{x^2} - 45$$

$$0 = \frac{1050000}{r_1^2} - 45$$

∴                $r_1$ = 152.75 mm

∴ Thickness of the shell = $r_1 - 100$
= 152.75 − 100 = **52.75 mm**

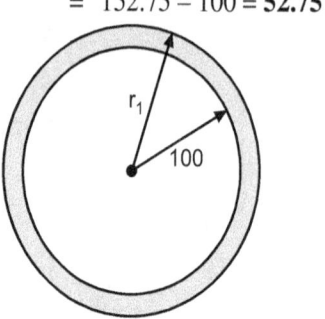

(All dimensions in mm)
Fig. 12.18

**Example 12.29 :** Determine the maximum and minimum hoop stress across the section of a pipe of 400 mm internal diameter and 100 mm thickness when the pipe contains a fluid at a pressure of 9 N/mm². Also sketch the radial pressure distribution and hoop stress distribution across the section.

**Solution :** We have,
$$\sigma_x = \frac{B}{x^2} + A \qquad \ldots (i)$$
$$p_x = \frac{B}{x^2} - A \qquad \ldots (ii)$$

When $x = 200$ mm, $p_x = 9$ MPa and when $x = 300$ mm, $p_x = 0$

Substituting in equation (ii),
$$9 = \frac{B}{200^2} - A \qquad \ldots (iii)$$
$$0 = \frac{B}{300^2} - A \qquad \ldots (iv)$$

Solving equations (iii) and (iv),
$$B = 648 \times 10^3 \text{ and } A = 7.2$$

Put in equation (i)
$$\sigma_x = \frac{648 \times 10^3}{x^2} + 7.2$$

For $x = 200$ mm, $\sigma_x =$ **23.4 MPa** and
For $x = 300$ mm, $\sigma_x =$ **14.4 MPa**

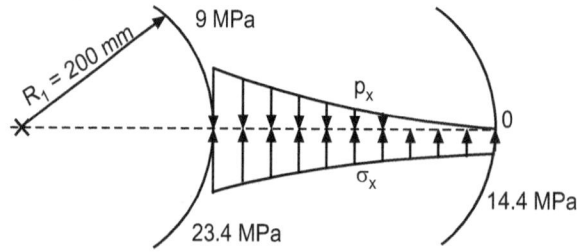

Fig. 12.19

**Example 12.30 :** A thick cylindrical shell has 175 mm internal diameter. It is subjected to an internal pressure of 9 N/mm². Determine the thickness of the shell if the permissible tensile stress is 21 MPa.

**Solution :** (i)
$$\sigma_x = \frac{B}{x^2} + A \quad \ldots (i)$$

$$p_x = \frac{B}{x^2} - A \quad \ldots (ii)$$

When $x = 87.5$ mm, $\sigma_x = 21$ MPa and $p_x = 9$ MPa

$$21 = \frac{B}{87.5^2} + A \quad \ldots (iii)$$

$$9 = \frac{B}{87.5^2} - A \quad \ldots (iv)$$

Solving equations (iii) and (iv),

$$B = 114843.75, \quad A = 6$$

(ii) Pressure on outer surface is zero.

$$\therefore \quad 0 = \frac{B}{x^2} - A$$

$$\therefore \quad 0 = \frac{114843.75}{x^2} - 6$$

$$\therefore \quad x = 138.35 \text{ mm}$$

$$\therefore \quad t = 138.35 - 87.5 = \mathbf{50.85 \text{ mm}}$$

**Example 12.31 :** A thick wall cylinder is made of steel, has an inside diameter of 20 mm, and an outside diameter of 100 mm. The cylinder is subjected to an internal pressure of 300 MPa. Determine the radial and hoop stresses at radial distances (i) 10 mm and (ii) 50 mm. Sketch the variation of these stresses across the cross-section.

**Solution :**
$$\sigma_x = \frac{B}{x^2} + A \quad \ldots (i)$$

$$p_x = \frac{B}{x^2} - A \quad \ldots (ii)$$

We have, when $x = 10$ mm, $p_x = 300$ MPa and when $x = 50$ mm, $p_x = 0$

$$300 = \frac{B}{10^2} - A \quad \ldots (iii)$$

$$0 = \frac{B}{50^2} - A \quad \ldots (iv)$$

Solving equations (iii) and (iv),

$$B = \mathbf{31250} \text{ and } A = \mathbf{12.5}$$

$$\sigma_{10} = \frac{31250}{10^2} + 12.5 = \mathbf{325 \text{ MPa}}$$

$$\sigma_{50} = \frac{31250}{50^2} + 12.5 = \mathbf{25 \text{ MPa}}$$

**Example 12.32 :** A thick-walled steel cylinder having an inside diameter 150 mm is subjected to an internal pressure of 40 MPa. Find the outside diameter required if the hoop tension in the cylinder wall is not to exceed 125 MPa. Calculate the actual hoop stresses at the inner and outer surfaces and plot a graph of variation of hoop tension across the wall.

**Solution :** (i)
$$\sigma_x = (B/x^2) + A \quad \ldots (i)$$
$$p_x = (B/x^2) - A \quad \ldots (ii)$$

We have when $x = 75$ mm, $p_x = 40$ MPa

$\therefore \quad 40 = (B/75^2) - A \quad \ldots (iii)$

When $x = 75$ mm, $\sigma_x = 125$ MPa

$\therefore \quad 125 = (B/75^2) + A \quad \ldots (iv)$

Solving equations (iii) and (iv),

$$B = 464062.5 \text{ and } A = 42.5$$

(ii) On outer surface, $p_x = 0$

$\therefore \quad 0 = (464062.5/x^2) - 42.5$

$\therefore \quad x = 104.5$ mm

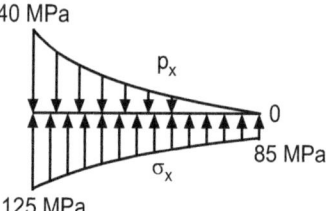

**Fig. 12.20**

$\therefore \quad$ External diameter $= 2 \times 104.5$
$= 209$ mm

(iii) $\sigma_{104.5} = (464062.5/104.5^2) + 42.5$
$= 85$ MPa

**Example 12.33 :** A cylindrical vessel whose ends are closed by means of rigid flange plates, is made of steel plate 3 mm thick. The internal diameter and length of vessel are 25 cm and 50 cm respectively. Determine the longitudinal and circumferential stresses in the cylindrical shell due to an internal fluid pressure of 3 N/mm². Also calculate increase in length, diameter and volume of the vessel. Take $\dfrac{1}{m} = 0.3$ and $E = 200$ GPa.

**Data :** $d_i = 25$ cm $= 250$ mm, $t = 3$ mm, $E = 200$ GPa $= \mu = 0.3$, $L = 50$ cm.

**Required :** Hoop stress, circumferential stress, change in length, change in diameter, change in volume.

**Solution :** (i) Hoop stress :
$$d = d_i + 2 \times 3 = 250 + 2 \times 3 = 256 \text{ mm}$$
$$\sigma_h = \dfrac{pd}{4t} = \dfrac{3 \times 256}{4 \times 3} = 64 \text{ MPa}$$

(ii) Circumferential stress:

$$\sigma_L = \frac{pd}{2t} = \frac{3 \times 256}{2 \times 3} = 128 \text{ MPa}$$

(iii) Change in dimensions:
(a) Circumferential strain:

$$\varepsilon_h = \frac{1}{E}(\sigma_h - \mu\sigma_L)$$

$$= \frac{1}{200 \times 10^3}(64 - 0.3 \times 128) = 1.28 \times 10^{-4}$$

$$\therefore \quad \frac{\delta d}{d} = \varepsilon_h$$

$$\therefore \quad \delta d = d \times \varepsilon_h = 1.28 \times 10^{-4} \times 256 = 32.76 \times 10^{-3} \text{ mm}$$

$\therefore$ Change in diameter = **32.76 × 10⁻³ mm**

(b) Longitudinal strain,

$$\varepsilon_L = \frac{1}{E}(\sigma_L - \mu\sigma_h)$$

$$= \frac{1}{200 \times 10^3}(128 - 0.3 \times 64) = 5.44 \times 10^{-4}$$

$$\frac{\delta l}{l} = \varepsilon_L$$

$$\therefore \quad \delta l = \varepsilon_L \times l = 5.44 \times 10^{-4} \times 500 = 0.272 \text{ mm}$$

$\therefore$ Change in length = **0.272 mm**

(c) Volumetric strain,

$$\varepsilon_V = 2\varepsilon_h + \varepsilon_L$$
$$= (2 \times 1.28 \times 10^{-4} + 5.44 \times 10^{-4}) = (8 \times 10^{-4})$$

$\therefore$ Change in volume = $\delta V = \varepsilon_V \times V$

$$= 8 \times 10^{-4} \times \frac{\pi}{4} \times d^2 L$$

$$= 8 \times 10^{-4} \times \frac{\pi}{4} \times 256^2 \times 500$$

$$= \mathbf{20.59 \times 10^3 \text{ mm}^3 \text{ (increase)}}$$

## EXERCISE

1. A thin spherical shell of internal diameter 800 mm and thickness 10 mm is subjected to an internal pressure of 15 MPa. Determine the principal stresses and principal strains. Also find change in diameter and volume. Assume E = 200 GPa and $\mu$ = 0.3.

   ($\sigma_1 = \sigma_2 = 300$ MPa (tensile); $\delta d = 0.84$ mm increase, $\varepsilon_1 = \varepsilon_2 = 1.05 \times 10^{-3}$ (tensile), $\delta V = 844.46 \times 10^3$ mm³ increase)

2. A 500 mm diameter pipe has 12 mm wall thickness. It connects reservoir at A with generating station at B. B is 100 m below water level at A. Determine maximum normal stress and maximum shear stress under static conditions. Take density of water as 10 kN/m³.

$$(\sigma_h = 20.83 \text{ MPa (tensile)}; \; \sigma_L = 10.41 \text{ MPa (tensile)}, \; \tau_{max} = 5.2 \text{ MPa})$$

3. A thin cylinder of 150 mm internal diameter and 2.5 mm thick is filled with water. When external axial pull of 55 kN is applied, the internal pressure is observed to fall. If E = 140 GPa, K = 2.2 GPa and μ = 0.3, find fall in internal pressure. (0.15 MPa)

4. A steel cylinder 2.5 m long, 0.8 m diameter and 10 mm thickness is filled with fluid at atmospheric pressure. The additional quantity of fluid is pumped in so as to have the internal pressure of 2.4 MPa. On releasing the pressure, the fluid let out measured 2.8 × 10⁶ mm³. If for the shell material E = 200 GPa, μ = 0.3, estimate the Bulk modulus of fluid. (1.82 GPa)

5. A cylindrical shell 110 mm diameter, 900 mm long and 4 mm thick is filled with an incompressible fluid at atmospheric pressure. If an additional quantity of fluid equal to 10 cm³ is pumped in, calculate (i) the pressure developed within the cylinder (ii) the stresses induced.
Assume E = 200 GPa and μ = 0.3.

$$(p = 8.95 \text{ MPa}, \; \sigma_h = 123.06 \text{ MPa (tensile)}, \; \sigma_L = 61.53 \text{ MPa (tensile)})$$

6. The change in volume of thin walled cylinder 1250 mm long, 135 mm internal diameter and 3 mm thickness of metal is 14050 mm³. If E = 200 GPa and μ = 0.28, find the internal fluid pressure and the principal stresses.

$$(p = 3.59 \text{ MPa}, \; \sigma_1 = 80.95 \text{ MPa}, \; \sigma_2 = 40.47 \text{ MPa})$$

7. A thin cylindrical shell has 1.35 m diameter and 4.75 m length. It is subjected to internal fluid pressure of 3.5 MPa. If the maximum shear stress is not to exceed 38 MPa, find (i) thickness of shell, (ii) change in diameter, (iii) change in length, (iv) change in volume. Assume E = 200 GPa and μ = 0.3.

(t = 15.54 mm say 16 mm; δd = 0.847 mm increase, δL = 0.701 mm increase, δV = 9.53 × 10⁶ mm³ increase)

8. A thin spherical shell with hemispherical ends is subjected to internal fluid pressure of 2.1 MPa. The length of cylindrical portion is 1.2 m and internal diameter of cylindrical as well as spherical portion is 450 mm. If E = 200 GPa and μ = 0.3, find change in volume of the shell assuming 14 mm wall thickness for the shell. (69.64 × 10³ mm³)

9. A cylindrical shell 85 mm diameter, 7 mm thickness and 1.35 m long is subjected to internal fluid pressure of 12 MPa. If the efficiency of circumferential joint is 86% and that of longitudinal joint is 96%, find (i) the stresses induced and (ii) the change in volume. Assume E = 200 GPa and μ = 0.3.

$$(\sigma_h = 75.89 \text{ MPa}, \; \sigma_L = 42.35 \text{ MPa}, \; \delta V = 5.59 \times 10^3 \text{ mm}^3)$$

10. A copper tube having 55 mm internal diameter and 3.2 mm wall thickness is closed at its ends by plugs which are 515 mm apart. The tube is subjected to an internal fluid pressure of 3.5 MPa and an axial pull of 6.5 kN. Compute (i) Change in length between the plugs, (ii) Change in internal diameter of tube.

    Assume E = 100 GPa and $\mu$ = 0.3.

    ($\delta L$ = 0.09148 mm increase, $\delta d$ = 0.01212 mm increase)

11. A spherical vessel of 550 mm diameter is made from 10 mm thick steel plate and is just filled with water at atmospheric pressure. Find the pressure rise when an additional 0.0004 m³ of water is pumped inside. Assume Bulk modulus of water K = 2.2 GPa and E = 140 GPa, $\mu$ = 0.28 for shell material. (6.88 MPa)

12. A thin spherical copper shell of diameter 200 mm and 2 mm thickness is just full of water at atmospheric pressure. Find how much the internal pressure will be increased by pumping in 31500 m³ of water ? Assume E = 100 GPa, $\mu$ = 0.3 and K = 2.2 GPa.

    (7.67 MPa)

13. A spherical vessel with a diameter of 6 m contains a corrosive gas at pressure of 1.5 MPa. The vessel can withstand a maximum tensile stress of 85 MPa. Due to corrosion, metal wall is eaten at the rate of 0.4 mm per year. If thickness of metal used initially is 30 mm, determine the life of the shell. (8.825 yrs)

14. A thin cylinder 125 mm internal diameter, 2.25 mm thickness has its ends closed rigidly. It is filled with water. When an external pull is applied to the cylinder axially the internal water pressure drops by 0.085 MPa. If E = 200 GPa, $\mu$ = 0.3 and K = 2.2 GPa, find the value of pull. (26.92 kN)

15. A cylindrical pressure vessel is having 250 mm internal diameter, 10 mm thickness and 4.3 m length. If the normal stress in plate is limited to 140 MPa, determine the change in length of vessel. Assume E = 200 GPa and $\mu$ = 0.3. (0.602 mm increase)

16. A thin cylindrical shell of length 2.75 m and internal volume 3.15 m³ is subjected to an internal fluid pressure of 3.3 MPa. If maximum permissible tensile stress is 200 MPa, find the change in volume of the shell. Assume E = 200 GPa and $\mu$ = 0.3.

    ($5.985 \times 10^6$ mm³ increase)

17. A spherical shell of 515 mm internal diameter and 7.5 mm wall thickness is filled with water under a pressure of 5 MPa. The pressure is gradually reduced by letting out some water to reduce the pressure to atmospheric. The volume of water let out was $2.15 \times 10^5$ mm³. If Bulk modulus of water is 2.2 GPa and E = 200 GPa for shell material, estimate the Poisson's ratio. (0.43)

18. A thin spherical shell of 1.4 m diameter is 7.5 mm thick. It is filled with liquid at internal pressure of 2.8 MPa. Find hoop stress, change in diameter, change in thickness and change in volume. Assume E = 200 GPa and $\mu$ = 0.3.

    ($\delta d$ = 0.64 mm increase, $\delta t = 2.94 \times 10^{-3}$ mm decrease, $\delta V = 1.971 \times 10^6$ mm³ increase)

19. A thin cylindrical shell 3.2 m long, 0.9 m diameter is subjected to an internal fluid pressure of 2 MPa. If the thickness of the shell is 12 mm, find (i) circumferential and longitudinal stress, (ii) maximum shear stress and (iii) changes in dimensions of the shell. Assume E = 200 GPa and $\mu$ = 0.3.

($\sigma_h$ = 75 MPa, $\sigma_L$ = 37.5 MPa, $\tau_{max}$ = 18.75 MPa, $\delta d$ = 0.286 mm increase, $\delta L$ = 0.24 mm increase, $\delta t$ = 2.025 × 10$^{-3}$ mm decrease)

20. A riveted boiler 2.5 m in diameter is subjected to internal fluid pressure of 1.1 MPa. The efficiency of longitudinal riveted joint is 80% and maximum allowable stress for the material is 110 MPa. Find thickness of shell and pitch of rivets assuming 22 mm diameter rivets and rivets to be in single shear.  (t = 15.625 mm, pitch = 110 mm)

21. A cylindrical boiler is subjected to an internal fluid pressure of 1.8 MPa. The thickness of the boiler is 8 mm and maximum permissible stress is 160 MPa. Find maximum permissible diameter when the efficiency of longitudinal joint is 90% and that of circumferential joint is 65%.  (1280 mm)

22. A steel cylinder 240 mm internal diameter is to withstand an internal pressure of 4 MPa. The increase in area of the bore due to the resulting radial expansion is limited to 0.1% of the nominal area. Calculate the necessary thickness of the cylinder and hoop stress induced in the section, assuming E = 210 GPa and $\mu$ = 0.3.

(t = 3.88 mm say 4 mm, $\sigma_h$ = 120 MPa)

23. A cylindrical shell of 300 mm internal diameter, 3 m long and 6 mm thick is subjected to an internal fluid pressure of 3 MPa. Calculate the change in length, diameter and volume of the cylinder if the efficiencies of longitudinal and circumferential joints are 80% and 50% respectively. Assume E = 200 GPa and $\mu$ = 0.285.

($\delta d$ = 1.084 mm increase, $\delta L$ = 0.724 mm increase, $\delta V$ = 204.45 × 10$^3$ mm$^3$ increase)

24. A boiler drum consists of a cylindrical portion 4 m long, 1.5 m internal diameter and 22.5 mm thick. It is closed by hemispherical ends. It is filled with water at atmospheric pressure. How much additional quantity of water can be pumped in to cause internal pressure of 5 MPa ? Assume E = 200 GPa, $\mu$ = 0.3 and Bulk modulus for water = 2.13 GPa. The circumferential strain at the junction of cylinder and hemisphere may be assumed same for both.  (35.69 × 10$^6$ mm$^3$)

www.ingramcontent.com/pod-product-compliance
Lightning Source LLC
Chambersburg PA
CBHW080402300426
44113CB00015B/2383